THE UNUSUAL AND THE UNEXPECTED ON BRITISH RAILWAYS

A CHRONOLOGY OF UNLIKELY EVENTS
1948-1968

DAVE PEEL

FONTHILL

FONTHILL MEDIA
www.fonthillmedia.com

First published 2013

Copyright © Dave Peel 2013

ISBN 978-1-78155-234-6

Dave Peel has asserted his rights under the Copyright, Designs
and Patents Act 1988 to be identified as the Author of this work

A CIP catalogue record for this book is available from the British Library

Typeset in 10pt on 13pt Sabon LT Std
Typesetting by Fonthill Media
Printed in the UK

Contents

Acknowledgements

NRM – National Railway Museum (Staff and resources)

NMM – National Media Museum (Staff and resources)

SSPL – Science & Society Picture Library (Staff)

Bournemouth Railway Club

Barry Fletcher, Alan Wild, Melvin Haigh for individual contrbutions

Key Publishing Ltd (various issues of *Trains Illustrated/Modern Railways*)

Railway Correspondence and Travel Society (various issues of *Railway Observer*)

Mortons Media Group Ltd (various issues of *The Railway Magazine*)

Photographers are individually credited. While every effort has been made to ensure that the attributions are accurate, if this is not the case, the author would welcome contact from the true copyright holder.

Introduction

Prior to the nationalisation of the railways on 1 January 1948, Britain's rail network was operated almost exclusively by four private Companies. The 'Big Four' as they were called – the Great Western, the Southern, the London Midland & Scottish and the London & North Eastern – had been formed by an amalgamation of several smaller companies in 1923, and these four were themselves not only nationalised in 1948 but consolidated into one large concern, British Railways.

Each of the Big Four had built up its own system of working in its own geographic area, with its own rolling stock (locomotives, coaches, wagons), its own staff, its own distinctive corporate image and recognisable livery. Thus BR inherited a diverse mix, not only of physical plant, but of traditions and loyalties developed over generations. Its first task therefore was to attempt to allay some of the misgivings and prejudices created by the transition to a single national company, though on the ground changes would inevitably be made slowly. Not only was capital investment in short supply, but much of the equipment was old, run down and in urgent need of attention before any national improvements could even be planned much less implemented.

As a move towards even-handedness, the 1948 Locomotive Interchange Trials were arranged, and new livery schemes for both engines and rolling stock exhibited, and these publicity moves brought BR into the public's awareness as a single nationwide company, as well as giving rise to some of the first 'unusual and unexpected' entries in these pages. Its intention to design and build new steam engines based on the best practise of the previous Companies (as identified by these Interchange Trials) also helped railwaymen gain a more positive view of their new employer, and dispel some of the bias that staff felt to be present in the new BR hierarchy.

Additionally management had to grapple with many and varied constraints in its desire to improve efficiency and create a nationally recognisable system. It was common knowledge that, alone of the Big Four, the Great Western engines were right-hand drive, and that consequently all the signals were on the opposite side of the track compared to other railways. This alone mitigated against 'free' use of GW engines elsewhere, but a further factor was the fitting of the GW's Automatic Train Control system, whose magnetic shoe had to be lifted for safety when off GW lines. Particularly restricting however was the loading gauge, which was slightly more generous in width, making platform edge clearances too risky in many places outside the GW area, though clearly incoming locos were free to run onto GW territory. As a result of this lack of ability to roam freely far and wide, there are probably a smaller number of references in these pages to GWR engines, relative to the overall territorial size of the former Company.

Further, all the major Railway Companies had a large number of restrictions as to which engines (and stock) could go where, even on their own system. Axle loading was often the deciding consideration and this governed which engine types could run on specific lines over which bridges and at what speed. This was a bureaucratic nightmare for BR, and in not a few instances resulted in 'foreign' locos being impounded by the local Civil Engineer as being 'unfit' to travel over the route they had just travelled! Hence the sphere of working of all the major (heaviest) classes was effectively confined only to those main lines that were passed to take the greatest axle loads, all the LNER Pacifics being banned entirely from East Anglia for instance.

The consequence of all this was that, for many of the years considered here, former Company engines tended to run almost exclusively on the lines they'd always run on, and could not be readily transferred round the country to where they might best be used, and clearly if a 'stranger' was seen 'out of bounds' this got reported! (Except in wartime, the only instance in which a sizeable number of engines was reallocated to a distant area in LNER/BR days, was that of 25 B12 4-6-0s from East Anglia to the Great North of Scotland area where only a light axle load could be tolerated).

All these considerations impinged on BR's desire to introduce a modern range of steam engines of its own, so that these would have the widest route availability and could be allocated anywhere in the country. This, by and large, they successfully achieved, though in later years even the new BR diesels had more restrictions placed upon them than was originally envisaged.

Another restraint on any drive towards more efficient working was the parochial way in which in which many services operated. Although BR set up, almost immediately, six Regions that corresponded geographically to the Big Four (the Scottish and North Eastern were the 'extras') the boundaries of these Regions were intended to be (or at least to become) much less rigid than the Company boundaries. Traditionally, the majority of each Company's services (freight or passenger) were self-contained movements within that Company's boundaries, which contained a multiplicity of small depots working localised services. Consequently both locos and crew were 'confined' to small operating areas. Within the new Regions that continued to be so, at least initially. However, much long-distance freight, and cross-country passenger services obviously crossed these boundaries and had previously changed engines where they did so; Oxford, Carlisle, Newcastle being but three places of many in this category. Other criteria for replacing engines often applied however. Grantham for instance (105 miles from King's Cross) was a convenient exchange location as it enabled the footplate crew to work the engine out and back from London in a single shift, and many engine diagrams (at every shed) were arranged in this manner. Leeds was another place where long distance trains swapped engines, though here change of direction was the main cause. Midland line trains ('Thames-Clyde Express', 'Waverley', 'Devonian') reversed in City station, as well as many of the Liverpool – Newcastle services, which ran via Harrogate rather than York. Leeds was also a Regional boundary with these cross-country expresses replacing LMS power with LNER power and vice versa. Across at Central (a purely terminal station) the 'Queen of Scots' Pullman train also reversed direction.

Gradually therefore, 'through engine working' (and stock of course) became more prevalent and these workings would be just one component under the 'unusual and unexpected events' heading this chronology seeks to catalogue. Much of this 'through working' was to be seen (especially in summer) on excursion trains which, right through to the mid-1960s were plentiful in number, and reached a multitude of destinations, where many 'foreign' locomotives arrived, and were duly reported.

As most of these excursion locos had to remain in steam to head the return working, it was frequently the case that the local shedmaster would use these incoming engines on one or two 'fill-in' turns before it did so. These 'extra' turns were not of course restricted to excursion locos; all unbalanced workings for instance created a 'spare' loco, and any working that had a long turn-round time was also fair game. The practice of 'borrowing' engines was therefore rife, especially when the visiting engine was in better condition than locos currently available locally.

To the enthusiasts of the day (and the travelling public in general) surprising sights did of course spring from many other sources. Freight engines pressed into service on passenger workings; engine failures - followed by 'exotic' replacements have always featured strongly, and diverted traffic frequently provided a rich supply of the unusual. Workings such as troop trains, circus trains, farm removal specials, extra boat trains, freight trains with special loads, and various locomotive test trains added to the variety of traffic that could (and often did) throw up an engine not commonly seen.

Running-in turns after an engine had been outshopped from one of the major Works provided some of the best spectacles of engines from distant parts, especially if they'd been repainted, and thus appeared in 'as new' condition. Railtours organised by and for enthusiasts also became increasingly popular as the years went by and these almost always had 'special request' locos. Sometimes these would be old types about to become extinct, but often as well as a 'strange' itinerary an engine from another Region would be provided. If, additionally this engine was to be piloted over part of the route, some rarely-seen combinations could be created and these are of course reported here.

The fact that an engine, be it steam or diesel, was not 'local' was not only revealed by its number or name, but also by its shed allocation. This was displayed on an oval plaque low down on the smokebox door (on steam engines) and was in an alpha-numeric code according to the district and then the particular depot within that district. For instance 6A always denoted Chester depot; '6' being the district code number and 'A' denoted the 'mother shed' for the district, usually the one with the largest allocation and best facilities in the group, of which 6J (as an example) was always Holyhead. (In many cases however, codes changed over the years, often following Regional boundary changes. Individual locomotives had their depot allocation changed much more frequently, as the traffic demands dictated, though as remarked earlier not with quite the freedom of movement desirable.) Hence it was immediately obvious that if a 'Black Five' appeared in Newcastle bearing a 60A shedplate (denoting Inverness), this was a rare event, even though there were 842 members of this class, and others of the same class allocated more locally (such as Carlisle) would not be given a second glance! Indeed, the same engine could well re-appear at Newcastle at a later date when its allocation had been changed to a Carlisle depot, in which case its presence would not be a significant event any more!

The fact that an engine was well off its beaten track is frequently indicated in these pages by the simple expedient of an exclamation mark after the shed code. 32B! expressing surprise that an Ipswich engine has reached Birmingham, for example. Within the text, an explanation as to how and why such a working came about is given, if it is known, but on most occasions it wasn't as the original correspondent simply reported the fact.

Engines could be out of place however, and still be close to home! At Aberdeen it would be regarded as most unusual to find a Kittybrewster loco on Ferryhill and vice versa, despite the relatively short direct connection between the depots. Here it was a case of 61A supplying northbound power for the GNS system, and 61B engines heading exclusively south towards Perth, Glasgow or Edinburgh. The two Leicester sheds, Midland and Central, were only a couple of miles apart as the smoke drifts, but twenty or more by rail, so to find 15C or 15E engines at the 'wrong' shed would be a notable event! Again, Leeds Holbeck depot was within sight of Copley Hill, but for the ex-Midland shed to allow its motive power to cross to the ex-Great Northern depot was almost unthinkable, and the same was true in reverse of course.

Some entries refer to future BR plans which, though published in good faith at the time ultimately turned out to be either not implemented at all, or in a modified form. Others are news items reporting progress on current projects, many of which are themselves history now, though it all makes interesting reading!

These then are the basic types of observations that constitute the bulk of the information listed. They found their way into the popular magazines of the day – *Trains Illustrated/Modern Railways,*

Railway Observer, Railway Magazine etc. – where, suitably edited they became the newsworthy items for that month; one-liners that were of interest at the time, but were superseded by another batch next month. Together they constitute, here, a snap-shot of recent history that many readers will be able to associate themselves with, though clearly the detail will have escaped the memory. It should be borne in mind however that throughout these pages entries can only be as accurate as the original published information. Very occasionally, a correspondent 'got it wrong', but this was usually corrected in the next month's issue. Text is printed in the present tense (as reported) and only a tiny number of 'with hindsight' or 'future development' comments are inserted, and only if strictly appropriate. A large number of entries do however have some simple extra comment added, to give a hint as to why the entry is surprising, unusual or unexpected. At the time, this would have been self-evident to those reading the reference, but today a gentle reminder would seem to be helpful.

The author's assiduous trawl through the relevant sources to re-create this series of observations is precisely that, a personal selection. Others would doubtless make different choices, and no attempt has been made to 'balance' any particular aspect with any other. After all, the original magazine editors could only pick, for publication, whatever was sent to them, and if their correspondents were thinner on the ground in some quarters than others, then that's the way it was. This book is not an easy, straightforward, read. Though the years could be regarded as chapters and the months as paragraphs, each entry can be thought of, with a little imagination, as a mini-story in its own right! The book is therefore probably best read a few entries at a time, sequentially, but be prepared to jump geographically to anywhere on the BR network from one entry to the next.

Enjoy!

BACKGROUND NOTES

1. For the purposes of these pages, the full BR numbering system has been adopted right from the outset, to avoid confusion. In reality it was clearly many months before every SR/LMS/LNER engine had been re-numbered.
2. Named locomotives are assumed to have retained their names throughout their working lives (even though many did not), for ease of identification.
3. Entries are largely in note form, and there are many abbreviations.
4. It will be noticed that, although the early months/years have relatively few entries, by the mid-1950s onwards each month contains a much larger number. This simply reflects both a severe paper shortage in the first 3 or 4 years, and later an increasing number of correspondents and photographers submitting their observations for publication.
5. Captions to photographs are not necessarily in the present tense and sometimes give a wider, more historical slant to the event which only hindsight can give. Some illustrations have a matching reference in the text, others do not, and are 'events' extra to those listed. The photographs themselves are not arranged chronologically though most pages are however 'themed' in some way, often geographically, or by engine type or by Region, for instance. In many cases the caption is also quite brief, as cross-reference to the date-entry will provide further details.
6. An extensive Appendix is located at the end, giving the sort of background information familiar to enthusiasts of the day, but which the reader may wish to be reminded of in order to better appreciate the significance of the entry.

The Entries,
January 1948 – December 1968

JANUARY 1948

1ˢᵀ First BR train out of Euston is the 12.2am to Crewe, with 'Patriot' 45508.
First out of Paddington is 12.5am to Birkenhead, with 5032 *Usk Castle*.

1-14 'Silver Princess' experimental lightweight coach runs in the 'Flying Scotsman' for two weeks. Vehicle is built by Budd (in Philadelphia, USA) in stainless steel on behalf of Pressed Steel Co. of Cowley Oxford.

6-31 Romney, Hythe & Dymchurch 4-6-2 *Dr Syn* is on exhibition at Waterloo station concourse. Substantial funds are raised for the SR orphanage.

13,14,15. LMS 1600hp Co-Co diesel 10000 comes out of Derby paint shop for local trials (13th). Undergoes further test runs Derby/St Pancras/Manchester (Central)/Derby on 12 coaches (with dynamometer car), 14th/15th

15 H2 4-4-2 32423 *The Needles* hauls 4-COR unit 3055 from Waterloo to Portsmouth and back (on oscillation tests), a surprising sight.

30 Official livery inspection at Kensington (Addison Road) sees:
LMS 4-6-0s
      44762 in SR malachite green, unlined
      44763 in LNER green, with black/white lining
      44764 in GWR green, with gold/black lining
      45292 in black, lined red
SR Co-Co
      CC 2 in pale blue, lined silver/black/silver
all lettered BRITISH RAILWAYS but lined out on one side only.

U/D 'Tilbury' tanks, 4-4-2Ts 41971-74 are transferred to Dundee(!) for local work. The last two are used (briefly) by Carstairs before going north.

FEBRUARY 1948

8ᵀᴴ (from) WD 2-10-0s ex-store at Longmoor, are transferred to store at Ringwood. These are 73774/76/84/89/94/95, becoming 90750/52/60/65/70/71.

15 SEC Royal Saloon 7930 appears at Littlehampton. (*See also September*).

16 61731 (Boston), ex-Cowlairs Works, heads a Berwick – Newcastle stopper, which it will probably never do again!

16   The 'Royal Scot' name is restored to the 10am express from Euston to Glasgow, to mark the centenary of the completion of the West Coast route. The title was introduced in 1927, but has been suspended since 1939.

27   The 'Yorkshire Pullman' arrives in King's Cross behind the unexpected pairing of 61107 + 61208, instead of the usual Pacific.

28   One of four football excursions from Waterloo to Southampton consists entirely of LMS stock, including two 'Grampian Corridor' 12-wheelers, surely never seen on this route before!

28   'Coronation' beaver-tail observation car 1729 arrives at Waverley on a parcel train from York. It is then attached (tail first) to the rear of the 4.20pm to Aberdeen, bound for Inverurie Works.

U/D   C12 4-4-2T 67374 works Finsbury Park – Alexandra Palace auto trains. It is more than 20 years since this class was employed on passenger turns so close to London.

MARCH 1948

2ND   De-streamlined 46225 *Duchess of Gloucester* arrives at Nine Elms shed for clearance tests prior to the Locomotive Interchange Trials.

4,11   5.36pm Redhill – Reading is worked by 4-4-0 31504, the first E1 seen at Reading for many years (4th). The same train a week later has I3 4-4-2T 32027, new ground for a loco of this class.

11   60530 *Sayajirao*, newly allocated to King's Cross, works running-in turns to Cambridge, few A2s ever reach here.

11-13   MSWJ 2-4-0 1335 works the Lambourn branch, usually railcar operated.

13   Semi-final of the FA Cup at Hillsborough brings 15 specials to Wadsley Bridge or Sheffield (Victoria). However, 60 freights have to be rearranged for this to happen!

27   41184 appears on Forres shed from Lochgorm Works (Inverness). Believed to be the first LMS Compound to be repaired there.

29   Nine specials are run from Leeds (City) for the Easter Monday race meeting at Wetherby, with the racecourse station open for the first time since the war.

U/D   D3 4-4-0 62131 arrives at Nottingham (Midland) with a train from the M&GN system, D3s are a real rarity here.

APRIL 1948

The 1948 Interchange Trials begin on 19 April and last for 20 weeks until the end of August. These are followed by four further weeks of supplementary tests (using Welsh coal) during November, December. See separate pages for schedules.

6TH   Exhibition of locomotives and rolling stock repainted in experimental liveries is held at Marylebone station and includes

   60091 *Captain Cuttle* painted royal blue, lined yellow
   61661 *Sheffield Wednesday* painted light green, lined yellow
   45292 painted black, with full LNW lining
   8-coach LMS corridor set in maroon & white
   7-coach LMS non-corridor set in crimson, yellow at waist
   2 GW coaches in GW livery.

13   M7 0-4-4T 30672 falls down the lift shaft at Waterloo that is used for raising, lowering Waterloo & City line underground stock. Engine is cut up on site.

| 14 | 2-6-4Ts 42198/9 are transferred to the SR for trials between Waterloo and Basingstoke (42198), Victoria and Tunbridge Wells (42199) in the first instance. |

14 2-6-4Ts 42198/9 are transferred to the SR for trials between Waterloo and Basingstoke (42198), Victoria and Tunbridge Wells (42199) in the first instance.

18 46162 *Queen's Westminster Rifleman* arrives at Top Shed (34A) prior to commencement of the Interchange Trials next day.

19 61001/09 *Eland/Hartebeeste* are on view at Liverpool Street with different versions of a proposed BR emblem on the tender.

22 90324 observed under repair at St Blazey, first WD seen west of Plymouth since the war.

26 A3 60091, B17 61661 seen on show at King's Cross station; as at Marylebone on the 6th but with lining re-done.

MAY 1948

5TH 46200 *The Princess Royal* runs into Princes Street (where they are not often seen) from Glasgow and returns there with the 3.43pm local.

6,8 J2 4-6-2T 32326 is trusted with a special from Brighton – Eastleigh for the Chairman and Officials of the Railway Executive, who visit the Works. Two days later 32326 heads the 4.36pm Brighton – Tunbridge Wells West, consisting of a 2-coach LBSC motor set with a 'Devon Belle' observation car at the rear, an eye-catching combination!

10,11 Each 14-car 'Devon Belle' Pullman set is taken for a trial run between Waterloo and Basingstoke. 35005 *Canadian Pacific* (with mechanical stoker) is used on both days, coupled next to the observation car on the return journey.

11 The King and Queen travel between Euston, Birmingham and back in the LNER Royal Train, headed by 45606 *Falkland Islands*.

13 Special from Victoria to Tunbridge Wells West is powered, most unusually, by W 2-6-4T 31918 as this class rarely works passenger trains.

13,14 L1 2-6-4T 67709 heads the 8.24am Buffet Car and the 5.54pm Restaurant Car expresses between Liverpool Street and Cambridge and their return workings. 67708 takes the 3.44pm Liverpool Street – Yarmouth non-stop Restaurant Car express next day (68¾ miles on 2650 gallons water capacity).

19 Craigentinny carriage sidings (Edinburgh) contains the following stock, all from the pre-war LNER streamlined trains;
- a full set of 'Coronation' coaches
- a triplet and twin from 'Silver Jubilee'
- at least one twin from the 'West Riding Limited'

19,20 O1 0-6-0 31048 works the Maidstone – Redhill passenger turn on both days, an unusual choice of power for this service.

23,25 Leith rolling stock exhibition includes the 'Silver Princess' coach, shortly to cross to Ireland for the Cork – Dublin service (suitably re-gauged!)

30 CR 'Pug' 0-4-0ST 56020 arrives back at Burton for internal shunting duties within the breweries, after overhaul at St Rollox, a long round trip.

U/D LNER J50 0-6-0T begins yard-shunting trials at Cricklewood.

U/D 'Tilbury' 4-4-2Ts 41971-74, ex-Dundee are put into store at Durran Hill.

U/D Parts for the gas turbine loco 18000 arrive at Swindon from Brown-Boveri of Switzerland in an SNCF boxcar, unusual freight!

Week Comm.	ex LMS No.1 car	loco	ex LNER car
19 Apr	10am Euston – Carlisle 12.55pm Carlisle – Euston	46236	1.10pm King's Cross – Leeds 7.50am Leeds – King's Cross *do.*
26 Apr	–	–	1.10pm King's Cross – Leeds 7.50am Leeds – King's Cross *do.*
3 May	10am Euston – Carlisle 12.55pm Carlisle – Euston *do.*	46162 35017	1.10pm King's Cross – Leeds 7.50pm Leeds – King's Cross
10 May	10am Euston – Carlisle 12.55pm Carlisle – Euston	35017	*1.10pm King's Cross – Leeds* *7.50pm Leeds – King's Cross*
17 May	*10am Euston – Carlisle* *12.55pm Carlisle – Euston*	60034	1.10pm King's Cross – Leeds 7.50pm Leeds – King's Cross *do.*
24 May	10am Euston – Carlisle 12.55pm Carlisle – Euston	60034	1.10pm King's Cross – Leeds 7.50pm Leeds – King's Cross
31 May	10.15am St Pancras – Manchester 1.50pm Manchester – St Pancras	45253	10am Marylebone – Manchester 8.25am Manchester – M'bone *do.*
7 June	*10.15am St Pancras – M'chester* *1.50pm M'chester – St Pancras*	61251	10am Marylebone – Manchester 8.25am Manchester – M'bone *do.*
14 June	10.15am St Pancras – Manchester 1.50pm Manchester – St Pancras *do.*	61251 34005	10am Marylebone – Manchester 8.25am Manchester – M'bone *do.*
21 June	10.15am St Pancras – Manchester 1.50pm Manchester – St Pancras	34005	10am Marylebone – Manchester 8.25am Manchester – M'bone

INTERCHANGE TRIALS 1948 : WEEKLY PROGRAMME

Note 1 60022 fails at Savernake 27 April; replaced by 60033
Note 2 60033 fails at Andover 31 May; replaced by 60022
Note 3 60022 fails at Salisbury 9 June; replaced by 60034

loco	ex GWR car	loco
60034	1.30pm Paddington – Plymouth 8.30am Plymouth – Paddington	6018
46162	*do.*	*35019*
46162	1.30pm Paddington – Plymouth 8.30am Plymouth – Paddington	35019 *60022/60033*
46236	*do.*	*(Note 1)*
46236	1.30pm Paddington – Plymouth 8.30am Plymouth – Paddington	60033
6018	*1.30pm Paddington – Plymouth* *8.30am Plymouth – Paddington*	*46236*
6018	1.30pm Paddington – Plymouth 8.30pm Plymouth – Paddington	46236
35019	*do.*	*46162*
35017	1.30pm Paddington – Plymouth 8.30pm Plymouth – Paddington	*46162*
61163	10.50am Waterloo – Exeter 12.37pm Exeter – Waterloo	35018
34006	*do.*	*60033/60022* *(Note2)*
34006	10.50am Waterloo – Exeter 12.37pm Exeter – Waterloo	60022/60034 (Note3)
45253	*do.*	*46154*
45253	10.50am Waterloo – Exeter 12.37pm Exeter – Waterloo	46154
6990	*do.*	*46236*
6990	10.50am Waterloo – Exeter 12.37pm Exeter – Waterloo	46236

Details in italics are of familiarisation runs on Monday to Thursday.
Other details are of test runs on Tuesday to Friday with dynamometer car.

Note 4 48400 (poor condition) replaced by 48189 for 1/2 July
Note 5 6001 with 2-row superheater, 6022 with 4-row.

28 June	10.40am Brent – Toton 9.30am Toton – Brent	48400 48189 (Note 4)	–
5 July	10.40am Brent – Toton 9.30am Toton – Brent	90490	4pm Perth – Inverness 8.20am Inverness – Perth *do.*
12 July	10.40am Brent – Toton 9.30am Toton – Brent *do.*	90752 63789	4pm Perth – Inverness 8.20am Inverness – Perth *do.*
19 July	10.40am Brent – Toton 9.30am Toton – Brent	2-8-0 63789	4pm Perth – Inverness 8.20am Inverness – Perth *11.20am Acton – Severn T Jct* *2.40pm Severn T Jct – Hanwell*
26 July	7.30am Ferme Park – New England 8.5am New England – Ferme Park	2-8-0 63773	11.20am Acton – Severn T Jct 2.40pm Severn T Jct – Hanwell
9 Aug	7.30am Ferme park – New England 8.5am New England – Ferme Park *do.*	90750 48189	11.20am Acton – Severn T Jct 2.40pm Severn T Jct – Hanwell
16 Aug	7.30am Ferme Park – New England 8.5am New England – Ferme Park *do.*	48189 3803	11.20am Acton – Severn T Jct 2.40pm Severn T Jct – Hanwell
23 Aug	7.30am Ferme Park – New England 8.5am New England – Ferme Park	3803	11.20am Acton – Severn T Jct 2.40pm Severn T Jct – Hanwell *do.*
30 Aug	7.30am Ferme Park – New England 8.5am New England – Ferme Park	90490	11.20am Acton – Severn T Jct 2.40pm Severn T Jct – Hanwell
22 Nov	Additional		–
29 Nov	Tests		–
6 Dec	using		–
13 Dec	Welsh coal		–

–	1.45pm Bristol – Plymouth 1.35pm Plymouth – Bristol	6990
	do.	*61251*
44973	1.45pm Bristol – Plymouth 1.35pm Plymouth – Bristol	61251
34004	do.	*45253*
34004	1.45pm Bristol – Plymouth 1.35pm Plymouth – Bristol	45253
61292	do.	*34006*
61292	1.45pm Bristol – Plymouth 1.35pm Plymouth – Bristol	34006
48189		
48189	9.45am Bristol – Eastleigh 11.36am Eastleigh – Bristol	2-8-0 3803
3803	9.45am Bristol – Eastleigh 11.36am Eastleigh – Bristol	90101
	do.	*63789*
90750	9.45am Bristol – Eastleigh 11.36am Eastleigh – Bristol	63789
90101	9.45am Bristol – Eastleigh 11.36am Eastleigh – Bristol	90750
63773	do.	*48189*
63773	9.45am Bristol – Eastleigh 11.36am Eastleigh – Bristol	48189
	1.30pm Paddington – Plymouth 8.30am Plymouth – Paddington	6001 (Note 5)
	1.45pm Bristol – Plymouth 1.35pm Plymouth – Bristol	6961
	11.15am Acton – Severn T Jct 8.40am Severn T Jct – Hanwell	2-8-0 3864
	1.30pm Paddington – Plymouth 8.30am Plymouth – Paddington	6022 (Note 5)

JUNE 1948

9TH 60033 *Seagull,* running-in on the 3.10pm King's Cross – Cambridge after failing at Andover the previous week, is detached at Hitchin and runs light engine to Nine Elms depot to replace 60022 *Mallard* in the Interchange Trials.

10 1028 *County of Warwick* works between Bristol and Stratford-on-Avon with a Penzance – North of England train. First 'County' seen on this route.

12 Up 'Cornish Riviera' passes Liskeard with 'Bulldog' 4-4-0 3445 *Flamingo* piloting 1009 *County of Carmarthen.* Ancient and modern in tandem.

14-25 Waterloo centenary exhibition provides a rare view of preserved Adams 4-4-0 563, which had run up to London on the 11th after re-tubing at Eastleigh.

23,24 Highland Agricultural Society's Show brings 61323 to Inverness on a special from Aberdeen, the first B1 to appear here. The day of the Royal visit (24th) sees two further B1s on Inverness shed, 61242 *Alexander Reith Gray* and 61307.

U/D 6985 *Parwick Hall* appears in the Midland shed at Gloucester to use the wheel-drop facility.

U/D Summer timetable. Special 7-coach excursion trains, including an observation car, run to Llanberis (branch closed to passengers in 1932), three days a week. Certain trains between Llandudno and Bettws-y-Coed also operate with observation cars, one of L&Y, one of LNW origin.

JULY 1948

2ND 34004 *Yeovil* leaves Euston piloting 46159 *The Royal Air force* on the 5.5pm to Holyhead as far as Crewe, and works the 9.25am Crewe – Perth next day. 34004 will commence its Interchange Trials, Perth – Inverness, next week.

7 K 2-6-0 32343 heads the 6.15am Brighton – London Bridge, a class rarely seen on business trains.

11 Sunday excursion from Cheltenham (St James) to Weston-super-Mare consists of ten LMS coaches hauled both ways by Compound 41058. Possibly the first time an LMS loco has been seen in St James.

14 As a trial, Ivatt 2-6-0 43018 works express freight between King's Cross (Goods) and Peterborough. 43011 is sent to Stratford for similar trails.

15 Non-stop 'Flying Scotsman' stops at Pilmoor for crews to change over as the corridor tender of 60033 *Seagull* had jammed.

17,18 34004 *Yeovil* works the 8.55am Perth – Euston unassisted to Carlisle, and as pilot to 46163 *Civil Service Rifleman* as far as Crewe. Then heads the 5am Crewe – Euston (solo) before transferring back to the SR next day.

20 34065 *Hurricane* catches fire at Rochester on the 5.15pm Cannon Street to Ramsgate. Chatham fire brigade called out and two fire officers ride the footplate to Gillingham, as the cab floor had been set alight.

20-23 To mark the centenary of Robert Stephenson's tubular bridge at Conway, LNW 2-2-2 *Cornwall* of 1847, LNW 2-4-0 *Hardwicke* of 1874, the replica *Rocket* and Queen Adelaide's saloon of 1842 are exhibited at Conway.

21 The last 'Claughton' 4-6-0 46004 reaches Huddersfield on the 10.50am Copley Hill – Crewe goods, an engine type not seen here since 1941.

26 62667 *Somme* surprisingly brings the 'South Yorkshireman' into Marylebone.

27	E4 0-6-2T 32514 works a 4-coach troop special between Kemp Town station and Brighton. Kemp Town has been closed to passenger traffic since 1932.
31	0-6-0PT 9601 (coupled inside!) assists 6027 *King Richard I* from Castle Cary over Bruton bank, and perhaps further. A most unusual double-header.

AUGUST 1948

2ND	700 class 0-6-0 30690 works from Three Bridges into Tunbridge Wells West, an almost unknown class here.
12-15	George Stephenson died at Chesterfield on 12 August 1848. This centenary is marked by an exhibition, and the following are on display; MR 4-2-2 118, MR 2-4-0 158A, L&M *Lion*, the replica *Rocket*, 61058, D10 62658 *Prince George* and the newly-named 45529 *Stephenson*, all at Market Street station.
15	A similar Memorial display is held at Manors station, which includes a 2-6-4T built for the Burma Railway by Robert Stephenson & Hawthorn Ltd in Newcastle during 1948, plus 60016 *Silver King*, 60036 *Colombo*, A2/3 60512 *Steady Aim*, 61100, L1 2-6-4T 67728 and other rolling stock.
13-16	Flooding in the Borders causes the 'Aberdonian' to be five hours late into King's Cross (13th). Extensive damage to track between Berwick and Edinburgh requires diversions, and the up 'Queen of Scots' arrives in Carlisle (from Carstairs) behind 61116 (Eastfield) (14th). On the 14th, 16th the up and down 'Flying Scotsman' is run via Selby, Leeds, Settle & Carlisle, Carstairs to reach Waverley. Down train reaches Carlisle behind 60964 (14th), 60025 *Falcon* on 16th. Aberdeen fish trains run via Carlisle, Rugby, Northampton, Bedford and Hitchin to reach King's Cross (Goods).
28	61180, 61336 appear at Troon, both with 12-coach specials from Kirkintilloch. First B1s seen on the Ayrshire coast.
U/D	Extended service runs on the Bisley branch for the Olympic Games. Through cheap tickets from Waterloo are advertised on a 'Small Bore Train' poster.
U/D	(29 April-26 August) The Thursdays-only 6pm Watford – Clapham Junction and 10.38pm return, runs in connection with the Wembley Speedway meetings, which are held at Wimbledon instead of Wembley, due to the Olympic Games.

SEPTEMBER 1948

2ND	J15 0-6-0 65448 works the up 'East Anglian' through Stratford complete with headboard on the smokebox lamp bracket, having taken over at Chelmsford.
6	F4 2-4-2Ts 67151, 67164 work the light railway between Fraserburgh and St Combs, equipped with cow-catchers back and front, essential on this line.
6,7	62657 *Sir Berkeley Sheffield* is noted passing through Sudbury & Harrow Road on the return empty milk tanks for Dorrington.
9	C2X 0-6-0 32547 heads the 1.50pm Tunbridge Wells West – Eastbourne, a rare class to be seen on a passenger turn.
22	S15 4-6-0 30842 is sent from Exmouth Junction to Newton Abbot for weighing, a type that not often reaches here.
23-27	The Duke of Sutherland's private saloon (from Dunrobin, north of Inverness) arrives at Willesden Junction in an ECS train from Euston (23rd) and proceeds to Marylebone for

storage in the carriage shed (with LNER beaver-tail coach). Four days later the saloon is viewed at Marylebone by Railway Executive members, thence to Neasden carriage sidings.

U/D   'Crab' 42865 is unusual power for the 'South Yorkshireman' between Bradford (Exchange) and Sheffield (Victoria).

U/D   A B12 4-6-0 unexpectedly reaches Leicester (Midland) on a Birmingham train from Yarmouth. Engines are normally changed well before here.

U/D   (winter timetable) New service between Cleethorpes, Birmingham is worked by ER B1s throughout. This is the first working of an LNER-type engine over the level crossing with the East Coast main line at Newark, and first regular working of ER locos into New Street.

U/D   SEC Royal Saloon 7930 is sold for use as a bungalow. Pullman Car Works at Preston Park are to carry out the conversion.

OCTOBER 1948

8TH   An N7 0-6-2T works along the Felixstowe branch from Ipswich, the first to do so since evacuation specials from London, 2 September 1939.

9   3.42pm Liverpool Street – St Ives unusually arrives at Cambridge with 61621 *Hatfield House* piloting streamlined 61659 *East Anglian*. The pilot is detached, 61659 works to destination. (Only two B17s are streamlined, 61670 *City of London* being the other, both specially converted in the 1930s to haul the 'East Anglian' express between London and Norwich.)

14   The 'Master Cutler' exits Marylebone behind double-headed B1s on 14 coaches, traffic being swollen by the Motor Show at Earls Court.

19   Rugby Locomotive Testing Station is opened by the Minister of Transport, the Rt Hon. Alfred Barnes. 60007 *Sir Nigel Gresley* is put through its paces 'on the rollers' for the benefit of those present and in honour of the late Sir Nigel Gresley who inspired the project.

28   An A4 Pacific hauls the 5.15pm semi-fast, Sheffield (Victoria) – Doncaster. A4s rarely venture to Sheffield.

30   'Saint' 4-6-0 2937 *Clevedon Court* and 6905 *Claughton Hall* both reach Bromsgrove with football excursions from Hereford. (Last previous visit of a GWR engine was that of 'Star' 4021 *British Monarch* in 1942).

U/D   SR coach 3773 in spotless malachite green stands in the sidings at…Melton Constable, of all unexpected places.

U/D   During the course of the month, both 30928 *Stowe* and 30929 *Malvern* work boat trains between Victoria and Newhaven – first time on record for the 'Schools' class to be diagrammed to this task.

U/D   Q1 0-8-0Ts 69925/7 surprisingly appear at Cowlairs for banking duties out of Queen Street, up the 1 in 42 out of the station. (On loan from Frodingham, not an obvious transfer).

U/D   The East Coast main line, which had been blocked by landslides and bridge damage between Berwick, Dunbar since 12 August re-opens; to freight 25 October, to passengers 1 November. Numerous speed restrictions apply over repaired sections, which include seven temporary bridges.

NOVEMBER 1948

6TH   34049 *Anti-Aircraft Command* heads a football special (to Bristol) between Bournemouth, Bath over the S&D line. First Pacific seen on this route.

9   4.23pm Sidmouth – Exeter (Central), usually two coaches, puzzlingly consists of; brake 3rd/corridor 3rd/two new Restaurant Cars/'Devon Belle' observation car, all hauled by M7 0-4-4Ts 30025/124.

11   Newly-built L1 2-6-4T 67733 powers the 12.5pm Waverley – Dunbar. Others later follow this route south to take up their allocations.

16   7007 *Great Western* + WR coaching stock make a special test run from Plymouth (North Road) to Devonport (SR) as a preliminary to a Royal visit.

20   Further new L1s 67735/6/7, from North British Locomotive Works, are run-in from Hamilton depot and are seen working into Glasgow (Central).

28   Down 'Golden Arrow' is diverted from Victoria, via Clapham Junction to Redhill, due to Sevenoaks tunnel being close for repairs. 5 December also.

U/D   'Pug' 0-4-0ST 56027 (used for quarry shunting at Trench Crossing) is housed at Wellington shed, the only Caledonian Railway engine allocated to a GWR depot.

DECEMBER 1948

7TH   St Margarets shed (Edinburgh) is allocated LMS 4-4-0 40666 from Carstairs to work local goods trains to Berwick and act as station pilot at Dunbar. A surprising move, since 40666 is the only one of its type at this depot.

20   46201 *Princess Elizabeth* is exhibited at Marylebone, painted black and lined red/cream/grey, with a 'Lion & Wheel' emblem on the tender. 46201 is coupled to 11 coaches, three of which are light red, others maroon, all for inspection by the Railway Executive.

24   Up Leeds express departs from Hitchin behind C1 4-4-2 62881 on 14 coaches for King's Cross, the Atlantic having replaced ailing 60917, and providing quite a sight on entering the terminus.

24   6913 *Levens Hall* is surprise WR power for the 2.35pm Plymouth (Friary) to Exeter (Central) SR service, and the 7.30pm return working.

28   Up 'Royal Scot' is diverted between Glasgow and Carlisle via Kilmarnock, due to a blockage at Cambuslang, adding interest to the journey.

U/D   New England – Darnall freight working has, surprisingly, the unique K1/1 2-6-0 61997 *MacCailin Mor* (Eastfield) as power.

JANUARY 1949

3RD   4.45pm ex-Leeds reaches King's Cross behind 61099 piloting 60014 *Silver Link,* the B1 being attached at Hitchin. An unusual pairing.

8   48003 seen at Dunkeld with a down Highland line freight, rare class here.

9   Liverpool (Central) closed due to engineering works at Brunswick. This brings D9 4-4-0s 62301/7/15 into Lime Street on diverted trains, where LNER locos are rarely seen.

10   Railway Executive inspects proposed new liveries at Kensington Addison Road;
   30853 *Sir Richard Grenville* in malachite green
   5067 *St. Fagans Castle* in GWR lined green
   46201 *Princess Elizabeth* in black, lined red/cream/grey
   46244 *King George VI* in 'Coronation' blue
plus LMS coaches in carmine & cream.

16   11.55pm Plymouth – Paddington sets off behind 6000 *King George V* + 6020 *King Henry IV* double-heading, a combination recently thought to be absolutely prohibited!

25   7.37am Didcot – Southampton (Terminus) is hauled by 0-6-0PT 5750, the first pannier tank to be seen in Southampton.

29   Down 'Flying Scotsman' is *cancelled* – an extremely rare event – due to a collision in dense fog at Holloway.

FEBRUARY 1949

7ᵀᴴ   Stanier 2-6-2T 40140 undergoes trials between Peterborough and Grantham on the 6.38pm, returning with ECS. 40180 repeats these trials next week.

13   Five GWR 0-6-0PTs are seen either in Crewe Works or around the yard, including 2127 (from Taunton!).

16   5962 *Wantage Hall* + GWR brake van tours the Aston area of Birmingham on clearance trials and visits Windsor Street Goods Depot.

22   V1 2-6-2T 67668 works the 6.50am Liverpool Street – Ipswich, a type not seen on these trains before.

26   GWR railcar W13W operates a special excursion from Swansea to Bristol, most unusual.

27   Kittybrewster shed hosts locos from five pre-Grouping Companies. NBR represented by D31, J36 classes; MR by 4-4-0s, NER by J72, GER by B12, F4 classes and GNS by D40, D41.

U/D   WD 2-10-0s arrive at Willesden from store on the SR before working north to their new allocations in Scotland.

MARCH 1949

1ˢᵀ- 26ᵀᴴ   Activity at Dunkeld, Highland main line: 90071 passes north and south on goods, J37 0-6-0 64536 heads up freight (1ˢᵗ); WD 2-10-0 90774 takes a down freight on 5ᵗʰ and returns light on the 6ᵗʰ; J38 0-6-0 65921 heads north on freight and 42833 (12A) passes south, light engine (19ᵗʰ); J35 0-6-0 64523, 90228 both seen on down freights and 64536 (again), 90149 both travel south on the 26ᵗʰ. All unusual workings on this line!

5   U1 2-6-0 31891 powers a Brighton – Watford football special throughout.

7   46126 *Royal Army Service Corps* (specially cleaned) is filmed at Willesden shed for Pinewood Studios' picture *Train of Events*.

7   U1 2-8-8-2T Beyer-Garratt 69999 arrives at Bromsgrove for Lickey incline banking trials, vacating its usual haunt on the Worsborough bank.

12   'Wemyss Bay' 4-6-4T 55352 (68D Beattock) heads the 1.50pm Muirkirk to Ayr, running-in after repair at Kilmarnock Works.

16   2.20pm New Street – Worcester is double-headed by 3P 4-4-0s 40758 + 40745 in a spectacle reminiscent of twenty years ago.

18   Three WD 2-10-0s are noted at Redhill *en route* from the Longmoor Military Railway to Pluckley, near Ashford (Kent).

U/D   8am Yarmouth (South Town) – Liverpool Street (and 3.44pm return workings) are seen several times hauled throughout by D16 4-4-0 62517 with the 'chocolate & cream' set of the 1948 experimental colour scheme.

APRIL 1949

15TH   2-6-2T 6123 (Slough) works a Good Friday Paddington – Birmingham special, a very rare if not unique, class to visit Snow Hill.

18   The 'Flying Scotsman' arrives into King's Cross behind N2 0-6-2T 69582 (bunker first) after 60097 *Humorist* had failed at Hatfield.

19   N 2-6-0 31865 heads the 6.10am Newhaven – Victoria and the 9.5am return working, a rare appearance on boat trains for this class.

20   0-6-0PT 2079 runs light all the way from Tyseley to Derby Works for repair.

22   The green-liveried Liverpool Street pilot J69 0-6-0T 68619 is pressed into service on a rush-hour train to Chingford.

26   D16 4-4-0 62531 arrives at Oxford with a train from Bletchley, an experimental working for an ER passenger engine to reach WR territory.

27   34059 *Sir Archibald Sinclair* is sent on loan to Stratford depot from Nine Elms and works test trains to Witham on the next two days.

U/D   An E4 2-4-0 has a one-week trial on Cambridge – Kettering passenger services. ER engines do not normally work onto the Midland main line.

MAY 1949

1ST   For a weekend excursion to the Channel Islands the Waterloo – Weymouth route is used. Previously all this traffic had been handled by the GWR/WR.

1   4902 *Aldenham Hall,* 4958 *Priory Hall* both work into Bournemouth (Central) with excursions from Oxford, Acton respectively. Unusual arrivals.

2   5.8pm arrival from Norwich reaches Liverpool Street – amazingly – behind O2 2-8-0 63959 (March), as 8-coupled engines are thought to be banned from Bethnal Green Bank.

3,4,5   2-6-4T 42689 (66A), on loan to the GNS Section, works the Aberdeen to Keith line and the Ballater, Peterhead branches on a trial basis.

11   C1 4-4-2 62881 runs light through Wood Green, reaches Palace Gates yard, and two days later goes to Stratford, the first and last Atlantic scrapped here.

15   'Crab' 42812 unexpectedly reaches Southend, on a special from Reading.

15   Hull (Paragon) rolling stock exhibition includes 60121 *Silurian* and 60534 *Irish Elegance,* A1 and A2 Pacifics are rarely seen here.

18   34059 *Sir Archibald Sinclair* heads the 'Norfolkman', Liverpool Street to Norwich and back, near the end of its trial period.

21   Peterborough Arts Week puts on an exhibition of rolling stock that includes LNER diesel shunter 8000, GNR Atlantic 251 (from York Museum) and a former 'Coronation' beaver-tail observation car.

23   (week ending) LMS diesel units 10000/1 work as a pair on the Midland main line before transferring to the Western Division of the LMR.

23   (from) The 'West Riding' now contains three articulated twins from the pre-war 'West Riding Limited' streamlined train, repainted in carmine & cream.

24   Q6 0-8-0 63415 works a special freight between Darlington and Eckington & Renishaw, using the Midland main line from Rotherham (Masborough), an extremely rare class to be seen in these parts.

28   E5 0-6-2T 32404 heads the 9.36am Southampton (Terminus) – Winchester (Chesil). First
        E5 to visit Southampton?

U/D   Ivatt 2-6-0 43036 (22A) works from Bath to Bournemouth (West) and a 'Crab' heads the
        'Pines Express' over the S&D, both most unusual.

U/D   61514 hauls a 9-car Shenfield EMU to Liverpool Street for inspection by Officials from
        the Railway Executive.

U/D   Eight 'Buttery' (Tavern) Cars S7892-99 painted in carmine & cream and 'brickwork'
        emerge from Eastleigh Carriage Works named as follows;

>   At the Sign of the White Horse (92)
>   At the Sign of the Jolly Tar (93)
>   At the Sign of the Dolphin (94)
>   At the Sign of the Bull (95)
>   At the Sign of the Salutation (96)
>   At the Sign of the Three Plovers (97)
>   At the Sign of the Green Man (98)
>   At the Sign of the George & Dragon (99)

JUNE 1949

1ST   LMR diesel units 10000/1 make a demonstration run on the down 'Royal Scot'. On
        arrival at Glasgow (Central) the crew are given 'film star' treatment, posing for photos
        and signing autographs!

2   L1 4-4-0 31786 works ECS from Lancing to Eastleigh, a type rare here.

4   V4 2-6-2 61700 *Bantam Cock* makes the first visit of an LNER engine to Ayr. Next week
        61701 arrives with a Sunday School excursion from Kilsyth!

6   The 'Fenman' passes Bishop's Stortford on time heading for London behind L1 2-6-4T
        67709. It is rare to entrust titled trains to tank engines.

8   6822 *Manton Grange* travels between Exeter (Central) and Templecombe on clearance
        trials, towing one coach and stopping at all stations. (Found to be too tight at both
        Chard and Sidmouth Junctions).

10   61066 (Wakefield) seen in Swindon Works yard, surprisingly.

11   B16 4-6-0 61461 takes the 'South Yorkshireman' forward from Leicester (Central) to
        Marylebone, an unusual class on express work.

14   0-6-0PT 3622 is in charge of the 10.50am Didcot – Eastleigh and back, not a type
        expected to be seen on this service.

15   Audition of whistles! Sentinel Y3 0-4-0T 68169 is rigged up at Stratford Works with a
        rack of all types of whistles to select a standard model.

18   The Lauder Light Railway (from Fountainhall), closed in August 1948 due to flooding,
        requires specialised engines of low axle loading.
        These are GER J67 0-6-0Ts 68492, 68511 – now at Galashiels – but when on the branch
        their side tanks are emptied and a tender is attached to keep the weight down.

20   Tavern car 'Dolphin', together with new Restaurant Car, enters service on the 'Master
        Cutler' between Marylebone and Sheffield (Victoria).

20   (from) Fowler 2-6-2Ts 40044, 40002 then 2-6-4T 42577 all work local trains from
        Leamington Spa into Snow Hill for a trial period, thus breaking the monopoly of GWR
        types into this station.

U/D 60959 runs through Stanley Junction tender first on a freight from Blair Atholl, where the turntable is too short for a V2 to turn.

U/D The 'Fife Coast Express' consists of five coaches from the pre-war 'Silver Jubilee' streamlined stock; twin 1581/2 and triplet 1586/7/8, now repainted in carmine & cream.

JULY 1949

2ND 60114 *W. P. Allen* reaches Rotherham on the 8.5am Newcastle – Paignton.

2 Ivatt 2-6-0 46413 (24E Blackpool), on trial on the WR, works locals from Didcot to Swindon, Reading and Oxford for two weeks.

2 C1 4-4-2 62877 makes a rare appearance for an Atlantic at Scarborough, with the 1.40pm (SO) to Sheffield as far as York.

2 62009 (new) is seen at Ayr, to general interest.

4 Ivatt 2-6-2T 41200 is loaned to Ipswich to work on the Aldburgh branch, the only engine of this type to be seen in East Anglia.

6 'Dean Goods' 0-6-0 2568 arrives in Plymouth on a fish train, an engine class not seen here for ten years or so.

9 Southbound freight passes through Dunblane double-headed by the 0-6-0 pairing of J37 64607 + 44330, most unusual.

10 A8 4-6-2T heads a return excursion from Scarborough to Jarrow via York and Darlington, rare to see this class on the main line north of York.

16 GWR railcar W12W forms a Paddington – Worcester – Droitwich chartered special to convey Stage & Screen celebrities to the Film & Theatrical Garden Party at Droitwich. Railcar also works the return trip.

16 46130 *The West Yorkshire Regiment* is surprise power for a Perth train from Buchanan Street.

18 34016 *Bodmin* runs a special trial goods train of loaded clay wagons from Exeter (Riverside) to Truro and back.

19 D20 4-4-0 62373 + B16 4-6-0 61430 double-head the 4.15pm Newcastle to Liverpool between Ripon and Leeds, an uncommon pairing.

19 D2 4-4-0 62151 reaches Marylebone with a 2-coach Railway Executive Officers' Special. Any 4-4-0 is a notable arrival at Marylebone.

24 J39 0-6-0 64860 + 90346 power a Bertram Mills Circus train between Harrogate and Leeds, returning light engines. Unusual train, and locos.

30 'Saint' 4-6-0s 2946 *Langford Court* + 2979 *Quentin Durward* double-head a Bank Holiday special from Penzance to Sheffield, between Plymouth and Newton Abbot, a rare combination nowadays.

30 2-8-0 4701 pilots 5056 *Earl of Powis* on the 9.30am Paddington – Newquay throughout, an unusual duo, especially over this distance.

AUGUST 1949

1ST T9 4-4-0 30304 works the 7.55pm Tunbridge Wells – Eastbourne, a rarity on this line, first since pre-war days.

4 An E4 2-4-0 brings the ECS of the 'East Anglian' into Liverpool Street, unusual work for this class.

5	90552 pulls the 3.28pm from Haywards Heath via Oxted into London Bridge, unexpected power!
6	45626 *Seychelles* heads a Derby – Scarborough excursion throughout. First 'Jubilee' to reach this resort?
9	No fewer than 1,200 people load onto two Sunday School specials at Leckhampton for a day trip to Weston-super-Mare and back.
15	90508 (complete with express passenger headcode!) arrives at Ipswich with an excursion to Yarmouth. (Engine replaced at Ipswich).
18	The experimental 'Leader' 0-6-6-0T 36001 hauls its first test train, from Brighton to Eastleigh.
21	L&Y 0-8-0 49500 (25D Mirfield) is spotted on shed at Carlisle (Durran Hill) looking rather out of place here.
22	L1 2-6-4T 67721 arrives at Harwich Parkeston Quay running bunker-first with the 'Day Continental' headboard on the top bracket. 67721 had replaced 61605 *Lincolnshire Regiment* at Gidea Park.
U/D	Cheap Day tickets at pre-war prices between Ipswich and Felixstowe (1s 6d return; 1s evening excursion) bring extra traffic, and two C12 4-4-2Ts 67367/85 are drafted in to help – a type not seen at Ipswich for many years.
U/D	Tavern Car 'Salutation', plus SR Restaurant Car, are included in the formation of the 12.40pm from Leeds, and the 3.50pm King's Cross – Leeds.
U/D	Tavern Cars 'White Horse' and 'Jolly Tar' are both employed on the Harwich/Lincoln/Manchester/Liverpool boat trains, accompanied by SR Restaurant Cars, bringing Eastleigh-built rolling stock to NW England on a regular basis for the first time.

SEPTEMBER 1949

1ST	First Ian Allan excursion for the 'Locospotters Club' runs from Paddington to Swindon (for the Works and shed). 6021 *King Richard II* heads the train.
3	61313 is repaired at Old Oak Common shed after failing with a Sheffield to Kent Coast through train. Few B1s reach 81A, whatever the cause!
3	Two excursions, each of ten SR coaches, are run from Baldock to Brighton. SR stock is rarely seen on the East Coast main line.
3	60525 *A. H. Peppercorn* (62B, and in olive green) surprisingly works the 12.38pm Sunderland – York.
3	Beyer-Garratt 2-6-6-2T 47997 heads a down coal train at least as far as Cheadle, a class uncommon beyond Gowhole.
5	D10 4-4-0 62657 *Sir Berkeley Sheffield* works Marylebone – High Wycombe locals, a real rarity.
6	MSWJ 2-4-0 1334 passes West Ealing, light engine on the down main line. It's some time since a 2-4-0 was in the London area on a WR route.
8,9	L&Y 0-8-0 49516 (25A) leaves Bristol with a northbound freight. LNW 0-8-0 49261 (3D Aston) works the same turn next day. 0-8-0s are usually very rare in Bristol!
10	WD 2-10-0 90757 appears at Perth on, surprisingly, a local passenger train.
10	44096 is observed between Hamworthy Junction and Broadstone running towards Wimborne with six LMS coaches. What's it doing on this stretch?
13	48376 reaches Stranraer with an ammunition train for Cairnryan. 8Fs are not normally permitted west of Dumfries or south of Ayr.

17	61245 *Murray of Elibank* (64B) and V1 2-6-2T 67612 (65C Parkhead) both arrive at Sunderland with excursions for the illuminatons!
19	One of the LMR diesel units (10000 or 10001) appears on the 1.35pm 'Bon Accord' out of Buchanan Street. A unique occurrence?
21	LBSC D3 0-4-4T brings ECS for the Newhaven boat train into Victoria, a most unusual class on this duty.
24	'Stars' 4022 + 4059 *Princess Patricia* double-head the noon Gloucester to Paddington, as far as Swindon.
26	The ceremony to mark the departure of the first electric passenger train to Shenfield is performed by the Minister of Transport at Liverpool Street. Services are increased progressively to the full electric service by 7 Nov.
28-30	11.40am Liverpool (Lime Street) – New Street is headed by 46200 *The Princess Royal* three days running. A rare class to appear in Birmingham.
U/D	By turning the turntable at Liverpool (Central) the other way to normal, it has been discovered that larger engines can be turned! Hence Trafford Park Compounds can be used instead of D9s.

OCTOBER 1949

2ND	An Eccleshill – Morecambe excursion travels the single-track line through Idle to reach Shipley behind an N1 0-6-2T + B1 4-6-0. Passenger services on this GNR line ceased in 1931, Eccleshill being opened specially for this train.

8,9,16	International Timetable and Through Carriage Conference is held at the Royal Pavilion, Brighton. Special excursions for delegates are run as under;
	        8th electric 20002 + 11 Pullmans, Brighton – London Bridge (visit docks)
	        9th same formation, to Windsor & Eton Riverside (visit Castle)
	        16th same formation, to Portsmouth (visit Isle of Wight).

10	E6X 0-6-2T 32407 is used, surprisingly, on pilot duties at Victoria.
12	7901 *Dodington Hall* runs light engine Salisbury – Portsmouth for clearance tests at Harbour station.
12	61602 *Walsingham* starts vigorously from Manor Park station on a down Southend excursion, beneath a bridge. The exhaust lifts the overhead wires which rebound to hit the engine's chimney, resulting in a terrific flash!
12	10am Marylebone – Manchester (London Road) has a *loaded* cattle truck at the rear (!) - seen passing through Harrow.
13	90308 undergoes trial trips between Salisbury and Exmouth Junction each way, with 65 loaded wagons. WDs are strangers here.
23	U1 2-6-0 31910 is attached to the front of DC electric 20003 to pilot the Newhaven – Victoria boat train through floods to Lewes, but…at the last minute current is restored and this unique steam/electric combination did not actually move!
24	L1 4-4-0 31789 works the Brighton – Plymouth through to Salisbury, returning on the Cardiff – Brighton. First L1 to visit Salisbury?
27	When 60061 *Pretty Polly* fails, A5 4-6-2T 69800 steps up to work the 12.15pm Marylebone – Manchester to Leicester, losing only 11 minutes.
29	90533 is seen, most unusually, on ECS duties at Cannon Street.
29	44417 works through to Boscombe (to/from Templecombe) on a football special from

Paignton for the Bournemouth v Torquay match. S&D engines rarely venture (even slightly) beyond their own patch.

U/D   Early Sunday morning Epping – Ongar through trains to Liverpool Street are worked by push/pull fitted F5 2-4-2Ts 67193/200/202/203, the first such trains in/out of this terminus on a regular service.

U/D   Blackpool Illuminations (first since 1939) attract no less than 909 specials over the period mid-September to late October.

NOVEMBER 1949

2ND   Since April, 16 GWR 0-6-0PTs have been repaired at Derby Works.

2   48055 (19C Canklow) appears on Haymarket (64B) shed, far from home!

2   SR double-deck electric multiple units (sets 4001/2) enter regular service.

8   Queen Victoria's Royal Saloon arrives at Leicester on the rear of the 5.50pm Manchester (Central) – St Pancras, and is then transferred to the 9.20pm local to Rugby. Vehicle is in transit to Wolverton works.

12   61512 (in LNER green) arrives at Harrow & Wealdstone on a football special from Colchester, the B12 arousing much public comment.

24   61729 (65C Parkhead!) noted at Finsbury Park after working south with a train that is moving an entire farm from the Glasgow area to the Fens.

25   34092 is named *Wells* at that City, though the trackbed of the S&D route from Templecombe to Glastonbury and Wells has to be strengthened in several places for the engine to reach Wells safely!

29   60065 *Knight of Thistle* (64A) in immaculate blue, passes Nottingham (Victoria) on an up coal train – an Edinburgh Pacific is an extreme rarity!

U/D   T9 4-4-0 arrives at Tavistock on an Officer's special comprising generator car, brake composite, Sleeping Car, Refreshment Car and saloon, a surprising formation. Train is berthed overnight and leaves for Plymouth next day.

U/D   WD 2-10-0s 90773, 90774 both carry the same name *North British*, after the manufacturer. (*As later does 60161, after the Railway Company*). 90732 bears the name *Vulcan*, after the builder, Vulcan Foundry. (*As later does 70024, after the god.*)

DECEMBER 1949

3RD   'Crab' 42812 (1A) heads a Watford – Brighton football special of ten LMS coaches throughout. First complete 'LMS' train to reach Brighton.

9   C15 4-4-2T 67464 (64E Polmont) works ECS into Edinburgh (Princes Street) instead of the usual local engine of LMS origin.

15   J39 0-6-0s 64732, 64918/66 arrive at Cricklewood for trials, the latter soon reaching Stewarts Lane on a cross-London freight.

16   90228 passes Prestwick on an up freight, the first WD noted here.

17   46227 *Duchess of Devonshire* (66A) uses the wheel-drop facility across Glasgow at Eastfield depot.

19   60121 *Silurian* arrives at Sheffield (Midland) on a special parcels train from York and turns on the Dore & Totley triangle.

24   'Flying Scotsman' retimed (this day only) to leave at 10.5am, breaking an 87-year old

record of departing at 10am (other than in emergency/war situations). Special Christmas traffic arrangement is the cause.

28   10.5am Eastbourne – Brighton is hauled by I3 4-6-2T 32086 on an 11-coach train. Stops at Lewes for assistance and is banked in the rear by K 2-6-0 32347 right through to Brighton. Unheard of!

U/D   D16 4-4-0 62535 is loaned from the Eastern Region to Trafford Park for Cheshire Lines work.

U/D   V1,V3 2-6-2Ts work between Middlesbrough and Scarborough, prohibited from this line until recently. These engines have only been seen once before, at Scarborough in 1946.

U/D   New 0-6-0PT 1608 is acquired by Penzance for a few days whilst 0-6-0PT 2148 has a snowplough fitted for work on the Princetown branch.

U/D   The four 'Tilbury' 4-4-2Ts 41971-74 stored at Carlisle (Durran Hill) for nearly 18 months are transferred to Skipton (on paper, 19/6/48) but haven't moved an inch!

JANUARY 1950

7TH   FA Cup match brings 61198, 61289 (both 51A) to New Street for the Aston Villa v Middlesbrough game. B1s go to Bournville for servicing. Also 61079 (40B) works through to Luton from Cleethorpes for a similar occasion, Luton Town v Grimsby Town.

12   J39 0-6-0 64732 leaves St Pancras with a boat train for Tilbury docks.

12   Due to a last-minute change in sailing arrangements, 30765 *Sir Gareth* heads an Ocean Liner Express from Waterloo round to Victoria Docks London, rather than the usual embarkation point of Southampton.

12   30857 *Lord Howe* takes a football special for the Norwich v Portsmouth FA Cup replay through to Tottenham, where an ER loco takes over.

14   Brown-Boveri gas turbine A1A-A1A 18000 leaves Switzerland for Harwich, arriving there on 4 February.

20   5.11pm St Enoch to Beith overruns Beith station and the buffer stops 100yd beyond, and crosses the main road (!) before stopping. All the passengers are unhurt, but re-railing 2-6-4T 42194 (67A) proves difficult!

28   4-6-0 61434 hauls the 2.55pm Retford – Lincoln. First time a B16 has been seen on local passenger services in this area.

28   L&Y 2-4-2T 50622 (20E Manningham) and L&Y 0-6-0 52252 (20C Royston) appear together on Heaton Mersey (9F) shed. First 2-4-2T here for 25 years or so.

U/D   45650 *Blake* (14B Kentish Town!) is a surprise arrival in Chester (Northgate) on the 5.8pm from Manchester (Central).

FEBRUARY 1950

4TH   2-6-2T 6129 is, amazingly, found under repair at 34A! (Neasden engine sub-shedded at Aylesbury.)

4   Last of the HR 'Clan' 4-6-0s 54767 *Clan Mackinnon* finds itself on St Rollox shed, *en route* to Kilmarnock Works for scrapping.

5   Imported gas turbine 18000 is hauled as far as Acton (from Harwich) by 61003 *Gazelle* and from there to Swindon by 7901 *Dodington Hall*.

6   N7 0-6-2T 69689 noted on station pilot duties at King's Cross, unusually.

6   60048 *Doncaster* arrives in Manchester (London Road) on the 7.35am from Leicester (Central). A3s rarely work north of Sheffield.

7   7908 *Henshall Hall* works a trainload of 28 prefabricated schools destined for Australia, from Weston-super-Mare to Avonmouth docks.

15   10.35am arrival at Paddington from Fishguard comes in behind 2-6-2T 6132 piloting 0-6-0PT 3681. 4091 *Dudley Castle* had failed at Maidenhead, 3681 hauled the train solo to Slough, with 6132 onwards.

16   60121 *Silurian* is noted at Normanton with a brake van. Later leaves on a loaded mineral train. Most unusual for an A1 to reach here.

16,17 45516 *The Bedfordshire and Hertfordshire Regiment* runs from Willesden to Eastleigh to work a special troop train carrying its namesake Regiment from Southampton New Docks throughout to Bury St Edmunds the following day. First 'Patriot' to Southampton (or Bury!).

19,26 Polmadie (66A) hosts D11 4-4-0 62682 *Haystoun of Bucklaw* on the 19th and 61823 (64A) a week later, both waiting repair at Cowlairs.

20-23 61263 heads the 'Bon Accord' both ways between Glasgow and Perth (1.35pm ex-Buchanan Street, 6.25am ex-Aberdeen).

21   61115 is the first B1 to run between Whitby and Scarborough, on a special test train.

25   60900 (34A) is surprise power for the 5pm Bristol – York from Derby, having arrived with the 4.3pm Sheffield – Derby stopper.

26   35005 *Canadian Pacific* travels light-engine to Rugby, from Eastleigh via Willesden, the first time this class has been seen so far north on the West Coast main line.

MARCH 1950

3RD   Strange sight between Rugby and Peterborough is that of an L&Y 2-4-2T (retaining its LMS number 10897) hauling the LMS test train of No.3 dynamometer car and all three Mobile Test Units. The loco had been withdrawn from traffic in 1945 and transferred to the Testing Department.

7   Closure of Liverpool Street – Ipswich main line due to collision, results in down 'Day Continental' and 'Scandinavian' boat trains to Harwich running as one train behind 61645 *The Suffolk Regiment*. This passes Ipswich in the UP direction, having travelled via Bury St Edmunds. The up 'East Anglian' is diverted via Cambridge, both most unusual workings.

8,16 35005 *Canadian Pacific* works the LMS test train of dynamometer car No.3 and two Mobile Test Units from Rugby to Willesden and back. Travels south to Stewarts Lane with No.3 and all three MTUs (16th).

16   62039 makes a debut appearance for this class on the M&GN section by working between South Lynn and Melton Constable.

20,21 Duke of Sutherland's 0-4-4T *Dunrobin* and 4-wheeled private saloon leave Golspie for the Romney, Hythe & Dymchurch Railway, reaching Perth via the Highland main line. Departs Perth on 21st with Captain Howey (RH&D Chairman) on the footplate, as far as Carlisle, reached at 4.55pm.

24   Special train from Liverpool to Newbury (one coach, one horse-box) is worked throughout by Compound 41124 (7C Holyhead).

25   Excursion train for the Grand National is run from Newcastle to Aintree utilising the 'Tees-Tyne Pullman' set of coaches.

26 Works shunter at Crewe is CR 'Pug' 0-4-0ST 56032 still wearing a 31E, (LMS code for Dawsholm) shedplate.

26 61651 *Derby County* runs into Marylebone with the 9am from Woodford Halse, a 6-coach non-corridor set. B17s are rare at this terminus.

22-31 35005 *Canadian Pacific* conducts test runs between Stewarts Lane and Salisbury with the LMS test train to evaluate its mechanical stoker.

30 3-cylinder 2-6-4T 42532 (33A) passes Bedford, southbound, light-engine, returning from Derby Works *en route* to the London, Tilbury & Southend, these engines normally being confined to this line.

APRIL 1950

1ST Stanier 0-4-4T 41900 (22B) – the Tewkesbury branch engine – works the 9.35am Ashchurch – Birmingham throughout to New Street, surprisingly.

6 (Maundy Thursday) Nine trains are booked to arrive and depart from Broad Street in an attempt to alleviate congestion at King's Cross over the Easter period, as an experiment. 61624 *Lumley Castle*, 61640 *Somerleyton Hall* both arrive here on Cambridge Buffet Car expresses.

6, 11 Compound 41058 heads a Gloucester – Manchester forces-leave special all the way. 41058 returns to Gloucester working the southbound 'Pines Express' from Manchester on the 11th, most unusual motive power.

7 4903 *Astley Hall* reaches Portsmouth on an excursion formed of LMS stock.

8 6006 *King George I* + 6020 *King Henry IV* are noted double-heading the 4.10pm Paddington – Wolverhampton out of Banbury. A rare pairing.

9 45430 visits Brighton on an excursion from Rugby (ten LMS corridors).

12 Railway Officers' special (one coach, one observation saloon) works from Liverpool Street to Southend (Central) behind 3-cyl. 2-6-4T 42532 (33A). First sighting of a Plaistow engine in Liverpool Street?

14 3P 4-4-0 40741 arrives in Bournemouth (West) on a train from Bath. First engine of this type to work over the S&D.

15 J39 0-6-0s 64901, 64954 reach Crewe from Northwich on football specials for the Cheshire Senior Cup Final, a type uncommon at Crewe.

15 34040 *Crewkerne* hauls a Brighton – Wembley Schoolboy's Cup Final special. 34084 *253 Squadron*, 34085 *501 Squadron* work two others from Canterbury and Strood respectively. First through workings of Bulleid light Pacifics from SR to LMR.

16 4958 *Priory Hall* (81A) heads an Acton – Bournemouth excursion throughout. Old Oak Common engines rarely reach Bournemouth.

18 The BBC makes a radio broadcast from Rugby Locomotive Testing Station while 45218 is running at 70mph 'on the rollers'.

19,20 A2/2 60503 *Lord President* runs through Lutterworth northbound with four vans and a brake. 60501 *Cock o' the North* is seen at Nottingham (Victoria) on an ECS train of 17 vehicles next day. At least one of 60501/3 or A2/3 60524 *Herringbone* visits Marylebone on passenger trains, strangers here.

20 V4 2-6-2 61700 *Bantam Cock* + 44957 double-head the 'Granite City' (10am to Aberdeen) out of Buchanan Street. Another rarely seen pairing.

24 A1A-A1A gas turbine 18000 reaches Oxford on a 6-coach clearance-test train, arriving at 1.6pm and departing at 1.45pm.

U/D   D16 4-4-0s 62568/88/99 from Norwich, and 62536 from Cambridge join 62535 at Trafford Park shed. Later 62532/87 arrive from Stratford (30A) as does 62609, ex-Colchester (30E). A unique transfer of locos from East Anglia to Manchester.

MAY 1950

1ˢᵀ-6ᵀᴴ   Experimentally, Bristol (22A) 'Jubilees' handle the 7.40am Bristol to Newcastle and 8.10am Newcastle – Bristol expresses throughout and are serviced at Heaton depot. The 7.40am is worked by 45682 *Trafalgar* on 1/3/5 May, by 45569 *Tasmania* on 2 May, and by 45690 *Leander* on 4/6 May. The 8.10am has 45682 on 2/4/6 May, 45569 on 1 May and 45690 on 5 May. 61013 *Topi* and 44962 share the 8.10am on the 3ʳᵈ.

1   The 'Master Cutler' leaves Marylebone without a guard! Train is halted at Wembley Hill until guard catches up. Now ¼ hour late 60054 *Prince of Wales* still brings the 12-coach train into Rugby a minute early!

5   46243 *City of Lancaster* works the 'Bon Accord' both ways between Buchanan Street and Perth. Unexpected class on this service.

6   60821, unusually, heads the up 5.20pm Buffet Car express out of Cambridge.

6   61294 (37C) brings the 10-coach Rugby League Cup Final special from Bradford (Exchange) into King's Cross NON-STOP, a unique performance.

13   Ivatt 2-6-2T 41200 returns to Ipswich for another summer season on the Aldburgh branch, having run light engine all the way from Bangor (?).

14   62769 *The Oakley* + 62770 *The Puckeridge* double-head a Whitby to Scarborough excursion. Consecutively numbered pairings are a rarity.

27   46209 *Princess Beatrice* is strangely employed on the 8.20pm Manchester (Mayfield) – Wilmslow, a 3-coach load!

27   Lochgorm Works contains LNER Y9 0-4-0T 68108, a most surprising transfer to Inverness.

28   Whit Sunday excursion from Kidderminster to Portsmouth is worked throughout by 5063 *Earl Baldwin*, only the third 'Castle' to arrive here.

29   North British Locomotive Company 827hp Bo-Bo diesel 10800 is delivered new to Polmadie depot (66A) in workshop grey.

U/D   J65 0-6-0Ts 68211/14 (the last examples of their class) operate as 2-4-0Ts in Ipswich docks to give more flexibility in rounding sharp curves.

U/D   V4 2-6-2 61700 *Bantam Cock* is put in charge of the 'North Briton' from Edinburgh to Glasgow, an unusual choice of locomotive.

JUNE 1950

1ˢᵀ   NBL Bo-Bo 10800 works to Ardrossan on a trial trip.

1   King and Queen visit Sherborne School and 35019 *French Line CGT* hauls the five vehicles over the 118.2 miles from Waterloo, a record distance for a non-stop run on a SR route as there are no water troughs.

1   U 2-6-0 31624 pilots 44839 between Bournemouth (West) and Bath (Green Park) on the 'Pines Express'. This is a trial run with tablet exchange apparatus fitted specially to 31624, a type new to the S&D.

2   Surprise of the month at Oxford is the visit of J11 0-6-0 64390 on the Hull to Marston sidings fish train, usually a B1 turn.

4	Sunday excursion from King's Cross to Clacton utilises the Pullman rake from the 'Queen of Scots'. N2 0-6-2Ts 69576/89 double-head the train as far as Bowes Park, with 61361/3 taking the train onwards.
4	61620 *Clumber*, 61636 *Harlaxton Manor*, both fresh from Gorton Works, reach Southport on excursion trains from Manchester, running-in.
8	A2/3 60500 *Edward Thompson* heads a southbound parcels train over the GC Sheffield – Nottingham main line.
10	L11 4-4-0 30409 double-heads T9 4-4-0 30283 on a 12-coach troop train between Bude and Exeter (Central). First L11 seen on a passenger working in this area since the war.
10	Co-Co electric 20002 catches fire in Eastbourne station. Fire brigade arrives when loco has been towed to a non-electrified siding.
17	Ivatt 2-6-0s 43017 + 43036 (both with double chimneys) are rare power to head the 10.35am (SO) Manchester – Bournemouth over the S&D.
18	62739 *The Badsworth* heads a Scarborough – Derby excursion throughout to Derby. First 'Hunt' seen here?
18	Two steam-hauled specials are run to New Brighton over the Wirral electrified lines; 2-6-4T 42455 with a 7-coach train from Chester, plus C13 4-4-2T 67428 with six coaches of very mixed origin.
18	61552 + 61539 double-head a circular tour from Aberdeen via Keith, Craigellachie, Boat of Garten, Aviemore, Perth and Forfar. B12s are rare sights on the Highland main line, and work through to Perth.
24	C4 4-4-2 62900 (40F) is an unexpected arrival at Sheffield (Victoria).
26	V1 2-6-2T 67607 (64A) comes into Scarborough with a train from Middlesbrough. Edinburgh tank engines should not reach this resort!
30	60003 *Andrew K. McCosh* fails on the up 'Capitals Limited' at Hitchin. 61850 takes its place – a first for a K3 – for the run up to King's Cross.
U/D	5.35pm King's Cross – York has a vestibule fire between 2nd/3rd coaches. Communication cord pulled; passenger and guard fight blaze with extinguishers, engine driver and fireman supply buckets of water, light engine stops on slow road and uses hose to add water, fire brigade chop away smouldering wood and canvas. Delay of 26 minutes caused. (!!)
U/D	Derby Works overhauls ER J39 0-6-0s – six are in evidence plus the unique U1 2-8-8-2T Beyer-Garratt 69999 and GWR 0-6-0 diesel shunter 15100.
U/D	'Star' 4058 *Princess Augusta* painted green, acquires bright blue tender from 6022 *King Edward III*.

JULY 1950

3RD	46232 *Duchess of Montrose* (66A) works through to Liverpool (Exchange) on the 1.40pm from Glasgow. First 'Coronation' seen in Exchange.
3	Up goods leaves York with Compound 41197 + J39 0-6-0 64737 pairing!
3	2-coach push-pull service between Rhyl and Llandudno is titled 'The Welsh Dragon'. The 2-6-2T engine has a large headboard on the buffer-beam. Welcome enterprise by the Chester Division management.
2-9	60533 *Happy Knight* is on loan, New England to Annesley – a freight shed!
5	61110, 61366 haul excursions to the Royal Show at Oxford throughout from Louth,

Cleethorpes respectively.

8   2-8-0 3856 (displaying express headlamps) works a Royal Show special for the Metropolitan Police (complete with horses) from Kidlington to Kensington.

8   L&Y 0-6-0 52094 + 'Crab' 42843 strangely double-head a down express at Stockport (Edgeley) composed almost entirely of L&Y saloons.

9   An excursion from Eastbourne to Windsor is formed of 6-PUL set 3014. Rare.

11-13   60012 *Commonwealth of Australia* arrives at Polmadie depot (66A) on loan. Staff investigate the mysteries of its corridor tender. 60012 then works the 10.10pm Glasgow (Central) – Euston sleeper as far as Carlisle on 12th/13th.

13,14   60118 *Archibald Sturrock*, 60119 *Patrick Stirling*, 60123 *H. A. Ivatt* all have their nameplates unveiled by H.G. Ivatt (son of H.A. Ivatt) at a ceremony at Doncaster. 60123 then heads (14th) the 6.25am to Leeds from Sheffield (Victoria), its first working after naming. A1s are rare engines in Victoria.

15   6021 *King Richard II* is provided for the Royal train between Paddington and Exeter, and the return. Most unusual not to see a 'Castle' on these workings.

16   To celebrate 100 years of the Great Northern Railway, A1/1 60113 *Great Northern* is chosen specially to work an excursion from King's Cross to York, outwards via Lincoln and Knottingley, returning direct on the main line.

18   61164 (34E Neasden) leaves Doncaster Works equipped with a chime whistle. Reason for this is obscure, and it is replaced fairly quickly.

22   61992 (64A) appears at Ferryhill (61B). K3s are uncommon in Aberdeen.

22   Stanier 2-6-0 42926 (5B) brings a relief from Newcastle into Glasgow (Central), a type rarely seen here.

28   4-4-0 62470 *Glen Roy* unexpectedly arrives in St Enoch, with a horse-box. D34s are rarely seen here also.

28   N1 0-6-2T 69475 makes a surprise appearance in Victoria station, London.

29   The Saturdays-only Sowerby Bridge – Scarborough reaches the resort behind 61899 piloting 44288, a strange combination.

U/D   C15 4-4-2T 67474 is taken out of store and used as the Carlisle station pilot.

U/D   B16 4-6-0 61418 + a 'Jubilee' double-head the 7.54am from Worcester to York forward from Sheffield (Midland), another really odd pairing.

U/D   2-8-0s 2890, 3860 appear on five occasions working freights over the CLC line between Chester and Northwich, a first for GWR locos over this route.

U/D   LNW 0-8-0 49335 works a 12-coach express from Manchester into Llandudno Junction – on time!

AUGUST 1950

4TH   U 2-6-0 31624 (with tablet exchange apparatus), sets off from Blandford with a forces leave special for Waterloo.

5   2-8-0 4708 heads a 12-coach express up Hatton bank, rare engines in the Birmingham district.

5   N15X 4-6-0 32327 *Trevithick* works as far north as Banbury on the Bournemouth to Sheffield. 32332 *Stroudley* appears a fortnight later, same train.

6   Shortage of coaching stock results in a relief Fishguard – Paddington boat train having five Restaurant Cars in use as ordinary coaches!

7	60126 *Sir Vincent Raven* fails on the 'Northumbrian'. N2 0-6-2T 69566 (bunker first) reaches King's Cross with the headboard proudly on the bunker!
8	8.10am stopping train from Hellifield arrives at Carlisle behind CR 4-4-0 54443 (66B Motherwell!). Unique, surely?
9	61800 (40B) reaches Banbury with the up fish train for Exeter and Penzance. An uncommon type to be seen here.
9	34050 *Royal Observer Corps* hauls a special 5-car all-Pullman sight-seeing excursion (including a 'Devon Belle' observation car) from Waterloo to Waterloo via Dorking, Chichester and Southampton.
10	6017 *King Edward IV* uses the wheel-drop at the LMR depot at Barrow Road.
12	Buffet Car in the 11.15am (FSO) Queen Street – King's Cross is replaced by a twin-set of pre-war 'Coronation' stock still in two-tone blue.
19	Saturday 'Cornish Riviera' (second part, 10.35am ex-Paddington) is double-headed by clean blue 'Kings' 6023 *King Edward II* + 6010 *King Charles I* between Newton Abbot and Plymouth. Quite a sight.
19	End of Stockport Wakes week sees the 8.15am relief Newquay – Stockport arrive with six coaches behind 46220 *Coronation* (66A). First Pacific to work a train that terminates at Stockport; Polmadie engines are rare as well!
20	N 2-6-0 31812 (73A) works a ramblers' excursion from Victoria to Stonegate, continuing to Robertsbridge with the ECS, a unique occurrence.
22	60873 on the 10.15am King's Cross – Leeds fails at Grantham and is replaced by the last Ivatt C1 4-4-2 62822 (built 1905), which proceeds to keep time to Doncaster with the 15-coach, 504 ton load and goes forward unchanged to Leeds (Central). A remarkable exploit with an Atlantic!
23	'Leader' 0-6-6-0T 36001 works a test train with the ER dynamometer car from Eastleigh to Guildford. Two strange sights in one train!
24	Lewes – Hastings special of eight GWR coaches is hauled by I3 4-6-2T 32030 over the electrified route, in place of the electric loco originally planned.
26	E4 2-4-0 62789 heads the 'Holiday Camps Express' of nine coaches (from Liverpool Street and with appropriate roofboards) between Lowestoft (Central) and Gorleston on Sea, a most unexpected task for an old, modest engine.
27	45072 (8B) arrives at Whitby (Town), piloted by G5 0-4-4T 67330 from Malton, on an excursion originating in Sheffield. First '5' to Whitby?
30	D41 62246 (61C) heads a football special from Peterhead to Aberdeen. Keith 4-4-0s are rarely seen on the Buchan line.
U/D	0-6-0 52414 (84G) is still regularly employed working Hereford – Brecon trains, not territory usually associated with L&Y engines.

SEPTEMBER 1950

2ND	12.10pm Manchester (Victoria) – York includes four MR clerestories, even one in a train would be noteworthy nowadays.
4	2-8-2T 7242 is seen on the 6-coach 2.25pm Aberdare to Pontypool Road. Most unlikely engines to be employed on passenger work.
5	60112 *St. Simon* fails at Grantham on the 'West Riding' and is replaced by 61553 which takes the 14-coach express up to King's Cross unaided.

5	45509 *The Derbyshire Yeomanry* (1A) is mis-used on the 3.40pm Bletchley to Bedford (St Johns) and the 6.15pm Bletchley – Woburn Sands 2-coach push/pull set!
9	9am St Pancras – St Enoch is made up entirely of LNER stock!
9	61554 (35B) arrives at Scarborough with an excursion from Grantham. Only the second B12 to visit the resort (last was in 1938/9).
10	44218 appears on Grantham shed for repairs. First known loco of this type seen here, sent from Peterborough due to labour shortage there.
16	'Saint' 4-6-0s 2920 *St. David* + 2937 *Clevedon Court* double-head a ½ day excursion from Hereford to Bournville via Droitwich Spa, banked up the Lickey incline by 'Big Bertha' 0-10-0 58100. First recorded GWR engines up the bank.
17	90172 crashes tender-first through Marsh Lane Goods depot (Leeds), having 'run away' from Neville Hill shed, without crew. Tender drops twenty feet onto the road. Engine rests at 45 degrees to depot wall and road.
17	34067 *Tangmere* heads a Victoria – Lenham ramblers' special via Crystal Palace. First time since the war that Maidstone (East) – Ashford line has been used for these excursions, and first known instance of a Pacific on the Crystal Palace line.
23	Ivatt 2-6-2T 41272 (the 7,000th Crewe-built engine) works the Bedford to Hitchin push/pull train, a first. Much interest is shown by Hitchin staff.
24	Q1 0-6-0 33013 noted in Stratford shed (30A). SR visitors are uncommon.
28	CR 'Jumbo' 0-6-0 57389 (66A) heads a PW train at Kittybrewster, presumably running-in after repair at Inverurie Works.
30	Crewe North shed (5A) surprisingly houses 'Star' 4040 *Queen Boadicea*.
U/D	34030 *Watersmeet* pilots an unidentified 'Merchant Navy' on the 1pm from Waterloo, at Yeovil Junction. A rare pairing.
U/D	E4 2-4-0 62791 heads the 12.53pm (SO) Liverpool St – Malden (East), which is non-stop to Shenfield. An 1896-vintage engine on a passenger train alongside the Shenfield electrics!

OCTOBER 1950

1ST	London Transport 0-6-0T L30 noted at Wimbledon sorting sidings, where it had been employed on bridge renewal work. A rare visit to BR tracks.
1	34040 *Crewkerne* runs northbound through Bushey tender-first and returns ½ hour later (from Watford Junction) with SR ECS bound for Wembley, in connection with the Catholic Centenary celebrations.
2	61353 (61B) runs solo from Darlington Works to the Locomotive Testing Station at Rugby for a stint 'on the rollers'.
5	Twin diesels 10000/1, for the first time, head 'The Mid-day Scot' between Euston and Carlisle (rather than 'The Royal Scot'), reaching Carlisle in a net time of 4hr 49min.
10	The 'Flying Scotsman' arrives in King's Cross behind L1 2-6-4T 67743, substituting for 60002 *Sir Murrough Wilson,* removed at Gifford.
14/15	61288 (50A) works a Scarborough – Blackpool illuminations special throughout and returns to Scarborough at 4.57am next day.
15	No fewer than fourteen ER J39 0-6-0s are seen at Derby Works for repair.
22	61513 is a surprise occupant of Ferryhill shed (61B), Aberdeen. Engines with GNS-section allocations rarely cross the city.

28   Crewe North depot contains 60012 *Commonwealth of Australia* which had worked in from Glasgow up the West Coast main line.

30   CR 'Pug' 0-4-0ST 56027 is despatched from Wellington (Salop) under its own steam to Crewe, *en route* to Preston (10B) for work in the docks.

U/D   Work starts to convert the line between Lancaster, Morecambe and Heysham from 6600 volt, 25 cycle single-phase AC (introduced in 1908 by the MR) to 1500 volts DC system (overhead), the new standard for further electrification. Stanier 0-4-4Ts 41900/02 are drafted to Lancaster to provide a temporary push/pull service.

U/D   Blackpool Illuminations this year see the arrival of 723 excursion trains between 15 September and 23 October, 388 ex-LMR plus 335 from other regions.

NOVEMBER 1950

2ND   'Leader' 0-6-6-0T 36001 performs its last and heaviest trials between Eastleigh and Woking with a 15-coach test train of 480 tons (including the ER dynamometer car). Test curtailed at Basingstoke, and 36001 retires to Eastleigh to await a decision on its future.

7-14 NBL 827hp Bo-Bo diesel 10800 works a demonstration run from Euston to Watford. Then on view at BTH, Rugby (8th-12th); back to London on 14th.

13   The 'Master Cutler' leaves Marylebone behind L1 2-6-4T 67785. Engine loses 45min on schedule before being replaced at Woodford Halse.

15   Princess Elizabeth names the last-built 'Castle' 7037 *Swindon* inside the Works. The Borough coat of arms decorates the splasher beneath the name.

16   L&Y 'Pug' 0-4-0ST 51207 (25C Goole) is observed in the formation of a goods train passing south through Wembley behind 44441.

19   61367 returns to Derby with an excursion to/from Cambridge. Not many B1s are to be seen at Derby.

19   Trials begin of Bo-Bo 1500V DC electric locos 26001/2 between Ilford and Shenfield, on both coaching stock and coal trucks. Former NER Bo-Bo electric 26510 also seen at Seven Kings with a 9-coach EMU set.

20   Fountainhall – Lauder light railway re-opens after being closed since August 1948 due to flood damage, still worked by its specialised locomotives.

24   Exceptionally, 30786 *Sir Lionel* visits Neasden on a transfer freight from Feltham. (Engine is 'officially' in store at Nine Elms (70A)).

25   Two D34 4-4-0s 62498 *Glen Moidart* + 62474 *Glen Croe* double-head the 3.46pm to Mallaig out of Queen Street. An uncommon sight nowadays.

25   'Saint' 4-6-0s 2944 *Highnam Court*, 2937 *Clevedon Court* haul two excursions for the FA Cup match between Bromsgrove Rovers and Hereford City. Engines then run light up the Lickey incline to Bournville shed, coming back to Bromsgrove about two hours later.

26   On its last run, C1 4-4-2 62822 hauls the BR-sponsored Ivatt Atlantic Special from King's Cross to Doncaster, a 9-coach train of 330 tons.

29 Oct; 5,12,19,26 Nov Track relaying between Lancaster and Preston causes diversion of the 'Ulster Express' (Heysham – Euston) through Hellifield, Bolton, Manchester (Victoria) and Stockport.

U/D   For one week, the 8.12am Liverpool Street – Cromer/Sheringham Restaurant Car express is powered by L1 2-6-4T 67789 between Ipswich and Norwich. 67788 repeats this the next week, unusual employment for tank engines.

U/D   60152 *Holyrood,* 60160 *Auld Reekie,* 60161 *North British* and 60012 *Commonwealth of Australia* all work on the West Coast main line between Glasgow (Central), Carlisle and Crewe whilst temporarily transferred to 66A (Polmadie) from 64B (Haymarket).

DECEMBER 1950

8TH   J20 0-6-0 64684 (31A) heads the Peterborough portion of the 5.52pm to Cambridge north from Hitchin. J20s rarely work passenger trains at all.

9   Fowler 2-6-4Ts 42309/46 double-head the 4.50pm New Street – Stoke, a 9-coach train running with express headlamps.

9   Fowler 2-6-2T 40040 (22B) seen shunting at Evesham bearing a 'Flying Scotsman' headboard!

10   Five-coach DEMU built by EE/BRCW for the Egyptian State Railways' service from Cairo to Alexandria, visits Worcester on a demonstration run from Birmingham via Kidderminster and Droitwich Spa.

13   A8 4-6-2T 69882 is employed on the 5.28pm 'all stations' from Leeds (City) to Ilkley via Arthington, probably the furthest west an A8 has ever travelled.

15   Former NER 1800hp 2-Co-2 electric loco 26600 is towed away for scrap behind 62058, seen at Pelaw Junction, Newcastle.

20   60135 *Madge Wildfire* reaches Sheffield (Midland) on the 7.25pm parcels from Newcastle. A1s not often seen this far south on the Midland line.

25,26   Eastbourne to Hailsham service consists of one coach, but this corridor/2nd/brake composite holds the distinction of providing neither 1st nor 3rd class accommodation! *(Only boat train stock offered 2nd class at this time, pre-empting BR's 1956 decision to rename 3rd class as 2nd).*

26,27   B16 4-6-0 61454 works the 4pm Newcastle – Birmingham through to New Street (rare here), returning next day as pilot on the 2.15pm Bristol – York.

29   K1/1 2-6-0 61997 *MacCailin Mor* (65A) + A4 60018 *Sparrow Hawk* run through Newark, southbound as a light-engine pair. An eye-catching sight.

26 Nov; 3,10 Dec 44764, fitted with the special LMS corridor tender (still in red) followed by dynamometer car No.3 and Mobile Test Unit No.1, conducts trials over the Oxford – Bletchley line. Reaches London on 10th, ex-Bletchley.

U/D   Tavern Car S7894 'At the Sign of the Dolphin' (formerly in the 'Master Cutler' set) enters Eastleigh Works for conversion, the last to do so.

U/D   (pre-Christmas) Unpainted Ashford-built 1750hp 1Co-Co1 diesel 10201 works its first trial trips between Ashford and Ramsgate on six and ten coach trains.

U/D   (Christmas period) Traffic at King's Cross reaches such confusion and congestion as has never been known before! During this period 60095 *Flamingo* (68E Carlisle Canal) sneaks into King's Cross for (probably) its first ever visit to London (21st). Another A3 rarity, 60057 *Ormonde* (64B) arrives on the 23rd.

JANUARY 1951

4TH   First BR Standard design, Pacific 70000 makes its initial trial runs between Crewe and Carlisle, then Crewe to Shrewsbury. First public outing is on the 12.50pm Crewe – Carlisle service train on the 12th, with dynamometer car.

4,17	Ashford-built 1Co-Co1 1750hp diesel 10201 arrives at Derby for a series of trials having run LE from Ashford. Returns there on 17th to receive exhibition finish in preparation for display at the Festival of Britain.

4,17 Ashford-built 1Co-Co1 1750hp diesel 10201 arrives at Derby for a series of trials having run LE from Ashford. Returns there on 17th to receive exhibition finish in preparation for display at the Festival of Britain.

5 46115 *Scots Guardsman* appears at Kidderminster (first 'Royal Scot' here?) with the Liverpool – Plymouth, diverted via Wolverhampton and Worcester.

6 46121 *Highland Light Infantry* (66A) heads a Coventry – Sunderland excursion as far as York. First Polmadie engine to reach York?

6 Boothferry Park Halt (for Hull City FC ground) – a new halt – opens for the day of the FA Cup tie with Everton. Shuttle service from Paragon brings 5,000 people at 6*d* return in four sets of suburban stock (labelled 'Potters Bar') brought specially from London.

8 61657 *Doncaster Rovers* heads the 6.20pm local from Nottingham (Victoria) to Northampton, first LNER loco seen here for six years.

8 44991 + 45122 double-head a football special from Inverness throughout to Aberdeen, first '5's east of Elgin since nationalisation.

9 'Fell' 2000hp diesel-mechanical 4-8-4 10100 makes trial runs from Derby.

20 BBC broadcasts the recording made last December at the Rugby Testing Station whilst 44862 was 'on the rollers'.

30 70000 is named *Britannia* by Sir Eustace Missenden (Chairman of the Railway Executive) at a ceremony at Marylebone station. 45700 loses its name *Britannia* – to be replaced by *Amethyst* in September.

U/D 'Campaign to save coal' results in Worcester – Honeybourne/Kidderminster services (Saturdays only) being cancelled. These are worked by diesel railcars!

U/D J10 0-6-0 65160 (9F Heaton Mersey) works a freight from Walton through to…Skipton! Not a type seen here before (or expected!).

U/D J37 0-6-0 64570 pilots 60535 *Hornet's Beauty* out of Queen Street on the up 'North Briton'. As odd a combination as you'll find!

U/D LMS Garratts occasionally reach Over Junction (near Gloucester) on the GW line to South Wales, well off their beaten track.

FEBRUARY 1951

2ND 6000 *King George V* heads the Plymouth – Liverpool between Bristol and Shrewsbury. First 'official' working of a 'King' through the Severn Tunnel. (Trial runs had been made previously).

2 6.40pm Eastbourne – Polegate freight is inadvertently diverted into the Eastbourne engine shed, colliding violently with two locos standing at the water columns. These two, plus the C2X 0-6-0 32543 + 2-6-4T 42074 double-heading the freight, are badly damaged.

3 34019 *Bideford* works a 9-coach special from Torrington to Exeter (Central) and the 11.20pm return. Rare use of a Pacific to Torrington.

3 Scotland v Wales Rugby International produces 18 specials into Princes Street and one into Waverley. This is brought in by the extraordinary pairing of D31 4-4-0 62281 piloting 60530 *Sayajirao* having traversed the Waverley route from Carlisle.

11 60810 arrives in Derby with the 6.30pm from Sheffield and returns on the 11.30pm to York. V2s do not normally reach Derby, to put it mildly.

17 60081 *Shotover* pilots 90098 on the 11.30am freight out of Neville Hill yards (Leeds), another extraordinary combination.

17-19	3.46pm Queen Street – Mallaig with 61784 + 61764 *Loch Arkaig* becomes stuck in a 15-foot snowdrift at Corrour, is stranded for 28 hours and reaches Fort William at 1am on Monday (19th). The rescue train sent out on Sunday afternoon is also snowbound on Rannoch Moor and not released until Monday morning.
18	L&Y 0-4-0STs 51207 (25C Goole), 51253 (27A Bank Hall) are noted on Bow shed, both on loan to Bromley Gas Works, and appearing rather lost.
18	Bo-Bo electric 26020 (brand new, with chromium handrails) is towed from Gorton to Neasden then Charing Cross, finally arriving at the Festival of Britain site. 1Co-Co1 diesel 10201 is already there.
22	Northbound goods train suffers engine failure near Bushey. Loco is removed, and a 'Royal Scot' 4-6-0 on the following Euston – Manchester express buffers-up to the engine-less freight train and pushes this, and pulls its own 15-coach load towards Watford Junction.
24	W 2-6-4T 31923 observed at Willesden Junction, and looks out of place here.
24	FA Cup tie special from Bristol brings 45607 *Fiji* to Newcastle. One of the other six specials includes a Sleeping Car!
27	2-6-2T 5571 works a WR engineers' inspection train Exeter – Barnstaple Jct., a 'first of kind' for the SR Ilfracombe line.
U/D	61554 (35B Grantham) comes into Leeds (Central) on a Saturday excursion. A B12 is an extreme rarity here.
U/D	Stanier 0-4-4Ts 41902/4 both work the Worth Valley branch from Keighley during January and February, a short-lived experiment.

MARCH 1951

3RD	Excursion is run for the FA Amateur Cup match between Weybridge and Bishop Auckland utilising the 'Tynesider' coaches i.e. entirely Sleeping Cars!
12	N1 0-6-2T 69442 works the Chingford branch – unprecedented?
14	34109 *Sir Trafford Leigh Mallory* begins a series of trials on the S&D with a view to their regular employment over this line.

15	Display of five brand new BR Mk1 coaches is put on at Marylebone:
	      3rd/corridor (TK) with roofboards 'The William Shakespeare'
	      Restaurant/1st open (RFO) with roofboards 'The Heart of Midlothian'
	      Composite/corridor (CK) with roofboards 'The Royal Wessex'
	      Brake/3rd corridor (BTK) with roofboards 'The Red Rose'

None of these named trains are running yet! Five titles are to be introduced for the Festival of Britain, these four plus 'The Merchant Venturer'. All will start on 3 May, when Festival opens. Stock removed by 2-6-2T 6129.

16	Derailment just south of Doncaster causes diversions between Retford and Doncaster via Mexborough and Sheffield. Hence a 20-coach train passes Darnall behind N4 0-6-2T 69234 piloting 60017 *Silver Fox*. Amazing!
17	45458 + 60159 *Bonnie Dundee* bring ECS into Waverley, rare pairing.
22	Forces leave extra departs Blandford for Waterloo behind 34107 *Blandford* (specially requested) which had worked the ECS from Bournemouth.
22	62039 (31B) arrives in King's Cross (where K1s are rare) ex-Cambridge.
22	60015 *Quicksilver* is a real surprise at Millhouses shed after working a Newcastle – Bristol train from York to Sheffield.

23	D16 4-4-0 62609 reaches Rowsley, arriving from Manchester (Central).
24	46223 *Princess Alice* (66A) makes a rare visit to Haymarket shed (64B) having hauled a rugby special for the Scotland v Ireland match.
26	60003 *Andrew K. McCosh* is observed at Wakefield (Kirkgate) on the 5pm Newcastle – Liverpool via York. Engines are usually changed at York!
28	LNER-liveried 61528 (61A!) creates a sensation at Waverley, with fish ex-Aberdeen.
U/D	'Coal-saving' cuts to train services made in January/February are restored for the Easter holidays (and thereafter), having saved 10,000 tons of coal per week whilst the cuts were in force.
U/D	Several A5 4-6-2Ts recently transferred to Norwich from the NER, gain temporary work on Liverpool Street – Southend turns while the Liverpool Street turntable is under repair. V1,V3 2-6-2Ts also drafted in, same purpose. These are classes not usually seen in East Anglia at all.
U/D	'Crab' 42742 is surprise power for a football special from Waverley to Kirkcaldy, a rare class in these parts.
U/D	(by 23rd) 60152 *Holyrood*, 60160 *Auld Reekie*, 60161 *North British* return to Haymarket from being on loan at Polmadie.
U/D	Good Friday. 46220 *Coronation* arrives in St Enoch – not a common class here – with a special originating in London.
30 March-14 April	D16 4-4-0 62590 (32B!) conducts clearance tests on LMR routes, including Rugby/Wellingborough/Saltley/Leicester/Derby/Birmingham. A surprising sight everywhere!

APRIL 1951

1ST	70004 *William Shakespeare* – brand new and in exhibition finish, arrives at Neasden and transfers to the Festival site at South Bank next day.
5	'Patriot' 45510 (8A) makes an unprecedented appearance on the 9.15am Buchanan Street – Dundee (West).
6	Ivatt 2-6-0 43089 works a Peterborough – King's Cross (Goods) freight train. First time for this class since 14 July 1948, when 43018 came up.
7	U 2-6-0 31893 and U1 2-6-0 31908 both reach Wembley with excursion trains of green SR stock for the Schoolboys' International football match.
9	42756, on cross-London freight, arrives at Hither Green – first 'Crab' here.
9	45506 *The Royal Pioneer Corps* is very unusual power for the 5.10pm St Enoch – Stranraer.
10	35022 *Holland America Line* travels LE to Newton Abbot for weighing.
14	60029 *Woodcock* finds itself on 38D (Staveley (GC)) shed on its way to Doncaster for repairs. It is sent via Annesley (38B) in order to test the newly-installed turntable at this depot.
17	At Stockport the northbound 'Comet' detaches two GWR coaches in full GWR livery (Special Saloon W9006 and special duties coach W7377). These vehicles convey the Queen Mother to Stoke-on-Trent for the opening of the University College of North Staffordshire.
19	61353 (61B) pilots 46159 *The Royal Air Force* on the 10.40am Euston to Carlisle from Rugby onwards. The B1 is on its way from the Rugby Testing Station to undergo further trials over the S&C main line.
21	61622 *Alnwick Castle* is a surprise choice to work ECS between Manchester (London

Road) and Longsight carriage sidings.

26   Brand new 73000 makes its public debut, exhibited at Marylebone.

28   30792 *Sir Hervis de Revel* leaves Cricklewood (where this class is rarely seen) on a coal train for Feltham.

28   60919 is uncommon power for the 'Bon Accord' from Aberdeen to Perth.

U/D   Famous 60103 *Flying Scotsman* works a York – Swansea train between Leicester (Central) and Banbury, thus meeting 'Castles' and 'Kings' at Banbury in ordinary service. 60103 returns on the Swindon – Sheffield mail.

U/D   SR Pacifics begin to reach Oxford regularly on the two through trains from Bournemouth. (First occasion was an isolated instance on 22 January 1947).

U/D   J20 0-6-0s 64678/9 both work into Feltham on cross-London freights, a class not often seen on these duties.

U/D   (March-April) Coaching stock seen in Gloucester Old Station sidings include the following veterans; two GSW 3^{rds}, one CR 12-wheeled 3rd, one North Staffordshire non-corridor, one HR corridor composite, two L&Y 'Club' cars and various LNW vehicles.

MAY 1951

1ST 61353 + 46239 *City of Chester* reach Crewe on the Windermere – Euston. 61353 is returning to Rugby again after test runs on the S&C.

6   44953 pilots the twin 1600hp diesels 10000/1 between Carstairs and Beattock summit – a rare triple-header due to generator failure on 10000.

8   M7 0-4-4T 30252 is at Taunton (first seen here) with ECS for Barnstaple.

8,9   34039 *Boscastle* (75A) arrives at Stratford (30A) on loan and works the 8.20am Liverpool Street – Cambridge next day.

10   Swedish Lloyd boat train leaves Tilbury for St Pancras behind the unexpected form of 45589 *Gwalior* (20A Leeds Holbeck!).

11   'Dukedog' 4-4-0 9022 is a surprise arrival at Crewe with an 8-coach special from Tonfanau, via Whitchurch. This class rarely reaches Crewe.

12   'Crab' 42743 is also a surprise at Arbroath, on the 12.10pm from Dundee. This class is uncommon on Scottish passenger turns, much less at Arbroath.

12   At the south end of Cambridge station, 70000 *Britannia*, an A4 Pacific and 34039 *Boscastle* are seen simultaneously. Photos please!

14   Half day 8-coach excursion leaves South Shields for Barnard Castle and Middleton-in-Teesdale, where 60801 is the first V2 seen since the war.

15   (Whit Sunday) 60900 (34A) – and King's Cross crew – work through to Scarborough unchanged, both surprised to find themselves at the seaside!

17   45683 *Hogue* + 62764 *The Garth* are a rare combination to double-head the 1.30pm York – Scarborough.

19   34073 *249 Squadron* + 34075 *264 Squadron* are noted running coupled together LE tender-first through Neasden, south from Cricklewood. Odd sight.

19   61166 (36B) heads a Newcastle – Marylebone Festival of Britain special into London. Only the second time a Mexborough B1 has reached London.

23   Exhibition for private viewing is held at Marylebone. On show are newly-built Standards 70009 *Alfred the Great*, 73001, 75000 and the 4-8-4 2000hp Fell diesel-mechanical 10100.

23,25	34065 *Hurricane* works the down 'Norfolkman' from Liverpool Street. Also the down 'Day Continental' to Harwich, and the up 'Scandinavian' on 25th.
24	New 1st class Pullman cars *Pegasus* and *Perseus* are towed through Tyseley heading for the SR and inclusion in the re-equipped 'Golden Arrow'.
26	2.56pm Fort William to Glasgow has 61344 piloting D11 4-4-0 62675 *Colonel Gardiner,* a most unusual pairing. Pilot is detached at Cowlairs.
29	60012 *Commonwealth of Australia* is on exhibition at…Ayr!
30	9.10pm arrival at St Enoch from St Pancras comes in behind double-headed Compounds 41135 + 40919, a rare sight nowadays.
30	45672 *Anson* descends to Liverpool (Riverside) with a troop train, also rare.
30	The Fell loco 10100 is unexpectedly found at Stewarts Lane (73A) depot.
U/D	2-6-4T 42689 (66B!) works the Aberdeen – Ballater branch, on a trial basis.
U/D	60151 *Midlothian* is chosen as a regular engine on the Festival train 'The Heart of Midlothian'. All five newly introduced 'Festival' titles receive brand new BR Mk 1 coaches in carmine & cream. The 'Royal Scot', 'Norfolkman' expresses are similarly re-equipped, and 'Golden Arrow' gets new Pullmans.
U/D	34039 *Boscastle*, 34057 *Biggin Hill*, 34065 *Hurricane* are loaned to Stratford. SR gain 70009 *Alfred the Great*, 70014 *Iron Duke* in return, plus 70004 *William Shakespeare* at the end of the Festival.
U/D	HM The Queen Mother and HRH Princess Margaret visit Belfast. Trains are worked throughout to Liverpool (Riverside) by '5' and 'Royal Scot' respectively.

JUNE 1951

1ST	Exhibition at Eastboune in connection with the International Union of Railways Conference sees 73001 arrive LE, 75000 towing the Fell diesel 10100 and 70009 *Alfred the Great* hauling four coaches from Battersea yard. Next day Co-Co DC electric 20001 works a Conference special (12 LMR corridors) taking delegates to Bath, as far as Reading spur.
3,4	V4 2-6-2 61700 *Bantam Cock* (65A!) heads the 7.24pm arrival into Newcastle from Carlisle, returning on the 10.30am (4th). A rare loco in either place!
3,4	Liverpool & Manchester Railway *Lion* 0-4-2 (of 1830) is steamed between Hertford and Welwyn Garden City for the film *Lady of the Lamp*. The 0-4-2 had left Crewe Works on 30 May hauling three replica coaches.
3	61554 reaches Scarborough on an excursion, repeating its visit of September 1950.
3	4082 *Windsor Castle* works through from Worcester to Bournemouth, and takes the ECS to Hamworthy Junction before retiring to 71B. First ever 'Castle' to reach here and the Authorities are not pleased!
4-16	Exhibition at York brings *Locomotion*, GNR Atlantic 251, 60022 *Mallard*, 70000 *Britannia* and Bo-Bo electric 26014 inside the City walls to the Old Station. 70000 arrived on 29 May with the 8.30am ex-King's Cross, returning thence on 18 June – first 'Britannia' in or out of King's Cross.
9	60132 *Marmion* fails at Doncaster on the 'Flying Scotsman'. 61635 *Milton* takes charge as far as York – an unprecedented choice!
11	D11 4-4-0 62690 *The Lady of the Lake* is a rarity in Newcastle, ex-Hawick.
12	A 'Canberra' jet bomber crashes near Bulwell Common station, blocking the down GC main line. Breakdown crews have normal working resumed by 6pm!

13   61998 *Macleod of Macleod* is a surprise choice for the 9.43pm Queen Street to Colchester. K4s are generally confined to the West Highland line.

16   0-6-0 64432 (36B) arrives into Scarborough on an excursion. No J11s have been seen here since before the war, so this is highly unusual.

16   0-6-0 2222 stops for water at Reading whilst working the 13-coach up 'Torbay Express'(!) due to an engine failure at Newbury.

17   2-6-2T 4525 (83G Penzance) is a very rare visitor to Southall depot, running-in from Wolverhampton Works. 0-6-0T 47348 (1D) is also a stranger here.

17   H2 4-4-2 32421 *South Foreland* works two Eastbourne – Hailsham trips, first Atlantic seen here for many years, on the one-coach Sunday service.

20   60089 *Felstead* has injector trouble on the down 'Flying Scotsman' and is piloted by D20 4-4-0 62396 from Alnmouth to Tweedmouth, a rare pairing.

23   'Devon Belle' includes Pullman car No.36 wearing the 'Fleche D'Or' and 'Golden Arrow' insignia. Portion of the up 'Atlantic Coast Express' departs Ilfracombe behind 34052 *Lord Dowding* wearing 'Devon Belle' headboards!

23   CR corridor-brake SC7366M seen in a Plymouth-Bristol train.

30   61521 (61A!) heads an up freight out of Doncaster. Jaws drop in disbelief!

U/D   'Star' 4054 *Princess Charlotte* makes a trial trip with one coach from Exeter to Plymouth via Okehampton on a clearance test.

U/D   7808 *Cookham Manor* heads a train of wagons through Bromsgrove and up the Lickey incline. Former GWR engines rarely work up this bank.

U/D   All the Crewe-built 'Britannias' 70000-70018 appear in Manchester (London Road) on running-in turns, (except 70004 which went straight to the Festival of Britain). 70015-18 bring the rare sight of GWR-pattern lamp-irons and lamps to the LMR as this batch is destined for the WR, such fittings being incompatible with those of other Regions.

JULY 1951

1ST   The last L&Y 4-6-0 50455 heads a Blackpool – York special both ways.

1   61163 works an excursion from Wembley Hill throughout to Windsor & Eton (Central).

1   2-6-0 6360 is the first GWR loco to work to Portsmouth via the Netley route since pre-war days with an excursion from Cheltenham.

1   Up 'Torbay Express' is hauled by 'Star' 4007 *Swallowfield Park*, few titled trains are headed by these engines nowadays.

1   45353, 45250 pass through Ipswich on Bedford – Clacton excursions. Both engines are serviced at Colchester, where this class is rare.

2,3   70016 *Ariel* (on temporary loan WR to 20A Holbeck) works the 3.12pm Leeds (City) – Morecambe on both days. First 7MT to reach Morecambe.

6   'Brighton Belle' unit runs between Waterloo and Portsmouth, conveying the Queen and HRH Princess Elizabeth.

8   N7 0-6-2T 69694 (34A) operates a Leeds (Central) – Bradford (Exchange) local. 69698 is also briefly allocated to Ardsley, a class not seen here before.

11   Triple-headed LE combination of K2s 61742/43/53 passes northbound through Tweedmouth. Heading for Cowlairs works?

12   70014 *Iron Duke* (with a wheel defect) is towed by an Atlantic (!) from Stewarts Lane to Brighton Works for attention. Seen on Brighton shed on 18th.

14	61647 *Helmingham Hall* (32B!) reaches Southport (Lord Street) with an excursion from Gorton; back via Widnes and Manchester (London Road).
16	34039 *Boscastle* is the first ever Pacific to reach Bury St Edmunds, arriving on the 12.45pm local from Ipswich (with only three shovelsful of coal left!)
18	Up 'Capitals Limited' reaches Newcastle behind D20 4-4-0s 62351 + 62383, which had taken over from A4 60024 *Kingfisher*. A rare pairing on any train!
20	ECS is brought into Waverley from Criagentinny by the highly unexpected 2-6-2 combination of 60822 piloting V4 61701.
24	60977 makes a rare appearance on Millhouses shed (Sheffield).
26	11.32am Perth – Glasgow is seen at Bonnybridge with V4 61701 being piloted by CR 'Jumbo' 0-6-0 57423 running tender first. Astonishment all round!
26	L1 4-4-0 31787 works the 10.42am Tunbridge Wells – Eastbourne, despite this class being prohibited from this route.
28	The 2.8pm stopping train from Carlisle arrives in Glasgow (Central) behind a WD 2-10-0, a type which rarely appears here under any pretext.
30	A2/2 60502 *Earl Marischal* passes through Horbury (between Wakefield and Huddersfield) with a fitted freight in the Manchester direction. Surely a first?
30	Up 'Granite City' departs Aberdeen behind 45574 *India* (28A Blackpool!), which is the surprise of the month here.
U/D	Norwich Festival Week railway exhibition includes an electric motor coach which had been towed from Ilford by 61611 *Raynham Hall*.
U/D	July novelties in Edinburgh; Compound 41138 reaches Waverley with an excursion from Ayr, 45703 *Thunderer* (1B) visits Dalry Road (64C), 'Crab' 42836 works the down 'Queen of Scots' Pullman train to Glasgow.
U/D	Ivatt 2-6-0 43111 works into King's Cross, whist 43137 is transferred from South Lynn to Eastfield for trials on the West Highland line. A far-flung class.

AUGUST 1951

4ᵀᴴ	Holbeck's Caprotti valve gear '5' 44754 somehow reaches...Bournemouth!
5	Edge Hill's 46135 *The East Lancashire Regiment* somehow reaches...Dundee!
5	61552 heads a circular tour from Aberdeen via Craigellachie, Aviemore, Perth and Forfar, with 61552 working throughout. B12s are rare on the Highland main line.
5	L&Y 'Pug' 0-4-0ST 51253 (27A) seen shunting at West Ham, of all places.
7-10	70016 *Ariel* (on loan to 20A) works the 'Thames-Clyde Express' from Leeds to St Pancras, the Ian Allan Locospotters Special Euston – Crewe and back (9ᵗʰ) and returns to Leeds with the 11.45am from St Pancras on the 10ᵗʰ.
8	2-6-4T 42190 (67A) noted heading south through St Albans complete with red-backed smokebox number plate and shed plate and a Caledonian route indicator on the buffer beam! (See U/D below also).
8	6016 *King Edward V* fails north of Taunton on the 'Cornish Riviera'. Replacement 2-6-0 7316 works the train (and the loco headboard!) through to Plymouth, assisted by a 'Castle' from Newton Abbot onwards.
9	61353 pilots 46236 *City of Bradford* on the 10.40am Euston – Carlisle northwards from Crewe. The B1 is returning to the S&C (again) for further tests after a spell at Rugby Testing Station.

10	61950 heads over Slaithwaite viaduct with a York – Manchester freight. K3s are uncommon visitors to this route.
10	48343 (2A Rugby) observed at Retford with a southbound coal train. These locos are uncommon visitors here also.
14	46223 *Princess Alice* (66A) arrives in New Street on a holiday train from Glasgow. Only the third or fourth visit of a 'Coronation' here, ever.
17	3P 4-4-0 40728 is a rare sight in London, arriving as pilot from Sheffield on the overnight Carlisle – Cricklewood milk train.
18	4-6-0 30833 (70B) is the first S15 seen at Dover since the war.
19	Excursion is run from Kidderminster to Barry Island via (and picking up at) Upton-on-Severn, Ripple and Tewkesbury. First advertised service from the Tewkesbury branch to South Wales.
20	70019 *Lightning* works to/from Penzance on the 'Cornish Riviera', first 7MT to reach the end of the line!
21	70009 *Alfred the Great* makes a rare (unique?) appearance on the up 'Royal 'Wessex' from Bournemouth (Central) to Waterloo.
25	60800 *Green Arrow* arrives to take a troop train southwards from Barnard Castle, where few V2s ever reach.
31	Fell 2000hp diesel-mechanical 4-8-4 arrives in Leicester on a test train.
U/D	'Britannia' Pacifics (70009 or 70014) twice work between Salisbury and Exeter (Central) – not their customary route!
U/D	'Crab' 42800 surprisingly works the 'Postal' between Forfar and Aberdeen.
U/D	3-cyl. 2-6-4Ts 42530/35 are sent for trials, from Plaistow to Greenock and 2-cyl. 2-6-4Ts 42190/91 are sent in exchange from Corkerhill to Plaistow.
U/D	D16 4-4-0 62568 reaches Southport (Lord Street) with a Bank Holiday excursion from Manchester. Probably a unique occasion.
U/D	(Late July to late September) Hunslet 0-8-0 diesel shunter, one of three destined for Peru, works a daily shift in Stourton Yard (Leeds); is engaged on freight work to Guiseley and the Yeadon branch, or on Leeds – Lancaster freight workings. Instances of non-BR locos undertaking 'regular' BR turns are few and far between.

SEPTEMBER 1951

2ND	61283 is a rarity at Shrewsbury, on an excursion from Nottingham.
6	2.22pm arrival in Waverley from Corstorphine comes in behind 60011 *Empire of India* running tender first, unusual power for a local!
7	2-6-4T 42103 commences work on the Bude branch from Halwill Junction. 42099/102/105 are also drafted to Exmouth Junction for a short period from Tunbridge Wells, mainly for Exeter (Central) – Plymouth (Friary) services.
7	N7 0-6-2T 69692 heads a King's Cross – Edgware goods train. Steam is not normally allowed over LT lines between East Finchley and Mill Hill East.
7,17	WD 2-10-0s 90767/74 (68A) appear at Mirfield, resectively. Rare workings.
9	61662 *Manchester United* works the 9.50am Nottingham (Victoria) – Marylebone throughout. B17s are not often seen in this London terminus.
12	70011 *Hotspur* (32A) is towed through Lincoln and is then seen on Gorton shed two days later on its way to Crewe for attention.
15	4-6-2T 69802 arrives in Hull – first A5 to work south of Scarborough.

22	'Royal Scot' arrives into Glasgow (Central) 1½hr late behind 45714 *Revenge* running tender first, not the prestige power usually associated with this train.
23	2.12pm Bristol – Bradford with 45685 *Barfleur* on ten coaches is diverted (due to a derailment) via the Severn Tunnel and Gloucester. First 'Jubilee' through the Tunnel? Express is 3hr 33min late into Bradford.
24	Changeover to the new No.5 signal box at Carlisle causes chaos. Delays of 2-4 hours occur outside the station whilst points are switched by gangs of men with crowbars! On the last day of the Glasgow autumn holiday, with many extra trains running, this is good news for the coach firms!
27	60160 *Auld Reekie* heads the 1.45pm Carlisle – Perth, first use of an A1 on this former LMS route.
27	J1 0-6-0 65013 is a surprise arrival at King's Cross with the 14-coach 5.15pm from Leeds after 60014 *Silver Link* is removed at Hatfield.
29	9-coach football special runs from Bath to Glastonbury behind an LMS 4-4-0 piloting 44523 – one of the longest trains seen at Glastonbury!
29	Another surprise at King's Cross is the arrival of Ivatt 2-6-0 43061 (35A) on a semi-fast working from Peterborough.
U/D	Several O4 2-8-0s are drafted from the NER to the WR on a temporary basis. These include 63673, 63835 sent to Oxley; 63770 to Southall, 63816 at Worcester shed on 7th, 63881 at Exeter with a down goods on 8th and 63812 (allocated to Taunton) observed at Bridgwater on the 9th. All are soon passed back to the NER and replaced by WD 2-8-0s.
U/D	'5' + B12 combination noted double-heading a freight from Blair Athol towards Druimuachdar summit. Unprecedented pairing on this Highland line.
U/D	60159 *Bonnie Dundee*, 60160 *Auld Reekie*, 60161 *North British* are again transferred to Polmadie for work between Glasgow and Crewe. This only lasts from 21 September to first week of November inclusive.
U/D	Loadings of 25, 30 or 40 vehicles seen on the 9.20am ECS working from Newcastle to Holloway, double-headed as far as Thirsk.
U/D	Festival of Britain closes 30 September, having opened on 3 May. Over 10 million people pay to see the six main exhibitions, 8½ million of these at the South Bank where 70004 *William Shakespeare*, 10201, 26020 etc. are stabled. Of this 8½ million, 36½% are Londoners, 56% other UK residents, 7½% are from overseas.

OCTOBER 1951

3RD	60034 *Lord Faringdon* is found on shed at Bradford (Hammerton Street) having new wheels fitted. Two further A4s, two A1s and an A3 have also been recent visitors for the same purpose. Any Pacific is rare at Bradford.
3	Former Furness Railway 0-6-0 52499 (12D Workington) hauls a 3-coach ex-Works electric set (M28644/5/6) south through Newton-le-Willows, well off its beaten track.
6	L1 2-6-4T 67733 speeds through Colchester on the down 'Day Continental' and 67737 appears on the down 'Scandinavian', both usually 'Britannia' turns.
10	2-8-2T 7236 works two auto-trailers between Moretonhampstead and Paignton instead of the usual 0-4-2T. A large increase in power and a unique instance!
11	44991 (60A) takes the 2.5pm to Perth out of Waverley, where Inverness engines are rarities.

12	45318 (84G) heads a train from Carlisle into Newcastle, where Shrewsbury engines are also rarities.
13	W1 4-6-4 60700 heads the down 'Northumbrian' to Grantham, returning with the up 'Flying Scotsman', both unusual turns for this locomotive.
14	L&Y 0-8-0 49547 (27B Aintree) appears, surprisingly, on Kingmoor depot.
16	Four engines – 32124/30670 at the rear, 30847/30232 at the front – are required to haul 16 loaded milk wagons up the 1 in 37 between St Davids and Central stations in Exeter. Spectacular!
17	MR 40383 (17A) brings one coach plus an engineer's saloon from Penrith to Keswick and back. First 4-4-0 at Keswick for many years.
20	Boat train from Tilbury Docks brings L1 67737 into St Pancras. A class first?
21,22	70004 *William Shakespeare* breaks a connecting rod at Headcorn whilst travelling at speed on the 'Golden Arrow'. This is due to the driving wheels shifting on the axles, and all 'Britannias' are withdrawn from service on completion of their runs next day. All are sent to Crewe for attention.
22	61996 *Lord of the Isles* noted at Dunkeld on the Highland line, a surprising location for a K4, which usually work the West Highland line only.
27	The independent North Sunderland Railway (not nationalised in 1948) closes. Y7 0-4-0T 68089 (hired from BR and sometimes bearing a 'Farne Islander' headboard) works the last train from Seahouses to Chathill. (The Y7 is later sold to work for contactors building an outfall sewer next to Morecambe Pier).
29	61650 *Grimsby Town* seen at Cricklewood on oil tanks from Stratford. Inappropriate power for this class of work?
29	61664 *Liverpool* heads the up 'Norfolkman', normally a 'Britannia' turn.
U/D	2-6-0 9304 unexpectedly arrives at Bletchley on a service from Oxford, as former GWR locos are not often seen on the West Coast main line.
U/D	70004 *William Shakespeare* leaves the South Bank site (1st) and is towed to Eastleigh to be steamed for the first time on the 5th. Works local trains until heading the 8.35am Victoria – Ramsgate on the 9th, and starts regular service on the 'Golden Arrow' with an official send-off from Victoria on the 11th.
U/D	Extra 'Pacifics' 34076 *41 Squadron*, 34089 *602 Squadron* and nearly-new 73000/2 are drafted to the GE Section to replace some of the temporarily withdrawn 'Britannias'.
U/D	On rebuilding with a taper boiler, the parallel boiler on 46134 *The Cheshire Regiment* is removed at Crewe and transferred to Ashford Works, to see several more years' service as a stationary boiler.

NOVEMBER 1951

3RD	On loan 73002 heads the 'East Anglian' out of Liverpool Street. Notable!
5	90170 observed working the up 'Aberdonian' at Kirkcaldy, presumably (hopefully!) due to engine failure further north.
5	Compound 41040 arrives into Leeds (City) solo on the up 'Thames-Clyde Express'. It had been pilot to 46133 *The Green Howards* from Carlisle, but the 'Scot' failed at Skipton.
6	4-6-0 30332 (72B Salisbury) visits Brighton on a banana special from Avonmouth Docks. First H15 to reach Brighton?

8	10.40am Euston – Carlisle is double-headed from Rugby onwards by 73008 + 46240 *City of Coventry*. The 5MT is on its way north for dynamometer car tests over the S&C after its stint at Rugby Testing Station.
11	D11 4-4-0 62660 *Butler Henderson* is a stranger to obtain light repairs at Longsight depot (9A).
11,17	K1/1 2-6-0 61997 *MacCailin Mor* (65A) noted on (38C Leicester (GC)) shed ex-Doncaster Works. Also visits Gorton depot on 17th after working the 6.4am Annesley – Motram freight.
13	61767 is surely 'desparation power' for the 'Day Continental' out of Liverpool Street?
16	48531 (26G Belle Vue) appears at Yate with a special train from Openshaw (Manchester) to Avonmouth Docks consisting of two 3' 6" gauge 4-8-2s built by Beyer-Peacock for the West Australian Government Railways to be loaded onto the ss 'Durban Bay' bound for Fremantle.
15-18	46154 *The Hussar* + 46117 *Welsh Guardsman* (both in spotless green) double-head a Toton – Brent train of loaded coal wagons, on braking tests. A really unexpected sight, even on a test train!
24	T9 4-4-0 30726 + 30750 *Morgan le Fay* combine to bring the 8.15am from Plymouth (Friary) into Waterloo, where double-headed trains are usually prohibited.
29	44762 arrives in Euston from Northampton still wearing the SR malachite green it was given experimentally in January 1948.

DECEMBER 1951

1ST	Hythe – Sandling branch closes and the last train leaves Hythe at 4.20pm to the customary accompaniment of exploding fog signals and continuous engine whistling. However, local populace assumes 'accident' up at the station and alert Doctor and Ambulance service, whilst a police Inspector, Sergeant and Constable are despatched to the station to investigate!
9	WD 2-8-0 undergoes high-speed (80mph!) 'slipping tests' on specially greased rails on the Faringdon branch. Photos are taken of 'wheel lift' on the leading driving axle. Wheel balancing is under review.
10	46203 *Princess Margaret Rose* is stripped down in Derby works to receive new front-end frames. Sent to Derby (rather than Crewe) on the instructions of the Mechanical Engineer.
12	70002 *Geoffrey Chaucer* (30A) comes into New Street on an overnight train from Glasgow; ex-Crewe Works as Stratford engines never normally reach New Street!
15,16	New 3000hp Co-Co gas turbine from Metropolitan-Vickers 18100, is towed from Trafford Park to Swindon.
18	70012 *John of Gaunt* + 70013 *Oliver Cromwell* coupled together and running LE pass through Peterborough heading for Crewe Works via Retford.
21	61883 (53A) arrives in King's Cross. Only the third visit of a Dairycoates engine to the terminus since nationalisation, 61883 each time!
21	N15X 4-6-0 32331 *Beattie* (70D Basingstoke) takes over the North Cornwall portion of the up 'Atlantic Coast Express' at Exeter (Central), a rare sight!
21	Shortage of power over the holiday period results in 61251 *Oliver Bury* (recently ex-Works) having to take a 515 ton Sleeping Car train out of King's Cross unaided.
22	CR 4-4-0 54454 pilots 73006 between Forfar and Aberdeen on the 'Granite City'. A real 'ancient & modern' pairing.

29   10.30pm Waterloo – Southampton has GWR special saloon W9006 and a composite brake added to the front of the train for the conveyance of the Prime Minister (Mr Churchill) who is *en route* to the USA.

31   'Clan' 72000 (as yet un-named) appears at Shrewsbury on a running-in turn from Crewe. 72001 works into Manchester (London Road) same day.

U/D   70022 *Tornado* is seen passing through Oxford light engine returning to Swindon from Crewe Works.

U/D   70004 *William Shakespeare* (73A Stewarts Lane) arrives at Swindon Works for further attention to driving axles.

JANUARY 1952

3RD   J67 0-6-0T 68525 (61A) brings the rare sight of a Kittybrewster shedplate to York as it passes through in the course of being transferred to Lincoln. Nearly as rare is G5 0-4-4T 67269 (31A!) on shed and in steam.

6   44667 + 45342 work Toton – Brent test runs with 52 loaded wagons of coal plus LMR dynamometer car No.3. (See also 20th, below).

12   Four football specials are run for the Norwich City v Arsenal FA Cup tie, the first hauled by B17 61648 *Arsenal*, the second by B2 61639 *Norwich City*.

12   61667 *Bradford* works through from Romford with a football supporters' train as far as Brent, where engines are belatedly changed.

12   Brush-designed BR-built 0-6-0 360hp diesel shunter 15004 is seen on Wood Green flyover working ECS out of King's Cross, a rare turn. Also noted on transfer freights between Ferme Park and Hither Green.

12   GWR 2-6-0 heads a special freight from Tidworth to Southampton Docks. First GWR loco between Andover, Basingstoke on the LSWR main line?

15   Coach 81061 is observed at Ipswich still lettered M&GN (i.e. pre-1923)!

16   Derby v Middlesbrough FA Cup replay brings 61198 (51A) through to Derby. Evening paper last Saturday had announced this special train within 1½ hours of the game ending at Middlesbrough!

16   72000 is officially named *Clan Buchanan* at Glasgow (Central) by the Lord Provost of Glasgow, with representatives from that Clan in attendance.

19   72001 *Clan Cameron* arrives in Euston with a train from Wolverhampton, the first of the new 6MT class to reach the terminus.

19   61172 (36B Mexborough) is a surprising shed to be represented at Oxford, coming in on a football special from Crook, Co. Durham.

20   70023 *Venus* + 70020 *Mercury* (both 81A!) double-head a train of 72 loaded coal wagons – 1200 tons – between Toton and Brent. (Investigation into the fitting all freight wagons with automatic brakes). An unprecedented sight.

23   The 'Granite City' reaches Aberdeen behind the powerful combination of 60532 *Blue Peter* piloting 45007 (65B), a most uncommon pairing.

24   70005 *John Milton* piloting 46249 *City of Sheffield* from Rugby on the 10.40am from Euston is also uncommon, but here 70005 is transferring from Rugby Testing Station for further tests on the S&C line.

26   An Alloa – Duns football special arrives in Edinburgh (Waverley) behind a pair of 4-4-0s D30 62426 *Cuddie Headrigg* + Compound 40924, changes engines and leaves

with a pair of Ivatt 2-6-0s, 46462 piloting 43136 both combinations being worthy of note.

31 Runaway steer careers up & down the track for 5 hours at Exeter (St Davids). Signalman is 'treed' up his own signal post and his bicycle tossed in the air. Crowded platform of on-lookers clears in a flash as the beast mounts the end ramp and approaches at speed! Steer is finally enticed into a pen.

U/D 45245 (61B) seen at Inverurie Works – an unusual class here.

U/D Ivatt 2-6-0 43138 (65A) unexpectedly works a Dundee – Aberdeen freight. This type is a rarity on this line.

U/D 72002 *Clan Campbell* heads the 12.5am Chester – Holyhead throughout on a running-in turn from Crewe.

U/D Due to steel shortages, the 1952 BR building programme suffers cuts of 45% in freight wagon production, 50% in locos and 100% in passenger coaches!

FEBRUARY 1952

2ND Portsmouth v Lincoln FA Cup tie specials arrive behind 6816 *Frankton Grange*, 6835 *Eastham Grange* and 6926 *Holkham Hall*, 6979 *Helperly Hall*. Unusual to find four GWR locos in Portsmouth at once.

2 Double-chimney 44765 (5A) is rarely-seen power at Aberdeen with a football excursion from Ayr.

6 61657 *Doncaster Rovers* works another football special, from Doncaster to Middlesbrough for the postponed Cup match, most appropriately.

10 Stanier 0-4-4T 41907 reaches Manchester (Central) on ECS – believed to be the first 0-4-4T at Central for 40 years!

11,15 Funeral train of King George VI is worked non-stop from Kings Lynn to King's Cross by 70000 *Britannia*. First appearance of a Pacific at Kings Lynn. 4082 *Windsor Castle* (having exchanged identities with 7013 *Bristol Castle*) heads the Paddington – Windsor leg on the 15th.

15 70012 *John of Gaunt* (running-in from Crewe Works with new axles) pilots 46245 *City of London* on the 8.30am Euston – Liverpool from Crewe onwards.

17 O4 2-8-0s 63809/49 noted on Reading shed *en route* from Gorton to Southampton Docks for shipment to Suez via Port Said. 63580, 63627, 63778 follow – all five converted to oil firing and given WD numbers. (92 other such engines were sent to the Middle East in 1942, none have since returned).

17 72001 *Clan Cameron* is a surprising loco to be found on Swindon shed (82C).

17,25 35030 *Elder-Dempster Lines*, 34012 *Launceston* (25th) conduct ferry vehicle tests Dover (Marine) – Chislehurst on 700 ton trains; 30 loads + 2 brake vans.

18 0-6-0 2263 (85A) works the 7.54am Worcester – York into New Street. First GWR engine seen in New Street on an ordinary train.

19 The 4.20pm from Penzance arrives into Plymouth at 7pm and collides with a hand-trolley carrying bullion. An extensive hand-lamp search recoups all but £4 16s 6d of the £2,500 scattered around!

21 Just south of Kings Langley station, on the up slow line, 5 corridor coaches are seen stationary, with passengers, but with no engine!

22 0-4-2T 1470 (83A) surprisingly appears at Marylebone on auto-train tests. Back working the Totnes – Ashburton branch on the 26th, where it belongs!

22,23 Sleeping Car train (one of 8 specials) conveys 168 Newcastle supporters to the FA Cup match at Swansea for £4 (fare/berth/breakfast/supper on return).

23 70014 *William Shakespeare* (73A) – released from Crewe works – is sent to Stratford (30A) in error, and has to be forwarded to Stewarts Lane depot.

23 Luton Town v Swindon FA Cup match brings 2-6-0s 6377 (83B Taunton), 7300 (82D Westbury) and 6360 (82C Swindon) right through to Luton (Midland Road) and these engines take the ECS on to Ampthill and Oakley.

26 Meteor jet fighter – trying to land at RAF Full Sutton – crashes into a Hull to York goods train at Fangfoss near York. Train is cut in two, 20 wagons are derailed and thousands of fish scattered on track and embankment. Track torn up, both lines blocked. Single line working in force by 8.30am next day!

U/D 70006 *Robert Burns* is towed from Gorton to Crewe Works by O2 2-8-0 63972, an extremely rare type to reach Crewe.

U/D 60095 *Flamingo* (68E Carlisle Canal) heads an express freight from Gateshead to King's Cross Goods, only its second ever appearance in London.

U/D Three times in the month the buffer stops at the end of platform 7 at Cannon Street are demolished, the last two so soon after each other there was no time to repair the platform in between!

MARCH 1952

2ND 72002 (66A) *Clan Campbell* arrives in Southport with the 9.40am from Manchester (Victoria), the first of this class to appear in this resort.

4 35022 *Holland America Line* is seen at Willesden on its way to the Rugby Testing Station.

8 International hockey match attracts specials from Shrewsbury, with 5097 *Sarum Castle* working through to Wembley Hill, and 61604 *Elvedon* (in immaculate condition) arriving at Neasden without change, from Ipswich.

8 Eight specials are put on for the Portsmouth v Newcastle FA Cup tie and A2/2 60501 *Cock o' the North*, 61026 *Ourebi*, 61125, 61258 and 60802 all arrive, and change engines at, Banbury. Two of the eight are composed entirely of Sleeping and Restaurant Cars, only the fourth occasion on which Sleeping Cars have been made available for football supporters, and probably the first time Portsmouth has seen these vehicles in public use.

9 Gas turbine Co-Co 18100 undergoes load tests on the 1 in 42 of Hemerdon bank, restarting a train of 18 coaches (610 tons) from rest, successfully.

10 62725 *Inverness-shire* is an unprecedented type for the 9.25am stopping train from Perth to Blair Atholl.

10 70014 *Iron Duke*, working the down 'Golden Arrow' halts at Tonbridge, short of steam. 'Schools' 30903 *Charterhouse* is attached as pilot to Dover, an extremely rare instance of double-heading on this train.

13 2-6-4T 42085 observed at Hornsey heading for the North-East after its transfer from 73A. Later works 55 empty wagons from Peterborough to Grantham. Tank engine workings are uncommon on this stretch, especially on freight.

16 'North Briton' leaves Queen Street with a B1 piloting D11 4-4-0 62682 *Haystoun of Bucklaw*, an odd combination.

16 70004 *William Shakeapeare* (73A) receives attention in Swindon Works 'A' shop, but is back on the 'Golden Arrow' on the 22nd.

16	34073 *249 Squadron* conducts further Continental ferry tests (see February).

16 34073 *249 Squadron* conducts further Continental ferry tests (see February).

21 46203 *Princess Margaret Rose* – now repainted green – noted on Derby shed after being outshopped from the Works with new front-end frames.

22 35002 *Union Castle* in green, is seen at Waterloo paired with a blue tender!

24 90464, coupled to the LMS corridor tender (still in red), LMR dynamometer car No.3 plus two Mobile Test Units, begins trial runs from Carlisle to Kilmarnock. Tests subsequently continue with WD 2-10-0 90772.

24 4-4-0 40543 (15C) heads the Birmingham – Cleethorpes through to Lincoln, where LMS types like this are strangers.

29 34069 *Hawkinge* gets through the blizzard and delivers Brighton fans to Watford (1 hour late, but a rare sight) for the match – which is then postponed!

31 LNER 1500V DC Bo-Bo electric 6000 returns from Netherlands Railways via Harwich to Ilford, to become BR class EM1 26000. (See also June 30th).

U/D (Good Friday) 61304 (53B) is a surprising arrival at Liverpool (Lime Street) with a special from Hull. Former LNER classes rarely reach here.

U/D (Easter Monday) Grassington – closed 1930 – is host to three excursions from Blackburn, Bradford and Leeds. Room is found (just) to stable 31 coaches!

APRIL 1952

2ND Gas turbine Co-Co 18100 works a 10-coach stock train to Old Oak Common consisting entirely of Kitchen Cars and Restaurant Cars.

2 61938 (31B) brings a horsebox special to Liverpool for the Grand National. 61626 *Brancepeth Castle* (31B) brings another the following day. March locos only appear in Liverpool at this time of year!

3 61606 *Audley End* (30A!) pulls into Derby (Friargate) with a west-bound goods, looking very much out of place, as Stratford engines shouldn't be here!

5 34047 *Callington* and 34069 *Hawkinge* reach Watford Junction in connection with the Schoolboys' International at Wembley.

6 WR-allocated 70015 *Apollo* and 70016 *Ariel* arrive on loan at Stratford (30A).

6 6009 *King Charles II* appears on clearance tests at Newport and Cardiff.

9 60816 heads a northbound freight out of Kittybrewster. First V2 on GNS lines.

11 48321 (68A) is a most unusual choice for the 5.55am Buchanan Street – Perth, especially as it has no steam-heat provision.

12 46225 *Duchess of Gloucester* works the 'Saint Mungo' both ways between Aberdeen and Perth, rare power for this express.

14 6870 *Bodicote Grange* surprisingly works an excursion from Newport through to New Street, and Walsall.

16 72009 *Clan Stewart* heads the 3.35pm Bradford (Forster Square) – Carlisle stopper in place of the usual '5'.

16,17 WD 2-10-0 90751 hauls a down goods through Shipley, whilst sister loco 90761 + 48454 run coupled LE southbound. 90751 also appears on an up freight next day. Three sightings of 2-10-0s in two days on a line that hardly ever sees any at all!

18 J17 0-6-0 65545 (30A) is a stranger at St Pancras, arriving with a Tilbury Docks boat train. First J17 seen here?

18   Because of the derailment at Blea Moor, the following 4pm St Enoch – Leeds is reversed
      between Appleby West and East, and proceeds to Kirkby Stephen (East) where the 'Royal
      Scot' runs round and takes the train, tender first, to Tebay then via Low Gill, Sedburgh
      to Hellifield. Here the loco turns on the turntable before completing the run to Leeds.
      Improvisation!

19   6840 *Hazeley Grange* (86G Pontypool Road!) works the 5.20pm from Oxford to
      Bedford, where observers understandably ask 'How on earth…?'

19   Rugby League Cup Final brings 20 specials into Euston from the North-West. One is
      headed by 45184 (64C) – surely a first for a Dalry Road engine to reach Euston, another
      by 45079 (25G Farnley Junction), a further shed rarely represented in Euston, having
      worked through from Leeds.

28   1750hp diesel-electric 10202 departs Waterloo on the 1pm service with the GWR
      dynamometer car behind the locomotive.

28   Lightweight 4-wheeled 3-car AEC diesel unit commences trial runs between Didcot and
      Newbury.

29   All-Pullman 8-coach special complete with a 'Devon Belle' observation car at the
      rear leaves Charing Cross at 9.6am for Port Victoria (on the Isle of Grain) headed by
      N 2-6-0 31827. Train is chartered by the Anglo-Iranian Oil Co.

30   72005 *Clan Macgregor* pilots 46109 *Royal Engineer* on the up 'Thames-Clyde Express'
      from Carlisle to Leeds, an unusual pairing.

30   CR 0-4-4T 55265 actually sets off from Glasgow (Central) with the 'Mid-day Scot', only
      to be relieved by 46227 *Duchess of Devonshire* at Polmadie!

MAY 1952

4TH   L&Y 'Pug' 0-4-0ST 51253 *en route* from Bromley Gasworks runs LE to Rugby,
      undergoes repairs and proceeds to Liverpool (27A Bank Hall).

6   60845 is seen passing Maidenhead on its way to Swindon Test Plant.

7   61641 *Gayton Hall* (31B) heads a horsebox special from Newmarket between
      Manchester (Central) and Chester (Northgate) on the CLC line.

13   B16 4-6-0 61432 (50B) works a British Industries Fair excursion through to Castle
      Bromwich, where NER locos are not common.

14   Ivatt 2-6-0 46433 (1A) is an extraordinary sight at Victoria (London!) on a parcels train
      from Willesden.

14,15 Five coach train, including four LMS Sleeping Cars is run from Bournemouth (Central)
      at 10.3pm to Victoria (arriving 12.20am) for a party of delegates attending the Anglo-
      French Conference. One of the very few occasions on which Sleeping Cars have ever used
      the Bournemouth line.

19-23 AEC lightweight 4-wheeled 3-car diesel unit runs trials between Marylebone and High
      Wycombe.

20,21 61239 (50A), and 61256 (50B) next day, both work southbound ECS trains of LNER
      vehicles through New Street, possibly in connection with the British Industries Fair.

21   Educational excursion from Cambridge arrives at Southampton Docks hauled by
      6933 *Birtles Hall* on a train of LNER stock; odd setting for this combination.

24   46212 *Duchess of Kent* (5A) works the West Coast Postal from Aberdeen, a most
      unusual type of engine to be found on this train.

| 26 | 72006 *Clan Mackenzie* (68A) heads the 'Bon Accord', the 6.25am Aberdeen to Buchanan Street, another unusual class at Aberdeen. |

26 | 72006 *Clan Mackenzie* (68A) heads the 'Bon Accord', the 6.25am Aberdeen to Buchanan Street, another unusual class at Aberdeen.

28 | Ivatt 2-6-0 43121 (14A) arrives at Hither Green on a cross-London freight, the first of this class to reach here.

30 | Three special trains carrying US servicemen direct from Southampton Docks pass over the M&GN line to Melton Constable. All are of green SR coaches, the first two also include Pullman cars; *Carmen* in the first and *Daphne*, *Mimosa* in the second. First appearance of Pullman cars on the M&GN. All trains return the same evening.

31 | 61541 is a big surprise at Bridlington, arriving with an excursion. Thought to be the first example of this class (B12) to reach here.

U/D | (May/June) Ealing Studios makes the film *The Titfield Thunderbolt* on the Limpley Stoke – Camerton branch, closed 15 months previously, plus scenes at Bristol (Temple Meads). Film features 0-4-2Ts 1401/56 and Liverpool & Manchester 0-4-2 *Lion* of 1830.

U/D | 1500V DC Bo-Bo electrics 26001/3/5/6/7/20 observed running trials in pairs between Ilford and Shenfield, in preparation for use on the Manchester/ Sheffield /Wath scheme.

JUNE 1952

5TH | 1750hp diesel-electric 10201 is removed from the 'Royal Wessex' at Beaulieu Road as it is on fire. Q 0-6-0 30548 on the following train proceeds to push the stranded express, and pull its own, to Brockenhurst where Q1 0-6-0 33024 and T9 4-4-0 30285 (a unique combination?) take the 'Wessex' forward.

12 | 72005 *Clan Macgregor* brings the 'Saint Mungo' from Buchanan Street into Aberdeen.

12 | 80037 powers the Brighton – Cardiff as far as Salisbury, a rare appearance for this class here.

14 | 62044 pilots 60158 *Aberdonian* on a troop special at Barnard Castle.

14 | 45400 + J37 0-6-0 64638 double-head a Clyde coast excursion through Paisley, a most unlikely combination.

15 | The eight D16 4-4-0s are returned to the GE section from the CLC lines. Seven, in a group of 3 and another of 4, are seen passing through Sleaford coupled LE in the direction of March.

15 | 61139 (34A) makes the first visit of an ER engine to Eastbourne, with an excursion from Hitchin. Caprotti 44748 (9A) also makes a class debut at Hastings on a special from Watford.

18 | 45692 *Cyclops* (66A!) is an astonishing visitor to Oldham (Lees) shed, to be used on Wakes Week specials.

21 | 61138 reaches Brighton – first B1 to do so – on a special from Cambridge.

22 | 73028 arrives in Hull – first 5MT to do so – with a special from Blackpool.

26 | D20 4-4-0 62388 (51J Northallerton) somehow makes it to Mirfield shed.

26 | L&Y 0-8-0 49578 (26B Agecroft) also makes it to Wolverhampton (Low Level)!

27 | WD 2-10-0 90751 provides a startling spectacle at Greenock (Princes Pier) when it arrives on a sheep train special.

27 | Glasgow (Central) – Manchester (Victoria) express arrives behind L&Y 2-4-2T 50852 double-heading 45702 *Colossus*, a remarkable choice of pilot engine from Preston!

28 | GWR diesel railcar W14 is provided for a special from Solihull to Buxton, outward via Uttoxeter, returning via Derby. A fascinating sight at these places, which are a long way from usual railcar territory.

29 | 80039 works through from Brighton to Bournemouth – a class debut here.

30   1500V DC Bo-Bo electric 26000 (the LNER prototype of 1941) is named *Tommy* at
            Liverpool Street by the President of the Netherlands Railways.
U/D   Seen in the Aberdeen area;
            61552 in black running with a green tender,
            45576 *Bombay* in green running with a black tender!
U/D   Ivatt 2-6-0 46460 (61A) is fitted with a cowcatcher on both the front buffer beam and
            tender buffer beam, for working the St Combs branch from Fraserburgh. The first tender
            engine so fitted on BR.

JULY 1952

1ST-5TH   The 'Fife Coast Express' between Queen Street and St Andrews, usually a B1 working,
            enjoys a week of mixed LMS power; Ivatt 2-6-0 43132, 45117, 45400 before reverting
            to D30 4-4-0 62442 *Simon Glover* on the 5th (down train). The service is formed of 5
            vehicles from the pre-war 'Silver Jubilee' set, an articulated twin + triplet, all now in
            carmine and cream.
4,5   72002 *Clan Campbell* (66A) leaves Colne at 7.35pm with a special Isle of Man boat
            train to Fleetwood. First ever Pacific to reach Colne. Returns and hauls another special
            to Euston next day.
5   2-6-2T 6142 works a High Wycombe – Southampton Docks excursion throughout. First
            of this class to reach Southampton since the war.
5   Ivatt 2-6-2T 41313 – on its way to Bude – pilots 34036 *Westward Ho* on the 11.49am from
            Exeter (Central) as far as Okehampton. 82011 pilots 34060 *25 Squadron* between Plymouth
            (Friary) and Exeter (Central). Both are uncommon pairings of small tank + Pacific.
6   60115 *Meg Merrilies* heads an excursion from Newcastle into Hull, where A1s are rare,
            working via Hessle as there is no Sunday service on the York to Hull direct line.
6   44994 pilots 46212 *Duchess of Kent* between Princes Street and Carlisle on a pilgrimage
            special, loading to 17 bogies from Symington where a portion from Paisley is added.
11   61166 (36B) works through to Chester (Northgate) with excursion traffic from
            Mexborough. B1 fails, and return is hauled, all the way, by D10 4-4-0 62650 *Prince
            Henry* (9G Northwich). This is then used by Mexborough to work a subsequent
            excursion to Bridlington, the first D10 at the resort.
11   E4 2-4-0 62789 operates a 'Station Gardens Judging Special' – a single Inspection Saloon
            – over the Ipswich to Yarmouth line. It's at least five years since an E4 passed this way.
11   Exeter (Central) sees the surprise arrival of N15X 4-6-0 32327 *Trevithick* (70D
            Basingstoke) on the 5.35pm from Waterloo, usually a Pacific turn.
12   2-8-0 53809 departs Bournemouth (West) on the 3.35pm to Bristol (St Phillips), which
            it works throughout. A rare trip off the S&D for this class.
12   Ivatt 2-6-0 46409 (25C Goole!) works the 8.45pm ex-Plymouth, from Crewe into
            Manchester (London Road).
13   Excursion from Brighton to Bedford arrives at platform 10 at Victoria – in error. Train
            reverses and is eventually sent the right way!
14   60081 *Shotover* double-heads A2/3 60512 *Steady Aim* on the 22-vehicle Newcastle –
            Holloway ECS train between Stockton and Northallerton. Pairings of ER Pacifics are rare.
15   G16 4-8-0T 30494, ex-Works, hauls a 2-car electric set from Eastleigh to Streatham Hill,
            a most unusual task for a hump-shunting tank.

16	On temporary transfer from the SR, 500hp diesel-mechanical 0-6-0 shunter 11001 receives attention at Hunslet Works in Leeds before commencing trials in Stourton yard. Later works coal trains between Stourton and Lancaster.
19	61875 (52B Heaton) is rare power for the 3.10pm Aberdeen – Edinburgh.
19	6019 *King Henry V* + 6002 *King William IV* double-head the second part of the 'Cornish Riviera' westward from Newton Abbot. Twin 'Kings' are rare.
19	70018 *Flying Dutchman* reaches Torquay, to general consternation. Taxi driver declares it to be a 'Southern'!
19	The 3-car AEC unit begins trials on the Watford – St Albans branch.
21	7.26am Edenbridge – London Bridge via the Crowhurst loop is worked by 34076 *41 Squadron*, the first time a Pacific has been routed this way.
22	*Titfield Thunderbolt* scenes are shot at Bristol (Temple Meads) alias 'Mallingford', with *Lion* in steam and a large crowd surrounding it.
26	U 2-6-0 31633 surprisingly heads the 10.28am Poole – Bradford through to Woodford Halse, as engines are usually changed at Banbury or Oxford.
26	Up 'Granite City' (14 bogies) leaves Aberdeen behind the unique (?) pairing of 45535 *Sir Herbert Walker, K.C.B.* + 73007.
27	61310 (37A Ardsley) works a military special throughout from Otley to King's Cross, and returns LE all the way back to its home depot.
28	9.20am Newcastle – Holloway ECS train arrives in London behind 60022 *Mallard* with 5 vans, one 1st class Sleeping Car, one Pullman car. Odd sight!
29	6819 *Highnam Grange* works the early morning one-coach auto-train from Leamington Spa to Banbury, deputising for a 14xx 0-4-2T.
29	D11 4-4-0 62687 *Lord James of Douglas* pilots 45356 between Stirling and Buchanan Street on the 12.5pm from Oban, an interesting duo.
30	41167 works right through to Brighton from Northampton on a 10-coach excursion. First ever LMS Compound to reach Sussex.
31	45518 *Bradshaw* (12A Carlisle Upperby) heads the 'Saint Mungo' out of Aberdeen. Unrebuilt 'Patriots' are rarely seen here.
U/D	45245 (61B on loan to 61A) works several services on the Aberdeen – Keith section of the GNS, where LMS engines are uncommon.

AUGUST 1952

1ST	45503 *The Royal Leicestershire Regiment* works throughout from Southampton Docks to Quorn, carrying men of this regimental name home from Korea.
2	Peak holiday traffic causes all 5 remaining SR class H2 Atlantics to arrive at Willesden with trains to/from the South Coast.
2	N15X 4-6-0 32327 *Trevithick* is noted running eastwards through Wool (where this class is rarely seen) and returns later, piloted by a T9 4-4-0.
2	5093 *Upton Castle* (81A) takes over the 1.11pm Portsmouth Harbour to Birmingham at Basingstoke and heads for Reading. 'Castles' are most unusual on this stretch of line.
9,10	Ivatt 2-6-0 43136 (65A) works the fortnightly provisions train (one coach) from Blair Atholl to Aviemore and back, a class debut on this line. Another surprise is 90049 (64A) working a special freight from Perth to Inverness. (The WD heads the 5am southbound goods the next day).

9   61625 *Raby Castle* hauls two 8-coach sets of suburban stock to Hull for use on football shuttle trains to Boothferry Park Halt on Hull City's home match days. Six 8-coach sets are required for the season; two more arrive same day behind 61951 (35A New England). Both locos are rare in Hull.

9   Three GWR 4-6-0s reach Leicester (Central) – a record for one afternoon.

9,23,30   46242 *City of Glasgow*, 46240 *City of Coventry*, 46241 *City of Edinburgh* respectively, work the down 'Welshman' west of Chester, the load being 17 coaches on each occasion. Normally Pacifics are rarely seen here.

11   SR 3rd class corridor coach S804S is attached to a local train arriving into Paddington, a novel sight at this terminus.

11   3.55pm Newcastle – Birmingham appears at Darlington double-headed by 46144 *Honourable Artillery Company* and a '5'. First 'Royal Scot' north of York on the East Coast main line?

14   35025 *Brocklebank Line* bearing the 'Atlantic Coast Express' headboard descends between Exeter Central and St Davids on a down goods train!

14   30915 *Brighton* is surprise power for the 9.20am Weymouth – Waterloo.

15   The former LMS 'Turbomotive' 46202 (now rebuilt conventionally) is officially named *Princess Anne* on the occasion of her second birthday.

17   61539 works a round trip excursion from Aberdeen, via Boat of Garten to Perth. Return is via Forfar. Another rare visit of a B12 to the Highland line.

20   A sightseeing special of 7 Pullman cars plus a 'Devon Belle' observation car is run from Waterloo to Dorchester via Wimborne (1½ hour stop). Road coaches take passengers to the coast and the re-boarding point at Wareham. 34008 *Padstow* is used throughout.

21   72007 *Clan Mackintosh* heads the 11.20am Inverness – Edinburgh as far as Perth. First 'Clan' to work over the Highland main line.

23   Excursion is seen passing through Manchester (Victoria) headed by 90568 piloted by L&Y 0-6-0 52343 – scraping the barrel for motive power!

24   GWR railcar W20W makes four return trips between Leeds and Harrogate on a trial basis.

24   D20 4-4-0 62360 (52D Tweedmouth) appears at Cudworth on a railtour.

U/D   GNR clerestory saloon and a HR corridor 3rd both noted in Waterloo to Bournemouth train formations!

U/D   46210 *Lady Patricia* departs Waverley on the 2.5pm to Perth in mid-August. A rare class to appear in Edinburgh.

SEPTEMBER 1952

6TH   K2 61735, K3 61924 both reach Ayr with excursions from Glasgow. LNER types are uncommon on the Ayrshire coast.

8   D11 4-4-0 62690 *The Lady of the Lake* (in LNER green) surprisingly appears at Dunkeld heading a southbound freight.

8   72006 *Clan Mackenzie* pilots the 12noon Perth – Inverness as far as Dalwhinnie, and returns light engine.

9   61900 (64A) leaves Perth with a northbound goods for Blair Atholl.

9   W1 4-6-4 60700 is a stranger at Lincoln on the 6.20pm from Grantham.

13   F3 2-4-2T 67127 (last of class) hauls the Lowestoft portion of the 'Easterling' forward from Beccles, with express headcode!

17,18	Freight Handling Exhibition at Battersea Wharf includes 70025 *Western Star*, 75019 and new 0-6-0 diesel shunter 12120, ex-Darlington Works.

17,18 Freight Handling Exhibition at Battersea Wharf includes 70025 *Western Star*, 75019 and new 0-6-0 diesel shunter 12120, ex-Darlington Works.

18 70004 *William Shakespeare* is a surprise visitor to Reading (South) shed yard.

18 WD 2-10-0 90774 is a notable sight on the Midland main line, heading into London on freight. ScR 2-10-0s are not supposed to reach London!

20 A1/1 60113 *Great Northern* works the 'Northern Rubber Special' throughout from Retford to Blackpool (North) for the illuminations. First LNER Pacific to reach Blackpool.

24 5927 *Guild Hall* arrives in Southampton Docks with an Institution of Mechanical Engineers' tour from Birmingham.

24 19-coach 'Mid-day Scot' departs from Euston with 46106 *Gordon Highlander* piloting 46210 *Lady Patricia*. Trains of this length are infrequent nowadays.

24 N1 0-6-2T 69445 is amazed to find itself shunting at...Clapham Junction!

25 34044 *Woolacombe* arrives in Swindon on the diverted Bournemouth – York. Level crossing accident and signal box damage cause these detours via Gloucester. 30742 *Camelot* also appears at Swindon on a northbound working to Birkenhead.

28 GWR railcar W13W is hired to convey members of the Light Railway Transport League from Paddington to Swansea and back. Longest ever run for a British railcar!

30 GWR railcar W20W begins 4-day trial working from Boston to Grimsby, Skegness and Mablethorpe, having previously been seen around Wakefield and Doncaster.

U/D WD 2-10-0 90757 is transferred from the ScR to the WR shed at Banbury for two weeks of trials. Then sent on to Ashford, and is seen hauling Continental freight traffic between Dover and Bricklayers Arms, and on Tonbridge to Redhill freight workings.

U/D 72006 *Clan Mackenzie* (68A) passes Rotherham (Masborough) with a cattle special from Carlisle to Sheffield. 'Clans' rarely reach these parts.

OCTOBER 1952

5TH H2 4-4-2 32424 *Beachy Head* hauls a Brighton Works Centenary Special from, and to Victoria. Special is re-run on 25th with 32425 *Trevose Head*.

6 2-6-0 5323 surprisingly arrives in Guildford with an excursion from Cambridge for the Farnborough Air Show consisting of ER stock.

7 GNR 4-2-2 No.1 (from York museum) and GNR 4-4-2 251 (from Doncaster Works) are towed up to London for the King's Cross Centenary Exhibition 13-18 October. 60022 *Mallard* makes its own way!

8 A2/3 60510 *Robert the Bruce* is a rare arrival at Dundee (West), ex-Glasgow.

8 Harrow & Wealdstone accident occurs at 8.19am. 112 die in the tragedy. Up Euston trains diverted to Paddington from 2pm include

'The Midlander' 9.45am from Wolverhampton behind 5954 *Faendre Hall*

'The Mancunian' 9.45am from Manchester behind 4960 *Pyle Hall*

'The Merseyside Express' from Liverpool behind 4092 *Dunraven Castle*

Return workings all call at Leamington, Snow Hill, Wolverhampton (LL).

9 'Midlander' arrives in Paddington behind 7927 *Willington Hall*, plus boat train from Liverpool (Riverside) behind 5066 *Wardour Castle*. 'Mancunian' arrives in St Pancras behind 45595 *Southern Rhodesia*.

16 4-4-0 40464 is a stranger at Banbury, arriving on a cattle special.

18 72005 *Clan Macgregor* heads a Perth train out of Waverley, a rare class here.

21	60130 *Kestrel* propels observation car E1719 – still in its 'Coronation' livery – from King's Cross to Huntingdon. Urgent ATC trials after Harrow.
23	9.50pm Paddington – Plymouth Sleeping Car train is diverted via Okehampton due to flooding at Plympton. Newspaper and TPO trains are similarly diverted.
23	35022 *Holland America Line* seen passing LE through Oxenholme to begin four weeks of testing between Carlisle and Skipton.
23	Royal train from London reaches Llandrindod Wells behind 7030 *Cranbrook Castle* + 7036 *Taunton* Castle, rare sights on the Central Wales line.
25	34051 *Winston Churchill* is observed passing through Reading (General) with an eastbound coal train!
26	73000 + 73001 commence trials on fitted coal trains from Toton to Brent.
27	NLR 0-6-0Ts 58854/57 are towed through Rugby by LNW 0-8-0 49164, *en route* from Birkenhead to Bow Works for overhaul. An unexpected trio.
29	Compound 40934 works the LMR No.3 dynamometer car and all three Mobile Test Units from Derby to Wath (Central), in connection with the Woodhead electrification scheme.
U/D	60854 acquires an experimental (Doncaster made!) copper-capped chimney with special blast-pipe (connected with steaming trials at Swindon with 60845), and begins an extensive 3-month ER trial with this device.
U/D	1026 *County of Salop* is an unusual arrival at Weymouth with the 12.30pm from Paddington.
U/D	New 7MTs 70025-30, ex-Crewe Works, all head Birmingham – Glasgow trains as running-in turns; as does 70021 *Morning Star* (83D Plymouth Laira).
U/D	In the aftermath of the Harrow crash, Stafford Road shed (84A) finds itself host to LMR power including 45527 *Southport*, four 'Jubilees' and '5's, as locos coming in from Manchester, Liverpool are changed at Wolverhampton.
U/D	At the same time, down freights from Camden to the north receive ER engines and gain the East Coast main line via Canonbury, eg. Grantham A1s on the 9.30pm Camden – Leeds. Up freights arrive by the same route behind LMR power, with several '5's being noted.

NOVEMBER 1952

1ST	3-coach electric set, ex-Watford/Richmond services but now with pantograph, is seen at Lancaster (Castle) for experimental working on the Morecambe line.
5	D11 4-4-0 62680 *Lucy Ashton* is an unlikely visitor to St Enoch.
5	72007 *Clan Mackintosh* paired with 45724 *Warspite* is observed running LE through Ilkley, from Leeds to Skipton. A most unexpected sight at Ilkley.
8	A football excursion from Hendon to Dartford is worked throughout by Fowler 2-6-2T 40033, hauling six non-corridors via Kentish Town, the widened lines and Metropolitan Junction. First publically advertised train to pass through Snow Hill tunnels since the war.
12	4967 *Shirenewton Hall* + 34095 *Brentor* are an odd pair to be seen double-heading a goods train between Weymouth and Dorchester.
16	60103 *Flying Scotsman* is used to haul a wagon containing the turntable from King's Cross (station yard) to Gorton Works for repair. Not the customary load for any A3!
20	30928 *Stowe* (73B) is a rarity at Exeter (Central) on the 5pm from Waterloo.
22	34039 *Boscastle* heads a football special from Brighton all the way to Yeovil Junction via Eastleigh. First through working over this route.

22	L1 2-6-4T 67792 + 60835 *The Green Howard* double-head a troop train into Barnard Castle carrying men of this Regiment home from Malaya. The name-sake V2 is specially provided, freshly painted, in immaculate condition and worked York to Northallerton solo, then with L1 as pilot.
22	Trials with Bo-Bo electric locos take place from Wath with 26030/34 topping and tailing 40 loaded wagons, both LMR and ER dynamometer cars and a Mobile Test Unit. Similar tests have 50 loaded wagons, locos double-heading.
29	35022 *Holland America Line* noted passing through Warrington on its way back to the SR after trials on the Settle & Carlisle.
U/D	First set of automatic lifting barriers to be installed at a level crossing in the UK are brought into use at Warthill on the York – Hull line.
U/D	BR hires a brand-new SNCF Mauzin track testing car, at £500 for 28 days. Vehicle runs 2,000 miles on the WR, in the company of W139, the WR's own track testing car, for comparison of the readings obtained over four different types of permanent way. Runs are made from Paddington to Hatton; Denham (for Uxbridge branch), Bristol, Frome, and Reading, the latter being for the benefit of the Press, BBC, Pathe News and Paramount News representatives. Vehicle arrives at Old Oak Common on 21 November, and leaves on 13 December. (*Information courtesy of Alan Wild*).

DECEMBER 1952

2ND	46104 *Scottish Borderer* heads the up 'Saint Mungo' out of Aberdeen, very unusual for 'Royal Scots' to work this train.
6	Newcastle – Holloway ECS leaves Stockton behind 60081 *Shotover* + 60157 *Great Eastern* pulling 20 bogies, six 6-wheelers, four 4-wheelers!
10	70009 *Alfred the Great* is the first Pacific to appear at Yarmouth (South Town) this year, working the 9.29am arrival from Ipswich.
12	Jersey cow being unloaded at Saltash breaks free and dashes across the Royal Albert Bridge into Cornwall. Captured two hours later in St Budeaux station. Some delays are caused!
13	34089 *602 Squadron* brings a football special from Slough into Eastbourne where Bulleid Pacifics are uncommon visitors.
14	48724 (87K) reaches Carlisle on a freight working. Extremely rare for a Swansea engine to appear here.
16	A2/2 60503 *Lord President* seen on a down special freight on the East Coast main line consisting of two empty cattle wagons plus brake van – a train barely longer than the engine!
18	8.20am Inverness – Perth is routed via Aberdeen (snowdrift at Dalnaspidal) and extended from Perth to Buchanan Street, this sector being worked by Compound 41125, rare on a Perth – Glasgow express nowadays.
19	48645 (15B Kettering) somehow materialises at Harrogate with the York breakdown crane.
23	D11 4-4-0 62692 *Allan-Bane* pilots 60972 to Dundee on the 7.30pm Aberdeen to London relief, a noteworthy combination.
23	Bradford (Forster Square) welcomes 46109 *Royal Engineer* on a stopper from Leeds and 46117 *Welsh Guardsman* on the previous night's 11.50pm from St Pancras to Leeds, extended to Bradford. 'Scots' hardly ever reach this station!

24	61655 *Middlesbrough* (30A) arrives at King's Cross with the 12.5pm relief from Newcastle which it had taken over at Stevenage from A2/3 60520 *Owen Tudor*. Stratford locos are rarities in King's Cross.
24	Down 'Tees-Tyne Pullman' is composed entirely of the stock of the up 'Northumbrian'. The late-running Pullman cars are forwarded as ECS later.
24	60093 *Coronach* (68E Carlisle Canal) heads the 7.10pm parcels to York out of King's Cross, the last of Carlisle's A3 quartet to reach London in 1952.
25	Passengers arriving at Brighton from Eastbourne find the 10.10pm connection (and last train) to London already gone. This train is recalled from Hassocks back to Brighton to pick them up!
25,26	46235 *City of Birmingham* (5A) works the 'Saint Mungo' into Aberdeen from Perth on Christmas day, and returns south with the 'Bon Accord' on the 26th.
29	New 70037 *Hereward the Wake* is found running-in on the 3.10pm fish train from Fleetwood. Unexpected!
31	The 'North Briton' departs from Queen Street (Low Level) behind Ivatt 2-6-0 43133, as High Level is out of action this day.
U/D	60152 *Holyrood* and 60161 *North British* are back at Polmadie working between Crewe, Glasgow (Central) on the 11.15am from Birmingham.
U/D	2-6-4Ts 42071/75/88/98 are drafted to Bournemouth to work trains to Weymouth whilst the turntable there is repaired. Tanks begin work on the 7th and are returned to the South Eastern Division from the 19th onwards.
U/D	70031 *Byron* and 70032 *Tennyson* – on loan to 8A – both work the 9am Lime Street to Leeds (City) during December. 7MTs are uncommon in Leeds (City).

JANUARY 1953

4TH	10.15am Glasgow – Aberdeen arrives at journey's end behind 61243 *Sir Harold Mitchell* + 72009 *Clan Stewart*, a most unlikely combination.
5	'Ian Allan Locospotters Club Special' consisting of a 7-coach suburban set departs from London Bridge for a circuitous run to Stratford, Works and shed, behind Fowler 2-6-2T 40034 (14B). Return, with same engine is to Victoria.
10	FA Cup tie at Liverpool brings an overnight excursion from Ipswich into Central behind 61961 (31B), which worked from Lincoln. On the return, the K3 is piloted to Dunford Bridge from Stockport by 'Crab' 42788.
11	The LMR Royal train is seen at Cambridge returning to Wolverton ECS behind 44916 + 45353, an uncommon class in Cambridge.
17	0-6-0PT 1501 noted at Newton Abbot awaiting entry to the Works – first of this type to be seen so far west.
18	70030 *William Wordsworth* heads a brake test train of 40 loaded coal wagons plus recording car, between Toton and Brent. One in a series of such trials.
22	Surprisingly, J6 0-6-0 64251 is on the 8.12am King's Cross – Cambridge!
24	45563 *Australia* (10C) works the 12.30pm Euston – Liverpool 'Red Rose'. Highly unusual for a Patricroft engine to be seen in Euston.
24	Cross-London football excursion from Gidea Park to Carshalton includes a working Restaurant Car!
28	90271 (26C Bolton) heads a trainload of new Rhodesian Railways carriages (3' 6" gauge) from Gloucester C&W Works towards Oxley.

30	N7 0-6-2T 69621 is unexpected power on the 10.4am from Banbury to Woodford Halse.
31	Floods put Yarmouth (South Town) station and shed out of action beneath six feet of water.
31	FA Cup tie specials: five B1s arrive at Bolton from Nottingham; 61964 + 61096 arrive into Warwick Road with an excursion from London for the Manchester United v Walthamstow Avenue game, and three '5's and 45656 *Cochrane* are serviced at Blaydon after bringing in fans for the Newcastle v Rotherham match.
U/D	All the new-build 'Britannias' 70030-37 are observed at New Street during the month on various running-in turns from Crewe.
U/D	Route restrictions on 'Britannias' working on the SR bar them from working on the Isle of Wight!

FEBRUARY 1953

1ST	Flooding maroons much of the LTS rolling stock at Shoeburyness, and…
2	…diversions cause Liverpool Street – Shenfield electric units (9-car sets) to use Fenchurch Street. First passenger carrying electric trains here.
3	B16 4-6-0 61475 powers a Waverley route freight from Carlisle, unusual class.
5	Canterbury & Whitstable Railway (closed 1 December 1952) re-opens for coal traffic to Whitstable – otherwise cut off by the floods.
7	1.55pm express from Ramsgate is observed at Rochester behind 34079 *141 Squadron* + 34092 *City of Wells,* probably the first such tandem pairing of this class seen in this area.
7	Scotland v Wales rugby match brings 27 specials to Edinburgh, resulting in Dalry Road hosting two 'Crabs', ten 'Jubilees', eight 'Royal Scots', with a further four 'Jubilees' sent to Carstairs overnight. Excursions from Carlisle also bring 44711/59/74/75 to Haymarket depot for servicing, a rare event.
7	Two football specials from Walthamstow to Harrow & Wealdstone are headed by L1 2-6-4T 67739 (30A), 61664 *Liverpool,* both serviced at Watford.
9-18	Augmented services between Southend (Victoria) and Fenchurch Street bring B17s 61601/10/13/30/50/60/66 (plus B1s, B12s also) into a terminus that has rarely, if ever, seen them before.
10,12	GWR railcar W14W appears at Welshpool for platform clearance tests, and at Moat Lane Jct. two days later.
13	7821 *Ditcheat Manor* (89A Oswestry) is a rarity at Paddington, firstly on ECS and then taking out the 7.10pm to Wolverhampton.
14	60152 *Holyrood* arrives into Glasgow on the 11.50pm ex-Euston, having come on at Crewe. First LNER-type Pacific seen at St Enoch.
14	Burnley v Arsenal match attracts three specials from London through to Burnley (Manchester Road) headed by 46131 *The Royal Warwickshire Regiment,* 46144 *Honourable Artillery Company* and 46146 *The Duke of Wellington's Regiment,* all receiving WD 2-8-0 bankers over Copy Pit.
17	GWR railcar W16W runs between Reading and Southampton (Central) on platform clearance tests.
19	60081 *Shotover* (50B Neville Hill) makes its first appearance in London since 1948 on a King's Cross – York parcels.
19	62011 (63D Fort William) is an eye-catching arrival at Aberdeen, on freight from Perth.
21	61661 *Sheffield Wednesday* and 61373 both reach Southall with football specials from Gidea Park for an FA Amateur Cup match.

24	1750hp 1Co-Co1 10201 descends the 1 in 37 from Central to St Davids in Exeter, and then returns. First main line diesel to reach St Davids.
26	A2/3 60513 *Dante* surprisingly arrives at Cambridge on a freight.
28	61010 *Wildebeeste* and 61074 bring football specials from Hull through to Barrow, where LNER-types are rarely seen.
28	The station at Kirk Smeaton (closed 1931) is briefly re-opened for a football excursion to Leeds. Upton & North Elmsall enjoys the same privilege.
U/D	Gas-lamp standards at Harrow & Wealdstone damaged in the crash, are replaced by columns bearing the words 'Midland Railway Company'. (30 years after the Grouping the Midland still encroaches on LNW territory!).

MARCH 1953

1ST	CR 4-4-0 54454 (63C) brings the 10.15am ex-Buchanan Street into Aberdeen.
2	Reading shed is host to 60845 (with indicator shelter) in connection with Swindon Test Plant controlled road tests.
3	SR light Pacific makes a trial run from Exeter to Barnstaple via the Exe Valley and Dulverton – a surprising sight on this WR route.
7	76021 + 60047 *Donovan* head the Newcastle – Holloway ECS train near Thirsk, an exceedingly rare combination.
10	46169 *The Boy Scout* + 46152 *The King's Dragoon Guardsman* power the 12.58pm Leeds – Liverpool into Huddersfield, an unusual same-class pairing.
12,13	45718 *Dreadnought* (63A) passes Bonnybridge on the 12.12pm Buchanan Street – Oban and again on the 9.12am from Oban next day, the return working. Did 45718 reach Oban for a first ever 'Jubilee' visit?
13	76002 (66B) brings the unique (?) sight of a Motherwell engine into Peterborough, on a Doncaster running-in turn.
14	Specials for the womens' International hockey match at Wembley bring 5073 *Blenheim* (from Shrewsbury), 30934 *St. Lawrence* (Dover), 34096 *Trevone* (Rye) and 61564 (Felixstowe) to Neasden for servicing.
14	Ivatt 2-6-0 46514 appears at Bath on a running-in trip from Swindon. Only 46413 of this type has been seen before, when on trials from Swindon 1948/9.
17	70032 *Tennyson* is named at Euston by Sir Charles Tennyson, who then drives the engine along the platform to the buffer stops.
19	60536 *Trimbush* (64B), a rarity, enters King's Cross on the 'White Rose'.
20	30931 *King's Wimbledon* leaves Weymouth on the 9.20am to Waterloo as LMS diesel 10000 arrives from Waterloo, both uncommon in Weymouth.
21	Football special from Crook to Stockton is routed via the Shildon – Stillington North section, which has not seen a passenger train since pre-1923!
21	Unusual A3/A1 combination 60086 *Gainsborough* + 60144 *King's Courier* heads the Newcastle – Holloway ECS between Stockton and Thirsk.
22	L&Y 2-4-2T 10757 (still with LMS livery and number), appears at Slaithwaite on a departmental working. A type not usually seen on this line at all.
22	44732 visits Snow Hill (rare here) on a Blackpool – Birmingham excursion.
22	34071 *601 Squadron* heads a ramblers' excursion from Victoria to Sheffield Park via Crystal Palace and Horsted Keynes. Only Pacific here since 1945.

23	GWR railcar W32W runs between Worcester and New Street via Bromsgrove on platform clearance tests, an unexpected sight along here.
25	61800 reaches Aintree with a horsebox special from Newmarket.
29	62733 *Northumberland* (64B) is found out of its usual territory, at Aberdeen.
31	46212 *Duchess of Kent* is unusual power for the 'Postal' from Aberdeen.
31	61289 (51A) is the first LNER-type to reach Worcester since the war, when provided for the 4.25pm to Sheffield.
U/D	'Coronations' 46252/54/55 all work the 9am Dundee – Perth stopping passenger train whilst the Perth turntable is out of action.
U/D	Next to the coaling tower at Ardsley shed is a large tip for refuse and ashes, which has been burning by spontaneous combustion for ten years. Now threatening the foundations of the tower, a barrier of steel piling is being inserted into the ground to isolate the fire.
U/D	The brickwork and stone frontage of King's Cross is cleaned for the Coronation – first clean in 101 years!

APRIL 1953

1ST	9.55am to Edinburgh leaves Aberdeen behind 45729 *Furious* + 60972, the LMS pilot coming off at Montrose.
2	45612 *Jamaica* (14B!) brings 'The Mid-day Scot' into Euston, most unusual.
3	72001 *Clan Cameron* (66A) provides Aberdeen with its first sight of a Polmadie 'Clan' when taking out the 'Saint Mungo'.
3	62718 *Kinross-shire* (64A) is unaccustomed power for the 10.20am Perth to Buchanan Street, returning with the 5.8pm relief to Dundee (West).
4	60039 *Sandwich* appears LE at Sheffield (Midland) after turning on the Dore & Totley triangle. Later seen on Millhouses shed, first A3 to reach here.
4	60973 + 60525 *A. H. Peppercorn* is a most unusual combination to power a football special into Buchanan Street.
5	Stanier 2-6-0 42979 hauls the 9.5am Manchester (Central) – Sheffield, a rare type to be seen on the Midland Division.
7	45735 *Comet* (1B) makes a striking appearance in Leeds on a Liverpool to Newcastle express. Camden engines hardly ever reach Leeds.
8	60526 *Sugar Palm* is a big surprise at Wakefield (Kirkgate) working the 5.5pm Newcastle – Liverpool (Exchange). Locos are usually changed at York.
10	72008 *Clan Macleod* makes a class debut visit to Ardrossan (Town) on the 5.59pm local from Dalry, and the 8.38pm return to Kilmarnock.
10	70040 *Clive of India* reaches Barrow on the 3.55pm from Manchester (Exchange). Class is allegedly barred beyond Carnforth!
12	Adams 4-4-2T 30583 works Exeter (Central)/Sidmouth Jct./Exmouth/Exeter in connection with an Ian Allan railtour from London. This engine is usually confined to the Lyme Regis branch only.
13	An LNW 0-8-0 arrives in Euston with the 10.10am from Liverpool, as 46207 *Princess Arthur of Connaught* fails at Watford. An odd sight.
15	60835 *The Green Howard* heads a special troop train carrying this Regiment throughout from Barnard Castle to Harwich. First V2 seen at Ipswich and on the Colchester main line. Troops are *en route* to Germany.

19	41180 works right through from Birmingham to Lincoln on a three-coach special. Compounds rarely reach this far east.
20	Due to a strike of tug-men at Southampton, RMS *Queen Mary* from New York docks at Plymouth, resulting in three 'Cunarder' boat trains leaving Millbay for Waterloo, via Okehampton to Exeter. All are 'Pacific' hauled with T9 4-4-0s as pilots to Salisbury; 30715 + 34061 *73 Squadron* on the first, 30708 + 34057 *Biggin Hill* the second, 30709 + 34066 *Spitfire* the third.
21	T9 4-4-0 30719 heads an Inspection train to Ilfracombe from Exeter. Special stop is made at Lapford to view the Coronation display there.
21,22	H2 4-4-2 32421 *South Foreland* is rare power for the 11.6am Salisbury to Yeovil and 4.5pm back, both days. 'Atlantics' are most unusual this far west.
24	35020 *Bibby Line* breaks a driving axle at Crewkerne whilst travelling at speed. (See next month).
29	Compound 41199 works a postal special from Market Harborough to St Pancras carrying 1 million samples of gravy powder in 3,900 mailbags loaded onto 26 fitted wagons. BBC broadcasts an interview with the Head Postmaster whilst train is being loaded. All part of the Coronation effort!
U/D	'Starlight Specials' are advertised between St Pancras and St Enoch, and from Marylebone to Waverley. These Friday and Saturday overnight Refreshment Car trains run from the 10th; fare 70s, 3rd class return booked in advance.

MAY 1953

2ND	60883 works a 7-coach special originating at Waterhouses (which closed in 1951) to Ripon races. The V2 is the first seen here and runs tender first to Durham where reversal is necessary.
3	H2 4-4-2 32425 *Trevose Head* reaches Portsmouth (where 'Atlantics' are a rarity) on an excursion from Waterloo organised by the SLS.
3	72001 *Clan Cameron* (66A) works through to York from Liverpool (Exchange). First 'Clan' at York; second Polmadie engine (see 6 January 1951).
6,7	W1 4-6-4 60700 heads the 6.5am King's Cross – Cambridge and 10.50am back on both days. The W1 is very seldom seen at Cambridge.
9	Veteran MSWJ 2-4-0 1336 works a few days light passenger and goods trains in the Swindon/Bristol area preparatory to hauling, by special request an excursion from Gloucester to Andover Jct. and back to Swindon (Town).
11	40632 is an interesting visitor to Kirkby Stephen (East) on the Lancaster Engineer's Inspection train. An LMS 4-4-0 wouldn't normally ever reach here.
12	Ex-'Coronation' observation car is included at the rear of an excursion from Saltburn to Stirling chartered by the NE Coast Women's Institutes. Not a route that has previously seen such a vehicle.
13	A 'Hall' pilots 70027 *Rising Star* between Swindon and Gloucester on the diverted 'Red Dragon'. 'Britannias' are rarely double-headed in these parts.
15	'South Yorkshireman' arrives at Marylebone behind 61077 + 60102 *Sir Frederick Banbury*, paired from Leicester. Unusual to double-head this train.
16	'Crab' 42769 (16A) pilots Q6 0-8-0 63458 through Durham on a southbound goods, a most improbable combination.

16	GWR railcar visits Welshpool forming a day excursion from Birmingham.
18	AEC 3-car lightweight diesel unit begins Bangor – Amlwch trials.
24	'Crab' 42931 (1A) works through to Hunstanton on a Whit Sunday special from NW London.
25	Astonishingly, D11 4-4-0 62667 *Somme* (40F) makes the first appearance of its class at King's Cross for over 20 years when arriving on a special parcels train from Grimsby.
26	62053 (31B) is a surprise visitor to Manchester (Central) working through on an excursion from Cleethorpes.
26	Excursion to Cleethorpes starts at Idle, picks up at Eccleshill and reverses at Laisterdyke before proceeding towards Leeds. Passenger services at Idle, Eccleshill had ceased in 1931!
27	CR 4-2-2 123 leaves St Rollox Works in Glasgow towed by 44670 to Carlisle *en route* to the 'Royal Journeys' Exhibition at Battersea. 123, which had not been south of Carlisle before, arrives at Stewarts Lane two days later.
28	'Brighton Belle' set passes Surbiton forming an excursion from Waterloo to the Isle of Wight. These sets are normally confined to the Brighton line.
29	44026 (21A) surprisingly arrives at Ripon on a pigeon special. Very few LMS engines are seen here.
29	61370 (30D Southend!) – ex-Gorton Works – heads an Ashburys to Rhyl excursion via Stockport (Tiviot Dale) and Chester (General), and back. Also reaches Scarborough next day, where a 30D shedplate is equally unknown.
30	D16 4-4-0 62530 pilots 70041 *Sir John Moore* out of Cambridge on the 11.50am Liverpool Street – Norwich. Rare to see a 'Britannia' piloted at all.
31	45404 takes an excursion from Tring through to Hastings, only the second appearance of a '5' here.
U/D	Coronation Decorations for Regent Street (large illuminated Tudor Roses) are transported from the Berkhamsted factory to Euston suspended from the luggage racks of non-corridor suburban coaches! Two pairs of coaches used on alternate days between 29 April and 19 May.

Following the Crewkerne incident on 24 April, all 30 'Merchant Navy' Pacifics are withdrawn for inspection from 12 May. Hence 38 locos are loaned to the SR allocated as follows; 16 to Nine Elms (70A), 16 to Stewarts Lane (73A), 3 to Exmouth Jct. (72A), 2 to 72B (Salisbury) and one to Dover (74C). These come from all other BR Regions and comprise 7 x 7MTs, 6 x V2s, 7 x '5's, 3 x 5MTs, 15 x B1s. Examples of these never to be repeated workings are as follows;

14	60928 reaches Dorchester on the 10.30am from Waterloo, despite being prohibited west of Bournemouth.
16	70030 *William Wordsworth* appears on the up 'Night Ferry'.
16	70024 *Vulcan* works the up 'Atlantic Coast Express' through Esher.
19	60896 heads the 'Bournemouth Belle' both ways.
23	'5' works a boat train to Southampton Docks.
23	45051 seen on the second portion of the 3pm Waterloo – Exeter.
24	60893 undergoes trials in Southampton Docks.
27	60917 powers a Pullman sightseeing excursion; Waterloo to Yeovil Jct. (for Wells).
30	61015 *Duiker* hauls the 11.35am Victoria – Ramsgate.
June 9	70028 *Royal Star* noted hauling a milk train west of Salisbury.

10   Pullman sightseeing special to Templecombe (for Bath Abbey etc.) is worked by 70029 *Shooting Star* from/to Waterloo.

13   73003 arrives in Brighton on an inter-regional excursion.

16   61148 (62A!), which had been on loan to the SR, heads the 6.58am Aylesbury – Marylebone, then the 3am to Crewe (17th) on its way back north.

JUNE 1953

2ND   'Tees-Tyne Pullman' is cancelled on Coronation Day, but runs as a special (at Pullman fares), departing Newcastle 11.48pm (1st) calling at Darlington, York arriving at King's Cross 5.48am. Breakfast is served *en route* and Luncheon boxes made available. Not a unique all-night Pullman journey, because...

2   'Yorkshire Pullman' portions leave Harrogate 11.55pm (1st), Bradford (Exchange) 12.3am and 12.20am from Hull. Combined train reaches London at 5.14am and returns at 5.30pm as booked.

2   Two specials run from the Isle of Wight to London via Ryde, leaving Ventnor at 3am and Cowes at 3.15am. Unique – only passenger carrying trains to run through the night on the island.

5   44883 (68A), complete with snowplough, makes a conspicuous appearance on the 3.35pm Bournemouth (West) – Bath (Green Park). Carlisle engines should not be reaching the south coast!

6   D11 4-4-0 62666 *Zeebrugge* works through from Retford to Bourne End on the 'Northern Rubber Special'. Engine takes the ECS to Windsor (Central), party re-boards for Willesden, with J19 0-6-0 64665 as pilot to Canonbury, where engines are changed. D11s are unknown in these parts!

6   4-4-0s 40542 + D16 62535 form a rare MR/LNER partnership on a Peterborough – Leicester local.

7   45503 *The Royal Leicestershire Regiment* (5A) is probably a unique sight at Doncaster, arriving with a troop train, leaving northbound LE straight away.

7   GWR railcars W33W/ 'swinger'/ W36W form an excursion from Southall to Weston-super-Mare, hired by the Accountants' Dept AEC (Southall), where the cars were built in the first place.

4,8   Ivatt Atlantic 251, ex-storage at Doncaster Works, hauls stock trains between Doncaster and Lincoln in preparation for working an excursion in September.

10   V4 2-6-2 61701 operates the Arrochar – Craigendoran push-pull service, a most surprising substitute for a C15 4-4-2T.

10   B16 4-6-0 61443 is an unusual class to power the Harrogate portion of the 'Yorkshire Pullman' north from Leeds.

10,28   A1X 0-6-0T 32662 appears on the Lyme Regis branch and pilots Adams 4-4-2T 30583. This is repeated on 28th when an RCTS railtour visits.

13   Ivatt 2-6-0 43022 + B16 4-6-0 61417 is a really odd LMS/LNER partnership to bring the 'Scarborough Flyer' into Scarborough.

13   61524 + 61528 head a circular tour from Aberdeen via Craigellachie, Boat of Garten, Aviemore and Perth, back via Forfar. Rare class on the Highland line.

13,30   The diesel hauled (10000 or 10001) 11.30am to Waterloo is double-headed out of Weymouth by a U class 2-6-0. Normal practise is to bank SR trains as necessary, so piloting is therefore rare.

13	Compound 40916 + 60152 *Holyrood* form an amazing and possibly unprecedented pairing on the 4-coach Carlisle – Glasgow (Central) stopper.
14,15	Newhaven boat train leaves Victoria behind U1 2-6-0 31892 + E1 4-4-0 31504 on the 14th, and next day behind 30915 *Brighton*, whilst the usual electric locos worked the Spithead Review trains.
15	The AEC 3-car diesel train now moves to Ayr for trials on the Dalmellington branch and on some Kilmarnock turns.
15	Ivatt 2-6-0s 43135/37 double-head tender-first the 1pm from Mallaig to Fort William. 43132/33 also work this section at this time while the ash-pits at Mallaig are repaired, isolating the turntable there. These locos have rocking grates (and have less need of ash-pits) and are better suited to tender-first running as they also have tender cabs.
16	Portsmouth – Windsor & Eton Riverside Royal train is a 5-car 'Brighton Belle' unit 3052, a unique Royal working.
16,17	60974 makes two consecutive appearances in New Street on the 3.55pm from Newcastle. Engines are usually changed much earlier.
16,19	SR runs 1st class-only Ascot race specials at 12.40pm from Waterloo, surprisingly composed of ER and LMR vehicles (six open firsts, three Kitchen Cars) plus two SR utility vans, with 'Pacific' haulage.
19	Ballast train from Meldon Quarry ascends the 1 in 37 between St Davids and Central stations, Exeter with no less than four engines; E1R 0-6-2T 32135 + S15 4-6-0 30829 in front, and 82018 + E1R 32124 behind 10 hoppers!
20	Evening excursion is run from Rhyl to Nantlle. 2-6-4T 42444 hauls the 8-coach train, forming the first passenger train on this branch since 1932.
22,23	D11 4-4-0s 62666 *Zeebrugge* and 62667 *Somme* both work excursion traffic into Hull (Paragon), where this class is an extremely rare sight.
23	D30 4-4-0 62419 *Meg Dods* (62A) – sent to Inverurie Works for repair – is 'borrowed' by Kittybwester for the 6.10pm Aberdeen – Keith. 'Scott' class locos are not normally seen on the GNS system at all.
23	2-6-4T 42226 (33A), ex-Works, reaches Manchester (London Road) on the 7.53am from Crewe. First Plaistow engine seen in Manchester?
23	On her State Visit to Scotland, HM the Queen arrives into Princes Street behind 46220 *Coronation*, appropriately.
25	90513 (62C) works freight from Kittybrewster to Keith, the first WD noted north of Aberdeen.
26	V1 2-6-2Ts 67600/60, heading back to Scotland after overhaul at Darlington, are pressed into service on a Newcastle – Tweedmouth freight working. First use of such a type for this purpose on the East Coast main line.
26	'Saint Mungo' leaves Aberdeen behind 45597 *Barbados* (20A). Leeds 'Jubilees' are 'never' seen in Aberdeen!
27	Former 'Coronation' beaver-tail observation car E1729E labelled 'Laisterdyke to Newcastle' is the focus of attention seen in a down parcels train at York.
28	Three train sets of green SR stock find their way to Aberdeen! All had formed troop trains, one from Aldershot to Inverness, and two to Aberdeen from Ludgershall and Tidworth. One of these sets (from the Southampton boat train pool) forms the 7.20pm departure to King's Cross. Interesting sights!

28   1.15pm Cardiff – Snow Hill via Hereford arrives behind 4984 *Albrighton Hall* (87G Carmarthen), and is composed entirely of LNER stock.

30   AEC lightweight diesel unit observed at York *en route* from Scotland to Hull.

30   70000 *Britannia* (30A) heads a parcels train from Finsbury Park to Doncaster, a most unusual working for a Stratford 7MT.

U/D   BR mounts a 'Royal Journeys' travelling exhibition, putting on display five vintage Royal vehicles plus CR 4-2-2 123. Exhibition opens at Battersea on June 19, but travels widely thereafter. (See also October U/D).

U/D   Notice board on reclaimed marshland between St Helen's and Bembridge (IOW) reads: 'British Railways - Shooting, Fishing and Egging prohibited by Order'.

JULY 1953

2ND   70000 *Britannia* is provided for the Institution of Locomotive Engineers' Special train (including the ER dynamometer car) from Sheffield (Victoria) to Doncaster and back. 70000 overnights at Darnall, returning to King's Cross from Doncaster on 3rd. (See 30 June also).

3   D11 4-4-0 62666 *Zeebrugge* causes a sensation at Whitby (Town) by arriving on a 4-coach school's special from Stow Park (near Lincoln) via Doncaster and York. This loco had been specially requested.

4   45021 arrives in Brighton with the 11.40am from New Street. Only the second appearance here of a '5' on an ordinary service train.

4   44882 (68A) reaches York (Harrogate bay platform) on a 6-coach school special routed via Skipton, Arthington and Harrogate. Carlisle '5's rare here.

4-10   76018, new, and on a devious route from Horwich to Eastleigh turns up at Bath, and is immediately employed on local freights.

6-25   AEC lightweight diesel unit works trials from Hull to South Howden, Filey and Market Weighton.

7   72005 *Clan Macgregor* + 46117 *Welsh Guardsman* pair up to head the 'Thames-Clyde Express' from St Enoch to Carlisle. 'Clans' are hardly ever seen carrying titled train headboards.

7   46201 *Princess Elizabeth* exits Manchester (London Road) with a train for Shrewsbury. This class is rarely seen anywhere in Manchester.

8   7826 *Longworth Manor* (87G) noted on a Swindon – Portsmouth excursion via St Denys, Fareham. Only second 'Manor' routed this way in two years.

11   D40 4-4-0 62270 seen working the St Combs branch from Fraserburgh with no cow-catcher, in place of the regular Ivatt 2-6-0 46460, which has two!

14   M7 0-4-4T 30025 + U 2-6-0 31841 + Co-Co 10000 triple-head the 1pm from Waterloo into Exeter (Central), after the diesel had failed at Broad Clyst.

16   76018 (now with tablet exchange apparatus) works from Bath (Green Park) to Bournemouth (West). First 76xxx over the S&D route.

18   D11 4-4-0 62675 *Colonel Gardiner* reaches Fort William, a rare visitor here.

18   2-8-2T 7242 (88A Cardiff Cathays) presents itself at Birkenhead (Woodside), to general consternation, as this class is previously unknown here.

18   53808 + 53802 head the 10.5am Bournemouth – Cleethorpes over the S&D, an extremely rare duo, especially of both large- and small-boilered types.

19   61203 operates a day excursion to Southend originating, surprisingly, at High Barnet on London Transport electrified lines.

20	O2 2-8-0 63974 (36A) is a very unusual sight at Shotton on a breakdown train.
22	60865 reaches Todmorden on a York – Liverpool express before being replaced by a 'Crab'. Doubtful if a V2 has been here previously at all.
23	E4 2-4-0 62785 (31A) breaks new ground for the class by plying the Midland main line with the 8.35pm Kettering – Leicester local.
25	B16 4-6-0 61476 heads the 2.21pm King's Cross – Cambridge. This class is extremely rare at both places, being more or less confined to the NE Region.
29	A2/3 60507 *Highland Chieftain* makes a jaw-dropping visit to Cleethorpes with a 17-coach ECS train. Has a Haymarket engine ventured here before?
U/D	D11 4-4-0 62666 *Zeebrugge* appears at least twice at Leeds (Central) on stopping trains from Doncaster. D11s are practically unknown in Leeds.
U/D	Popularity of the 'Starlight Specials' puts much pressure on stock. On three weekends 3/4, 10/11, 17/18 July they carry 9624, 6576 and approximately 17,000 passengers respectively.

AUGUST 1953

1ST	45650 *Blake* brings a relief express into Euston consisting of GN corridors, four LNER Tourist coaches (with bucket seats), some ECJ and GE stock! Quite the weirdest train set seen here for some time. (See also U/D July).
1	D34 4-4-0 62472 *Glen Nevis* works a special to Ayr. NB locos are rare here.
8	45595 *Southern Rhodesia* works an excursion throughout from Manchester (London Road) to Brighton – first 'Jubilee' to be seen here.
8	4-6-0 61420 heads the 2.30pm King's Cross – Harrogate as far as Grantham, and returns with the up 'White Rose'! First recorded instance of a B16 on a titled express south of Doncaster.
8,9	Due to the derailment of the 'Royal Scot' in the Clyde Valley, northbound trains are diverted over the Waverley route, causing 46200 *The Princess Royal* and 46224 *Princess Alexandra* to appear at Hawick, and 46210 *Lady Patricia* next day. 46200 is also seen on the 8th at Portobello returning south with the 5.40pm Glasgow (Central) – Euston.
8	D11 4-4-0 62681 *Captain Craigengelt* + 45214 exit Queen Street on the 3.46pm to Fort William, an interesting and unusual pairing.
8	80052 passes through Huddersfield with a relief train for Newcastle, a surprising use of a 2-6-4T engine.
10	61996 *Lord of the Isles* (65A) arrives in Aberdeen on a freight from Perth. K4s are infrequent visitors to the Granite City.
12	CR 4-4-0 54454 pilots D30 4-4-0 62418 *The Pirate* on a goods train from the south into Craiginches yard, Aberdeen. Double-headed 4-4-0s on freight turns are almost unheard of.
15	K1/1 61997 *MacCailin Mor* (65J Fort William) is somewhat out of bounds hauling the 12.52pm Waverley – Hawick, and 4pm return goods.
15	70030 *William Wordsworth* works the Sheringham portion of the 'Broadsman' through to Sheringham. Only the second 7MT to run onto the M&GN system.
16	44830 (71G Bath) is found on Mirfield shed. Rare indeed for an S&D loco to venture this far north.
17	20kV AC electric units (converted 1914-built LNW stock) begin work on Morecambe and Heysham trains from Lancaster.
17	AEC lightweight diesel train is now running trials from Snow Hill to Solihull, Wolverhampton, Knowle and Henley-in-Arden.

19   N15X 4-6-0 32332 *Stroudley* works a Brighton excursion between Reading (South) and Redhill. First record of an N15X between these places.

19   62034 (65A) is surprise power for the King's Cross Goods – Doncaster Works stock train. Ivatt 2-6-0 43100 (53A) also powers this train during August, both of which are rare events.

20   T9 4-4-0 30724 heads the Bournemouth – Birkenhead from Basingstoke to Oxford, after 34018 *Axminster* fails. 30724 also works the return from Oxford, through to Bournemouth. Most unusual for T9s to work expresses solo.

21   MR 4-4-0 40326 (tender first) runs south through Rugby (Central) with an Inspection Saloon. These are rare engines on the GC main line, on any train.

24   35024 *East Asiatic Company* seen running east LE between Newton Abbot and Exeter, presumably after being weighed at Newton Abbot.

28   5.53pm Exeter (Central) – Waterloo is double-headed all the way with 34064 *Fighter Command* + 1750hp diesel 10202 (unable to produce full power).

30   5912 *Queen's Hall* leaves Marylebone with a troop train for…Chester, not a destination usually associated with this terminus.

SEPTEMBER 1953

1ST   6001 *King Edward VII* heads a Paddington – Bristol 2hr test train (10 coaches, with the WR dynamometer car). New 'Bristolian' timings in mind.

2   A2/3 60524 *Herringbone* and 60091 *Captain Cuttle* are both noted on the Midland main line north of Sheffield; 60524 on the 7.24am from Sunderland, 60091 the 8.15am from Newcastle. Unusual power for both trains at this point.

4   70008 *Black Prince* brings the 1.32pm Norwich – Liverpool Street into King's Cross (accident at Bethnal Green), and returns at 6.30pm as the 5.54pm from Liverpool Street. 'Britannias' are uncommon at King's Cross on any train.

5   N15X 4-6-0 32327 *Trevithick* is a surprise arrival at Weymouth, where appearances of 'Remembrance' class locos are few and far between.

5,6   Morecambe illuminations attract 30 extra trains over the weekend.

6   7903 *Eaton Mascot Hall* heads a military special from Chester into Marylebone. (Return working of that which 5912 took out on 30 August).

9   Ivatt 2-6-0 43136 (65A) leaves Aberdeen on the 2pm fish train for New England, an unusually small choice of power for this working.

11,12   46122 *Royal Ulster Rifleman* (9A) is a surprise arrival at Bath (Green Park) on the 'Pines Express', returning north on the same train next day.

12   12-coach train of Portsmouth line stock arrives at Chessington on a day excursion from Gillingham (Kent), an unusual sight here.

12   34015 *Exmouth* runs through Reading (General) on an up excursion. SR Pacific workings east of Reading on the WR main line are a novelty.

12   45594 *Bhopal* comes off the up 'Thames-Clyde Express' at Ampthill (firebox problem). 48177 is substituted, and headboarded, and runs Luton – St Pancras in one minute less than the express's schedule!

12   J15 0-6-0 65464, painted with the CIE emblem on one side of the tender, works the 6.5am Stratford – Hertford (East) between filming stints for the motion picture *O'Leary Night*, shot on the Buntingford branch.

12 46209 *Princess Beatrice* (5A) is an unexpected guest at Eastfield (65A) to use the wheel-drop facility. LMS 4-6-2s are decidedly 'foreign' here.

13 70020 *Mercury* (81A), on an excursion from Paddington reaches Barry Island, first Pacific seen here.

15 Compound 41060 is, on the face of it, a very unsuitable engine to work freight between Lincoln and March.

15 The 'Flying Scotsman' arrives in Waverley behind 62721 *Warwickshire*, 60024 *Kingfisher* having succumbed at East Linton.

16 Three specials are run from Southampton Docks for POWs returning from Korea on board the 'Asturias'. First special goes to Crewe via Bristol and Birmingham, second to Edinburgh (schedule 11hr 20min), third to Waterloo.

16,17 Preserved GNR 4-4-2s 990 *Henry Oakley* + 251, double-head the 12-coach 5pm King's Cross – Peterborough. Familiarisation runs prior to 20,27 September.

19 Compound 41085 (24E) is a very rare arrival at Bradford (Exchange), having worked an excursion through from Blackpool.

20,27 4-4-2s 990 + 251 work the northbound 'Plant Centenarian' from King's Cross to Doncaster via Lincoln. Exhibition at the 'Plant' includes Stirling 4-2-2 No.1, 70000 *Britannia*, 60022 *Mallard*, 60862, plus Bo-Bo 26020. A4 60014 *Silver Link* heads the return to London. On the 27ᵗʰ, 990 + 251 run a second special from Leeds and Doncaster to King's Cross, including beaver-tail observation car E1729E. 60014 takes the train back to Leeds.

21 61627 *Aske Hall* is surprise power for an up freight out of York.

24 Leicester (Central) sees, in the same evening, Ivatt 2-6-0 43111 (31D South Lynn) on the 6.15pm to Nottingham, and 6966 *Witchingham Hall* waiting to take out the Hull – Swindon fish train, which arrives behind the immaculate ex-Works 61665 *Leicester City* (32A). First recorded visit of this particular B17, post-war.

25 72001 *Clan Cameron* (66A) makes a class debut appearance on the North Wales coast with the 10.50am Euston – Holyhead, returning next day on the 9.10am Llandudno – Euston.

26 Remarkably, S&D 2-8-0 53801 (71G Bath) pilots the 'Pines Express' right through to New Street, and appears on Saltley shed next day.

26,27 More than 80 specials arrive at Blackpool bringing visitors to view the sea-front illuminations.

26/27 GWR railcar W13W is chartered by the Talyllyn RPS, and works through from Paddington (6.45am) to Towyn (12.34pm), with a fuel stop at Leamington. Return departure is 11.3pm; W13W breaks down at Lapworth, 2-8-0 2830 tows it to Leamington (5.25am), passengers transfer to W22W and arrive Paddington 7.45am. Longest ever railcar special, and first overnight!

29 45664 *Nelson* (19B Millhouses), very rare in Euston, works a 7-coach special to Lancaster (Castle), returning from Morecambe (Promenade), for an inspection by overseas railway representatives of the AC electrification scheme. Sir George Nelson of the EE Co. is joint host with BR for the occasion, hence this particular engine. (45664 is named after the Admiral!).

30 60814 is towed dead into Liverpool Street by 61555 to undergo platform clearance tests. First V2 seen here, for any purpose!

U/D AEC lightweight diesel train operates the Southminster – Wickford branch from 21 September to 9 October, then moves to Romford – Upminster Branch.

OCTOBER 1953

1ST   61207 (35A) works through to Bournville with a 'Cadbury's Special' from Harringay, via the East Coast main line as far as Peterborough.

6   61664 *Liverpool* brings a troop special to East Rudham, between South Lynn and Fakenham – first recorded 'Sandringham' here on the M&GN.

9   Q 0-6-0 30548 reaches Bath – a first for this class – over the S&D from Poole. Returns to Bournemouth with the 9.55am from Green Park on the 15th.

10   7013 *Bristol Castle* works into Crewe on a Worcester – Blackpool excursion. 'Castles' are infrequent visitors here.

11   U1 2-8-8-2T Beyer-Garratt 69999, now oil-fired, undergoes trials between Mottram yard and Crowden with 600 ton trains to test the new system.

14   Three new boilers for 84xx 0-6-0PTs are seen on a goods train at Bushbury, in transit from Swindon to Bagnall's at Stafford, an uncommon sight.

17   Up 'Cornish Riviera' is powered by green 6029 *King Edward VIII* paired with a blue tender from 6025! A short-term expedient.

19   44983 tows 61543/32/01 (ex-61A) past Polmadie *en route* to Kilmarnock Works for scrap. (That's GER locos from the GNS system running via CR lines to GSW Works behind an LMS engine, masquerading as a straightforward BR movement!).

21   0-6-0 diesel shunter 13014 visits Southampton Docks for clearance tests.

23   GWR railcar W16W appears at St Pancras, chartered by the Solihull Society of Arts, running via Stratford-on-Avon, Olney and Bedford.

25   'Thames-Clyde Express' leaves St Enoch behind 72008 *Clan Macleod* piloting 46103 *Royal Scots Fusilier*. An unusual combination.

U/D   'Clans' are passed to work to Lymington Pier, but SR 2-6-0s and Bullied Light Pacifics are forbidden! (SR route restriction Regulations).

U/D   Beattie well-tanks are diagrammed to work the 11.50am (SO) Padstow to Wadebridge, their first scheduled passenger workings for many years.

U/D   AEC lightweight diesel train works the Gravesend – Allhallows branch.

U/D   Motive power shortage at Kittybrewster leads to D11s 62679 *Lord Glenallan*, 62680 *Lucy Ashton*, D34 62477 *Glen Dochart*, D30 62423 *Dugald Dalgetty*, D40 62273 *George Davidson* – all 4-4-0s, and 90097/455 being used on trains to Keith, all drafted in for the purpose. D40 62276 *Andrew Bain* also works to Ballater on the 8.11am from Aberdeen. Interesting workings!

U/D   L1 2-6-4-Ts 67729/37 (30A) are loaned to Toton (18A) for use on air-braked coal train tests to Trowell and back.

U/D   'Royal Journeys' exhibition (including the CR 4-2-2 123 and 5 ex-Royal coaches), tours BR starting at New Street 17-21 July, and ending at Cardiff 7-12 November, visiting 11 other cities in between. It was at Battersea Wharf from 19 June to 11 July initially.

NOVEMBER 1953

5TH   60028 *Walter K. Whigham* propels ex-'Coronation' observation car E1729E from King's Cross to Huntingdon on ATC tests.

11-13   Two 625hp diesel hydraulics built by the North British Loco Co. for the Mauritius Government are tested on BR, including a 3-coach train from Glasgow (Central) to Lanark (11th) and 5-coach trains between Glasgow and Princes Street on the other two days.

14	'Santa Special' says the engine headboard, as 30850 *Lord Nelson* works from Eastleigh to Southampton (Terminus). 700 children are guests of E. Mayes & Sons' Department Store.
18	60102 *Sir Frederick Banbury* (38C Leicester GC) arrives at King's Cross with the 'Master Cutler' diverted due to a derailment near Leicester.
19	60022 *Mallard* is chosen for a special, chartered by the British Iron & Steel Research Corporation, throughout from King's Cross to Sheffield (Victoria), where A4s are rarely seen.
21	0-6-0 64511 heads the 1.10pm Silloth – Carlisle, most unusual to see a J35 on a passenger working.
U/D	AEC lightweight diesel train is bought by BR w/e 14 November, new insignia being applied while still working on the Gravesend – Allhallows branch. Leaves for Southall (AEC Works) on 16th before going into BR service on the Watford – St Albans branch.

DECEMBER 1953

1ST	60527 *Sun Chariot* (62B!) heads the 5.30pm King's Cross – Leeds.
2	'Crab' 42865, on loan for the seed potato traffic, is a strange sight departing Waverley on the 8.45am to Perth.
3	Dual air/vacuum-braked 70043 (9A) appears in St Pancras with the 12.5pm express from Derby.
3	4056 *Princess Margaret* heads the 'Merchant Venturer' from Bristol. 'Stars' are rarely turned out for titled expresses nowadays.
5	4-4-0 62490 *Glen Fintaig* reaches Newcastle, ex-Hawick. D34s are rare here.
9/10	Striking tugmen at Southampton cause the 'United States' to dock at Plymouth where delayed disembarkation means the 'Statesman' boat train to Waterloo travels overnight – a first – arriving 5.15am on 10th. Also affected is the boat train for the 'Arawa' which now runs to London Docks from Waterloo, but still has Pullman cars and Pacific haulage by 34011 *Tavistock*.
10-12	Air-braked locos 73031 and 70043 work coal train tests between Toton and Brent, either singly or as a pair.
13	Due to track repairs WR expresses between Exeter and Plymouth, including the 'Cornish Riviera', are diverted via Okehampton.
22,24	70022/27 *Tornado/Rising Star* double-head 8am Penzance – Paddington through Totnes, first pairing on a passenger working? 70028/25 *Royal Star/ Western Star* also double-head the 'Red Dragon' into Paddington, 24th.
24	8.54am Waterloo – Salisbury, an 'extra' for Christmas, changes engines at Salisbury and proceeds as a relief train through to Cardiff. Flexible working!
25,26	72000 *Clan Buchanan* heads the 'Granite City' out of namesake Buchanan Street on both days. 'Clans' rarely work titled trains (except at Christmas!).
U/D	Three 'Crabs'(on loan for the seed potato traffic) are noted working on the East Coast main line from Edinburgh to Heaton – exceptional sights here.
U/D	80110 works St Boswells – Tweedmouth, *en route* (new) to Aberdeen.

JANUARY 1954

| 2ND | 46229 *Duchess of Hamilton* is surprise power for the 3-coach 10.54am Nuneaton – Stafford local, having failed the previous night on the down Perth. |

8,19,22 1000 *County of Middlesex* noted running tests between Swindon and Reading (equipped with indicator shelter and stovepipe chimney) following draughting modifications at Swindon.

9 'Big Bertha' 0-10-0 58100, ex-Derby Works, appears on Saltley depot (21A).

9 61664 *Liverpool* (32B) heads the 3.39pm to Cleethorpes out of Scunthorpe, where this class is rarely seen, especially Ipswich examples.

9 N2 0-6-2T 69500 (65C Parkhead) undertakes station pilot duties at Aberdeen, after repair at Inverurie Works – both firsts for this class.

9 45664 *Nelson* (19B) works a 12-coach excursion (including Restaurant Car) from Leicester to Middlesbrough for an FA Cup tie. Not many 'Jubilees' reach here.

12 Ivatt 2-6-2T 41304 (71A) awaits Works attention at Swindon. (Why not Eastleigh, it's allocated next door?).

12 Fowler 2-6-4T 42316 is observed at Clapham Jct. at 6.45pm with a horsebox special for Norwood or East Croydon. An unexpected engine in these parts.

17 44947 (24E) and 44741 (9A) both reach Snow Hill on excursions from Blackpool and Manchester respectively. Both go to Tyseley shed.

18,19 60528 *Tudor Minstrel*, 60532 *Blue Peter* each visit Inverurie Works for weighing, firebox repairs respectively. Rare for A2s to run on the GNS at all.

19,22 N1 0-6-2Ts 69464 (19th), 69447 (22nd) appear on ECS workings at Liverpool Street after repair at Stratford! Both are 37C (Bradford) engines – surely a shed not previously represented at this terminus?

24 73030 + 73031 undergo Westinghouse air brake trials on 50 loaded coal wagons plus recording car, between Toton and Brent.

25 A5 69806 (38A) makes a rare trip to Cambridge, heading for Stratford Works.

26 Amazingly, 46125 *3rd Carabinier* works the 9.15am Manchester (London Rd) to West of England/Swansea right through to Cardiff (General), due to chaotic snow conditions. Has a 'Royal Scot' ever reached Cardiff before?

30 34066 *Spitfire* heads a return Kensington Olympia – Folkestone excursion that has two Pullman cars for meal service, after a trip to see Bertram Mills Circus.

30 Arsenal v Norwich City FA Cup match attracts five specials from Norwich and one from Hunstanton into King's Cross (!) pulled by 70006 *Robert Burns*, 70009 *Alfred the Great* and 61877, 61918/39/53 – a most unusual sextet to arrive at this terminus.

U/D J11 0-6-0 64348 pays two visits to Darlington, a type rarely seen here.

U/D 0-6-2T 56xx (81C Southall) is surprisingly seen on ECS duties at Paddington.

U/D Camping Coach W9930W is on display at Paddington, painted in malachite green livery.

FEBRUARY 1954

3RD, 4TH Derailment at Watford causes diversion of three Euston-bound trains, from Bletchley via Oxford to Paddington. Consequently the 'Red Rose' appears at the WR terminus behind 45591 *Udaipur*, 46152 *The King's Dragoon Guardsman* with the 8.55am from Perth and 45050 on the 4.12pm from Liverpool. Next day, the up 'Mancunian' is formed of a scratch set of mostly GWR stock with no Refreshment Car, though a tea urn, sandwiches and packed lunches are made available. It does however go to Euston.

5 Due to labour troubles at Southampton, Shaw Saville Line's 'Dominion Monarch' embarks all passengers at London's King George V Dock. Boat train still departs

Waterloo for the 31 mile run via Neasden, taking 2 hours for the journey, 7 miles from Waterloo as the crow flies!

8-14 1750hp diesel 10202 is loaned to Dover for trials on the 'Golden Arrow' and 'Night Ferry', the first occasions these expresses have been diesel hauled.

9-11 Co-Co 1500V DC electric 27000 (new) pilots a 26000-series Bo-Bo on the 2.55pm Wath – Mottram freight, an unexpected pairing.

11,19 60093 *Coronach* (11th) and 60095 *Flamingo* (19th), both Carlisle Canal (68E) engines, are rare visitors to Lincoln, running-in from Doncaster Works.

15 GWR railcars W33W + W38W (with trailer car between them) are seen on clearance tests from West to Central stations in Bournemouth.

18 77000/1, brand new, pass through Woodford Halse in transit from Swindon to Darlington.

19 Middlesbrough – Stockton 15-coach (mostly non-corridor) special, conveys 1,750 schoolchildren plus staff to a matinee performance by Sadler's Wells Ballet. A J21 0-6-0 heads the train; fare 5d child return, 10d adult.

20 60015 *Quicksilver* works throughout between King's Cross and Crook (assisted by A8 4-6-2T 69851 from Darlington). Both locos take the ECS to Bishop Auckland. Train is a football special for Hitchin Town supporters to the FA Amateur Cup tie v Crook Town.

20 Football excursions from Leicester reach Norwich behind 45221, 45263, 45342 and 73046 – first 5MT seen here since 73000/02 were on loan in 1951. '5's are not exactly commonplace either at Norwich.

21 60108 *Gay Crusader* + 60111 *Enterprise* double-head (from Leicester) the 3.50pm ex-Manchester (London Road) into Marylebone. Unprecedented pairing of Pacifics on the GC main line.

21 5055 *Earl of Eldon* makes an extremely rare appearance at Birkenhead (where 'Castles' are almost unknown), to work the 7.45pm fast freight to Paddington.

22 GWR railcar W3W heads west out of Salisbury on clearance tests to Exeter.

21-25 BRCW A1A-A1A 955hp 3'6" gauge diesel for the Commonwealth Railways of Australia is tested – on standard gauge bogies – between Smethwick and Banbury. ER supplies two quintuplet sets of suburban stock as load.

23 6961 *Stedham Hall* pilots a 'Royal Scot' on the (diverted) 2am Crewe – Penzance, from Worcester to Hereford. An astonishingly rare pairing.

24 Two 1st class and three 3rd class Sleeping Cars are provided at Snow Hill as a hostel for contestants in the WR Boxing Championships.

25 'Canberra' jet bomber crashes and explodes onto the Midland main line embankment near Napsbury station. Much disruption to traffic ensues.

26 Adams 4-4-2T 30583 reaches Newton Abbot – a first – for weighing.

U/D 48616 tows Longmoor Military Rly WD 2-10-0 600 + USA 2-8-0 700 to Bagnalls at Stafford for repair. Locos to 'work their passage' south.

MARCH 1954

1ST-6TH U 2-6-0 31621 undergoes trials on the S&D (complete with tablet exchange apparatus) heading the 11.40am Bournemouth (West) – Bath (Green Park), and 4.25pm return working.

2 Scarborough – Leeds Pantomime excursion calls specially at some intermediate stations that closed more than 20 years ago.

3	46105 *Cameron Highlander* (66A) heads the 9.35am Aberdeen – Glasgow, the 'Saint Mungo', first 'Royal Scot' in Aberdeen since June last year.
5-6	70020 *Mercury* performs all night on the set of the Ealing Studios film *Lease of Life* at Windsor & Eton (Central). First 'Britannia' at Windsor?
6	'Patriot' 45550 (8A) steams up the Cleckheaton branch towards Low Moor with the ECS of a supporters special for the Huddersfield v St Helens RL match. Doubtful if this class has ever been in this neck of the woods before.
8	U1 2-6-0 31895 works a 'Billy Graham Crusade' excursion throughout from Redhill to Harringay Park. Further specials run over the next two weeks with light Pacific haulage, all SR engines being serviced at Stratford.
8-13	U1 2-6-0 31906 works the same trials over the S&D as 31621 did.
9,10	60900 brings the down 'Saint Mungo' into Aberdeen and returns south with the up 'Bon Accord' next day. Uncommon power for these trains.
10	92007 heads a 1070 ton test train from Bidston Dock to Shotton.
11	61611 (30A) *Raynham Hall* is a stranger to the East Coast main line, heading a Doncaster – King's Cross train, then returns with a loose-coupled freight.
15	45367, 45247 (on loan to 61A) head the 7.2am Aberdeen – Keith and 2.20am Aberdeen – Inverurie goods. LMS locos are rare on GNS routes.
15	AEC (now BR) lightweight diesel unit works the Harrow – Belmont branch.
16	10.5am Newcastle – Holloway ECS train seen near Thirsk behind the rare combination of B16 4-6-0 61434 + 60020 *Guillemot*.
18	Fowler 2-6-4T 42374 (on loan to 34A) brings the ECS of the down 'Aberdonian' into King's Cross – first of this class seen here.
20	34047/48 *Callington/Crediton* both arrive at Ashton Gate with football specials for the Bristol City v Brighton match. First 'West Country' class in Bristol since 34006 *Bude* in the 1948 Interchange Trials.
21	Fell 2000hp diesel mechanical 10100 runs trials on the CLC lines between Manchester (Central) and Liverpool (Central). New ground for this engine.
24	Derailment between Exeter and Taunton causes WR freight diversions via Yeovil (Pen Mill and Junction) and along the SR main line to Exeter. GWR locos using this route are; (up direction) 2-6-0 9305, 6908 *Downham Hall*, 6874 *Haughton Grange*, 6856 *Stowe Grange*; (down direction) 2-6-0s 7302/3, 6830 *Buckenhill Grange*.
25	Piloting over the South Devon banks produces the contrasting combination of 'Dukedog' 9023 + 7031 *Cromwell's Castle* at Newton Abbot on the 8am Penzance – Paddington.
27	1st class Sleeping Car M484 is surprisingly noted on the rear of the down 'Pembroke Coast Express' at Paddington.
U/D	Ivatt 2-6-0s 43133/35 (65A) both work to Heaton with seed potato traffic from Edinburgh. Eastfield engines of any type are noteworthy at Newcastle.

APRIL 1954

2ND	Stanier 2-6-0 42948 (1A) reaches Marylebone (first of this type seen here) with a parcels train from Bletchley.
3	42374 is promoted from ECS trains to the 6.54am King's Cross – Cambridge!
3	60809 *The Snapper...* (52A) arrives in Queen Street – where Gateshead engines rarely appear – on a football special for the Scotland v England game.

3	60103 *Flying Scotsman* heads a King's Cross – York Westminster Bank excursion of six GNR coaches + Cafeteria Car + beaver tail observation car!
4	N7 0-6-2T 69713 (complete with headboard – very rarely seen on tank engines) pilots 61399 on the up 'Scandinavian' diverted via Witham.
7	A2/3 60515 *Sun Stream* heads the 9.20am Hull – Liverpool, to Leeds. Unusual.
12	61214 pilots 60016 *Silver King* from Sunderland through Haswell with the diverted 5pm Newcastle – Liverpool. No regular passenger trains run here.
14	HM the Queen Mother, Princess Margaret, Prince Charles and Princess Anne leave Waterloo for Portsmouth in 'Brighton Belle' unit 3052.
16	Surprisingly, 61911 (64A) is trusted with the 4pm Aberdeen – Perth.
17	Easter Saturday, Buchanan Street. 46243 *City of Lancaster* heads the 'Saint Mungo' both ways between Glasgow, Aberdeen and 45673 *Keppel* + 45731 *Perseverance* double-head the 1.15pm from Aberdeen – abnormal workings.
17	Bletchley shed hosts, on adjacent tracks, 6138, 80081, 62585, 90423. Variety!
19	'Cauliflower' 0-6-0 58412 (12C Penrith) works the 3.35pm Penrith to Darlington as far as Kirkby Stephen (East), an exceptional appearance here.
19	34040/42 *Crewkerne/Dorchester* double-head the northbound 'Pines Express' at Evercreech Jct., a same-class pairing not seen before on the S&D.
19	Seven specials, all for Belle Vue, all 8F hauled, all with class 'A' headcodes pass within 15min on the Huddersfield – Manchester trans-Pennine route!
21	J19 0-6-0 64643 (31B) is an inexplicable sight heading an up freight on the Trent Valley main line north of Rugby.
21	Ivatt 2-6-2T 41318 + C2X 0-6-0 32545 arrive in Victoria bunker-to-tender on the 5.15pm boat train from Newhaven, 20001 having failed at East Croydon.
22	J38 0-6-0 65925 (62A) causes some consternation by appearing on the Deeside line (Aberdeen – Ballater) with a special goods train.
24	Low Moor (Bradford) has five 'Jubilees' on loan to work Halifax – Wembley specials for the RL Cup Final. Later, Neasden has seven 'Jubilees' on view!
25	'Dukedog' 4-4-0s 9023 + 9011 double-head an RCTS special from Victoria to Swindon Works. First departure of GWR locos from Victoria since 1915!
25	30932 *Blundells* pilots 4-4-0 40601 from Bournemouth (Central) to Bath on a railtour special – first 'Schools' class to run over the S&D. 40698 + 40601 double-head the return to Evercreech Jct., 40601 solo to Templecombe, 30932 works back to Waterloo.
26	60815 brings the Ampleforth College start of term special (nine corridors including Cafeteria) throughout from King's Cross to Gilling.
27	Compound 41188 works the 3.50pm Leeds – Northallerton to Harrogate, then pilots 90481 on a Newport – Neville Hill goods. Unprecedented pairing!
28	46131 *The Royal Warwickshire Regiment* arrives at York at 3.37am on a mail train from Crewe. 'Scots' are a big rarity on any train reaching York.
29	44700 (64D) departs northwards from Aberdeen with a forces leave train. New territory for a Carstairs engine.
30	First of the 2-car DMU sets for West Riding local services runs from Marylebone to Bradford under its own power. Test runs to Beaconsfield and back had taken place on both previous days.

MAY 1954

1ST   61540 seen at Melton Mowbray on the through Lowestoft – Leicester.

1   45696 *Arethusa* (66A) passes LE through Waverley. Noticeable!

3,4   70004 *William Shakespeare* (73A) works the 6.35pm Chester – Rhyl stopper on both days (a far cry from 'Golden Arrow' duty!) running-in from Crewe.

8   Diversion of several West Coast trains over the S&C causes the unique side-by-side occurrence of the down 'Royal Scot', behind 44900 + 45317, taking water at Hellifield alongside the down 'Thames-Clyde Express', also halted there to attach a pilot over Ais Gill. A further notable spectacle at Hellifield is the pairing of 75044 + Compound 41152 on a Morecambe – Leeds train.

8   0-6-0 diesel shunter 13064 (36B) heads an inspection train inside the new Woodhead Tunnel – an Official Saloon plus two flat wagons with benches.

9   As Leeds (Central) is closed for PW work, the up 'Harrogate Sunday Pullman' runs from City, via the Midland route to Normanton, thence to Wakefield (Kirkgate, Westgate – reversal). They blinked at Normanton!

9,16   'Cornish Riviera' is diverted via Bristol, due to bridge repairs at Newbury.

10   46247 *City of Liverpool* takes the diverted 'Royal Scot' round Manchester (London Road) on the MSJ&A line to head north. 46210 *Lady Patricia* passed the same way ten minutes earlier on the 11.15am Birmingham – Glasgow.

11   61116 (34E Neasden) passes Bushbury on a return special of LNER stock ex-British Industries Fair at Castle Bromwich. First B1 at Wolverhampton?

13,14   4056 *Princess Margaret* powers the 'Cornishman' from Bristol to Wolverhampton, and the down train next day. Rare work for a 'Star' nowadays.

15   (Week ending) Brand-new 2-car DMUs 79000/79500 and 79001/79501 run trials between Bradford (Exchange), Leeds (Central) and Harrogate; also Leeds (Central)/Ardsley/Castleford, prior to public service.

16   75039 reaches Clacton-on-Sea with an excursion from Berkhamsted. First of this class to be seen in East Anglia.

16   Compound 40935 is a stranger at Lincoln, arriving on a train from Nottingham

19   Royal train noted at Euston, most unusually, behind 46247 *City of Liverpool* + 46229 *Duchess of Hamilton* as a pair, quite a sight.

19,20   WR footplate strike means boat trains from Plymouth Millbay Docks run up to Waterloo for the French liners 'Colombie' (19th) and 'Liberte' (20th), WR Ocean Liner stock being used on the first date.

20   46100 *Royal Scot* itself heads a special train of 13 vehicles (inc. 7 Sleeping Cars), conveying Restaurant Car staff and supplies, for 7 works-outings from Huddersfield to Llandudno on 21st. Train runs from Euston to Low Moor carriage sidings via Stockport and the Cleckheaton branch – first 'Scot' here?

20   Airline Terminal at Southampton Docks is used by commercial passengers for the first time since the war, when Aquila Airways inaugurate their flying boat service to Capri. Two Pullman cars are detached from a boat train and worked to the Terminal station.

20   Co-Co DC electric 20003 operates a special 12-coach Pullman train (including a 'Devon Belle' observation car) from Victoria to Brighton on a 58 minute schedule, for delegates to the International Railway Congress (IRC).

20,21   D11 4-4-0 62690 *The Lady of the Lake* heads the 6.13pm Carlisle – Riccarton Jct. two days running, a surprising class to be seen on this service.

| 21 | Princess Margaret arrives at Plymouth (North Road) in the Royal train headed by 34037 *Clovelly*, tender-first with the 4-lamp headcode on the tender. Train had been re-routed from Paddington to Waterloo at the last minute, and so is 'wrong way round' on arrival at Plymouth! |

21/22 A Sleeping Car train is run from Scarborough in connection with the ICI Directors' Conference. Four cars (plus brake) leave for York and are attached there to the 1.16am to King's Cross.

22 Final 'Billy Graham' meeting at Wembley brings five Bulleid Pacifics and a SR 2-6-0 through Kenton. Another excursion from Brighton to Charing Cross is formed of 4-COR + 4-BUF + 4-COR units.

22,23 Two 1st class-only specials for delegates to the IRC run from King's Cross to Edinburgh on non-stop 6¾ hour schedules, 10min apart – an historic first. A4s 60022/34 *Mallard/ Lord Faringdon* head the 7.55/8.5am departures, both 8 coaches + two Kitchen Cars + beaver-tail observation car. Delegates return to Euston (23rd) from Wemyss Bay (after sailing the Clyde), meaning former 'Coronation' cars travel the West Coast line!

29 61645 *The Suffolk Regiment* is noted in the carriage sidings at Clapham Jct., first of this class to be seen here.

29 L3 2-6-4T 69060 passes through Cambridge *en route* from Frodingham to Stratford for modification as a stationary boiler to pre-heat the stock in Stratford carriage sidings.

30 Troop train stock stored in sidings between Trowbridge and Romsey includes 4 x CR Pullmans, 2 x LNER Buffet Cars and a HR coach – all in carmine & cream livery.

31 The eye-catching combination of 78023 + B16 4-6-0 61431 double-heads a train of 16 non-corridors south through Ripon. 78023 is (probably) in transit, brand-new from Darlington Works to the LMR.

U/D The Whit Sunday 6.54pm Waterloo – Basingstoke is graced by the surprise pairing of 34020 *Seaton* + 30788 *Sir Urre of the Mount*.

U/D Pullman cars 27/171/166/96/169/17 and a 'Devon Belle' observation car provide restaurant facilities for exhibitors at the British Industries Fair.

U/D 25 May-6 June. Rolling stock exhibition is held at Willesden depot in conjunction with the IRC. Locos on display are 71000 *Duke of Gloucester*, 70037 *Hereward the Wake*, 73050, 77009, 92014, 80084, 84019, diesels 10203 and 10100, gas turbine 18000 and DC electric 27002 plus much coaching stock and wagons. 71000 is so named in commemoration of the Duke's Presidency of the IRC London meeting.

JUNE 1954

1ST-3RD New Street's centenary exhibition features 46235 *City of Birmingham*, along with veteran 2-4-0s *Hardwicke* (LNW) and 158A (MR).

2,3 60062 *Minoru* (34A ex-Works) is borrowed by Neasden for the 'Master Cutler' out of Marylebone, strengthened with additional Kitchen, Restaurant Cars for the Minister of Transport and officials. The new Woodhead Tunnel is opened by the Rt Hon. A. Lennox-Boyd next day, with Bo-Bo 26020 on the inaugural special, then 3-car EMU runs four public trips.

2 72006 *Clan Mackenzie* reaches Barrow (a first) at 1.13pm from Manchester.

2 Chessington South hosts 34011 *Tavistock* + Pullman train as the Queen returns from here to Waterloo, after attending the Epsom race meeting.

4	61230 (37C) + Bradford crew, work the 12-coach 'Bradford Flyer' right through to King's Cross, an exceptional event.
8	Whit-Tuesday excursions from Bradford (Forster Square) to Bridlington bring Compounds 41061, 41104 to the seaside, where these are uncommon locos.
12	60534 *Irish Elegance* (64B) arrives at King's Cross on the through train from Filey holiday camp. This Haymarket Pacific is a rarity in London.
12	GWR railcar works through from Wolverhampton to Towyn as an excursion to the Talyllyn railway.
13	45725 *Repulse* is a surprise arrival at Tynemouth on a special from Sheffield.
13	41156 reaches Westbury (class debut here) on an SLS special from New Street.
12,14	Last day of all-steam operation of Bradford (Exchange) – Leeds (Central) services sees J6 0-6-0 64203 work the 8.50pm ex-Bradford using GNR, NER, and LNER coaching stock. First scheduled DMU services introduced on 14th. Only five 2-car sets available, so three push/pull sets from London supplement these, and N7 0-6-2Ts 69691/4/5/6 are drafted to 37A (Ardsley).
14	Summer timetable begins. All trains over Woodhead now electrically hauled.
14	92014 makes a class-first visit to Cambridge heading GE mainline freight towards Bishops Stortford.
16	C13 4-4-2T 67438 passes through Mirfield (rare here) with ECS for Bradford.
19	N7 0-6-2T 69673 (30E Colchester, ex-Works) brings the 6.42am from Luton into King's Cross – neither a class, nor a shed, normally represented here!
19	45319 (60A) reaches Aberdeen from Inverness, usually a B1 turn.
20	61792 + 61539 power a circular tour Aberdeen/Craigellachie/Boat of Garten/Aviemore/Perth/Forfar. K2s are unknown on Highland main line!
20	'Crab' 42939 – rarely seen in Norfolk – passes Thetford on a down troop train.
21	61638 *Melton Hall* spotted between Hull, Beverley with a lone brakevan.
23	61749 visits Swindon – first K2 to do so – on the fish train from Hull.
25	4-4-0 30728 heads a schools' special to Stalbridge on the S&D, T9s rare here.
29	0-6-0 3202 (89C) appears at Rhyl on a 2-coach special, to general surprise.
29	D1 4-4-0 31509 is unusual power for the 10.16am Redhill – Reading.
29	D11 4-4-0 62691 *Laird of Balmawhapple* arrives in Newcastle with ECS then heads the 4.30pm to Hawick. D11s are infrequent sights in Newcastle.
30	61060 works through from Driffield on a day excursion to Shrewsbury, territory that B1s rarely invade.
U/D	Whitsun period; LMS Co-Co diesel 10000 arrives at Hastings with ECS from Brighton, where it had been under repair at the Works.
U/D	For King Edward VI school's Thanksgiving service in Winchester Cathedral, the Southampton school organises two special trains to Winchester (Chesil). 76007, 76027 head the trains, each of 12 coaches.

JULY 1954

2ND	D11 4-4-0 62666 *Zeebrugge* heads a Lincoln – Windermere (Lakeside) school special throughout. New ground for a D11! Seen on Carnforth shed on the 4th.
2	Beattie 2-4-0WT 30586 seen working the 11.55am Padstow – Wadebridge. Unusual task for these diminutive engines, also tried out last October.

3   4950 *Patshull Hall* reaches Bletchley with a Swindon Works staff holiday ('Trip') special to Yarmouth (Vauxhall). GWR engines are rare at Bletchley.

3   77011 finds itself newly-delivered from Swindon to Dalry Road (64C), instead of Darlington, and is sent on to its correct shed the following week!

3   H2 4-4-2 32425 *Trevose Head* works private charter from Clapham Jct. to Portsmouth via Three Bridges and the mid-Sussex line, returning same way.

7   2.15pm fish train leaves Aberdeen behind 61786 + 45673 *Keppel*, a highly unusual combination of LNER/LMS types.

8   A5 4-6-2T (!) arrives at Huddersfield with the diverted 9.30am Liverpool (Central) to Sheffield (Victoria). Departs for Penistone piloted by a 2-6-4T.

10   11.39am from Exeter (Central) is often triple-headed to Yeoford, but today sets off with four locos (!), 32124/30712/34013 *Okehampton*/31846 – the lead engine being a banker going down to St Davids.

10   45665 *Lord Rutherford of Nelson* arrives in Scarborough on the 8.46am from Bradford (Forster Square), leaves with the 12.24pm to York, then the 3.10pm to Leeds. Pastures new for a 67A (Corkerhill) 'Jubilee'!

10   41113 passes Thetford on a Northampton – Yarmouth excursion. First sighting of a Compound in Norfolk?

10,14   '5' seen at Rhyl in grey-pink undercoat without numbers. (45659) *Drake* appears in this guise (14th) on the 2pm Birmingham – Liverpool. Entertaining!

11   75035 (1E) reaches Ipswich on a Bletchley – Felixstowe special, and 2-6-4T 42221 works the Sunday milk train, both classes new to Ipswich.

17   (Glasgow Fair Saturday) 61772 *Loch Lochy* + 61733 head the 8.48am Milngavie – Bridgeton, which today is extended to…London! Also, 48756 is noted at Bonnybridge on the 8am Buchanan Street – Oban (all the way?).

17   45569 *Tasmania* pilots 90049 on a 67-wagon northbound freight through Kilmarnock, an astonishing pairing!

17   8.5am Wadebridge – Waterloo seen at speed near Crediton behind '0395' 0-6-0 30564 piloting 34004 *Yeovil*. Even more astonishing!

18   60074 *Harvester* arrives in Scarborough with a troop train from Birtley, avoiding York by using the Gilling branch. Pacifics rarely reach this resort.

18   D16 4-4-0 62551 is a surprise sight at Rugby (Midland), ex-Peterborough.

22   Special to convey 400 German people, runs Dover (Marine) – Chigwell. All coaches in SR green livery with J15 0-6-0s 65450 + 65476, an odd sight.

26   60016 *Silver King* passes through Wetherby (a most unusual location for an A4) working the 8.45am Leeds (City) – Newcastle.

29   8P 71000 *Duke of Gloucester* appears at Perth for the first time on the 7.20am ex-Euston, from Crewe. Returns south on the 9pm from Perth.

29   62749 *The Cottesmore* takes an Inspection Saloon as far west as Huddersfield, exceedingly rare for this class to reach here.

30   W 2-6-4T 31921 brings the ECS of the Brussels boat train into Victoria.

31   4-4-0 40491 (18C Hasland!) pilots 72001 *Clan Cameron* out of Carlisle on the 9.15am Glasgow (Central) – Liverpool (Exchange), a very unexpected pair.

U/D   ER B1s cleared to run to Lymington Pier! (says SR Route Restriction book).

U/D   The 1-coach Mound Jct. – Dornoch branch train is a WR corridor composite!

AUGUST 1954

1ST   45658 *Keyes* visits Tilbury, of all places, where Holbeck 'Jubilees' are rare.

3   30907/26 *Dulwich/Repton* power the 12.25pm Charing Cross – Hastings, an unusual same-class pairing on any train.

5   2-6-4T 42221 (33A) surprisingly reaches Sheringham on a Norwich train.

5   60104 *Solario* makes an unprecedented appearance at Banbury on the 7.30pm Marylebone – Shrewsbury milk empties.

5,6   61539 (the last Scottish example) arrives in Inverness, but is held to repair leaking tubes. An Elgin D40 4-4-0 also arrives (6th) on a special, returning as eye-catching pilot to 44975 on the 12.45pm ex Inverness.

7   Leicester (Central) hosts a most interesting engine, 30790 *Sir Villiars*, which had worked in with a special from Portsmouth.

7,8   60063 *Isinglass* pilots 61136 into Marylebone on the 10.40am from Manchester, and 60111 *Enterprise* + B1 61369 combine next day on the 4pm ex-Manchester. Double-heading had previously been rare on the GC!

8   72008 *Clan Macleod* reported seen at Crewe Works with tablet exchange apparatus fitted.

9   GNR preserved 4-4-2 251 noted in steam on Doncaster shed. Later in the month, 251 heads 3.5pm Retford – Lincoln, 5.31pm Lincoln – Sheffield trains prior to use on the 'Northern Rubber Special' to Liverpool on 4 September.

9   Fowler 2-6-2T 40056 is an unprecedented sight on a goods train at Neville Hill, Leeds, in course of transfer to Hull (Botanic Gardens).

11   4905 *Barton Hall* (85C Hereford) causes some astonishment by running light engine through Warrington towards Chester.

12   71000 *Duke of Gloucester* works 'The Mid-Day Scot' out of Euston for the first time.

13   E3 0-6-2T 32462 hauls the 5.19pm Horsham – Brighton, a rare class on passenger turns in this area.

14   Ivatt 2-6-2T 41313 (72A) seen on a Westbury – Swindon pick-up goods, running-in after a visit to Swindon Works.

14   U1 2-6-0 31894 works the 8.56am Ramsgate – Birkenhead throughout between Redhill and Reading via Kensington and the WR main line. Diversion is due to an obstruction at Guildford, and the 7.35am Birkenhead – Margate runs via Clapham Jct. to Redhill where, to general consternation, 5956 *Horsley Hall* is still at the head of the train. 5956 is promptly impounded and not allowed to regain the WR for a week!

14   60094 *Colorado* (64B) is a rarity on 66A, having arrived on freight from Perth.

15   70004 *William Shakespeare* is on view at Eastleigh Works open day, receives Works attention and then hauls (on the 15th) the 9am Channel Islands boat train from Waterloo, and derails in Southampton Docks. Eventful day!

15,16   76039 (34E Neasden) arrives at King's Cross Goods on the Aberdeen fish train, but heads the 8.8am King's Cross – Hitchin next day, both unusual workings for this class.

16   Derailment at Wolverton diverts the up 'Lakes Express' / 'Royal Scot' / 'Manxman' / 'Welshman' and 'Irish Mail' through Luton, as well as the down 'Mancunian' and 'Merseyside Express'. The up 'Mid-day Scot' (17 coaches) travels via Wolverhampton, arriving in Paddington behind a pair of 'Halls'.

17   Coaching stock for the 9.50pm King's Cross – Newcastle extra comprises an LMS 3rd Open, two GW composites and seven GW 3rd Opens branded 'Craven Arms No. 4'!

| 18 | 73042 takes a public excursion to Crewe Works from Euston right into the Works itself, as far as the loading dock adjacent to the Paint Shop. |

18   73042 takes a public excursion to Crewe Works from Euston right into the Works itself, as far as the loading dock adjacent to the Paint Shop.

18   2-6-2T 4165 is strange motive power choice for the 9.25pm Chester to Llandudno, where GWR locos are rarely seen.

18   Budd-built coach 'Silver Princess' emerges from storage at Pressed Steel Co. (Cowley) and is worked into Marylebone on the 11am parcels from Princes Risborough for official inspection.

19   The 3-car ex-AEC diesel unit now works the Foxfield – Coniston branch.

25   'Bomb Train' departs Hitchin for Scotland behind 90559. This conveys bombs from the airfield at Royston to the MOD base at Cairnryan.

27   'Crab' 42859 pilots 73014 (84G) into Ripon on a pigeon special from the WR. First 5MT, and first Shrewsbury loco noted at Ripon.

28   O4 2-8-0 63574 works 'under the wires' Sheffield (Victoria) – Penistone with an express to Manchester, three weeks before the introduction of electric working between Sheffield and Penistone. O4 returns on the 3.15pm Manchester (C) – Cleethorpes. Rare to see an O4 with class A headlamps!

28   3F 0-6-0 43201 (originally S&D 64) celebrates 100 years of the Glastonbury to Highbridge line of the Somerset Central by hauling a 12-coach excursion from Glastonbury to Burnham-on-Sea. Train is organised by Clarks (boot and shoe manufacturer) and filled to capacity.

28   61658 *The Essex Regiment* (31B) is a shock arrival at Newcastle on a York to Heaton goods, but is then kept busy working a special to Morpeth (!) before returning to York on a parcels train. Has a B17 ever reached further north than Morpeth?

31   LNW 0-8-0 49105 is an even bigger shock at Retford, with freight for Doncaster, surely a first for this class on this stretch of line?

U/D   2-6-4T 42085 brings a race special into Ripon from Middlesbrough, rare engines indeed to reach Ripon.

U/D   A2/2 60505 *Thane of Fife* visits Mexborough (!) and works B1 duties.

U/D   The southbound 'Saint Mungo' leaves Aberdeen for Perth behind the arresting combination of V4 2-6-2 61700 *Bantam Cock* piloting a '5'.

SEPTEMBER 1954

2ND   Compound 40921 pilots CR 4-4-0 54467 on the 9.25am Perth – Blair Atholl (what a pairing!). 40921 then works the fortnightly 'provision train' on to Aviemore and back, 'stocking up' the signal boxes along the way.

4   Compound 40930 (22B Gloucester!) reaches Cleethorpes (highly unusual) on the through train from Bournemouth.

4   6018 *King Henry VI* pilots 70015 *Apollo* between Newton Abbot and Plymouth on the second portion of the 'Cornish Riviera', a rare combination.

4   GNR preserved 4-4-2 251 double-heads D11 4-4-0 62663 *Prince Albert* from Retford to Edge Hill on the 'Northern Rubber Special'. Train proceeds to Liverpool (Riverside) top & tailed by LNW 0-8-0s 49082/49314. Memorable!

4   45719 *Glorious* (27A) heads the 10.12am York – Yarmouth as far as Lincoln, a rare occurrence for a 'Jubilee' to work over any part of the East Coast line.

7   62702 *Oxfordshire* works one of the periodic Eyesight Test Specials (one coach/one van) from York to Pilmoor. The 'Test Signals' are about ¾ mile west of the main line at Pilmoor South, on disused trackbed.

8,9	V4 2-6-2 61701 heads an Aberdeen – Aboyne special for the Highland Games. 61700 *Bantam Cock* arrives at Banchory tender first on the 8.45am goods from Aberdeen next day. Rare to see either of these locos on the Deeside line.
8	T9 4-4-0 30724 runs non-stop from Portsmouth Harbour to Waterloo with a special for BTC officials and Sir Brian Robertson. The two coaches had earlier been worked Cirencester – Eastleigh by 'Dukedog' 4-4-0 9022.
11	30788 *Sir Urre of the Mount* arrives at Ashton Gate on a football special from Eastleigh. 'King Arthur' class engines rarely appear at Bristol.
12	251 + 62663 (see 4th) haul the 'Farnborough Flyer' (for the Air Show) from Leeds (Central) to Basingstoke and back. Train includes ex-'Coronation' beaver-tail observation car. Outstanding visitors for Basingstoke to savour.
13	Bognor Regis despatches four circus trains to Worthing, which had arrived three days earlier from Portsmouth – worth watching!
14	60008 *Dwight D. Eisenhower* heads the King's Cross – Manchester (London Road) special forming the first official train to be electrically hauled from Sheffield, where 60008 gives way to Co-Co 27000 whistled away by Sir Brian Robertson. Full electric working starts 20 September (winter timetable).
17	5.45pm slow train from Derby to Nottingham has the stunning combination of 'Crab' 42769 piloting D11 4-4-0 62663 *Prince Albert* !
18	T9 4-4-0 30724 departs Oxford with the 9.20am Birkenhead – Bournemouth, most unusual power for this important cross-country service.
18	61620 *Clumber* + 61633 *Kimbolton Castle* are a rare sight heading the Liverpool – Harwich boat train along the GN/GE Joint line.
20	First Sleeping Car to operate regularly on the Birkenhead – Paddington service since 1922 (W9091W), reported at Shrewsbury on the 7.15pm ex-Birkenhead.
21	61629 *Naworth Castle* takes the first ever Sleeping Car out of Liverpool Street on the 3.33pm to Yarmouth, conveying a private party, who will return early next morning.
23	'Night Ferry' comes into Victoria 2½ hours late behind 2-6-0 31815 + 0-6-0 31713 after the failure of the train engine 35027 *Port Line*.
23	A G5 0-4-4T leaves Leeds (Central) on the Harrogate portion of the 1.18pm from King's Cross. G5s seldom wear a class 'A' headcode nowadays.
24	62706 *Forfarshire* (64B!) heads the 7.10am Northallerton – Leeds (City) via Wetherby, not where you'd expect to find a Haymarket engine.

OCTOBER 1954

1ST	8P 71000 *Duke of Gloucester* heads a special train for 300 members of the Institution of Locomotive Engineers from Euston to Stechford, to visit the Metro-Cammell Works at Saltley. 71000 also powers the return working.
2	V4 2-6-2 61701 reaches Elgin on the 3.40pm from Aberdeen, most unusual.
2,15	70044/43 (with air pumps) both work the 7.55am Derby – St Pancras in between employment on Toton – Brent coal train tests.
3	Taff Vale 0-6-2T 205 (withdrawn) leaves Oxford shed for Oswestry via Shrewsbury, heading for Moat Lane as a temporary pumping engine.
6	G16 4-6-2Ts 30494/5 arrive (separately) at Liss, on loan to the Longmoor Military Railway. Engines return to the SR a week later. Rare movements.

9	76002 (66B Motherwell) arrives in Aberdeen on the 'Saint Mungo', the 5pm from Buchanan Street. A 4MT 2-6-0 is very unexpected power on this train!
9	O4 2-8-0 63821 + J39 0-6-0 64824 is equally unexpected power to be seen on the York – Banbury express north of Nottingham!
10	D11 4-4-0 62679 *Lord Glenallan* (64B) is a rare find at Blaydon shed.
10	T9 4-4-0 30729 journeys as far north as Tring, on a ramblers' excursion from Blackfriars, a unique visit to these parts for this SR class.
16	GWR railcars W33W + W36W (with trailer W1096 between) are used for the Westminster Bank Railway Club's special from Paddington to Southampton.
16	62708 *Argyllshire* (62A!) works a pick-up goods to Bedale, running-in from Darlington Works. New ground for a Thornton engine.
18-23	60087 *Blenheim* and 60096 *Papyrus* conduct a one-week trial working the 9.50am Edinburgh – St Pancras and 9.5pm St Pancras – Edinburgh between Edinburgh and Leeds throughout, via the Settle & Carlisle route.
20	70005 *John Milton* (30A) visits Workington with the Whitehaven portion of the 11.5pm from Euston – first 'Pacific' to reach Workington.
25	46112 *Sherwood Forester* is excessive power for the 9.33am 2-coach local from Bradford (Forster Square) – Leeds (City).
28	70018 *Flying Dutchman* is a rare sight on the 'Cambrian Coast Express' from Paddington, as 'Pacifics' are hardly ever used on the WR Birmingham route.
28	Both ex-'Coronation' observation cars are seen tail-to-tail as part of a King's Cross – Doncaster ECS train, a noteworthy sight.
28	8P 71000 *Duke of Gloucester* pulls one open truck and a brake van through Snow Hill, bound for the Swindon Test Plant. Interesting!
28,29	44665 + 45186 (with whitewashed coal!) work the Royal train from Bradford (Manningham), and take the Queen as far as York. Next day, V3 2-6-2Ts 67653/89 head the Royal train as the Queen visits Tyneside and Sunderland.
29	30920 *Rugby* pilots 34074 *46 Squadron* on the up 'Night Ferry'; rare pairing.
30	70051 *Firth of Forth* works into Aberdeen with the 7.15am from Buchanan Street, and returns on the 3.30pm 'Postal'. 7MTs don't often reach Aberdeen.
U/D	D11 4-4-0 62674 *Flora MacIvor* (65A) is found in…Gorton Works!

29-31	Both the CR and GSW main lines between Carlisle and Glasgow are closed by floods and landslips. LMR traffic is therefore diverted *either* via Glasgow – Edinburgh – Newcastle – York – Leeds i.e. ECML Route *or* via Glasgow – Edinburgh – Carlisle i.e. the Waverley Route. A selection of significant workings are as follows:
29	ECML Route

up;   9.20am St Enoch – St Pancras 'Thames-Clyde Express' ('TCE')
         9.5pm St Enoch – St Pancras
down; 9.5pm St Pancras – St Enoch
         10am Euston – Glasgow 'Royal Scot' 46221 into Newcastle

Waverley Route

up; 60100 on 'Royal Scot'	70052 on Glasgow – Manchester
down; 'Royal Scot' 2 x '5's	46253 on 'Mid-day Scot'
46210 Birmingham – Glasgow	60510 on 12.20am Euston – Glasgow

30	ECML Route

up;   'TCE' leaves St Enoch behind 60535

10am 'Royal Scot' 46221 to Newcastle, 60981 to Leeds

1.30pm 'Mid-day Scot' 60840 from Glasgow (Central)

Garelochhead – Portsmouth special has 45729 to Newcastle

45661 10.40am Glasgow – Manchester

45118/72003 9am Perth – Euston, from Edinburgh

down; 10am St Pancras – St Enoch 'TCE' 46108 Leeds – Glasgow

46230 2.3pm King's Cross – Niddrie freight

46232 10pm Thames Wharf – Niddrie freight

both freights from Newcastle, both Pacifics having brought overnight trains into Newcastle from Glasgow.

Waverley Route

up;   46210 10.5am Glasgow – Birmingham

46243 11am Coatbridge – Euston

down; 46227 on the 'Royal Scot'

45704 on 9.25am Crewe – Perth

31   ECML Route

down; 46210 seen at Alnmouth with class E freight, from Newcastle.

46221 heads 11.30pm (30th) Dringhouses – Niddrie, from Newcastle.

29,30 Hawick witnesses the passage, on various trains over these two days, of

'Coronations'	46222/27/43/48/52	'Royal Scots'	46107/08/20/57
'Jubilees'	45640/61/91, 45701/04	'Britannias'	70050-54
'Clans'	72001/2/3/7		

Newcastle sees LMS Pacifics for the first time.

NOVEMBER 1954

2ND   45720 *Indomitable* (67A) heads the 7pm to Birmingham out of Euston, where Corkerhill engines are rarely seen. 72000 *Clan Buchanan* (66A) works the 10.50am from Edinburgh into Leeds, where Polmadie engines are also rare.

3   Ivatt 2-6-0 46482 works a train of cripple wagons from King's Cross Goods to Conington, returning north after being on loan to 34A from West Auckland!

6   2-6-0 6304 arrives at Redhill on a football special from Oxford to Tunbridge Wells West. 2-6-0s U 31627 + U1 31894 take the 10-coach set of WR stock (including Restaurant Car) forward, a strange vision at Forest Row!

11   'Night Ferry' arrives at Victoria 217 minutes late just as the 'Golden Arrow' is about to depart – a rare juxtaposition.

12   J88 0-6-0T 68341 is unable to brake its train of wagons, and falls into the Firth of Forth at Kirkcaldy Harbour. Loco is recovered on the 14th.

13   46239 *City of Chester* and 46249 *City of Sheffield* both sent to Bushbury (3B) four days prior to the Duke of Edinburgh's visit to Birmingham, to prepare one of them to head the 3.55pm Wolverhampton – Euston, his scheduled return train. 46249 worked the train, the Duke flew!

16,17 D16 4-4-0 62574 (31A) ventures onto the West Coast main line to work the 8.30am Bletchley – Wolverton School train.

17   Down 'Royal Scot' (46237 *City of Bristol*) and 'Mid-day Scot' (46210 *Lady Patricia*)

pass through Wellington, diverted via Stafford/Shrewsbury/Crewe.

18   70026 *Polar Star* (86C) reaches Barrow on a relief to the 6.40am from Euston.

20   80025 (67A) makes a surprise light engine visit to Grange-over-Sands.

20   30917 *Ardingly* heads a Pullman football special through from Hastings to Hounslow for the FA Cup match.

26   T9 4-4-0 30719 is surely unsuitable power to work a 450 ton train of empty hopper wagons between Redhill and Woking?

29   Overnight train (14 coaches) from Fakenham to Southampton Docks for USAAF personnel returning to America, passes Eastleigh double-headed by 4944 *Middleton Hall* + 5935 *Norton Hall*.

30   9.5pm Derby – Nottingham has the unlikely combination of D11 4-4-0 62663 *Prince Albert* piloting 2-6-4T 42174.

DECEMBER 1954

5TH   70023 *Venus* (81A), ex-Crewe Works, finds itself on Patricroft shed (10C).

11   Excursion is run from Kirbymoorside, Nawton, Helmsley, Gilling and Coxwold – all closed stations – to York and Leeds, for Christmas shopping.

11   9-coach football special runs from Hastings to Selby, consisting of SEC 'Continental' stock, plus Pullman buffet car. Heads turn at Selby!

11   The Bradford (Park Avenue) v Southend FA Cup tie brings 61155 + 61267 to Horton Park station on a supporters' special. The Bradford City v Merthyr Tydfil match attracts two excursions, which return from Exchange station behind 44834 (5B) on 10 WR coaches, and 73013 (84G) on 8 WR coaches including a Cafeteria Car. Rare events all round.

12   Brand-new 80112 arrives at 61B in error. Sent to 66A next day!

15   80016 pilots H2 4-4-2 32424 *Beachy Head* on the London Bridge – Brighton van train, a strange pairing.

16   W 2-6-4T 31911 found on Hornsey shed – a rare visitor here – after working a transfer freight to Ferme Park.

18   Brand-new 80113, running-in from Doncaster Works, appears at Sheffield (Victoria) – a new location for this class.

19   80033 (75A) found ex-Works on Derby(!) shed. 80019 (also 75A) due shortly.

21   30917 *Ardingly* works (by request) Ardingly College's end of term special to Victoria. These engines are exceptionally rare at East Grinstead.

25,26,27   Three consecutive days of Sunday Service. (Sat/Sun/Mon)

27   (Boxing Day) First four coaches of the 'Royal Scot' are in Southern green!

27   70023 *Venus* (81A) now appears at Polmadie (66A) – see 5th.

28   S&D 2-8-0 53805 rolls into Birmingham with fish wagons from the West Country, a rare outing for this class, usually confined to the S&D only.

29   44923 (65B St Rollox!) leaves York on the 2.35pm ECS to Neville Hill.

29   62755 *The Bilsdale* + 62752 *The Atherstone* power the 2.5pm Darlington to Manchester from Ripon to Leeds; same-class pairings are always unusual.

30   O2 2-8-0 63954 (36A) is a rare sight at Ripon with an up goods.

U/D   Ivatt 2-6-2Ts 41301, 41308 are unexpected visitors to Dover Marine.

JANUARY 1955

1ST,6TH   34073 *249 Squadron* pilots 30915 *Brighton* on the up 'Night Ferry'; on 6th, 30915 pilots 34074 *46 Squadron* on the down service. Worth watching!

5   E4 0-6-2T 32509 heads the 7.58am Fareham – Alton, a most unusual type on the Meon Valley line.

7   Fowler 2-6-4T 42328 is employed on the 5.10am King's Cross – Baldock parcels, and outer suburban work. LMS locos are rare in King's Cross.

7   D11 4-4-0 62679 *Lord Glenallan* reaches Newcastle on an Alnmouth train. Not many 'Directors' travel the East Coast main line into Newcastle.

8   Football special runs from Hastings to Wadsley Bridge (Sheffield) composed of 10 SR coaches, and has A4 haulage south of Grantham, both ways.

8   60048 *Doncaster* is specially chosen to work the supporters' train from Thorne South to King's Cross for the Watford v Doncaster FA Cup match.

8   Four Bulleid light Pacifics retire to Bath Road shed for servicing after bringing football specials for the Bristol Rovers v Portsmouth Cup tie.

13   Q6 0-8-0 63344 with a J39 0-6-0 as pilot, work a Shell oil tank train from Skipton to Harrogate via Ilkley and Arthington, a rare sight on this line.

15   77019 pilots 72009 *Clan Stewart* on the 12.15 St Enoch – Carlisle, an unexpected combination of 'Standards'.

20   70004 *William Shakespeare* heads the 8.10am Windermere – Manchester (Exchange). Surely a 73A engine has not been to Windermere before?

21   SR Co-Co electric 20003 visits Hither Green depot for tyre turning, running LE from Selhurst and requiring steam haulage to get in/out of the shed.

23   45571 *South Africa* (24E) works an excursion from Blackpool through to Snow Hill – a rarity here – going to Tyseley for coal and water.

24-28   Camping coach W9930W, in green, is on exhibition at Snow Hill.

25   BTC's £1240 million modernisation plan for BR is announced.

26   4-4-0 40602 is a surprising type to be on shed at Hawick, probably the first.

28   Six cars of new electric stock for Tyneside – built at Eastleigh – head north on the East Coast main line, hauled (from Canonbury) by J6 0-6-0 64256.

29   N7 0-6-2T 69694 powers a 2-coach DMU replacement train on a Leeds to Bradford service. C14 4-4-2T 67446 does the same on the 4.16pm Leeds to Castleford train. Bad weather (frost) is affecting the DMUs.

29   45611 *Hong Kong* (16A) reaches West Hartlepool on a football special. Nottingham 'Jubilees' are rarities on the North East coast.

29   Mobile Test Unit No.1 seen outside the erecting shop at Kilmarnock Works.

30   7006 *Lydford Castle* undergoes clearance tests between Gloucester and Kings Norton, prior to working the excursion booked for 16 April.

FEBRUARY 1955

5TH   20 specials run from South Wales to Edinburgh for the Scotland v Wales rugby match. At least three have limited sleeping accommodation, at 25s extra on top of the fare of 56s return.

6   Crewe Works shunter, CR 'Pug' 0-4-0ST 56032 still bears a 31B shedplate, the old LMS code for Stirling.

6,10	4-4-2T 'Tilbury' tanks 41971/2/3/4 which had been in store outside Durran Hill shed at Carlisle since June 1948 are moved inside the depot to prepare them for the final journey to Derby for scrap. WD 2-10-0 90769 hauls the quartet south towards Leeds on the 10th.
6	T9s 30301 + 30732 double-head the 'Hampshireman' railtour over the Meon Valley line, which had officially closed the day before.
7	J68 0-6-0T 68662 is seen on a pick-up goods at Aylesbury, and similar J69 tank 68527 shunts the yard at Harrow. Both 30A locos – on loan?
10	Ivatt 2-6-0 43063 breaks the class's duck at Southend (Victoria) by arriving on a local from Shenfield, and leaving on the 8.55pm to Liverpool Street.
10	N7 0-6-2T 69692 works the Bradford portion of the 'Yorkshire Pullman' from Leeds to Bradford. First time that an N7 has hauled a Pullman car train?
13	60002 *Sir Murrough Wilson* provides an unprecedented sight at Hull, coming in on an excursion from Newcastle.
14	61577 (32B) and 61633 *Kimbolton Castle* (31B) both reach King's Cross, probably because the Cambridge turntable is out of action.
17	46229 *Duchess of Hamilton*, 46231 *Duchess of Atholl* and 70051 *Firth of Forth* – all 66A – appear at Corkerhill (67A) for coaling, unusual locos here.
19	G5 0-4-4T 67327 is a unique sight at Polmadie, *en route* from Kittybrewster to Kilmarnock for scrapping.
19	Nottingham (Victoria) is an unusual destination for 60138 *Boswell*, which arrives there on a football special from the North East.
20	70041 *Sir John Moore* (30A) passes through Walsall on the diverted 2.30pm Manchester – Birmingham. Has a Stratford engine been seen at Walsall?
21	70045 *Lord Rowallan* (6J) heads the 3.53pm Manchester – Barrow, where few Holyhead engines ever reach!
22	J21 0-6-0 65091 works the 7.15pm St Boswells – Tweedmouth, a rare class to be found on passenger services nowadays.
24	60100 *Spearmint* (64B) brings the 5pm Leeds – Newcastle into Sunderland, where Haymarket engines are notable visitors.
25	70001 *Lord Hurcomb* (32A!), in ex-works condition, graces Rhyl shed, an unaccustomed watering hole for Norwich locos.
25	78018 becomes stuck in a snowdrift at Bleathgill, 7½ miles from Kirkby Stephen on the Stainmore line.
25	Farm Removal Special run between Lenzie and Tunbridge Wells West is the first train carrying passengers over the Bricklayers' Arms branch since 1939.
26	75029 brings the 7.10am from Oxford into Paddington where, other than 'Britannias', standard engines are not common.

MARCH 1955

2ND	61606 *Audley End* brings an excursion from Bury St Edmunds through to Kensington Olympia. This class is rarely seen here.
2	2-6-4Ts 80007 and 42277 – both 66A! – arrive at Hawick to work Newcastle trains as far as Wall, where trains terminate. Buses complete the journey to Hexham, where the Border Counties viaduct is under repair.
4	Ivatt 2-6-2Ts 41292/2, 41302/15/16, all SR engines, in Swindon Works yard!

6	2-6-4T 42685 works a 2-coach special from St Pancras to Leicester at 2am, to clear passengers who missed the 12.15am due to problems on the tube.
8	60084 *Trigo* arrives in Hull (where Pacifics are rare) on the 2.57pm from Bradford (Forster Square), and leaves on the 7.10pm.
10	72000 *Clan Buchanan* powers the 2.15pm London fish train out of Aberdeen.
12	Announcement heard at Newcastle: "Passengers should note that the parcels train standing at Platform 8 is not the 'Flying Scotsman' "!
12	76027 appears at Evercreech Jct. on a Bournemouth (West) – Bath (Green Park) working, the second of this class to be seen on the S&D. (See 16/7/53)
12	46 extra trains run through/to/from Nottingham (Victoria); 8 for Notts County v York, 8 to Wembley Hill (womens' hockey), 5 to Bishop Auckland for Amateur Cup match v Wycombe plus 2 from Shrewsbury = 23 each way!
15	2-6-2T 6109 (81A) hauls the 7.15am west out of Swindon, with two Camping Coaches attached to the rear – these being bound for Devon and Cornwall.
18	D20 4-4-0 62384 pilots A2/3 60517 *Ocean Swell* from Ripon to Leeds on the 8.55am Newcastle – Liverpool, a notable combination.
19	J37 0-6-0 64603 (64A) is a rare sight between Blaydon and Heaton, as these freight engines don't usually work this far south.
25	92049 tows two Longmoor Military Railway locos south from overhaul at Bagnall's at Stafford, WD 2-10-0 *Gordon* and an Alco 2-8-0, both in Works grey and un-numbered.
26	7025 *Sudeley Castle* is provided for the Grand National special from Paddington through to Birkenhead (Woodside). Train has 9 coaches (including 4 Restaurant Cars!). 3 x double-deck Crosville buses take the clientele to Aintree via the Mersey Tunnel.
26	For the FA Cup semi-finals at Villa Park (Sunderland v Manchester City) and Hillsborough (York v Newcastle United) the NER operates no fewer than 52 specials. This demands the provision of 587 coaches, the cancellation of over 100 freight trains (over a 3-day period) and alterations to a similar number.
26,27	62721 *Warwickshire* and 62706 *Forfarshire* – respectively – appear at Ferryhill, the class being generally unusual visitors to Aberdeen.
30	61402 (61A) makes a particularly rare trip to Glasgow, working through to Buchanan Street from Aberdeen on a 'Billy Graham Crusade' special.
31	R 0-4-4T 31666 heads a special van train for school baggage from Bexhill to Eastbourne, and is also used on the Hailsham push/pull service before beating a hasty retreat to St Leonards and heading home to Tonbridge.

APRIL 1955

2ND	'Flying Scotsman' arrives in Waverley with J83 0-6-0T 68449 piloting the (failed) A4 train engine, and V1 2-6-2T 67629 banking at the rear!
4	60925 gets as far as Derby on a special from Saltburn to Bournville. The V2 transfers to 17A for servicing and works the return to Saltburn.
4,5	D1 4-4-0 31743 heads a special from Victoria to Grain, which includes two ER Sleeping Cars + ER brake. These are for the benefit of the catering firm's staff who are supplying the fare when the Queen opens a new oil refinery at Grain the following day. First BR Sleeping Cars seen in Kent?

7	61354 + 60027 *Merlin* enter Newcastle on a relief to the up 'Flying Scotsman' and the up 'Queen of Scots' also has 61357 + 60162 *Saint Johnstoun* as far as Newcastle. The B1s are for Easter 'extras'.
9	The solitary Aviemore '5' (45136) makes its first visit to Aberdeen, ex-Perth.
9	J69 0-6-0Ts 68607 + 68549 head an Easter Saturday football special from Shoeburyness, through Deptford towards New Cross Gate. Unusual power!
9	60002 *Sir Murrough Wilson* (tender first) + K1 620xx head an up coal train through Newcastle – a most unusual sight!
9,11	45610 *Gold Coast* (17A) arrives in Newcastle with a relief from Birmingham. Returns on the 12.40pm to Bristol (11th) – first time since 1949 that a 'Jubilee' has worked a regular service train from Newcastle.
11	(Easter Monday) Wetherby race specials from Leeds contain several London suburban sets, displaying 'Potters Bar' and 'King's Cross' destinations!
11	Q6 0-8-0s 63355 + 63373 travel over the Kirkby Stephen – Tebay line as a pair. Civil Engineer allows passage over Deepdale and Belah viaducts on a train, to reach Kirkby Stephen. First time engines of this size seen here.
11	J6 0-6-0 64276 (37B Copley Hill) is seen on a 4-coach Leeds – Harrogate extra, a type not previously used on this route at all!
13	45726 *Vindictive* heads the 7.15am Buchanan Street – Aberdeen and the up 'Postal' return working. (1950 since a 5A 'Jubilee' was last in Aberdeen).
14	70025 *Western Star* (86C) powers the 7.55am Leamington Spa – New Street through Kenilworth. Cardiff Canton engines are rare in New Street!
14	Stanier 2-6-2T 40170 (one of the regular Kirkcudbright branch locos!) is noted at Bonnybridge on the 8.5am Buchanan Street – Stirling, and return working.
15	7017/25 *G. J. Churchward/Sudeley Castle* are stabled overnight on the Wallingford branch near Cholsey, with the Royal train.
16	'Patriot' 45550 reaches Liverpool (Riverside) with a Cunard line boat train.
16	34057/58 *Biggin Hill/Sir Frederick Pile* head the 8.20am Plymouth (Friary) to Exmouth Jct. freight. 34058 catches fire at North Tawton. 34057 continues alone whilst fire brigade deal with 34058. Eventful trip!
16	7017 (81A) works over the Midland main line from Bristol and up the Lickey incline – a first – banked by 0-10-0 58100, which buffers-up carefully to an ex-'Coronation' observation car! From Bournville a '5' takes the train into New Street, 7007 *Great Western* returns the Ian Allan special to Paddington.
17	Perth shed hosts 15 LNER locos (!) amongst the more usual candidates.
19	2-6-4T 42073 and 60968 meet and derail each other at Newcastle Central!
19	46237 *City of Bristol* commences a 4-week loan to the WR by working from Paddington to Bristol. Subsequently heads the 'Merchant Venturer' and 'Cornish Riviera' expresses, and works the Birmingham/Wolverhampton line.
20	T9 4-4-0 30719 heads another Ian Allan special, Victoria/Eastleigh/Swindon/ WR main line/Kensington/Victoria. Plenty of new ground here for a T9!
22	Fell 2000hp diesel-mechanical 10100 arrives at Kingmoor depot to begin dynamometer car trials over the Settle & Carlisle, commencing 25th.
23	44917 (71G) brings an excursion into Wembley Central for the Schoolboys' Soccer International. Unique visit to London by an S&D based loco?
24	Vale of Rheidol narrow-gauge 2-6-2T 7 seen under repair at Swindon Works.

26	80116 works the 5.30pm Leeds (City) – Scarborough throughout, surprisingly.
26	0-4-4T 58072 is a rare sight nowadays on the 6.5pm Bath – Binegar local.
28	60156 *Great Central* reaches Gilling from King's Cross with the beginning of term special for pupils at Ampleforth College.
28	72007 *Clan Mackintosh* departs from the passenger platform at King George V Dock (Glasgow) with a troop train to Crail. Unusual start/finish points!
28	V1 2-6-2T 67630 takes out the 4.10pm to Hawick from Waverley – a first appearance of this type on this line with a timetabled working.
29	60010 *Dominion of Canada* (34A) heads the 'Queen of Scots' from Leeds (Central) to Harrogate/Ripon/Northallerton, a surprisingly rare route for an A4.
30	61576 exits St Pancras, the first seen here, on a 'Hertfordshire Rail Tour'.
U/D	32 loaded coke wagons are worked from West Auckland to Kirkby Stephen by Ivatt 2-6-0s 43056/57/51, two leading and one banking, as trial runs.
U/D	A Bradford (Exchange) – Leeds (Central) service is late into Leeds and misses the London connection. The DMU then 'chases' the express to Wakefield (10 miles in 11min), where the London train is held, with a 5 minute delay only!

MAY 1955

2ND-13TH	Catering facilities for exhibitors at the British Industries Fair at Castle Bromwich are provided on site by Pullman cars 54/55/166/171/249.
5	46220 *Coronation* is highly unusual power for the 'Thames-Clyde Express' between St Enoch and Carlisle.
6	60002 *Sir Murrough Wilson* (52A) arrives at Cambridge from Ferme Park with empty cattle wagons, not the customary load for an A4!
6	Carlisle Canal's 60093 *Coronach* makes one of its few trips to London with freight from Doncaster, and 60041 *Salmon Trout* (64B) takes the 7.15pm parcels train out of King's Cross on the same day, both rarities in the capital.
6	V3 2-6-2T 67606 pilots 60537 *Bachelor's Button* out of Edinburgh on a 15-coach schools special back to Appleby. Corstorphine Zoo has been visited.
7	A2/3 60515 *Sun Stream* (50A) appears at Marylebone on a Cup Final special.
8	0-6-0 30700 pilots 34012 *Launceston* between Alton and Medstead on a Waterloo – Weymouth troop train, an unexpected combination.
8	61554 works an enthusiasts' special from Nottingham (Victoria) to Crewe, penetrating right into the Works itself, as far as Stone Yard Bank.
9	A5 4-6-2T 69824 surprisingly reaches Cromer, on the 7.51am from Norwich.
10	Oxford University Railway Society charters GWR railcar W21W for a special to Eastleigh, returning via Newbury and Didcot.
10-20	46237 *City of Bristol*, on loan to the WR, reaches Plymouth (10th) and subsequently makes two up runs on the 'Cornish Riviera' with the WR dynamometer car on the 18th and 20th.
12	C16 4-4-2T 67496 is a most unusual pilot to 44794 on the 6.35am Aberdeen to Laurencekirk local.
14	Opening meeting of the 'Billy Graham Crusade' at Wembley Stadium attracts 13 specials, with locos from WR/SR/ER in charge.
14	Beattie well tank 30587 heads a REC railtour from Andover to Bulford.
15	C2X 0-6-0 32550 is a rare sight at Poole, on a Portsmouth – Weymouth goods.

15	T9 4-4-0 30719 takes a ramblers' excursion from Waterloo up the GC line to Amersham and Great Missenden, quite an adventure for a SR engine!

15 T9 4-4-0 30719 takes a ramblers' excursion from Waterloo up the GC line to Amersham and Great Missenden, quite an adventure for a SR engine!

15 45505 *The Royal Army Ordnance Corps* finds its way to Ilkley, and looks out of place at this location, as Longsight (9A) engines should!

18 U1 2-6-0 31893 reaches Oxford, having worked an East Croydon excursion throughout via Redhill and Reading, which returns on the WR main line as far as Old Oak Common, then Kensington and the West London extension.

19 61794 *Loch Oich* (65A) heads the 7.17pm St Boswells – Carlisle goods. Rare!

20 60128 *Bongrace* arrives in Cleethorpes to test the new turntable, having run LE from Grantham via Retford. A1s do not normally reach Cleethorpes!

21 72007 *Clan Mackintosh* heads the 1-coach 4.24pm Carstairs – Lanark. Excess!

21-25 Farm removal train sets off from Edenbridge Town for Inverurie (21st) with 30 wagons of equipment. Second train runs on 25th with everything else, behind K 2-6-0s 32351 + 32346, as far as Willesden.

22 61805 (30A!) brings a down freight into Blaydon, a rare bird indeed.

22 45515 *Caernarvon* (8A) makes it to Hull with an excursion from Liverpool.

24 46164 *The Artists' Rifleman* + first coach part company from the remaining 13 coaches of the 2.30pm Euston – Liverpool just south of Crewe, both sections coming to a stand ¼ mile apart. 46164 proceeds to Crewe, and 2-6-4T 42431 (hauling No.3 dynamometer car, one coach and an engineers' saloon full of officials) buffers up to the rear and pushes/pulls everything into Crewe.

25 70010 *Owen Glendower* reaches Cromer on the 7.51am ex-Norwich (see 9th).

25 T9 4-4-0 30718 heads the 5.18pm Brighton – Victoria via the East Grinstead and Lewes line (in its last week of existence). First known working of a T9 on a scheduled train on this line, which includes Pullman car *Savona* returning from Preston Park works.

28 6001/14 *King Edward VII/King Henry VII* double-head the 2.10pm Paddington – Birkenhead into Leamington Spa, a rare sight on this route.

28 2-6-4T 42200 passes through Craigendoran (Upper) on a Sunday school excursion from Motherwell – first loco of this type seen on the West Highland.

28 ASLEF strike begins (ends 14 June). 'Aberdonian' loses its Sleeping Cars for the duration, as does the 'Night Scotsman' six cars from which form a hostel for Headquarters' officials at platform 17 at King's Cross. Remaining 'Night Scotsman' cars are placed at platform 18 at Liverpool Street for same purpose.

29 Due to the strike, 203 engines reside on shed at Doncaster – a record?

U/D 'Dukedog' 4-4-0 9023 (82C) arrives at Plymouth with an empty fish train, and a few days later brings a passenger train from Cornwall into Plymouth. This class is rarely seen this far west nowadays.

JUNE 1955

ASLEF strike period is from midnight 28 May (Whit Saturday) to 6pm 14 June.

2ND 70037 *Hereward the Wake* reaches Southend – first 7MT here – on the 5.15pm from Liverpool Street, others follow.

5 360 locos are to be seen around Stratford Works and shed.

5,6,7 The one daily Leeds (Central) – King's Cross is worked by 60865 manned by Bradford men to Grantham, the engine working from/to Hammerton Street, probably the largest engine to work from this depot. 60938 (31B) performs the same duty 12/13/14 June, as strike is 100% solid at Copley Hill.

15	Compounds 40930 + 41156 take the down 'Pine Express' through Mangotsfield, a most unexpected (though attractive) pairing.
16	45320 (60A) is a rarity on the up 'Saint Mungo', leaving Aberdeen.
18	61009 *Hartebeeste* (34E Neasden) noted at Burton Salmon with ECS from York to Sheffield. (Probably returning after a 'Starlight Special' working).
22	Budd stainless steel car 'Silver Princess' seen at Willesden in carmine & cream livery, effectively hiding the 'stainless steel'!
23	34095 *Brentor* reaches Clifton Down (for Bristol Zoo) with an excursion from Pokesdown – first SR Pacific on the Avonmouth line.
23	72003 *Clan Fraser* powers a Highland Show special between Ardrossan and Princes Street. 6MTs rarely reach the Ayrshire coast.
25	61865 + 61910 double-head a Skegness – Oldham excursion into Clegg Street. 61910 then works the ECS via Rochdale to Newton Heath, the first K3 over the Oldham/ Rochdale route.
25	'Crabs' 42787, 42870 appear at Southend (Victoria) on troop trains of WR stock (including Cafeteria Cars), and return the ECS the same afternoon.
26	4-4-0 40501 (3C Walsall) heads the 2-coach Birmingham portion of the CTAC Scottish Tours Express (Wemyss Bay – Manchester) south from Preston, and runs non-stop (?) to Birmingham.
29	L&Y 2-4-2T 50752 pilots the down 'South Yorkshireman' between Huddersfield and Halifax, an odd choice of 'assisting' loco!
U/D	(Strike period) GWR railcars W24W + W25W run in tandem on the Bristol to Avonmouth branch, a unique occurrence. Streamlined car W13W, an exceptionally rare type in Bristol, works a Bristol – Cardiff shuttle service.
U/D	Camden 'Coronations' work through to Morecambe from Euston with 6.20pm 'Ulster 'Express', overnight at Carnforth and return on the up 'Ulster Express' next day. First time 8Ps have appeared regularly in Morecambe.
U/D	Two J37 0-6-0s double-head the Royal train at Inverkeithing, *en route* to Rosyth shipyards.

JULY 1955

1ST	73059 pilots 72000 *Clan Buchanan* on a 'Starlight Special' which originates at Gourock, rather than St Enoch.
2	48266 – complete with headboard – brings the down 'Thames-Clyde Express' into Trent after two engine failures *en route* from St Pancras.
2,6,16	71000 *Duke of Gloucester* arrives in Aberdeen with a special from Buchanan Street and returns the ECS to Perth (2nd). Works 4.35pm Perth – Aberdeen and 9pm goods (6 vans only!) back again (6th). Then heads 7.15am Buchanan Street – Aberdeen and 3.30pm up 'Postal' put of Aberdeen (16th).
4	46203 *Princess Margaret Rose* is a surprise arrival at Dumfries with the 4pm St Enoch – Leeds. 'Princess Royals' are rare on the GSW line.
4	61730 (40B), ex-Cowlairs Works, reaches Ayr on a running-in turn. Few Immingham engines ever get to Ayr!

5-7	Nottingham Royal Show uses 35,000 old railway sleepers laid side-by-side to form water-proof roadways between the stands!
8	(Week commencing) A pair of Lincoln-based DMUs 79032/3 undertake crew training on the GNR lines between Bradford/Halifax/Keighley via Queensbury. As passenger services on these lines had only been withdrawn on 23 May, this exercise is not well received locally!
9	62718 *Kinross-shire* (64A), ex-Darlington Works, appears on the 7.10am Northallerton – Leeds (via Wetherby) running-in turn. A rare specimen!
9	7820 *Dinmore Manor* (83D) is equally rare power for the 2.35pm to Reading out of Paddington. 'Small' Laira engines are uncommon in London.
10	7.20pm Bristol – Birmingham and the 10.37pm thence to Newcastle are worked by 45707 *Valiant* (67A). First Corkerhill 'Jubilee' seen in Bristol?
10	73031 (with air pumps) reaches Hull with an excursion from Manchester.
11	The two 'Britannias' with air pumps, 70043/44 both appear in New Street on the same day, on the 9pm to Derby and 11.25am for Glasgow respectively.
11	62709 *Berwickshire* (64B) is unexpected power for the up 'Postal' between Carstairs and Carlisle, travelling on the CR main line.
14	61993 *Loch Long* (65A) mysteriously inhabits Tweedmouth shed.
16	L 4-4-0 31771 – a rare visitor to Victoria – heads the 1.20pm to Ramsgate.
16	L&Y 2-4-2T 50777 pulls into Leeds (Central) with the 7.48am from Manchester, a vintage loco for such a service. A failure somewhere perhaps?
16	J11 0-6-0 64417 (36D Barnsley) does reach Scarborough on an 11-coach excursion, though surely this is not the first choice of motive power?
16	80119 (new) is used for both the up and down Whitby portions of the 'Scarborough Flyer' to and from York. Tank engines rarely work titled trains.
16	46225 *Duchess of Gloucester* is a surprise pilot to 73006 on the up 'Granite City' out of Aberdeen. This means that both *Duke* and *Duchess* appear in Aberdeen on the same day! (See 2,6,16 above).
17	34066 *Spitfire* heads the 9.37am Victoria – Heathfield ramblers' excursion, and takes the ECS on to Polegate. First SR Pacific over the 'Cuckoo' line.
17	61820 (30A) somehow finds its way to...Scarborough! First Stratford engine to reach this resort, certainly.
18	Budd coach (M7585M) starts a week's trial in the 'Ulster Express' rake.
20	44538 (17B Burton) takes over the 11.45am St Pancras – Bradford at Leeds and works the 12-coach train to Forster Square. Unusual power!
22	8.55pm St Enoch – St Pancras includes six SR 2nd class coaches, i.e. boat train stock (*as only these could be designated thus at this time*).
23	11.9am ex-Newcastle arrives in Scarborough behind 60078 *Night Hawk* (from Darlington). 60078 leaves LE tender first, for York as A3s cannot be turned on Scarborough's turntable. Only the 4th Pacific here since 1948.
23	62721 *Warwickshire* + 73007 take the up 'Granite City' out of Aberdeen, a most unusual pairing.
24	C2X 0-6-0 32554 (73B) hauls the Ashburton Grove refuse train in both directions – commandeered by Hornsey from a cross-London freight. Rare!
24	Spectacular sight in Kent as the late-running 'Golden Arrow' is seen side-by-side with the 'Kentish Belle' between Bickley and Bromley South – two Pullman expresses in parallel!

22,29	3pm Dundee (West) – Buchanan Street is headed by the notable combination of V4 2-6-2 61701 (61B) + 45319 (60A) on the 22nd, and by the even rarer pairing of 61140 + 44677 (the only two ScR engines equipped with self-weighing tenders!) on the 29th.
29	60532 *Blue Peter* (61B) makes a rare foray to London and heads back with the 7.15pm King's Cross – York parcels.
30	60154 *Bon Accord* (52A) departs Aberdeen with the up 'Aberdonian', first Newcastle Pacific to reach Aberdeen so far this year.
30	Compound 41142 + 2-6-4T 42229 double-head the 'Empress Voyager' boat train between St Enoch and Greenock (Princes Pier). Interesting pair.
30	Trouble at King's Cross when passengers refuse to enter the very dirty inner suburban 8-coach set provided for the 2.21pm to Cambridge!
30	N7 0-6-2T 69694 works a 4-coach train from Leeds (Central) to Harrogate and Knaresborough to supplement the DMU service over the Bank Holiday, repeated on 2 August. First N7 seen on this route.
31	(Sunday) Two troop trains are run from Trawsfynydd! The first (11 coaches) is for Blackpool at 7.50am, the second (10 coaches) for Liverpool at 8.45am conveying 850 passengers in total. Both are double-headed, the stock running ECS from Wrexham.
31	3 x 14-coach rakes of SR stock are run up the West Coast main line from Glasgow to Stewarts Lane and Barnstaple – returning troop specials?
U/D	Unidentified K4s reported occasionally working over the Highland main line north of Perth, as far as Aviemore.

AUGUST 1955

1ST	61779 (61C) reaches Aviemore with freight from the Speyside line.
1	3MT + 4MT combination 77008 + 80030 brings the 'Cunarder' boat train into Greenock (Princes Pier) from St Enoch, an unusual pairing.
3,9	61610 *Honingham Hall* (30A) appears at Hull on a running-in turn from Doncaster Works. 61620 *Clumber* (31B) repeats this on the 9th.
5	78023 (19B) is surprise power for the morning Leeds – Otley goods.
5	O1 2-8-0 63975 is a rare class at Scarborough, on ECS from Mexborough.
5,6	70052/54 *Firth of Tay/Dornoch Firth* (both 66A) reach Morecambe on consecutive days, presumably on excursion traffic from Glasgow.
6	J6 0-6-0 64186 works the 4.3pm Broad Street – Cambridge, and returns on the 8.50pm to Kings Cross, where eyes widen at the ancient motive power.
6	'Dukedog' 4-4-0 9023 + 2-6-2T 5148 double-head the 8.10am Manchester to Penzance between Newton Abbot and Plymouth. Scraping the barrel?
6	L&Y 0-6-0 52290 pilots 45642 *Boscawen* from Preston to Bolton on the 10.50am Glasgow – Manchester (Victoria). Strange sight; odd choice of pilot!
7	6879 *Overton Grange* (84B) is an extreme rarity at Colwick, where it turns on the triangle and heads for Nottingham around 8pm.
8	U1 2-8-8-2T Beyer-Garratt 69999 commences work as an oil-burner on Lickey incline banking duties.
8	48309 + 48728 head the Royal train on its tour of South Wales, and are seen approaching Pembroke on the line from Whitland. Unusual power!

10 W1 4-6-4 60700 makes a rare appearance at York, having worked the 4-coach 3pm local from Doncaster, possibly running-in after Works attention.

12 6.50pm King's Cross – Aberdeen contains stock displaying 'Master Cutler' and 'Cambridge Buffet Express' roofboards!

12 62714 *Perthshire* (63B Stirling!) heads the 7.10am Northallerton – Leeds via Wetherby, running-in from Darlington, but a rarity nonetheless.

13 61070 reaches New Street on the Yarmouth train, but is then employed as pilot to 45738 *Samson* (3B) on the 4.37pm ex-Euston, to Wolverhampton!

13 L1 2-6-4T 67800 is surprise pilot for 0-6-0PT 7736 on the 3.45pm auto-train from Princes Risborough to Aylesbury.

13 61464 powers the 9.50am Grantham – Doncaster, a rare passenger duty for a B16 4-6-0 on this stretch of the East Coast main line.

13 73061 (66A!) arrives at Scarborough with the 8.45am from Bradford, and returns on the 1.10pm for Leeds. Has a Polmadie loco been here before?

14 61031 *Reedbuck* passes through Driffield with an excursion from Dudley Hill composed entirely of SR stock, including some still in malachite green.

14 34075 *264 Squadron* finds unexpected employment on a special coal train from Newhaven to Ashford via Hastings.

14,21 Two scenic excursions are run from Newcastle to Rothbury via Reedsmouth, returning via Morpeth with stops at Riding Mill and Stocksfield to view prize-winning station gardens. Line had been closed to passengers 3 years earlier.

16 61996 *Lord of the Isles* is noted on an engineers' train near Dunkeld on the Highland main line north of Perth, a K4 is a most unlikely class here.

17 V4 2-6-2 61701 (61B) makes a rare appearance in Waverley.

17 76001 (66B) is an even rarer sight at York shed, on an unknown mission.

18 2-6-4T 42388 powers the 'Pembroke Coast Express' between Whitland and Carmarthen. Has an LMS loco worked this train before?

18 2-6-4T 42374 (34D Hitchin) is an unexpected visitor to Colchester shed.

19 61565 runs into Rugby (Midland) on a train from Peterborough.

19 D11 62671 *Bailie MacWheeble* (65A) reaches Ferryhill before heading south on a special goods. An uncommon class in Aberdeen.

20 45563 *Australia* (10C) departs Waverley – where Patricoft 'Jubilees' rarely reach – with the 2.33pm to Carlisle via Hawick.

20 62718 *Kinross-shire* passes through Dunkeld LE southbound; why?

23 K 2-6-0 32342 pilots H2 4-4-2 32426 *St. Alban's Head* on the 9.41am Brighton – New Cross Gate van train, an unusual pairing.

23 45585 *Hyderabad* passes Richmond on an excursion from Derby to Kew Gardens. The engine is serviced at Feltham, where a 'Jubilee' is a rarity.

23 45506 *The Royal Pioneer Corps* works the Appleby – London milk train over the Settle & Carlisle to Leeds. 'Patriots' are infrequently seen on this route.

24 Ivatt 2-6-0 46460 hauls an Inspection Saloon throughout from Aberdeen to Inverness, arousing much interest here – a novelty arrival in Inverness.

25 Doncaster Works turns out its first ever 4-6-0 (73100) after 102 years!

27 Polegate, 12.30am. 2-NOL EMU forming the 10.46pm Brighton – Eastbourne is pushed into the station by Co-Co electric 20002, pulling its own 30-wagon Norwood – Eastbourne freight. E4 0-6-2T 32511 tows the EMU onwards.

27	2-6-4T 42586 (3C Walsall) heads an 8-coach Wolverhampton – New Brighton excursion throughout. Quite a journey for a tank engine!
27	J39 0-6-0 64767 is provided for the 7.10pm arrival at Southend ex-Liverpool Street, an unlikely class to work a timetabled passenger train from a major London terminus.
28	D11 4-4-0 62664 *Princess Mary* is observed passing Abergele (of all places) on an unidentified 5-coach train.
29	Fareham – Hayling Island 5-coach excursion is headed throughout (i.e. from Fareham) by A1X 0-6-0Ts 32640 + 32650 exceptional work for these locos.
U/D	90027 (51B Newport) works the 7.42pm Thirsk – Harrogate stopping passenger train, unlikely work for this class of heavy freight engines.

SEPTEMBER 1955

1ST,2ND	USA 0-6-0T 30061 passes through Acton *en route* to Kentish Town for shunting trials at Somers Town Goods depot (1st). 30066 appears at Willesden (2nd), and heads north to Bank Hall (27A) Liverpool, for similar trials there.
4	4-4-0s D20 62360 + Compound 41102 head an SLS special between Hawes and Garsdale, an attractive and photogenic pairing on this scenic route.
4	70018 *Flying Dutchman* powers the 2.55pm Birkenhead – Paddington, the first 7MT for 10 months on the Birmingham line.
5	60101 *Cicero* works in/out of Aberdeen on the down/up 'Granite City'. Most unusual to find an A3 on this express.
5	Unbelievably, 44783 (60A) is on Grantham shed. Rarity of the month!
6	72001 *Clan Cameron* (66A) heads the down 'Thames-Clyde Express' from Leeds, where Polmadie engines are infrequent visitors.
6,10	46123 *Royal Irish Fusilier* noted at New Street (6th) masquerading as 46121 *Highland Light Infantry*, this Regiment had specifically requested troop train haulage Holyhead – Glasgow (10th) by 'their' loco, currently in Crewe Works, hence 46123 (recently shopped) swapped identities on a temporary basis.
7	Crosti-boilered 92028 runs LE from Wellingborough to Brighton, to be inspected by Works staff and officials. First 9F seen in these parts.
8	70054 *Dornoch Firth* takes the up 'Saint Mungo' out of Aberdeen, unusually, as 'Britannias' are rarely to be seen on this train.
9	7822 *Foxcote Manor* reaches Weymouth on a pigeon special, and brings an 84K(Chester) shedplate to Weymouth for the first time?
10	44266 (22A) brings another pigeon special, from Bristol, into Ripon – first Bristol engine to work right through?
11	G6 0-6-0T 30162 shunts Southampton Docks, first time in 25 years, as USA's 30061/66 are on loan to the LMR.
11	'Farnborough Flyer' (14 coaches inc. Sleeping Car + observation car E1729E) is headed by D11 4-4-0s 62666/67 *Zeebrugge/Somme* between Doncaster and Basingstoke, where E1729E is removed and train reversed. Train originated at Leeds; 60133 *Pommern* works it to Doncaster.
11	45703 *Thunderer* reaches Marylebone on a parcels train from Bletchley. Crewe North (5A) 'Jubilees' are rare specimens in this terminus.
15	70015 *Arrow* (81A) works the 7.30am Euston – Holyhead before returning to the WR on the 18th. (Still running-in from Crewe Works).

16	62749 *The Cottesmore* pilots Compound 41075 on a Leeds (City) – Bradford (Forster Square) service. Another attractive combination.
16	Two Ocean Liner expresses are run from Southampton Docks to Victoria. Excess boat train traffic causes Waterloo to overflow to Victoria (Eastern).
20	45478 (60A) is a great rarity in Carlisle, arriving with the 9am Perth – Euston, to be relieved by 46146 *The Rifle Brigade*.
21-24	T9 4-4-0 30304 is used on the 6.5pm Basingstoke – Reading (21st), then runs LE to Tyseley (22nd), then LE to Shrewsbury (23rd) and finally heads the Talyllyn Railway Preservation Society special Welshpool – Towyn (24th).
24	J38 0-6-0 65925 (62A) is rare power for a Springburn – Ibrox football special.
29	60824 takes the up 'Postal' out of Aberdeen – first recorded occurrence of an LNER engine leaving the Granite City on this working.
U/D	Between 30 July and 10 September relief boat trains from Holyhead to London are run to Paddington (with reversal at Chester).
U/D	Smokeless Zone Act comes into force – but does not apply to locomotives!

OCTOBER 1955

4TH	LTS 4-4-2T 419xx is a short-notice substitute for a B17 on the 9.45am Southend (Victoria) – Liverpool Street, where a 4-4-2T is a rarity nowadays.
4	6910 *Gossington Hall* (in black livery) is seen at Paddington paired with a green tender complete with the initials 'GW' and the company crest!
5	2-car DMU 79006/79506 fails on reaching Ripon, from Bradford. On the return trip this is pushed (!) to Harrogate by the Ripon pilot J39 0-6-0 64859.
6	J37 0-6-0 64573 (65C Parkhead) is a rare sight at Heaton, arriving with freight from Edinburgh. This class almost never leave Scotland.
7	73100/01/02 form a unique consecutively numbered trio working three football specials from St Enoch to Stranraer.
7	D20 4-4-0 62387 pilots A2/2 60501 *Cock o' the North* between Ripon and Harrogate on the 8.55am Newcastle – Liverpool, an impressive combination.
10	35017 *Belgian Marine* runs along the sea wall at Teignmouth, towards Exeter. Few 'Merchant Navy' class locos pass over this WR route.
15	41137 (20A) is employed on the 2.10pm St Enoch – Kilmarnock, the first English Compound north of Carlisle for some years.
16	62760 *The Cotswold* is seen at Golcar, heading the NER Inspection Saloon between Leeds and Stalybridge – rare engines west of Leeds.
20	B2 61671 *Royal Sovereign* + B17 61657 *Doncaster Rovers* double-head the 7.57pm King's Cross – Cambridge Buffet Car Express, a pleasing sight.
20	0-6-0 diesel shunter 11108 runs LE down the East Coast main line in the course of transfer from King's Cross to Immingham, an odd working.
23	Lichfield (Trent Valley) sidings hold 'out of gauge' export freight from Loughborough to Merseyside. This includes a Brush-Bagnall 1000hp diesel for the Ceylon Gvt Rly on accommodation bogies, with its own 5' 6" gauge bogies on separate wagons.
24	61992 unexpectedly reaches Buchanan St on the 3pm from Dundee.
27	35029 *Ellerman Line* is noted on Brighton shed before becoming the first MN to go into Brighton Works, not leaving there until 7 December.

28   34063 *229 Squadron* enters Reading (General) on the 3.20pm ex-Basingstoke. SR Pacifics are infrequent visitors to the station itself.

29   'Crab' 42774 (20A) works a football special from Bradford (Forster Square) to Darlington, via Harrogate. An unusual class in the North East.

U/D   The closed signalbox at Harbledown Jct. (instruments removed) is purchased and demolished by a railway employee for £2 10s 0d, for the timber.

U/D   Diesel shunting locos 13162-66 arrive at King's Cross coincidentally at the same time as brand new 1st class coaching stock FKs E13162-66, which had been hauled from Swindon via Oxford and Cambridge.

U/D   Constructed during 1955 at the Dick Kerr Works at Preston, 'Deltic' was originally painted in EE's house colours of green & cream before repainting in 'French blue' (or 'Powder blue') prototype loco livery. It was then transferred by road to the EE Netherton Works for static tests and moved under its own power for the first time on 15 September. 'Deltic' is allocated to Speke Jct. shed, close to the Napier Works at Netherton on 24 October. Various tests take place here before working ECS trains between Edge Hill and Preston.

NOVEMBER 1955

4TH   Up goods passes Flitwick with a newly painted road parcels van (conveyed on a wagon) with the legend 'LNER' at the top and 'London and North Eastern Railway Company' at the bottom, both in bright blue!

8   Co-Co 'Deltic' works LE to Crewe and powers an Officers' special to Shrewsbury and back.

12   46203 *Princess Margaret Rose* runs-in from Crewe Works on the 4.32pm Chester – Llandudno Jct., only the second time this year that a Stanier Pacific has been seen on the North Wales Coast.

12/13   O4/5 2-8-0 63726 (36D Barnsley) works an overnight freight throughout from Wath to Rose Grove, the furthest an O4 has travelled into L&Y territory.

13   34090 *Sir Eustace Missenden, Southern Railway* reaches Weston-super-Mare (first SR loco seen here?) on an excursion from Brighton, worked throughout.

13   D20 4-4-0 62387 heads the 5.20pm York – March as far as Doncaster, a rare class to work over this stretch of line.

15   A8 4-6-2T 69882 (50B Neville Hill) appears at Ripon on the 7.10am Northallerton – Leeds via Wetherby; first A8 to reach Ripon for some years.

16   72000 *Clan Buchanan* takes the 3.30pm up 'Postal' out of Aberdeen, 'Clans' are an uncommon sight on this working.

18   R.O.D. 2-8-0 3038 (86G Pontypool Road!) heads a freight along the MSJ&A line through Timperley, in the Altrincham direction. Astonishing!

19   V3 2-6-2T 67680 pilots 44848 between Darlington and Crook, on a football special for the Crook Town v Derby County FA Cup tie.

25,26   E68000 – a new 3rd rail electric parcels car for Tyneside – undergoes trials between London Bridge and Brighton with 6 or 9 empty coaches.

28-30   'Deltic' 3300hp prototype diesel electric works its first revenue-earning trains, the 7.30pm Edge Hill – Camden express freight, arriving 3.7am (29th) and departing with the 7.35pm return working reaching Edge Hill 1.7am (30th).

U/D   80xxx series 2-6-4Ts from 61A occasionally work right through to Inverness

U/D   34026 finally receives its name – *Yes Tor* – the last West Country to do so.

DECEMBER 1955

2ND   46203 *Princess Margaret Rose* (up 'Comet'), 46239 *City of Chester* (6pm to Crewe) and 46257 *City of Salford* (6.25pm Mayfield – Crewe) all seen together in Manchester (London Road) around 5.50pm, a real surprise!

3   34014 *Budleigh Salterton* with 8 loaded hopper wagons from Meldon Quarry requires Ivatt 2-6-2T 41306 as pilot and E1/R 0-6-2Ts 32135/24 in the rear to mount the bank between the two Exeter stations.

13   'Deltic' heads first passenger services; the up 'Merseyside Express' from Liverpool (Lime Street) to Euston and the down 'Shamrock'. Heads turn at Euston and much Press attention is given to the event.

17   'Father Christmas' is conveyed into Llandudno by special 1-coach (decorated) train. Loudspeaker fixed to tank engine plays 'Jingle Bells' and loco carries a headboard, all sponsored by a local, prominently named, firm!

17   90539 works a goods from Kittybrewster into Keith – first WD seen on the GNS system for over a year.

19   B2 61671 *Royal Sovereign* (31A) is surprisingly at the head of the down 'Norfolkman' out of Liverpool Street.

19   An E4 2-4-0 is unexpected substitute power for the 4.55pm Cambridge to Kettering, followed by the 8.15pm to Leicester over the Midland main line!

20   Disruption caused by heavy snow sees 62062 work the 'Yorkshire Pullman' and J39 0-6-0 64861 the 11.50am to King's Cross, between Harrogate and Leeds (Central). The down 'Tees-Tyne Pullman' avoids York altogether, routed via Burton Salmon, Tadcaster, Harrogate and Northallerton.

23,24   61553 (35B Grantham) is a sensational visitor to Gateshead depot, leaving for York with a freight on Christmas Eve.

24   Compound 40927 is paired with D11 4-4-0 62663 *Prince Albert* to work the 3.5pm Lincoln (St Marks) – Derby, a contrasting combination.

24   72009 *Clan Stewart* is noted on the Calder Valley line near Mirfield with a lightweight goods. Later returns LE and spends Christmas on Normanton shed.

27,28   Compound 41160 grinds to a halt within Sough Tunnel and then runs backwards, with the 8-coach 11.55am Colne – Euston. A rebuilt 'Patriot' is provided the following day for safety!

29   Ayr's Sentinel Y1 0-4-0T 68138 is towed through Waverley to reach St Margarets (64A), leaving for Darlington works next day. An interesting sight.

30   After a mishap at Leicester the 'Master Cutler' arrives at King's Cross behind 60049 *Galtee More* (38C), a rare engine at this terminus.

30   Two Southampton – Ripon troop trains consist of SR stock, some of which is still in malachite green.

U/D   LMS Co-Co diesel 10000 is fitted with a bi-directional water scoop (as per 'Deltic'). Trials take place on Kegworth troughs, (Derby/Loughborough).

U/D   Successful tests are held on the Lancaster/Morecambe/Heysham line with a germanium rectifier-equipped electric train. Developed by BTH this is the first railway application of this device anywhere in the world.

JANUARY 1956

4TH	61058 (32A!) makes a surprise appearance on Cricklewood depot, and pays an equally surprising visit to Kentish Town shed two days later.
5	0-4-4T 58051 hauls Templecombe's G6 0-6-0 30274 to Bournemouth (71B) for attention, 58051 also making a class debut here.
7	Sheffield (Victoria) sees 60016 *Silver King*, 60038 *Firdaussi*, 60045 *Lemberg* and 60083 *Sir Hugo* plus 60884, 60942 arrive on football specials for the Wednesday v Newcastle FA Cup match.
9	LTS 4-4-2T 41943 (16D Mansfield) runs LE through Luton its way to Bow Works for overhaul, a most unusual type to pass this way.
14	W class 2-6-4T 31916 observed still lettered 'Southern' on its side tanks.
14	ECS of returning rugby special from Murrayfield is hauled out of Glasgow (Central) by WD 2-10-0 90756 – a rare sight in this terminus.
15	'Golden Arrow' is diverted via Eynesford between Swanley and Sevenoaks.
15	Stanier 2-6-0 42954 heads the 4.20pm Carlisle – Preston, very infrequent on passenger services over Shap.
16	T9 4-4-0 30728 is a rare visitor to the S&D line from Bournemouth to Bath, working the 11.40am between West and Green Park.
18	70022 *Tornado* is employed on the 7pm Newton Abbot – Acton freight, the first recorded appearance of a 'Britannia' on freight in the London Division.
18	O2 0-4-4T 30183 works (uniquely) the Seaton Branch, 'always' an M7 duty.
26	2-8-0 3831 is an unusual climber of the Lickey bank with a ballast train from Droitwich, hauled as far as Kings Norton.
27	L&Y 0-8-0 49662 brings freight from the North Wales Coast into Chester. 'Austin Sevens' are rarities in these parts.
29	30859 *Lord Hood* heads the 4.45am London Bridge – Brighton, the first ever 'Lord Nelson' on passenger work on this line. 30859 then enters the Works.
29	70051 *Firth of Forth* (66A) appears on York shed and later heads off to Manchester with a parcels train.
31	4-4-0 40652 (17A) is surprise power for a transfer freight between Cricklewood and Neasden – the first of this type seen here.
U/D	73118 is used on the 'Bournemouth Belle' out of Waterloo, and gains time on schedule!
U/D	23rd; 27 of the 30 'Kings' are withdrawn for immediate attention to bogie frames, hence 46254 *City of Stoke-on-Trent* works the 9.10am Paddington to Wolverhampton. 27th; 46257 *City of Salford* heads the 11.15am 'Merchant Venturer' to Bristol. 30th; Entire class withdrawn as main frames also need inspecting. 46207/10 arrive on loan plus nine 5MTs from SR and LMR. (See February).

FEBRUARY 1956

Observations of LMR Pacifics on WR trains whilst 'Kings' out of action. All four Pacifics are returned by the end of the month.

1ST	46257 *City of Salford* heads 'Cornish Riviera' out of Paddington.
7	46207 *Princess Arthur of Connaught* works the 6.7pm ex-Wolverhampton.

9	1015 *County of Gloucester* pilots 46254 *City of Stoke-on-Trent* on the 'Cornish Riviera' between Newton Abbot and Plymouth.
10	46210 *Lady Patricia* seen on Dainton with the down 'Cornish Riviera'.
14	46254 *City of Stoke-on-Trent* noted on the up 'Torbay Express'.
15	6834 *Dummer Grange* pilots 46210 up Rattery bank.
U/D	73114 (also on loan) heads the 6.5pm Paddington – Oxford.

2	Crosti-boilered 92027 works into Oxford on freight from Bletchley.
8	80098 (33A) brings the ECS of the 10.24am to Norwich into Liverpool Street, a rare class to be found here.
9	K 2-6-0 32333 leaves Bournemouth on the 6.30pm Weymouth – Waterloo.
9	35018 *British India Line* – the first rebuilt 'Merchant Navy' – is outshopped from Eastleigh Works for official inspection and photographs in the yard.
10-15	B4 0-4-0T 30084 is abandoned in a snowstorm at Dover Eastern Docks (10th). P 0-6-0T 31027 is sent to the rescue and fails but A1X 0-6-0T 32670 succeeds on the 15th, and works the daily sea-front train on subsequent days, the first 'Terrier' to be employed in Dover docks.
11	30740 *Merlin* is 'blown up' for the TV cameras filming *Saturday Night Out*. This takes place on the Longmoor Military Railway, and the engine is towed to Brighton for scrapping.
14	46109 *Royal Engineer* + 46143 *The South Staffordshire Regiment* double-head the up 'Comet' into Euston, a conspicuous same-class pairing.
16	12.50pm Ipswich – Colchester is surprisingly headed by 4-4-2T 41949 (30A).
17	73071 heads the 6.5am, 44911 the 2.5pm King's Cross – Cambridge. Both engines are on loan to 34A, testing ATC equipment on the main line.
19	Liverpool Overhead Railway coach No. 9 is hauled to/from Southport to turn on the Chapel Street triangle, a rare movement away from its usual confines.
20	4.30pm from Liverpool Street arrives in Norwich behind a 'Britannia' as usual but runs into the Royal Dock platform, as all others are blocked due to a derailment at the station approaches.
22	L&Y 2-4-2T 50650 travels LE from Royston (20C) to Bedford, transferred there to work the push/pull service to Bletchley. 50646 joins a few days later.
23	2-6-6-2T Garratt 47967 passes Harrow & Wealdstone with an up freight.
26	60539 *Bronzino* + 46105 *Cameron Highlander* (66A) form an astonishing partnership on a heavy westbound parcels train out of York.
26,27	Co-Co DC electric 27002 is seen being towed through Cambridge *en route* to Southend, for display at the Tilbury Centenary Exhibition. 70038 *Robin Hood* (30A) travels to Hornsey (27th) to pick up 60022 *Mallard* and hauls it to Southend for same purpose – first A4 seen at Southend, dead or alive!
U/D	Hard water at Shoeburyness causes scale in loco boilers and hence shortage of steam. ICI provides 'tablets' to add to water tanks, some tanks being so clogged as to require two doses!
U/D	Excursion notice dated Feb 1956 and displayed at Hessle, is headed 'LNER'!

MARCH 1956

1ST   90444 (rare on the Highland line) is seen at Blair Atholl.

1-3   Rolling stock exhibition is put on at Southend (Central) for the Centenary of the LTS line; locos on view are 60022 / 70038 / 27002 / 80080 / 0-6-0 diesel 12134 plus LTS 4-4-2T 41966 (as No.80), which hauls special Centenary train to Liverpool Street (3rd).

3   70015 *Apollo* + 70027 *Rising Star* head the up 'Capitals United Express'.

8   73124 visits Alnwick – a rare class here – with a cattle train from Heaton.

10   Womens' Hockey International brings six SR light Pacifics to Wembley (Central), four going to Watford for servicing, plus three 'Schools' class to Wembley (Stadium), these engines retiring to Neasden depot.

15   45546 *Fleetwood* appears at Marylebone (first 'Patriot' here) on the 3.19am parcels train from Bletchley.

17   45642 *Boscawen* reaches Euston, where Newton Heath 'Jubilees' are scarce.

17   FA Cup semi-final day. Spurs v Manchester City at Villa Park brings 61663 *Everton* and 61227, 61384 (all 30A) to Monument Lane depot. Sunderland v Birmingham City at Hillsborough sees two A1s, five A2s and two A3s arrive on specials into Sheffield (Victoria).

17   7913 *Little Wyrley Hall* (84G) works in/out of Marylebone with an excursion from Snow Hill. Shrewsbury engines rarely reach Marylebone.

17   72008 *Clan Macleod* is routed via Hawick on the Aberdeen – Manchester fish train. This class is not often seen in Edinburgh, or on the Waverley route.

21   92061 (15A) reaches Tilbury to turn after working a bulk haul of soda ash to West Thurrock. A notable arrival at Tilbury.

21   0-6-0PT 9610 on the 7.55am Temple Meads – Bath stopper suffers brake failure at Keynsham, but reaches the loop at East 'box. Here the following Weymouth train is drawn up alongside on the main line and all the 7.55's passengers transfer to it by means of a step ladder, with only 15min delay.

22   A8 4-6-2T 69890 (50G Whitby) takes the York engineers' saloon to Clayton West, the first visit of an NER loco to this remote outpost of the L&Y.

27   44911 (34A on loan) works the 8.45pm King's Cross – Hull freight lodging turn, and heads south next day with the 3.32pm fish train.

28   Up 'Royal Scot' arrives in Carlisle (2 hours late) behind, astonishingly, tender first 45090...of Inverness! Surely a first for a 60A loco to haul this train.

29   62745 *The Hurworth* powers the York – Lowestoft through to March, where this is probably the first D49 to be seen here.

30   (Good Friday) 60016 *Silver King*, 60021 *Wild Swan* are both rare visitors to Hitchin shed, for attention. Even more so is W1 4-6-4 60700 a few days later.

30   75002 (82C) heads a relief Bristol express out of London Road. Swindon engines are unknown in Manchester (or were!).

30   62721 *Warwickshire* + 45673 *Keppel* form a most interestingly diverse pairing on the 5.32pm Perth – Glasgow.

30   46211 *Queen Maud* (8A!) arrives in Aberdeen on the 3.21pm from Perth.

U/D   Both 73071 and 44911 visit Doncaster Works for modifications to the ATC equipment. First Stanier 4-6-0 inside Doncaster Works?

U/D   Newcastle – Manchester (Red Bank) parcels leaves York behind the very strange pairing of 60835 *The Green Howard* + 45702 *Colossus*.

U/D 46225 *Duchess of Gloucester* is worked over the Settle & Carlisle for the first time on record, on dynamometer car trials following static tests at Rugby.

U/D BR announces future electrification to be 25kV AC (and vacuum braked!)

APRIL 1956

1ST 77011 (52C) reaches Edinburgh (Waverley) on the 9am from Hawick.

2 L&Y 2-4-2T 50650 works the 5.40pm Wellingborough (Midland Road) to Northampton – a first appearance here for this class. (Easter Monday).

2 61653 *Huddersfield Town* reaches Bridlington, from Mexborough. Rare!

2,6 72002 *Clan Campbell* (66A) running-in from Crewe, finds itself at Southport, and on the 6th works the 6.35pm Chester – Rhyl.

4,6 D11 4-4-0 62681 *Captain Craigengelt* (65A), fresh from overhaul at Inverurie, works south with the 2.52pm freight from Aberdeen. Even more unusually, 43922 (68A) heads the 11am southbound goods on the 6th.

7 60526 *Sugar Palm* is spotted at Neasden, after working to Wembley Hill.

7 9.35am Newcastle – Holloway ECS train includes 1st class Pullman car with 'Ocean Liner Express' roofboards (Waterloo – Southampton Docks boat train stock!)

7 70032 *Tennyson* (9A) is the first of its class to traverse the Lickey incline, working south with a schools' rugby international special to Bristol.

9 'Dukedog' 4-4-0s 9021 + 9017 power the up 'Cambrian Coast Express' between Welshpool and Shrewsbury. A nostalgic sight! Contrastingly…

12 72004 *Clan Macdonald* (66A), ex-Crewe Works, also reaches Shrewsbury.

13 Derailment at Aylesbury causes the unprecedented sight of J20 0-6-0 64689 (30A) passing through Chalfont with the Woodford Halse breakdown train.

15 0-6-0 diesel shunter 13219 operates a special 300 ton freight from Horsham to Guildford and back, with a view to their use on diagrammed goods trains.

15 Detonator tests are carried out between Tamworth and Burton whereby an up train is run at high speed over 200 detonators in rapid succession. 73054 plus five coaches performs the task and the fragments collected by PW staff to assess prototypes of several new designs for the safest (least fragmentation).

16 46135 *The East Lancashire Regiment* + 46104 *Scottish Borderer* head the 10.30am Workington – Euston, to Lancaster. Unprecedented sight in Furness!

17 34008 *Padstow* arrives at Temple Mills with a banana train from Southampton.

19 L1 2-6-4T 67784 works a returning special from Hitchin, to… Bournville!

23-4 May British Industries Fair at Castle Bromwich provides seven Pullman cars from the spare 'South Wales Pullman' set + Buffet Car No.5, as catering vehicles. (These return down the Lickey bank on 7 May, a rare sight in itself).

25 60041 *Salmon Trout* enters Princes Street on 3.32pm ex-Stirling. LNER Pacifics are rarities at the 'other' Edinburgh station.

27 LNW 0-8-0 49005 surprisingly heads the 8.20am Castlethorpe – Wolverton.

27 34020 *Seaton* + 34054 *Lord Beaverbrook* bring the 5.53pm from Exeter into Waterloo, where double-heading is supposedly banned!

28 62727 *The Quorn* + 61339 power a Knaresborough – Edinburgh excursion as far as Newcastle. D49s are rare on East Coast main line work.

28	A2/1 60509 *Waverley* works into St Enoch from Edinburgh with the overnight 'Starlight Special'. The Glasgow train (usually a separate working) has been combined with the Marylebone – Edinburgh on this occasion.
30	92052 is noted working ECS out of Euston.
30	D11 4-4-0 62664 *Princes Mary* arrives at Newton Heath ex-Gorton Works, to be run-in on local services prior to working the 'Pennine Pullman' on 12 May.
U/D	6024 *King Edward I* is an unusual visitor to Barrow Road shed (22A) to use the wheel-drop facility (and is there nearly a month).
U/D	(Easter period). Heaviest traffic since the war reported at Huddersfield where 57 relief trains plus 51 excursions pass through in addition to normal services.

MAY 1956

1ST	73004 takes a train of specially treated ash to Immingham for shipment to Australia, for use on the Olympic Games track in Melbourne.
1	45642 *Boscawen* (26A) is a surprise arrival in Aberdeen; 5.55pm ex-Dumfries.
1	34063 229 *Squadron* hauls a special train of five Pullmans to Fawley in connection with an official function at the Esso refinery.
2-9	D11 4-4-0 62664 *Princess Mary* works a ballast train to Ashton under Lyne (2nd); 6.2am Greenfield – Huddersfield, 7.4am Huddersfield – Leeds (City), 9.15am Leeds – Manchester (Exchange) on 3rd/4th/5th. Then 8.35am M/C (Victoria) to Blackburn, 1pm Bolton – Royton Jct. freight (7th) and 7pm Mytholmroyd to Stockport parcels (8th). 62662 *Prince of Wales* arrives Newton Heath (6th), works 7pm Mytholmroyd – Stockport parcels (7th) then 6.2am Greenfield to Huddersfield etc. (9th), all in preparation for the 12th.
4	60090 *Grand Parade* heads the 'Bon Accord' into Aberdeen and takes out the 7.45pm fish train to Carlisle. Unusual motive power for both trains.
7	4-4-0s 40454 + 40489 work an enthusiasts' special from Nottingham into Swindon via the MSWJ line, returning via Didcot and Oxford.
9	N 2-6-0s 31830 + 31845 bring the Royal train from Launceston into Exeter.
10	J39 0-6-0s 64821 + 64942 take the up 'Queen of Scots' out of Ripon; A2/3 60524 *Herringbone* fails there with leaking tubes. Unique Pullman power?
11	62760 *The Cotswold* (50A) reaches as far west as Stanhope (on the Wearhead branch) with a signal engineers' special. This class is rare here.
11	'Valiant' jet bomber crashes and explodes on the railway line just east of Southwick station on the Brighton – Portsmouth main line. This rips up rails and blows a large hole in the embankment at 12.35pm. Trains are running again over the affected sight by 5am next day.
12	L&Y locos 50647 (2-4-2T) + 52438 (0-6-0) double-head an enthusiasts' special up the 1 in 27 Werneth incline – the steepest in Britain for passenger use.
12	'Pennine Pullman' excursion (including a 'Devon Bell' observation car) leaves Marylebone behind 60014 *Silver Link* as far as Sheffield (Victoria), then Co-Co electric 27002 to the outskirts of Manchester. Here 62662/64 head the special over the L&Y main line through Rochdale, Todmorden to Mirfield and Barnsley, with 60014 returning the train to King's Cross, via Retford. A memorable day out!
17-21	New 80135 carries out ECS duties at Liverpool Street, unusual type here.
19-22	73007 (63A Perth!), complete with snowplough and cab-side tablet exchange apparatus is a real surprise working local trains between Leeds, Manchester on Whit Saturday.

Also seen at Southport on Whit Monday (21st) and Blackpool next day, working from Huddersfield depot!

21 45711 *Courageous* (67A) is an extreme rarity at St Pancras on a night relief for Glasgow. Almost as rare is…

22 'Crab' 42920 (5B) seen heading 13 bogies out of York, to Newcastle!

24 D16 4-4-0 62551 nearly reaches Birmingham on freight from Peterborough, but fails and is drawn back to Nuneaton shed for attention.

26 62752 *The Atherstone* + 62762 *The Fernie* power a pigeon special of 20 vehicles (going back to the WR) south out of Ripon, towards Harrogate.

27 Boat train from Southampton Docks is run into Victoria, conveying several hundred West Indian immigrants. Very large amounts of luggage causes delay both to the 4pm and 4.30pm Continental boat train departures!

U/D 'Dukedog' 4-4-0 9015 is highly unusual substitute power for the Fairford branch passenger trains on several days in early May.

JUNE 1956

1ST D16 4-4-0 62551 (35C), having been on Nuneaton shed for several days is towed south on the West Coast mainline by a Stanier 8F.

1,2,3 46139 *The Welch Regiment* (1B) works an ECS train of seven dining cars Euston – Nottingham (Midland) on the 1st. Seven excursions are run to Blackpool (2nd) in connection with the Raleigh Industries Works Outing. Each train contains one of these dining cars, all are 'Jubilee' hauled including 45639 *Raleigh*. 46139 takes the dining cars back to Euston ECS on the 3rd.

3 3rd class abolished and renamed 2nd class throughout BR.

3 45685 *Barfleur* (22A) and 45719 *Glorious* (24E) both visit Whitley Bay on excursions from Wath, Normanton respectively. Rare locos on the NE coast.

3 For the ramblers' excursion from Crystal Palace to Chesham, C2X 0-6-0 32543 hauls SR stock to New Cross Gate, where LTE train with electric loco 14 takes passengers onwards. First Metropolitan electric at New Cross Gate.

3 G5 0-4-4T 67254 pilots 60154 *Bon Accord* on the 5pm Newcastle – Liverpool diverted via Haswell from Sunderland. A rare pairing of locos.

3/4 60007 *Sir Nigel Gresley* heads the Royal train King's Cross – Redmarshall (East); stables overnight, A4 going to Stockton shed (51E). 60147 *North Eastern* takes train on to Redcar (4th).

7 61113 (35A) becomes the first B1 to descend the Lickey incline when hauling an excursion from Peterborough to the Wye Valley, with 61113 working at least as far as Gloucester.

7 U 2-6-0 31629 (71A) is an unexpected sight at Gloucester in the loop line.

9 72001 *Clan Cameron* noted at Fort William, and works the West Highland line throughout the following week to familiarise crews prior to the 16th.

9 6009 *King Charles II* works the 9am Paddington – Pwllheli through to Ruabon as neither Stafford Road nor Shrewsbury could provide a replacement.

9 5081 *Lockheed Hudson* arrives in Bournemouth with an excursion from Great Malvern. The visitor is not welcomed by the SR authorities, is returned LE with a severe speed restriction, and 'Castles' duly banned south of Eastleigh.

9 34037 *Clovelly* makes the first appearance of an SR Pacific on the Torquay branch, and the return excursion from Churston approaches Paignton with 34037 piloted by 6860 *Aberporth Grange*, quite a sight!

9,12 44831, 45430 (both 2A Rugby) arrive at Chingford with excursions from Coventry for a Boy Scouts' Rally at Gilwell Park – unique workings. 44831 is a stranger on Stratford (30A) shed (12th), presumably some mishap befell it three days earlier.

10 All seven main line diesels (10201/2/3, 10000/1, 10100, 10800) are to be seen either inside Derby Works or Works yard. Meanwhile, inside the south shed 48153 deposits itself into the turntable pit; tour group members stand aghast!

11 Summer Timetable commences and 'Royal Scot'/'Merseyside Express'/'Mancunian'/'Midlander' expresses all receive maroon-liveried stock with distinctive roofboards. On the WR 'Cornish Riviera Limited' and 'Torquay Express' are the first to gain 'chocolate & cream' painted coaches.

11 Waverley – Galashiels and the Gleneagles, Crieff, Comrie branches are worked temporarily by twin-unit diesel railcars, but only until 21 July.

15 61185 works a school's excursion from Barnsley and Penistone throughout to Windsor, and is serviced at Slough before returning north.

16 46156 *The South Wales Borderer* heads a special train between Saltley and Crewe conveying coaching stock built at the Metro-Cammell Works for the Nigerian Railways, for export through Birkenhead.

16,20 60959 works to Ayr on an excursion. 60836, 60965 do the same on 20th. At least three years since V2s ventured here previously.

16 A gathering of the Clan Cameron is held at Achnacarry Castle near Spean Bridge, and 72001 *Clan Cameron* is provided to haul the 7-coach special from Queen Street to Spean Bridge. Driver, fireman and guard are all Camerons (by stipulation), and 61995 *Cameron of Lochiel* is sent ahead on a special freight to cover any failure. 72001 works the ECS to Fort William, is serviced and heads the returning train to Glasgow.

21 New BR emblem is first worn by 70016 *Ariel*, inspected at Marylebone.

23 Rare A2/A1 combination 60539 *Bronzino* + 60127 *Wilson Worsdell* heads north through Durham with a Birmingham – Newcastle express.

23 Q1 0-6-0 33017 is an unexpected choice for ECS workings into Waterloo.

23 45324, 45372 work excursions throughout from Berkhamsted, Tring to Hastings, visiting Ashford shed for coal and water. One of the 11-coach trains is stabled empty at Rye Harbour – an exceptional sight.

23 46201 *Princess Elizabeth* is used on the 9pm goods from Aberdeen to Perth!

26 46229 *Duchess of Hamilton* noted at Macclesfield on the down 'Comet'. Princess Margaret is in one of two GWR vehicles included in the train, saloon 9001 and brake composite W7377W, both in GWR livery.

27 72008 *Clan Macleod* works through Huddersfield on the 8.55am Newcastle to Liverpool. First 'Clan' to travel the LNW route between Leeds, Manchester.

29 48543 + 53804 double-head a Bristol to Bath freight. Rare to see an S&D 2-8-0 away from its own 'patch'.

30 61574 (35B) appears at Todmorden with a special of ER stock which it works right though to Blackpool! Joint surprise of the month with…

30 Three 'Sandringhams' all reach York, 61600 *Sandringham* itself and 61613 *Woodbastwick Hall* (both 30A), B2 61616 *Fallodon* (30E Colchester). Additionally, 70015 *Apollo* (81A) arrives, bringing the unique sight of an Old Oak Common engine to York!

30	4-4-0 62539 (31A) works the Southminster branch, first D16 for many years.
U/D	75065 heads the 5.5pm Ramsgate – Victoria, the 'Kentish Belle'; a surprising choice of motive power for a Pullman train.
U/D	The 'Welsh Dragon' (Rhyl – Llandudno) is now formed of two twin-unit diesel railcars, with roofboards but no headboard.
U/D	Budd stainless steel car (now maroon), 1st class Lounge Car M7585, resumes work in the 'Ulster Express'.
U/D	Inverurie Works (north of Aberdeen) scraps coaching stock sent to it from Willesden (MR clerestory), Annesley (LNW vehicles), Nottingham (CLC coaches) and Heeley (a North Staffordshire relic).
U/D	Vale of Rheidol locos all receive names; 7 *Owain Glyndwr*, 8 *Llywelyn* and 9 *Prince of Wales* – carriages gain chocolate & cream WR livery.

JULY 1956

1ST	61283 heads a Nottingham – Margate excursion as far as Reading, and is serviced at the SR shed there, a rare sight here.
1	62738 *The Zetland* brings an excursion from Harrogate into Morecambe, a debut appearance for this class at the West Coast resort.
1	45524 *Blackpool* is a notable sight at Keswick to work the 7pm special to Manchester. Another unrebuilt 'Patriot', 45543 *Home Guard* arrives at Windermere (Lakeside) with a train from Coventry.
3	73014 (86C!) also reaches the Furness district on excursion traffic.
3	70053 *Moray Firth* heads the Royal train into Ardrossan (Town) where 'Britannias' are rarely seen. (So are Royal trains!).
4,5	Willesden (1A) hosts 61287 (31A), Compound 41187 (27A) on the 4th, and 61669 *Barnsley* (32B) next day, all three unlikely visitors.
5	2-6-2Ts 84005 + 41269 double-head a heavy goods train between Bedford and Hitchin, a strange sight on such a train.
6	5.32pm Fenchurch Street – Shoeburyness breaks in two at Chalkwell. First section proceeds behind the original engine, the detached portion is pushed by the following train to Southend. Chaos reigns behind all this; many passengers climb out of their trains, walk back along the line and catch buses!
6	80120 observed at Dingwall, having worked the Fortrose branch freight. First 'Standard' to work north of Inverness?
7	Royal train is hauled from Portobello to Berwick up the East Coast main line by 44994 + 45161, very rare indeed for this class to be seen here.
7	72006 *Clan Mackenzie* (68A) arrives at Wolverhampton (Low Level) with a troop train from the north and hands over to 4089 *Donnington Castle*. 72006 goes to Stafford Road for servicing.
9	(from) Beaver-tail observation car E1729E is attached to the rear of the 10.24am Fort William – Mallaig and 1pm back for the duration of the summer service. A fee of 2s 6d is charged for its use during the journey.
10	60537 *Bachelor's Button* provides a remarkable spectacle by piloting (tender first) D34 4-4-0 62467 *Glenfinnan* between Queen Street and Cowlairs on a Kirkintilloch train.
10	Royal train (with Prince Philip) arrives in Oxford behind 45278 + 45324 and departs for London with 5060 *Earl of Berkeley* + 5055 *Earl of Eldon*.

12   D11 4-4-0 62688 *Ellen Douglas* (65A) is a decidedly uncommon specimen to reach
             Hawick on the 8.35am from Edinburgh, returning with the 12.20pm.

14   Glasgow Fair holiday traffic produces the remarkable sight of 73100 (67A) on the
             11.5am relief Glasgow – Euston passing through Carlisle, non-stop, on 15 bogies!
             Further, the 12.5pm Glasgow – Liverpool is worked throughout by 45692 *Cyclops* (63A
             Perth), surely a 'cop' in Liverpool!

15,22   5018 *St. Mawes Castle* + 5042 *Winchester Castle* as a LE pair, make a series of clearance
             and stress-measuring tests on the Severn Bridge connecting Lydney and Sharpness.

16,18   D11 4-4-0 62681 *Captain Craigengelt* surprisingly heads the 3.6pm Stirling to Callander,
             and appears in Glasgow (Central) two days later.

16   350hp diesel shunter 13301 drags the ECS of the 'East Anglian' into Liverpool Street, a
             most unusual sight at this terminus.

17-19,25   0-6-0 2237 visits Rhyl on an excursion (17th and 19th); 2202/33/55/89 are on Rhyl shed
             (18th), and 2209 + 'Dukedog' 9028 double-head an excursion into Rhyl from Denbigh
             on the 25th.

20   A rare combination of motive power is seen at Leeds (Central) on the 5.15pm to King's
             Cross; 60525 *A. H. Peppercorn* piloting 60027 *Merlin*!

24   7018 *Drysllwyn Castle*, complete with 'Torbay Express' headboard and still coupled to
             the WR dynamometer car, works the 5.45pm Goodrington to Hackney freight as far as
             Newton Abbot, an odd sight indeed.

24,25   70004 *William Shakespeare* (73A) heads the 7.20pm Waterloo – Southampton Docks *en
             route* to Eastleigh Works open day 24 hours later, after which it runs to Romsey to haul
             an Army Cadet special to Farnborough.

28   76056 (75B Redhill) finds its way, somehow, into Euston!

28   N 2-6-0 31413 is seen heading south through Harrow & Wealdstone with a troop train
             from Bushey to Ashford. SR engines rarely trespass onto the LMR.

28   'Crab' (number unknown) works over the S&D – first since 1949.

28   62734 *Cumberland* (68C) appears – looking out of place – at Queen Street on the
             7.52pm relief to Edinburgh.

28   Wakefield portion of the 7.24am Bradford (Exchange) – King's Cross is specially started
             at Keighley to coincide with that town's first day of annual holidays. 11.52am King's
             Cross – Leeds has its Bradford portion replaced by one for Marsden, detached at
             Wakefield (Kirkgate). Neither Keighley nor Marsden are normally connected directly
             with London via the East Coast line.

29   N15 30789 *Sir Guy* reaches Nottingham (Victoria) – a first – on an excursion from
             Bournemouth. 30789 has 4951 *Pendeford Hall* as pilot from Banbury to Leicester, and
             61079 onwards to Nottingham. 30789 retires to Annesley depot, then has 61066 as pilot
             as far as Banbury on the return journey.

29   H2 4-4-2 32425 *Trevose Head* powers a ramblers' special from East Croydon to Marlow
             as far as High Wycombe. Goes to Slough for servicing, then works the return train from
             Bourne End to Maidenhead and up the WR main line.

30   73087 (71G) brings the 'Pines Express' into New Street from Bath (Green Park). Unusual
             for Bath engines to work through to Birmingham.

31   'Sheffield Holiday Express' arrives in Whitby with 62747 *The Percy* piloting 'Crab'
             42937 of …Willesden (1A)! – a depot debut for Whitby.

31   45066 (60A) is surprise power for the up 'Granite City' out of Aberdeen.

U/D	61326 (36A) receives Works attention at Crewe (!) and runs-in on the 8.40am Crewe – Shrewsbury (where B1s are rare) and the 12.10pm back.
U/D	Polmadie 'Britannia' is used on the 7.45pm Perth – Edinburgh (Waverley) and returns next day. First trips for this class over the Forth Bridge (surprisingly).
U/D	7818 *Granville Manor* works right through to Redhill on the (summer Saturdays) 10.20am Birmingham – Margate.
U/D	46130 *The West Yorkshire Regiment* undergoes casual repairs at Horwich Works. Being too large for the erecting shop traverser, it is dealt with in the electric car shops.
U/D	C 0-6-0 31280 makes a surprise appearance on the 4.20pm London Bridge to East Grinstead, ten bogies as far as East Croydon!
U/D	Swindon-built diesel sets bound for the ScR are tested on the Malmesbury branch, which closed to passengers 10 September 1951.
U/D	Surprise of the month…Astonishingly 45360 (60A Inverness!) arrives in Wolverhampton (Low Level) with a 2-coach portion of a CTAC train.
U/D	Monthly Hull – Newcastle excursion runs via Market Weighton/Pocklington to reach York (instead of Selby/Church Fenton). No previous case of this route being used on a Sunday is known, and is contrary to an agreement between the NER and Lord Londesbrough that no train shall use this line on Sunday.

AUGUST 1956

1ST	'Mid-day Scot' arrives at Euston behind the unusual combination of Compound 40926 + 44761.
1	9.15am Nottingham (Victoria) – Skegness is worked throughout by 2-6-4T 67771 (38A Colwick), which also heads the return. First L1 seen at Skegness.
4	(Bank Holiday Saturday). Down 'Atlantic Coast Express' draws into Exeter (Central) behind 35003 *Royal Mail* + 35030 *Elder Dempster Lines*. Rare!
4	61849 (30A!) works the 10.37am York – Filey Holiday Camp.
4	D20 4-4-0 62343 is employed on the 'Yorkshire Pullman' between Harrogate and Leeds (Central) – a real throwback to earlier days.
4	90621 finds itself working the 12.10pm Huddersfield – Manchester (Victoria), and the 3.15pm from Exchange to Leeds as far as Huddersfield.
4	New 76064 (allocated to 71A in July but not yet sent!) heads the 8.25am Leicester (London Road) – Scarborough from York. Train consists entirely of 1st class stock, mostly labelled 'For use of 3rd class passengers' (*sic*).
4	Notable 'same-class' double-heading combinations seen at York include 60895 + 60935 on the 9.40am to King's Cross; 60903 + 60839 on the 8.35am Bristol – Newcastle, B16 4-6-0s 61430 + 61439 on a Leeds local and 45195 (1E!) + 45234 on the Clifton – Red Bank Sidings ECS/parcels.
5	61911 (64A) is observed on shed at Beattock, surprisingly.
6	45698 *Mars* heads a ramblers' special from Liverpool (Exchange) to Kirkby Lonsdale, on the Clapham – Low Gill line, closed to passengers in 1954.
6	'Patriot' 45508 (10B Preston) reaches Weston-super-Mare with an excursion from Bristol, and heads the return working.
7	Due entirely to local pressure, East Grinstead – Lewes line reopens to passenger traffic after being officially closed from 13 June 1955. First train, the 9.30am from Lewes, is hauled by K 2-6-0 32342. Service is 4 trains daily.

10	34078 *222 Squadron* is noted in Stratford shed yard, and 80070 (33B) takes the ECS of the 'Hook Continental' down to Liverpool Street.
10	BTC is convicted and fined under the Smoke Abatement Act at Clerkenwell Police Court for smoke nuisance at Camden depot – engine proved to be working with a defective damper.
11	Eight ER non-corridors labelled 'Manchester (London Road) suburban set' are sent to Barmouth for a Church Lads' Brigade special train to Scunthorpe!
11	12-coach Wolverhampton express charges through Yatton behind 2-8-0 2860!
12	York shed contains, surprisingly, 62012 (65J Fort William) and 61395 (38E Woodford Halse).
13,14	61665 *Leicester City* (specially requisitioned from Yarmouth) works the 'City of Leicester Holiday Express' through to Windsor, and is serviced at Slough shed. 61665 takes another 'CoLHE' from Leicester to Marylebone and back next day.
14	34012 *Launceston* hauls a boat train from Waterloo, complete with Pullman car and roof boarded 'Ocean Liner Express', via Willesden Jct. and South Tottenham to King George V Dock, North Woolwich – as far as Stratford.
16	EE 'Deltic' travels from Crewe to Carlisle (Kingmoor) prior to a series of tests over the Settle & Carlisle line commencing on the 20th, and lasting to 27 September.
17	New 76068 (ex-Doncaster Works, *en route* to the SR) is used by Neasden on the 9pm Marylebone – York parcels, as far as Leicester.
18	60016 *Silver King* works a 'Starlight Special' non-stop from Edinburgh to York. 'Elizabethan' excepted, all trains normally stop at Newcastle.
18	61620 *Clumber* (31B) appears on the 1.25pm York – Leeds stopper, an exceptionally rare class in Leeds (City). 61288 pilots 61620 on the return.
20	4-car Inter-City diesel set built at Swindon for the Edinburgh – Glasgow service passes north through Lancaster on the main line.
25	70019 *Lighting* (83A) heads the 11.15am Newquay – Wolverhampton through Cheltenham. First trip for a 7MT over the Stratford-on-Avon route?
25	11.35am Plymouth – Waterloo passes Cowley Bridge Jct. triple-headed by 0-6-0 30691 + N 2-6-0 31838 + U 2-6-0 31635, an astonishing sight!
25	70003 *John Bunyan* (30A), ex-Works, heads the 3pm Doncaster – York local service. 'Britannias' are rarely seen on this stretch of line.
25	Ivatt 2-6-0 43094 (31D South Lynn!) somehow appears at King's Cross (a class almost unknown here) on the 3.24pm ex-Grimsby, from Peterborough.
29	44911 (34A on loan, ATC trials) works the 4pm King's Cross – Cleethorpes throughout.
U/D	BR Mk1 coach W21164 is modified, and sent via the channel ferry to France and Germany for riding trials. On its return, it spends time on the LMR accumulating mileage and is then sent abroad again for repeat trials.
U/D	Up 'South Yorkshireman' departs Sheffield (Victoria) behind – amazingly – D11 4-4-0 62664 *Princess Mary*, complete with headboard!

Heavy rain and subsidence cause closure of both the East Coast line (at Granthouse) and the Waverley Route (between Melrose and Galashiels). The following is a selection of the interesting diverted workings that resulted, 28-30 August.

28	Up 'Flying Scotsman' – already on the Waverley route – is forced to retreat to Edinburgh and go via Carstairs and Carlisle, thence to Newcastle, and is seen going up Beattock

7 hours after leaving Edinburgh behind 60145 (arriving in King's Cross 1am). Other diverted trains ascending Beattock include 60967 on the Edinburgh – St Pancras, 60027/33 on the up 'Queen of Scots' and down 'Elizabethan' respectively, 60080 (down 'North Briton'), 60534 (up 'Heart of Midlothian'). 'Queen of Scots' is worked in/out of Princes Street, 5.15pm to Leeds starts here and the 'North Briton' from Leeds ends here.

29   Waverley route now open and sees the passage of A4s 60004/11/19/27/31/33, A1s 60137/50/54 and A3s 60040/92. At Carlisle, V2s 60973/55 (both 61B) arrive from Newcastle on down expresses and D49 62724 (53B!) + A2 60529 come in from Newcastle on a down parcels train. 45692 *Cyclops* (63A!) arrives in Newcastle from Carlisle on the Aberdeen – London fish train.

30   Single line working (down line only) operates at Cockburnspath and sees the passage of the 'Elizabethan' with A4 60011 banked by D49 62721 and the 'Flying Scotsman' with A4 60023 banked by J37 64576.

Up line also reopens (afternoon) and sees the passage of

	J36 65329	piloting	A3 60092 on the 'Heart of Midlothian'
	do.	do.	A4 60004 on the fish train from Aberdeen
	D34 62487	do.	A4 60023 on a fitted freight
and	D34 62494	do.	A4 60033 on the 'Elizabethan'

On the Waverley route A2 60525 (61B) heads the St Pancras – Edinburgh.

SEPTEMBER 1956

2ND   78029 works an excursion from Leicester right through to Clacton.

2   70033 *Charles Dickens* (9A) appears at Darlington on an enthusiasts' special.

4   70031 *Byron* (9A) arrives in Leeds (Central) on the 3.3pm local, ex-Doncaster.

4   60033 *Seagull* (34A) found in Fife working the 1.31pm Leven – Edinburgh!

8,10   60527 *Sun Chariot* (62B) makes a rare visit to Leeds (Central) on the 2.18pm ex-King's Cross, and brings the 'White Rose' into London (10th).

8   61815 finds surprise employment on the 'Hook Continental' from Liverpool Street to Harwich. K3's rarely work titled trains/carry headboards.

8   A2/3 60511 *Airborne* pilots 60126 *Sir Vincent Raven* through Northallerton on the 8.5am Birmingham – Newcastle. A powerful combination.

8   2.35pm York – Cambridge passes Selby behind 60005 *Sir Charles Newton* piloting 60938, another train with excess power. A4s rarely pilot anything.

9   Diversion through Ripon of a main line express provides the unexpected pairing of 62736 *The Bramham Moor* + 60011 *Empire of India*.

12   61658 *The Essex Regiment* noted on Heaton shed – only the third appearance of a 'Sandringham' at Newcastle in six years.

15   10.50am Frome – Bristol via Radstock has Ivatt 2-6-2T 41294 (74A), ex-Works, in charge. Ashford engines should, theoretically, never reach Bristol!

16   61575 observed on Cricklewood shed (14A), with some surprise.

16   'The Docks Express', an Ian Allan/Trains Illustrated special, has 5014 *Goodrich Castle* Paddington – Salisbury, 34106 *Lydford* on to Weymouth via Fordingbridge and 0-6-0PT 1370 through the streets to Weymouth Quay, new ground for the ex-'Devon Belle' observation car attached at the rear. 34106 returns the special to Paddington (!) via Bournemouth, Southampton.

17	D34 4-4-0 62480 *Glen Fruin* reaches Inverness (a great rarity here) and pilots a '5' on a morning train to Elgin, a most unusual sight in itself – anywhere.
21	0-6-0 3217 works the 9.24am Great Malvern – New Street and the balancing working, the 1.55pm to Worcester. First time that a GWR engine has brought a passenger train into New Street since 18 February 1952.
22	D 4-4-0 31075 pilots 'Dean Goods' 2538 between Shrewsbury and Towyn on the Talyllyn Railway Preservation Society's special from Paddington. The only lodging turn ever worked by Reading South men?
23	Another D, 31577, heads a ramblers' excursion from Waterloo to Flitwick (for Woburn Park) throughout and is serviced on Bedford shed!
23	Derailment just north of Crewe causes many trains to be diverted via Chester and Warrington. Frodsham therefore witnesses 'Coronations' 46236/39/29, 'Patriots' 45514/32/35, 'Princess Royal' 46204, 'Jubilee' 45623 and others.
24	CCTV is provided on an excursion train for the first time in Europe when the 'Glasgow Evening Citizen' runs two 7-coach trains at 8.50am/9.20am from Queen Street to Oban, screening a variety show throughout the train.
25	5.54pm Brighton – Victoria is formed of a 4-COR unit and two 4-SUB units. First recorded occasion that express, suburban units have worked together?
25	'Deltic' noted turning on the Shipley triangle with only the LMR No.3 dynamometer car, after a test run over the S&C.
27	'Crab' 42884 brings the sleeper from St Pancras, into St Enoch.
28	Compound 40937 heads the 11-coach Glasgow – Liverpool out of Carlisle. Many years since a 4-4-0 has taken a train of this weight south over Shap.
U/D	9,16,23,30 Steam push/pull service operates out of London Bridge to Sevenoaks, calling only at Swanley. Westerham branch set used + H 0-4-4T.

OCTOBER 1956

2ND	61570 is unusual power nowadays for the 10.5am Liverpool Street – Harwich 'Scandinavian' boat train.
4	2-6-2T 5501 provides a rare glimpse of a GWR loco on the SR route to Barnstaple Jct. with an engineer's train from Exeter.
5	45675 *Hardy* (20A) is an unprecedented sight on a Battersea – Cricklewood train of coal empties, seen passing through Clapham Jct.
6	45673 *Keppel* (63A) is a surprise choice for the 3.40pm Inverness – Edinburgh (from Perth), noted at the Dunfermline stop.
8	76033 is a 'small' engine to work the 8.50pm Liverpool Street – Ely.
11	Duke of Sutherland's 0-4-4T *Dunrobin* is steamed at New Romney for the first time since 1950, when it arrived from Scotland.
12	30859 *Lord Hood* appears at Reading South shed, looking lost.
20	Second CCTV excursion sponsored by the 'Glasgow Evening Citizen' is a 12-coach special to Blackpool headed by 70050 *Firth of Clyde*.
21	60071 *Tranquil* reaches Sheffield (Midland) on the 6.25pm for Bristol.
22,23	A boat-launching special is run from King's Cross to Haverton Hill and guests return to Harrogate for the night behind 60157 *Great Eastern* (34A), which overnights at Starbeck (where King's Cross engines are unknown), before returning to London via York the day after.

26	70028 *Royal Star* (86C) works the 5.12pm Crewe – Llandudno followed by the 7.35pm ex-Holyhead back to Crewe. (The last WR 7MT to be overhauled at Crewe, repairs now transferred to Swindon).
27	45278 is a rarity at Southend (Victoria), on a football special from Watford.
28	L&Y 0-6-0 52138 is seen at Bolton still boasting 'LMS' on the tender.
28	Crosti-boilered 92023 runs LE on the Bedford – Sandy branch for bridge testing purposes, at speed varying between 1-67mph.
U/D	Main line diesels 10000/1 run trials as a twin unit between Derby and Cricklewood with a 14-coach load, mainly of Kitchen Cars.
U/D	Early October; 'Deltic' noted heading Edge Hill – Preston ECS trains before resuming work on Liverpool – Euston expresses.
U/D	(21 September-10 October) 35018 *British India Line* runs down to Brighton from Nine Elms (21st) and enters Brighton Works for piston examination between 27 September and 4 October – the first time a rebuilt 'Merchant Navy' has received attention at these Works. (See also 27/10/55). Returns to Nine Elms on 10th, with the 1.45am Hassocks – Selhurst special ECS (a 4-car EMU and a goods brake van).

NOVEMBER 1956

7TH	48056 heads a northbound freight from York to Heaton, an uncommon class to be seen on this stretch of the East Coast main line.
7	'Pug' 0-4-0ST 51235 (ex-17A) arrives at York to replace the withdrawn Y8 0-4-0T Departmental No.55 (ex-68091). First L&Y loco to be allocated to York.
9	62744 *The Holderness* (62B) is a rare engine to reach Carlisle, departing on the 1.5pm to Newcastle.
11	Crane engaged in bridge work topples over and blocks both lines near Newton Abbot. WR trains take the SR route from Exeter to Plymouth, including the Truro – Paddington Sleeping Car train (rare on this line), as is a 'Castle' on the Plymouth – Liverpool.
14	A8 4-6-2T 69877 (bunker first) propels an Officer's saloon north through Ripon, an odd sight.
14	TV-equipped excursion stock is used for a 'Christmas Shopping Special with Music' from Girvan to Glasgow behind immaculate 45707 *Valiant* bearing a large headboard.
16	75073 works a ballast train between Eastbourne and Heathfield. First 4-6-0 of any sort to penetrate onto the Heathfield line.
17	Up 'Mid-day Scot' leaves Carlisle behind 46251 *City of Nottingham* with three milk tanks at the rear. Does any other titled train convey milk tanks?
17	60123 *H. A. Ivatt* spotted at Bradford (Hammerton Street) minus the leading pair of driving wheels. Most unusual for an A1 to be at Bradford at all!
18	70036 *Boadicea* (30A) passes through Hitchin with a diverted Liverpool Street to Norwich running via Hertford (North) and Cambridge.
20	92022 (Crosti) + 92108 double-head a train of 56 empties north through Flitwick – first reported train hauled by two 2-10-0s in the UK.
21	Ministry of Supply WD 0-6-0STs 106, 157 run from Marchwood Royal Engineers' depot to Southampton to turn on the Northam triangle. Rare sights.
23	45162 makes a class debut on the Deeside line when working a ballast train from Aberdeen to Culter and back.

26	60012 *Commonwealth of Australia* (64B) puts in a very rare appearance at Aberdeen, heading the 3.40pm to Edinburgh.
27	61327 (39B Sheffield Darnall!) heads a freight of Government stores throughout from Woodford Halse to Old Oak Common.
27	'Golden Arrow' arrives in Victoria an hour late with 73082 (tender first) towing 70014 *Iron Duke* (failed) plus Pullmans.
29	5-BEL Pullman set is used for the 4.22pm special (chartered by Unilever) from Blackfriars to Eastbourne via Herne Hill and Streatham Common.
U/D	Clee Hill quarries (near Ludlow) relinquishes the LMS Sentinel 47181 (84G) for scrap. Replacement is LNER Sentinel Y3 0-4-0T 68164.
U/D	New 0-6-0PT 3409 is put into traffic. This is the last engine to be built to a pre-Nationalisation design, part of a GWR order placed in 1947, built by Yorkshire Engine Co. as sub-contractor to Hunslet Engine Co. (Leeds).

DECEMBER 1956

5TH	J10 0-6-0s 65153 + 65181 pass north as a LE pair through Northallerton. 8 x J10s are transferred, LMR to NER, 5 travelling via Tebay and Stainmore, to Darlington, where any ex-GC engine is a rarity.
6	7819 *Hinton Manor* works up the Lickey incline with a 20-hopper train of ballast to Barnt Green. 'Manors' have not been seen on the climb since 1951/2.
7,11	61821 enters Sheffield (Midland) with the 1.23pm arrival from York. Sister engine 61982 repeats this on the 11th, both rare appearances here.
8	34070 *Manston* visits Swindon with a 9-coach Cafeteria Car special from Bournemouth for the FA Cup match.
13	Special trials are conducted with a 2-car DMU, which runs non-stop from Sheffield (Victoria) to Marylebone. Unit returns, again non-stop at 2.51pm.
17	Owing to restrictions on motoring due to petrol rationing (Suez), Felstead School end of term special grows to six coaches and runs as a separate train through to Liverpool Street via Bishop Stortford behind 61535.
18	48672 passes through Market Harborough towing 2-6-4T 42680 + Tilbury 4-4-2Ts 41951/70/76 (30D Southend), these last for scrap at Derby.
19	L 4-4-0 31776 heads the 11.30am Brighton – Plymouth through to Salisbury, the first time this class has reached here.
19,21	Stanier 2-6-2Ts 40139, 40112 (21st) haul Bradford (Forster Square) to Harrogate trains and the 8.40pm on to Ripon, a class not seen here previously.
20	'Star' 4056 *Princess Margaret* appears at Salisbury, on the 1pm to Bristol.
21	46161 *King's Own* pilots 46257 *City of Salford* into Euston on the 7.45am ex-Crewe, and 45389 (63A!!) is a shock arrival piloting another '5' on a relief.
21	Fog-bound Paddington displays most trains as '99min late' since the Arrivals Indicator has no provision for 3-figures under the 'Minutes Late' column!
22	11.50pm (21st) Euston – St Enoch sleeper reaches Carlisle at 4.35pm (10 hour 25 minutes late) behind Fowler 2-6-4T 42317 + 46236 *City of Bradford* fog having prevailed over the entire journey. However, the Euston – Glasgow (Central) sleeper finally arrives 11 hour 10 minutes late, (not a record, as on 13 March 1947 overnight trains were nearly 24 hours overdue!)

22	'Tynesider' Sleeping Car train reaches Newcastle from King's Cross 252 minutes late behind W1 4-6-4 60700 – a very rare visitor – having worked throughout.
22	44942 takes the up 'Queen of Scots' between Glasgow and Edinburgh.
22	Torrington – Torquay excursion is worked throughout from Barnstaple Jct. by a 'West Country' Pacific, which is serviced at Newton Abbot shed.
23	B16 4-6-0 61440 (52B) is an unprecedented sight at Perth, on a down freight.
24	A2/3 60519 *Honeyway* (64B) enters Leeds (Central) on a relief from London.
27	61995 *Cameron of Lochiel* (65A) heads the 11am Carlisle – Niddrie freight over the Waverley route.
28	45544 (8A) comes into Leeds (City) from the south with the day-time St Pancras – Edinburgh, unusual class ('Patriot'), and shed (Edge Hill).
29	62731 *Selkirkshire* exits Manchester (Victoria) on the 9.15pm to Leeds. First time a member of this class has been in Manchester since 1927!
30	SR 1Co-Co1 diesels 10201/2 (as a pair) work a 15-coach test train to Derby.
31	Through electric working Liverpool Street – Southend (Victoria) begins. Like schemes to Shenfield (1949) and Chelmsford (11 June 1956) this uses 1500V DC overhead, but is convertible to the recently adopted 25kV AC system.
U/D	Inverness (60A) receives the novelty of adding 78052 to its allocation.
U/D	Polmadie (66A) receives (surprisingly) three J36 0-6-0s 65216/32, 65304.

JANUARY 1957

2ND	Due to petrol shortages, two football specials travel from Larkhall to Bo'ness (closed May 1956), and return behind 73062 and 45008.
2	7.11am Maidstone (East) – Victoria EMU is hauled by C 0-6-0 31694 to Otford Jct., tender first, as the conductor rail is iced up at Maidstone.
3	Up 'Cornish Riviera Limited' is sent back from Truro to Chasewater and diverted via Perranporth to Newquay, thence to Par, to avoid mine-shaft subsidence near Burngullow. Bus service runs St Austell – Truro section.
5	Fowler 2-6-4T 42327 heads the 1.55pm New Street – Worcester only the second time since the war that this class has visited Worcester.
5	FA Cup day. For the Spurs v Leicester match, Caprotti 5MTs 73141/2/3 all work specials from Leicester (via Cambridge) to Northumberland Park, locos being serviced at Stratford. A Fulham supporters special arrives at Ipswich with 45147 (1A) in charge, and 44769 (8A) takes Liverpool fans right through to Southend (Victoria), where the emergency store of coal has to be used to fuel 44769 as the line is now worked by EMUs.
7	The unlikely pairing of L1 2-6-4T 67791 (bunker first) piloting 60149 *Amadis* is seen on the 7.21pm King's Cross – Peterborough slow, via the Hertford loop, to avoid the accident site at Welwyn Garden City where the 'Aberdonian' had rammed the back of the 6.18am Baldock – King's Cross.
8	GWR 4-4-0 3717 *City of Truro* passes through Rugby (Central) *en route* from York Railway Museum to Swindon for restoration. (Loco withdrawn in 1931).
10	GWR flag is flown over Paddington to honour the appointment of Harold MacMillan as Prime Minister, who was a former Director of the GWR.
11	Up 'Night Ferry' is unusually diverted via Gravesend (Central) where both engines take water.

12	Two football specials are run from High Wycombe to St Albans, worked throughout by 2-6-2T 6142 + 4939 *Littleton Hall*, big surprises at St Albans. On the same day, 2-6-2T 6117 heads a circus special into Harringay Park from Aylesbury, all three GWR engines going to Neasden for servicing.
13	61982 reaches Washwood Heath (Birmingham) – a rare visitor – with the overnight freight from York, diverted due to repairs in Milford Tunnel.
13	B2 61607 *Blickling* (30E Colchester) makes a rare appearance north of Hitchin when working the King's Cross breakdown train to Sandy.
13	0-6-0PT 9401 is loaned to Stratford (30A) for trials in Bishopsgate Goods yard and Spitalfields yard at Bethnal Green, a most unexpected transfer.
14	SR 2000hp diesel 10203 works a 15-coach test train, Cricklewood to Derby.
15	Special children's excursion is run to Kensington from Westerham, where the 11-coach ECS arrives with D1 4-4-0 31487 in front and 34017 *Ilfracombe* in the rear to form the 12.15pm departure. Return terminates at Dunton Green. The most impressive passenger train seen at Westerham for many years!
15	A2/3 60523 *Sun Castle* works a single-coach special for the Ministry of Transport's Inspecting Officer, from Peterborough to Finsbury Park. (See 7th).
17	61580 runs LE Grantham to Lincoln to see if it will fit on their turntable.
18	45727 *Inflexible* (63A) is a surprise choice to power the 'Queen of Scots' Pullman train from Edinburgh to Glasgow.
19	45741 *Leinster* (3B Bushbury) is a rare visitor to Leeds (City) with a football special ex-Walsall piloted the last 34 miles by LNW 0-8-0 49428!
21	45677 *Beatty* (1B Camden) is an even rarer sight on the Cleckheaton branch, heading the 3.20am freight from Normanton to Bradford (Adolphus Street).
21	New 'Hastings' 6-car DEMU set 1001 makes trial runs from Eastleigh to Weymouth and back. A novelty attraction at the resort!
22	Fell 2000hp diesel mechanical 10100 makes test runs between Derby, Cricklewood.
23,24	61854 (68E) enters Aberdeen with a horse-box special from Perth. Another special freight arrives next day behind WD 2-10-0 90760 (66B).
26	45741 *Leinster* is again seen on a football special, this time to bring Aston Villa fans to Middlesbrough, for the FA Cup tie. An even rarer sight here!
26	For the 4th round FA Cup tie between Huddersfield Town and Peterborough United, 20 specials are run, carrying 10,400 supporters; 10 from Peterborough (East) via Derby, and 10 from Peterborough (North) via Retford, all B1s, inc. 61001 *Eland* (34E).
26	Due to a blockage at Warrington, some overnight West Coast trains run via Manchester (London Road) and Eccles. These include the 'Postal' (71000 *Duke of Gloucester*), 9.10pm Euston – Glasgow (pair of diesels) and the 11.10pm Birmingham – Glasgow (46251 *City of Nottingham*).
28	Baildon reopens (closed 5/1/53) due to petrol shortages. New nameboards and lighting provided and first train is 7.8am Skipton – Bradford (Forster Square) via Ilkley. *(Closes again 29/4/57 – reopens yet again 5/1/73!)*.
28	Inaugural run of the 'Royal Duchy' (Paddington – Penzance) stops at Saltash for a short civic reception!
28,30	5.5pm Dumfries – Aberdeen fast freight is worked throughout by 45661 *Vernon*, and 45706 *Express* (30th), both Newton Heath (26A) engines, not a shed represented at Aberdeen before?

30   Newly repainted in green livery, SR DC electric loco 20002 visits Waterloo for an official inspection.

31   61580 arrives at Derby (Midland) on the 3.5pm from Lincoln. (See 17th).

U/D   62738 *The Zetland* appears at Low Moor for repairs. First LNER engine to be sent here for attention.

U/D   (from 31 December 1956) Blue 'Deltic' normally works the 1.35pm Euston – Perth as far as Carlisle, being stabled at Upperby and refuelled at Kingmoor.

FEBRUARY 1957

2ND   Scotland v Wales rugby international attracts 30 specials to Edinburgh from Wales; 2 arriving Wed 30 January, 7 on Thursday 31 January and 7 on Friday 1 February, all to Princes Street, plus 14 on Saturday 2 February; 9 to Princes Street, 5 to Waverley.
Strangers on Dalry Road include 45733 *Novelty* (3B), special ex-Swansea, 45686 *St. Vincent* (1A) ex-Treherbert, 45644 *Howe* (9A) ex-Neath (all on 31st) 45672 *Anson* (1B) ex-Swansea on the 1st, and 45569 *Tasmania* (55A) on 2nd.
15 more come in from Glasgow and SW Scotland, 6 from NE Scotland also.

2   34030 *Watersmeet* arrives at Torquay with a rugby special from Exeter.

2   Largest consignment of scooters to date reaches Wimbledon. A special SNCF train of 20 vans comes in double-headed via the East Putney line.

3-9   Subsidence between Hinton Admiral and Christchurch causes the 10.30pm Waterloo – Weymouth to run via Ringwood, Poole, Bournemouth (Central, reverse), thus calling at Poole twice.

4   K 2-6-0 32347 (75E Three Bridges) is an unexpected arrival at Dover (Priory) on the 3.40am from London Bridge.

5   Daily Mirror 'Bill Haley Special' exits Waterloo at 12.35pm to Southampton (Terminus) behind 34007 *Wadebridge*, with a full-size headboard on the engine and roofboards on all coaches (including 2 Pullmans).

6   Compound 40907 (19B) visits Darnall – uniquely – for wheel turning.

7,11,16   In the course of transfer from Croes Newydd (Wrexham) on the 7th, to Helmsdale (60C) for use on the Dornoch branch, 0-6-0PT 1646 reaches St Margarets (11th) and is seen shunting at Inverness (16th). First GWR-type to be allocated to Scotland in BR days.

8   'Hastings' unit 1003 makes a trial run from Eastleigh to Bournemouth (West) via Ringwood.

9   'Suffolk Hunt Special' is run from Bury St Edmunds to Mellis, returning from Elmswell. D16 4-4-0 62615 in spotless condition works the two Gresley brake-corridors separated by a string of horse-boxes.

13   Down 'Mid-day Scot' is (uniquely?) headed by two unrebuilt 'Patriots' 45511 *Isle of Man* + 45517 (both 1A) between Crewe and Glasgow.

15-17   BBC Film Unit is at Baynards using T9 4-4-0 30310 as part of *The Railway Children* by E. Nesbit, to be shown on *Children's Hour* (TV, Sundays). T9s are usually banned from the Guildford – Horsham line and special permission had to be obtained for its use.

16   30753 *Melisande* passes through Reading (General) on an up coal train to Sonning Power Station, a previously unknown occurrence!

16   Bournemouth v Spurs FA Cup tie brings four specials to Boscombe including two of ER stock (with Restaurant Cars) from South Tottenham headed by 73088/89 (both 73A).

16   61250 *A. Harold Bibby* (36A) is seen at Hull, painted green!

16   Inverness plays host to two rare English visitors, 45230 (11A Carnforth) and amazingly, 44951 (25F Low Moor!). How on earth...?

16   60028 *Walter K. Whigham* is noted working tender first with the complete 'Queen of Scots' Pullman train, to test the braking effect of the new ATC equipment on Pullman stock. Tests run Finsbury Park – Welwyn and back, extended to Hitchin on the 23rd.

17   Monthly winter excursions from Blackpool, Liverpool/Manchester to Birmingham bring 44947 (24E) and 45401 (8A) into Snow Hill.

19   75021 powers the 'Red Dragon' from Cardiff to Swansea. Unusual.

21   72004 *Clan Macdonald* brings three coaches of the Royal train out of Bellahouston Carriage Sidings. These had been standing by in case the Queen's flight from Portugal was diverted from London to Prestwick.

22   7.48am from Peterborough (East) provides the astonishing sight of a Kittybrewster (61A) engine entering Leicester (Midland) – 61348!

24   6806 *Blackwell Grange* finds itself heading a train of oil tank wagons from Saltley to Stanlow, running round its train near Frodsham, and working it tender first into the refinery.

24   *City of Truro* (in Swindon Works) undergoes a number change from 3717 to 3440, a boiler change, and receives 1903 GWR livery, retaining top feed and copper capped chimney – never having previously appeared in this condition. 5995 *Wick Hall* is also observed still displaying GWR lettering!

25   6-car 'Hastings' unit 1003 works a General Manager's special non-stop from Waterloo to Bournemouth (Central) in 116min.

27   Troop train carrying the 2nd Battalion Scots Guards on their return from Germany is run from Parkeston Quay to Victoria. 61375 is piloted by 61280 from Stratford to Victoria, a spectacle not previously seen here.

28   D16 4-4-0 62571 (31A) reaches Derby on the 3.5pm from Lincoln.

U/D   BMW 'Isetta' bubble cars are to be assembled in part of Brighton Works, with the first cars due out in May.

MARCH 1957

1ST   Ex-Works 60532 *Blue Peter* (61B) is found, amazingly, on Lincoln shed.

2   Six B1s visit New Street on football specials for the Birmingham City v Nottingham Forest FA Cup match, a rare haul in one day.

2   Bournemouth v Manchester United Cup tie brings 73111/115 (both 70A) through to Boscombe from Willesden, but the majority of specials run overnight via the Somerset & Dorset line.

3   5pm Newcastle – Liverpool is diverted over the Wellfield line and 60019 *Bittern* is piloted by G5 0-4-4T 67265 between Sunderland and West Hartlepool, a most unusual combination.

6-9   C12 4-4-2T 67363 (33A) noted on ECS duties at Liverpool Street. Rare!

7   J38 0-6-0 65916 is an unlikely station pilot at Glasgow (Central).

9   'Deltic' enters EE's works at Netherton for attention to various components.

9   Women's Hockey International at Wembley brings numerous strangers to Neasden, including two B17s, one B12, one A3, one V2, many 'foreign' B1s, seven 'Halls', three 'Schools' and five SR light Pacifics. Variety!

12   The tailboard on the rear vestibule of the 11.10am Paddington – Birkenhead reads...'The Talisman'!

12-15 D16 4-4-0 62571 (31A) reaches Sheffield (Victoria) four days running on the 2.30pm from Lincoln. It is at least 20 years since a D16 worked a passenger train into Sheffield. (Then you get four on the trot!)

15 2nd class Sleeping Car E1286E, with roofboards reading 'King's Cross – Aberdeen' is observed in a Colchester – Cambridge train and subsequently in the 8.50pm Cambridge – King's Cross. Strange.

16 60815 (38E) brings 12 WR coaches into York. Heads turn at the audacity!

16 4-4-0 40631 pilots 46229 *Duchess of Hamilton* (surely unnecessarily) on the 10.40am Euston – Windermere.

17 45624 *St. Helena* is also superfluous piloting 71000 *Duke of Gloucester* on the 11.5am Euston – Carlisle.

17 Railcar W16W is used for a special between Paddington and Portskewett (on the Sudbrook branch), organised by Imperial College Railway Society to view the Severn Tunnel and the Sudbrook Pumping Station.

18 10.15am St Pancras – Manchester (Central) arrives at Derby with 92052 piloting 45561 *Saskatchewan*, which had injector trouble.

18 DMU works a trial from Norwich (Thorpe) to Norwich (City) and back, via Cromer and Melton Constable.

18-25 'Cornishman' is diverted via Worcester (Shrub Hill) and over the Midland line to Bristol, GWR engines from 85A working the train.

25,30 *City of Truro* works two return trips to Bristol from Swindon prior to going to Wolverhampton to head (on the 30th) the Festiniog Railway's Paddington to Portmadoc special as far as Ruabon, its first excursion use.

29 5035 *Coity Castle* powers the Paddington – Birkenhead (Woodside) Grand National Restaurant Car special, throughout.

30 3.25pm Perth – Edinburgh is headed by 72007 *Clan Mackintosh*, working over the Forth Bridge into Waverley, a rare route for a 'Clan', later seen on 64B.

30 RH&D narrow gauge railway operates a Royal train when a 6-coach special from New Romney to Hythe conveys HM the Queen, HRH the Duke of Edinburgh and HRH Princess Anne.

U/D Adams 4-4-2T 30583 spotted shunting the carriage sidings at Exeter (Central), rather than working the Lyme Regis branch.

APRIL 1957

2ND Dockers refuse to handle RMS *Queen Mary* at Southampton, so passengers land at Plymouth. WR uses the SR 'Cunarder' boat train sets between Millbay Docks and Paddington, the first leaving behind 4077 *Chepstow Castle* + 4088 *Dartmouth Castle* (9 Pullmans, 5 coaches) the first Pullmans to run over the WR West of England route since the 'Torquay Pullman' in 1930!

2-10 Dynamometer car trials are held with four A3s, King's Cross – Newcastle on the up/down 'Talisman' and 'Tees-Tyne Pullman', with extra coach in mind.

3,9 D16 4-4-0s 62599 and 62568 six days later, both reach York, surprisingly.

5 61789 *Loch Laidon* (65A) arrives in Newcastle on freight from the north. First named K2 to appear here since the war.

5 'Glasgow Evening Citizen' TV train departs St Enoch behind 45728 *Defiance* piloted by 2-6-4T 42124, as an overnight football special to London for the match against England. 45620 *North Borneo* (16A) returns the train on Sunday.

6   D11 4-4-0 62666 *Zeebrugge* noted in Manchester (London Road), ex-Works.
6   J39 0-6-0 64740 is a strange choice for the 4.52pm Irlam – Liverpool (Central). Many
         years since a J39 seen on a passenger working over these CLC lines.
7   30799 *Sir Ironside* heads a theatre special from Brighton to London, first time in years
         that an N15 has run up to Victoria – a nostalgic sight!
12   EMU derails in Southend, resulting in an L1 2-6-4T operating a shuttle service of 'dead'
         electric stock between Prittlewell and Southend.
13   J21 0-6-0 65110 heads a well-filled race special from Newcastle to Rothbury, a branch
         closed to passengers on 15/9/52, stopping at Scots Gap both ways.
14   Birmingham – Newhaven 14-coach special is double-headed from Willesden onwards by
         E 4-4-0 31506 + 30911 *Dover*.
15   48430 (82B) observed crossing the Royal Albert Bridge into Cornwall, light engine. Is it
         a BR first, for this class to reach Cornwall?
15   (Week beginning) SR 2000hp diesel 10203 works the down 'Mancunian' from Euston,
         returning on the 10.28pm parcels from London Road.
18   61253 (32B Ipswich) is a surprise arrival at Newcastle with a parcels train.
19   First 'Starlight Specials' of the season head out of St Enoch; 60812 sets off for
         Marylebone via Edinburgh, and 45697 *Achilles* + 45573 *Newfoundland* leave for
         St Pancras, running via Barrhead. (Good Friday).
19   46117 *Welsh Guardsman* piloted by a '5' heads the 2.43pm Clifton Sidings to Red Bank
         ECS train. A 'Scot' is an unexpected class in the Calder Valley.
23   3440 *City of Truro* works a 7-coach special Pontypridd – Swindon both ways.
24   60029 *Woodcock* exits Paddington on an Ian Allan excursion to Doncaster, the first time
         since the 1948 Interchanges that an A4 has been in Paddington. 61008 *Kudu* returns the
         train to Marylebone, coming on at Nottingham.
28   Ivatt 2-6-2Ts 41202/3 double-head the RCTS North Somerset Railtour onto the Bristol
         Harbour line – first passenger train on the branch since 1931.
28   With all three electric locos out of action, a Newhaven – Victoria boat train leaves behind
         34047 *Callington* piloting (!) D1 4-4-0 31743, on 16 vehicles.
30   0-6-0 diesel shunter 12079, the Carlisle Viaduct yard pilot, returns to Carlisle from
         Cowlairs Works by travelling LE over the Waverley line, quite a detour.
30   73167 reaches Hornsea with an Inspection Saloon, first visit by a 5MT here.

MAY 1957

1ST   46170 *British Legion* + 46167 *The Hertfordshire Regiment* are used to double-head a
         Euston – Bletchley service, most unusual.
1   4-4-0 40501 enters Wolverhampton (LL) on the 6pm from Snow Hill – rare!
1   'Merseyside Express' gets in to Euston a record 25 minutes early behind 45398 piloting
         45525 *Colwyn Bay*.
2   46229 *Duchess of Hamilton* works through to Wolverhampton (HL) on the 8.50am
         from Euston with the Queen Mother in a Royal Saloon at the rear. 46229 goes to
         Bushbury shed (3B), and the Queen Mother returns from Snow Hill (in the Saloon) on
         the 'Inter-City', headed by 6005 *King George II*.
4   2-8-0 3865 (84B Oxley) hauls a pigeon special from Gloucester into Bath (Green Park),
         an unusual loco to reach here.

4 The Framlingham branch receives an unprecedented train when 61571 plus five 1st class coaches and a Buffet Car, arrive with a wedding special from Liverpool Street. Line closed to passengers on 3/11/52.

4 York B16 4-6-0 reaches Stratford-on-Avon (surely a first) with a troop train.

4 D11 4-4-0 62666 *Zeebrugge* is a surprise arrival at York, ex-Sheffield.

4 D11s 62675/82/84/88 all seen on St Rollox shed, enjoying a very(!) short transfer from Eastfield. 62675 *Colonel Gardiner* even wears a 65B shedplate.

6 J20 0-6-0 64694 takes the 10-coach York – Lowestoft onwards from Norwich!

7 60161 *North British* (64B) is a rare and welcome sight at Leeds (Central) with the 1.18pm from King's Cross.

7 0-6-0PT 2069 is spotted shunting at Wolverton Carriage Works, deputising for one of the LNW 0-6-0ST locos under repair.

10 BMW 'Isetta' bubble cars make their first appearance from Brighton Works.

12 D16 4-4-0 62571 powers the RCTS 'East Midlander' railtour from Nottingham (Midland) via Cudworth, Hull, Beverley, York, Selby and Doncaster – a D16 is exceptionally rare at most of these places.

14 5.15pm Norwich – Liverpool Street reaches the terminus with 44143 (14B) dragging 70012 *John of Gaunt* plus train, the 4F being a unique sight here.

14 4095 *Harlech Castle* is weighed at Caerphilly Works, first 'Castle' seen here.

15 Bo-Bo 827hp diesel 10800 is surprise power for a Harrogate – Lincoln special.

15 'Deltic' reverts to hauling Liverpool – Euston trains.

15 CR 4-4-0 54491, running-in after repair at Inverurie, is an unusual engine to work the 8.45am Aberdeen – Banchory goods.

16 45584 *North West Frontier* (24E) noted on the turntable at Stafford Road shed.

18 3440 *City of Truro* + 2-6-0 4358 work the Ian Allan 'Daffodil Express' from Newport to Swansea, which also sports a 'Devon Belle' observation car.

19 Trackwork at Ferryhill Jct. causes Kittybrewster to host its first 'Clan' Pacific.

20 34046 *Braunton* is engulfed by 50' flames at the buffer stops at Brighton when a conductor rail short circuit flash sets alight the motion oilbath. Dramatic!

25 45688 *Polyphemus* (3B) enters Weston-super-Mare; special ex-Birmingham.

25 Two excursions reach Littlehampton; 61329 (30A) works through from Chingford, and 34068 *Kenley* from Harrow. Both serviced at Brighton and run back coupled LE to Littlehampton for the return workings. Unique pairing?

U/D Derby-built DMUs for Snow Hill suburban services are seen on trial at Cleobury Mortimer, on the Bewdley – Tenbury Wells line.

U/D (Three weekends). Up 'Flying Scotsman' is diverted via Lincoln and has a timetabled stop here on these days – first time ever.

JUNE 1957

1ST 61808, 61910 both head Blackpool excursions through Preston.

3 D8000 – an English Electric 1000hp Type 1 diesel – is the first Modernisation Plan loco to be handed over to BR.

4 Ivatt 2-6-0 46443 (17A) runs south through Rugby (Central) hauling LMS Officer's Saloon (M45058).

6 D16 4-4-0 62543 (31E Bury St Edmunds) reaches Newark on the 3.45am New England

– Doncaster freight, a type rarely if ever seen here.

6   46114 *Coldstream Guardsman* ventures down to Liverpool (Riverside) with passengers for the Isle of Man celebrating 50 years of the TT races.

7   30939 *Leatherhead* takes the Royal train from Victoria to Tattenham Corner for 'Oaks Day', the train being held by signals for 3 minutes at Battersea Park for a Norwood – Battersea freight to cross in front of it . Heads will roll!

7   'Hunter' jet fighter crashes near the Epping – Ongar railway line, partially derailing the push/pull set working the service.

7   60531 *Barham* heads the 'Saint Mungo' from Perth to Aberdeen, an uncommon class to work this service.

7   L1 4-4-0 31777 (75A) finds highly unusual employment as the Parkstone banker between Poole and Branksome.

8   A startling arrival at Polmadie shed is Longmoor Military Railway's WD 2-10-0 No. 601 resplendent in blue livery, and on loan for some months.

8   (Whit Saturday). Astonishingly, 60020 *Guillemot* pilots Fort William's 62011 out of Neville Hill yard (Leeds) on freight, whilst 61111 (34E Neasden) is seen on the shed. This later pilots 60096 *Papyrus* (64B), ex-Works and carrying a 'CTAC Scottish Tours Express' headboard, on a train of 17 parcels vans to Newcastle.

9   2-6-0 5337 (85A) reaches Redhill on a Kidderminster – Brighton excursion.

9   5925 *Eastcote Hall* reportedly works through to Swanage on a special from Lye, near Stourbridge.

10   60031 *Golden Plover* (64B) works freight into Leeds from the east, a rare engine to reach Leeds at all, especially from this direction.

10   2-8-0T 4262 piloting 0-6-0PT 3758 is a barrel-scraping combination to handle a Whit Monday excursion from Bristol to Weston-super-Mare.

10   70035 *Rudyard Kipling* (32A) is unexpectedly seen at Spalding on the 5.55am Doncaster – March slow.

11   Haymarket's 60043/90/100 *Brown Jack/Grand Parade/Spearmint* all appear in Leeds, plus 60804, 60937 (both 62B), the latter appearing on the up 'North Briton', piloted by 73166 – an eye-catching combination.

11   One of the ex-'Devon Belle' observation cars is attached to the rear of the 4.35pm Edinburgh – Glasgow slow, *en route* to Buchanan Street to commence work (on 17th) on the 7.55am to Oban and 5.15pm return working.

12   P 0-6-0T 31325 (75A) has a short stint on the Hayling Island branch, and is seen shunting at Winchester later in the month.

12   73169 (50A) heads a York – Great Malvern excursion throughout.

13,14   D8000 – the first 'pilot scheme' diesel – works a one-coach special from Earlestown – Chester, and then ECS between Liverpool (Lime Street) and Manchester (Victoria) and back, next day.

15   72009 *Clan Stewart* is the first 'Clan' to reach St Pancras, heading the 3.25pm arrival from Bradford (Forster Square), having worked from Leeds.

16   B16 4-6-0 61439 makes a rare visit to Oxford on the Bradford – Poole train.

16   35017 *Belgian Marine* is sent LE from Redhill to Newhaven to work the 6.40pm boat train to Victoria, first recorded 'Merchant Navy' to do so.

16   Liverpool Street – Cambridge main line is closed for bridge work, and 70003/9/42 travel via Audley End/Saffron Walden/Bartlow on diverted services. Some Norwich trains

go via Crystal Palace/Bounds Green/Hertford North and Hitchin, 70002/13 are seen running north this way.

16 Hull (Paragon) witnesses its biggest ever exodus to the coast, with 11,000 leaving between 9am and 1pm, the Hornsea and Withernsea services alone requiring 8 Booking Office windows to be open!

17 34110 *66 Squadron* arrives at Harwich (Parkeston Quay) with a special from Southampton consisting of 14 WR coaches, uncommon engine, and stock.

17 D8000 heads an 8-coach ECS train from Preston to Penrith, scheduled to become the regular running-in turn for subsequent new diesels as well.

20 77016 makes a class debut at Ferryhill *en route* to Inverurie for repair.

21 'Deltic' passes through Kensington (Olympia) light engine. (See also 28-2 July).

21 45523 *Bangor* (1B) enters York on an excursion from Liverpool, rare, if not unique, for a Camden engine to visit York.

21 5071 *Spitfire* (83A!) reaches Crewe on the 8.5am Kingswear – Manchester.

22,25 Due to a strike by French Engineering Officers, the French Line ship *Flandre* terminates its voyage from America at Southampton, from where passengers to France go by two special trains to Newhaven (via Haywards Heath, reverse) and catch the ferry for Dieppe. Two further trains run in the opposite direction on the 25th for French passengers embarking for the USA.

22 Caprotti 44753 (55A!) travels the Somerset & Dorset line with the 9.10am New Street – Bournemouth (West), an unprecedented sight.

22 73170 heads the up 'Scarborough Flyer' to York; unusual class on this service.

23 Last surviving N15X 4-6-0 32331 *Beattie* is chosen to head a ramblers' special from London Bridge to Windsor & Eton (Riverside).

26 61205 (35C) is a 'first of type' at Worcester (Shrub Hill), on ER stock.

26 34066 *Spitfire* makes another 'first recorded visit' by reaching Tilbury with a rake of SR stock that includes three Restaurant Cars.

28-2 July Exhibition of modern rolling stock is put on at Battersea Wharf. 'Deltic', D8000 and shunter 13354 are the only locos, plus several prototype coaches.

29 61619 *Welbeck Abbey* is highly unusual power on a York – Scarborough.

29 60132 *Marmion* enters Sheffield (Midland) on the 9.42am York – Bristol.

30 72003 *Clan Fraser* makes a rare (first?) visit to York with an excursion from Blackpool via Skipton, Otley and Harrogate.

30 45363 comes into Windsor & Eton (Riverside) with an excursion from Rugby, and 45004, 45188 work over the mid-Sussex line to Bognor via Dorking, with further specials from Tring and Bletchley, all rare workings.

U/D 75029 (with double chimney, and dynamometer car) heads the 8.5am Bristol to Weymouth over several days.

U/D 84029 is the last steam engine to be built at Darlington Works.

U/D 73154 is the last steam engine to be built at Derby Works.

U/D (Two weeks following Whitsuntide – in dead of night). Track and vehicle tests are carried out between Redhill and Three Bridges to examine riding at high speeds. Engaged are; 8-COR + 4-BUF, 2-EPB suburban unit, 'Hastings' 6-car DMU, 1Co-Co1 10203, Co-Co 20003, 35017 *Belgian Marine* – which reportedly touches 98mph (see also 16th).

JULY 1957

1ST 9.55am Newcastle – Liverpool leaves Leeds (City) behind 45735 *Comet* (1B) + 45520 *Llandudno*. Camden engines are very rare in Leeds.

1-5 One of the specials for the Open Golf Championship at Gleneagles is headed by the unusual pairing of D30 4-4-0 62442 *Simon Glover* + 45359.

5 61229 + 61230 (37C) work a Bradford (Exchange) – Whitley Bay excursion throughout. No staff at Heaton recall having serviced a Bradford loco before!

5 76060 + D1 4-4-0 31247 provide an eye-catching 'ancient & modern' combination on the 5.20pm Maidstone – Reading (South).

6 46230 *Duchess of Buccleuch* (66A) is spectacular power for the 4.45pm London-bound fish train out of Aberdeen.

6 Visitor of the month to Paddington is 5928 *Haddon Hall* (87J Goodwick).

6 2.20pm Charing Cross – Hastings (two 6-car 'Hastings' sets) noted at High Brooms running 30 minutes late with C 0-6-0 31280 banking at the rear!

6,14 61638 *Melton Hall* (6th) and 61657 *Doncaster Rovers* (14th) make guest appearances at Skegness – first B17s seen here for some years.

7 English Electric gas turbine (later GT3) finally arrives at Rugby Testing Station – by road! It had set off on 19 May from Vulcan Foundry hauled by a '5' but sustained axle problems near Crewe and returned north.

9 34104 *Bere Alston* cause a stir at Tilbury (Riverside) by arriving with a 10-coach ECS train at mid-day.

9,10 45507 *Royal Tank Corps* (9th) and 45503 *The Royal Leicestershire Regiment* next day, both work on the Bletchley – Bedford (St Johns) branch, this class never having been previously recorded here.

10 L1 2-6-4Ts 67766/77 (bunkers first) head the Royal train at Catterick Camp.

10 Preston 1.29pm; down 'Royal Scot' is halted in platform 5, and up 'Royal Scot' is halted in platform 7. Unique? (Preston is not a booked stop).

12 Interesting cutlery and crockery set for four at the dining room on platform 9 at Leeds (City) - soup spoon, LMS hotels; sugar bowl, LMS Dining Car; tablespoons, York Station Hotel and Station Hotel Perth; 4 x dessert spoons, MR Hotels/LNWR Hotels/SR/ NER Middlesbrough; vegetable dish, NER Refreshment Room Selby.

13 Rare sightings at York: 60035 *Windsor Lad* (64B) on a Cardenden to Marylebone 'Starlight Special' as far as York; 60093 *Coronach* (68E) with the 7.5pm Newcastle – Bristol; 73158 (34E), off a northbound 'Starlight' works a York/Hull/York round trip, then 5.20pm to Harrogate; 'Crab' 42816 (21A) + 61842 (38E) head for Scarborough, as does 61801 (31B) with the 'Queen of Scots' tailboard on the last coach's vestibule!

14 45020 works through to Yarmouth (Vauxhall) on a special from Bletchley.

14 SHT 0-4-0ST 1142 arrives at Clee Hill quarries (Ludlow) to replace Y3 0-4-0T Sentinel 68164, but two days later is at Shrewsbury for attention.

16 70045 is named *Lord Rowallan* by the Chief Scout himself in a ceremony at Euston. 46169 *Boy Scout* is also on show, having been named by the then Chief Scout in December 1930.

17 80121 reaches Inverness on a Girl Guide special from Elgin.

18 G5 0-4-4T 67338 is taken dead up the 1 in 50 section between Lees Moor Tunnel and Ingrow (East) on the Keighley – Halifax branch. It is then twice allowed to run down by gravity until being deliberately derailed on a stretch with concrete sleepers. This is an impact test on two types of concrete sleepers with bullhead, flat-bottomed rail.

19   72000 *Clan Buchanan* heads the 2-coach 6.2am Greenfield – Leeds (City)!

20   60018 *Sparrow Hawk* makes a rare appearance in Sheffield (Midland) on the 7.40am Sunderland – Bristol.

20   Southbound 'Devonian' comes into Bristol behind 45720 *Indomitable* (67A). Second Corkerhill 'Jubilee' to reach Bristol (see 10 July 1955).

20   61472 (50A) arrives in Marylebone with a 'Starlight Special' that originated at Dundee (Tay Bridge).

21   70009 *Alfred the Great* brings a special from Norwich into Southend (Victoria), first view of a Pacific here since the 1955 ASLEF strike.

21   J21 0-6-0s 65033 + 65103 (both 52C) haul a ramblers' excursion from Newcastle to Hawick over the Border Counties Line.

22   Because of the bus strike in Coventry, so many people travel from Kenilworth by the (strengthened) push/pull service, that a ticket window not used since 1930 has to jemmied open and brought into use!

23   Tilbury 4-4-2Ts 41949/75 seen on station pilot duty at Liverpool Street.

24-26   Royal Welsh Agricultural Show is held at Llanbadarn (on the Vale of Rheidol line) near Aberystwyth. Because of the local bus strike, the VoR maintains a 12 min-interval shuttle service, top & tailed, with 8-coach trains between 8.30am and 10.30pm! In the three days, the 2' gauge line carries 50,520 passengers at 6d return – special fare – as well as maintaining the timetabled service to Devil's Bridge. An incredible feat.

27   Crosti-boilered 92022 is an unusual spectacle at York, arriving on a stopping passenger train, probably the 3.2pm from Sheffield.

27   11.10am Clacton – Birmingham is worked from Colchester to Ipswich by E4 2-4-0 62785 (of 1891 vintage!), on an 11-coach express.

27   7.30am Glasgow – Scarborough has 61355 + 60004 *William Whitelaw*
8.30am Glasgow – King's Cross has 61221 *Sir Alexander Erskine-Hill* + 60024 *Kingfisher*
12.36pm Glasgow – King's Cross has 61241 *Viscount Ridley* + 60886, the B1 pilots working as far as Newcastle, in order to head relief trains back to Edinburgh at the end of the Scottish holiday fortnight.

30,31   60803 (31B) appears at Ripon on the 2.20pm Liverpool – Newcastle, unprecedented for a March engine to reach here (?). Almost as rare is New England's A2/3 60514 *Chamossaire* on the 9am Liverpool – Newcastle next day.

31   D34 4-4-0 62475 *Glen Beasdale* (62A) is a highly unlikely choice to head a luggage special on the Paisley Joint line.

U/D   LMR WD 2-10-0 No. 601 (on loan) works the 4.45am freight from Polmadie to Ardrossan.

U/D   Ex-'Coronation' observation car seen at work on the 10.24am Fort William to Mallaig and 6.20pm back, using the shed turntable to turn round in between.

U/D   73106 (60A, recently allocated) noted working the Kyle of Lochalsh line, a class new to this route.

U/D   BR is submitting plans to electrify Waterloo – Bournemouth on the overhead system with pantograph pick-up.

AUGUST 1957

World Scout Jamboree, Sutton Park, Birmingham runs from 1-12 August.
Pre-opening. 29-31 July. Scouts begin to arrive from all parts of Britain to Sutton Coldfield, Sutton Park, Streetly and Four Oaks stations; also from the Continent via Dover, Folkestone and Newhaven. In all, 54 special trains bring scouts to the Jamboree.

1ST	Jamboree opens with 70045 *Lord Rowallan* bringing the Chief Scout and VIPs from St Pancras to Sutton Park, returning from Streetly.
2	46168 *The Girl Guide* arrives with Guides from camp at Windsor to visit the Jamboree, having worked LE Willesden – Windsor (WR) to pick up the train, then running via Oxford – possibly the first 'Scot' to be seen here.

During the event, 135 extra trains are put on, either to take scouts on special day trips to Swindon/ Crewe/Derby Works etc, or to bring in visitors. Sutton Park and Streetly stations are repainted and equipped with loud speakers. 26 extra engines are drafted in to cope with all the additional workings.

1	Up 'Comet' boasts double-headed, consecutively-numbered 'Britannias' 70032 *Tennyson* + 70033 *Charles Dickens*, a doubly rare event!
1	62057 passes through Gerrards Cross with southbound ECS in SR green livery. K1s are a very unusual sight on this line.
2	75067 heads the 10.10am Hastings – Charing Cross, probably the first 4-6-0 ever to traverse the Hastings to Tonbridge line.
3	45384 (62B) makes an infrequent appearance for this class on the Waverley route, when working the 12.5pm Edinburgh – Carlisle.
3	44096 (71G Bath Green Park) is the outstanding Bank Holiday Saturday arrival at Melton Constable, with a Leicester – Yarmouth (Beach) excursion.
3	61306 (53B) surprisingly reaches St Pancras, working in from Leeds with a 'Starlight Special'. First time a B1 has been here since the 1948 Interchanges.
3	Crosti-boilered 92024 arrives at York on holiday traffic, returning south on the 1.18pm Darlington – Birmingham, but relieved at Sheffield by another unlikely engine, 45440 (71G!).
3	Due to a bomb hoax at Sandy, several East Coast expresses are diverted via Cambridge and Hitchin, including the 'Elizabethan' and 'Flying Scotsman'. Cambridge therefore sees A4s 60003/5/22/25 and A1s 60123/53 in a day.
3	73157 (34E) heads a Blackpool – Saltburn relief throughout via Skipton, and Harrogate. Neasden engines are unheard of at Blackpool (or Skipton).
4	61890 (31B) reaches Ripon, tender first, with a horsebox special from Newmarket, via Thirsk, (reverse). Two March locos in a week at Ripon!
5	92080 on a 20-coach express! This stock was being worked as ECS from Cricklewood to Derby, but the 8.15am St Pancras – Nottingham is cancelled in error (Bank Holiday Monday) leaving stranded passengers. The ECS train is therefore 'turned into' the 8.15 from Market Harborough onwards, though only the leading ten coaches are available to passengers.
5	The 'Welsh Dragon' (Rhyl – Llandudno) is worked as a six-car DMU. Three new 2-car sets bound for Scotland are 'acquired' to cope with holiday traffic!
6	44831 (2A) makes a surprising sight at Ripon on the 10am ex-Sunderland.
10	4997 *Elton Hall* is a stranger to be found on Bath (Green Park) shed.

1. Locomotive naming ceremonies were always special occasions; this is for 61379 to have its nameplate unveiled at King's Cross on 13 July 1951 by Commander Harold L. Goodwin (US Navy) of Boston, Massachusetts. (*NMM/SSPL*)

2. ScR preserved locos 49 *Gordon Highlander* piloting the 'Jones Goods' 103 pull away from Stevenston with a Largs – Glasgow excursion on 7 September 1959 in conjunction with the Scottish Industries Exhibition. (*W. J. Verden Anderson/Rail Archive Stephenson*)

3. Only one Royal funeral train operated during the years 1948-68, that for King George VI. The King died at Sandringham on 6 February 1952 and after lying in state at Westminster Hall was buried at Windsor on the 15 February. This is the scene at Paddington, with the late King's coffin being placed on board the black Royal funeral saloon as Guards of Honour stand in silence and solemn music accompanies the proceedings. (*NRM/SSPL*)

4. The funeral train for King George VI, running from Paddington to Windsor, passes Southall behind 4082 *Windsor Castle*. Note the Royal crests on both sides of the engine and also that the upper lamp is topped by a crown. (See also 15 February 1952). (*R. E. Vincent/transporttreasury.co.uk*)

5. Another unusual Paddington departure was that of 46237 *City of Bristol* heading the 'Cornish Riviera' on a 4-hour time trial to Plymouth, 17-20 May 1955. The GWR dynamometer car is behind the tender. (*NRM/SSPL*)

6. 34107 heads a funeral train for guests, on 25 October 1961 (see text also), entering Blandford Forum. The occasion was the funeral of Alan Cobham, founder of Flight Refuelling Ltd. (*G. A. Richardson, author's collection*)

7. In addition to the A4s, two other LNER locos were streamlined in the 1930s in the same style, and dedicated to working the 'East Anglian' express to Norwich. Here 61659 *East Anglian* brings the service into Liverpool Street in 1949. 61670 *City of London* was the second, both losing their streamlining in April 1951. (*R. E. Vincent/ transporttreasury.co.uk*)

8. 'Hastings' DEMU conducts riding tests near Stevenage, southbound, on 6 January 1968. (*David Percival*)

9. Easingwold, terminus of the 3-mile line from Alne, was not nationalised and hired-in J72 0-6-0 68294 to work the branch. Vintage GC 6-wheeled coach boasts 'ER' and '2nd' class (in 1948 – eight years ahead of BR!). (*E. E. Smith, author's collection*)

10. Before completion of the Trans-Pennine scheme some electrics ran trials on the Shenfield line where 26002 is on 19 November 1950. (*NRM/SSPL*)

11. 4472 *Flying Scotsman* heads the Manchester – Marylebone 'GC Railtour' on 16 April 1964, allowed through Woodhead Tunnel (in steam but doing no work) hauled by 26001, a very rare event! (*Gavin Morrison*)

12. Warwick; old steam shed now full of DMUs yet to enter service, new from Derby 4 April 1959. (*D. Horne/transporttreasury co.uk*)

13. On 27 March 1960, Bournemouth traffic was diverted via Ringwood, bringing the rare sight of 30862 *Lord Collingwood* passing through Broadstone, a type usually banned here.

14. The rerouting also caused the 'Bournemouth Belle' to approach Poole from the west, with 34061 *73 Squadron* coming off the S&D line at Holes Bay Jct. (*Both Colin Boocock*)

15. 35002 *Union Castle* + 30934 *St. Lawrence* head out of Weymouth and attack the climb to Bincombe Tunnel. Rare to see a 'Merchant Navy' piloting any train whatsoever! 12 June 1962. (Martyn Thresh)

16. On 8 June 1963 – for only the second time – a 'Jubilee' (45597 *Barbados*) reached King's Cross; see text, plus 23 March 1961. (*David Loveday*)

17. 46460, the only BR tender engine fitted with a cow-catcher fore & aft, stands at Fraserburgh on the branch train to St Combs, 16 May 1952. (*J. L. Stevenson*)

18. 4.40pm Bournemouth – Eastleigh surprisingly departs Christchurch behind Ivatt 2-6-0 43007, borrowed by Eastleigh after Works attention, 27 May 1965. (© *Carl Symes*)

19. 61375 (piloted from Stratford by 61280) brings a troop train from Harwich towards Victoria, passing Longhedge Jct. on 27 February 1957. (*R. C. Riley/ transporttreasury. co.uk*)

20. Brighton Works shunter tows 10001 into the Works, 27 April 1954. (Midland Railway Trust)

21. D7041 appears at Derby on acceptance trials from Cardiff on 27 June 1962. (*Alec Swain/ transporttreasury. co.uk*)

22. 16 August 1948 was one of only two days on which, due to flooding in the North East, the down 'Flying Scotsman' was diverted to run via Leeds and Carlisle. Here Grantham's *Falcon* passes the prominent signalbox on its circuitous route north. (See text for 13/16 August 1948). (*NRM/SSPL*)

23. Although 35019 (in original form) reached Leeds (Central) during the 1948 Interchange Trials, 35012 *United States Line* was the first rebuilt engine seen in Leeds. On 13 June 1964 it is about to depart City station for Carnforth, Shap and Carlisle with driver Bert Hooker (Nine Elms), who had taken 34004 *Yeovil* to Inverness in 1948 via Shap, as fireman. (See text for 12/14 June 1964). (*Gavin Morrison*)

24. The farthest-flung engine in the 1948 Trials was 34004 *Yeovil*. On 8 July during crew familiarisation week, 34004 is at Inverness with the 8.20am to Glasgow, as far as Perth. (*A. C. Sterndale, courtesy Mrs S. J. Sterndale*)

25. 3440 *City of Truro* at Glasgow (Central) having come in from Aberdeen (!) on 10 July (see text U/D September 1959). (*J. L. Stevenson*)

26. Another out-of-place loco was J88 0-6-0T 68341, just fished from Kirkcaldy harbour, having run away down the branch, January 1955. 68341 did not return to service. (The crew jumped clear). (*W. J. Verden Anderson/ Rail Archive Stephenson*)

27. 'Golden Arrow' was very rarely piloted, but on 10 March 1952 30903 *Charterhouse* did so from Tonbridge to Dover – see text also. (*NRM/SSPL + bottom*)

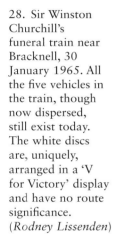

28. Sir Winston Churchill's funeral train near Bracknell, 30 January 1965. All the five vehicles in the train, though now dispersed, still exist today. The white discs are, uniquely, arranged in a 'V for Victory' display and have no route significance. (*Rodney Lissenden*)

29. 'At the sign of the Jolly Tar' was one of eight 'Tavern Cars' (see text for May 1949) with longitudinal seating and top-light windows, seen at Waterloo.

30. Sights at Shipley. (top) Preserved 7029 *Clun Castle* passes Bingley Jct. on 21 August 1967 (see text also) on a Steeton – Leeds run, towing a 4-wheeled converted horsebox as gauging saloon.

31. The Engineer's saloon behind 77013 heads for Leeds on 18 July 1963. The General Manager (pointing) is on the balcony with NER Board members flanking him.

32. On 5 July 1963 a Bradford – Lancaster goods derailed, blocking all passenger lines. As the Wakefield breakdown crane clears up, the 7.35am Bristol – Bradford (42093) stops on the goods lines where passengers detrain by ladder! (*All, Robert Anderson*)

46. On 20 September 1953 a very special train left King's Cross, headed by Atlantics 990 *Henry Oakley* + 251. Both usually resided in York Museum, but were put back into working order for the centenary of the opening of Doncaster Works. Train is passing Holloway – see text for 20/27 September 1953. (*R. E. Vincent/transporttreasury.co.uk*)

47. In the 1950s Richard Dimbleby presented the BBC TV programme *Down Your Way*, one of which was broadcast live from Top Shed. With the camera on a very low-tech trolley, the man himself is seen in the cab of 60155 *Borderer*, whilst technicians look on. (*Collection of Peter Townend*)

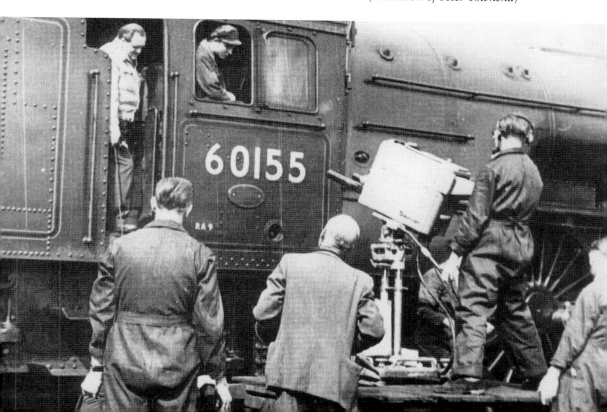

48. The 'Pennine Pullman' of 12 May 1956 set off from Marylebone and brought the triple rarity of an A4 (60014 *Silver Link*, doyen of the class), Pullman cars, and an observation car to the GC's London terminus.

49. Still at Marylebone, but on show between 11-14 May 1961 is the EE/Vulcan Foundry gas turbine GT3 4-6-0 of 2750hp based on the chassis (and tender) of a 5MT. Despite several tests on BR being successful in themselves, BR lost interest and the loco was scrapped in 1966. (*Both NRM/SSPL*)

50. As the prototype English Electric 'Deltic' was out of gauge on the NER, it travelled for tests in Scotland via Carlisle to reach Edinburgh. Operating out of Leith depot, this distinctive engine stands in Waverley station (east end) prior to a trial run. (See text for 8-15 June 1959). (*Author's collection*)

51. Believed to be the only DMU ever to run over the M&GN line, this Ian Allan special on 4 October 1958 had set off from King's Cross and is seen here at Wisbech (North) on its way to Yarmouth Beach. (*John Spencer Gilks*)

52. 72001 *Clan Cameron* climbing Glen Falloch *en route* to Spean Bridge – see 16 June 1956. (*J. Robertson/transporttreasury.co.uk*)

53. 61552/39 head a Sunday excursion south past Luncarty on the Highland main line – see text 18 June 1950. (*W. J. Verden Anderson/Rail Archive Stephenson*)

54. On 25 August 1964, hours before leaving, 6858 *Woolston Grange* sits on shed at...Huddersfield! See text for 15 August for the remarkable details.

55. Nine new 0-4-0 Sentinel shunters work their passage (first three are under power) near Mirfield on 25 July 1963, an arresting sight. (*Both Robert Anderson*)

56. Pairings of both types of WD locos were exceedingly rare, but here's 90774 + 2-8-0 variety on an up goods at Beattock Summit in June 1957. (*W. J. Verden Anderson/Rail Archive Stephenson*)

57. 41123 pounds up Hatton Bank working the 'Talyllyn' special between Paddington/ Shrewsbury, 27 September 1958. (*NRM/SSPL*)

58. On 28 September 1957, the equivalent train was powered west of Shrewsbury by the outlandish pairing of 50781 + 9021, seen between Welshpool/Abermule.

59. Even more exotic was the previous year's combination of 31075 + 2538, also west of Welshpool, on 22 September 1956 (*Both Ivo Peters, © Julian Peters*)

60. The 'Pennine Pullman' had both significant locos and coaches – see text for 12 May 1956. At the Sowerby Bridge stop, 62664/2 pays a rare visit to the L&Y main line. (*NRM/SSPL*)

61. 7017 *G. J. Churchward* at Bromsgrove with another Ian Allan special is the first 'Castle' to ascend the Lickey, 16 April 1955. (*R. C. Riley/ transporttreasury. co.uk*)

62. Climbing the Lickey's 1 in 37 is the (unique?) pairing of 69999 + 58100 'Big Bertha' – the regular banking engine for many years. (*NRM/SSPL*)

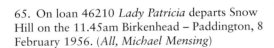

63. Birmingham area. 48430 + 34046 *Braunton* bring a 12-coach football special through Old Hill – see text for 27 April 1963.

64. Up 'Inter-City' at Snow Hill behind 6005 *King George II*, with the Queen Mother descending the steps to board the Royal saloon, 7 May 1957 – see text.

65. On loan 46210 *Lady Patricia* departs Snow Hill on the 11.45am Birkenhead – Paddington, 8 February 1956. (*All, Michael Mensing*)

66. 5.20pm Eastleigh – Southampton (Terminus) is hurried out of Eastleigh by… a Swansea 2-8-0 2821 on 7 May 1959. (*Colin Boocock*)

67. 9Fs were frequently used on passenger work, but rarely a Crosti-boilered variety. 92024 (15A) is near Pontefract with the Leicester – Scarborough, 3 August 1957. (*Peter Cookson*)

68. 1pm to The Mound waits at Dornoch behind 0-6-0PT 1646 on September 1959. This, and partner 1649 (both 60C) were the only WR pannier tanks (GWR-designed, BR-built) to see BR service in Scotland. (*Brian Stephenson*)

69. French 0-4-0 p.w. diesel inside Eastleigh Works 20 Sept 1966, see U/D April 1968. (*B. I. Fletcher*)

70. The 4.40pm Severn Tunnel car carrier (rarely photographed) climbs towards Pilning on 9 May 1958. Small car 15s 5d, Bentley 18s 7d, waterproof sheets 3s 2d per sheet. (*Michael Mensing*)

71. After flooding affected the East Coast main line in Southern Scotland, the track, once repaired, was subjected to severe temporary speed restrictions. Hence on 31 August 1956, 60033 *Seagull* on the up non-stop 'Elizabethan' passes slowly over the section at Cockburnspath with pilot 62494 *Glen Gour* restraining speed to observe the limit, a rare sight nonetheless. (*C. J. B. Sanderson/Armstrong Railway Photographic Trust*)

72. Two or three Haymarket Pacifics were occasionally transferred within the ScR to Polmadie to work the heavy Sleeping Car trains between Glasgow and Crewe, returning on the 11.25am from Birmingham. On this train, 60161 *North British* is seen on the unfamiliar climb to Shap. (*NRM/SSPL*)

73. East Anglia. 'Suffolk Hunt', arriving by train for the last time, is stabled in Mellis yard – see text for 9 February 1957.

74. Even in the 1950s of 2-4-2T pairs were rare when F6 67231 + F5 67216 were spotted near Lowestoft.

75. Tram engines operating the Wisbech & Upwell tramway (such as J70 0-6-0T 68217) were an unusual sight, complete with cow-catchers and 'side skirts' on the freight-only branch. (*All, I. C. Allen/ transporttreasury. co.uk*)

76. E2001, the ex-WR gas turbine converted into an AC electric for driver training, passes East Didsbury, 17 May 1960. (*Alec Swain/ transporttreasury.co.uk*)

77. E5003 heads to Brighton from Three Bridges after rail-stress tests on 4 April 1960; two each of 'Hastings' coaches/bogie wagons/coal wagons/hopper wagons/ brakes! (*The late Derek Cross*)

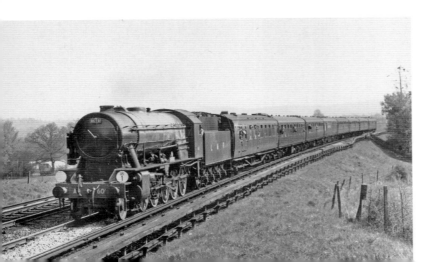

78. LMR 2-10-0 600 *Gordon* works an RCTS special between Woking, Liss on 30 April 1966. (*Rodney Lissenden*)

79. In its rebuilt form (as here) 46202 bore the name *Princess Anne* but was previously the LMS's 'Turbomotive' built 1935. Most unfortunately, the rebuild only lasted two months, being destroyed in the dreadful crash at Harrow & Wealdstone on 8 October 1952. When active, 46202 pulls out of Crewe with a northbound express.

80. During the change-over period from steam to diesel, coaching stock remained largely steam-heated. Hence the early mainline diesels were fitted with train heating boilers, and with water pick-up scoops to enable these to be replenished *en route*. D214 *Antonia* heads a down express over Dillicar troughs in the Lune Gorge, 1963/4. (*Both NRM/SSPL*)

81. 60062 *Minoru* (34A!) is an unlikely sight at Bradford (Exchange) – see text for 5/12 April 1959 for further details. (*Robert Anderson*)

82. Equally uncommon was the pairing of 40461 (16A) + 60910 on a Bristol – Newcastle, near Pontefract on 27 May 1958. (*Peter Cookson*)

83. Strange vision at Harrogate on 24 August 1952 is W20W, doing a spot of shunting! See text also. (*Harry Whitby, Stephen Askew collection*)

84. This is the 'White Rose' express standing at Doncaster with the up service on 12 April 1962, only 60107 *Royal Lancer* bears the special headboard in support of 'The Yorkshire Campaign' to promote woollen products. Both the Leeds, Bradford portions carried such headboards for the duration of the campaign. (*NRM/SSPL*)

85. 60008 has, literally, just left English soil at Southampton bound for America. (See text 24/27 April 1964 for details). (*NMM/SSPL*)

One of a kind – or W, X, Why? Z for short!

Left: 86. 10800 (N.B. Loco Co.) 827hp Bo-Bo leaves Euston on a test run 14 November 1950.

Right: 87. Brand-new 2750hp Co-Co 'Lion' leaves BRCW's works for the first time, 28 May 1962. (*NMM/SSPL*)

Left: 88. Another 1950 test train is ready to depart from Brighton, with contrasting power – Bulleid's ill-fated 'Leader', with driver (front) separated from fireman (centre door). (*Both NRM/SSPL*)

Right: 89. Hawker-Siddeley 4000hp Co-Co 'Kestrel' stands at Marylebone for inspection, 27 January 1968. Sold to the USSR in 1971! (*Alec Swain/transporttreasury.co.uk*)

10   An urgent request for a lightweight loco to shunt Littlehampton Wharf means that Brighton turns out the Works (departmental) shunter A1X 0-6-0T S377 for the job. Stroudley's 'Improved engine green' brightens up the Wharf!

10,16   V4 2-6-2 61701 is pressed into service on the 'Saint Mungo' from Aberdeen to Perth, and works into Waverley from Thornton Jct. six days later.

13   A 'Bristol' cargo plane overshoots the runway at Southend airport, runs down the railway embankment stopping a yard (!) from the overhead support gantry.

16   Compound 40925 (5A) is a rare sight at Perth piloting 44650 (also 5A) on the 9pm Perth – Euston sleeper.

16,17   70026 *Polar Star* penetrates to Banbury on the 8.10am Swansea – Newcastle, returning south on the 4.12pm to Oxford. First visit of a 7MT for some years, but the second visit is next day, when 70018 *Flying Dutchman* comes in on the Cardiff – Sheffield relief to the 8.10am!

17   Crosti-boilered 92022 (15A) reaches Blackpool on the 8.50am from Sheffield, returning with the 2.15pm back to Leicester.

17   73050 (71G) gets as far as Castleford, having worked a relief train from Bournemouth throughout from Bath!

17   44249 (18D Staveley) is an unexpected guest on Gateshead depot.

18   48259 finds unusual work on Paddington ECS movements.

20   Down 'Elizabethan' passes through Newcastle behind 60538 *Velocity*, as 60012 *Commonwealth of Australia* had failed near Gateshead.

23   11.30am Peterborough – Edinburgh fails near Dunbar. 60087 *Blenheim* is removed and the train proceeds behind the unusual combination of 61787 *Loch Quoich* (65J Fort William) + 62721 *Warwickshire*.

24   60007 *Sir Nigel Gresley* (34A) works both the 11.40am Newcastle – Carlisle and the 12.17pm ex-Stranraer back from Carlisle, where 'Top shed' engines are rarely seen.

24   73168 penetrates as far south as Grantham on the up 'Norseman', a surprise choice of power in the first place.

24   Most unusually, two boat trains from Southampton Docks are worked into London Bridge, running via Tulse Hill from Wimbledon.

24   2.35pm to Cambridge leaves York headed by the unlikely pairing of 60043 *Brown Jack* (64B) piloting 61972 (31B).

25   The annual Gloucester – Portsmouth (Harbour) excursion is worked through by 2-6-0 6373, giving the Netley line its first sight of a WR loco this year.

29   61972 (31B) passes Horsforth with the up 'Yorkshire Pullman', most unusual.

31   62046 (51A) enters Marylebone on the 1.15pm from Brackley, one of the few appearances of a K1 on passenger duties in this area.

U/D   61535 is a stranger at Oxford, arriving on a service from Cambidge.

U/D   An unusual transfer is of N5 0-6-2Ts 69267/90 to Tyne Dock from Wrexham.

U/D   Stanier 2-6-2T 40150 is transferred to Wick. The closest sister loco is in the Glasgow/Edinburgh region, about 300 miles away!

SEPTEMBER 1957

1ST   46136 *The Border Regiment* is a notable visitor to Keswick, from Newcastle.

3   3F 0-6-0 43742 is surprise power for the 4.15pm Ilkley – Leeds (City).

5	45156 *Ayrshire Yeomanry* (26A) passes through Clapham Jct. on a cross-London freight, first named '5' south of the Thames (?).
6	61947 works through from Nottingham to Newcastle with the Continental Car Sleeper from Dover – a rare duty for a K3.
7	60116 *Hal o' the Wynd* pilots A2/3 60511 *Airborne* on the 8.5am Birmingham – Newcastle from York. Double-headed ER Pacifics are rare.
7	61276 (51A) pilots 45708 *Resolution* into Liverpool (Lime Street) on an express from Hull. B1s are seldom seen in Lime Street.
8	61010 *Wildebeeste* (53B) is serviced at Bournville shed after bringing an excursion from Hull to visit Cadbury's factory. B1s seldom seen here either.
8	A Southend – Farnborough excursion (for the Air Show) is a 4-coach train of Stratford railcars, stabled at Basingstoke until the return working.
9	34091 *Weymouth* works through to Brandon (Norfolk) on a troop train, turns at Ely and heads the ECS back to the SR. A rare penetration of East Anglia.
12	3440 *City of Truro* is worked as 'train engine' on the 5.30am Paddington to Plymouth (from Didcot onwards) with a 'King' as pilot!
13	B16 4-6-0 61469 (52B) appears at Bathgate shed, tries to turn on the turntable but is too long, and disappears in the Edinburgh direction.
13	45509 *The Derbyshire Yeomanry* is a surprise arrival at St Pancras with the 'Thames-Clyde Express', which is almost always 'Jubilee' hauled.
14	A Hull – Morecambe charter is headed throughout by 61306 (53B).
14	This time A2/3 60511 pilots 60126 *Sir Vincent Raven* on the 8.05, see 7th.
15	3440, having arrived at Laira on the 12th, now heads a Plymouth – Penzance special and back, thus visiting its 'home' town Truro for the first ever time.
17	N2 0-6-2T 69564 is noted at Haltwhistle on the pick-up goods from Carlisle.
18	Wandering 5A Compound 40925 reaches Cambridge, from Bletchley.
19	Metro-Cammell power car M50136 is coupled to the LMS No.3 dynamometer car and one Mobile Test Unit for performance trials over the Settle & Carlisle.
20,22	35017 *Belgian Marine* travels LE from Stewarts Lane to Darnall (Sheffield) via the GC main line, in connection with high-speed hammer-blow tests to be conducted on the 1500V DC line between Deepcar and Wharncliffe Wood on the 22nd, current being switched off on this section. During the period 14-28 September other locos involved are diesels D8001, 10000, 10203, 10800, electrics 27000, 26000/24 and an EMU.
22	30909 *St. Paul's* heads a Hitchin – Worthing excursion through from Canonbury, first known instance of a 'Schools' on the North London Line.
22	8-car diesel set forms an excursion from Birmingham to Ramsgate, longest DMU day trip yet run.
28	48354 (84G), tender first, brings southbound empty horseboxes into York.
28	44703 heads a 10-coach football special from Brechin to Glasgow – first passenger train to use the Brechin to Bridge of Dun line for 5 years.
28	Talyllyn Railway Preservation Society's AGM special is hauled from Paddington to Shrewsbury by 3440 *City of Truro*. 'Dukedog' 9021 piloted by (of all engines) L&Y 2-4-2T 50781 take the train on to Towyn. Remarkable!
U/D	BR confirms electrification of Waterloo – Bournemouth on the overhead system. Planned to begin 1962.

OCTOBER 1957

1ST   'Patriot' 45517 (1A) reaches Aberdeen with an overnight freight from Dumfries, first of this class in Aberdeen since summer 1952.

5   York's 73167 is turned out for the 12.12pm King's Cross – Cambridge.

5   Up 'Capitals United Express' comes into Swindon behind 70016 *Ariel* (with headboard) piloting 2-6-2T 6155, an unexpected sight!

6   61306 (53B) works a Hull – Windermere cyclists' special both ways, and retires to Carnforth depot between journeys.

8   61234 (30A) heads a troop train from Harwich through to Dover (Marine) and returns with the empty ER stock.

10   The 'Cunarder' boat train from Waterloo to Southampton Docks is powered by 30906 *Sherborne*, rather than the usual light Pacific.

17   76114 is the last steam engine to be built at Doncaster Works. However, 76047/8 (of Kirkby Stephen) arrive for repair at…Stratford!

18   Dislocation of workings at Preston bring no fewer than 5 'Coronation' Pacifics (46236/41/42/46/54) to Carnforth shed for servicing.

19   Crosti-boilered 92020 (15A) is an unlikely engine to appear on the Carlisle to Birmingham freight passing through Apperley Bridge, towards Leeds.

19   44907 (8A) heads a Donnington (Salop) to Oswestry football special, working tender first from Gobowen. First '5' to reach Oswestry shed.

19   0-6-0PT 1605 works the ex-Midland branch to Dursley from Coaley.

23   New 800hp Bo-Bo diesel D8200 noted on a trial run with one coach from the Yorkshire Engine Co. (Meadowhall) to Chinley and back. Consternation reigns amongst the crowds at Sheffield (Midland) waiting the arrival of the Duke of Edinburgh in the Royal train, mistakenly thinking the diesel special might be his train!

24   Special high-speed test takes place between Paddington and Birmingham with 5082 *Swordfish* + 5 coaches + the track-testing car. Train is at Snow Hill in 111min and returns in 107min (on a 110min schedule), with the introduction of Pullman diesel units in mind.

25   Collapse of a signal gantry at Darlington causes the down 'Flying Scotsman' to be diverted via Shildon, Bishop Auckland and Willington to reach Durham.

26   76114 (newly allocated to 65B), instead works into London on freight!

29   O4/3 2-8-0 63686 (39A Gorton) passes through Birmingham on an overnight freight from Chester to Ashchurch, via Manchester, Derby. Returns on special freight next day, being serviced at Gloucester in between. A rare movement!

29   Swindon Carriage Works paints four of its new cross-country cars in experimental livery; beige/pale blue, red/black, pale green/yellow lining, being three.

31   70019 *Lightning* reaches Neyland and heads the 3.50pm Milford Haven to Gloucester fast fish train (appropriately!).

31   7928 *Wolf Hall* heads a troop train into Southampton Docks.

31   72002 *Clan Campbell* is seen on the down 'Queen of Scots' at Falkirk (High). (72000/2/5/6 are transferred to 64B to release V2s for seed potato traffic).

31   Experimental Davey-Paxman powered converted twin LM coaches covers Sheffield (Victoria) – King's Cross in 161min, with brief stop at Retford.

U/D   LMR WD 2-10-0 No. 601 is converted to oil burning at the Hyde Park Works (Glasgow) of the North British Locomotive Co.

U/D   72005 *Clan Macgregor* is observed at Tweedmouth heading north on a freight from Newcastle. The four 64B 'Clans' also work over the Waverley route.

NOVEMBER 1957

2ND   72002 *Clan Campbell* works into Newcastle on freight from Edinburgh. 72000 *Clan Buchanan* also appears the following week.

3   Fowler 2-6-2T 40057 is a surprising loco to be working the 10.10am fromManchester (Central) to Sheffield, and the 2pm return.

5   73157 leaves Sheffield (Victoria) on the up 'South Yorkshireman', having worked the down 'Master Cutler' the previous evening.

5   Crosti-boilered 92026 brings the 2.25pm arrival into St Pancras when 46152 *The King's Dragoon Guardsman* fails at Wellingborough.

5   Up 'Lancastrian' strikes the wreckage of a 10-ton articulated lorry that had plunged 30' onto the West Coast main line at Kilsby, dragging parts of the lorry into the tunnel. Both lines are blocked, but cleared by 3am next day.

7   73144 heads the Duke of Edinburgh's Royal train to Edmondthorpe & Wymondham station. First Royal train, and 5MT, on the Saxby – Bourne line.

9   61577, ex-Works, is employed on the 5.10pm Cambridge – Mark's Tey comprising two LNER coaches and 4 loaded cattle wagons!

10   5912 *Queen's Hall* is seen on clearance tests at Washwood Heath sidings.

10   D11 4-4-0 62690 *The Lady of the Lake* (64B) arrives in Newcastle towing A2/2 60507 *Highland Chieftain* to Doncaster for repair.

13   2-6-4T 42091 stalls on Grosvenor bank (out of Victoria) on the 5.50pm to Groombridge, and is eventually banked away by electric loco 20002. Unusual!

13   70029 *Shooting Star* (86C), running-in from Crewe Works, heads a freight from Carnforth to Leeds, where Cardiff Canton engines are surely unknown?

14   48472 is the first 8F seen at Aberdeen for some years, with freight from Perth.

14   Express from Newcastle enters King's Cross behind 60134 *Foxhunter* piloting 60005 *Sir Charles Newton* (short of steam at Sandy). Rare sight.

21   Immaculate 30915 *Brighton* hauls a 6-coach special train (including two Restaurant Cars) from Victoria to Swale Halt on the Sheerness branch. Train conveys representatives of the Press to view the progress of electrification works, and is *propelled* back to Sittingbourne from Swale Halt.

23   35017 *Belgian Marine* appears on Guildford shed, making a class debut here.

23   73110 (70A) arrives in Parkeston Quay on a special from Southampton Docks, and returns the ECS (which includes a Pullman car) to Clapham.

23-30   ScR TV train is used to exhibit the goods of a Glasgow Woollen firm. Train tours between Ayr and Aberdeen, films shown and the Buffet Car is popular.

24   Oil-burning LMR WD 2-10-0 No. 601 is noted at Kingmoor depot.

25   Derby-built 3-car suburban DMU (with Rhymney on the blind!) turns up at Liverpool Street for official inspection.

25   Gas turbine 18000 makes its first trip through the Severn Tunnel on ECS in preparation for the following day's special working. (See December).

25-29   7.43am York – King's Cross and the 2.10pm back is hauled by 60136 *Alcazar*, complete with indicating shelter, and dynamometer car in the consist.

| 29 | New Brush A1A-A1A 1250hp diesel D5501 heads up ECS at Hitchin. |

29 New Brush A1A-A1A 1250hp diesel D5501 heads up ECS at Hitchin.

U/D 7029 *Clun Castle* is the first of its class to receive a Heavy General overhaul at Wolverhampton Works, and 1029 *County of Worcester* undergoes the same treatment at Caerphilly Works, again a first-of-class occurrence.

U/D D600 *Active,* the first 2000hp A1A-A1A diesel hydraulic (from North British Loco. Co. Glasgow) heads 3-coach special to Kilmarnock (25/27 November) and eight coaches to Dumfries and Gretna Green, 2/3/4 December.

DECEMBER 1957

Canadian Trade Mission Special Train starts its 1129 mile tour on 26 November, leaving Paddington at 9.15am for Didcot, Bristol and Cardiff behind gas turbine 18000, which spends the night at Canton. Mission then visits Margam, Coventry, Birmingham, Sellafield, Edinburgh, Glasgow, Manchester, Leeds and reaches Marylebone at 5.58am on 7 December. 'Deltic' works the 12.45am Liverpool (Lime Street) – Glasgow (Central) on 3rd to work the leg to Manchester (over Beattock) on 4th. On 7th train leaves Doncaster for Leicester (Central) behind 60114 *W. P. Allen* Formation is seven vehicles, plus six Sleeping Cars (three nights spent on the train).

4TH Serious accident occurs in fog at Lewisham when 34066 *Spitfire* runs into the rear of the 5.18pm Cannon Street – Hayes EMU which is standing at signals. The wreckage damages the supports to the Nunhead railway flyover bridge, which crashes onto the Pacific's train. 90 die in third worst railway accident.

5 Overnight sleeper from King's Cross is surprisingly powered by 62733 *Northumberland* (64B) on arrival at Aberdeen.

8 46245 *City of London* freshly painted red with yellow and back lining, is at Euston for official comparison with 46250 *City of Lichfield* in green livery.

10 Derailment near Oxenholme causes diversions over the Settle & Carlisle line between Carlisle and Hellifield, bringing a pair of main line diesels over this route for the first time, probably on the 9.25pm Glasgow – Euston.

11 Crew-training run from Southend (Victoria) is seen at Shenfield headed by D5500 + D5501, but not in tandem, as D5501 had failed at Wickford.

15 0-6-0PT 7428 noted still bearing 'GWR' on its tanks and 7429 still lettered 'British Railways' in full, both at Stourbridge.

16 Failure of District Line services between Upminster and Bow Road causes the 12.10pm Shoeburyness – Fenchurch Street (2-6-4T 42531 + 11 coaches) to traverse the District Line from Upminster to East Ham, calling at all stations.

21 61147 (62A) heads a Carlisle – Perth parcels train, rare for a B1 to work on the ex-Caledonian main line.

21 Compounds 41078 + 41143 are a stunning combination to head the up 'Palatine' at Leicester, where both engines take water.

24 62040 (31B) exits Liverpool Street on the 1.20pm relief to Ipswich. This class are uncommon sights at this terminus.

24 72000 *Clan Buchanan* (64B) powers the 7.28am Berwick-on-Tweed to Newcastle, and the 6.25pm return working. Standard Pacifics are still rare on this stretch of the East Coast main line.

27 1pm Barrow – Euston sets off behind a brace of 'Royal Scots' 46151 *The Royal Horse Guardsman* + 46161 *King's Own*, a most unusual pairing.

28   44976 (65J Fort William) finds its way, somehow, to Hawick shed.

28   60535 *Hornet's Beauty* (64B) is an eye-opening arrival in Leeds (Central), ex-Works, on the 10.19am from King's Cross.

29   Due to an engineering blockage at St Mary Cray, three Chatham line trains are 'topped & tailed' out of Victoria, routed via Ludgate Hill and the Dartford loop. The leading engine is removed at Ludgate Hill, where trains reverse.

30   D8014 runs LE from Devons Road to Nine Elms for tests out of Waterloo.

U/D   70016 *Ariel* (86C) works into Salisbury, is 'borrowed' by that depot for a train to Winchester, where it derails, and is sent back to 72B for examination.

JANUARY 1958

1ST   D11 4-4-0 62690 *The Lady of the Lake* works into Hawick on a day excursion from Edinburgh (Waverley). D11s are infrequent visitors to Hawick.

2   L&Y 0-4-0ST 51204 (8D Widnes) noted on Oxley shed (84B). Loco is on loan to Courtaulds at Wolverhampton for internal shunting.

2,3,15   D8014 makes morning round trips from Waterloo to Farnborough having run LE from Devons Road to Nine Elms. Also makes trial run from Victoria to Brighton to test ATC equipment (15th).

3   3-car Derby DMU is at Sheffield (Victoria) in pea-green + off-white lining!

3   D16 4-4-0 62529 (31B) brings a parcels train into Liverpool Street, unusually.

4   C 0-6-0 31244 is an odd choice for the 1.38pm Tonbridge – Oxted.

4   Two Aberdeen – King's Cross meat trains depart at 10.12am, 10.45am behind ex-Works J37 0-6-0s 64626 (65C), 64617 (62C) respectively. Rare sights!

4   45662 *Kempenfelt* (82E) works right through from Bristol to Accrington with a football special. Barrow Road 'Jubilees' are extreme rarities at Accrington.

4,5   72008 *Clan Macleod* finds itself working the up 'Thames-Clyde Express' through from St Enoch to Leeds, returning north next day on a Leeds to Newcastle excursion.

6   (Week beginning). 60081 *Shotover* makes daily visits from Low Moor to the 7/8 mile long Lees Moor Tunnel (between Ingrow and Cullingworth), an unprecedented loco on this line, closed to passengers in 1955. It is joined in this cloak & dagger experiment by D8010/11, sent up specially from Devons Road shed, Bow! St Bartholomews Hospital, London is testing emissions from steam, diesel locomotives and using this tunnel for the purpose!

7   Stanier 2-6-2T 40159 (64A) turns up at Ferryhill (61B) for trials on the GNS section lines to Keith, Elgin and Lossiemouth.

8   J17 0-6-0 65564 is a surprise visitor to Clapham Jct. on the Stratford – Hither Green goods, diverted this way due to the collapse of Nunhead viaduct.

9,10   2-6-2T 5540 (82C) heads the 4.38am Banbury – Southall freight, and 5561 (82A) has the 7.45am freight between the same two points, with 5543 (83B) on the 12.30pm Banbury – Basingstoke goods next day. Any 55xx class loco in the London area is rare, but three…All are ex-Wolverhampton Works.

11   72005 *Clan Macgregor*, 72002 *Clan Campbell* (both 64B) both seen in Newcastle, 72005 on the 2pm ex-Carlisle, 72002 to Edinburgh on freight.

13   Brand new A1A-A1A 2000hp D600 *Active* travels from Glasgow to Crewe and on to Stafford Road (84A), moving to Swindon next day to enter service.

14	72002 heads the late afternoon Aberdeen – Edinburgh express out of Dundee. 'Clans' do not often cross the Tay, Forth bridges.
17	800hp Bo-Bo D8202 undergoes trials over the S&C working an 11-coach train from Sheffield to Carlisle and back.
17	70021 *Morning Star* works a Cardiff – Paddington rugby special and takes the ECS to Henley, first Pacific here. Serviced at Reading prior to working back.
18	New D55xx diesel heads the 10.30am Liverpool Street – Norwich, where it is met with a civic reception!
18	72006 *Clan Mackenzie* takes the Aberdeen portion of the 'Night Scotsman' through to the Granite City from Waverley.
19	10am Plymouth (Friary) – Waterloo fails to stop at Basingstoke but is brought to a halt by the guard. Train reverses through the station on the *down* main line and re-enters on the up main line, finally leaving 17 minutes late.
20	Part of Scarborough station roof collapses under the weight of snow. Some of the shed roof follows suit four days later.
21	Gas turbine 18100 is transferred from Metropolitan Vickers' Works at Dukinfield to their Works at Stockton, being hauled dead via Stalybridge, Huddersfield and Leeds, making first appearances all the way.
24	6.48am Clacton – Liverpool Street starts at Colchester (due to heavy snow) and comprises five coaches, with a ScR 2nd class Sleeping Car, a Kitchen Car and a Buffet Car in front of them – all thrown open to passengers! The station announcement says it is a 'special formation'.
25	30863 *Lord Rodney* and 30856 *Lord St. Vincent* haul two football specials from Portsmouth (for the FA Cup tie against Wolves) via Guildford as far as Reading, where they await the return working on South shed.
25	Chelsea v Darlington Cup tie brings 60078 *Night Hawk* (52A), 61224 (51A) into King's Cross on through workings from Darlington, which are rare occurrences.
31	Very strangely, L1 2-6-4T 67730 (40E Colwick) passes northbound through Berwick and subsequently receives attention at Haymarket shed (64B).
31	D5501 makes a class debut at Sheffield (Victoria) on the 8am Harwich to Liverpool boat train, working this from March.
31	82026 heads the NE Region Officers' saloon over the circuit Darlington/Tebay/Penrith/Kirkby Stephen/Darlington.
U/D	44255 is a surprise transfer to Fort William shed.
U/D	0-6-0 Dock Tank 47166 is on loan to BICC (British Insulated Callandars' Cables) at Preston to investigate the corrosive properties of locomotive smoke on 25kV AC overhead wiring.
U/D	New Underground cars for the Piccadilly line are seen being towed south through Birmingham (Snow Hill).

FEBRUARY 1958

3RD	Derailment at Hartford causes the down 'Caledonian' to be diverted via the Midland main line to Leeds, and the S&C line. Most unusually, 'Patriot' 45528 (complete with headboard) works Euston – Carlisle throughout.
4	45658 *Keyes* (55A) is a surprise choice to head the up 'Caledonian' out of Glasgow (Central), presumably again diverted via the S&C and Leeds.

4-6	1016 *County of Hants* works two up, two down trips on the 'Cambrian Coast Express' between Shrewsbury and Paddington. 'Castles' then resume control.
5	0-6-0PT 3711 (86H Aberbeeg) reaches Robert Stephenson & Hawthorn's works at Newcastle, hauled by a J27 0-6-0, to be converted to oil-burning.
7	Stanier 2-6-2T 40159 (15C) is a rare type at Hitchin, working to/from Bedford.
8	92169 (36A) finds itself marooned at Heaton for the weekend. No freight is moving at all in the North East due to heavy snow.
8	N7 0-6-2T 69614 (Liverpool Street pilot) enters Southend on a parcels train.
9	T9 4-4-0 30719 makes a rare appearance in Victoria on the 12.55pm from Brighton, returning to 70A after a Brighton Works visit. (See next entry).
9	Things don't always go to plan! Stewarts Lane diagram 509 is booked for a U1 2-6-0, but...

9.38am has 4MT 4-6-0 75065 (74C) on way to Eastleigh Works

12.55pm has T9 4-4-0 30719 (70A) ex-Brighton Works,

4.38pm has L 4-4-0 31778 (75A) and

7.55pm has 4MT 2-6-4T 80xxx

all on Victoria – Uckfield – Brighton, and return workings.

9	10.15pm (7th) 'Aberdonian' finally arrives in Aberdeen at 4.42pm – 20 hours late! Train was (only) 6 hours late at Newcastle due to heavy snow, but finds the line blocked between Montrose and Stonehaven.
10	61998 *Macleod of Macleod* (65A) leaves Aberdeen on the 9pm freight for Kilmarnock. K4s are uncommon sights in Aberdeen.
11	45658 *Keyes* (55A) again works the up 'Caledonian' out of Glasgow (Central).
11	Severe storm at Rayleigh damages the catenary and blocks both lines. At 7pm 3,000 passengers crowd the forecourt at Wickford for buses to Rayleigh.
15	61952 (52D) appears at Newark having worked from Grantham on the 5.15am parcels from King's Cross. Tweedmouth locos are rare so far south.
15	48350 (18A) is found on Darlington shed after working a pigeon special.
16	30859 *Lord Hood* heads the 8.14am Feltham – Wimbledon special freight.
17	V1 2-6-2T 67661 (65C) ex-Darlington Works is unusually employed on traffic between Edinburgh and Perth.
18,19	46112 *Sherwood Forester* + 46133 *The Green Howards* double-head the 10.15pm Sheffield (Midland) – Leeds on both days, an unusual pairing.
21	2-8-0 4707 pulls into Salisbury with freight from Bristol, surprisingly, since this class are thought to be banned from the Westbury – Salisbury route.
22	A5 4-6-2T 69824 (40B shedplate) finds itself on ECS duty at King's Cross.
23	Victoria – Cranleigh ramblers' excursion is powered by E1 4-4-0s 31506 + 31067. Locos go to Aldershot to turn as the Guildford turntable is out of action.
24	Compound 41078 is hosted by Bristol (Bath Road), most irregular!
25	2.25pm King's Cross – Cambridge stuck in a snowdrift near Royston is "rescued by airmen from RAF Henlow".
25	Heavy snowfalls cause arrivals indicator at King's Cross to read " 'Flying Scotsman' 5.3pm expected 10.55pm; 6.39pm ex-Aberdeen and 7.51pm ex-Leeds (the 'White Rose') – no information". However a chalked notice also reads "Cafeteria will remain open all night"!
25	Electrically-hauled down freight fails just inside Woodhead Tunnel. Steam engine is allowed to run wrong line through the tunnel from Woodhead and pull the train

through! Also, the 9.24am Hull – Liverpool arrives at Sheffield (Victoria) 1¾ hours late behind the unexpected combination of 62701 *Derbyshire* + N5 0-6-2T 69292. Train leaves towards Manchester in heavy snow behind a K3 hauling two dead electric locos and 10 coaches. Reaches Dunford Bridge (19 miles away) 678 minutes late at 11.3pm!! K3 works through Woodhead Tunnel as far as Guide Bridge. Exceptional workings.

25	Up 'South Yorkshireman' becomes snowbound at Denby Dale and terminates!
25	11.30am Scarborough – Hull and 10.35am Hull – Scarborough both run into large snowdrift at Speaton Cutting and are stranded for 14 hours despite vigorous attempts to release them. 11.30 finally reaches Hull at 3.40am (26th).
25	Heavy snow blocks the West Coast main line between Preston, Warrington forcing the up 'Royal Scot' (46226 *Duchess of Norfolk)* and up 'Caledonian' (46257 *City of Salford)* to divert through Manchester (Oxford Road).
25-28	Wensleydale roads are blocked by snow, hence the 7.35am and 4.5pm parcels trains from Northallerton are run as passenger trains to Hawes. Branch had been close to passengers in 1954.
25	Due to the bad weather, the down 'Golden Arrow' travels from Ashford to Folkestone via Canterbury (West), Minster, Deal and Dover. The 'Arrow' is seen at Wye at 3.35pm and the 'Man of Kent' at 7.20pm.
26	South Lynn – Fakenham (West) is cleared by snowplough pushed by four engines, J17 0-6-0 65582 + Ivatt 2-6-0s 43084/43104/43110. Quite a sight!
26	Ivatt 2-6-0 46467 (31A) makes a surprise visit to Bournville shed, returning east on the 3.15pm New Street – Cleethorpes.
26	WD 2-10-0 90763 (12A) looks out of place in Aintree shed.
28	Blizzard in Derbyshire means Ashbourne – Buxton line re-opens for the day (closed 1/11/54), one passenger train making a return trip. At Edale, the 8.55am Manchester – Sheffield is held until an expectant mother arrives requiring urgent transfer to Sheffield hospital (roads blocked). At Bamford a LE with snowplough breaks through drifts and picks up a child with appendicitis, and heads quickly back towards Sheffield Hospital.
U/D	D601 *Ark Royal* runs trials between Glasgow and Kilmarnock.
U/D	Railbus SC 79979 (AC Cars) is on show at Marylebone (13th) and Paddington (19th), then heads off for the Crieff – Gleneagles branch.
U/D	45716 *Swiftsure* (68A) appears at Scarborough with a train from Bradford.
U/D	30904 *Lancing* heads a Salisbury – Exeter slow, a rare type on this line.
U/D	Fowler 2-6-2T 40011 is an interesting transfer from Willesden (1A), seen on Ferryhill (61B) on 26th on its way to Keith (61C) to replace 40159, previously on loan, which is returned to 64A.
U/D	" Preliminary work has already started on the Doncaster – Hull electrification. Erection of catenary is hoped to start soon after 1960". (BR Official statement)
U/D	"Waterloo – Exeter to be electrified by 1973, dieselised by 1962" (do.)

MARCH 1958

1ST	SR stock in green livery reaches Crook behind L1 2-6-4T 67763 + 60925, forming a football special to the Crook Town v Wokingham Amateur Cup tie.
1	45317 most unusually takes a northbound freight through Carlisle (Citadel) station itself. Goods traffic always (!) uses the station avoiding line.

3	New DMU service starts between Leeds and Barnsley increasing traffic 900% in first week of operation. Ironically the General Manager of Yorkshire Traction Omnibus Co. is an invited guest on the first train.
3	D11 4-4-0 62690 *The Lady of the Lake* works through from Edinburgh to Aberdeen with the 2-coach portion of the 'Flying Scotsman' which had missed its connection in Waverley. A very rare working for an engine of this class.
7	A2/3 60518 *Tehran* springs a surprise by working the 'Talisman' into King's Cross. Surely not the diagrammed loco for this prestige train?
8	76114 (65B) is unlikely power for the 12noon Buchanan Street – Oban.
8	SR Pacifics 34046/89/91/92 bring excursions into Wembley Central for the womens' International Hockey match – one containing Pullman cars. All locos proceed to Watford to turn on the triangle there.
8	70010 *Owen Glendower* (32A) passes Boston on a coal train from Doncaster to New England. (7MTs are thought to be banned from crossing the Grand Sluice Bridge, north of Boston).
8	0-6-0 2270 (84C) is a rare type at Crewe, on a Hinksey – Manchester freight.
9	70017 *Arrow* (86C) is surprise power for the 8am Cardiff – Snow Hill. Only the second Pacific to pass through Kidderminster.
9	61131 (56F Low Moor) + A1/1 60113 *Great Northern* seen double-heading south from Hitchin, an unlikely combination! 61131 worked an excursion from Halifax to King's Cross on 8th, runs short of steam on the return working, and is to pick up a northbound goods from London.
10	60863 travels from Leicester GC shed to Leicester Midland shed via Nottingham, Trent and Loughborough. First V2 south of Derby on this line?
12-18	'Transport Treasures' exhibition at Hove includes LSWR 4-4-0 563 and A1X 0-6-0T *Boxhill*, both soon to be despatched to Tweedmouth (!) for storage.
14	Down 'Waverley' enters Waverley behind D30 4-4-0 62428 *Talisman*, which had taken over at Hawick. The D30 also proudly carries the headboard.
14	D200 (the first EE 2000hp 1Co-Co1 Type 4 diesel) passes through Sheffield (Victoria) *en route* from Vulcan Foundry (Newton-le-Willows) to Doncaster.
14	7.42am Bournemouth (Central) – Salisbury leaves Daggons Road behind T9 4-4-0 30313 + 34107 *Blandford Forum* pulling 1 horsebox + 1 coach!
15	45539 *E. C. Trench* seen heading through Goole on a football special returning to Chester. 'Patriots' rarely pass this way.
15	The 'Radio Train' – which can receive or relay BBC programmes – is used for an excursion between Snow Hill and Paddington.
16,23	60855 (34E Neasden) conducts clearance tests between St Pancras and Cricklewood, and (on 23rd) between Cricklewood and Wigston.
17	D601 *Ark Royal* passes Preston LE *en route* from Glasgow to Swindon.
18	CR 4-2-2 123 works its first train after 23 years of retirement when it heads the 2-coach 2pm special from Perth to Princes Street, both the restored coaches being in CR livery also.
20	D11 4-4-0 62690 *The Lady of the Lake* hauls A2/3 60509 *Waverley* from Edinburgh to Newcastle, the Pacific being on its way to Darlington Works.
23	60160 *North British* seems misplaced heading the 12.47pm local from Leven, whilst 72000 *Clan Buchanan* has the 10.40am Edinburgh – Dundee.
24	60033 *Seagull* heads a 6-coach Pullman special between King's Cross and Sheffield (Victoria) throughout for the Cutler's Feast. Return is next day.

24 Liverpool Street – Chelmsford Royal train is headed by 70000 *Britannia* but the LE ahead of it (to ensure a clear line) is 76046 (51F West Auckland)!

25 Fowler 2-6-4T 42411 enters Newcastle – a rare type here – on the 5.12pm from Sunderland. The engine is thought to be on short term loan.

25 76086 appears in St Pancras (Tilbury boat train?) – first of class here.

27 2am freight Mirfield – Barrow is worked throughout by L&Y 'Austin Seven' 0-8-0 49515 (26A), a rare sight in these parts.

29 WR Restaurant Car excursion to Birkenhead for the Grand National arrives at Woodside behind 5099 *Compton Castle*, which works the train both ways.

30 GSWR 12-wheeled dining car SC299M is noted at Leeds in the formation of a Liverpool – Newcastle express. Not many of these about!

U/D (First week). 35015 *Rotterdam Lloyd* is run in after repairs on the 11.28am freight between Hither Green and Feltham, and the 2.28pm return working.

U/D 2-6-4T 42110 (24A Accrington) is still lettered 'British Railways' in full, not having been repainted since new in 1949.

U/D Fowler 2-6-2Ts 40054/49 (both ex-1A) are surprisingly loaned to 62B Dundee Tay Bridge!

U/D Since Gourock Pier buildings were destroyed by fire (December 1957), the Caledonian Steam Packet Co. has been using 3 Camping Coaches as offices.

U/D 70001 *Lord Hurcomb* + 70013 *Oliver Cromwell* are unexpectedly seen on freight through Nottingham (Victoria), a rare same-class pairing.

U/D J83 0-6-0T 68464 sets a record by working the same actual turn from St Margarets depot ('Leith Walk No.3 Pilot') throughout its entire working life, from arriving new in 1901 to its withdrawal in March 1958!

APRIL 1958

1ST 5026 *Criccieth Castle* passes Ashchurch on the diverted 'Cornishman' – a rare event to see a 'Castle' here.

1,2 Derailment at Filton Jct. causes South Wales expresses to be diverted through Gloucester, where 70023 *Venus* is noted on the up 'Capitals United Express' and 5051 *Earl Bathurst* on the 'South Wales Pullman'.

3 80099 (33A) is surprise power on the 6.20pm Peterborough – Grantham stopper. Standard tanks are rarities on the East Coast main line.

3 0-6-0PT 3711 emerges from RS&H Works in Newcastle fitted for oil-burning. Engine remains at the rear of Central station until the 14th, when trials on the North Wylam branch are scheduled to commence.

3 (Maundy Thursday). At least six southbound departures leave Waverley with B1/Pacific pairings, the B1s to work northbound extras over Easter. These include; 61246/60507, 61099/60027, 61029/60004, 61307/60534 (on the 'Heart of Midlothian'), 61332/60094 and 61244/60162.

4,5 60093 *Coronach* (Carlisle Canal) is a rare visitor to Aberdeen, with a relief train ex-Edinburgh; 60082 *Neil Gow* (52B) heads the 10.30pm up goods, the first Newcastle A3 since summer 1954, 46120 *Royal Inniskilling Fusilier* (5A) also comes in on a special from Glasgow – all Good Friday events. Amazingly J39 0-6-0 64818 (50D Starbeck) appears in Aberdeen next day.

5   Ivatt 2-6-2T 41319 is entrusted with the 8-coach 8.20am Brighton – Victoria.

6   Another Easter surprise is 48138 (19C Canklow) at Dalry Road (64C).

7   61082 (40B) is a notable arrival at Buxton (from Scunthorpe); 62760 *The Cotswold* is an unusual class at Cleethorpes, both on excursion traffic, whilst 45558 *Manitoba* (26F) reaches Sunderland on a football special.

8   11.45am Harrogate – King's Cross starts from Ripon and 61892 (53A) works it to Leeds, a most unusual class on this line…and yet on the same day 61920 pilots 60081 *Shotover* through Ripon on the 9am Liverpool – Newcastle, itself an uncommon combination.

8   60910 + 60922 (52B) double-head a relief to the 8.30am Cardiff – Newcastle northbound out of Sheffield (Midland). Pairs of V2s are rare – anywhere!

9   Restored 4-4-0 3440 *City of Truro* pilots 70017 *Arrow* on the 8.43am from Cardiff as far as Pilning, a most unexpected, and contrasting, sight.

9-18   EE 2000hp 1Co-Co1 D200 makes trial run from Doncaster to Welwyn Garden City and back (9th); then runs to Stratford via Spalding (11th) and Stratford to Cambridge (15th-17th). Heads 9-coach demonstration run on 18th to Norwich from Liverpool Street, where D201 is also present for inspection.

12   70033 *Charles Dickens* (9A) is a surprise arrival at Glasgow (Central).

13   L 4-4-0 31776 makes two round trips between Newhaven and Willesden, piloting 30909 *St. Paul's*, then 30910 *Merchant Taylors* on 13-coach extras.

13   H2 4-4-2 32424 *Beachy Head*'s last public run is on the 'Sussex Coast Limited' from Victoria to Newhaven, a 7-coach special for the RCTS.

14   5.27am Ramsgate – Charing Cross is sent to Cannon Street in error, closely followed by a 'Hastings' DEMU, also bound for Charing Cross!

17   T9 4-4-0 30310 is a last minute substitute to work the 1.10pm Bournemouth (West) – Bath (Green Park). T9s are rarities on this route.

17   D5501 is seen at Plaistow operating driver training duties to Shoeburyness with 11-coach suburban sets.

19   60076 *Galopin* (51A) reaches Sheffield (Midland) with a football special from Middlesbrough. Darlington Pacifics scarcely ever appear in Sheffield.

19   60887 is observed at York in green, but paired with a lined black tender!

20   'Cornish Riviera Limited', diverted via the Okehampton route from Exeter to Plymouth is, most unusually, headed by SR Pacific 34079 *141 Squadron*.

20   Ramblers' excursion from Newcastle arrives in Keswick behind 45439 + 45512 *Bunsen*, probably the most powerful pairing yet seen on the CKP.

20   62031 (65J Fort William) is employed on Edinburgh suburban passenger workings, running-in from Darlington Works, an unlikely sight.

21   45684 *Jutland* (5A) makes a guest appearance in Norwood Yards on a cross London freight from Willesden.

21   0-6-2T 69453 (56B Ardsley) is very unexpected power on the 5.37am Normanton to Sowerby Bridge – first N1 seen here in years.

21   2-6-0 6306 is a late replacement for a SR Pacific on the 9.17am Weymouth to Waterloo, which it works as far as Bournemouth (Central). Most unusual.

21   York has the rare sight of a Plaistow loco when 80104 (33A) hauls A5 4-6-2T 69805 *en route* to Darlington Works.

23   D601 *Ark Royal* appears at Oxford on trials with a 10-coach train plus the WR dynamometer car.

24	After it last public run, H2 4-4-2 32424 works an ECS train from Lancing to Micheldever, then LE to Eastleigh Works for scrapping.
26	60157 *Great Eastern* heads the Trains Illustrated's 'Pennine Limited' from King's Cross into Leeds (City) from the east via Castleford and Garforth, complete with ex-'Devon Belle' observation car. Special is worked to Crewe by Compounds 41100 + 41063; by 8P 71000 *Duke of Gloucester* to Euston.
26	Restored 4-4-0 3440 *City of Truro* travels as far as Ruabon on the FRS special from Paddington. 'Dukedog' 4-4-0s 9017 + 9021 continue to Minffordd and back to Shrewsbury, where 3440 again takes over.
27,28	LSW 4-4-0 563 and A1X 0-6-0T *Boxhill* leave Brighton behind 30935 *Sevenoaks* to Stewarts Lane, bound for Tweedmouth. The pair is seen again next day at Heaton, hauled by 61353.
27	D8017 reaches Victoria with a van train from the LMR. Gawping is allowed.
29	D201 makes a trial run on six Pullmans between King's Cross and Sheffield (Victoria), prior to the inauguration of the dieselised 'Master Cutler'.
29	60964 is named *The Durham Light Infantry* in a ceremony at Durham, to mark the 200th anniversary of the raising of the Regiment.
U/D	J27 0-6-0 65894 turns up at Low Moor shed for repair, brought there from Wakefield. First North Eastern Railway type to be given attention here.
U/D	2-8-2T 7235 is trialled for 3 days as Lickey banker, but fouls the platform at Bromsgrove. Replaced a couple of weeks later by 2-8-0T 5226, also on trials.
U/D	8.34pm Peterborough (North) – Melton Mowbray arrives from Peterborough (East) behind the extraordinary triple combination of Compound + J39 0-6-0 + D16 4-4-0!

MAY 1958

2ND	76011 (71A) appears at Cole, an unusual type on an S&D working.
2	Caprotti 73139 (15C) works right through from Luton to Portsmouth Harbour with an educational excursion. First LMR loco here for a long while.
3	61749 (40E) is a stranger on the 1.40pm out of Marylebone.
3	Caprotti 73126 (84G) visits Paddington with an FA Cup Final special from Wrexham (General), a rare class to reach this London terminus.
5	D11 4-4-0 62660 *Butler Henderson* replaces failed A2/3 60517 *Ocean Swell* at Retford on the 15-coach Colchester – Glasgow, which it works as far as York. Astonishing. It must be many years since a D11 tackled a train of this weight.
6	30850 *Lord Nelson* enters Victoria (Eastern), a type rarely seen here of late, on an Ocean Liner Express from Southampton, diverted from Waterloo.
7	34075 *264 Squadron* (72A) arrives at Windsor (SR), where Exmouth Junction Pacifics are notable sights, with an excursion from Torrington.
8	An ex-'Devon Belle' observation car passes through Edinburgh (Waverley) on its way to Cowlairs Works.
10	44830 is replaced at Neasden on the down 'Master Cutler' by 44711 (1A). One Stanier 4-6-0 on this service is rare, two even more so, and surely a Willesden loco has not previously worked the express?
10	Gloucestershire Railway Society runs a 3-car WR cross-country DMU over the S&D to Bournemouth, the first of these vehicles to do so.

11	Restored 4-4-0 3440 *City of Truro* is noted at Wandsworth Common heading a ramblers' excursion from Greenford to Ardingly, as far as East Croydon.
12	LNW 0-8-0 49444 makes a class debut at Scunthorpe, working in on an iron ore train from the Northampton area.
13	77013 (50G Whitby) takes the NER Engineer's Saloon up the Worth Valley branch from Keighley.
14	U 2-6-0 31615 leaves Weymouth on a stopper to Dorchester (West), whilst new 'Hastings' unit 1032 arrives on a trial run from Eastleigh, unusual sights.
14	New 800hp Bo-Bo D8400 returns to North British in Glasgow after several days trials from Dumfries.
16	60024 *Kingfisher* is a rare sight on the 'Bon Accord', working the Perth to Aberdeen sector and returning on the 9pm Aberdeen – Kilmarnock fitted freight. (Which has now been worked by, amongst others, A4 and K4 classes, a 'Princess Royal' and 8P 71000 *Duke of Gloucester*!).
17	60964 (recently named *The Durham Light Infantry*) hauls a special from Durham to Brancepeth (the Regiment's HQ), conveying Princess Alexandra.
17	Caprotti 73137 (6J Holyhead!) reaches Brighton on excursion traffic.
17	5934 *Kneller Hall* is a surprise arrival at Bath (Green Park) on a pigeon special, first 'Hall' to reach this station for a year,
17	Preserved LNW locos *Cornwall* and *Hardwicke*, specially prepared, leave Crewe Works for exhibition at Carlisle. (See June 7-18).
20	60048 *Doncaster* is unusual, though appropriately named power, for the 8am stopping train to Doncaster from Sheffield (Victoria).
22,25	80074 (33B Tilbury) passes Clapham Jct. on an special to Windsor (SR), and three days later 45683 *Hogue* (41C Millhouses) is an even bigger surprise, reaching as far as Clapham with a Whit Sunday excursion.
23	D11 4-4-0 62664 *Princess Mary* causes a stir at York, on the Bournemouth to York; another stranger is ex-Works 61659 *East Anglian* (32D Yarmouth South Town) which leaves on the 3.34pm Newcastle – Birmingham.
23	62051 (31B) leaves Liverpool Street, a type infrequently seen here, on the 8.50pm to Ely.
23	Pigeon special arrives at Ripon behind the unlikely combination of B16 4-6-0 61427 piloting 45630 *Swaziland* (5A). These two are later joined on Starbeck by 45685 *Barfleur* (82E Bristol Barrow Road). Two 'Jubilees' on 50D!
24	76049 (51F) heads the 12.30pm Cambridge – Chatteris and back, and then the 3.50pm to Stratford, where it had been recently overhauled.
24	Stanier 2-6-0 42946 (3D Aston) mysteriously appears at Leeds (Central) with the 11.47am from Bolton (Trinity Street). Class debut here?
24	Restored CR 4-2-2 123 fails on a special and is towed to Ardrossan for repair, its demise causing immense satisfaction to the local ex-GSW railwaymen!
24,25	72007 *Clan Mackintosh* inhabits Millhouses shed for Whit weekend, having worked through to Sheffield from Carlisle. 'Clans' are rare south of Leeds.
25	Birmingham – Bournemouth (West) excursion is formed of four 2-car Derby sets, only the second DMU to traverse the S&D route.
26	Up 'Waverley' leaves Carlisle behind 44668 + 45538 *Giggleswick*. 'Patriots' are a rare type over the S&C line.

26	Fowler 2-6-2T 40011 (61C) is seen at Craigellachie with the 6.45pm to Boat of Garten – on trial in these parts.
27	The rare (possibly unique) pairing of 4-4-0 40461 (16A) + 60910 brings a Bristol – Newcastle express into York. Another rare arrival is 70030 *William Wordsworth* (32A) on the 8.5am from Birmingham; 70030 continues to Newcastle and is serviced on Gateshead depot.
29	13-coach special from Fishguard has S15 4-6-0 30835 between Redhill and Newhaven. First S15 on a Newhaven boat train?
29,30	72003 *Clan Fraser* (66A) heads the 2.52pm Hellifield – Liverpool (Exchange) on both days, a most unusual working.
30	First Car Sleeper to arrive at Eastbourne (from Glasgow) is met by the Mayor and various railway dignitaries!
31	10.35am Leeds (City) – St Enoch reaches Dumfries 20min late, where 45732 *Sanspareil* is removed and replaced by the odd duo of 4-4-0 40614 + 76098.
U/D	60128 *Bongrace* operates high-speed riding tests between Darlington and York with different tyre profiles on coaching stock (2 coaches only). Achieves start-stop times of 37min down and 34min up, with max speed of 101mph.
U/D	'Deltic' enters EE's Vulcan Foundry for a complete overhaul.

JUNE 1958

1ST	7-coach scenic and photographic excursion is run from Hull to Scarborough via Driffield, Malton and Whitby. Train is seen struggling up the incline from Whitby Town to West Cliff in rain and sea mist with 80116 in front and 61010 *Wildebeeste* + A8 4-6-2T 69861 pushing manfully in the rear.
1	WD 2-10-0 90763 finds itself on Hellifield shed, looking out of place.
2	80120 heads the 9-coach 4.25pm Leeds – Scarborough throughout.
2	204hp 0-6-0 shunter 11223 works the daily goods between Robertsbridge and Tenterden, and the early morning newspaper & passenger train Crowhurst to Bexhill (West) – a rare instance of diesel haulage on the Eastern Section.
3	Down 'South Yorkshireman' leaves Rugby (Central) behind, surprisingly, 60088 *Book Law* (52B Heaton), a rare NER intruder onto GC metals.
4	L1 2-6-4T 67740 noted on trial at Euston with ECS workings.
5	61063 reaches Windsor with an excursion from Bradford, via Oxford.
5	Thornaby MPD opens as 51L. D5510 (30A!) works a special VIP train to the new depot and, after the opening ceremony, heads the special to Saltburn for the VIP lunch at the Zetland hotel.
7-18	The 'Carlisle 800 years' celebrations include a railway exhibition with Furness Railway 0-4-0 *Coppernob*, LNW 2-2-2 *Cornwall*, LNW 2-4-0 *Hardwicke*, CR 4-2-2 123, MR 4-2-2 118 and replica *Rocket* all on show.
8	Q 0-6-0 30539 powers a ramblers' excursion from Charing Cross to Midhurst, first passenger train to traverse the branch from Pulborough since 6 Feb 1955.
9	'Royal Scot' empty stock is brought into Euston by L1 2-6-4T 67747.
9	WR 4-6-0s begin regular workings to Bournemouth from Weymouth, on the 8.4am ex-Dorchester (South) and the 5.4pm return freight to Weymouth, with a return trip to Poole in between.
9	73054 (82E!) is observed heading a Scarborough – York goods train.

10	92080 + 92113 double-head a fitted coal train (including a recording car) out of Nottingham towards Newark.
11	Double-heading tests take place on the South Devon banks between Newton Abbot and Plymouth, with 12-coach loads plus WR dynamometer car. D601 *Ark Royal* acts as pilot to 7000 *Viscount Portal* then 7813 *Freshford Manor*, and is also piloted by 4905 *Barton Hall*.
11	61151 (41A) works the 1.32pm Derby – Bristol parcels (via Worcester) throughout, unusual task for a Sheffield (Darnall) engine.
12	6-car Cross-Country DMU set forming the 5.40pm Snow Hill – Hereford has an additional GWR coach at the rear to increase capacity, a rare sight.
14	Some summer Saturday Winchester – Southampton DEMU services are diverted to start at Chesil.
14	73168 (+ headboard) works the up 'Scarborough Flyer' as far as York.
14	30861 *Lord Anson* is unusual power for the 12.5pm Waterloo – Ilfracombe.
14	K 2-6-0 32348 heads an excursion throughout from Three Bridges to Bournemouth (Central) – a rare type to arrive here.
14	34056 *Croydon* surprisingly arrives at Torquay with a train of SR stock.
14	70025 *Western Star* reaches Windsor (WR) on a special from Cardiff and is serviced at Slough next to 61380 (off an excursion to Bourne End).
14	10.20am Aberdeen – Euston arrives in Carlisle behind 45727 *Inflexible* (63A), working the train from Stirling. Perth 'Jubilees' are uncommon in Carlisle.
14	W 2-6-4T 31914 (73A) makes a very rare appearance in Margate piloting 73041 on a track repair train.
14	92139 heads a rake of 18 bogies (ECS) up the Lickey incline banked by 92079 + 0-6-0PT 8403, most of the stock being post-war LNER coaches in maroon livery and roofboarded 'Starlight Special'. Quite a sight.
14	V1 2-6-2T 67645 (52A) makes a foray to Carlisle, where this class is rare.
14	72008 *Clan Macleod* (12A) arrives in Bradford (Exchange) – a first here – on a working from Blackpool. It then spends the next week based at Low Moor working the 8.45am to Blackpool and 7.30pm back, before returning north.
15	61974 (40E) reaches Llandudno on a ½ day excursion.
15	60529 *Pearl Diver* (64B) is an extreme rarity at Harrogate, working the 5pm Newcastle – Liverpool.
16	6820 *Kingstone Grange* (85A) is also a rare sight at Nottingham (Victoria), arriving with the 1.20pm from Leicester (Central).
16	CR 4-4-0 54486 travels the Dundee (East) – Forfar branch with the BR Cinema Coach train.
16	D601 *Ark Royal* is the first diesel-hydraulic to leave Paddington, heading the down 'Cornish Riviera Express'.
17,18	73059 (66A) heads the 'Aberdonian' from Dundee to Aberdeen on both days, most unusual power for this train.
18	D5511 (30A, on loan to Inverness) passes through Waverley towards Glasgow and then on to Perth for tests on the Highland main line.
19	70014 *Iron Duke* (transferred to 9E Trafford Park) parts company with its tender, heading the down 'Palatine' between Hazel Grove and Cheadle Heath.
19	D 4-4-0 31737 (ex-store at Ashford Works) is moved to Stewarts Lane (73A). Ten days later it departs for Tweedmouth (and further storage), being seen on 30th approaching Heaton hauled by an A1 Pacific!

19,20	61090 brings the 'Tees-Tyne Pullman' into King's Cross, and arrives with the 'Flying Scotsman' next day, replacing failed locos on both occasions!
20	30909 *St. Paul's* (73A) makes a surprise visit to St Albans with a train of SR stock labelled 'Charing Heath Primary School, Lenham'.
20	73052 (82F Bath Green Park) raises eyebrows at Waterloo, arriving on the 4.9pm from Salisbury. Bath engines 'never' reach Waterloo!
20	73116 (71A, on loan to 82F) brings the 'Pines Express' into New Street, and even more surprisingly goes forward to Sheffield on the 2.45pm.
21	L&Y 0-6-0 52248 is trusted with the 10-coach special from Oldham (Clegg Street) to Skegness, as far as Guide Bridge.
22	Fowler 2-6-4T 42411 heads an excursion to Killingworth races and proceeds to Morpeth, with its train, to turn. A rare type on this stretch of the main line.
24	J39 0-6-0 64907 (56C Copley Hill) puts in to Hellifield for repairs, as does 73124 (67A), neither of which would be expected to be seen here.
25	Another 73A engine reaches St Albans in the shape of 73080, also on excursion traffic.
26	Inverurie Works Open Day attracts D40 4-4-0 62277 *Gordon Highlander* (in GNS green, scheduled for preservation); 73154, D2410 and a 2-car DMU.
26/27	Queen travels from King's Cross in the LMS Royal train behind 60149 *Amadis* to Sleaford. Train is stabled on the Bourne branch overnight, proceeding to Lincoln next day behind a pair of B1s.
27	45632 *Tonga* heads the 5.10pm Chester – Paddington as far as Wolverhampton (Low Level), where 'Jubilees' are decidedly uncommon.
28	D16 4-4-0 62511 arrives in Colchester from Ely the 8.5am Birmingham to Clacton. J15 0-6-0 65451 then takes over for the non-stop run to Clacton!
28	75046 (27A) most unexpectedly pilots 45635 *Tobago* into Carlisle on the 9.30am Manchester – Glasgow, the 4MT returning south piloting 45531 *Sir Frederick Harrison* on the 1.45pm Glasgow – Liverpool/Manchester.
28	V1 2-6-2T 67670 stands with a suburban train in Waverley station right next to the 'England – Scotland' border sign (!), newly repainted in Edinburgh.
29	0-6-0PT 8402 pilots a 'Jubilee' into New Street on the 2.10pm from Bristol!
29	92017 reaches Llandudno on an excursion from Castleton formed of a 10-coach set (938) of green-liveried Southern stock, which had arrived the previous day at Oldham on a relief from Eastbourne.
29	J11 0-6-0 64373 is given the unaccustomed task of reaching Hull on the 12.3pm from Sheffield (Victoria).
U/D	10½ years after nationalisation 2-6-4T 42110 is in Crewe Works with its side tanks still reading 'British Railways'. Elsewhere, 6870 *Bodicote Grange* still says 'Great Western' either side of the GWR arms on the tender.
U/D	0-6-0PT 1649 is sent to Helmsdale to work the Dornoch branch while 1646 is under repair.
U/D	Trafford Park (9E) receives six 'Britannias' to assist with summer traffic; 70004/14 (ex-73A), 70015/17/21 (ex-86C) and 70042 (ex-30A).
U/D	From the summer timetable (14/6/58) the 8.37am Newcastle – Bournemouth (West) is rostered for a 'Hall' through to destination, from Oxford.
U/D	end of June; D5511 on trials with 8-coach trains, Perth/Aviemore/Inverness.
U/D	61361 arrives at Southend with a 12-coach excursion from the Leeds area including a Refreshment Car, a Restaurant Car and two Sleeping Cars!

U/D   Tweedmouth shed now contains Wainwright SEC 4-4-0 31737, Adams LSW 4-4-0 563 and Stroudley LBSC 0-6-0 *Boxhill*, all in storage.

JULY 1958

2ND   Severe flooding occurs at Sheffield (Midland) due to a cloudburst and several thunderstorms. Station closed to all traffic, with rivers of water between the platforms, and much ballast dumped under the road bridge at the north end.

2   Up train of ER stock arrives in New Street behind 45720 *Indomitable* (67A), a shed rarely represented here, whilst 61374 (40B) leaves with a relief for Bristol. Immingham engines are also infrequent visitors to Birmingham.

2   45632 *Tonga* lurks on Reading shed (a rare sight here) having arrived from Chester on the 7.35am Birkenhead – Margate.

5   73010 (55A) is surprise power for the 7.15am Yaxley – York freight.

5   Events at York. 62751 *The Albrighton* (on 10 coaches of LMS stock) runs through non-stop on the 9.29am Scarborough – Manchester; the 8.25am Leicester – Scarborough goes forward behind 61841 (2F Woodford Halse); the down 'Scarborough Flyer' leaves with 2-6-4T 42073 and the up service comes in, amazingly, behind 44108 (21A) complete with headboard! Hardly express treatment for this once-famous train!

5   L1 2-6-4T 67783 (14D Neasden) mysteriously arrives in Newcastle on a parcels train from Carlisle.

5   48613 is spotted paired with a Fowler straight-sided tender in green livery, formerly behind 45742 *Connaught*.

5   On loan D5511 arrives in Perth on a fish/parcels train from Inverness.

5   60116 *Hal o' the Wynd* (52B) also reaches Perth, on the 2.5pm ex-Waverley. Heaton locos rarely venture this far north.

5   Restored CR 4-2-2 123 works a 3-coach special from Hamilton (Central) to Princes Street conveying troops for the Territorial Review.

6   Selby – Driffield line (soon to be axed) sees the passage of nine excursions to Bridlington totalling 94 coaches (all to be berthed, somewhere!)

6   A Ripon – Morecambe excursion has 61405 (40A) + 62738 *The Zetland* (50D) throughout. Lincoln engines are noteworthy on the west coast.

7   Derailment at Oxenholme causes the up 'Mid-day Scot' to reach Hellifield via Low Gill, Sedburgh, behind 46201 *Princess Elizabeth,* the engine returning LE to Carlisle next day. The up 'Caledonian' also comes this way with 45593 *Kolhapur*, as does the down 'Mid-day Scot' ('Patriot' 45551 + 'Crab' 2-6-0, a really odd combination!)

7   70040 *Clive of India* (30A) is seen at Newark heading north with a train of 27 ancient and decrepit brake vans (an ex-Works running-in turn).

7   New Metropolitan-Vickers 1200hp Co-Bo D5700 commences 14-coach trials between Stockton and Leeds, via Ripon.

9   7820 *Dinmore Manor* (83D) is an outstanding visitor to Portsmouth, on an excursion from Swindon. Laira engines are akin to hens' teeth at Pompey.

10   A2/2 60503 *Lord President* makes a proud entry into King's Cross on the 'Elizabethan', taking over from 60030 *Golden Fleece* (lost water scoop).

10   2.10pm Victoria – Wimbledon EMU is routed into platform 7 at Norwood Junction, which is not electrified, and so grinds to a halt. C2X 0-6-0 32551 pushes the train

forward to rejoin the juice!

10   D5511 works through to Fort William, and returns next day with the 9.31am to Queen Street.

10   92164 heads the 'Master Cutler' out of Marylebone, as far as Leicester.

10   8am Harwich – Liverpool arrives in Sheffield (Victoria) behind 70003 *John Bunyan* (30A), only the second known visit of a 7MT here.

11   92011 heads the 'South Yorkshireman' between Sheffield and Leicester.

11   Uniquely, the 'Cambrian Coast Express' heads out of Shrewsbury into Wales behind Fowler 2-6-4T 42388, with the headboard resting on a side tank!

11   60112 *St. Simon* + 60083 *Sir Hugo* double-head the 9.40am to King's Cross out of York. Pairings of Gresley Pacifics are rare events.

11,12 61600 *Sandringham* (30A) is seen at York with ECS, and at Darlington shed next day – the first B17 here since 1950. For scrap at the Works?

12   72006 *Clan Mackenzie* works the 9.50am Edinburgh (Waverley) – Sheffield unchanged from Carlisle, and is serviced at Millhouses depot.

12   L1 2-6-4T 67725 works the 9.56am Liverpool Street – Felixstowe throughout.

13   73139 (6J Holyhead) reaches Cambridge on an excursion bound for Yarmouth, providing Cambridge with a rare class, and an even rarer shedplate.

14   Swindon-built 2000hp B-B diesel hydraulic D800 is named *Sir Brian Robertson* by K.W.C. Grand, General Manager, Western Region, at Paddington. After which D800 works a 4-coach Press special to/from Reading.

14   Down 'Waverley' is powered out of Leeds by 72000 *Clan Buchanan* (66A) piloting 46109 *Royal Engineer* (55A), an uncommon pairing.

15   D8400/1 pass through Waverley station *en route* to Glasgow for maker's attention. D8402 does the trip in the reverse direction next day.

15   92164 reaches 86mph between Leicester and Nottingham whilst working the down 'South Yorkshireman'.

17   Recently-named 60964 travels to Barnard Castle to pick up a troop train of its namesake, The Durham Light Infantry, bound for Southampton.

17   A1X 0-6-0T 32640 appears at Midhurst to be filmed by the Boulting Brothers for the cinema. Very many years since a 'Terrier' was at Midhurst.

17,18 D5511 works goods trains of 35 'Minfits' round the Edinburgh suburban line.

18   92156 brings the 'Thames-Clyde Express' into Sheffield from Chesterfield.

18   First DMU leaves Buchanan Street for Aberdeen.

19   D11 4-4-0 62660 *Butler Henderson* (41A) is an unexpected sight on the main line with a short train of ECS, between Retford and Newark.

19   45591 *Udaipur* (5A) is a welcome sight at Bath (Green Park), to take out the 10.45am to Liverpool.

19   Q1 0-6-0 33007 arrives at Weymouth with a 10-coach excursion from Luton, having worked the train from London – a long journey for this class of loco.

19   6.5pm Bradford (Forster Square) – Derby arrives in Leeds (City) behind 44238 + 44577, whilst the 1.50pm Manchester – Leeds arrived earlier with the even stranger pairing of Fowler 2-6-4T 42310 + 48276.

19   5023 *Brecon Castle* (85A) provides excitement at Leicester (Central), arriving on a Swansea – Sheffield relief.

19   Shrewsbury's Caprotti 73133 finds itself on piloting duties between Newton Abbot and Plymouth, assisting 6004 *King George III* with the 8.15am Perranporth – Paddington

	and 5065 *Newport Castle* on the 11am Paddington to Penzance, to local astonishment.
21,22	The last remaining E4 2-4-0 62785 pilots 61575 on the 8.20pm arrival into Cambridge from Colchester, on both days. The old order soldiers on!
22	Cafeteria Car excursion, in connection with the British Empire and Commonwealth Games (opened on 18th by Prince Philip), runs from Cardiff to Llanberis (via Hereford and Chester), leaving Cardiff at 6.10am arriving Llanberis 12.45pm in time for the afternoon rowing events on Llyn Padarn.
23	0-6-0PT 1649 noted in Lochgorm Works (hot box after journey from Bristol).
23	60032 *Gannet* (34A) is observed at Ripon working the evening Newcastle to Neville Hill class D freight, of all trains.
24	Derby-built 1160hp Bo-Bo D5000 is inspected at Marylebone by Sir Brian Robertson, Chairman of the British Transport Commission.
25	61136 pilots 45627 *Sierra Leone* through Bedford on the 8.52am Bradford to St Pancras. First time since 1948 that a B1 has appeared on the southern end of the Midland on a regular timetabled working.
25	D5511 visits Aberdeen and heads south on the 8.15pm freight to Edinburgh.
25	WD 2-10-0 90764 (66A) surprisingly heads a down freight from Rugby (Midland).
26	30769 *Sir Balan* works into Eastbourne with a holiday relief from Coventry. First N15 to reach Eastbourne for many years.
26	H15 4-6-0 30521 is assigned to the 10.15am Waterloo – Ilfracombe, but loses time badly. Not a wise choice!
26	D800 *Sir Brian Robertson* takes a special Saturday working of the 'South Wales Pullman' out of Paddington for Cardiff. Train consists of nine cars, required for an extra working at the end of the British Empire Games.
26	12.5pm Newcastle – Colchester is headed out of York by the interesting pairing of 60930 piloting 70035 *Rudyard Kipling* (31B).
26	92174 is the first 9F to reach Scarborough, on the 4.40pm arrival from Glasgow, which it had worked from Newcastle via the Gilling branch. 9F has to go to the Filey Holiday Camp triangle to turn.
26	D5511 works the up and down 'Waverley' between Carlisle and Edinburgh, being stopped on the up run at Tynehead for a test start on the 1 in 70.
26	T9 4-4-0 30120 pilots 34041 *Wilton* over Masbury summit on the 7.35am Bournemouth (West) – Nottingham. A rare pairing on this line.
26	70027 *Rising Star* reaches Leicester (Central) on the Swindon – Sheffield, and returns on the 1.36pm Sheffield – Cardiff. New destination for an 86C loco?
26	62051 is unusual power for the 'Broadsman', Norwich – Cromer.
26	Two Norwich (!) B1s 61046 + 61146 head a Hull – Glasgow special through Armadale on the Bathgate line. How on earth…?
26	8-car formation of Metro-Cammell DMUs leaves Aberdeen at 12.30pm as a special to Edinburgh (Waverley).
28	Ex-'Devon Belle' observation car (M280) is in use as the 'Land Cruise Lounge' at the rear of a North Wales holiday touring train from Rhyl.
28	WR 3-car Cross-Country DMU set (on loan to the ScR) works the 8.5am Aberdeen – Inverness and the 12.45pm return working.
29	Exeter – Plymouth excursion is worked out via Okehampton and back via Newton Abbot with T9 4-4-0 30709 piloting U 2-6-0 31790 throughout.

31	D5511 works a 9-coach special including the NBR Directors' Saloon from Inverness to Wick, returning next day.
31	Outstanding visitor to Brighton is 44043 with an excursion from Luton, first of its class to reach here (not surprisingly!).
U/D	Ex-'Devon Belle' obs. car (Sc 281) in use between Buchanan Street and Oban, ex-'Coronation' obs. cars (E 1719/29) in use between Queen Street, Fort William and between Fort William, Mallaig.

AUGUST 1958

1ST	92098 (of Tyne Dock and complete with air pumps for working Consett iron ore traffic) heads a Gateshead – Neville Hill freight through Ripon.
1,2	As no stock is available for the 3.59pm King's Cross – Cleethorpes relief, a number of 2-car DMU sets are sent from Lincoln to form this train, becoming the first public DMU out of King's Cross. Next day, 5 x 2-car sets form the 6.50am Grimsby – King's Cross and 3.52pm return working.
2	CR 4-4-0 54476 pilots 46205 *Princess Victoria* out of Buchanan Street on the 4.25pm to Inverness, an unprecedented pairing.
2	92062 (52H Tyne Dock) works the 8.15am Newcastle – Heads of Ayr to Carlisle, returning with the 11.15am parcels train to Newcastle.
2	45565 *Victoria* (55A!) somehow reaches Aberdeen, and returns south on the 6.5pm to Buchanan Street. First Holbeck engine here since 45597 on 26/6/53.
2	60129 *Guy Mannering* (52A) is an unlikely choice for the 1.38pm Buffet Car express from Cambridge to King's Cross.
2	1019 *County of Merioneth* (82C) is an equally unlikely arrival at Leicester (Central) on the 11.5am Swindon – Sheffield.
4	(Bank Holiday Monday) 60036 *Colombo* on a Sunderland – York excursion hits the buffer stops in York's bay platform, partially mounting the platform. DMU also hits the buffers on arrival at Whitby Town!
5	D5511 heads the 1.45pm Inverness – Wick freight, another trial run.
5	A 9F passes southbound over Welwyn viaduct with a 24-coach ECS train comprising 3 x 8-car quad-art sets which had been used on Nottingham to Skegness day trips during the Bank Holiday weekend. Worth watching!
6	60836 (64A) heads an up special through Newark, the first ScR V2 seen south of York since the second world war.
6	L&Y 0-8-0 49508 (26A) is a rare arrival in the London area, passing Watford on a southbound freight about 9pm.
6	BRCW 1160hp Bo-Bo D5300 runs acceptance trials, Doncaster to Grantham.
6,7	WR 3-car Cross-Country DMU on loan to the ScR works an excursion from Aberdeen to Keith and back, and a return trip to Inverness next day.
7,8	92100 works a Chesterfield to Ashburys (for Belle Vue) excursion composed entirely of roofboarded 'Starlight Special' stock. This is used again the following day as a relief to the 'South Yorkshireman' between Huddersfield and Marylebone, headed by 92075 as far as Sheffield.
8,10	72004 *Clan Macdonald* (66A) is borrowed by Mirfield shed to work a Huddersfield – Torquay holiday week extra. 72004 + 44474 run LE to Low Moor to pick up the ECS, the pair work

as far as Stockport, with 72004 going on to Shrewsbury (8th). On the 10th 72004 works back to Manchester on the 12.40pm ex-Cardiff, running via Northwich and Altrincham.

9   Fog disrupts flights to the Channel Islands and an extra boat train is operated from Weymouth Quay to Waterloo – a rare working into this terminus.

9   Q1 0-6-0 33028 works an 11-coach inter-regional train through from Kensington to Brighton, an unusual choice of motive power for this train.

9   Stanier 2-6-0 42956 is an extraordinary engine to be seen slogging up the Lickey incline with the northbound 'Pines Express'.

10   H15 4-6-0 30476 is used to haul a troop special throughout from Portsmouth Harbour to Canterbury (West), via Clapham Jct., Orpington and Tonbridge.

11   73131 (84G Shrewsbury) arrives in Ayr (!) on a special from Wakefield.

15   34066 *Spitfire* works a troop train down the GE main line and heads for either Colchester or Parkeston Quay.

15   'Dukedog' 4-4-0 9004 heads the 6pm Afonwen – Portmadoc (the Pwllheli portion of the 'Welshman' from Euston), unusual power for this working.

16   'Cornish Riviera Express' arrives in Paddington behind the unexpected pairing of 5940 *Whitbourne Hall* + 7916 *Mobberley Hall*, due to a 'Warship' failure.

16   60129 *Guy Mannering* pilots 70035 *Rudyard Kipling* out of York on the 12.5pm Newcastle – Colchester, an eye-catching combination.

16   Huddersfield holiday week returning traffic produces 90680 on a Southport – Clayton West extra and 48311 on a Morecambe – Holmfirth special via Ilkley.

16   Interesting V2s at Scarborough include 60855 (14D Neasden) and 60894 (64A), plus 60846 (56B Ardsley) which works the 'Scarborough Flyer' throughout to Kings' Cross.

16   92192 heads the 3pm to Newcastle out of King's Cross, and 92184 takes the 1.52pm to Leeds as far as Grantham, returning with the 13-coach 1.10pm from Edinburgh and topping 90mph down Stoke bank in the process!

16/17   9.25pm Euston – Glasgow stalls on Shap and the 11.10pm Birmingham to Glasgow (46248 *City of Leeds)* is allowed to buffer-up to the rear of the 9.25pm (also with Pacific haulage). The 29 coaches being pushed/pulled by two Pacifics storming Shap is reported to have been 'spectacular'!

19   'Crab' 42781, complete with headboard, works the 'Caledonian' between Stafford and Rugby when 46231 *Duchess of Atholl* has to come off.

19   A2/1 60507 *Highland Chieftain* (64B) is most unusual power for the 2.20pm Liverpool – Newcastle, seen leaving Leeds (City).

20   9.25am Crewe – Perth passes through Larbert behind the exceptional pairing of 60053 *Sansovino* piloting 45704 *Leviathan*!

21   92177 (36A) is a rare arrival at Waverley on a parcels train ex-Newcastle.

22   72009 *Clan Stewart* is a surprise sight at Grange-over-Sands, towards Barrow.

23   70003 *John Bunyan* is 'borrowed' to work the 11.18am King's Cross – Hull, and 70037 *Hereward the Wake* (ex-Works) brings a parcels train into King's Cross, where 'Britannias' are still an unfamiliar sight.

23   60800 *Green Arrow* works the 'Scarborough Flyer' from coast to capital.

23   2-8-0 4706 charges out of Paddington on the 'Royal Duchy'. These locos are rarely used on titled express passenger trains.

24   61641 *Gayton Hall* makes a pleasant change by arriving at Skegness, where B17s are infrequent visitors.

25	8.30am Cardiff – Newcastle noted north of Gloucester headed by the highly unexpected combination of 61925 (36A) piloting 45725 *Repulse*!
26,27	5.18pm Nuneaton (Abbey Street) – New Street is headed by the wandering 61925 (36A), and by 75023 (85A) the following day – variety!
27	Most unusually, A2/3 60515 *Sun Stream* heads the up 'Fair Maid' and A2/3 60521 *Watling Street* is equally rare on the up 'Flying Scotsman'.
27	Heavy freight climbs the 1 in 66 from Bilton Jct. to Harrogate behind the extraordinary pairing of 62759 *The Craven* piloting 90426!
28	61215 *William Henton Carver* (53B) works an excursion from Hull through to Southport (for the Flower Show).
29	GT 18000 reaches Oxford from Paddington with an 8-coach special conveying delegates to the 7th International Symposium on Combustion. Loco returns LE.
29	60852 has the up 'Elizabethan' and 60950 the up 'Flying Scotsman', very rare for both prestige expresses to be without Pacific power.
29-31	70041 *Sir John Moore* exits King's Cross on the 12noon to Newcastle (29th) and is seen at Darlington on the 10.8am King's Cross – Glasgow (30th); then works the 10.25am Newcastle – King's Cross to Grantham on the 31st.
29	45448 (3D) heads the 5.5am Kyle of Lochalsh – Inverness, and 44739 (6G) is at Kyle on the same day, though just how Aston and Llandudno Jct. engines got so far north is a good question!
30	Derby Works Open Day has D5001 / D5700 / 92166 / 70017 *Arrow* on show.
30	CR 4-2-2 123 heads a 2-coach special from Princes Street to Carlisle to commemorate the 70th anniversary of the 'race to the north' of 1888.
30	61249 *FitzHerbert Wright* (30A) brings excursion traffic through to Bognor Regis – first B1 here – from Walthamstow and is serviced at Brighton.
30	A2/3 60524 *Herringbone* departs Sheffield (Midland) with the 8.45am Bristol to Newcastle. LNER Pacifics are uncommon at this Sheffield station.
30	4.47pm Selby – York stopper has, at the rear, an SR van labelled 'Newspaper Traffic Ilfracombe – Waterloo'.
30	D602 *Bulldog* appears at Slateford (Princes Street – Carstairs line) on trials.
30	4-4-0 40660 (5A) works all the way from Crewe to Carlisle with the 10.30am parcels train, a rare length of journey (141 miles) for a solo 4-4-0 nowadays.
30	L 4-4-0 31766 is still trusted with the 3.6pm Victoria – Ramsgate, the all-Pullman 'Kentish Belle'.
31	4-car DMU arrives in Bognor Regis as an excursion from Southend and Tilbury – the first appearance of a DMU at Bognor.
31	Big surprise at Darlington when 46143 *The South Staffordshire Regiment* arrives with a Sunday excursion from Manchester via Leeds and York.
31	2-6-0 6351 heads a PW train down the Swanage branch as far as Corfe Castle, a rare WR encroachment onto a SR branch.
U/D	46238 *City of Carlisle* uses the wheel-drop facility at Bescot shed, an unprecedented visitor.
U/D	Ivatt 2-6-2T 41224 still lettered 'British Railways'. Last on the LMR? 2-6-2T 6147 still labelled 'GWR' and 2-6-0 6344 has the GWR monogram on the tender!
U/D	72007 *Clan Mackintosh* powers the 9.50am (SO) Edinburgh – Sheffield from Carlisle to Leeds, where 72006 *Clan Mackenzie* takes over. A 'Clan-to-Clan' handover must be rare,

anywhere, and consecutively numbered even rarer!

U/D   Order is placed with NB Loco. Co. for a further 33 'Warships' (D605-37).

U/D   In connection with the electrification of the East Coast main line, three overbridges between Selby and York have been raised.

SEPTEMBER 1958

6TH   D5506 reaches Luton (Bute Street) on a football special from Upminster.

6   Robertsbridge/Bodiam/Northiam shuttle service (for hop pickers) – 2 coaches and a van – is worked by 0-6-0 diesel shunter 11223.

6   34048 *Crediton* travels through to Ashton Gate (Bristol) with a football excursion from Brighton.

6   45613 *Kenya* (6E Chester West) comes into Bristol on the 8.45am Liverpool to Penzance via the North & West route and the Severn Tunnel.

6   Flooding causes Queen Street – Waverley trains to be diverted through Bathgate (Upper). A3s 60089/96 and A2 60535 (on the 'Queen of Scots') pass this way, plus 72003 (most unusually) on an Edinburgh Festival special.

7   61203 takes an excursion from Cambridge through to Basingstoke for the Air Display, and D201 heads the 'Farnborough Flyer' from Leeds (Central) all the way to Farnborough.

8   61212 unexpectedly arrives in King's Cross on the 'Fair Maid'.

8   MR 0-6-0 58123 (11A Barrow) is a rare sight at Preston on a ballast train.

9-11   'Yorkshire Pullman' departs London on successive days behind 60914, 60800 *Green Arrow* and 60950. Choice, or shortage of available Pacifics?

10   L&Y 0-8-0 49515 (26A) is a rare visitor to Shrewsbury, on freight ex-Crewe.

10   Restored 4-4-0 3440 *City of Truro* hauls the WR General Manager (K.W.C. Grand) from Cardiff to Swindon, in the Bristol District Inspection Saloon.

12-14   14,000 people attend an exhibition of rolling stock at Wood Green (Borough Charter celebrations). On view; 60022/92196/68846/67352/D208/D5300.

13   5089 *Westminster Abbey* forms a rare combination, piloting 45632 *Tonga* into Shrewsbury from Wolverhampton on the 9.10am Paddington – Birkenhead.

13   92169 (36A) passes through Ripon on the 9.38am (SO) South Shields to Manchester, the first 9F on a passenger working on this line.

13   Last day of steam operation on the Gleneagles – Crieff line brings the sight of three CR 4-4-0s in Crieff at the same time; 54500 on the 8.50am from Gleneagles, 54495 on the 10.2am to Gleneagles and 54476 shunting the yard before departing on the 9.50am freight to Perth.

15   D207 takes the inaugural 6-car Pullman version of the 'Master Cutler' away from Sheffield (Victoria) to King's Cross. The new loco headboard is unveiled by Sir Frederick Pickworth, the current Master Cutler.

16   8.30am Cardiff – Newcastle is double-headed north of Chesterfield by the strange pairing of 62057 + 73011, seen passing Dronfield.

17   72009 *Clan Stewart*, on loan to Stratford (from Kingmoor) works the 'Essex Coast Express' out of Liverpool Street.

18   46123 *Royal Irish Fusilier* is noted at Upton-by-Chester heading an up freight off the Chester – Birkenhead line, new ground for a 'Royal Scot'.

19	LNW 0-8-0 49158 (5C Stafford) is unusual power for the 6.30pm Neville Hill to Red Bank ECS train, as far as Sowerby Bridge.
19,20	W1 4-6-4 60700 is a unique visitor to Sheffield (Victoria), bringing in the 6.40am from Doncaster on both days, returning light engine.
20	'Trains Illustrated' magazine 'Westcountryman' excursion runs Waterloo to Plymouth, back to Paddington; 35017 *Belgian Marine* to Exeter, T9 4-4-0s 30712 + 30726 to Plymouth (SR route), then 35023 *Holland-Afrika Line* to Paddington (WR route throughout – Pullmans over Hemerdon!) whilst the T9s work the 4.32pm North Road – Exeter (St Davids) service train (WR route). Exciting!
20	46102 *Black Watch* (Polmadie) pilots 45563 *Australia* into Leeds on the 5pm Liverpool – Newcastle. 66A locos are rare in Leeds, especially from this route.
20	2-6-2T 5509 works the 1.3pm Andover Jct. to Southampton (Terminus), a type not previously seen here before.
21	D11 4-4-0 62660 *Butler Henderson* appears at Wakefield (Kirkgate) on an enthusiasts' special, not a class to be seen here in normal circumstances.
21	Caprotti 73142 reaches Eastbourne on a special from Bedford.
22	C 0-6-0 31588 handles the 6.15pm London Bridge – Tunbridge Wells.
24	U1 2-6-0 31906 (73A) puts in a surprise appearance on ECS workings at Stonebridge Park Carriage Depot, outside Euston!
26	45706 *Express* is seen oddly paired with a black tender, ex-8F 2-8-0.
27	41123 (85E) takes the Talyllyn Railway Preservation Society special out of Paddington (first Compound here), as far as Shrewsbury.
27	Up 'Queen of Scots' arrives in Newcastle behind J39 0-6-0 64924, having replaced 60539 *Bronzino* at Alnmouth.
27	Fowler 2-6-4T 42477 pilots 60121 *Silurian* on the 9am Liverpool – Newcastle between Leeds and Harrogate, a really unusual combination! 42477 (now bunker-first) pilots 62759 *The Craven* back to Leeds via Wetherby on the 12.30pm from Harrogate.
27	45711 *Courageous* (67A!) reaches Scarborough on the 11.14am arrival from Bradford, returning west at 12.30pm piloted by 62747 *The Percy*.
28	Scarborough – Blackpool return excursion has problems! Although booked to set down at Cross Gates, the train is routed via the through road here, forcing passengers to detrain onto the ballast! Further on, at Kirkham Abbey, the signal box is found to be closed along with the level crossing gates, and the crew have to knock up the signalman before the train can proceed!
U/D	80103/137 are transferred to King's Cross for outer suburban work.
U/D	D5300 also works trials between Broad Street and Welwyn Garden City.
U/D	0-6-0PT 3711 (oil burner) is on loan to the CM&EE, Test Plant, Swindon.

OCTOBER 1958

1ST	D5700/01 take a test train from Hendon to Gushetfaulds (Glasgow), an overnight run of about 10½ hours, a prelude to the proposed 'Condor' service.
2	BTH 800hp Bo-Bo D8209 is seen on acceptance trials Sheffield – Appleby on 10 coaches. All the class undergo this procedure.
3	D5302 passes through Snow Hill *en route* to Doncaster from Smethwick for acceptance trials. Other class-members do the same.

4   60034 *Lord Faringdon* (34A) surprisingly arrives at Leeds (City) on the 5.10pm from York, leaving again on the 5pm Liverpool – Newcastle.

4   70004 *William Shakespeare* (9E) ex-Works, heads the Barrow/Workington portion of the 11.35am from Euston, staying overnight at Workington – a first.

8   D34 4-4-0 62471 *Glen Falloch* pilots 60068 *Sir Visto* between Edinburgh and Hawick on the 9.25pm Waverley – St Pancras, a nostalgic combination.

8   45725 *Repulse* (41C Millhouses) is an unexpected guest in Gorton Works.

9   D5700/01 appear at Manchester (Central) on the 12.5pm to St Pancras.

11   Three 'Top Shed' Pacifics are seen at Cambridge together; 60122 *Curlew*, 60021 *Wild Swan* and 60103 *Flying Scotsman*.

11-13 Ex-GT 18100 emerges from Metropolitan Vickers' works at Stockton (11th), now renumbered E1000 as an A1A-A1A 2500hp electric loco for driver training between Manchester and Crewe. Passes York towed by 90377 (12th), reaching Crewe in a freight train from Manchester on the 13th.

12   'Hampshire' DEMU sets are used on the Fawley branch for the first time.

13   92173 arrives in York on the down 'Talisman', having replaced 60025 *Falcon* at Newark, and surprisingly not replaced itself at Doncaster.

14   'Patriot' 45517 is a most unusual visitor to Bradford (Exchange) on the 10.31am from Manchester, returning there on the 2.15pm.

14-30 0-6-0PT 9770 (82D Westbury, on loan to the SR) goes to Hither Green, then on to Folkestone for successful tests on the Harbour branch, leaving on the 28th for ECS trials between Waterloo and Clapham Junction on 29th, 30th.

16   Royal train comes into Carlisle behind a brace of Perth '5's 44704 + 44721, the ECS being removed by an immaculate LNW 0-8-0 49392.

16   Fell 4-8-4 10100 catches fire in Manchester (Central) whilst waiting to take out the 12.25pm to Derby. Fire Brigade summoned, loco replaced by steam.

18   46102 *Black Watch*, 46222 *Queen Mary* and 70052 *Firth of Tay* (all 66A) work through to Shrewsbury from Glasgow, on football excursions to Cardiff for the Wales v Scotland match. Polmadie engines are rare in Shrewsbury.

19   E1 4-4-0 31019 leaves Paddington (!) with the LCGB-organised 'Rother Valley Limited' to Tenterden, Bexhill, Newhaven and back to Victoria.

20   Crosti 92022 noted at Luton with the 12noon Bradford – St Pancras.

20   CR 0-4-4T 55229 is a rare visitor to Waverley on an engineer's saloon.

22   Ex-Works 70043 *Lord Kitchener* brings the 7.43am from York into Leeds (a rare working for a 'Britannia') then pilots 46164 *The Artists' Rifleman* from Leeds to Manchester on the 9.55am Newcastle – Liverpool.

22   60117 *Bois Roussel* passes Ely on the diverted 8.25am Leeds – King's Cross.

22,23 D603 *Bulldog* conducts trials on the Carstairs line from Edinburgh.

23   60017 *Silver Fox* appears on Newark shed after failing on a fitted freight.

23   Stanier 2-6-4T 42553 works the 7.50am Leeds – Stockton and the 1.53pm return ex-Darlington. Has this type been to Stockton or Darlington before?

27   Cadbury's trade excursion from South Wales to Bournville is headed by 70018 *Flying Dutchman* via Gloucester and the Lickey, a 7MT first?

28   60029 *Woodcock* arrives in King's Cross with the all-Pullman 'Master Cutler' after a diesel failure earlier in the roster. Train had left Sheffield behind a B1, which also failed, at Grantham.

28-31   D5303 (34B, on loan to Leith Central) passes through Newcastle *en route* from Doncaster to Leith, works the 10.12am Waverley – Perth (29th), and arrives at Kyle of Lochalsh on the 31st.

29,30   0-6-0 shunter 15229 (73C, on loan to the ScR) is seen at work on the Speyside goods and the 4.10am Keith – Buckie freight next day. (Subsequently taken to Glasgow, and is noted passing Lenzie behind a CR 0-6-0 on 7 Nov.)

U/D   D8006 (1D, on loan to 61A) is tested on GNS territory including the Fraserburgh and Deeside lines. (Moves to southern Scotland in November.)

U/D   76001 (66B Motherwell) is briefly loaned to Skipton, and works to Ilkley, Leeds and Bradford, a previously unseen type at these places.

NOVEMBER 1958

1ST   0-4-2T 1462 arrives at 72A. Trials on the Lyme Regis branch take place 11th, 12th with 2-coach then 3-coach trains. Trials are unsuccessful.

1   30926 *Repton* heads Dover – Victoria boat train, unusual power nowadays.

3   On loan D8006 works the 3.35pm Dundee – Carlisle freight, then LE to 5B.

8   D16 62582 heads the 9am Liverpool Street – Bishops Stortford stopper. Sightings of 4-4-0s are increasingly rare in this terminus.

11,12   West Coast diversions are in force between Stafford and Crewe, trains running via Wellington, Shrewsbury. 'Caledonian/Shamrock/Emerald Isle Express/Ulster Express/Northern Irishman' all pass this way, with their normal motive power. Next day, down 'Royal Scot' runs via Stoke-on-Trent headed by 46224 *Princess Alexandra* (66A), a type usually banned from this route.

12   3-train collision occurs near Swindon, blocking all lines. 5.30am Paddington to Penzance via Bristol (6010 *King Charles I* + 7006 *Lydford Castle*) is diverted via Newbury, Devizes to Bathampton. 'Kings' rarely come this way, and this combination is uncommon east of Newton Abbot. Down 'South Wales Pullman' and up 'Capitals United Express' are both run via Evesham.

12   34089 *602 Squadron* slips to a stand on Grosvenor bank with the 6.10pm from Victoria and is pushed up by the following electric service.

12   Fowler 2-6-4T 42411 reaches Thirsk, unusually, on the 5.25am ex-Harrogate.

13   A5 4-6-2T 69820 arrives in Derby (Midland) with the 2.52pm from Lincoln. Former GC engines are not often seen in Derby.

15   'Crab' 42898 (24B Rose Grove) appears on Tyseley shed after working a football special from Blackburn for the match v West Bromwich Albion.

15   Lauder branch sees its 'first & last' train of bogie stock as 78049 heads a 2-coach special from Fountainhall to mark the closure of this Light Railway.

15   Kensington Olympia contains, at the same time, examples of all of the 'Big Four' Companies; GWR 'Hall'/ SR 'King Arthur'/ LMS '5'/ LNER B1.

16   0-6-0T 1505 turns up at Oswestry (!), displaying an 81A shedplate.

19   The unlikely pairing of 60825 + 46107 *Argyll and Sutherland Highlander* enters Carlisle (where the V2 is removed) on the 11am Glasgow – Manchester.

19,20   Blockage to the main line causes King's Cross trains to run from Peterborough via March, Ely and Cambridge to Stratford or Liverpool Street, from where the down 'Tees-Tyne Pullman' leaves behind D201 at its scheduled King's Cross time of 4.50pm, and the up 'Queen of Scots' arrives here. B2 61644 *Earlham Hall* is surprise power for the up 'Aberdonian' (10.11am at Temple Mills) as is 61840 on the up 'West Riding' (1.6pm). St Pancras puts on a non-Pullman substitute for the down 'Master Cutler' behind 73002 at 7.30pm (19th). Next day, the up 'Aberdonian' has 62016 at Temple Mills, 61653 *Huddersfield Town* has the 7.5pm from Aberdeen and 70011 *Hotspur* (32A) is noted at Knebworth in the afternoon.

20	Derailment at Liverpool Street causes the 8.30am to Norwich to be formed of an 8-coach Ipswich non-vestibuled suburban set!
20	E1 4-4-0 31019 backs onto a 3-coach Inspection train at Victoria, brought in by W 2-6-4T 31914, a notable sight.
23	Monthly excursion from Derby arrives in Newcastle behind 45610 without nameplates. Formerly *Gold Coast* it is scheduled to be renamed *Ghana* at a ceremony at Euston on 12 December.
27	Up 'Master Cutler' is worked throughout by a B1, and 60029 *Woodcock* heads the 11.20am down Pullman to Sheffield. (D2xx is rostered for these).
28	60531 *Barham* works the 4pm Aberdeen – Camperdown coal empties instead of the usual WD 2-8-0!
28	72004 *Clan Macdonald* (66A) brings an express from Barrow/Workington into Euston, where Polmadie 'Clans' rarely reach.
29	A pair of Co-Bo's is seen on both the up and down 'Thames-Clyde Express', the first such diesels seen on this service.
29	62718 *Kinross-shire* noted banking 62743 *The Cleveland* between Duddington and Morningside Road on the Edinburgh suburban line. Unusual!
29	Football excursion from Bristol to Birmingham is routed via Gloucester (Central)/Ledbury/Worcester/Stourbridge Jct., a unique occurrence for a Cafeteria Car train to be sent this way.
U/D	80117 pilots 60086 *Gainsborough* out of Leeds (City) on the 9.50am (SO) Manchester – Newcastle, a new double-heading variation?
U/D	2pm at King's Lynn station; four (!) D16 4-4-0s appear on passenger trains off the Ely and Hunstanton lines, 62566/82 and 62606/18. Unrepeatable?
U/D	SR 0-6-0 shunter 15229 (73C) is now noted at Eastfield, ex-Kittybrewster.
U/D	D5303 (on loan to the ScR), covers Glasgow – Fort William, the Highland lines from Inverness, plus Aberdeen – Glasgow/Edinburgh.
U/D	Special high-speed LE tests are made between Twyford and Maidenhead with D800 *Sir Brian Robertson*, D602 *Bulldog* and GT 18000 with speeds in excess of 100mph recorded. Damage to rail ends by diesel locos is being investigated by Derby Research Dept.

DECEMBER 1958

2ND	61875 (52B) unexpectedly reaches Perth on the 8.50am ex-Waverley.
3	45692 *Cyclops* (63A) leaves Rosyth Dockyard with the 5.5pm for Waverley.
3	45721 *Impregnable* (5A) works the 7.20am Carlisle – Newcastle and 12.20pm return, first 'Jubilee' to travel this line!?
5	Special Pullman train is run from Waterloo to Fawley when the Minister of Fuel opens new chemical plant.

6	A W class 2-6-4T appears at Rowfant with a special train of empty oil tanks from Norwood. The W is on its way to Brighton for weighing.
6	44713 (5B) reaches Newcastle with a Stockport – Blyth football special.
6	48080 pilots 61230 on a well-loaded freight on the Laisterdyke – Shipley (Windhill) goods branch, the heaviest train for years on this GN line.
6	4-4-0 40411 (16A) is a very unexpected guest on Tilbury shed.
7	72003 *Clan Fraser* (66A) heads a special freight from Garston to Dringhouses and is serviced on York shed – where Polmadie locos are extremely rare.
9	90693 undergoes clearance tests on the S&D line.
10	70053 *Moray Firth* (55A) works (on test, with an Inspector) the 8.42am Bradford (Forster Square) through to Scarborough – new territory for a 'Britannia', which only just fits on the 60' turntable. Returns on the 12.30pm to York, followed by the 3.10pm to Leeds and the 4.5pm slow to Bradford.
11	4-4-0 40643 is a rare sight passing through Waverley station, taking a crane from Thornton to St Margarets.
13	5.10pm Newcastle – Liverpool (Exchange) departs with 60091 *Captain Cuttle* piloting 60153 *Flamboyant*, a rare pairing of Pacifics.
13	NB Loco. Co. 1000hp diesel hydraulic B-B D6300 pauses at Cannock Road, Wolverhampton *en route* from Glasgow to Swindon, for acceptance tests.
13	K1/1 2-6-0 61997 *MacCailin Mor* (65J Fort William) is never-to-be-repeated power for the Immingham – Wath mineral empties!
13	(Week commencing) 'Jinty' 0-6-0T 47542 is used three times to handle the Templecombe – Blandford pick-up goods, an unprecedented experiment, not repeated!
14	92250 is the 7331st and last steam engine to be built at Crewe.
14	Monthly excursion from Derby to Newcastle brings the rare visit of 73167 (50A) to Tyneside, an under-represented class here.
16	H 0-4-4T 31279 heads a parcels special from Brighton into Portsmouth, a most uncommon type here.
16,20	60159 *Bonnie Dundee* (64B), ex-Works, is a welcome visitor to Leeds (Central) on the 10.20am from King's Cross. Four days later it makes a striking appearance at Lincoln on the 10.10am York – Yarmouth.
17	0-6-0 2279 is observed at Blisworth, on the West Coast main line, presumably having worked a freight over the SMJ connection.
18	NB Loco. Co. 1000hp Bo-Bo D6100 is towed north through Newcastle by 90047, heading back to the makers.
19	30939 *Leatherhead* is a surprise arrival at Horsham with an excursion to Kensington via Three Bridges.
20	62036 (30A) is a stranger spotted on Old Oak Common (81A).
20	Sentinel Y1 0-4-0T 68138 brings the rare sight of a 67C (Ayr) loco to Darlington, arriving for repair via Hurlford and Carlisle.
21	3.43pm to Euston leaves Northampton behind the unlikely pairing of 46105 *Cameron Highlander* (66A) + 46117 *Welsh Guardsman* (55A).
22	61008 *Kudu* reaches Swindon on a through working from the GC line.
22	70015 *Apollo* (9E), ex-works from Crewe, arrives in Sowerby Bridge with the 6.11pm Normanton – Red Bank ECS via Halifax, retiring LE to Huddersfield.
23	More clearance tests are carried out on the S&D, this time with 0-6-0PT 3604 and 0-6-0

	2215 running as a LE pair.
23	WD 2-10-0 601 (Longmoor Military Railway) is hauled south through Carlisle by 48722 (3A) after spending several months in store at Kingmoor.
24	45289 + 46228 *Duchess of Rutland* work the 10.5am to Birmingham through from Glasgow, it being most unusual for the pilot engine to do the entire run.
27,29	61013 *Topi* + 'Crab' 42733 form an unusual combination on the afternoon ECS from York to Manchester, and 61013 is seen two days later at Runcorn with, probably, a relief to the 2.50pm Liverpool – Plymouth.
28	60528 *Sun Chariot* (62B), ex-Works, takes the 8.20pm to Edinburgh out of King's Cross, where Dundee engines are always rarities.
29	A1/1 60113 *Great Northern* heads the up 'Master Cutler' through Newark in lieu of the diagrammed D2xx diesel.
29	4-4-0 40700 + 73047 (both 82F Bath Green Park) enter New Street with the down 'Devonian', S&D locos very rarely work through to Birmingham.
29	5.49pm Victoria – Groombridge is delayed for 20min at Sanderstead while police are called to remove an unauthorised person from the footplate.
30	Birkenhead 'Crab' 42778 finds itself at Doncaster at the head of an excursion for Belle Vue.
U/D	0-6-0PT 7428 still bears the legend 'GWR' in shaded letters.
U/D	Bo-Bo 2552hp DC electric E5000 is completed at Doncaster on the 24th, and is seen being towed through Newark by 60852 on 31st. Leaves Ferme Park hauled by C2X 0-6-0 32447 for the trip to Durnsford Road in early January.
U/D	Brighton Works is now devoted almost entirely to the motorcar industry (manufacturing 'Bubble Cars').

JANUARY 1959

1ST	New Year surprise at London Bridge when ECS arrives as a 16-coach rake and blocks platform road exits. (12-CEP unit had inadvertently coupled to a 4-HAP during shunting at Streatham Hill!).
1	Adams 4-4-2T 30584 is seen inappropriately engaged in the task of banking trains between the two Exeter stations!
2	'Deltic' is a total failure in traffic (for the first time?) and has to be removed from the 'Lancastrian' at Rugby, where a pair of 'Crabs' take over.
3	12.53pm Charing Cross – Deal via Dover is headed by a brace of 'Schools' 4-4-0s, most unexpectedly.
4	4-6-0 30476 runs Haywards Heath – Eastleigh via Hove with damaged 'Hastings' units. First H15 on the Brighton main line?
5	'Crab' 42933 (5B) is an unusual choice for the 5.25pm Carlisle – Niddrie freight over the Waverley route.
5	The newly introduced Sleeping Car service between Paddington and Milford Haven runs non-stop (in each direction) between London and Swansea, the first service on record to cover this journey without intermediate stops.
5	Diesel shunter D3496 works one of the services on the Witham – Braintree branch when the railbus fails.
5	2.50pm to Northampton leaves Euston with 80043 piloting 70031 *Byron*.

6   60137 *Redgauntlet* (52A) reaches Boston on a New England – Frodingham train of empty bolster wagons. Returns LE to Peterborough.

7   MR 0-6-0 58115 (11A Barrow) works through Shipley on a Neville Hill to Skipton freight, a rare sight here.

7,12   D8208 also passes through Shipley LE from Toton to Polmadie, and later sets off from 66A towards Kittybrewster on freight (12th). Subsequently on loan to Thornton Jct. (62A) at the end of the month.

8,9   Passenger trains run again between Crook and Tow Law for the first time in two years as roads are blocked by snow. L1 2-6-4T and 76049 employed on 8th, 77003 + 78016 double-head next day – a rare combination.

10   In connection with the FA Cup tie at Norwich, the 11.30am ECS Melton Constable – Weybourne, 12.13pm Weybourne – Norwich (City) and 1.35pm City – Melton (usually 2-car DMUs) are worked by 61654 *Sunderland*. First visit of a B17 to Norwich (City)? More football excursions arrive at Norwich (Thorpe) behind 44776, 44809 and 'Crab' 42903, unusual types here.

11   Diversions cause the down 'Royal Scot' and 'Mancunian' expresses to pass through Wolverhampton (High Level) behind 10201/3 and 70033 *Charles Dickens* respectively.

12,14,16   'Deltic' transfers from West Coast to East Coast and takes two brakevans between Manchester and Leeds (via Huddersfield) *en route* to York. Appears at Leeds (Central) on clearance tests (14th) and at Berwick on 16th hauling an observation saloon. Proves to be out gauge on the NE Region!

13/14   61163 sets off from Newark with a 'removal special' to Grampound Road with the complete stock of a farm, due 3.50am next day in Cornwall. 3-hour stopover at Chippenham allows cattle to be milked, fed and watered.

13   Ferryhill shed (61B) contains three Carlisle engines, 61239/90 (12C) and 'Crab' 42907 (12A). 45478 (60A) is also an unusual visitor.

13,14   61145 (36A) works 8.20am Blackpool (Central) – Rochdale, and 3.10pm Manchester (Victoria) – Blackpool on both days, most unusual on regular, non-excursion traffic.

13,14,17   Full train loads of fuel oil from Hutton Cranswick (NER) to Massingham (M&GN) are worked from Spalding as follows; 13th 2-6-0s 43082 + 61766, 14th 61766 + J6 0-6-0 64265, 17th 61766 + 43110 each train consisting of 20 tanks, 4 runners, two brakevans.

14   WR track testing vehicle covers the New Street/Redditch/Ashchurch route, and the following day a Cravens 3-car DMU is tested over this line.

14   A DMU also undergoes trials on the South Devon banks – rare sight here.

16,17   Exhibition of rolling stock held at the new Lincoln Holme Goods Shed runs to 45 vehicles, including 60022 *Mallard*, 60881, 92201, 67352, D5309 and, surprisingly DC electric 26015, plus coaching stock. 7,600 people attend.

19   Extraordinary conditions of sea fret and mist, without parallel in the Scarborough Station Master's 45 years experience, produces rails so greasy that the service on the coastal line to Whitby comes almost to a standstill. The 7.28am ex-Middlesbrough slips to a stand near Hawsker, despite the 2-car DMU (both power cars) being piloted by 62751 *The Albrighton*. Even 2-6-4T 42084 (on 2 coaches) + 62751 run out of sand attempting to climb Ravenscar bank. Northbound, the 12.52pm from Scarborough departed with 62770 *The Puckeridge* on 2 coaches, but eventually reached Whitby at 4.40pm with one coach and 62770 + 62751!

20   Fare-paying passengers have their first trip in a BR 25kV EMU when a derailment at Longsight causes the prototype Tilbury line set (on loan to the Manchester – Crewe scheme) to be used for an improvised service between Wilmslow and Mauldeth Road.

21	90732 (36A) and still carrying the name *Vulcan*, is seen at Saltley.
22	90125 has a trial on the S&D with the 11am freight from Bath.
23	10.52am from Crail is worked between Thornton Jct. and Waverley by 'Crab' 42837 (12A), ex-Works from St Rollox. Unusual arrival at Waverley!
24	30906 *Sherborne* reaches Alton on a 10-coach football special (of WR stock) from West Drayton. 30906 is turned and watered at Aldershot.
25	'0395' class 0-6-0 30567 is a strange sight at Victoria, with an excursion to Gosport (which includes two Pullmans). Loco only reaches Guildford!
27	A2/1 60509 *Waverley* (64B) heads the 3.30pm 'Postal' from Aberdeen. First time on record that a Haymarket Pacific has been used on this train.
28	A Renfrew school makes history by chartering the ScR's TV train for an educational tour routed Glasgow/Oban/Callander/Stirling/Glasgow, with commentary by the school staff.
28-7 Feb	Queen Victoria's Saloon is shown at the Furniture Exhibition at Earls Court. Moved by rail from Wolverton, then by road for the final stage.
31	Ivatt 2-6-0 43083 enters King's Cross on the 9.25am from Peterborough.
U/D	80117/8 (both bunker-first) bring the up 'Harrogate Sunday Pullman' into Leeds (Central), and 2-6-4T 42553 is seen on the 'Yorkshire Pullman' between Harrogate and Leeds, highly unusual workings.
U/D	D6300-2 are tested as twin units between Swindon and Gloucester.
U/D	Lincoln shed receives MR 0-4-4Ts 58065/85 an interesting transfer!
U/D	'Deltic' is re-allocated to Hornsey; is prohibited from several platforms at King's Cross, and is confined to King's Cross – Leeds workings. Any major problems to be rectified at Stratford. Suffers engine failure and is sent back to EE for a replacement No.1 power unit.
U/D	Residents at Eaglescliffe are notified that they will lose part of their gardens due to electrification of the line!

FEBRUARY 1959

2ND	J15 0-6-0 65457 (31A) breaks new ground by working the 10.30am stopping train from Nottingham (Midland) to Leicester (London Road), via Trent.
2	D8208 passes southbound through Hawick on freight after trials in Fife.
3	61193 hauls new Bo-Bo DC electric E5001 through Newark, bound for the SR. (E5002 also heads south on the 24th, ex-Doncaster Works).
3	7818 *Granville Manor* (84B Oxley) makes an unusual trip to Birkenhead (Woodside) on the 11.43am from Chester.
3	Q6 0-8-0 63397 (51C West Hartlepool) is a surprise at Newark with up freight.
5	42271 (64C) appears on Ferryhill shed. Last LMS 2-6-4T here was in May 1949.
5	10.5am Bristol – Swindon has D6301/2 (in tandem) hauling 2 coaches, 2 vans.
5-8	20 specials for the Scotland v Wales rugby match arrive in Edinburgh from the south, 15 at Princes Street, 5 into Waverley. Those into Princes Street did not change engines at Carlisle and bring eleven '5's and seven 'Jubilees' from diverse English sheds to Dalry Road. CR 4-4-0 54478 is brought out of store to heat the Sleeping Cars for the returning specials. The most interesting arrival in Waverley is from Queen Street, powered by 44975 (65J) + J36 0-6-0 64636 (64E Polmont) – a spectacular combination! The return to Pantyffynon is headed out of Shrewsbury by 0-6-0 2220 + 48760, and the return to Treherbert leaves Crewe behind 5992 *Horton Hall* (83B Taunton!). Scheduled Waverley

Route services during this period are worked largely by '5's donated by Carlisle depots, 44901/39/93, 45248/96, 45351 being noted.

6   60845 (50A) shows up at Low Moor shed after working a special train of 17 bogie vans ex-Aberdeen to Bradford (from York).

6   6.10pm Paddington – Birkenhead is wrongly routed at Ashendon Jct and proceeds to Grendon Underwood (8 miles 'off course' on the GC line) before the crew realise they don't know where they are! Train is hauled back to the junction and then heads off in the right direction.

6   61993 *Loch Long* (65A) is a rarity on the Waverley route, with the 10.15am Portobello – Carlisle freight.

9   10.25am from St Pancras arrives in Manchester (Central) with 45712 *Victory* unexpectedly piloted by 61053 (50A).

9   62056 is most unlikely power for the 7.35am Nottingham – Bristol.

9   Manchester (Oxford Road) station is adorned with the 16' long, 58-letter name board from Llanfair PG on the forecourt canopy. This University Rag stunt is removed with difficulty on the 12th, as non-reversible screws are used!

10   61652 *Darlington* is a surprise visitor to Broad Street on the 7.29am from Hertford (North), as this class is not thought to be passed to work into here.

10   Two brand-new Co-Bo diesels from Metropolitan Vickers Works at Stockton pass through York station LE *en route* to Derby.

13   Van train on the London – Brighton main line is powered by the consecutive pairing of 30900 *Eton* + 30901 *Winchester*, heading south. Rare!

13   D603 *Conquest* + D604 *Cossack*, returning to their Glasgow makers for attention, are towed through the Midlands by a 'Hall'.

14   5th Round FA Cup matches give rise to the following; 45137/9 reach Ipswich for the tie with Luton, 61141/77 and 61381 appear at New Street with Notts Forest fans. The Spurs v Norwich game attracts 17 specials for away supporters, 7 x B1s, 7 x K3s, 2 x B17s , 1 x 7MT are used . 173 coaches are required to carry over 10,000 people. Match drawn, Norwich win the replay and go to Sheffield in the next round (see 28th).

15   O4 2-8-0 63626 (36C Frodingham) is found, distinctly out of place, on King's Cross shed! Heads a rake of empty wagons north next day.

15   2-6-2T 5153 (83A!) works the 4.53pm High Wycombe – Aylesbury 7-coach train, most unusual.

16   WR 3-car DMU is at Weymouth for a week on crew training.

16   D801 *Vanguard* works the up and down 'Bristolian' – its first diesel haulage.

17   60920 (64B) heads the 3.25am Niddrie – Oxley freight, but is not relieved at Carlisle and works through to Warrington and, eventually to Chester, where the spectacle is treated with some disbelief by shed staff!

21   N 2-6-0 31880 is an extremely rare sight on the Oxted line (north of Birchden Jct.) with the 9.55am Brighton – Victoria.

22   HR 4-4-0 54398 *Ben Alder* is noted intact on Forfar shed along with *Gordon Highlander* (ex-62277) and about a dozen others, mostly in store.

22   44906 (8A) pays an infrequent visit for this type to Snow Hill, on an excursion from Liverpool.

23   61838 (2F) penetrates the southern end of the West Coast main line when working a down train of iron ore hoppers through Leighton Buzzard.

27   Engineering works dictates that a 2-car DMU connection is provided between Polegate and Eastbourne – first passenger carrying DMU to reach Eastbourne.

28   FA Cup 6th round match Sheffield United v Norwich City brings 12 specials to Sheffield. Five go to Midland (4 x B1s + K3) having been routed over the M&GN on its last day of operation. Seven go to Victoria (B1 + 6 x K3s) the last to arrive being entirely 1st class. 130 coaches required. Match drawn, Norwich win replay and meet Luton at White Hart Lane. (See March).

28   (Week ending) Stanier 2-6-0 42983 (5B) seen on the 10.8am Sheffield (Victoria) – Nottingham (Victoria). A first on this route for this class?

U/D   60836/63, appear at Wellingborough shed for repair, from the GC line.

U/D   Ex-'Devon Belle' Pullman observation car (M280M in maroon/cream) is exhibited for a few days in Euston. Evidence of its previous use as the 'Land Cruise Lounge' on North Wales excursion trains is obliterated by plain cream.

MARCH 1959

2ND   45486 (62B) puts in a rare appearance for this class on the Ballater branch with ECS (Only 45162 (61B) previously reported here, 18 months ago).

4   60532 *Blue Peter* heads the up 'Postal' between Aberdeen and Perth, returning on the 5.30pm ex-Buchanan Street, the 'Saint Mungo'.

4   D5003, running light, fails near Canterbury and is pushed to Faversham by a 3-coach instruction train, which is following. Cab of D5003 is full of men under training, one of whom accidentally turned off a main switch. The fitter from Ashford, sent next day, simply switches the engine on, starting at once!

5   3F 0-6-0 43394 (9G Gorton) is a strange visitor to Brackley (Central).

6   Derailment at Inverkeithing diverts Edinburgh – Aberdeen services via Alloa. 60161 *North British* passes on the 10am ex-Waverley, and 60532 *Blue Peter* on the 7.5am from Aberdeen, welcome sights at Alloa.

6   Ivatt 2-6-0 46467 heads the 2.15pm Liverpool Street – Cambridge parcels. Rare type to be seen in this London terminus.

7   W 2-6-4T 31920 is noted between Wimbledon and West Croydon with 21 French and Italian vans loaded with Lambretta scooters.

7   Caprotti 73139 (15C Leicester Midland) makes an unlikely appearance at York with the 7.23pm Birmingham – Newcastle.

7,8   'Deltic' pays a visit to Stratford diesel depot for bogie examination following derailment in Hornsey yard.

8   Due to resignalling work at Glasgow (Central) the up 'Royal Scot' departs from Buchanan Street behind the unexpected combination of Caprotti 5MT 73153 piloting 46223 *Princess Alice*.

9   Press special to inspect the modernisation works in Kent is seen parked up at Sittingbourne, guests being served lunch in a 4-coach (1[st]class only) train that includes Restaurant Car, Inspection Saloon. L1 4-4-0 31749 heads the stock.

9   61930 enters Newcastle on the up 'Queen of Scots' (Pacific failure).

13   D602 *Bulldog* works a 15-coach test train from Newton Yard, Glasgow to Kingsnowe, Edinburgh after attention at North British.

13   E5002 hauls a test train from Victoria to Newhaven, making two round trips.

14   Women's Hockey International match brings 30937 *Epsom* to Wembley (Central), which then works the ECS to Harrow (!) before proceeding to Watford to turn. Six SR Pacifics 34008/19/67/77, 34101/105 also reach Wembley as do four 'Halls' 4988, 5966, 6944 and 7909.

14   Four 64B A4s are seen at Ferryhill at the same time! 60009 *Union of South Africa*, 60011 *Empire of India* to work expresses to Edinburgh; 60027 *Merlin* and 60031 *Golden Plover* to head express fish trains.

14   Meldon Quarry ballast train climbs between the two Exeter stations with four locos; M7 0-4-4T 30044 piloting N 2-6-0 31833, with M7s 30668/9 pushing!

15   0-6-0 shunter D3102 is stated as being 'on Swindon Test Plant'!

16/17   Overnight 'Condor' freight service commences between London (Hendon) and Glasgow (Gushetfaulds), hauled by a pair of Co-Bos, both ways.

17   'Master Cutler's Special' (for the Cutler's Feast) leaves King's Cross behind 60017 *Silver Fox*, non-stop to Sheffield (Victoria), returning next day.

17   A fire at Ilford close to the railway tracks means the 7.30pm Restaurant Car express to Norwich is announced at Liverpool Street as starting from Goodmayes with bus connection from Ilford. The Ilford EMU train connecting with the bus has refreshment trolleys provided on the platform prior to departure from Liverpool Street – thoughtful!

17   Troop train from Bury St Edmunds to Farnborough arrives at its destination behind 62069 (31B), which heads the ECS to Basingstoke before returning LE to Stratford.

18   Norwich City v Luton Town FA Cup semi-final replay at Villa Park brings five 32A B1s 61046/8, 61270, 61317 and 61204 (31F) to New Street.

20   Main line diesels 10000/1 are seen in tandem on the 9am Euston – Bletchley.

21   Grand National special to Aintree leaves Sheffield (Victoria) as a 13-coach train with a Pullman car and ex-'Devon Belle' observation car (M280M) – 'for Mr Pegler's party' – bringing up the rear. Co-Co 27000 works to Guide Bridge where 44554 + 44501 take over. A strange power transition!

21   46100 *Royal Scot* reaches Wakefield (Kirkgate) on a football special. This class is rarely seen here.

21   Twelve WR 0-6-0PTs are surprisingly allocated to the SR, five to Folkestone Jct. and seven to Nine Elms.

21   'Deltic' heads a braking trial between Doncaster and Ferme Park consisting of 50 loaded mineral wagons plus dynamometer car, 1146 tons.

23   D6102/5, as a LE pair, are seen heading north through Darlington.

24   61535 heads Framlingham College's end of term 6-coach special to Liverpool Street.

24   Main line diesel 10203 works, unusually, an up fitted freight near Tring.

24   D5012 (in pale green livery) is noted on a 15-coach test train to Cheadle.

25   0-6-0PT 9770 (on loan from Nine Elms) arrives at Wadebridge for trials to Padstow, Bodmin (North).

26   Ivatt 2-6-0 43090 (31C) appears in Liverpool Street with the 2.49pm arrival from King's Lynn, presumably having worked throughout.

27   (Good Friday). First 'Starlight Special' of the season leaves St Enoch for Marylebone via Edinburgh behind 60150 *Willbrook* (52A). (This year these trains will only operate regularly 22 May-11 September).

27   72000 *Clan Buchanan* works into Blackpool (North), leaving LE soon after.

27   45545 *Planet* (5A) is an Easter visitor to Aberdeen, seen on Ferryhill.

28	60084 *Trigo* (50B) is a rare sight at Waverley on the down 'North Briton'. Neville Hill locos are 'always' changed at Newcastle!
28	61002 *Impala* (50A) reaches Temple Meads with a York – Bristol express, having worked through, most unusual.
30	'Six Lochs Land Cruise' – first DMU excursion of the year in Scotland – runs from Buchanan Street/Stirling/Callander/Killin/Crianlarich/Queen Street (LL), all for 10s. Train is formed of 4 x 2-car sets (all brand new!).
30	King's Cross – Newcastle relief arrives in York behind Ivatt 2-6-0 43033 of Bournville depot, hopefully due to a failure further south!
U/D	During the month, 'Deltic' makes several test runs with the ER dynamometer car; to Grantham (5th) 106mph recorded, to Leeds (Central) on 9-12 March, and to Newcastle on 16-19 March – though trains terminate at Gateshead northbound and restart in the goods lines near Central station as loco fouls platform edges in Newcastle station.
U/D	Ivatt 2-6-2T 41224 is still lettered 'British Railways' on its tank sides.
U/D	Bluebell Line Preservation Society is formed to purchase the line between Horsted Keynes and Sheffield Park.

APRIL 1959

1ST	J36 0-6-0 65277 (64F) finds itself, inexplicably, at Aviemore!
1	10.35am Leeds (City) – St Enoch is taken out of Leeds by 45665 *Lord Rutherford of Nelson* + 45687 *Neptune* (both 67A), a pairing that would be rare, even around Glasgow!
2	The spectacular combination of 70004 *William Shakespeare* piloting 45598 *Basutoland* is seen at Luton on the 10.25am St Pancras – Manchester (Central).
4	44843 noted with an unidentified westbound train between Norwich and Ely. A most unusual type on this line.
4	8.20pm Eastleigh – Reading is double-headed by the uncommon duo of 75079 piloting 30905 *Tonbridge*.
5,12	Bridge repairs at Copley Hill cause diversions of King's Cross – West Riding services near to Leeds. 60148 *Aboyeur* is seen on the down 'Harrogate Sunday Pullman' at Horbury & Ossett *en route* from Wakefield to Low Moor; 60141 *Abbotsford* passes Heckmondwike Jct. with the 10.45am from King's Cross, 60062 *Minoru* climbs out of Bradford (Exchange) on the 10.56am to London and 60033 *Seagull* passes through Cleckheaton (5th). On the 12th, 60117 *Bois Roussel* is noted at Thornhill on the 10.45am from King's Cross and the up 'HSP' is double-headed from Leeds to Low Moor by 61115 + 'Crab' 42862 – an unlikely pairing on a Pullman train.
7	'Baby Deltic' D5903 surprisingly passes Sheffield (Victoria), LE southbound.
8	Up 'Condor' from Glasgow to Hendon suffers diesel failure at Dent (of all remote places) and is worked forward by 45081 + 45100, both 12A.
9,10	D34 4-4-0s 62471 *Glen Falloch* + 62496 *Glen Loy* double-head the ScR's TV train from Glasgow to Fort William on a schools' special. This train is used next day as an overnight football special from St Enoch for the soccer match at Wembley, leaving behind 45490 + 45665 *Lord Rutherford of Nelson* (Scotland lose 1-0).
9-12	Compound 41157 (17A) works the Barnt Green – Ashchurch line for four days being filmed for the BBC TV programme *Railway Roundabout*, to be shown on 5 May.

10	CR 4-2-2 123 plus the two restored CR coaches, and D603 *Conquest* with 15 coaches, are both in action on the Holytown – Edinburgh line, being filmed by a BBC unit.
11	RL Cup semi-final at Odsal stadium brings 61904/22/45 into Bradford (Forster Square) with excursions from Hull. First K3s seen here?
11	73073 (41C) is a rare sight on the East Coast main line heading a Doncaster to Grantham freight.
12	60046 *Diamond Jubilee*, 60100 *Spearmint* both work Marylebone – Edinburgh returning football specials routed via Leeds and the S&C line due to the resignalling at Newcastle.
12	With the new signalbox at Newcastle being commissioned, Gateshead shed is not available. Engines work through from Doncaster to Edinburgh, bringing A3s 60036/74/84, A1 60128, A2s 60502/22 as notable visitors to Waverley.
18	61216 + 61259 double-head a schools excursion from Leeds to Edinburgh (via Wetherby) throughout, and the return, a most unusual occurrence.
18	D5709 + D5710 work the 5.30pm (SO) St Enoch – Carlisle. (On Fridays Co-Bos also work the 10.20pm sleeper as far as Carlisle and 7.15am return).
20	45154 *Lanarkshire Yeomanry* (26A) makes a rare visit of a Newton Heath loco to Euston, seen on a relief to the 8.20am down service.
20	12noon Bradford – St Pancras is surprisingly taken south out of Leeds by Corkerhill's 45665, which returns the same evening on a parcels train.
20	D34 4-4-0 62469 *Glen Douglas* enters Cowlairs Works, leaving as NBR 256.
21	4-4-0 40504 pilots 73010 out of St Pancras on the 6.33pm to Leicester. 73010 runs a hot-box at Kettering and is replaced by 92125, amazingly marshalled in front of 40504, surely a unique combination!
21,22	O4 2-8-0s 63775, 63577 (respectively, both Gorton) are unexpectedly seen working freights along the North Wales coast.
25	45090 (60A!) reaches Carlisle as pilot on the 11am Glasgow – Liverpool.
25	34020 *Seaton* heads down the Lymington branch as far as Town station with a pigeon special, returning LE to Brockenhurst. A surprise working.
25	Troop train from Southampton Docks to East Grinstead is taken forward from Clapham Jct. by U1 2-6-0s 31904 + 31907, which also return with the ECS.
26	70051 *Firth of Forth* (66A) heads the 1.30pm to Glasgow out of Aberdeen.
26	'Scandinavian' leaves Liverpool Street behind 61572, rare nowadays.
27	Tweedmouth V2 60926 unusually brings the 'Granite City' into Aberdeen.
28	D34 4-4-0s 62496 *Glen Loy* + 62471 *Glen Falloch* work the 5.45am Queen Street – Mallaig as far as Fort William and 2.56pm return, as a prelude to the special event on 8,9 May.
29	60099 *Call Boy* (64B) is a rare visitor to King's Cross, working through from Waverley on the afternoon 'Talisman'.
29	Diminutive 0-4-0T 41528 is noted passing through Sheffield (Victoria) hauled by an O4 2-8-0. 41528 is on hire to Batchelors Peas Ltd at Wadsley Bridge.
29	Royal train reaches Weymouth for the Queen and the Prince of Wales to inspect HMS Eagle. Train is taken to Portland dockyard by 0-6-0PTs 4689 + 3737. Royal party re-boards here, providing the unusual spectacle of a Royal train on a closed branch line hauled by two 0-6-0 tanks boasting the 4-lamp headcode, to Weymouth, where 34046 *Braunton* + 34048 *Crediton* take over.
U/D	EE/Vulcan Foundry 500hp 0-6-0 shunters D226/7 (electric/hydraulic transmissions) act as station pilots at Doncaster; then go to Scunthorpe for two weeks with a further stint at Sheffield (Darnall) before returning to Hornsey.

U/D	D5902 is the first 'Baby Deltic' to run on BR, hauling a single coach from Vulcan Foundry to Chester (1st). At 75 tons D5900/01 were found to be 3 tons overweight and had to be 'dieted' before released to traffic. On 3rd D5902 works an ECS train Edge Hill – Penrith and back, on running-in trials.
U/D	D16 4-4-0s 62597, 62612/13 appear at Northampton (from Peterborough), following the closure of the M&GN line.
U/D	Ten sets of Timken roller bearings are reported to have arrived at Swindon for fitting to 'King' class locos.
U/D	To illustrate the improvement to passenger traffic resulting from modernised services BR releases the following as an example;

NER Leeds – Barnsley DMU service	Journeys	% increase
Steam service, final year	204,154	
Diesel service, year ended 31.3 59	740,531	263

MAY 1959

1ST	Royal Albert Bridge at Saltash is floodlit to commemorate the centenary of its completion.
2	7026 *Tenby Castle* appears on Neasden shed after working an FA Cup Final excursion from Wolverhampton. Also on shed are no less than 12 B1s that have worked in on other football specials.
2	5017 *The Gloucestershire Regiment 28th,61st* + 70024 *Vulcan* double-head the combined 1.55pm South Wales and 2.15pm Cheltenham out of Paddington.
2	To celebrate the centenary of the opening of the Royal Albert Bridge at Saltash, and the centenary of the year of Brunel's death, a special train is run from Paddington to Saltash. BBC TV *Childrens Newsreel* broadcasts a recording of the event on the 13th.
3	H 0-4-4T 31322 is a rare sight on the 2.2pm Faversham – Dover.
4,5	Rarity! 'Royal Scot' is double-headed out of Euston by pairs of 'Jubilees'; 45706 *Express* + 45722 *Defence*; 45592 *Indore* + 45676 *Codrington* (5th).
5	Shah of Persia visits this country and a special train of four Pullmans is run from Gatwick to Victoria behind 34010 *Sidmouth*.
5	New 'Baby Deltic' D5902 is exhibited at Harrogate station in connection with a conference held in the town, but departs for York in the evening.
6	61119 (30A) reaches Portsmouth (Harbour) with a schools excursion, arriving via the Portsmouth Direct and returning through Eastleigh.
7	46251 *City of Nottingham* fails on the down 'Mid-day Scot' at Oxenholme, and the train is proudly taken to Carlisle by Fowler 2-6-4Ts 42317 + 42345.
7	2-8-0 2821 (87E Landore) finds unusual employment on the 3-coach 5.20pm Eastleigh – Southampton (Terminus). A rare working indeed.
8,9	The 'Two Glens to Fort William' tour sees D34 4-4-0s 62496 *Glen Loy* + 62471 *Glen Falloch* power the 5.45am out of Queen Street and 2.56pm return on both days, filmed by the BBC TV for *Railway Roundabout*, due 13 July.
9	Rare sights at Paddington as 46154 *The Hussar* heads the Trains Illustrated excursion 'The Potteries Express' which includes an ex-'Devon Belle' observation car.
9	RL Cup Final at Wembley brings in a whole crop of NE Region B1s, the rarest being 61353 (51L Thornaby) on an excursion from Hull.

9,16	92200 (36A) heads the morning York – Edinburgh parcels as far as Newcastle. 92182 (34E) repeats this on the 16th. 9Fs are rare on this section.
10	60022 *Mallard* leaves Wakefield (Kirkgate) for York via Normanton, Castleford and Church Fenton on the diverted 12.30pm ex-King's Cross.
12,14	7.32am Lincoln – Sheffield is brought into Victoria by 61572 (31A), a class not seen here for 20 years at least! 61572 then works a special from Lincoln to Driffield for the Institute of Water Engineers, and proceeds to Bridlington with the empty stock. Here the engine fails and is taken to Hull (14th). Repaired, the B12 is seen (23rd) at Gainsborough on a pick-up goods.
15	The 'North Briton' bound for Leeds, leaves Queen Street behind the exotic combination of J37 0-6-0 64638 piloting 60162 *Saint Johnstoun*!
15	Gloucester's 4085 *Berkeley Castle* + 5094 *Tretower Castle* (in sparkling condition) head the 11.45am Cheltenham – Paddington, and both return on the down 'Cheltenham Spa Express'. Steam at its best!
16	Liverpool Street is treated to the (probably unprecedented sight) of 70007 *Coeur-de-Lion* + 70034 *Thomas Hardy* arriving double-headed on the 3.45pm from Norwich, having worked as a pair from Ipswich, at least.
17	N7 0-6-2T 69629 (34B Hornsey) is a most unusual visitor to Lincoln.
18	Whit Monday. 5,500 people arrive at, and 8,500 depart from Ilkley – a record since the second war and a 200% increase over 1958. Most are carried in DMUs with some steam hauled extras.
16,18	*Gordon Highlander* (ex-D40 4-4-0 62277) is noted in Inverurie Works being restored as GNS 49, and HR 'Jones Goods' 4-6-0 103 is seen under repair at St Rollox two days later, both destined for use on excursion traffic.
19	D5716 pilots 45694 *Bellorophon* on the 1.15pm St Pancras – Bradford as far as Leicester. First recorded steam/diesel pairing on the Midland main line.
22	A2/3 60515 *Sun Stream* very surprisingly reaches Saltburn hauling ECS.
22	4pm from Manchester (London Road) arrives in Euston behind 70031 *Byron* + 70043 *Lord Kitchener*, another unusual pairing of 'Britannias'.
23	44771 + 45324 (both 1A) work through from London to Burnley with a special freight of 53 container wagons, a parcels van and a Sleeping Car!
23	61783 *Loch Shiel* is an exceptional sight at Aviemore on the 8.25am goods to Elgin via Craigellachie.
23	The SLS runs its 'Golden Jubilee' railtour between King's Cross and Doncaster. 60007 *Sir Nigel Gresley* (the 100th Gresley Pacific) is provided and reaches at least 110mph down Stoke bank!
24	5079 *Lysander* heads the diverted 3.20pm Wolverhampton – Paddington over an overgrown stretch of line between Bearley station and Bearley North unused by a passenger train since 1939!
25-29	Track tests on the SR Central Section just short of Balcombe Tunnel (south-bound only) are conducted as follows;

25th	DC electrics 20001/2 coupled LE	10 runs at	2 - 40mph
26th	do.	10 runs at	45 - 80mph
27th	D5309/12 coupled LE	12 runs at	2 - 75mph
28th	4-CEP/baggage car/4-CEP	5 runs at	20 - 90mph
29th	DC electrics E5003/4 coupled LE	18 runs at	2 - 108mph

29   70022 *Tornado* + 70029 *Shooting Star* double-head the down 'Red Dragon'(strengthened to 15 coaches as the 5.50pm service is cancelled). Another unusual instance of paired 7MTs.

31   45658 *Keyes* reaches Whitley Bay on a 13-coach excursion from Cudworth, and is serviced at Heaton before working the return.

U/D   Melton Constable – Norwich (City) line sees 90559, a J20 0-6-0 and D5524, all first examples of these classes on this line, since withdrawal of passenger services.

JUNE 1959

3RD 46239 *City of Chester* and 46253 *City of St. Albans* depart Chester for Euston within ten minutes of each other on two specials chartered by the Bowater Group in connection with a visit to a paper mill at Ellesmere Port.

3   60066 *Merry Hampton* (34A) is seen briefly at Holbeck shed (55A) – rare here – after running LE from Leeds (Central), soon departing for Neville Hill.

5   45537 *Private E. Sykes, V.C.* (12B) brings a pigeon special from Stirling into Worcester, and 45596 *Bahamas* (12B) brings another into Cheltenham from Glasgow, Carlisle engines being rare at either destination.

5   61661 *Sheffield Wednesday* works an excursion from Purfleet to Windsor & Eton (Riverside) throughout, a class seldom seen here.

6   D201 travels through from Retford to Windsor (WR) with a Northern Rubber Co. special, the train including an ex-'Devon Belle' observation car.

6   46114 *Coldstream Guardsman* (8A) reaches Weston-super-Mare on excursion traffic from Coventry with stock roofboarded 'London – Rugby'!

8-15   'Deltic' travels over the Waverley Route from Carlisle to Leith (Central) (8th), and works repeated round trip trials (9-12 June) between Craigentinny and Berwick with various loads up to 18 coaches. Returns to Carlisle on 15th.

15   Kent Coast electrification commences full service. Preliminary dates are
    2nd 1st electric loco Victoria – Ramsgate throughout, E5004
    3rd 1st EMU Cannon Street – Ramsgate throughout, units 7138/41/42
    8th 1st public electric, down 'Night Ferry', Victoria – Dover, E5003
    9th 'Inaugural' run 9.55am Victoria – Margate for Sir Brian Robertson, SR Officials, Civic Officials and Press.

16th 1st letter of complaint published in Evening News re-lateness on 15th!

9   D5015 + D5016 work into York on the 8am Birmingham – Newcastle, coming back on the 12.48pm Newcastle – Bristol, a rare consecutively-numbered duo.

11   61329 (32B) passes through St Albans (where Ipswich engines are a rarity) on a return excursion from Whipsnade Zoo.

11   D11 4-4-0 62670 *Marne* is the surprise pilot to 61369 on the up 'South Yorkshireman' out of Sheffield (Victoria). (See also U/D August 1956). 90400 works the 10.18am to Skegness, another surprise.

12   3.50pm from Wolverhampton arrives in Euston with 72009 *Clan Stewart* piloting 45742 *Connaught*, an unexpected combination.

12   0-6-0 2207 leaves Gloucester with an out-of-gauge load of two Rhodesia Railways coaches, bound for export through Tilbury.

12,15   9.25pm York – West Hartlepool stopper is headed by 45519 *Lady Godiva* (82E) on both days. First Bristol engine at West Hartlepool?

13   49 *Gordon Highlander* (ex-62277) makes its first run since restoration from Glasgow to Dumfries and back (4 coaches + 'Devon Belle' observation car).

14   61161 is an extreme rarity in Paddington with a special from Leicester that is visiting both London and Windsor.

14   73116 (70A) astonishingly finds itself at Longsight depot (9A)!

15   Restored MR Compound 1000 undergoes steaming trials between Derby and Trent, painted in 'base red'.

15   D5717 passes through New Street heading to the Freight Transport Exhibition at the Central Goods Station.

15   Kent Coast – see above.

16,20   An unprecedented sight at Exeter (St Davids), where the engine is changed, is that of 30850 *Lord Nelson* working a British Legion special from Southampton to Newton Abbot. 30850 having 'broken the ice', 30859 *Lord Hood* arrives on the 20th (Strong's Brewery special).

16   60040 *Cameronian* (52B) makes a rare appearance in Hull working the 7.30am Hull – Skelton Sidings freight.

17   The last two London-based T9 4-4-0s 30338 + 30719 depart for Exmouth Jct. by double-heading an 8-coach troop train for Farnborough and Yeovil.

19   14-coach school special departs from Blairgowrie (closed 10 January 1955) for Glasgow behind 44960 + 45483.

20   D5300 (34B) is observed at Boston on a northbound stopping service.

20   30902 *Wellington* (by special arrangement and very sprucely turned out) heads the 12.5pm Reading – Redhill and 3.4pm back to mark the centenary of Wellington College.

21   Reading–Weymouth excursion is worked throughout via Southampton and Bournemouth by 6968 *Woodcock Hall*. Return is booked via Ringwood, but 'Halls' are not permitted and 34006 *Bude* substitutes, with 6968 working 34006's diagram starting with the 7.12pm Weymouth – Eastleigh.

26   4.52pm York – Doncaster local (5 coaches) has the excessive power combination of B16 4-6-0 61439 + 60119 *Patrick Stirling*.

27   61164 surprisingly arrives at Bath (Green Park) at the head of the 9.8am from Birmingham. B1s are rare visitors here.

27   'Patriot' 45517 (27A) is supplied by Polmadie to work an excursion to Ayr from Grangemouth, where this type has not been seen before.

27   EE 500hp 0-6-0 shunters D226/7 reach Stratford and soon commence ECS duties at Liverpool Street.

28   Lincoln based 3-car Cravens DMU runs an excursion from Nottingham to Bournemouth (West), first time a DMU has worked between Eastleigh and Bournemouth. Unit spends the day in West station. Very unusual working!

28   6820 *Kingstone Grange* makes a class debut at Bath (Green Park) with an excursion from Ledbury to Bournemouth, returning north with the same train.

30   7.52pm arrival at Waterloo from Salisbury is double-headed by 30912 *Downside* + 30916 *Whitgift*, a most uncommon pairing at Waterloo.

U/D   Glasgow 'Blue Train' 3-car EMU arrives in the Manchester area for testing on the Styal line.

U/D   Ex-'Coronation' beaver-tail observation cars E1719E, E1729 rebuilt with new rear windows, operate on 10.20am Queen Street – Fort William and 4.40pm back (3s 6d extra); 7.50am Fort William – Mallaig and 6.10pm back (2s 6d).

U/D   'Castle' and 'Grange' 4-6-0s run clearance tests between Exeter (Central) and Basingstoke.

U/D   0-6-0PT 4613 (from Folkestone Jct.) works Deal – Margate local services.

U/D   Majority of the engines displaced from the South Eastern Division of the SR by the Kent Coast scheme are allocated *en masse* (106 locos) to Nine Elms (at least on paper) doubling the depots allocation, for which there is no room!

JULY 1959

4TH   61306 (53B) reaches Rhyl with an excursion from the East Coast.

4   45717 *Dauntless* is the first Bank Hall (27A) 'Jubilee' to be seen in Aberdeen.

4   'Crab' 42856 (6C) arrives at Wolverhampton (LL) with the 9.20am Birkenhead – Paddington, which it has worked through from Chester.

4   V3 2-6-2T 67684 is an unusual class to visit York, on the 12.8pm from Hull.

4   Up 'Waverley' comes into Carlisle with 61307 (64A) piloting 70053 *Moray Firth* (55A). Derailment at London Road Jct. causes engines to be changed at Canal Junction with 70053 coming on there, the loco for the 2pm Carlisle – Newcastle acting as pilot into the station.

4   Crosti-boilered 92024 (15A) is a remarkable visitor to Carlisle, departing with the 5.47pm Carlisle – Cricklewood milk train.

4   10.35am from Paddington leaves Newton Abbot with 6018 *King Henry VI* piloting D602 *Bulldog*, an unusual combination.

5   0-6-0PT 1369 noted at Reading shed as breakdown crane stand-by engine, a most unlikely class to be seen so far east.

5   61661 *Sheffield Wednesday* (30E Colchester) is spotted on Darlington shed after hauling L1 2-6-4T 67717 + 90424 from York to the Works.

6   Frome witnesses the highly unexpected appearance of Q 0-6-0 30535 (71A), working a special parcels train from Weymouth to Westbury.

6   D5901 fails near Knebworth on the 3.57pm Baldock – King's Cross. J6 0-6-0 64197 tows D5901 and stock south as passengers have got out and walked!

9   Cambridge B1 61171 is an equally unusual sight at Buxton, arriving from Ely.

11   12.40pm Cardiff – Manchester is worked throughout to Chester by 70029 *Shooting Star* (86C), Canton locos rarely reaching here.

11   8.4am Newquay – Newcastle breasts Dainton behind 4944 *Middleton Hall* + 92225. 11am Newquay – York has 7818 *Granville Manor* + 92222!

12   Prototype 'Peak' 2300hp 1Co-Co1 D1 travels to Carlisle from Derby for a local naming ceremony – *Scafell Pike* – after which it returns to Derby.

12   D16 4-4-0 62613 is a type rare to Fenchurch Street, heading an LCGB special.

12   N7 0-6-2T 69694 (31C Kings Lynn) appears on Darlington shed, prior to Works attention (or scrap?).

13   J10 0-6-0 65177 performs station pilot duties at Wigan (North Western), an incongruous juxtaposition when a 'Coronation' passes on the 'Royal Scot!

15   62065 double-heads Ivatt 2-6-2T 41253 on the 2.57pm Bradford (Exchange) to Penistone stopper, new ground for a K1.

15   61002 *Impala* (50A) finds itself to be a last-minute replacement for a 'Britannia', heading the 'Palatine' between Manchester (Central) and Derby!

17   Tilbury shed plays host to an unexpected loco in the shape of Q1 0-6-0 33018.

17	60923 (52A) makes a unique visit to Gourock on a special ex-Newcastle.
17	Co-Bo D57xx is noted heading an Isle of Man boat train into Ardrossan, a fill-in turn between 'Condor' express freight duties.
18	2-6-0 5384 brings the rare sight of a Weymouth engine (71G) to Paddington, having worked though on the 11.12am from Weymouth. Returns on the 6pm departure, piloted to Newbury by 6003 *King George IV* – an interesting pair!
18	An 8-car DMU set is provided as the 9.4am relief Whitley Bay – Edinburgh. Has a DMU covered this stretch of the main line before?
20	45724 *Warspite* (12A) appears in Queen Street on the 3.36pm from Thornton.
20	Stanier 2-6-0 42980 (5B) exits Scarborough, on the 11.45am to Manchester.
20	61641 *Gayton Hall* reaches Cleethorpes with an incoming excursion.
20	Due to a temporary blockage of the main line, 60022 *Mallard* takes the down 'Talisman' through…Bishop Auckland!
22	72000 *Clan Buchanan* (66A) heads the 7.47am Todmorden – Manchester, surprise power for this local service.
23	3.35pm relief boat train Weymouth (Quay) – Paddington is diverted via Bournemouth, Basingstoke and Reading, worked throughout by a 'Hall'.
24	Restored NBR 4-4-0 256 *Glen Douglas* (ex-62469) emerges from Cowlairs Works and is taken to Dawsholm shed, 65D.
25	61910 enters Llandudno on a relief from Stretford, but 61161 heads even further west to Pen-y-chain (for Butlins) with another ex-Manchester (Central).
25	61875 works a 13-coach relief King's Cross – Edinburgh forward from Newcastle, booked non-stop to Waverley.
25	92177 (36A) heads the 11.15am (SO) to Llandudno out of Newcastle.
25	45565 *Victoria* (55A) works an Aberdeen – London fish train between York and Grantham, first 'Jubilee' seen on a main line train south of York.
25	10.45am Victoria – Newhaven is headed by E5000, first working for this class on a passenger service on this route. Loco is a 2552hp DC Bo-Bo.
26	Lincoln – Blackpool excursion passes through Rochdale with the unusual combination of 48469 + 61145 in charge.
27	'Warship' D807 heads the up 'Torbay Express' and D808 heads the down service, its first day of diesel haulage.
27	8.15am Newcastle – Cardiff arrives in New Street behind D5709 + 73069. D5709 returns north piloting the 9.14am Paignton – Sheffield.
27	T9 4-4-0 30711 (72A) works local services around Brighton before going to Ashford for scrapping.
28	'Crab' 42783 (2B) works an excursion from Nuneaton/Coventry throughout to Yarmouth (Vauxhall), which may well not have seen this type before.
28	6028 *King George VI* + 92247 are seen double-heading between Newton Abbot and Plymouth. (See 11th for other combinations involving 9Fs).
28	The three SR preserved locos are moved from Tweedmouth to Eastleigh (82, 563) and Ashford (31737), and are noted at Durham and Sheffield (Victoria).
31	Compound 41101 is sent to Gorton Works for a special paint job (yellow, red, black!) for the *Daily Mirror* 'Andy Capp' Blackpool special.
31	Gas turbine 18000 fails at Bath on the 1.55pm Paddington to Weston-super-Mare. 0-6-0PTs 7729 + 3720 haul the train into Temple Meads.

U/D   46232 *Duchess of Montrose* + 46235 *City of Birmingham* double-head LE from Perth to Dundee for turning. Perth turntable is out of action.

U/D   Closure of Forres shed results in more frequent appearances at Inverness of 76xxx and 80xxx standards from Kittybrewster, previously rare types.

U/D   LTS 4-4-2T 41949 seen on extra Kings Lynn – Hunstanton holiday trains, not a class used previously on this branch.

U/D   Brighton Works opens its doors to steam engines again – to store some of the 'spare' locos released by the completion of the Kent electrification scheme.

U/D   Neasden shed acquires 0-6-0PT 6413, on loan from…Aberdare!

U/D   Kilmarnock Works closes (beginning of the month), as does Lochgorm (last engine to leave is 45477). Gateshead had already closed in early March, last engine being J94 0-6-0ST 68036.

U/D   WR single unit railcar takes part in Daily Mail's London – Paris air race! Route: Marble Arch/Paddington(bus)/Ruislip Gardens (rail)/Northolt (car)/Le Bourget (Comet)/Arc de Triomph (road). Time 61¼ minutes overall!

AUGUST 1959

1ST   Bank Holiday Saturday at Carlisle. 44960 (63A!) arrives with the 11.55am from… Hellifield! 12noon Glasgow – Manchester enters behind CR 0-4-4T 55234 bunker first on 10 coaches (45710 *Irresistible* replaced at Lockerbie), and the down 'Thames-Clyde Express' has 'Crab' 42760 (17C Rowsley!) as tender first pilot to 46112 *Sherwood Forester*. Interesting sights.

1   61076 (64A) reaches Ardrossan (Montgomery Pier) on an Irish boat train. 61246 *Lord Balfour of Burleigh* (64A) comes into Winton Pier an hour later with an Arran boat train.

1   Channel Islands boat train from Paddington arrives in Weymouth behind WR 0-6-0PT + SR U 2-6-0 after 5082 *Swordfish* fails at Yeovil.

1   2-8-0 4706 arrives in Exeter (St Davids) on the 1.25pm Paddington to Kingswear, passing 4704 at an adjacent platform heading the 3.20pm Kingswear – Paddington, both bearing the express passenger headlamp code.

1   70025 *Western Star* heads the 9.35am Swansea – Birmingham via Gloucester, a 7MT being almost unknown on the North Warwickshire line.

1,2,4   45503 *The Royal Leicestershire Regiment* (8B) surprisingly heads the portion to Bradford of a King's Cross – Leeds train out of Wakefield (Westgate) on the 1st, then works an excursion from Bradford to Southport and back (2nd). Also noted at Cleckheaton on a 20-coach train towards Bradford (4th).

3   'City of Plymouth Holiday Express' is worked through to Sidmouth by 34104 *Bere Alston*. Tender engines of any class are normally unknown at Sidmouth.

3   Compound 41101, grossly disfigured with yellow boiler/tender, red cab, splashers and rods, plus white wheels (and a chime whistle from a 'Clan'!) works the Daily Mirror sponsored 'Andy Capp' special between Manchester and Blackpool. (Derby Works refused to do the paint job!).

5   44712 reaches Margate and is serviced at Ramsgate, despite both dieselisation and electrification in Kent.

5   A2/3 60512 *Steady Aim* heads a Newcastle – Gloucester extra into Sheffield (Midland) and is turned on the triangle at Dore & Totley.

6   60918 (50A) is seen at Cleckheaton with ECS for Bradford that carries roofboards reading 'Starlight Special'.

7   D5710 (with 'Condor' headboard) found on Manningham shed after failing.

7,18   New Bo-Bo D6305 (ex-North British) passes through Snow Hill bound for Swindon. Same engine is hauled dead through Preston (18th), going back to Glasgow from Swindon!

8   92206 (83D) is noted solo on the up 'Mayflower' at Newton Abbot.

8   92240/44 both arrive at Snow Hill on passenger workings from the south, and 92104/37/64 also head passenger trains over the Lickey.

8   76003 (66B) is surprise power for the 3pm Queen Street – Crianlarich.

10   45241 (24L Carnforth) contrives to work the down 'Postal' into Aberdeen!

15   11.38am Brighton – Sheffield leaves behind D1 4-4-0 31743, which takes the 9 coaches as far as Kensington, a surprising class for such work nowadays.

15   Pre-grouping locos at Carlisle; MR 4F 0-6-0 44008 heads an Appleby to Carlisle, NBR D34 4-4-0 62471 *Glen Falloch* comes in from Hawick and NER B16 4-6-0s 61459/19 work in/out from Newcastle.

16   Birmingham – Minehead excursion is formed of a six-coach Buffet Car DMU set – the first diesel working on this branch from Taunton.

16   1.22pm Cambridge – Colchester is headed by the unlikely pairing of 61000 *Springbok* piloting J15 0-6-0 65468 on 3 coaches and a van.

17,18   Frodingham (36C) Q1 0-8-0Ts 69928/34 turn up at Northallerton shed, but only *en route* to Darlington for scrap. Another, 69929 passes next day through Burton Salmon, for the same purpose. Probably their longest runs ever!

18   6.45pm Norwich – Liverpool Street provides an amazing sight at Flordon headed by D5532 (dead) and being propelled (hard!) by 70011 *Hotspur*, which it did as far as Forncett, where another diesel replaced D5532.

18   73050 brings the rare sight of an 82F shedplate to York, the Bath loco arriving on the 2.15pm Bristol – York!

19   E5000 leaves Waterloo for Portsmouth (Harbour) with a 4-coach Pullman special for a ship launching ceremony at Cowes.

21   6822 *Manton Grange* reaches Bournemouth on the 8.55am from Newcastle, and 2-6-0 7303 is noted on the 6.35am Weymouth – Brockenhurst, having taken over at Dorchester when T9 4-4-0 30707 failed. 7303 is later seen heading the 9.37pm Southampton (Central) – Wimborne, an unusual working.

22   0-6-0s 44207 + J39 64824 combine to make an unexpected pairing on the York – Manchester (Red Bank) ECS train.

22-24   6979 *Helperly Hall* startles everyone by arriving, uniquely, at York on the 11.16am Bournemouth (West) – Newcastle having been piloted from Nottingham (Victoria) to York by B16 4-6-0 61450. 6979 spends the weekend on shed and leaves (24th) on freight. An astonishing incursion by a GWR loco!

23   J39 0-6-0 64930 (8E Northwich) is a big surprise at Barrow Road shed, Bristol and is later seen arriving at New Street with a passenger train to Derby.

23   44715 arrives at Eastbourne with an excursion from Coventry, and on the return is piloted by U 2-6-0 31797 – a most unusual combination.

25   L&Y 0-8-0 49674 leaves Embsay with a ballast train. Rare loco type here.

25,26   45585 *Hyderabad* is engaged in high-speed trials with a 3-coach train between St Pancras and Manchester (Central) prior to introduction of 'Blue Pullmans'

26,28	Crewe entertains two 'Castles'; 7018 *Drysllwyn Castle* arrives (26ᵗʰ) on a freight ex-Weymouth, and 5081 *Lockheed Hudson* heads a freight from Oxley.
26	Restored 4-4-0 3440 *City of Truro* passes through Sheffield (Victoria) LE *en route* to Glasgow to work specials in Scotland.
28	92170 brings the 'Master Cutler' into King's Cross after taking over from D206 at Biggleswade. Has a 9F headed a Pullman train before?
29	Stranger of the month at Scarborough is 80076 (33B Tilbury), used by York as an ex-Works running-in turn from Darlington before heading south.
29	WD 2-10-0 90763 appears on Birkenhead depot for possible trials on the Bidston – Shotton iron ore workings.
29	73002 (41D) is seen on Crimple Viaduct (Harrogate) with a 16-coach pigeon special heading for Treherbert. 5MTs are rare visitors to Harrogate.
29	Derby Works Open Day features MR 1000, 70004 *William Shakespeare*, 92165, D2 *Helvellyn* on display.
29	Restored NBR 4-4-0 256 *Glen Douglas* works its first special, from Waverley to Penicuik and other lines around Edinburgh.
30	Newly restored MR Compound 4-4-0 1000 heads its first public outing, from New Street to Doncaster (for the Works) and York (for the Museum).
U/D	4-4-0 40618, instead of a railbus, heads from Aviemore to Boat of Garten.
U/D	4-coach EMU for the ER is borrowed by the ScR to test newly installed overhead equipment on the Milngavie – Westerton branch.

SEPTEMBER 1959

1ˢᵀ	4.25pm Buchanan Street – Inverness leaves behind A2/1 60507 *Highland Chieftain* (64B). Haymarket Pacifics are only occasional visitors here.
3	61002 *Impala* (50A) works a Cadbury's Trade Special into Bournville.
3	'Scandinavian' enters Liverpool Street behind Immingham's 61912, rarity!
4,5	2-8-0 63906 (36C Frodingham) is the first O4 to visit Newcastle, on freight from York. Also used next day to head empty wagons to Morpeth.
5	46205 *Princess Victoria* works from Perth into Buchanan Street, rare type here.
5	Pigeon special reaches Gosport (freight only) branch behind 2-6-0 7308 (84C).
5	CR 0-6-0T 56325 (61B Ferryhill!) is allocated on loan to…Wolverton Works!
6	30794 *Sir Ector de Maris* turns the clock back by arriving at Brighton on excursion traffic from Bedford.
6	8-car DMU forms an RCTS Leeds (City) – Towyn scenic railtour via Chester/Ruabon/Oswestry/Welshpool/Aberdovey and Barmouth.
7	46204 *Princess Louise* (8A) is an unlikely sight at Manchester (Victoria), coming in on the 7.30am ex-Aberdeen, leaving on the 8.55pm to Heysham.
7	Caprotti 73144 (17A) heads a special conveying Rolls-Royce personnel from Derby through to Farnborough for the Air Show.
8	Fowler 2-6-4T 42346 (5D Stoke) is short-notice replacement power for a Kentish Town – Stratford parcels train, and is serviced on 30A at 6am.
8	78030 (5A) is a rare sight at Wellington with an LMR Inspection Saloon from Crewe via Market Drayton.
9	10.55am Princes Street – Carstairs has the unusual pairing of 44952 piloting CR 4-4-0 54505.

9	L&Y 0-8-0 49624 (26A) appears in Washwood Heath sidings – a type not seen in Birmingham for several years.
10	N7 0-6-2T 69614 (Liverpool St pilot) works a Chingford evening rush hour train, and J69 0-6-0T 68619 (the other pilot) headed the 7.19am to Chingford.
10	Restored 4-4-0 3440 *City of Truro*, heading north LE, is called upon to haul the brokendown Crieff branch railbus from Gleneagles to Perth for attention!
10	J39 0-6-0 64787 (31F Spital Bridge, Peterborough) somehow finds its way to Barrow Road shed (82E) Bristol. Even more strangely, 0-6-0PT 4666 (wearing an 87C Danygraig shedplate) appears on Exmouth Jct. depot.
12	92208 heads the 'Merchant Venturer' from Bristol to Weston-super-Mare.
13	Special workings for the Farnborough Air Show bring D5512 in from Southend, and 61066 (31A) into North Camp from Cambridge.
15	61629 *Naworth Castle* (32B) pays a surprise visit to Frodingham depot.
17	D5512 now wanders off to Bournville on a Cadbury's special from Upminster.
19	Football special from Hebden Bridge to Barnsley is a 13-car DMU no less!
20	Enthusiasts' excursion from Nottingham to Eastleigh arrives with 2-6-0 7307 in charge, which works the entire train into the Works yard.
20	61629 *Naworth Castle* and 61637 *Thorpe Hall* both arrive at Darlington shed in error and are sent on to Doncaster for scrapping a few days later.
20	Beginning of term 8-coach special for Cranbrook College is worked out of Charing Cross by C 0-6-0 31723, an unusual sight on passenger work here.
22	70026 *Polar Star* (86C) is a surprise at Hereford on the 'Cathedrals Express'.
23	4073 *Caerphilly Castle* arrives for light repairs at Caerphilly Works – most unlikely to have even visited its 'home' town before, much less the Works!
24	Restored MR Compound 1000 takes an Institute of Engineers special from New Street to Berkeley Road to visit a new Generating Station.
24	U1 2-6-0 31901 heads the 1pm Cardiff – Brighton from Salisbury, uncommon power for this service.
26	Glasgow – Blackpool special brings 72000 *Clan Buchanan* (66A) through Blackburn, where Polmadie locos are always notably scarce.
26	60951 (64B) piloted by an LMS 4-4-0 form a spectacular pair to arrive in St Enoch. The V2 later departs with the 9am relief to St Pancras.
26	Caprotti 44749 (9A) reaches Cardiff on the 8.55am parcels from Crewe, a rare through working for a Manchester engine.
27	E50xx on the down 'Night Ferry' damages an overbridge near Faversham when its pantograph is accidentally raised at speed, damaging this also.
27,28	Rolling stock exhibition at St Botolph's station goods yard, Colchester includes D5537, 70010 *Owen Glendower*, 68619 (in GE royal blue livery) and D8402 (a local product by Davey Paxman).
29	60928 enters King's Cross on the 'Sheffield Pullman' after a diesel failure.
29	Ivatt 2-6-0 46469 (30E) arrives in Southend (Victoria) with freight, first recorded appearance of this class here.
U/D	Pullman Camping Coach (blue external livery) is on show in Liverpool Street.
U/D	E1 4-4-0 31497 – newly displaced from the SE Division – heads the 7.15am Salisbury – Bournemouth (West) via Fordingbridge, a new type on this line.
U/D	Ashford Works shops 0-6-0PTs 4601 (201,295 miles since last general repair!) and 4601

(187,543 miles).

U/D   60146 *Peregrine* (50A) heads the up 'North Briton' out of Queen Street.

U/D   60027 *Merlin* records 31 round trips working the (Mon-Fri) 'Elizabethan' (King's Cross – Edinburgh) between 15 June, 12 September (24,000 miles).

U/D   In connection with the Scottish Industries Exhibition at Kelvin Hall, Glasgow, an extensive series of special excursions runs 3-19 September. These utilise five pre-1923 veterans in various combinations over several routes the locos being CR 4-2-2 123, HR 4-6-0 103, GNS 4-4-0 49 *Gordon Highlander*, NBR 256 *Glen Douglas* and GWR 4-4-0 3440 *City of Truro*. Prior to their workings the Scottish examples were on show to the public at Princes Street (103), Dundee (123), Ayr (256) and Aberdeen (49) during 25-27 August.

OCTOBER 1959

3ʀᴅ   D5309 fails on the 8.20am King's Cross – Hitchin at Knebworth. Passengers transfer to other service; 90349 + D5309 + quad-art set head north, odd sight. As is that of 0-6-0 D2029 at Hitchin on the Saturday RAF leave train from Henlow Camp to Broad Street (though engines will be changed at Hitchin!).

3   CR 123 + 2 restored CR coaches form a special from Edinburgh to Alloa via the Forth Bridge, returning via Larbert.

4   61379 *Mayflower* is seen heading out of King's Cross with a special train (including two Kitchen Cars) whose roofboards read 'The Ancient and Honourable Artillery Company of Massachussets Express' – the longest yet?

6   Main line diesel 10203 undergoes tests between Crewe and Carlisle with a dynamometer car, two Mobile Test Units and 13 coaches.

7   Up fish train leaves Carlisle behind 45504 *Royal Signals* (82E) ex-Works. Bristol engines are not often seen in Carlisle.

7   70053 *Moray Firth* (55A), also ex-Works, heads the 5.30am Scrooby – New England freight. Holbeck 'Britannias' are rarities on the East Coast main line.

10   45301 (3E Monument Lane) is noted on Cardiff (Canton) shed, whilst 45556 *Nova Scotia* (9A) leaves the same shed LE for Pontypool Road.

10   School special of 7 standard-width coaches leaves Charing Cross non-stop to St Leonards via Tonbridge, Ashford and Hastings behind 30929 *Malvern*.

12   73170 (55A) is noted on the 4.30am New England – Ranskill freight.

13   61317, 61372 haul two troop trains throughout from Brentwood to Southampton Docks – first B1s to reach here. Return is one train, double-headed.

14   B16 4-6-0 61448 (50A) provides a rare sight at Cambridge, working in from Hitchin with a daily goods, and returning with a freight back to Hitchin.

14   E1R 0-6-2T 32697 is an unusual type to work a Guildford – Redhill service.

17   Padstow and Plymouth portions of the ACE (four coaches only) leave Exeter (Central) behind 34057 *Biggin Hill* + 34033 *Chard* – superfluous power!

18   Preliminary trials of the new 'Midland Pullman' (for St Pancras – Manchester service to commence mid-Jan 1960) take place between the Metro-Cammell Works in Birmingham and Aldridge (via Castle Bromwich).

24   Last LMR loco still lettered 'British Railways' in full is Ivatt 2-6-2T 41224.

25   60108 *Gay Crusader* is a notable visitor to the Grantham – Nottingham line, and is seen

on Colwick depot.

28   D5331 takes over from an A4 at Longniddry on the 2.25pm Waverley to Newcastle, first appearance of this type on passenger duty on Tyneside.

28   L 4-4-0 31760 heads the 5.25pm London Bridge – Reading (South), several years since any 4-4-0 worked this train.

29-3 November   Harwich – Liverpool boat train is diverted from Lincoln over the LDEC line via Tuxford to reach Sheffield (Victoria). 'Britannias' 70000, 70005/10/39 are therefore rare sights over this route.

30-1 November   D16 4-4-0 62612 (31F) is hauled south from Leicester (Midland) shed and is seen on Cricklewood next day, later going on to Stratford.

31   76114 (piloted by a '5') works the 9.31am Fort William – Glasgow. First sighting of this class north of Crianlarich.

U/D   92250 emerges from Rugby Testing Station fitted with a Giesl oblong ejector and is allocated to Banbury to work iron ore trains to South Wales. First BR usage of this device, though the Talyllyn bought one in 1958, and the NCB is conducting trials at Baddesley Colliery with an 0-6-0ST.

NOVEMBER 1959

2ND   Winter timetable begins, delayed due to printing strike. New augmented hourly service introduced between Paddington and Snow Hill. All equivalent services from Euston cancelled for the electrification works.

2   61255 heads the inaugural 'Tees-Thames' between Saltburn and York.

3   72002 *Clan Campbell* appears on Gateshead depot, booked to work to York.

3   13-coach special for a ship-launching at Barrow passes Ulverston behind a brace of 'Scots' 46111 *Royal Fusilier* + 46144 *Honourable Artillery Company.*

6   4-coach special is run from Basingstoke to Bournemouth (West) behind 30918 *Hurstpierpoint* as the 9.20am from Birkenhead is running an hour late.

9   Two cows are killed on the line at Broxbourne in the morning peak period, causing much disruption to commuters.

11-14   70053 *Moray Firth* (55A) – with speedometer – seen on Darnall shed (11th). 70001 *Lord Hurcomb* arrives at Sheffield (Victoria) on the westbound Harwich boat train and proceeds (on loan) to Holbeck, whilst 70053 goes forward to Harwich on the eastbound boat train (13th). 70001 noted at Skipton on the down 'Thames-Clyde Express' (14th). 70053 undertakes speed braking trials between Stratford, Norwich and Ipswich on the 20th.

12   D6130 (on loan from the ER) is tried on the 5.45am Queen Street – Mallaig, arriving 1½ hours late and delaying the steamer service. The return working is 2½ hours late into Glasgow. Engine's performance is said to be 'lamentable'.

13   8.15am St Enoch – Largs Inter-City DMU is formed with the driving cabs coupled nose-to-nose and the corridor connections at the outer ends!

14   4922 *Enville Hall* (82B) is unusually employed on the 2.35pm Plymouth (Friary) to Exeter (Central) via Okehampton.

14   34046 *Braunton* passes through Barking with the ECS of a football special from Bournemouth to Walthamstow. Proceeds to Tilbury for servicing and to turn, being the first rebuilt Bulleid Pacific on the LTS section.

14   Shrewsbury's 45406 reaches Peterborough (East) with a football excursion from its hometown for an FA Cup tie. Engine refuels at Spital Bridge (31F) where considerable interest is caused by the WR reporting number frame and plates fitted to 45406, the first seen here.

15   C2X 0-6-0 32535 is noted running with 3 WR coaches on the Midhurst branch near Fittleworth; 'Horizon Films' are shooting some scenes.

15   West Coast main line is shut for engineering works at Garstang and Carnforth. Up 'Ulster Express' passes Giggleswick with 46226 *Duchess of Norfolk* ; up 'Royal Scot' runs via Low Gill and Ingleton behind 46242 *City of Glasgow* but down train goes over the S&C with 46211 *Queen Maud*, as do the 9.25am Glasgow – Birmingham (46252 *City of Leicester*) and the 11.10am Birminghamham – Glasgow (45189 + 46200 *The Princess Royal*). Between Wigan and Hellifield both 'Royal Scots' have pilots; 2-6-4T 42436 + 46242 and 42484 + 46211.

15   East Coast main line traffic also diverted via March, Ely and Cambridge due to engineering works. Cambridge sees no fewer than 24 Pacifics of various types including 60138 *Boswell* on the up 'Harrogate Sunday Pullman'.

16   60954 (50A) breaks new ground for the class by arriving at Bristol with a Washwood Heath to Westerleigh freight. Seen on Bromsgrove shed on 17th.

16   6-car unit makes first appearance, on trial runs Leicester – Luton.

16   6pm Minehead – Taunton runs into a herd of bullocks just beyond Dunster, killing 8 outright, plus another put down on the spot.

18   2-6-4T 42182 (15C) is a surprise arrival at Stoke Gifford yard on freight.

19   2-6-4T 42336 + 6839 *Hewell Grange* form an unlikely combination to head the 1.58pm from Banbury into Paddington.

21   0-6-2T 6655 works an Oxford – Bletchley parcels, a new class here where GWR visitors have included 'Castle', 'Grange' and 'Hall' 4-6-0s (four of the latter); 2-6-0 7341 and 2-6-2T 4148 over the last 16 months.

21   L&Y 0-8-0 49624 (26A) is a loco type rarely seen on York shed.

21   61961 (36A) reaches Stoke Gifford on freight, returning north LE.

21   Restored HR 4-6-0 103 works an SLS special from Buchanan Street to Blair Atholl, consisting of a stove van, the two restored CR coaches and ex-'Devon Belle' observation car SC281M.

22   West Coast line again closed and 46233 *Duchess of Sutherland* takes the up 'Royal Scot' over the Low Gill – Clapham route.

23   43957 (31F) is an unexpected arrival at Newark on freight from Colwick.

25-27   E5009, fitted with experimental anti-wheelslip equipment, operates tests between Victoria and Dover (Marine) with simulated 'Night Ferry' loadings. Train comprises the LMR No.3 dynamometer car and 10 loaded hopper wagons sandwiched between two bogie brake vans, 695 tons, and is a strange sight departing from Victoria at 10.43am on three successive days.

26   Ivatt 2-6-0 43083 (40F Boston) heads a down freight through Finsbury Park.

27   E3001, the first of the AC lines electric locos to be delivered, is handed over to BR at Sandbach, for use (initially) on the Styal line.

28   LNW 0-8-0 49130 (24L Carnforth) is a surprise visitor to March (31B).

29   Colwick depot surprisingly hosts 60067 *Ladas*, 60109 *Hermit*, 60015 *Quicksilver* and 60983 – apparently the shed is helping out with GN main line repair work.

29	B16 4-6-0 61468 noted at Saltley, a class not normally allowed west of Burton.
30	The 'Robin Hood' enters St Pancras with 61136 piloting 45532 *Illustrious*, an extremely rare combination. Very few B1s reach St Pancras at all.
U/D	At least six GWR pannier tanks still bear pre-BR insignia, including 8769 and 9710, which both display the monogram abandoned prior to 1939!
U/D	Four 66A 'Clans' are loaned to Edinburgh depots to release V2s for seasonal work on seed potato and sugar beet traffic. 72001/2 go to 64B, 72003/4 to 64A.
U/D	BTC is charged by the Scottish police with permitting a train of 30 wagons to pass along Camperdown Street (in Dundee) on 25 August. Byelaw (of 1931) restricts trains to 20 wagons. Also, train was not accompanied by a pilotman. BTC is admonished on first charge and fined £2 on the second!

DECEMBER 1959

2ND	E6 0-6-2T 32418 arrives in Brighton from Tunbridge Wells for fitters' attention and is then sent to work at Newhaven – an exceptional sight here.
3	J19 0-6-0 64669 brings the 8.30am from Stansted into Liverpool Street, unaccustomed work for this class!
5	D5513 heads a football special through to Southampton from Southend, and takes the ECS into the New Docks – the first main line diesel to enter these.
5	J69 0-6-0T 68619 (the Liverpool St pilot in GE livery) appears at New Cross Gate with a Newmarket – Epsom horsebox special.
5	Football special carrying Crystal Palace supporters to Margate is a 12-coach EMU formed of three Portsmouth line 4-car sets – a most unusual working.
5	Another football special from York to Crook Town comprises a DMU formation of 12-cars, the longest rake seen so far in this area in public service.
5	61653 *Huddersfield Town* is a rarity at Selby, heading northbound freight.
8	N 2-6-0 31846 (72A) works a special freight from Tavistock Jct., Plymouth, to St Austell, and is serviced at St Blazey, before returning LE to Friary shed. An unprecedented incursion into WR territory by a SR engine.
8	35002 *Union Castle* travels LE to Newton Abbot for weighing, back next day.
10	Stanier 3-cyl. 2-6-4T 42512 is a rare sight at Liverpool Street on a parcels train.
11	Another V2 60839 appears in Bristol (Barrow Road) after working a freight into Westerleigh yard. Stays for six days before heading off to Gloucester.
11	45538 *Giggleswick* noted on a pick-up freight at Stamford, strange choice!
12	46256 *Sir William A. Stanier, F.R.S.* makes a guest appearance in Princes Street on the 6.12pm to Glasgow.
13	W 2-6-4T 31919 pays an annual visit to Tattenham Corner to collect parcels vans for the Christmas traffic.
14	1007 *County of Brecknock* provides a variation in power at the head of the 'Red Dragon' out of Paddington – rare indeed to see a 'County' on this train.
15,21	60083 *Sir Hugo* heads the morning Hull – Liverpool; 60074 *Harvester* repeats this on 21st, though steam has become uncommon recently.
15	43893 is observed heading north through Leeds hauling 61743 + 61750 from Lincoln to Motherwell for scrapping.
17	First of the 1550hp BRCW Bo-Bo Type 3s D6500 arrives at Hither Green.

19	61123 (56B) works throughout from Bradford (Exchange) to King's Cross with an excursion train, most unusual for B1s to work unchanged to London.
21	60012 *Commonwealth of Australia* – running at speed on the morning 'Talisman' – parts company with the train! 60865 (52D) pushes the coaches into Morpeth to be reunited with the waiting A4.
22	70006 *Robert Burns* – immaculately turned out – heads the Royal train from Liverpool Street through to King's Lynn. 70006 returns the ECS to Wood Green via Cambridge and Hitchin, reaching Stratford by way of Palace Gates.
24	2-6-0 5351 heads the 6.15pm Portsmouth – Salisbury van train. First GWR engine over this stretch of line since 26 March.
24	1.49pm arrival into Liverpool Street surprisingly brings 61158 (36A) into the City of London, whilst even more of a shock is 61075 (34A) on the up 'East Anglian'. Locos from 'Top Shed' are extremely rare in this terminus.
24	Northbound 'Pines Express' comes into Bath (Green Park) behind the unlikely combination of 'Jinty' 0-6-0T 47496 + 34028 *Eddystone*.
24	70025 *Western Star* reaches Wrexham on the 8.55am Cardiff – Manchester.
24	Tweedmouth A3 60069 *Sceptre* is a surprise choice for the up 'Aberdonian' out of the Granite City.
25	60020 *Guillemot* (52A) is another surprise arrival into Aberdeen from Edinburgh in mid-morning. First Gateshead A4 to reach Aberdeen since 1952.
27	A2/3 60511 *Airborne* + 44891 form a rare partnership on the 2.41pm York (Clifton Sidings) to Manchester (Red Bank) ECS train.
28	Hatfield diesel shunter D3490 heads the 12.45pm Luton (Bute Street) to Leighton Buzzard passenger train and return working, rare usage for this type.
28,29	70035 *Rudyard Kipling* is engaged in a special Liverpool Street – Cambridge trial, making the run in an hour. D5545 (uprated to 1600hp) is similarly tested next day.
29	Special train of tankers, Fawley – Leicester via Reading (West), is worked through to Didcot by 30905 *Tonbridge*, a 4-4-0 being a strange choice!
29	Vale of Rheidol 2-6-2T *Prince of Wales* noted under repair at Swindon Works.
30, January 1,2	A2/3 60522 *Straight Deal* is provided to work a train of empty bolster wagons from Healey Mills to the North East. 60008 *Dwight D. Eisenhower* and 60158 *Aberdonian* perform the same duty on 1,2 January respectively, each a rare working in itself.
U/D	61068 (of Scarborough) brings a parcels train from Leicester into Bedford, where a V2 is also found on shed, both unexpected visitors to the Midland.
U/D	D16 4-4-0 62612, *en route* from Leicester to Stratford for cutting up, puts in a spell of work at St Albans on the way, a local Christmas treat?
U/D	'Lord Nelson' 4-6-0s are expected to have a further life of 15 years (says BR).
U/D	45009 (63A) and 73122 (67A) both work into Heaton on freights from Scotland, both strangers south of the Border.
U/D	Stationary boiler in use at Ashford Works is a 250psi parallel boiler 'Royal Scot' type, built Crewe Works 6/1937, number 9882. Removed from 46134 (15/9/51), converted to saturated type and fitted with new firebox, commencing work at Ashford 27/10/51, but still going strong!
U/D	Lightning strike by railwaymen causes down 'South Yorkshireman' to leave Marylebone (V2 hauled) composed of 'Yorkshire Pullman stock'!

U/D Wrong Crest! College of Heralds dictates that the lion within the current BR crest must always face to the left. Transfers on hundreds of locos, and thousands (?) of carriages require replacement.

JANUARY 1960

1ST 'Deltic' is spotted inside Stratford Works.

3 T9 4-4-0 30120 reaches Swindon on an enthusiasts' special from Southampton.

5 48319 (18A) arrives in Salisbury on a Kineton – Bulford ammunition train.

5 CR 0-4-4T 55221 (61C) occupies the wheel drop facility at Ferryhill depot.

6 1450 emigrants to Australia leave Plymouth on the Panama registered vessel 'Fairsky'. Four special 14-coach trains arrive at Millbay Docks carrying them; 1028 + 4976, 4936 + 5940, 6829 + 6026, 7808 + 6004 power the trains.

6 A2/2 60502 *Earl Marischal* (50A) is surprisingly in charge of the 'Tees-Tyne Pullman' as the up train passes Newark – a type rarely seen on any Pullman.

8 84021 heads the 9.7am Fareham – Netley freight, a class debut here.

8 80152 is noted at Southampton working the 11.10am Plymouth – Brighton, first time for many months that this class has done so.

8 34010 *Sidmouth* (70A) is a most unexpected visitor to Kentish Town (14B), and 73110 (70A) is a surprise arrival at Tilbury on a special boat train.

9 FA Cup day. Rotherham v Arsenal brings 60137 *Redgauntlet*, 60022 *Mallard*, 60029 *Woodcock* into Sheffield (Victoria). 45543 *Home Guard* (9A) reaches Lincoln from Accrington and 'Crab' 42898 comes in from Burnley. 45540 *Sir Robert Turnbull* (3B) arrives at York and Sunderland receives 45580 *Burma* (24E) ex-Preston and Stanier 2-6-0 42961 from Darwen. All rare engine workings at these destinations.

10 73156 (41B) finds itself spending the weekend on Cardiff Canton shed.

12 D5094 – the first main line diesel built at Darlington – emerges from the Works driven by the local 'Railway Queen'.

13 Wolves v Sunderland Cup (evening) replay brings one 12-car and one 8-car DMU to Wolverhampton from the North East on match specials.

14 30917 *Ardingly* works the 5.37pm London Bridge – East Grinstead, a first for this class, and returns with the 7.26pm to Victoria.

15 4078 *Pembroke Castle* (84A) puts in a rare appearance at Leicester (Central), leaving with the 8.15pm fish train from Hull.

15 45739 *Ulster* (green) is seen paired with a lined black tender, an odd sight.

15 82009 (84H Wellington) is an extreme rarity at Reading, heading freight towards Didcot. Type not seen here since 1954, new ex-Swindon, running-in.

15,19,20 60151 *Midlothian*, 60075 *St. Frusquin* and 60947 all appear on Mirfield shed after working through from the North East on freights.

16 D5579 is exhibited at Liverpool Street painted 'bronze/gold' at the request of the ER. It is said that green blends into the countryside in East Anglia and you cannot see trains coming at a distance.

16 60915 (51L Thornaby) is a strange loco to work the 4.8pm Sheffield – Derby, returning north on a Bristol – York.

16,23 Berwick – Newcastle fish train has 60152 *Holyrood* on two vans, and D244 on one van a week later. Superflous power!

18	Fitters are sent from Scarborough to Whitby by taxi to attend a DMU which, it turns out, has run out of fuel. This is therefore purchased at a local garage and transported to the DMU in tins, by taxi!
18	Camping Coach W9877W in chocolate and cream is on display at Snow Hill.
18	For the second replay of the Arsenal v Rotherham cup-tie at Hillsborough, 60015 *Quicksilver* works through to Wadsley Bridge, with a supporters' special, booked non-stop from King's Cross.
20	90021 traverses the S&C line towing 61731/48/51/62 towards Motherwell for scrap. K2s were never seen 'live' on the S&C.
22	2-6-2T 8108 (84E Tyseley) is rare, possibly unprecedented power for the 8.50am Shrewsbury – Hereford.
23	7.5pm Aberdeen – King's Cross departs behind the unusual combination of 44955 piloting 60004 *William Whitelaw*.
29	5-BEL Pullman unit is used for a special from Waterloo to Portsmouth for the launch of the new Channel Islands steamer 'Caesarea' at Cowes.
30	Thirteen specials are run from Peterborough to Sheffield for the Cup tie. Five A2s, three A3s and five V2s provide the power. Four are run to Wadsley Bridge, nine go to Sheffield (Victoria).
30	Signalling work at Victoria causes the 'Brighton Belle' to depart from London Bridge, and the 'Golden Arrow is re-routed via the Redhill – Tonbridge line headed by 34085 *501 Squadron*.
31	'Golden Arrow' runs from Victoria to Folkestone Harbour via Edenbridge behind 34068 *Kenley*, unusual routing.
31	H15 4-6-0 30331 reaches Redhill depot, a type not previously recorded here.
U/D	46153 *The Royal Dragoon* (3B) is noted pulling one parcels van at Walsall, as the usual Parcels Railcar is away for repair.
U/D	45588 *Kashmir* and 45703 *Thunderer* (both 12B) visit Aberdeen, unusual here.
U/D	45506 *The Royal Pioneer Corps* heads the 6.30am Hereford – Cardiff and 5.10pm back to Crewe. First foray of this class into South Wales.
U/D	Machynlleth (89C) receives Stanier 2-6-2Ts 40086/110/205 from Wrexham, a type new to the Cambrian coast.
U/D	Royal train working from Sandringham to Romsey (for a wedding), and return, uses no fewer than eight locos; 3 x 'Britannias', 2 x B1s, 2 x '5's and a 'Merchant Navy'!
U/D	WR organises a staff competition for the most suitable name to grace 92220, the last steam engine to be built at Swindon. *Evening Star* is chosen.

FEBRUARY 1960

1ST	J36 0-6-0 65258 makes a rare trip to Tweedmouth hauling 60529 *Pearl Diver* which is *en route* to Doncaster Works.
1	Q 0-6-0 30533 is an unexpected sight at Hornsey shed.
2	44097 (31F) heads the 5.9am Doncaster – Grantham freight, most unusual.
3	E5003 fails on an up coal train at Bekesbourne and is rescued by E5012, providing the rare sight of 'double-headed' electrics, as far as Faversham.
3	New WR 8-car Blue Pullman makes a trial run from Saltley to Mangotsfield.
3	60909 heads the afternoon 'Talisman' into Newcastle (A4 fails, Doncaster).
4	80046 works the 6pm Carlisle – St Enoch, a lengthy trip for a 2-6-4T.

| 5 | 45562 *Alberta* (55A) leaves Canton shed LE to Pontypool Road, having arrived in Cardiff with the overnight parcels from Crewe. Rare class at 86C. |

5   45562 *Alberta* (55A) leaves Canton shed LE to Pontypool Road, having arrived in Cardiff with the overnight parcels from Crewe. Rare class at 86C.

6   60007 *Sir Nigel Gresley* (34A), after repair at Colwick, works the 6.50am freight to Doncaster, a new task for a 'Top Shed' A4!

7   Q1 0-6-0 33039 heads the 7.55pm Brighton – Victoria, giving a sprightly run!

8   WD 2-10-0 90763 (12A) passes Bury towards Heywood on a breakdown train.

8   Bo-Bo electric E3036 (first build from NBL, Hyde Park, Glasgow) undergoes trials between Milngavie and Singer before being towed south.

9   D8032 (61A) is surprise power for the 9.20am Perth – Inverness.

10   'Hampshire' diesel unit 1115 makes a special speed trip from Waterloo to Dorchester South, 3 hours being allowed. Later seen on trials to Oxted, also.

10   60004 *William Whitelaw* (64B) is the first A4 to work the West Coast Postal from Aberdeen to Perth.

10   73084 (70A) brings a troop train of SR stock through to Parkeston Quay.

10   61138 (41D Canklow) is a rare sight on the Settle & Carlisle line, working the 6am Carlisle – St Pancras freight.

12   'Baby Deltics' D5903 + D5905 double-head a coal train from Whitemoor to Bury St Edmunds, most unusual use of these locos.

14   70003 *John Bunyan* (32A) passes Newark on special freight, pleasant surprise.

15   LTS 0-6-2Ts 41991/2/3 appear at Kingmoor, for scrapping in Scotland.

17-19   60020 *Guillemot* heads the 7.52pm Haymarket – Carlisle freight on three successive nights. On the last, 60023 *Golden Eagle* also works the 7.44pm Carlisle – Waverley passenger, this route having previously been an A4-free zone (except in emergencies).

19   6006 *King George I* is unaccustomed power on the 4.55pm Oxford – Didcot.

20   Two football specials are proposed from Brighton to Preston for the FA Cup tie, but the LMR flatly refuses to accept them, pleading 'Staff shortages and congested freight traffic'.

20   Dundee's 60822 is an unusual sight in Glasgow (Central).

20   E4 0-6-2T 32470 is a rare choice on the 1.8pm Three Bridges – East Grinstead

24   O1 2-8-0 63676 makes a surprise appearance at Southall for an Annesley loco.

25   30923 *Bradfield* works a special train of 1st class and Pullman cars only from Victoria – Brighton in connection with the Quaker Oats Co. conference.

25   0-6-0PT 9620 sets off from Weymouth LE to Ashford Works via the coast line, arriving two days later.

26   Doncaster Works departs from tradition and accepts 4 x LMS locos a week for scrapping. 40025, 40582, 43665, 43759 are the first, from Derby.

26   48422 overruns its Watford termination point with its 65 wagons of coal. Train is halted at Bushey and reverses, wrong line, back to Watford yard.

26   The 'Northumbrian' reaches King's Cross behind D5569 + D5588, a first.

27   0-6-2T 32107 runs light engine between Fratton and Southampton Docks, first E2 seen on this route.

27   L1 2-6-4T 67750 pilots 60111 *Enterprise* from Darlington to Crook with a football special from London for the FA Amateur Cup match v Hayes.

27   61131 (56A) is serviced at Edge Hill after working a Wakefield RL special for the match at Widnes.

29   H16 4-6-2T 30516 is surprise power for the 4.20pm Eastleigh – Totton.

U/D	500hp EE 0-6-0 D0226 (82B) is used at Chippenham for shunting cattle trains on market day (Friday). (Loco renumbered from D226).
U/D	'Patriot' 45544 reaches Ayr on the 10.15am parcels train from St Enoch.
U/D	72005 *Clan Macgregor* is seen employed on Waverley route traffic.
U/D	60038 *Firdaussi* and 60077 *The White Knight* are, remarkably, transferred to Holbeck from Gateshead, for use over the S&C route.
U/D	Major expresses between Liverpool and Euston are routed via Earlestown and Warrington from January to early March to allow pre-electrification work at Runcorn. 'Foreign' locos at Earlestown include 'Princess Royals', 71000 *Duke of Gloucester* and ex-Works 46243 *City of Lancaster*.
U/D	'Buffer tests' at Manchester (London Road) entrance spectators, as firstly two coaches are fly-shunted into them at 10mph, and then a 2-8-0 with 15 coaches attacks the buffers twice, at 5mph and 8mph, with 'satisfactory' results.

MARCH 1960

1ST	D5586 surprisingly heads the 'Heart of Midlothian' out of King's Cross, and passes Hatfield on time.
4	St Pancras – Sheffield express is hauled by D57xx piloting a 'Jubilee' at least as far as Bedford. Not a combination seen before.
4	D6500/01 noted working an up 10-coach test train through Tonbridge.
5	J20 0-6-0 64692 (31B) is an unexpected arrival at Southend (Victoria) on the morning parcels train.
7	Beattie 2-4-0WT 30586 seen on 72B, returning from Eastleigh Works to Wadebridge, and is the first steam engine to have BR diesel-type numerals.
10	The last B12 61572 assists D5564 which fails at Littleport on the 7.20pm Liverpool Street – Kings Lynn. Unique pairing?
11	73141 (17C Rowsley) works the 1.5pm Tilbury boat train from St Pancras.
12	Neasden houses a cosmopolitan selection of locos having brought in specials for the womens' Hockey International; 4 x 'Castles', a 'Hall', a V2, 3 x B1s, 2 x SR Pacifics and D5000/04 that double-headed a train from Faversham.
12	45010 (67B) works through to Waverley with a football special from Kilmarnock to Eyemouth (!).
12	Stock of the 'Royal Highlander' noted at Beauly behind a '5', running through to Dingwall taking hoteliers and press reporters to a conference at Strathpeffer.
13	Track renewals at Waterloo cause 'Sitmar Line' boat train (34094 *Mortehoe*) and a troop train (34009 *Lyme Regis*) to terminate at Victoria (Central Section).
14	'Britannia' 70047 (9A) reaches Pontypool Road on the 9am Manchester (London Road) – Swansea, returning with the 7.30am Penzance – Manchester.
15	Neasden B1 61077 appears at Willesden and then heads a down freight on the West Coast main line, a most uncommon event.
15,16	4917 *Crosswood Hall* conducts clearance tests between Fareham and Southampton (via Netley) with a bogie brake van.
18	92220 – the last steam engine to be built by BR – is officially named *Evening Star* by K.W.C. Grand of the BTC. Loco is in full BR green and has copper-capped double chimney. Cash prizes are awarded to the competition entrants who chose this name. Attending guests

are conveyed to Paddington by special train headed by 7007 *Great Western*. Exhibition of rolling stock is also laid on and includes D817/D818/6003/5057/3440/CR 123 plus six coaches, all built at Swindon (except CR 123 of course).

18 D5303 fails at Hatfield with the 5.10pm King's Cross – Royston, and the train is worked forward by D8047, first use of this type on an outer suburban train?

19 D5314 takes over from 60533 *Happy Knight* south of Hatfield and brings the 'Tees-Thames' into King's Cross.

19 Ivatt 2-6-0 45619 (89A), ex-Swindon Works and in unlined green, arrives at Southampton (Terminus) with the 1.5pm from Andover Jct. First of this class seen anywhere near the English Channel!

19 61131 is a rare visitor to the Furness district with a rugby league excursion from Wakefield to Whitehaven. Piloted each way from Carnforth by 45306.

19 'Patriot' 45517, 45717 *Dauntless* and 45719 *Glorious* (all 27A) reach Hull on football specials, as do 'Crabs' 42721/45 (27B), all uncommon types in Hull.

20 34029 *Lundy* reaches Bristol on an excursion from Portsmouth; retires to 82A.

21 Ivatt 2-6-0 46483 enters Scarborough on a route learning train; 1st of class here.

21,22 4956 *Plowden Hall*, 4917 *Crosswood Hall* (resp'y) work the 10.30am Cardiff to Portsmouth throughout. (Salisbury turntable is out of action – see 15,16).

21 Minister of Transport (Ernest Marples) inspects the 'Midland Pullman' and makes a special trip from Cricklewood to St Albans and back in it. Other diesels put on show at St Pancras include D10 *Tryfan* and D255 – a rare type in this terminus.

22 76080 (24D Lower Darwen) is a highly unusual arrival in London, on the 9.20pm Hillhouse – Camden fitted freight.

23 D5503 passes Watford with a Cadbury's special from Southend (Victoria) to Bournville, the loco going to Saltley for refuelling.

24 Five SR engines arrive in Westbury, four heading banana specials from Southampton Docks (H15 4-6-0 30474, 30770 *Sir Prianius*, U 2-6-0 31809 and N 2-6-0 31813). U 31802 also comes in hauling the failed DMU forming the 11.40am Weymouth – Bristol.

26 73137 + 61026 *Ourebi* arrive at Aintree on a Grand National excursion from Cleethorpes.

27 Waterloo – Bournemouth trains are diverted via Ringwood, which sees 34061 *73 Squadron* on the down 'Bournemouth Belle', and 34009/10/18/20/39/42/46/48/98 besides, and, by special authority 30862 *Lord Collingwood*, the first of this class to take this line, travelling both ways.

29 92204 (82B) makes test runs between Bath and Bournemouth (West) with 11 coaches – very successfully.

29 60041 *Salmon Trout* (64B) brings the rare sight of a Haymarket engine to Stockton, at the head of the 10.30am Bristol – Newcastle.

29 46211 *Queen Maud* is most unusual power for the down 'Caledonian'.

30 72003 *Clan Fraser* is borrowed by Newton Heath to work the 7.47am from Manchester to Todmorden! (This is repeated on Good Friday April 15th).

31 0-6-0 3218 works the Templecombe – Blandford pick-up freight, first GWR loco south of Templecombe since the war.

U/D Following exhibition at Swindon, CR 4-2-2 123, 4-4-0 3440 *City of Truro* go on show at Bristol (Temple Meads), then Cardiff (Queen Street).

U/D 61998 *Macleod of Macleod* is an unexpected type to receive attention at Inverurie Works.

U/D   0-6-0PT 1369 is sent to Weymouth for work on the Quay still lettered 'Great Western' in pre-monogram style!

APRIL 1960

2ND   (Week ending). 60022 *Mallard* clocks up 3216 miles in 6 days on a diesel diagram working the 'Flying Scotsman' to Newcastle and 5pm return, daily.

2   Express leaves St Pancras with D5 *Cross Fell* + 46106 *Gordon Highlander*, a new combination, it is thought.

3   Caprotti 44743 (27A) passes through Northallerton towards Darlington with the ECS of a Blackburn – Ripon excursion.

3   Bournemouth services are again diverted via Ringwood, with the 12.10pm Eastleigh – Bournemouth (West) headed by 30910 *Merchant Taylors* though 'Schools' are not permitted over this line (?). Ringwood sees the passage of 8 x WC/BB Pacifics and 3 x 5MTs during the day as well, on other diverted traffic.

4   90130 / 90137 / 90174 / 90261 all surprisingly noted on Reading (South) shed.

4,6,7   E5003 takes part in rail-stress tests north of Balcombe Tunnel. D5714 also makes a number of trial runs over this section (6th), having been sent down from Cricklewood specially, returning to the LMR on the 7th. First time one of these locos has been seen so far south.

7   77013 passes over the Laisterdyke – Shipley (Windhill) single line freight branch (which lost its passenger services in 1931), making a class debut here.

7   61330 (62A) heads a Heaton – Haverton Hill freight through Stockton, where Thornton engines had not previously reached.

7   60023 *Golden Eagle* is surprise power for a freight working into Hull.

9   Ivatt 2-6-0 43085 (40F) works ECS through from Skegness to Heaton, first Boston engine to be seen here?

9   D5532/35/74 bring three football specials from Norwich through to Coventry, not a class frequently noted here.

9   92025 (15A) appears at Fleetwood on a special train of prefabricated track from Derby, and is serviced at Blackpool North shed, first Crosti to reach here.

10   Rare sight (nowadays) is that of consecutive 'Hunts'; 62743 *The Cleveland* arriving in Waverley on the 8.6pm from Hawick and 62744 *The Holderness* coupling on to the other end to form the 8.20pm back to Hawick.

11   D267 runs out of fuel at Watford on an up sleeper, leaving a 2-6-4T to take the train on into Euston.

11   60532 *Blue Peter* takes the West Coast Postal out of Aberdeen, working through to Carstairs.

11-13   Restored 4-4-0 3440 *City of Truro* and CR 4-2-2 123 are exhibited at Birmingham (Moor Street), being towed back to Tyseley each night.

12   J35 0-6-0 64499 is a rare type on the Carlisle – Haltwhistle pick-up goods.

12-14   61660 *Hull City* and 61657 *Doncaster Rovers* (both 31B) appear in Rugby (Midland) – a first for this class.

13   D254 heads the first diesel-hauled passenger train into Scarborough.

14   70042 *Lord Roberts* (26A) is a notable arrival in Newcastle on a relief from Manchester.

| 14 | 60073 *St Gatien* (52B) is a surprise occupant of Ferryhill depot, and 60074 *Harvester* (55H Neville Hill) is a rarity in London on a fish train from Hull. |

| 15 | (Good Friday) First 'Starlight Special' of the season leaves St Enoch for St Pancras (via Edinburgh) behind 60160 *Auld Reekie* (64B). |

| 15 | L1 2-6-4T 67743 reaches Stratford-on-Avon after propelling two brake vans over the SMJ line, and soon returns towards Blisworth. |

| 15 | 72003 *Clan Fraser* enters Morecambe with an excursion from Manchester. |

| 16 | 9.30am Aberdeen – Glasgow is taken out by 45520 *Llandudno* (9A), only the third visit by a 'Patriot' class loco since 1952. |

| 17 | 45616 *Malta G. C.* passes through Snow Hill (a rare type here) with an excursion from Manchester (Central) to Stratford-on-Avon. |

| 18 | 44277 (24G Skipton) hauls an Easter Monday excursion from Bradford (Forster Square) to Grassington, which lost its passenger service in 1931. |

| 18 | 61020 *Gemsbok* reaches Morecambe on excursion traffic from Wakefield. |

| 18 | Restored Compound 1000 enters St Pancras as pilot to 45569 *Tasmania* on the 12.25pm from Manchester (Central). (Returns to Derby on 27th, piloting 46106 *Gordon Highlander* on 1.55pm to Manchester. See 20, 26 April also). |

| 18 | Last working D16 4-4-0 62613 heads the 'Fenman', Cambridge – Kings Lynn. |

| 20 | Restored 4-4-0 3440 *City of Truro* pilots Compound 1000 on an Ian Allan special from King's Cross to Doncaster and back, though 3440 fails at Peterborough on the return leg. A memorable pairing. |

| 20 | In total contrast, the 'Midland Pullman' diesel set runs trials on the Cambridge to Kettering branch. |

| 20,21 | 2-8-0s 4706, 4701 both observed working Reading – Oxford locals. |

| 23 | 60859 heads along the Calder Valley as far as Mytholmroyd with a freight from Mirfield. Has a V2 been seen here before? |

| 25,26 | GWR 4-4-0 3440, CR 4-2-2 123 travel under their own steam from London to Oxford for two days' display at Rewley Road station. |

| 26 | Repeat railtour from King's Cross to Doncaster Works has the last B12 61572 piloting Compound 1000 in each direction. Another fascinating pair. |

| 27 | D603 *Conquest* noted on a 13-coach test train from Glasgow to Kilmarnock. |

| 30 | 61660 *Hull City* is surprisingly found receiving attention in Wellingborough shed (15A). |

| 30 | Schoolboys International soccer match at Wembley brings five 'Halls' and a 'Castle' in on specials, plus two 'Schools', all going to Neasden for servicing. |

| 30 | 20-coach ECS train – the longest seen for some time – is taken from Clapham Jct. to Southampton New Docks by 30902 *Wellington* piloting 34095 *Brentor*. |

| 30 | Doncaster Works receive, for scrapping, Compounds 41090, 41102 and surprisingly S&D 2-8-0 53802. |

| U/D | E6 0-6-2Ts 32410/15 are given a very brief spell on the Folkestone Harbour branch before being banned by the Civil Engineer. |

| U/D | 60039 *Sandwich* and 60077 *The White Knight* work the Hull – Aintree overnight freight throughout on two occasions during the month. |

| U/D | All Hornsey's NBL diesels D6100-09 are transferred to Scotland, travelling as LE pairs. Similar arrangements apply to Hornsey's BRCW diesels D5300-09. Hornsey receives brand-new Brush diesels D5602-15, and BRCW D5310-15 over the course of April/May/June, also in pairs. |

MAY 1960

2ND	

2ND   J15 0-6-0 65479 is provided for the M&GN Preservation Society special from Norwich (City) to Lowestoft.

2   Ivatt 2-6-0 46520 (89A Oswestry) makes a rare appearance at Neath (Riverside) heading the 4.10pm to Brecon.

3   Holbeck's 73170 reaches Malvern (!) on a special from Newcastle.

6   350hp shunter D3044 is on trial at Sheperdswell on the East Kent line.

6   D230 arrives in St Pancras with the 11.42am from Manchester, unexpectedly as its route availability on the Midland is not yet assessed! (See also 21 March).

7   J21 0-6-0 65033 visits Carlisle on an enthusiasts' special from Darlington, outwards via Tebay and Shap, returning via Penrith, Kirkby Stpehen.

7   46100 *Royal Scot*, 46153 *The Royal Dragoon* and 70015 *Apollo*, 70017 *Arrow* are sent to Rose Grove shed to work supporters' specials to the FA Cup final (Blackburn 0 Wolves 3). One of the returning specials is diverted up the Werneth Incline (1 in 27) to reach Oldham in the early hours of Sunday.

8   5.25pm St Pancras – Manchester is headed throughout by 'Crab' 42870 (1A)!

9   7.50am Taunton – Paddington produces the unprecedented pairing of D820 *Grenville* + D601 *Ark Royal*.

9,10   45600 *Bermuda* is noted at Sheffield working the up/down 'Condor' on successive days, a rare class to be seen on this express freight service.

10   73068 (82E Barrow Road) – in lined green livery – works between Doncaster and Grantham on a running-in turn from Doncaster Plant.

10   70038 *Robin Hood* (32A) brings a train of petrol tanks into Heaton, rare here.

10   60010 *Dominion of Canada* heads a special train throughout from King's Cross to Walker (Riverside) conveying officials of the Canadian Pacific Steamship Co. to the launch of the new liner 'Empress of Canada'. The A4 continues round the electrified line to Benton, then south to Heaton and reverses its train back to Riverside for the return journey.

10-13   Tests take place between Carlisle and Skipton with a 2-car BRCW DMU plus a 2-car Metro-Cammell DMU plus four coaches, plus a testing vehicle. Radiator and cooling systems of DMUs are being investigated.

11-24   Stoke-on-Trent celebrates its Golden Jubilee, and BR stages an exhibition where the star of the show is 46254 *City of Stoke-on-Trent*, which the LMR withdraws on 22 May quoting 'Shortage of motive power'!

12   72001 *Clan Cameron* (66A) is a startling arrival in St Pancras on the 11.42am from Manchester (Victoria), only the second 'Clan' to reach here.

12   D272 heads the 7.25pm Gateshead – King's Cross Goods fitted freight, 47 wagons plus the ER dynamometer car, on a timing trial. Meanwhile...

12   D210 becomes the first of its class to be named, becoming *Empress of Britain* at a ceremony at Euston.

12,18   75056 (16A) arrives at Windsor (WR) on an excursion from Nottingham, as does 61283 (31A) on one from Ely six days later.

13   0-6-0PT 4608 is a novel arrival in Marylebone on the 7.53am from High Wycombe having replaced a failed 2-6-4T at West Ruislip.

13   61930 (52D) is a rarity at Whitemoor, on freight from Cambridge.

14	RL Cup final at Wembley (Wakefield v Hull) brings several specials into St Pancras from unusually, Wakefield (Kirkgate). Sixteen specials run down the GC (9 from Hull) so that Neasden depot sees 12 x B1s, 2 x V2s and 2 x K3s from various NER sheds. One excursion train returning to Lancashire also goes up the Werneth incline, as did a football special last week.
14	4-4-0 3440 *City of Truro* works an enthusiasts' special from Gloucester to Southampton Docks, via the MSWJ line outward, and back via the DNS line.
14	61853 pilots 45662 *Kempenfelt* as a remarkable combination to enter Temple Meads on the 12.48pm York – Bristol, from Sheffield.
15	RCTS visit to Swindon Works includes, on the return to Paddington, a reserved coach (late of the Caledonian Railway!) on the 4.10pm which is then attached to the rear of a 6-car DMU at Didcot.
14,28	4-4-0 49 *Gordon Highlander* (with two restored CR coaches and observation car), runs from Queen Street to Oban for a University extra-mural course on transport. 4-4-0 256 *Glen Douglas* similarly goes to Dundee on 28th.
17	D5612/13, brand new and only delivered from Doncaster that morning, have charge of the 'Heart of Midlothian' between King's Cross and Peterborough!
17	CR 4-4-0s 54485 + 54486 head the 6.47am Perth – Inverness in preparation for filming the following weekend.
18,31	61152 (41C) reaches Bath (Green Park) with the southbound 'Pines Express', and 61027 *Madoqua* (41A) arrives on the same train on the 31st, leaving on the northbound 'Pines' the following day.
18	Compound 1000 works an evening excursion from New Street to Stoke and back to view the exhibition there. (See 11-24 May).
20	D11 4-4-0 62663 *Prince Albert* is a strange sight indeed at Bishops Stortford, being hauled by D8205 to Stratford for scrapping.
20-23	54485/6 again work the 6.47am Perth – Inverness, filmed by the BBC for their *Railway Roundabout* series. They also head the 2.5pm Inverness – Forres on 21st. 4-4-0 49 takes over the railbus working, the 10.27am Craigellachie to Aviemore and 12.18pm return, for 3 days' further filming. HR 4-6-0 103 hauls the 5.40pm Inverness – Kyle (20th) and 6.20am Kyle – Dingwall next day.
21,22	Three troop trains between Pembroke and Whitland are headed by the unusual pairings of 1001 *County of Bucks* + 2-6-2T 4594; 2-6-0 6306 + 2-6-2T 4550 and next day, 2-6-2T 4122 piloting 6909 *Frewin Hall*.
22	Bridge maintenance causes diversion of up 'Thames-Clyde Express' from Skipton to Leeds via Ilkley, where 46117 *Welsh Guardsman* is seen passing.
26	2-8-0s 2840/78/80 + 2-6-0 5319 are towed from Oxley to Killamarsh (near Sheffield) for cutting up, very strange apparitions here!
26/27	Royal train from King's Cross stables overnight at Picton, arriving behind 60032 *Gannet*. 60115 *Meg Merrilies* takes train on to Horden (Co. Durham).
28	46119 *Lancashire Fusilier* brings a long train of ECS into Worcester.
29	Five 'Midland Pullman' cars seen at Marylebone for an official photograph.
30	34059 *Sir Archibald Sinclair*, piloted by the branch engine, works Seaton Jct. to Seaton, bringing back an empty pigeon special. Pacifics rarely reach Seaton.
30	60038 *Firdaussi* works the 'Thames-Clyde Express' through from Leeds to St Enoch – first of Holbeck's allocation to do this.

30	45511 *Isle of Man* (8B) appears at Norwich – first 'Patriot' seen here? – with the 8.40am from Peterborough, returning on the 3pm freight to Whitemoor.
30,31	92188, 92202 arrive at Skegness (rare sights at the east coast) on successive days to remove rakes of coaches from winter storage.
U/D	J72 0-6-0s 68723, 68736 are repainted into NER livery for station pilot duties at Newcastle and York repectively.
U/D	D3 *Skiddaw*, D10 *Tryfan* both reach Aberdeen in the last two weeks, working the 2.15pm Aberdeen – Broad Street fish train as far as Perth.

JUNE 1960

1ST	M7 0-4-4T 30377 works the 9.27am Maiden Newton – Weymouth, first instance of an M7 on the WR Castle Cary – Weymouth line.
3	'Patriot' 45517 (27A) reaches Newcastle with an evening train from York.
3	D6510/11 pass through Snow Hill, newly delivered from Smethwick to the SR.
4	Of the 20 Co-Bo Type 2s, 17 are stored unserviceable at Cricklewood or Derby, with the 'Condor' now regularly worked by '5's.
4	2869 found stored at Llanymynech. First 2-8-0 on the Cambrian (in any state?)
4,11	Doyen of the B1s 61000 *Springbok* reaches Scarborough on a Whit Saturday relief train. 73000 comes in from Sheffield a week later.
5	73068 (82E) – in green livery – brings a Whit Sunday excursion from Leicester into… Brighton! Surely a first for a Barrow Road engine?
6	43948 reaches Hunstanton on a special from Ullesthorpe; 44572 arrives with trippers from Northampton, and 75040 gets to King's Lynn with an excursion from Hinckley, interesting motive power visitors to this district.
6	2.38pm Allhallows to Gravesend (two coaches) is (over-)powered by H 0-4-4T 31512 piloting C 0-6-0 31510.
6	44168 (16A) – with tender tablet catcher – is a surprise choice for the 3.40pm Bradford (Forster Square) – Carlisle slow. 4Fs are rare on passenger workings over Ais Gill.
7,8	61312 (41D) brings the 9am relief train from St Enoch into St Pancras and 61162 (41A) also arrives with the 12.50pm relief from Carlisle. Next day's 'Thames-Clyde Express' leaves St Pancras double-headed by 61162 + 45656 *Cochrane*, the headboard being on the B1 – definitely a first!
9	Stanier 2-6-2T 40085 approaches Barmouth on a train from Machynlleth, last of five transferred to 89C earlier in the year, the others soon moving away.
10-12	60022 *Mallard* arrives at Immingham depot in order to power, from Grimsby, the 'Lincolnshire Poacher' private excursion from Alford to Edinburgh via the S&C and Waverley routes. First A4 seen at Grimsby?
11	Last train on the Dornoch branch is headed by 0-6-0PT 1649 on three coaches.
11	3.50pm from Weymouth departs for Waterloo behind 34028 *Eddystone* piloting 35021 *New Zealand Line*, an unusual combination of Pacifics.
12	O1 2-8-0 63610 is recorded working both up and down the Lickey incline.
13	D5506 works the 7.32am Southend (Central) – Fenchurch Street, first diesel to work an LTS rush-hour duty from Shoeburyness.
13	30851 *Sir Francis Drake* reaches Reading (General) on the 7.38am ex-Basingstoke.
15	B16 4-6-0 61440 (50A) noted at Rugby, standing outside the Testing Station.

15,16 7.40am Bristol – Bradford arrives in Derby behind 61041 and attaches 72007 *Clan Mackintosh* as pilot! Next day 72007 pilots a 5MT on same train!!

17 84005 shunts the yard at Harrow, first of this class seen here.

17 'Warship' D833, the first NB Type 4 diesel hydraulic, passes through Wellington on its delivery run to Swindon.

18 'Crab' 42853 (2B Nuneaton) reaches York on an excursion from Birmingham.

18 8.45am Waterloo – Lymington Pier is headed by U 2-6-0 31634 after a 'Schools' failure on Nine Elms, unusual last-minute power.

18 60120 *Kittiwake* (56C Copley Hill) is a rare visitor to Newcastle on the 8.55am from Filey, as Leeds A1s almost always head south.

18 73011 (6J Holyhead) is a rarity at York on the 8.50am ex-Newquay.

18 61995 *Cameron of Lochiel* heads an SLS special from Queen Street to Fort William (last K4 here?), back to Buchanan Street via Stirling.

18 D253 reaches the coast on the 'Scarborough Flyer' first time diesel hauled?

18 60003 *Andrew K. McCosh* fails at Knebworth and the 8.10am from Newcastle enters King's Cross with A2/1 60508 *Duke of Rothesay*, running tender first!

19 4-4-0 62668 *Jutland* is a startling arrival at Hull on excursion traffic. Goes to Dairycoates for servicing before heading the return working.

20 60533 *Happy Knight* brings the 'Sheffield Pullman' into King's Cross.

21 61113 (34E) noted passing through Tamworth (LL) with ER stock.

21 60061 *Pretty Polly* comes into Sheffield (Victoria) on a schools' special from Brookmans Park. A3s are uncommon nowadays in Victoria.

21 7.50pm Girvan – Glasgow DMU fails and is propelled to Ayr by the following 'Lothian Piper' express freight (45086) at up to 40mph!

22 J19 0-6-0 64653 works into Liverpool Street on the 10.21am from Bury St Edmunds after D5521 collides with a lorry at Cheshunt.

22/23 Royal train conveying the Queen Mother spends the night stabled on the Delph branch prior to going to Stockport next morning.

23 61287 reaches Brighton on a party special from Newmarket.

23 'Midland Pullman' 6-car set is on exhibition at Marylebone; WR 8-car set gives the Press a run from Marylebone to High Wycombe and back.

23 60159 *Bonnie Dundee* appears in Princes Street at the head of the Scottish TV train, on an excursion to Aberdeen.

25 'Flying Scotsman' arrives in Newcastle behind B16 4-6-0 61455, 60006 *Sir Ralph Wedgwood* having failed at Thirsk.

25 Margate receives an excursion from Windsor composed of two 4-COR sets and a 4-RES unit, carrying roofboards 'Waterloo-Portsmouth-Isle of Wight'!

26 Compound 1000's safety valves lift and stick open in New Street. Three large panes of glass from the station roof smash onto the platform, and damage cars in the adjacent Queens Drive! 1000 is on an SLS special to Gorton Works.

26 D5346 (64B!) enters Crewe towing D1 *Scafell Pike*, which had failed.

26 Cravens 3-car DMU is chartered for a private excursion from Nottingham through to Portsmouth & Southsea.

27 Preserved Wainwright 4-4-0 (ex-31737) is towed from Ashford to Nine Elms, then by road to Clapham Museum (early on the 28th).

27 92220 *Evening Star* works both the up 'Red Dragon' and the down 'Capitals United

Express' between Cardiff and Paddington.

28   2.15pm from Bristol reaches York behind, amazingly, 75021 (82E)!

28   Fire breaks out in the roof of Preston shed, destroying the entire roof and some offices. 12 engines are damaged, and buckled track has to be relaid.

29   45687 *Neptune* (67A!) is an astonishing arrival at Bath (Green Park) on the southbound 'Pines Express', and takes out the northbound train next day.

29   1011 *County of Chester* arrives at Southampton (Terminus) with an excursion from Bristol. First 'County' to reach Southampton, serviced at Eastleigh.

29   60001 *Sir Ronald Matthews* works the 'Queen of Scots' between Leeds and Newcastle, a unusual class on the Leeds Northern line through Harrogate.

U/D   46212 *Duchess of Kent* exits Aberdeen on the 3.10pm, first 'Royal' this year.

U/D   D11 4-4-0 62664 *Princess Mary* reaches Cambridge *en route* to Stratford Works for scrap, but heads a freight to March and is returned to the GN lines!

U/D   Neville Hill puts into service a 3-car DMU comprising Met-Cam power car/BRCW trailer/Derby lightweight power car. Variety! (Or panic measure?).

U/D   76001 (66B) is loaned to Fort William to work the Mallaig extension.

JULY 1960

1ST   D6501 reaches Bedford (for Whipsnade Zoo) with a special from Kent.

1   61010 *Wildebeeste* (50B Hull Dairycoates) reaches Windermere (Lakeside) with a schools' excursion from Hull, having worked the train throughout.

2   82039 pilots 44559 between Bailey Gate and Templecombe on the combined milk train and 3.40pm Bournemouth (West) – Bath (Green Park).

2   7.30am ex-Penzance arrives at Newton Abbot with a 'Castle' + 2-8-0 4703. The preceeding 8.5am ex-Newquay has D6316 + 73041. More variety!

2   34055 *Fighter Pilot* works a load of fertiliser between Polegate and Heathfield.

2   9.29am to Manchester leaves Scarborough behind 75031 (6B), first of its class seen here. 61059 (31B), with self-weighing tender comes in on a relief.

2   Exmouth – Cleethorpes passes over the S&D behind 2-8-0 53808 piloted by 4-4-0 40696, routine except that 40696 is running tender first. Most unusual!

4   MR Blue Pullmans begin operating from Manchester (Central) to St Pancras and back, with a round trip to Leicester from St Pancras in between.

5   72009 *Clan Stewart* arrives in Sutton Coldfield, having worked the Car Sleeper through from Stirling. Returns in the evening on the down service.

6,7   'Crab' 42781 (2B) enters Windsor (Central) on an excursion from Nuneaton. 60890 comes in next day with a special from Sutton-on-Sea.

7   34088 *213 Squadron* heads a Royal train near East Croydon bringing the King of Thailand from Gatwick airport to Victoria.

8   2-6-4T 42556 (15E) brings the 6.5am Leicester – Manchester into Sheffield (Victoria), rare to see a tank engine on such a working.

8   C 0-6-0 31244 heads the 8.10am Tonbridge – Brighton, antediluvian power.

9   60138 *Boswell* is an unprecedented arrival in Scarborough on the 10.45am from Newcastle via Gilling, first A1 to reach here.

9   72005 *Clan Macgregor* (!) arrives in Bristol on the 8.45pm (FO) Bradford to Paignton, leaving with the 7.45am (SO) Paignton – Newcastle via Worcester.

9	46169 *The Boy Scout* (5A) is surprise power for an Aberdeen – Glasgow train.
9	1008 *County of Cardigan* (83G Penzance!) reaches Leicester on the Bournemouth – York, a real shock arrival!
9	'Patriot' 45549 (8B) enters Cambridge, from Leicester, and looks out of place!
9	73042 is a rare sight at Paddington on the 11.12am from Weymouth. Other than 'Britannias' standard types are uncommon in Paddington.
9	45605 *Cyprus* and 45608 *Gibraltar* (both 55A) work into Marylebone on 'Starlight Specials' ex-Waverley. Not the usual terminus for Holbeck locos.
9	D281 leaves Filey Holiday Camp on the 10.55am to Derby, piloted as far as Bridlington by tender-first 62717 *Banffshire*, an odd couple.
10	45536 *Private W. Wood, V.C.* (41C) arrives in Newcastle with an excursion from Chesterfield – first rebuilt 'Patriot' seen in Newcastle.
12	61005 *Bongo* (31B) works through to Birmingham (Curzon St Goods Depot) with a 'Birdseye' frozen food special from Yarmouth.
13	2-6-4T 42577 (2A) turns up at Hunstanton with a local from Kings Lynn.
13	D5122 (60A) reaches Waverley at 8.41pm, working through from Inverness.
14	35025 *Brocklebank Line* heads a Southampton – Milford Haven petrol tank train as far as Westbury, where 'Merchant Navy's' are notable arrivals.
15	45617 *Mauritius* (12B) is unusual power at Buchanan Street at the head of the 8.35pm to Dover.
16	60082 *Neil Gow* (55A) reaches Morecambe (Promenade) on the 8.35pm from Leeds (City), a class debut for an A3 at this resort.
16	10.5am ex-Filey, and 2pm ex-Bridlington are both extended from Leeds to Halifax, where 60952 and B16 4-6-0 61411 are both extreme rarities.
16	O1 2-8-0 63687 is a highly unusual visitor to Gunton, working the Norwich (City) to Norwich (Thorpe) freight service.
16	60077 *The White Knight* (55A), working a Newcastle – Bristol express fails near Burton and goes on shed there. First A3 on the Derby – Birmingham main line.
16	Remarkably, three successive arrivals at Carlisle, all from Heads of Ayr, are headed by 'Crabs' 42917, 42916, 42743 with trains bound for Newcastle, Manchester & Liverpool, Leeds – usually a rare type on passenger trains here.
16	Leeds (City) gets the rare sight of a Dalry Road (64C) engine when 45022 arrives on the 7.4am from…Huddersfield!
17	4-4-0 40620 + 60038 *Firdaussi* (55A) form an incongruous pairing at the head of the 9.5pm St Enoch – St Pancras sleeper out of Glasgow.
17	E5004 + 20001 + D6505 conduct track tests between Balcombe Tunnel and Three Bridges on the Brighton main line. A unique trio.
18	A London Transport aluminium coach and a LMR 2-car DMU are noted at Dunton Green returning from exhibition in France!
18	61045 (32A) and 60940 (52B) are both strange visitors to Holbeck.
19	Beattie 2-4-0WT 30587 works a special train between Exeter (St James' Park Halt) and Central, to mark the latter's centenary. GW panniers are hidden away for the day and replaced by M7s!
19	73039 (1A) heads the 8.7am Cambridge – Hunstanton, to Kings Lynn, a rare task for a Willesden engine, obviously 'borrowed' by Cambridge.
19-21	6-car 'Trans-Pennine' DMU runs trials Leeds (City) – Liverpool (Lime St).
20,21	'Deltic' conducts high-speed brake trials, King's Cross – Grantham, 12 coaches plus ER

21 43973 (8F Springs Branch) causes a minor sensation, arriving at Ferryhill shed *en route* to Inverurie Works, first time an engine from as far afield as Wigan has visited these Works.

22 60533 *Happy Knight* (34E) breaks new ground when seen standing on the Keighley – Bradford side of the Shipley triangle, light engine.

23 45516 *The Bedfordshire and Hertfordshire Regiment* (8B) brings the 9.25am from Birmingham into Norwich, a most unusual class to reach here.

23 73095 (84G), in green livery, and ex-Doncaster Works, arrives at Scarborough on an excursion. Has a Shrewsbury engine reached here before?

23 Westbound 'Devonian' comes into Bristol behind 46164 *The Artists' Rifleman* (41C), having worked through from Sheffield. 'Scots' rarely reach Bristol.

24 7pm Sheffield (Midland) – Chinley departs behind the amazing combination of 3F 0-6-0 43207 piloting 70017 *Arrow*!

25 62031 (65J), ex-Doncaster Works, brings the unique sight of a Fort William engine to Cambridge, taking out the 1.55pm to Birmingham.

26 9.17am stopping train from Carlisle is brought into Glasgow (Central) by 60077 *The White Knight* (55A), most unusual in this terminus.

27 Ex-Crosti 92021 takes a lightweight freight out of Marylebone.

30 61847 + 46104 *Scottish Borderer* (66A) form an eye-catching combination on the 4pm to Leeds out of Manchester (Exchange).

30 5.10am Queen Street – Mallaig is worked forward from Fort William by 76001 piloting 44255, a new pairing on the Mallaig extension.

30 D5100 + D5096 power the 10.50am Scarborough – Newcastle via Gilling, where few main line diesels have yet been seen.

30 92180 (34E) leaves South Shields (!) with the 9.10am to King's Cross.

31 Astonishingly, 45673 *Keppel* (63A Perth!) arrives in St Pancras on the 1.55pm from Manchester. Also seen next day working the 11.52am ex-Manchester, at Luton, piloted by 92080!

U/D 62718 *Kinross-shire* (64A!) works a Hull – Bridlington; jaws drop!

U/D 4-4-0 40646 works the Birmingham portion of the CTAC Scottish Tours Express through to Preston, a long solo working nowadays for this type.

U/D 'Welsh Dragon' (Rhyl – Llandudno) is a 4-car DMU fully roofboarded.

AUGUST 1960

1ST (Bank Holiday Monday). Two 8-coach specials run from Birkenhead (Woodside); 2-6-0 6366 (86G Pontypool Road) – sent specially – works 1X45 to Barmouth, 2-6-4T 42222 (14D) has 1X47 to Llangollen (non-stop!). First time the new 4-character reporting numbers have been seen here.

3 60933 (64A) arrives in Carlisle working a Comrie – St Pancras Cadet Force special, from Stirling via Beattock. An interesting working!

3,4 Stanier 0-4-4T 41900 performs the Coventry station cross-platform parcels shuttle (station being rebuilt, lifts out of action).

4 10.30am Euston – Blackpool noted at Bletchley with D7 *Ingleborough* piloting 46170 *British Legion*, not a combination so far seen at Euston.

4 6842 *Nunhold Grange* works the 9.40am 'Somerset Holiday Express' from Keynsham (via Yeovil, Axminster) to Sidmouth Jct. then to 72A for servicing.

6	5.15pm Queen Street – Oban has J37 0-6-0 64570 as far as Dunblane, where 61067 is attached as pilot before proceeding towards Oban, an odd pairing.
6	92059 (15A) appears in Leeds (Central) working a Fleetwood – Accrington extra, extended to Leeds. First 9F to reach here.
6	46228 *Duchess of Rutland* is the first 'Coronation' seen at Aberdeen this year.
8	61137 enters Brighton bearing a large circular headboard 'City of Leicester Central Holiday Express'. Any headboarded train is notable in Brighton!
8	Z 0-8-0T 30950 (72A) goes to Redhill for trials in the Holmethorpe sand sidings; shows no advantage over the 350hp diesel shunter and is returned.
9	1014 *County of Glamorgan* leaves Basingstoke on the 6.5pm to Reading.
9	2-8-2T 7252 heads an ECS working of LNER stock at Exeter (St Davids).
10	61975 is assigned to a Clayton West – Morecambe excursion, which it works through, then goes to Carnforth depot. First K3 at Morecambe?
12	ECS from Bedford to Lewes consists of 18 LMR coaches headed by U1 2-6-0 31895 + 34086 *219 Squadron* ex-Clapham Jct., an exceptional sight at Lewes.
12	J20 0-6-0 64692 (31B) is a rare type at York, on freight from Doncaster.
13	30927 *Clifton* appears at Tottenham on a Lydd – Brandon troop train, handing over to a B1.
13	Ivatt 2-6-0s 43014 (50A), 43003 (2F), 43146 (41B) all arrive in Scarborough on excursion traffic, as does 61756 (40E) piloted by a B16 on the 10.42am arrival from Normanton, interesting viewing for enthusiasts.
13	WD 2-10-0 90754 is a surprise visitor to Aberdeen to work the 9.12pm fast freight to Kilmarnock. First of this type in Aberdeen for some time.
13	45478 (63A!) is the second Perth engine to reach St Pancras in a fortnight, heading a relief from Bradford – remarkable!
14	D5600 works through to Brighton on a special from Hitchin.
14	Seamans' strike causes a special to be run from Southampton to Gatwick Airport with passengers for America off the *Queen Mary*. Another runs to Newhaven Harbour for cross-channel passengers, both unusual workings.
17	60011 *Empire of India* heads the 12.20pm Perth – Euston at Beattock, and re-appears on the same train 8 days later. A4s rarely grace this route.
17	92073 + 92091 power (!) a northbound GC line freight near Lutterworth.
18	48338 (18A) provides an eye-catching sight at Worcester, heading seven coaches of LT tube train stock for scrap at Hereford.
18	Co-Co diesel 10001 (1B) comes into St Pancras on the 8.20am from Nottingham. Camden engines rarely reach this terminus.
19	60077 *The White Knight* works the Stirling – Sutton Coldfield Car Sleeper throughout and is serviced at Aston. First A3 to reach Birmingham.
19	D211 enters Glasgow (Central) on the 4.15pm ex-Crewe, first of this type here.
19	45576 *Bombay* is the first 'Jubilee' to be seen at Cleethorpes for two years, on an excursion from Chesterfield.
20	73087 (82F) heads a relief train from Bournemouth right through to Lancashire, most unusual for Bath engines to reach so far north.
20	Exmouth – Cleethorpes seen traversing the S&D with 2-8-0 53801 piloted by 'Jinty' 0-6-0T 47275 bunker first – again, a most unusual occurrence.
20	75047/48 (27A!) both arrive at March on holiday trains from Leicester.
20	J69 0-6-0T 68619 (the Liverpool Street pilot in GER livery) works the 1.59pm to Enfield

Town from the ex-GER terminus.

21 7-car DMU excursion is run from Birmingham over the S&D to Bournemouth giving this line a rare sight of 'modern' power.

22 'Queen of Scots' Pullman train arrives in Leeds (Central) behind O2 2-8-0 63984 when 60134 *Foxhunter* fails at Wakefield.

23 60153 *Flamboyant* heads the 9am to Liverpool out of Hull – first A1 here for more than a year.

24 J37 0-6-0 64624 is a highly unusual type to reach Blair Atholl, on freight.

25 90689 works an 11-coach Southport – Sunderland excursion (including two Restaurant Cars) into Leeds (City). First WD recorded on a scheduled passenger train along the Calder Valley.

26,29 D57xx works trains of mineral empties from the Glasgow area to Oakley yard (between Dunfermline and Alloa) on both days, unusual sights here.

27 8P 71000 *Duke of Gloucester* is the star attraction at Derby Works Open Day.

27 61935 is a rare deputy (for the customary B1) on the Hull portion of the 'Yorkshire Pullman' from Hull to Doncaster.

28 DMU outing to Belle Vue is run from Rubery (on the Longbridge – Old Hill line, and closed in 1919!), the station re-opening specially for the day.

29 46135 *The East Lancashire Regiment* (5A) is a startling arrival in Cardiff on the 4.48pm from Pontypool Road. 'Scots' are extreme rarities in South Wales.

30 J39 0-6-0 64798 (16D) passes through Warwick heading freight towards Hatton, very strange engine in these parts.

U/D 'Jinty' 0-6-0T 47275 seen solo at Midford on the 6.5pm Bath – Binegar, rare indeed for this class to be seen on passenger work.

SEPTEMBER 1960

1ST 76018 reaches North Cornwall – a first – by working a Civil Engineers' special from Exeter to Bude and back.

1 60530 *Sayajirao* works the 12.20pm Perth – Euston to Carlisle, via Beattock.

2 Man crashes car into lamp-post outside New Street and dashes on foot into station and into the tunnel. Police requisition a Lichfield line DMU to give chase and capture him!

3 60087 *Blenheim* (64B) passes Motherwell on a relief to the 9.4am Dundee (West) – Manchester (Victoria). A3's over Beattock are as uncommon as A2s.

3 J39 0-6-0 64934 (55H Neville Hill) is observed ex-Works at…Stirling!

3 61940 (36A) arrives at Blackpool on an excursion from Ipswich whose Buffet Car is roofboarded 'Liverpool Street – Bury St Edmunds'.

3 U 2-6-0 31626 heads the 2.20pm Bournemouth (West) – Waterloo, after 30907 *Dulwich* steams no further than Bournemouth (Central).

3 75006 (6E Wrexham!) reaches Redhill on the 10.45am from Snow Hill.

3 W 2-6-4T 31920 brings troop train ECS into Caterham, which leaves for Devynock (near Brecon) behind Q 0-6-0 30549 with stovepipe chimney.

5 'Brighton Belle' unit leaves Waterloo on a special working to Portsmouth.

5,6 Stanier 2-6-2Ts 40126/171 arrive at Templecombe for projected use on the Highbridge Branch. 40171 heads Bailey Gate – T'combe milk next day.

6 D5074 makes a class debut on the WR by arriving at Reading with the Willesden breakdown train.

6	Caprotti 73142 (17D Rowsley) noted on Tilbury shed, stranger here!
7	6.22am Seaford – Brighton becomes defective at Newhaven, and 30900 *Eton* pulls the 4-BIL EMU into Lewes, where the train terminates.
9	U 2-6-0 31634 appears at Somers Town Goods depot, on cross-London freight.
9	Trials are held with DMUs over the South Tyneside electric line between Newcastle and South Shields.
9	Final run of last 'slip' coach takes place when the 5.10pm Paddington to Wolverhampton detaches a 3-coach portion at Bicester, an historic event.
10	10.12am York – Yarmouth is double-headed to Lincoln by the very strange pairing of 92066 (52H Tyne Dock) + D276.
10	J36 0-6-0 65316 takes the 7pm Waverley – Newcastleton out of Hawick.
10	Northampton – Skegness evening excursion reaches Peterborough behind 'Crab' 42779 formed of green SR set 468 plus SECR Continental brake!
10	42814 appears at Newport on the 11.45am Swansea – Birmingham via Hereford. First 'Crab' on a passenger train in South Wales since the war.
10	D5076 pilots 46140 *The King's Royal Rifle Corps* on the 7.50am Derby – St Pancras, an unexpected combination.
11	Air Display attracts D5631 (ex-Norwich), D5634 (Southend) through to Farnborough station, plus 61286 (31A) which passes through Reading with a Cambridge – North Camp special for the Air Show.
12	70031 *Byron* + 70032 *Tennyson* team up to power the 'Palatine' out of St Pancras with a track recording coach at the rear of the train. Consecutively numbered pairings are always rare and worthy of note.
12	(Winter timetable starts). Manchester – Crewe electric service begins. 'London Road' is renamed 'Piccadilly' and all services previously diverted to Victoria/Exchange/Central resume operating from Piccadilly.
12	WR 8-car Blue Pullman sets begin operating Paddington – Snow Hill and Paddington – Bristol routes, both twice/day in each direction.
13	O4 2-8-0 63837 (9G) works the 7.40pm freight from Lever Bros yard, Port Sunlight to Warrington – first LNER type seen here.
13	S15 4-6-0 30840 brings the 6.30pm from Waterloo into Weymouth, having replaced 34041 *Wilton* at Basingstoke.
13	D5584 arrives at King's Cross with the 'Fenman', diverted from Liverpool St.
13	80028 (61A) is a notable sight at Queen Street at the head of the 4.35pm to Perth via Alloa. Kittybrewster tank engines don't usually stray this far!
15	30858 *Lord Duncan* is a remarkable visitor to the South Coast, making two trips through Shoreham towards Brighton with empty stock.
16	61831 is a most unusual type to run east LE at Ealing Broadway.
17	Blackpool bound excursions bring 5042 *Winchester Castle* (81A) and 7007 *Great Western* (85A) into Crewe, where two 'Castles' in a day is noteworthy.
17	L&Y locos 2-4-2T 50850 and 0-6-0 52271 (front and rear) work a special up the Werneth incline (1 in 27) between Middleton Jct. and Oldham. Shades of pre-grouping days!
18	'Harrogate Sunday Pullman' is diverted into Leeds (City) and the Bradford portion is worked forward to Forster Square, where Pullman services originated in 1874 but have rarely appeared since those early days.

18	2-8-0 53804 exits Buckhorn Weston Tunnel on an LCGB special, rare to see these locos anywhere other than on the S&D.
18	Ivatt 2-6-2T 41297 runs trials on the Lyme Regis branch, with lively results!
20	5093 *Upton Castle* is a surprise arrival at Leicester (C) on the Bournemouth – York.
20	D211 *Mauretania* and D212 *Aureol* are both named at Liverpool (Riverside).
23	45110 (6J Holyhead!) leaves Peterborough (East) toward Rugby with 3-coach ER electric unit 309 sandwiched between two guards vans. Interseting!
23	National Trust Land Cruise train to the Highlands – a 1st class Sleeping Car train of 12 vehicles – exits Waverley with well-groomed 60530 *Sayajirao*.
23	60124 *Kenilworth* (52A) heads the 'Postal' from Aberdeen to Carstairs.
24	An 8F hauls three 25kV AC locos E3028/41/50 and a 3-car Glasgow 'Blue Train' unit through the London suburbs bound for exhibition at Battersea at BTC's Electrification Conference in early October.
24	60842 (50A) is a stranger found on Stockport Edgeley shed (9B).
24	Four of the new Pullman cars for use in the 'Master Cutler' formation visit Hatfield for an official photo. They commence service on 28th.
24	'Deltic' emerges from overhaul at EE and resumes work on the ER.
25	46240 *City of Coventry* is a welcome sight at Whitchurch with a perishables train from the Chester direction.
26	60857 hauls E3056 (also bound for Battersea) via the Hertford loop.
27	D6519 works a Victoria – Grain special of four Pullmans and a brake.
30	60014 *Silver Link* is chosen to head the 'Anglo-Scottish Car Carrier' between King's Cross and Newcastle since, as 2509 this engine had commenced work on the 'Silver Jubilee' exactly 25 years previously. (Then 4hr, now 4hr 35min by 'Talisman').
U/D	Freight ascends Beattock bank headed by a 'Crab' and banked by…46203 *Princess Margaret Rose* – astonishing!
U/D	Six 'Kings' are allocated to Cardiff Canton, first time any have been shedded in Wales (but are not to work west of Cardiff).

OCTOBER 1960

1st	73098 (66A) works the 4.10pm Heaton – Niddrie freight, unusual type.
1	44678 passes through Watford hauling the 3-car ER EMU set 309 back from trials on the Manchester – Crewe line.
2	(Week commencing). As Weymouth turntable is out of action nine 4MT 2-6-4Ts are on loan to work all local trains to, from Bournemouth. However 34029 *Lundy* works through on the 9.15pm Waterloo – Weymouth Quay (4th) and is sent to Yeovil Jct. to turn.
3	75061 (15C) is an unexpected arrival in King's Cross with the 9.15am from Cambridge; the bigger surprise is 75008 (81F) on outer suburban work!
3	D5311 undergoes freight tests (with dynamometer car) from Doncaster to Barnetby and Scunthorpe, and return.
3	82019 + 34023 *Blackmore Vale* together bring the 11.30am Brighton – Plymouth into Exeter (Central), a most unusual combination.
3-9	BTC Electrification Conference promotes an exhibition of motive power at Battersea Wharf. E5022 (DC) and E3008/28/41/50/56 (AC) are all on show.

5	60156 *Great Central* is a most unusual visitor to Sheffield (Victoria) on the 4.35pm Hull – Liverpool (Central), A1s rarely come this way.
5	61020 *Gemsbok* (50A) comes into Liverpool Street from Kings Lynn. York engines are extremely rare in the City of London terminus.
7	3.44pm East Croydon – East Grinstead is hauled by 80015 and includes three 1st class Pullman cars, to be used for filming purposes on the 11th.
9	Most unusually, the 'Golden Arrow' is worked via Chatham in each direction.
10	46201 *Princess Elizabeth* (66A) is a notable visitor to Newton Heath (26A) having worked in on a Glasgow – Manchester express.
13	60532 *Blue Peter* (61B) – not ex-Works! – heads the 5.24am Doncaster to New England goods. Aberdeen locos this far south are rare in normal service.
14	South African rugby team arrives at Eastbourne from Southampton Docks in a special train of two 1st class coaches, Restaurant Car plus van.
15	D802 *Formidable* + D813 *Diadem* take the 12.35pm ex-Manchester out of Newton Abbot, an uncommon 'same-class' double-header.
16	D5711 is engaged in coal train tests (with dynamometer car) between Toton and Brent on the Midland main line.
16	60092 *Fairway* (55A) passes through Ilkley on the diverted 'Thames-Clyde Express', first A3 seen on this line. On similar diversions on 2,9 October the 'TCE' is headed this way by 46113 *Cameronian*.
17	D240 is seen on the up 'Tees-Thames', first diesel to work this service.
20,21	Launch of the nuclear submarine HMS 'Dreadnought' at Barrow (21st) brings 46144 *Honourable Artillery Company* to Windermere with 9 of the 14 1st class coaches of the special from Euston, 5 going to Ulverston (20th). Royal train travels overnight with 46240 *City of Coventry* through to Arnside (!), is stabled on the Hincaster Jct. line, then to Barrow behind 45193 + 44904.
21	K 2-6-0 32353 heads an Engineers Dept train from East Grinstead to Horsted Keynes to lift sidings. First train here for many months.
22	9pm Glasgow (Central) – St Pancras sleeper is diverted into Euston behind 45575 *Madras* (14B). Kentish Town locos rarely appear in Euston.
23	More track testing takes place at Balcombe Tunnel Jct. with E5000/16 hauling 9 loaded iron ore wagons with 3-coach set 822 split either side of the wagons.
24	D299 (new) leaves Newton-le-Willows for Doncaster carrying large yellow boards proclaiming it the 100th Type 4 diesel built at Vulcan Foundry.
24	60093 *Coronach* (12C Carlisle Canal) mysteriously appears on Thornaby shed (51L).
25	Two oil barges sailing between Avonmouth and Gloucester collide in thick fog with a pier of the Severn railway bridge. The barges explode and catch fire, two spans collapse into the river, thus destroying the rail link.
26	61181 (41A) is a shock arrival at Euston on the 7.23am from Tring.
27	'Patriot' 45551 surprisingly reaches Hither Green on a cross-London freight.
29	61808 (41E Barrow Hill) reaches Bristol LE from Westerleigh after bringing a freight from Washwood Heath carrying concrete sleepers.
31	Stanier 2-6-2T 40075 (55E Normanton) arrives at Heaton on loan. Works trials on the Rothbury and Reedsmouth branches, but returns on 12 November.
31	0-4-4T L44, on two coaches, reaches New Cross. LT steam on SR territory!
U/D	60049 *Galtee More* is the first fitted with German-type smoke deflectors.

U/D   Both ex-'Coronation' beaver-tail observation cars are seen stored in sidings at Torphins (on the Ballater branch).

U/D   D10 *Tryfan* is unusual power for the 3.10pm Aberdeen – Glasgow.

U/D   'Britannias' 70018/22/25 are seen working the 'Cathedrals Express' between Worcester and Hereford.

U/D   'Deltic' suffers an engine failure (1ˢᵗ) and is despatched to Vulcan Foundry for a replacement, returning to Finsbury Park on the 17ᵗʰ.

Disruption due to flooding in Devon (diesel working west of Exeter discontinued).
Significant workings as follows:

Sept 30   2-8-0 2892 heads the 7.30am Paddington – Paignton.

Oct 1   'Torbay Express' routed via Tiverton Jct. – Tiverton and Exe Valley line to reach Exeter. Up 'Cornish Riviera Express' routed same way.
          Down 'Royal Duchy' 3 hours late into Exeter with 2-6-0 7316.

3   Brighton – Plymouth at Exeter (C) with 82019 + 34023 *Blackmore Vale*, which goes to Plymouth solo via Newton Abbot.

3   S15 4-6-0 30844 + 34049 *Anti-Aircraft Command* arrives Exeter (C) from Seaton Jct. with 14 coaches.

6   S15 30843 + 35016 *Elders Fyffes* 5.22pm Ex(C) – W'loo to Seaton Jct.

27   'Torbay Express' reaches Exeter via Yeovil with 4945 *Milligan Hall* from Heywood Road Jct. 'Royal Duchy' runs via Basingstoke to reach Exeter behind 5920 *Wycliffe Hall*. 4945, 5920 stand side-by-side in middle road at Central at 7.45pm!

27   Up 'Cornishman' terminates at Exeter. Up 'Cornish Riviera Express' runs SR route to Basingstoke (with SR locos). Stops at Templecombe for the 'Cornishman's Bristol passengers.

27   Brighton – Plymouth departs Newton Abbot at 8.39pm behind the unique combination of D827 *Kelly* piloting 34076 *41 Squadron*, carrying the 'ACE' headboard (!), which it had worked earlier.

NOVEMBER 1960

1ˢᵀ   60005 *Sir Charles Newton* reaches Sheffield (Victoria) on a New England to Manchester freight, and D5054 comes in on the Harwich – Liverpool boat train, substituting for 70035 *Rudyard Kipling* from Ipswich onwards.

1   61927 (50B) enters Liverpool Street on the 2.15pm parcels from Cambridge. First Neville Hill loco seen in this terminus.

2   D9000 is tested for the first time inside Vulcan Foundry, a 4-hour continuous full engine-load test.

3,4   61031 *Reedbuck* (51L) noted at Lancaster on a Heysham parcels train. Next day works, surprisingly, the 7.58am Skipton – Leeds via Keighley.

4   L&Y 0-8-0 49618 (26A) is a new type to be seen on Darlington shed, having arrived with freight, and is observed at Northallerton the following day.

4-7   Liverpool Street – Shenfield/Southend is changed over from 1500V DC to 6.25kV and 25kV AC system, originally electrified in 1949.

5   Severe flooding at Lewes means that only a restricted service is possible, steam-hauled. Thus 80153 leaves on the 12.12pm to Eastbourne and K 2-6-0 32341 heads the 9.12am Brighton – Eastbourne, amongst others.

6,7 Glasgow suburban electrification (with 'Blue Trains') is inaugurated on 7th after a dress rehearsal of the weekday service on 6th. First BR electrification scheme in Scotland.

7 70036 *Boadicea* is an unusual sight on the Felixstowe branch working a schoolboys' special.

7,8 Green-liveried 73094 (84G ex-Works) appears at Lincoln, and heads the 1.55pm Sheffield (Victoria) – Leicester (Central) next day.

11 7.5pm Fawley – Eastleigh freight is double-headed by the eye-catching pairing of 0-6-0PT 4616 + H16 4-6-2T 30516, first PT seen on the branch.

12 60049 *Galtee More*, 60007 *Sir Nigel Gresley* both appear at Sheffield (Victoria) on football specials from King's Cross to Wadsley Bridge.

12 0-6-0 2221 (81E) is an unexpected arrival at Brockenhurst, with a special train of loco coal from Eastleigh.

13 Ivatt 2-6-2T 41308 conducts load tests on the Lyme Regis branch with up to six coaches.

15 Haymarket 60161 *North British* (ex-Works) is a sight for sore eyes at Lincoln on a running-in turn, repeated a week later.

16 Channel Islands ferry promotional cruise uses the new ship 'Caesarea' between Weymouth and Southampton. Guests arrive at Weymouth Quay in five 1st class Pullmans – first appearance of such vehicles on the Quay tramway. ECS is taken to Southampton for the return trip to Waterloo.

18 O4/8 2-8-0 63675 (40E) brings a train of concrete sleepers into Stoke Gifford yard and runs LE to Gloucester for servicing, a very unusual loco here.

22 34092 *City of Wells* brings the empty stock of a troop train tender first into Caterham, runs round and takes the loaded train through to Parkeston Quay.

22 84020 is unaccustomed power for the 6.5am Brighton – Tonbridge.

23 70015 *Apollo* (9E) reaches Bristol on the 9.5pm from Newcastle, returning next day (to Sheffield) on the 10.30am Bristol – Newcastle. A rare working.

23 Up afternoon 'Talisman' and down 'Flying Scotsman' (among others) are diverted between Berwick and Edinburgh via Kelso and Galashiels, due to a blockage at Marshall Meadows. Both are powered by EE Type 4s.

24 'Thames-Clyde Express' enters St Pancras behind the incongruous pairing of a 9F piloting 45514 *Holyhead* – which had become short of steam at Bedford.

24 D5107 + D5108 team up to head the 'Heart of Midlothian' from Edinburgh to Newcastle. Consecutively numbered diesel pairs are even rarer than steam!

25 Wandering 61031 *Reedbuck* now appears on Bedford shed!

25 45665 *Lord Rutherford of Nelson* (67A) is a surprise arrival at Leicester having worked the 12.10am freight throughout from Carlisle.

26 61204 (31B) reaches Oxford with the 4.35am football special from Whittlesea to Torquay for Peterborough's FA Cup match there.

26 Crystal Palace v Watford Cup tie brings three specials to Norwood Jct. behind 44834, 45440 and 2-6-4T 42099. All take the ECS to New Cross Gate, locos going to Bricklayers Arms for refuelling.

26 D34 4-4-0 62484 *Glen Lyon* notably banks the up 'Waverley' out of Hawick.

27 Due to engineering work at Weaver Jct., West Coast traffic is diverted via Stockport, Manchester (Piccadilly) and the MSJA line to Patricroft. 'Coronations' 46223/38/46/53/54/57 pass this way, plus D7 *Ingleborough* on the up 'Ulster Express'.

30	45673 *Keppel* (63A) heads the 'Postal' out of Aberdeen, first 'Jubilee' for about two years on this train.
U/D	D69 reaches Perth on the 'Royal Highlander', having worked from Crewe.
U/D	Period 21 Nov to 5 Dec: two of the Newcastle – Liverpool (via Harrogate) expresses (each way) are routed daily through Wetherby, due to remodelling at Leeds (City). A3 60085, A1s 60124/151, A2 60538 all appear, though Neville Hill A3's predominate, a glut of Pacifics that Wetherby has not witnessed before.

DECEMBER 1960

3RD	Hawick shed hosts 43968 (55B) probably bound for scrap at Inverurie (?).
4	61356 + 61246 *Lord Balfour of Burleigh* are an unusual sight on the Aberdeen – Perth route, heading a special to the Smithfield Show in London.
4	Due to (yet more) flooding at Exeter, 'Cornish Riviera Express' leaves Yeovil Jct. for Salisbury with a 'County' 4-6-0, a type banned from the SR main line!
5	L&Y 0-8-0 49618 (26A) surprisingly reaches Shrewsbury, class debut here.
5	70039 *Sir Christopher Wren* arrives at Mansfield in the course of transfer to Immingham from Norwich. First Pacific allocated to 40B. More follow.
5-9	Landslip at Midford closes the S&D line and 'Pines Express' is diverted in both directions from Bournemouth to Salisbury, Westbury, Bath, Filton Jct. then its regular route from Yate South Jct. to Birmingham. 34102 *Lapford* works throughout to New Street, overnights at Saltley, returns with 'Pines' next day. 6th ; U 2-6-0 31805 is in charge to Westbury, 4942 *Maindy Hall* works to New Street, then Saltley, then 'Pines' to Westbury next day. 7th; 34053 *Sir Keith Park* is changed at Gloucester, working back to Bristol on freight. 8th, 9th SR Pacifics are changed at St Philips Marsh, where 45723 *Fearless* (12B) – itself a rarity – heads successive up/down 'Pines' to Birmingham.
7	2-8-0 3801 passes through Cardiff with a train of withdrawn LT Central Line tube stock, seven coaches with an adapter wagon and brake van at each end.
10	HR 4-4-0 54398 *Ben Alder*, now on the official list of locos to be preserved is moved from storage at Forfar, towed by D6126.
12	Due to Blockage at St Denys, up 'Bournemouth Belle' reverses back into Southampton, goes to Romsey (reverse), then Eastleigh (reverse again).
12	70052 *Firth of Tay* (66A) + 45525 *Colwyn Bay* appear at Huddersfield on the 9.55am Newcastle – Liverpool. Polmadie locos rarely venture this way.
13	Manchester (Piccadilly) – Crewe stopping train consists of non-corridor stock, including LNER coaches labelled 'Hertford East', hauled by an electric loco!
13	'Tees-Tyne Pullman' reaches King's Cross with 61207 as pilot to D207.
14	'Ulster Express' reaches Euston behind D5519 (31B)! (Earlier engine failure).
14	E1 4-4-0 31019 heads a 4-coach special (with Restaurant Car and observation car) from Victoria to Allhallows-on-Sea. TUCC inquiry into the closure of the line meets the day after; this is an inspection visit.
16	Up 'North Briton' departs Newcastle with 60036 *Colombo* piloted by A2/2 60502 *Earl Marischal*. ER Pacifics double-heading is quite a rare event.
18,19	Newly introduced (on the 7th!) Glasgow suburban electric service is suspended and replaced *next day* (!) by a substitute steam service again, an organisational feat without precedence.

| 21 | 70052 *Firth of Tay* (66A) arrives at Holyhead to take out a special, damages its bogie and is still on shed six days later. Polmadie locos are rarities at 6J. |

21 | 70052 *Firth of Tay* (66A) arrives at Holyhead to take out a special, damages its bogie and is still on shed six days later. Polmadie locos are rarities at 6J.

21 | D34 4-4-0 62484 *Glen Lyon* tows the failed DMU forming the 5.5pm from Perth into Waverley from Dalmeny.

22 | 0-6-0 2257 (84E) is an unprecedented sight on the West Coast main line, heading a freight from Northampton to Wolverton, and the return working.

24 | 75060 (15C) is a surprising type to appear on Ipswich shed.

27 | Caprotti 73144 (17A) is a rare visitor to Bradford (Forster Square) on a train from Morecambe (Promenade).

29,30 | WD 2-10-0s 90751/70 are highly unusual station pilots at Glasgow (Central).

31 | 30803 *Sir Harry le Fise Lake* reaches Temple Meads on an excursion sponsored by Vickers Armstrong. First N15 in Bristol since 11 September 1954.

JANUARY 1961

2ND | 'Trans-Pennine' 6-car Inter-City DMU service is introduced between Hull. Leeds, Manchester and Liverpool.

2 | 4.30pm Queen Street – Perth is booked to terminate at Dollar, and is worked forward from Alloa by 350hp shunter D3342.

3 | 46134 *The Cheshire Regiment* (5A) has charge of the 6.5pm Aberdeen to Glasgow, first 'Scot' in Aberdeen for six months.

4 | 70044 *Earl Haig* (55A) is an unexpected arrival in Perth at the head of the 9.50am ex-Euston. Holbeck engines rarely reach so far north.

4,9 | New Pullman cars for the 'Yorkshire Pullman' are on display to the public at Hull, Harrogate, Leeds and Bradford on the 4th, and enter service on 9th.

7 | CR 4-4-0 54486 pilots 45355 into Aberdeen on the 10.5am from Buchanan Street. Shades of yesteryear in terms of motive power.

7 | 70004 *William Shakespeare* heads a parcels train on the freight-only Leamington – Rugby branch, a far cry from the 'Golden Arrow'!

7 | Two B1s pass through Wolverton with football excursions from Peterborough to Portsmouth for the FA Cup tie behind 61048 (32A), 61052 (31B).

7 | 45728 *Defiance* + 45652 *Hawke* power the combined 10.50am Glasgow to Manchester/Liverpool (15 coaches) into Carlisle, a notable combination.

9 | An entire Car Sleeper train is chartered by a cigarette manufacturer to take sales staff and their cars from Euston to Glasgow to begin an intensive campaign in Scotland. 46144 *Honourable Artillery Company* heads the train.

9 | 6.55am Wolverhampton – Euston is Pacific hauled for the first time, by 46200 *The Princess Royal*. Last month 46248 *City of Leeds* headed the 9.42am departure, again a Pacific first from Wolverhampton.

11 | D5667 – embarrassingly – fails when heading the down 'Fenman' with the Queen conveyed in a special saloon. (See 16th).

12 | 'Patriot' 45513 reaches Frodingham with iron-ore empties, surprising power.

13 | D1 4-4-0 31739 heads the start of term special, Charing Cross to Cranbrook.

16 | 60977 makes a class debut visit to Farnley Jct. shed (55C), also the first LNER loco of any kind recorded here.

16 | 70009 *Alfred the Great* is in charge of the Royal train back from Kings Lynn to Liverpool Street!

16,17	New EE Type 5 3300hp Co-Co 'Deltic' D9001 passes through Sheffield (Victoria) *en route* to Doncaster (16th), and joins D8 *Penyghent* and D6539 at Stratford Works for a private exhibition the following day.
20	(Week ending). Steam works the up 'Master Cutler' Pullman for five days running; 3 x B1s, 2 x A3s, despite the 'rule' this train must be diesel hauled.
20	B16 4-6-0 61451 (50A) is most unusual power for the 1.30pm Leith (South) to Cadder yard freight, as this class rarely breaches the Scottish border.
20	O4/8 2-8-0 63728 is equally unusual on a Huddersfield – Bradford goods.
21	0-6-0PT 1507 (81A) works the 10.15am Wolverhampton (LL) – Leamington via Worcester, Stratford-on-Avon. (Running-in turn, ex-Stafford Road Works)
24	1.45am York – Liverpool parcels is devoid of power from Mirfield, so L&Y 0-6-0 52413 proudly deputises, right through to Lime Street! Edge Hill then keeps it for six days for the Wapping shunt. Amazing.
24	60065 *Knight of Thistle* heads the King's Cross – Gilling special taking pupils to Ampleforth College, from Grantham to Malton, where A3s never (!) reach.
25	0-6-0PT 6422 is 'stolen' from Stafford Road shed (84A) in an attempt to run LE to Worcester. Control stops the loco at Droitwich; civilian crew arrested!
26	'Trans-Pennine' DMUs are diverted via Dewsbury/Brighouse/Todmorden due to a blockage at Diggle. EE Type 4s on Newcastle – Liverpool trains also travel the Calder Valley despite having yet to receive clearance for this route.
27,28	92207, 92004 both reach Southampton (Terminus) on successive days on the 10.27am Salisbury – Portsmouth vans.
28	D5529/82 both work throughout from Norwich to Scunthorpe with football specials for the FA Cup match.
28	60058 *Blair Athol* (52A) heads the 12noon Perth – Euston to Carlisle via Carstairs and Beattock, where A3s used rarely to be seen.
31	J50 0-6-0T 68981 provides a big surprise by appearing at Victoria (Eastern Section) filling in time between cross London freight duties.
31	D5526 is startling power for the down 'Flying Scotsman' seen passing through Selby, as replacement for a failure further south.
U/D	'Princess Royals' appear on up coal trains at least three times in January at the southern end of the West Coast main line.
U/D	34039 *Boscastle* speeds through Reading (General), leading a diverted express towards London.
U/D	1.50pm Glasgow (Central) – Carlisle is headed by 45651 *Shovell* (82E Barrow Road) a novel shed to work out of Central.
U/D	'Queen of Scots' Pullman leaves Queen Street behind D5322/27, most unusual.
U/D	Two specials to London bring the startling sight of SR Pacifics to Sheerness!
U/D	GT3 noted on trials between Crewe and Shrewsbury.
U/D	Immingham depot (40B) receives 70039 *Sir Christopher Wren*, 70040 *Clive of India*, 70041 *Sir John Moore* to work the King's Cross turns.

FEBRUARY 1961

1ST	45381 (1A) noted on Ipswich shed, and 75060 (15C) works through Bury St Edmunds on a freight for Parkeston Quay, both unexpected sights.

1	6pm Braintree – Witham railbus hits a dog near Cressing. Dog unhurt, railbus injured and is towed away by shunter D3298 !
4	2-6-4T 42099 heads a Dunstable – Kensington special, carrying large circular headboard 'Vauxhall Motors Childrens Circus Train', with painted clown.
4	'Crab' 42827 (21A) reaches Barry with banana empties from Carlisle.
4	45248 comes into Swansea on the 7.55pm parcels from…Carmarthen!
6,7,10	0-6-0 PT 1368 is an unusual arrival in Bournemouth, light engine from Weymouth. Seen on 7th heading ECS to Hamworthy Jct. Returns to Bournemouth on 10th with freight and departs LE back to Weymouth in the evening.
7	46200 *The Princess Royal* is an unlikely choice as station pilot at…Chester!
7	45506 *The Royal Pioneer Corps* has the rare task of shunting the Carmarthen portion of the 'Red Dragon' onto the main train in Cardiff. Degrading job!
7-20	D6504 (73C Hither Green) travels to Derby for static tests of its electric train heating equipment with eight different types of vehicle, as one train. Works this stock Derby – Hornsey via Peterborough (10th). Conducts tests from King's Cross – Craigentinny carriage sidings, down 14/16 Feb, up 15/17 Feb. Returns to Derby 20th. First D65xx seen on the East Coast line.
9	3440 *City of Truro* is at Kensington Olympia with 'Westward TV' exhibition.
9	'Flying Scotsman' is routed via Stockton, West Hartlepool and Sunderland to reach Newcastle. 60007 *Sir Nigel Gresley* has pilotman from York.
10	Due to derailment near Swindon, down 'Bristolian' and the first up 'Bristol Pullman' are diverted via Newbury and Devizes, a first for the Pullman units.
10	46210 *Lady Patricia* pays a rare visit to St Enoch on a local from Carlisle.
11	6.40am Waverley – Carlisle leaves behind 60101 *Cicero* piloted by 61359, a rare instance of double-heading on this route. B1 to Hawick only.
11,12	Fourteen specials from the Scotland v Wales rugby match change engines at Shrewsbury, including 8.55am Edinburgh – Swansea and 9.5am Edinburgh to Port Talbot, leaving with 73094 + 0-6-0 3206, 73034 + 2-6-4T 42394 respectively, and Exeter's 1007 *County of Brecknock* heads the Newport train.
13	34100 *Appledore* heads a 3-car Pullman train from Gatwick airport to Victoria conveying the Greek Prime Minister to London.
17	Q6 0-8-0 63378 is a strange type at Berwick, on a coal train from Newcastle.
18	'Heart of Midlothian' runs from Peterborough to Newcastle behind 70038 *Robin Hood* (31B), replacing a defective A3. A unique occurrence for a GN line titled train to be 'Britannia' hauled?
18	45515 *Caenarvon* (26A) sets off from Cardiff on the 7.55pm Shrewsbury to Swansea parcels, fails *en route* and goes to Neath shed (87A) for repairs.
19	D8036 hauls a 'special load' 123-ton transformer (bound for the Trawsfynydd nuclear power station) along the Blaenau Festiniog branch, ex-Llandudno Jct.
21	61010 *Wildebeeste* (50A) is a stranger on the S&C line, on an up freight.
21	44333 (21A) appears in Cardiff, first 4F to do so?
22	'Night Scotsman' enters King's Cross behind 92038, replacing an A4.
23,28	D9001 is the first 'Deltic' to arrive at Doncaster Works for acceptance trials. Five days later D9000 is released from Vulcan Foundry, runs LE to Doncaster. (Original is languishing at Vulcan Foundry pending a decision on its future).
25	75022 (82E) is the largest loco yet recorded on the Yatton – Witham branch, heading the 2.45pm and 6.52pm return.

25	45559 *British Columbia* (24E) is, these days, a rarity on a Blackpool – Euston.
25	60851 brings the 9am Perth – Euston into Carlisle, an unusual 62B arrival.
25	Ex-Crosti boilered 92021 is a rare visitor to Heaton shed.
27	34007 *Wadebridge* works the 1pm Cardiff – Brighton from Salisbury at least as far as Southampton still bearing the 'Atlantic Coast Express' headboard!
U/D	S&C line is used to get the Glasgow 'Blue Train' sets to Manchester for repair.
U/D	73145 (65B!) works a Halifax – Manchester passenger train in the small hours of the morning (train ex-York via Wakefield (Kirkgate), reversal at Halifax).

MARCH 1961

1ST	LTE 'Chesham' coaches are worked from Neasden to New Cross Gate by a LT steam engine. (Stock is on its way to the Bluebell Railway).
1	10.50am Glasgow – Manchester has 45652 *Hawke* as train engine, piloted out of Carlisle by…46226 *Duchess of Norfolk*, very odd this way round!
2	70054 *Dornoch Firth* (55A) is a highly unusual arrival in Sheffield (Victoria) on the 7.30am from Leicester (Central). Holbeck locos 'don't run' on the GC!
2	60077 *The White Knight* (55A) leaves Ayr with a Carlisle bound freight, first visit of an A3 to Ayr, and another 'out-of-place' Holbeck engine.
4	'North Briton' requires D257 in front, and N15 0-6-2T 69181 at the rear, plus the station pilot D3277 – most unusual – to get out of Queen Street.
5	USA 0-6-0T 30073 arrives at Lancing Carriage Works for trials as Works shunter, but returns to Southampton on 11th.
5	34042 *Dorchester* heads an unidentified train out of Bath (Spa)!
5	45518 *Bradshaw* is a rare visitor to the North East coast, passing through West Hartlepool on a diverted York – Heaton freight.
7	2.15pm Aberdeen – Broad Street fish train produces the eye-catching spectacle of 60531 *Barham* piloting 45492 as far as Perth.
7	61000 *Springbok* (36A) is a stranger on Aston shed, having worked the 7.5pm Immingham – Soho freight.
8,9	'Westward Television' tour train is on show at Yeovil (Town), then moves to Weymouth behind T9 4-4-0 30120. Part of a 36-day tour that began on 13 Feb (ending 25 March) utilising 3440 *City of Truro* for much of the time.
10	70007 *Coeur-de-Lion* is a notable sight at Brough, heading westbound freight.
11	Womens' Hockey International at Wembley brings 34038/46 to Willesden, whilst 34086/90 work their ECS to Watford and turn on the Croxley triangle.
11	Rare visitor to London 60068 *Sir Visto* (12C Carlisle Canal), leaves King's Cross Goods with the 4.15pm northbound fitted freight.
12	5.15pm Bristol – York departs Derby behind the highly unusual pairing of 60812 + 45576 *Bombay*.
14	Q1 0-6-0 33002 is seen on the Ferme Park flyover with a cross-London freight.
14	2-6-0 7308 (71G Weymouth) works a Bournemouth (West) – Eastleigh freight via the Ringwood line, rare to find a WR loco on this route.
14	70051 *Firth of Forth* (66A) is an unprecedented arrival at Grangemouth with a freight from Perth.
14	0-6-0T 30073 heads the 6.25am Eastleigh – Fawley freight as far as Totton, first time a USA has been seen on freight outside Southampton Docks.

15	L1 2-6-4T 67707 is a rare visitor to the Calder Valley, reaching Mytholmroyd with the 4am freight from Normanton.

15,21,22 D9001 runs high-speed trials King's Cross – Doncaster (15th), followed by King's Cross – Newcastle (down 21st, up 22nd)

16 46120 *Royal Inniskilling Fusilier* is an unprecedented sight on the 6.5pm Broad Street – Tring, a type thought inadmissible to Broads Street's platforms.

16 Electric 'Motor Luggage Van' S68002 works as a 'locomotive' on the Stewarts lane – Lancing stock train consisting of two Pullmans plus van.

17 U1 2-6-0 31910 makes a noteworthy appearance at Staines on the 4.20pm Reading – Feltham freight.

17 0-6-0 64745 (9G) observed on Edge Hill shed, first J39 recorded there.

17,18 BR Amateur Boxing semi-finals are held in Hove Town Hall. Special train is provided as contestants' accommodation; 5 x Sleeping Cars, Restaurant Car plus open 2nd. 30907 *Dulwich*, 30901 *Winchester* provide steam heat.

18 46245 *City of London* powers the 4.30pm Carlisle – Willesden milk train, which loads up to 600 tons. 46238 *City of Carlisle* was used a week earlier.

18 FA Cup semi-final at Villa Park (Spurs v Burnley) brings D5618/35 to New Street with supporters' specials from Tottenham.

18 J20 0-6-0 64687 recorded at Stamford on the evening pick-up, rare here.

19 Salisbury's turntable is out of action and engines on east-west trains work through. 'Halls' 4999, 5984, 6944, 7927 all reach Portsmouth, as does 6816 *Frankton Grange* on the 11.10am ex-Plymouth, first 'Grange' here since the war. Heading west, 73085 gets to Bristol on the 11.20am ex-Portsmouth.

19 Adams 4-4-2T 30582 is provided by special request for a REC Waterloo/Windsor/ Guildford railtour.

20 Rear power car of the 3-car DMU forming the 12.50pm Leeds – Scarborough is removed at Malton. For the return at 4.5pm, lead driving car is detached, turned on the shed turntable, re-coupled to the trailer car. Train leaves on time.

20 O2 2-8-0 63972 (36E) is a rare visitor to Halifax.

21 70014 *Iron Duke* (26A) reaches Bath (Green Park) with the southbound 'Pines Express' – first time a 7MT has been seen here.

21 CR 4-4-0 54505 is a noteworthy arrival into Princes Street, from Lanark.

23 45561 *Saskatchewan* travels all the way from Keighley to…King's Cross, on a womens' organisation special. An unprecedented working to King's Cross!

25 Grand National day attracts 12 specials to Aintree amongst which are 78061 + 46146 *The Rifle Brigade*, 78063 + 45530 *Sir Frank Ree* and 4-4-0 40684 + 45534 *E. Tootal Broadhurst* all ex-Euston with pilots from Wigan. A special from Cleethorpes includes a new Pullman car (332) and ex-'Devon Belle' observation car M280M, headed by a very grimy 'Crab'.

26 Night expresses to Euston are diverted from Nuneaton into St Pancras where the 'Royal Highlander' arrives behind 92054, D320 having failed earlier.

29 First section (for small exhibits) of the Clapham Museum – a former LT bus Garage – is opened to the public. Admission 1s adult, 6d children.

29 D9002 reaches Neville Hill on a test train; returns to Gateshead via Harrogate.

30 Maundy Thursday diversions observed at Embsay station; 44852 + 60088 *Book Law* heading north, 45564 *New South Wales* on a Leeds – Morecambe, 60038 *Firdaussi* with southbound parcels. Up 'Waverley' has 60077 *The White Knight* and Ivatt 2-6-0 43030 + 45639 *Raleigh* head the down train. Up 'Thames-Clyde Express' has 45677 *Beatty* whilst the strange pairing of 2-6-4T 42138 + 46117 *Welsh Guardsman* powers the down service.

31   (Good Friday). First of the season's 'Starlight Specials' leaves St Enoch behind 60824 for St Pancras, via Waverley.

31   61242 *Alexander Reith Gray* heads a Perth – Queen Street train that conveys both ex-'Coronation' observation cars, coming out of winter storage.

U/D   73029 (71G Weymouth) is noted, unusually, on ECS duties at Waterloo.

U/D   Midnight Penzance – Paddington sleeper is now regularly double-headed by two D800-series 'Warships', to Newton Abbot.

U/D   Sentinel 0-4-0T shunter from the S&D line 47190 arrives on Saltley shed.

U/D   70026 *Polar Star* (88A Canton) is found, most unexpectedly, on Oswestry shed for repairs – first 'Britannia' to visit here?

U/D   'Deltic' is withdrawn from service as no further repairs are sanctioned.

APRIL 1961

2ND   (Easter Sunday). Brush Type 2s make their appearance in the Calder Valley, when Blackpool specials from Sheffield are headed by D5682/85/89.

2   Excursion from Manchester to Stratford-on-Avon is worked throughout by 45540 *Sir Robert Turnbull* (9E) 'Patriots' are a rare sight in Snow Hill.

2,3   Reamarkably, Blaydon shed hosts 45238 (14A!), on a day excursion from Derby to Newcastle. Next day it is at Scarborough on a special from Sheffield!

3   60002 *Sir Murrough Wilson* returns to Hull in the early hours, coming back with a day excursion to Newcastle. A4s are uncommon visitors at Paragon.

3   Race special brings 48129 (1A!) into Wetherby, and a return excursion to Sheffield leaves behind 61276 paired with 90127, surprisingly.

3   'Six Lochs Land Cruise' DMU operates a Glasgow – Killin round trip.

4   Trouble in the Carlisle area means the up 'Thames-Clyde Express' is over seven hours late into St Pancras; the 'Waverley' is a mere five hours down!

5   Astonishingly, 61894 (40E Colwick) penetrates into South Wales with an ammunition train from Leadenham to Milford Haven. Seen heading west through Port Talbot in the morning, and at Swansea (from the Carmarthen direction) paired LE with a 'Castle' in the afternoon. Overnights at Neath shed.

5   60882 (64A) is noticed on New England; Scottish V2s are rare this far south.

5   48007, working load trials from Brent to Norwood Jct. via Kew, Clapham Jct. is unable to restart from a signal stop between Herne Hill and Tulse Hill, and is pushed from the rear by a Holborn – West Croydon EMU!

5   Express from Blackpool arrives in Euston behind 92122 piloting diesel failure D7 *Ingleborough*, an unusual, if necessary pairing.

6   77015 (67B!) is surely the first Hurlford loco to be seen in York station?

7   30916 *Whitgift* graces the WR/SR transfer freight scene by working the late morning goods from Didcot.

8   Two troop trains from Edinburgh to Southampton Docks arrive behind 5926 *Grotrian Hall* (84A) and 30451 *Sir Lamorak* (72B), hauling ER/ScR stock that includes a Sleeping Car and a Kitchen Car.

8	Ex-Crosti 92026 forms a spectacular double-headed combination with 4967 *Shirenewton Hall* on the 4.15pm Salisbury – Bristol.
8	Ivatt 2-6-2T 41203 (82E) is a stranger found on Gorton shed, where there are no diesels on view whatsoever.
8	Holbeck A3s 60072 *Sunstar*, 60077 *The White Knight* found under repair at Eastfield (65A) and Polmadie (66A) respectively.
9	9am Liverpool – Newcastle (D257) is diverted over the Oldham, Ashton & Guide Bridge line, first main line diesel seen at Oldham.
10	'Crab' 42923 (2A) recorded at Reading on a special freight from Banbury.
10,11	46112 *Sherwood Forester* works two specials between Leicester and Swindon on consecutive days, organised by Ian Allan Ltd. First 'Scot' at Swindon?
12	0-6-0PT 3679 heads the 8.50am Exeter (C) – Exmouth (first PT since 12/59).
12	70020 *Mercury* runs through Cheltenham with a Cadbury's special from Porthcawl to Bournville. Not many 7MTs pass over the Lickey incline.
14	D800 *Sir Brian Robertson* takes the SR route between Exeter and Plymouth, noted at Tavistock on an evening freight. First D8xx seen on this line.
16	550 passengers cram into an 8-car DMU ramblers' excursion from Bradford (Forster Square)/Leeds (City) to Kirkbymoorside via York and Pilmoor.
17	LNW 0-8-0 49443 (1E) is a strange apparition at Aylesbury on a down goods.
17	34089 *602 Squadron* heads a Victoria – Portsmouth Royal train.
19	30796 *Sir Dodinas le Savage* is a notable visitor to Bath Road shed, Bristol.
19	72003 *Clan Fraser* (66A) travels through to Wolverhampton (HL) with a special from Glasgow for the Wolves v Rangers European Cup semi-final.
19-21	'Brighton Belle' unit 3051 works a Unilever Conference special from Blackfriars to Eastbourne. Party returns to Victoria on 21st.
20	45548 *Lytham St. Annes* (2A) arrives, most unusually, at Lincoln on the 7.15am Colchester – Newcastle. (Fails, and is replaced by a B1).
20	Former gas turbine E2001 goes for trials on the Glasgow suburban lines, but the thrush's nest and eggs in its bogies have to be carefully removed first!
21,22	K1/1 2-6-0 61997 *MacCailin Mor* (63B Stirling) is on Heaton shed, heading for Doncaster Works. Towed there next day by 60525 *A. H. Peppercorn* (61B), a rare pair to be trundling 112 miles up the East Coast main line.
22	6002 *King William IV* is granted permission to reach Ruabon working the Paddington – Portmadoc 'Festiniog Railway Special'. (6009 also got this far on 9 June 1956 on the 9am Paddington – Pwllheli service train).
22	Bluebell Railway Society tours Sussex branch lines with a 6-coach train 'topped and tailed' – an unprecedented feature over such a distance. E4 0-6-2Ts 32503, 32564, 32479 and E6 0-6-2T 32418 participate, with 32564/32479 double-heading the final leg from Horsted Keynes to Brighton.
22	(Week ending). A high-speed run with a test train of five coaches is worked between Paddington and Snow Hill for track testing purposes. 5056 *Earl of Powis* does the honours, making the down trip in 95 minutes.
24	60110 *Robert the Devil* is immaculately turned out to head a special from King's Cross to Consett where the Iron Co. is opening a new rolling mill.
24,26	45660 *Rooke* (82E) heads a 12-coach private special from Bristol to Scarborough throughout, bearing a large circular headboard reading 'Farmers Party visiting Barlby

BOCM'. 61200 (34A) also reaches York on another special for BOCM (British Oil Cake Manufacturers, north of Selby) on 26th.

27	D1 4-4-0 31489 works a Charing Cross – Ashford school special. Steam is not yet dead on the Eastern Section.
29	Schoolboys International at Wembley attracts 20 special trains, 18 of which are steam hauled, only D5580, D5628 representing 'modern' power.
30	Doncaster – Lincoln parcels is headed by 62011 (65J Fort William)! (Awaiting entry to the Plant).
30	USA 0-6-0T 30073 runs through Swaythling with an LCGB railtour.
U/D	45662 *Kempenfelt* (82E Bristol Barrow Road) is a surprise Easter guest at 67A.
U/D	Reading South turntable is out of action, and groups of up to five SR locos go to Reading West triangle to turn.
U/D	After its visit to St Rollox Works, 4-4-0 54398 *Ben Alder* is seen at Dawsholm shed.

MAY 1961

1ST	D5908 works the 3.5pm King's Cross – Ely, a first for this class here.
2	60026 *Miles Beevor* reaches Malton with the King's Cross – Ampleforth College special, relieved there by 2-6-4T 42477.
3	D832 *Onslaught* and D840 *Resistance* head two boat train specials to London between Plymouth and Exeter via the SR Okehampton route.
3	45581 *Bihar and Orissa* arrives at Doncaster, goes briefly into the Works – a 'Jubilee' first – in the morning, and goes on shed in the afternoon.
4	78000 (89C Machynlleth), ex-Works, is an unprecedented visitor to Reading, passing through on an up freight.
6	60103 *Flying Scotsman* works over Shap! Loco heads a Gainsborough Model Railway Society special; Lincoln to Carlisle via Newcastle, travels LE to Penrith (train goes to Keswick), then over Shap to Preston, back to Lincoln.
6	E2001 is observed in a siding on the Helensburgh line in the Glasgow suburbs.
7	8P 71000 *Duke of Gloucester* is a rare sight on GSW territory, working the 10.24pm Glasgow (Central) – Euston sleeper through Dumfries.
8	D9002 begins heading the 5.50pm Newcastle – York fitted freight on a regular basis. Not seen yet on scheduled passenger trains.
9	45540 *Sir Robert Turnbull* is a surprise on the 7.7pm Sheffield (Vict.) – Hull.
10	D5689 works both the up and down 'Sheffield Pullman', rather than a Type 4.
11-14	To celebrate the 50th Anniversary of the Institution of Locomotive Engineers, a rolling stock exhibition is held at Marylebone Parcels Depot. On display are MR 1000, 60022, 71000, 92220, D28, D867, D5699, D6553, D7000, D8400, D9003, E5014, E3059, GT3, new WR dynamometer car, and other vehicles.
12	30921 *Shrewsbury* (73A) reaches Oxford on an excursion from Redhill.
12,13	Sutton Oak shed (8G) prepares 'Royal Scots' 46120/61, 'Patriot' 45544 and 'Jubilees' 45554/93 to work specials to Wembley for the RL Cup final. On the 13th, 46160 *Queen Victoria's Rifleman* (14B) amazingly departs from Leeds (Central!) for St Pancras, via Wakefield, Pontefract and Chesterfield. In all, 34 specials are run for this event, requiring some 350 coaches.
15	70050 *Firth of Clyde* (66A) is shock power for the 7.15am York – Leeds.

16	1700hp B-B D7000 is handed over to the WR by Beyer-Peacock (Hymek) Ltd in a ceremony at Paddington.
16	The last B12 61572 is turned out by Norwich to head a schools excursion from Swaffham to Liverpool Street. Another unusual arrival here is Ivatt 2-6-0 43121 (14A) on a diverted Tilbury – St Pancras boat train.
16	EE 2500hp 4-6-0 GT3 arrives at Leicester (Central) from the Marylebone exhibition, to begin test runs southbound at 10.15am, 1.20pm each day.
17	WR DMU runs from Cheltenham to Andover on the MSWJ line for the benefit of the local TUCC Inspection Committee.
17	A Royal train is run from Waterloo to Guildford for the consecration of the new cathedral. 34089 *602 Squadron* takes three Pullmans plus the LNER Royal Saloon there, 34009 *Lyme Regis* heads the return. The same coaches form the Derby day special to Tattenham Corner behind 30926 *Repton* (31st).
18	45506 *The Royal Pioneer Corps* (82E) is a remarkable arrival at Eastleigh after working the Bromford Bridge – Fawley oil train. Only 45516 is known to have visited this area before, on 17 February 1950.
20	Unique sight at York is the simultaneous arrival of two 'Royal Scots'; 46151 *The Royal Horse Guardsman* on the 9.40am slow from Sheffield, and 46164 *The Artists' Rifleman* on the 7.48am Nottingham – Newcastle relief.
20	D5692 is the first of its class to reach Scarborough, with an excursion from Sheffield (after which they become frequent visitors!).
21	(Whit Sunday). D5690 makes a class debut at Southport on a special from Chesterfield. D5685/87/92 reach Blackpool same day on further specials.
21	45650 *Blake* becomes only the second of the class to visit Brighton, on excursion traffic from Leicester. It is promptly impounded by the Civil Engineer and remains on shed until 3 June, departing LE. (The special returns behind 30907 *Dulwich* – though not through to Leicester – and it was 45595 that arrived on 8/8/53). D8208/33 also reach Brighton, from Chingford.
21,22	14 excursions reach Hunstanton on the Sunday; 75041/44 (15C) are notable arrivals at Kings Lynn on Monday with further specials for the coast.
21	Two 4-COR EMUs form a special from Windsor & Eton to the Kent coast.
22	WR gas turbine 18000 is seen at Rugby Testing Station.
22	60859 sets a precedent by arriving at Huddersfield with the 9.45am Newcastle – Liverpool, replacing a failed diesel at Darlington. The V2 is relieved by 46152 *The King's Dragoon Guardsman*.
24	Brush Type 2 arrives in Grimsby (Town) with a cinema coach and Directors Saloon in tow.
25	70014 *Iron Duke* (26A) seen at Leeds (Central) on the 3.25am to Manchester.
25	'Brighton Belle' unit forms the 9am Victoria – Dover special for AEI Ltd.
27	45535 *Sir Herbert Walker K.C.B.* (8A) is an extreme rarity at Ayr on the 11.30am from St Enoch. First Edge Hill loco seen at Ayr?
28	L1 2-6-4Ts 67703/35 head a 12-coach rake of EMU stock into Shoeburyness.
29	D6537 is a first-of-class to arrive at Ely, on excursion traffic from Gillingham.
31	E5018 makes several runs between Waterloo and Guildford.
31	70034 *Thomas Hardy* (32A) brings the 10.20am York – Bournemouth into Sheffield (Victoria), rare for a 'Britannia' to enter from this direction.

U/D　Cardiff Canton (88A) 'Britannias' are despatched (on 5 May) for overhaul at Doncaster, via Crewe, Stockport and Wakefield shed (arriving on 10 May), proceeding four days later to Doncaster.

U/D　Oban – Buchanan Street train seen at Glenoglehead with 45049 piloting, most surprisingly, 61278 (62B) – a rare class on the Callander & Oban line.

JUNE 1961

1ST　BTC Chairmanship passes from Sir Brian Robertson to Dr Richard Beeching.

1　First revenue-earning Anglo-Scottish working of a 'Deltic' occurs when D9004 (64B) heads the 11am Waverley – Newcastle, and 4.24pm return.

3　60068 *Sir Visto* (12C) arrives in Whitley Bay on a private charter from Workington, a rare engine in Newcastle let alone Whitley Bay!

3　70037 *Hereward the Wake* (31B) heads the 10.5am York – Edinburgh as far as Newcastle, returning on the 1.25pm Glasgow – York relief.

3　Brush 'Falcon' 2800hp Co-Co D0280 is on display at the Company's Works at Loughborough. NBL Bo-Bo 10800 is also at these Works after a repaint.

4　'Festival of Rambling' produces three excursions to Ingleton; 73000 from Chesterfield and one each from Leeds and Bradford behind Ivatt 2-6-0s 43036/30 respectively, calling at all stations to Sedbergh, ECS to Tebay.

4　4073 *Caerphilly Castle* is hauled by road to the Science Museum.

4　'Deltics' make their first appearance at Lincoln when D9001 passes through on the diverted 8.20pm King's Cross – Edinburgh.

4　45233 (14A) surprisingly works through to Great Yarmouth and back with an excursion from Mill Hill. First Cricklewood loco seen at this resort?

4　76066 heads the 4pm Plymouth – Waterloo out of Exeter (Central), rare power.

6,7　72003 *Clan Fraser* works through to Windermere (Lakeside) on an excursion from Southport. Next day it heads the 2.30pm Liverpool (Exchange) to Bradford (Exchange) – first 6MT here – returning on the 7.15pm to Southport.

8　60028 *Walter K. Wigham* heads the LNER Royal train from King's Cross taking the Queen to the Duke of Kent's wedding in York Minster. 60003/15 *Andrew K. McCosh/Quicksilver* head specials for the guests. Reception is at Hovingham and return journeys start at Malton, again behind 60028/03/15 which run LE tender first from York, the latter as a pair. Interesting!

8　60036 *Colombo* is a stunning arrival at Manningham, bringing ECS into the carriage sidings. Definitely the first A3 seen here!

9　34055 *Fighter Pilot* reaches Luton (Midland Road) with a 16-coach schools' special from the Portsmouth area to Whipsnade Zoo, loco serviced at Bedford.

10　O1 0-6-0 31065 pilots 30934 *St. Lawrence* on the 4.58pm Dover (Priory) to Tonbridge. The 0-6-0 is on railtour duty next day from Paddock Wood.

10　46100 *Royal Scot* departs Bath (Green Park) with the northbound 'Pines Express', most unusual power.

10　E1 4-4-0 31067 works the Tonbridge – Brighton service, rare type nowadays.

11　'Trans-Pennine' set is used for an excursion from the West Riding to Towyn, for the Talyllyn Railway. Unit is serviced at Barmouth.

12　NER Bo-Bo electric shunter 26500 emerges from South Gosforth after overhaul turned out in lined NER green with both NER, BR crests.

13	New Channel Islands ship *Sarnia* arrives at Weymouth from Southampton with invited guests, who proceed to Waterloo in five 1st class Pullmans cars.
16	5990 *Dorford Hall* (84C) works into Southampton Docks with pigeons from York to the Channel Islands.
16	2-6-4T 42227 (33C) is a most unusual arrival at Mirfield on a Holyhead to Healey Mills cattle train, leaving for York next day on the 2.35am freight.
17	61764 *Loch Arkaig* is specially provided to work the 2.50pm Queen Street to Crianlarich and return. Last passenger run for a K2 on West Highland.
17	Brush Type 2 observed on the down 'Norseman' at York (usually a Pacific).
17	45545 *Planet* is a rare sight at Bridlington shed, off a Carlisle excursion.
17	92220 *Evening Star* takes the 'Merchant Venturer' out of Paddington.
17	30793 *Sir Ontzlake* is surprise power for the 'Bournemouth Belle' seen passing through Esher 45min late.
18	Cleethorpes receives Stanier 2-6-0 42963 on excursion traffic, most unusual.
18	34108 *Wincanton* is observed heading a ballast train on the Exmouth branch between Topsham and Exton, a very uncommon loco type on this line.
18	46248 *City of Leeds* brings a special into Aberdeen, making the first visit of this class so far this year.
19	60003 *Andrew K. McCosh* works into LMR territory with a Royal visit to Corby, and is noted at Manton station, *en route* Stamford to Peterborough.
20	New D7002, in paintshop grey, works a 10-coach ECS test train into Derby from Manchester, returning shortly after. Later examples repeat the process.
20,21	70018 *Flying Dutchman* (88A) passes through Huddersfield LE, heading for Doncaster Works. The following day 70032 *Tennyson* (1A) is also a surprise at Huddersfield heading the 9am Liverpool – Newcastle.
22	61954 (31B) is a noteworthy stranger to the West Coast main line, reaching Wolverton with ECS from the Northampton area.
22	60883 (64A) is surprise power for the 1.15pm Largs – St Enoch.
24	D8052 appears at Lincoln on the 5.18pm Boston – Sheffield, and makes a trial run Lincoln – March on ECS next day.
24	70030 *William Wordsworth* (31B) works the 8.45am Wakefield – Scarborough as far as York, leaving with the 12.52pm Newcastle – Colchester.
25,27	Stirling – Sutton Coldfield Car Sleeper is hauled throughout to New Street by 60088 *Book Law* (55A). Two days later 60038 *Firdaussi* works the same train as far as Derby.
26/27	The Queen Mother travels from King's Cross to Tyneside in three Royal Saloons attached to the rear of the 11.20pm, these being stabled overnight at West Gosforth on the Ponteland branch. After launching s.s.'Northern Star' at Vickers-Armstrongs V3 2-6-2T 67685 + 60033 *Seagull* bring the ECS of the guests' special plus Royal Saloons, from Heaton to Walker for the return run.
27	2.21pm EMU from Gidea Park is stopped at Forest Gate as a member of the public has deposited a push chair onto the overhead wires!
27	60084 *Trigo* is an outstanding arrival in St Pancras on the 'Thames-Clyde'!
28	70015 *Apollo* (26A) reaches Bradford (Exchange) on the 11.30am from Liverpool (Exchange). First 'Britannia' seen here?
29	L1 4-4-0 31786 works an inspection special from Portsmouth to Waterloo via Horsham and Epson.

29	Invalid saloon (E22026E, York 1911) is the lead vehicle on the up 'Tees-Thames' from York to Kings' Cross, its first use since September 1960.
30	34057 *Biggin Hill* heads ECS on the Bristol – Avonmouth line in the early evening, before being serviced at St Philips Marsh (82B).
30	44168 (21A) is a rare sight at Eastleigh yard, having arrived on a train of empty oil tanks.
U/D	0-6-0PTs 1646/49 are taken out of store for shunting duties at Inverness.
U/D	0-6-0PTs 1501/2/9 move on from Wellington (Salop) to Bagnalls (Stafford) for reconditioning before going to the NCB.
U/D	Ex-'Devon Belle' observation car SC280 begins work on the 10.30am Inverness – Kyle of Lochalsh and 5.30pm return working.
U/D	45151 (66B) and, more surprisingly, 45458 (63A) both appear in Liverpool (Exchange) during the month.

JULY 1961

1ST	46231 *Duchess of Atholl* (66A) arrives in Manchester (Exchange) with the 17-coach 10.45am ex-Glasgow. In contrast, 46244 *King George VI* reaches Buchanan Street on the 7.52am from Callander, having worked from Stirling.
2	34050 *Royal Observer Corps* having been in use for 12 years, qualifies for the ROC long service medal. Loco is presented with two plaques (in the colour of the medal ribbons) to be mounted on the cabsides, at a Waterloo ceremony. 34050 then heads an ROC special to Bournemouth at 11am.
3	61324 (61A) is noted on 66A, where Aberdeen B1s are infrequent visitors.
5	D9007 *Pinza* (named on 22 June) seen LE on Beattock (on clearance tests?).
6	Caprotti 44757 pilots 46120 *Royal Inniskilling Fusilier* (1A) between Leeds (City) and Bradford (Forster Square) – first ever Willesden loco here? – on the 12.10pm from St Pancras. 46120 then heads a freight to Cricklewood.
6	60088 *Book Law* (55A) is a remarkable visitor to Crewe South (5B) from Aston, where it had spent five days after working through to Sutton Coldfield on the car carrier from Stirling. Heads north to Carlisle the following day.
6,7	45579 *Punjab* (21A) arrives at Lydney on a schools' excursion, which next day heads off to Portsmouth reaching Eastleigh behind 7003 *Elmley Castle*, Portsmouth behind 73083. 7003 returns LE via Salisbury.
7,11	19-vehicle pigeon special from Newcastle reaches Newhaven (Harbour) headed by C 0-6-0s 31583 + 31714. Empties return on 11th from Norwood to Dalston headed by 34083 *605 Squadron* piloting C 0-6-0 31579! Quite a sight.
8	First 'Coronation' to visit Aberdeen this year is 46248 *City of Leeds*, coming in on a special.
8	70053 *Moray Firth* (55A) and 60893 (34E) both arrive in Marylebone with overnight 'Starlight Specials' from Glasgow/Edinburgh. 'Britannias' rarely reach this London terminus.
8	Tunbridge Wells (Central) – Worthing special is formed of a 6-car Buffet set of 'Hastings' stock, first use west of Brighton for this stock.
8	20003 powers a Portsmouth (Harbour) – Hastings excursion throughout and on to Ore with the ECS. The Hove – Preston Park section is steam-hauled (with 20003 at rear) into Brighton, to resume forward travel to Lewes.

8,15	Melcombe Regis is the starting point for the 1.55pm return to Swindon (of a Works holiday 'Trip' special) on both days. On 15th, a Channel Islands boat train (8 hours late) also sets off for Waterloo from Melcombe Regis.
9	46247 *City of Liverpool* works an RCTS special, Leeds – Carlisle, over the S&C route, where any appearance of this class is highly unusual.
9	Adams 4-4-2T 30583 runs LE between Eastleigh, Brighton (as LSWR 488) en route to the Bluebell Railway. Arrives on 12th; heads a special same evening!
10	1005 *County of Devon* (82B) is a most unexpected sight at Crewe South shed.
13	70053 *Moray Firth* (55A) heads an excursion from Castleford to Caernarvon.
14	(Glasgow Fair Friday). 10.35am Leeds – Glasgow arrives in St Enoch with D18 piloting 70044 *Earl Haig*; the 9.25pm overnight from St Pancras enters with D11 piloting 46109 *Royal Engineer*. Extra locos for excursion traffic.
15	70023 *Venus* (88A), ex-Doncaster Works, reaches Newcastle on the 8.40am King's Cross – Edinburgh. First Cardiff Canton loco in Newcastle, surely.
15	70003 *John Bunyan* (31B) is the first 'Britannia' to appear at Bridlington, taking over the 8.10am Cardiff – Filey Holiday Camp at Gascoigne Wood. It then works the ECS to Scarborough, becoming only the second 7MT to reach here, 70053 *Moray Firth* arriving experimentally in December 1958.
15,19	70027 *Rising Star* and 70023 *Venus* both appear, respectively, on March shed; more running-in for 88A 'Britannias', ex-Works, but rare just the same. March also hosts (15th) 60123 *H. A. Ivatt* (56C Copley Hill) another stranger here.
15	80099 (33B) is used by York for workings to Scarborough, Bridlington and Hull. Tilbury locos shouldn't be seen in these parts!
15	D24 heads a relief boat train, St Enoch to Stranraer, first 'Peak' seen here?
15	60076 *Galopin* (51A) is a surprise arrival at Wakefield (Kirkgate) on the 4.46pm Leeds (Central) – Doncaster.
17	Race traffic causes 60072 *Sunstar*, 60088 *Book Law* to reach Ayr on specials ex-Glasgow.
18	D9003 *Meld* (named on 1st July) conducts high speed tests from King's Cross to Leeds and back.
18	A remarkable sight at Stockport (Edgeley) is that of 0-6-0PT 3739 (82C), having travelled LE from Crewe. (Sold to Beyer Peacock at Gorton?).
22	The 'Welshman' passes through Llandudno Jct. with 14 bogies, (8min early) hauled by double-chimneyed 45596 *Bahamas*, working through from Euston.
22	Stanier 2-6-2T 40150 (ex-Thurso) is used on ECS workings at Inverness. The nearest sister engines are allocated to Glasgow sheds.
22	W 2-6-4Ts 31917/23 noted on Clapham Jct. – Waterloo ECS workings.
22	A year on, 4-4-0 40646 again works the 2-coach Birmingham – Preston portion of the 'CTAC Scottish Tours Express' in each direction.
23	D5909 turns up at Mablethorpe on an excursion from Biggleswade.
23	60879 (50A) is surprise power for a down parcels train through Wolverton.
24	60895 (50A) is sent to Sowerby Bridge for a special freight working to Garston, but is refused passage beyond Hebden Bridge by the LMR authorities.
26	Merton Park station is used by Associated Television as a setting for their programme *Summersing*. C2X 0-6-0 32549 (as 2549) is provided (clean!) with headboard 'Summersing Express', plus four elderly carriages.
27	30772 *Sir Percivale* arrives in Oxford and 45684 *Jutland* takes over its train of SR stock.

27   LNW 0-8-0 49104 tows 72002 *Clan Campbell* (with dismantled motion) over the CR
      main line from Carlisle to Polmadie, where the 0-8-0 is a rare sight. 49104 is also seen
      at Motherwell a few days later on an up train of steel pipes.

28   U 2-6-0 31628 is surprise power for the 1.10pm Bournemouth (West) – Bath
      (Green Park) and 7.15pm return. A most unusual class on this line.

28   822 *The Earl*, after overhaul at Oswestry, becomes No.1 of the Welshpool & Llanfair
      Railway, on its delivery to Welshpool on a low-loader marshalled in the morning
      Oswestry – Moat Lane goods.

29   30911 *Dover* is an unprecedented sight on...Camden (1B) shed!

29   D9008 is run-in between Carlisle, Newcastle on an Ayr – Newcastle express.

29   48134 brings a Saturday extra from Birmingham to Euston, and later heads the 2.45pm
      relief to Northampton. 8F's rarely work passenger trains at Euston.

29   46238 *City of Carlisle* works a Glasgow (Central) – Liverpool (Exchange) relief, but fails
      close to Liverpool, where the train arrives behind 90712 tender first. Last recorded visit
      of a 'Coronation' to Exchange was by 46232 *Duchess of Montrose* on 3 July 1950.

30   60019 *Bittern* heads the 11.5am to King's Cross out of Saltburn, where few A4s ever reach.

U/D   45546 *Fleetwood* (8B Warrington) is a big surprise at the head of the 8.45am Bradford
      (Exchange) – Blackpool on two days in the month.

U/D   70027 *Rising Star* noted on a stopping train at Boston, to everyone's surprise. (See 15, 19)

AUGUST 1961

1ˢᵀ   Northbound 'Devonian' arrives in Derby with 70017 *Arrow* as pilot to D80.

2   34017 *Ilfracombe* reaches Banbury with ECS; hands over to 92010.

3   D5696 (30A) brings a troop train into Southampton Docks, notable type here.

3   46128 *The Lovat Scouts* visits Cardiff by working through with the 9.30am
      Manchester (Piccadilly) – Swansea. Not many 'Scots' reach Cardiff.

3,5   2-6-0 7317 (82E) noted leaving Weymouth on the 3.50pm to Waterloo (3ʳᵈ).
      Also heads 11.4am Bournemouth (Central) – Sheffield to Basingstoke, returning on the
      9.9am Sheffield – Bournemouth (5ᵗʰ). Most unusual workings.

4   'Waverley' fails near Bedford and passes through Wellingborough behind 44381, with
      44667 pushing hard at the rear!

5   Tank engines 42616/42101/40132/40078/42487 all coupled, work LE from Caernarvon
      to Afon Wen to work returning Butlin's Holiday Camp traffic.

5   46158 *The Loyal Regiment* (9E) is the first 'Scot' to reach Scarborough, on the 1.52pm
      arrival from Leeds, returning with the 7.30pm to Wakefield.

5   2-8-0 3854 (86G) works the 8.50am Swansea – Paignton throughout.

5   'Patriot' 45510 is employed on an all-stations Chester – Birkenhead local!

6   11am Euston – Windermere is headed by a 'Princess Royal' throughout!

8   5.16pm arrival into Liverpool Street from Cambridge comes in with J15 0-6-0 65476
      (tender first) piloting D5666, a strange old/new assemblage.

8   Due to a derailment near Granthouse, D9006 on the up morning 'Talisman' is the first
      'Deltic' to be diverted via St Boswells and Kelso to Tweedmouth.

8   70037 *Hereward the Wake* (31B) appears in the Calder Valley at the head of ECS from
      Edinburgh to Luddendenfoot, where March engines are rarities.

9   70011 *Hotspur* is turned out to work the 3.15am Temple Mills to Hertford (East) goods and 9.43am return, first Pacific to be seen on this branch.

11   45581 *Bihar and Orissa* arrives in Scarborough with the 'City of Birmingham Holiday Express'. 'Jubilees' are always scarce at this Spa town.

12   44812 (21A) is provided by Tyseley to work the Snow Hill – Pembroke Dock as far as Cardiff, and the 5.10pm Cardiff – Birmingham via Gloucester.

12   61989 (41H Staveley GC) brings an up relief into New Street, unexpectedly!

13,14   46206 *Princess Marie Louise* is a highly unusual visitor to Patricroft shed (26F); used for the 1.18am Manchester – Bangor newspaper train next day.

13-19   45521 *Rhyl* (8A) pulls into Leeds (Central) on the 6.45pm ex-Manchester (Victoria). Works Bradford (Exchange) – Blackpool excursions on 14th, 16th and the 8.30am Leeds (C) – Blackpool on the 15th followed by the 9.45am B'ford – Llandudno on 19th. All rare work for an Edge Hill loco.

14   46117 *Welsh Guardsman* noted at Otley heading the 8.30pm Morecambe to Headingley return excursion, an uncommon class on this section.

14   70018 *Flying Dutchman* (88A), ex-Works from Doncaster, works both the 5.15pm Hull – King's Cross and the 6.26pm King's Cross – Hull to/from Grantham. 45116 (16D) is seen on the 5am King's Cross – York parcels and 60830 (31B) heads the up 'Tees-Thames', all unusual workings.

16   7.30am Edinburgh – Aberdeen leaves with five coaches behind 60027 *Merlin* whilst the 'connecting' portion from King's Cross, two Sleeping Cars + one through coach, forms a separate train 15min later with 73006 (63A).

19   Astonishingly, 46162 *Queen's Westminster Rifleman* (21A) is put on the 8.40am King's Cross – Edinburgh between Doncaster and Newcastle! Returns south LE an hour later to York, then pilots 60128 *Bongrace* to Doncaster, where it is removed. Explanation please!

19   0-6-0 3215 pilots 2-8-0 53806 over the Mendips on the 11.12am Bournemouth – Sheffield, rare to see a '2251' class on pilot work.

19   45519 *Lady Godiva* (82E) works into Southampton (Northam Yard) from Salisbury via Eastleigh with empty oil tanks from Bromford Bridge. 'Patriots' are extreme rarities anywhere near Southampton.

19   SR green 8-coach set 268 arrives in Wolverhampton from Bournemouth. Weeks later the set could not be located; SR sends a signal to all sections in order to trace it. Found in sidings at Westgate-on-Sea!

23   Surprise! S&D 2-8-0 53801 is found in Crewe Works, recently condemned.

26   70014 *Iron Duke* (26A) reaches Ayr on the 11.53am from St Enoch.

26   Up 'Cornish Riviera Express' (D867 *Zenith*) is amongst others diverted between Plymouth and Reading via Okehampton, Exeter (Central) and Basingstoke due to a landslip at Patney.

26   92001 departs Bath (Green Park) 53 minutes late on the Bradford – Bournemouth (West) and arrives at its destination ½ minute early!

26   Among exhibits at Derby Works Open Day are 46254 *City of Stoke-on-Trent* and 92220 *Evening Star* (88A), both unlikely to ever reach Derby normally!

26   92006 (71A) is a shock arrival at Manchester (Victoria) on a train from Bournemouth, and takes the ECS to Horwich. Eastleigh loco in Lancashire!

26   Red 46248 *City of Leeds* exits Waverley on a 5.30pm return football excursion to Perth.

'Coronations' are rare sights in Waverley.

26   46162 *Queen's Westminster Rifleman* works through to Newcastle (again!) on a relief from New Street.

27   11.50am Newcastle – Manchester (Red Bank) ECS arrives into Leeds behind 61032 *Stembok* + D5103/07. All treble-headers are noteworthy.

27   WR Blue Pullman set appears in Shrewsbury, having run there from Wolverhampton to turn. First visit to Shrewsbury?

29   N1 2-6-0 31876 (73J Tonbridge) works the 8.1am Eastleigh – Bournemouth (Central) freight, a most unusual class in these parts.

31   70011 *Hotspur* is an unexpected arrival at Hunstanton on excursion traffic.

31   New WR dynamometer car is seen for the first time in the West of England on the 8.30am Plymouth – Paddington behind D853 *Thruster*.

U/D   D77 conducts loaded coal trials on the Midland main line, with a 'diesel brake tender' next to the engine.

U/D   GT3 is seen on ECS workings at Woodford Halse.

U/D   Several 57xx 0-6-0PTs reach Beyer Peacock's Works in Gorton, Manchester for overhaul. (25 to be sold to the NCB?).

U/D   At least four GWR 0-6-0PTs are unpainted since Nationalisation; 9710 bears the circular GWR totem, 8783/9703 have large GWR initials, 8757 still reads 'Great Western'.

U/D   After a period of storage, the last L&Y 2-4-2T 50850 is back at work at Southport (Chapel Street) as station pilot for the heavy Flower Show traffic.

U/D   D11 4-4-0 62685 *Malcolm Graeme* supplies steam heat to the Caledonian Hotel on Princes Street, Edinburgh.

SEPTEMBER 1961

2ND   70034 *Thomas Hardy* is an unexpected arrival in Scarborough on the 11.1am from Sheffield. 61119 (30A!) is however an even bigger surprise, ex-Works.

2,9   Up 'Cornish Riviera Express' is routed via Bristol and Badminton behind D604 *Cossack* (2nd), and D808 *Centaur* the following week.

5   46227 *Duchess of Devonshire* (66A) successfully reaches Liverpool (Exchange) on the 1.45pm from Glasgow, returning with the 2.15pm next day.

6   J39 0-6-0 64747 (2F) is a stranger at Reading on eastbound freight.

7   70046 *Anzac* is seen heading north through Nuneaton hauling a 4-car EMU.

7   J37 0-6-0 64591 is an unlikely sight on the West Coast main line, heading southbound freight between Abington and Crawford in the Clyde Valley.

7   45593 *Kolhapur* is noted in Old Oak Common (81A) yard, unusual here.

8   In lieu of Pacific power, D8076/81 take a 'Starlight Special' out of St Enoch.

8   60009 *Union of South Africa* works the last up, and 60022 *Mallard* the last down, non-stop steam-hauled 'Elizabethan' expresses.

9   77018 finds itself at the head of the 11.40pm (8th) Euston – Glasgow sleeper, when a 'Coronation' is removed at New Cumnock.

11   D8027 heads the 3.5pm King's Cross – Ely throughout, a first for this class.

11   (Start of winter timetable). All Canton 'Britannias' are transferred to the LMR, Birmingham and Carlisle districts. Five pass through Snow Hill in one afternoon during the week, all on Tyseley turns.

11	'South Wales Pullman' becomes a Blue Pullman diesel unit, after a special trip Swansea/ Swindon/Swansea for BR Officials and Press on the 6th.
13	45577 *Bengal* runs LE from Cardiff to Barry to work the 7.10pm banana train to the north of England. Neither Cardiff, nor Barry see many 'Jubilees'.
13	46103 *Royal Scots Fusilier* comes into Scarborough on a freight from York, but returns on the 10.10am passenger working. Few 'Scots' reach this resort.
14	D207 heads the 8.10am Sheringham – Norwich. Rare locos north of Norwich.
14	6853 *Morehampton Grange* is seen reversing off the Derby main line into Saltley carriage sidings, and 6818 *Hardwick Grange* (87F Llanelly) travels to Eastleigh with oil tanks for Fawley, both unusual workings.
15	46130 *The West Yorkshire Regiment* departs Leeds (Central) – few 'Scots' reach here either – on the 8.55pm to Manchester, but returns next day on the 12.30pm from Liverpool (Exchange), surprisingly.
15	8.40am Nottingham (Victoria) – Marylebone is unusually double-headed, with 61271 piloting 70015 *Apollo*.
16	60103 *Flying Scotsman* is seen passing through Nottingham (Victoria), several years now since an A3 was noted here.
16	J52 0-6-0ST GNR 1247 (ex-68847), privately owned, works a 6-coach special from Welwyn Garden City to Hertford (North). Quite a sight!
16	44857 (55A Holbeck!) enters Southend-on-Sea (Central), having worked an excursion throughout from Leicester (London Road).
16	70018 *Flying Dutchman* (12C) works the 12.15pm Perth – Euston as far as Carlisle, complete with WR-pattern lamp brackets and WR lamps, therefore.
16	46137 *The Prince of Wales's Volunteers (South Lancashire)* is a surprise at Darlington heading the 12.43pm Newcastle – Bristol.
16	60044 *Melton* works the Royal train Hitchin – Newcastle, rare use of an A3. Last minute change of plan; high winds dictate rail rather than air travel.
18	'Master Cutler' Pullman arrives in King's Cross behind 60044 *Melton* which replaced D209 at Peterborough.
18	'Patriot' 45542 (12B) reaches Cambridge on freight ex-March, unusual loco.
19	2-8-0 2842 is a rare type to be found on Tilbury shed.
19	D18 works through to Morecambe on the 3.14pm from Leeds (City), a first?
21	45662 *Kempenfelt* (82E) heads a Fawley – Bromford Bridge oil tanks train through Southampton, first 'Jubilee' to work this service. On reaching Salisbury 2-8-2T 7242 is attached as pilot, an amazing combination!
21	46251 *City of Nottingham* appears at Manchester (Piccadilly) on the diverted 'Merseyside Express'.
23	D6306 is surprise power for a morning stopper from Swindon to Reading.
23	J11 0-6-0 64420 (9G) appears at Manchester (Victoria) at the head of the 'Four Counties' RCTS railtour. J11s are rare here on any pretext.
23	70023 *Venus* (12A, ex-WR) heads the 1.5pm Euston – Perth out of Carlisle with a pair of brakevan side lamps as headlamps, lights showing fore and aft!
24	30924 *Haileybury* is unusually employed on an early morning Didcot to Reading freight.
24	ScR TV train visits North Wales! Private day excursion utilises this on a run from Hazel Grove to Llanfair PG behind 2-6-4Ts 42372/16. Train is booked for a weekend trip to Blackpool; this is an extra charter in between.

24 10.20am Bradford (Exchange) – King's Cross leaves behind 60026 *Miles Beevor* (34A) and runs via Low Moor and the Cleckheaton branch to reach Wakefield. (D9003 *Meld* repeats this on 15 October). A4s are extremely rare in Bradford.

25 C 0-6-0 31229 brings ECS into Charing Cross, first steam here for months.

25 60835 *The Green Howard* (52B) works into Derby on the 7.5pm Newcastle to Bristol, returning with the 8.5am Birmingham – Newcastle next day.

26 'Birmingham Pullman' diesel unit is being serviced, and the spare loco-hauled set (usually a 'King') is headed by 5026 *Criccieth Castle* on this day.

26 45475 (63A) is a rarity at Hawick on the 5.30am freight from Portobello. 45475 returns tender first on the 9.53am goods back to Edinburgh.

29 D5142 catches fire on the down fast line at Carpenders Park on a Camden to Stockport freight, and D1 *Scafell Pike* also sets fire to itself on the up fast line south of Kings Langley on the 8.15am Manchester – Euston. The dislocation to services is considerable!

30 GWR 0-6-0PT L90 in London Transport red livery appears on 84A (Stafford Road), and later moves to Oxley. Sold to the NCB?

30 60022 *Mallard* heads the 'Northern Rubber Special' throughout from Retford to Blackpool (North), a train which includes M280, an ex-'Devon Belle' observation car. Compound 1000 pilots 45548 *Lytham St. Annes* on an excursion to Blackpool from Stoke Golding; 1000 then pilots the A4 (departing at 12.5am next day) as far as Stansfield Hall, with M280 replaced by two Sleeping Cars for the return journey. Fascinating workings!

30 TRPS AGM special is headed by 2-8-0 4704 both ways between Paddington and Shrewsbury, with 2-6-2T 5555 + 0-6-0 2217 (running as 2222 'in the interests of symmetry'!) on to Towyn and back.

U/D 'Horse of the Year Show 1961' includes 'Tom', aged 20, employed for the last 8 years shunting horseboxes at Newmarket.

U/D GT3 carries out a series of test runs with 8 coaches between Leicester and Marylebone.

U/D 45283 (89A Shrewsbury) powers the up 'Cambrian Coast Express' from Shrewsbury to Wolverhampton (LL) three days running.

OCTOBER 1961

1ST Glasgow 'Blue Train' suburban electric services resume.

5 70010 *Owen Glendower* is an unusual visitor to the Rugby – Peterborough line with a Restaurant Car excursion from East Anglia to Bournville.

8,16 0-6-0 2210 is a rare sight at Northampton, booked to work a train to Stratford-on-Avon. 2201 also visits on 16th.

11 6.20pm Bristol – Cardiff DMU catches fire inside the Severn Tunnel. Driver, plus some helping passengers, extinguish the fire. Guard breaks emergency wire and walks back to the east entrance. As a result, the 12noon Penzance to Crewe, is diverted via Gloucester, where the 'King' is removed.

13 Very surprisingly, the 12noon Bradford – St Pancras leaves Forster Square behind 45725 *Repulse* + 46132 *The King's Regiment Liverpool*, to Leeds.

13-18 Historic 0-4-2 *Lion* (Liverpool & Manchester Rly 1830) is extricated from storage at Crewe Works and taken to Rugby on a wagon in the 12.15pm Crewe – Bletchley freight. Then undergoes crew training on the Market Harborough loop in preparation for filming the TV programme *Look Around* at Dunchurch on 18th.

16,17	D0280 *Falcon* works two King's Cross – Cambridge round trips on both days.
17	'Crab' 42764 (15B Kettering) is a notable arrival at Eastleigh on 'Esso' oil tank traffic from the Midlands.
18	60848 (51A) heads a York – Edge Hill freight via Rochdale/Bolton/Wigan, which it surprisingly works through to Liverpool.
19	D7004 powers the up 'Bristolian', first of this type seen on this duty.
19	U 2-6-0 31793 + 34020 *Seaton* form an unusual pair to power a troop train from Southampton Docks to Ludgershall.
22	In the early morning, four Circus Specials reach Huddersfield (Hillhouse Yard). Later 60889 heads a Leeds – Huddersfield ECS train that includes five Sleeping Cars, another unusual working.
23	Outstanding visitor of the month to Ayr is 46252 *City of Leicester*, coming in on an early morning train from Glasgow.
25	4-car Pullman train is run from Brighton to Blandford Forum headed by 34107 *Blandford Forum*. Highly unusual to see Pullman cars on the Netley line, and a first for the S&D. Train is a Esso special to Flight Refuelling Ltd at nearby Tarrant Rushton conveying a funeral party.
25	84029 is observed on ECS work between Southampton (Terminus) and Eastleigh.
26	70006 *Robert Burns* is surprise power for the 3.44pm Norwich – Sheringham.
27	D9015 (recently named *Tulyar*) fails at Marshmoor on the 7.20am 'Master Cutler', replaced by D5646. 'Deltics' are rostered for one week only on the Sheffield Pullman trains, strengthened to 8-cars for Motor Show traffic. (D9009 *Alycidon* had also failed the day before!).
29	'Trans-Pennine' set (borrowed from Leeds) is used for a special from Scarborough to York and back.
30	'Peak' class loco hauling 5 x 1st class coaches and a Kitchen Car takes the place of the 'Midland Pullman' set between St Pancras and Nottingham.
U/D	L1 2-6-4T 67766 noted on station pilot duties at Leeds (Central), first L1 used in the West Riding for some years.
U/D	GT3 is engaged in 8 days of Crewe – Carlisle tests, with up to 12 coaches.
U/D	Brush Type 2s from Darnall work the 3.16pm Leeds (City) – Morecambe, and EE Type 4s resume crew training on the Leeds – Carlisle route.
U/D	All Metro-Vick Type 2s D5700-19 undergo modifications at Dukinfield.

NOVEMBER 1961

2ND	60974 (50A) takes a PW train over the CLC branch, Aintree – Southport.
3	9.50pm York – Liverpool/Swansea mail is headed by 73162 + 73169.
3	6.43am Gloucester – York fails to stop at Blackwell. An 0-6-0PT (Lickey banking engine) takes the eight stranded passengers in the cab (!) to Barnt Green to connect with a Redditch – New Street service.
4	12-car 'Hastings' set forms a football special, Ashford to High Wycombe.
4	61348 appears at Crewe on a football excursion from Lincoln.
4	60093 *Coronach* (12C) is a rare visitor to Darlington, again with football supporters, through from Carlisle.
4	D1 and E1 4-4-0s 31749 + 31067 double-head a PW special to Tonbridge in the course of their last journey to Ashford, for scrapping.

5	D29 (55H) heads the 10.25am King's Cross – Bradford (Exchange) via Lincoln, Cleckheaton and Low Moor, providing unusual sights at these places.
5	Thornaby depot (51L) hosts 60012 *Commonwealth of Australia* (64B), which brought a Scunthorpe – Middlesbrough football special from Doncaster.
6	The three Cornish beam engines (dating from 1866) that keep the Severn Tunnel dry are brought to a stand and taken over by modern electric pumps, in a short ceremony at Sudbrook (Monmouth) pumping station.
7	30929 *Malvern* is in charge of an up Ocean Liner Express from Southampton.
7	Motor train at East Croydon! H 0-4-4T 31005 + 2-coach set forms an up train from Forest Row in place of the 5.47pm Tunbridge Wells – Victoria and an 8.8pm substitute return working. Broken rail at Hartfield causes the disruption.
9	2-6-0 6378 (89C) works from Westbury (replacing a 9F) into Eastleigh on a Bromford Bridge – Fawley oil tank train. Machynlleth is thought to be the most distant shed to 'supply' an engine for these workings.
9	D0280 *Falcon* works the 8.36am Liverpool Street – Kings Lynn and 11.33am return. The 'on loan' loco is mainly engaged on Ipswich/Norwich expresses.
12	46170 *British Legion* is provided for the Armistice Day service at Rugby shed instead of 45500 *Patriot*, now withdrawn.
14	4.47pm Newcastle – Liverpool enters Leeds (City) with 60018 *Sparrow Hawk*. A4s rarely show up at City station.
18	45699 *Galatea* (89A) reaches Swansea (High Street) with the Carmarthen parcels train from Cardiff. Has a 'Jubilee' been this far west before?
18	Surprise! Ivatt 2-6-2T 41261 pulls the 8.20am Brighton – Victoria all the way.
19	60009 *Union of South Africa* (64B) is noted in Buchanan Street heading the 9.30am to King's Cross. (Queen Street is closed on Sundays).
21	D5606/09 double-head the up 'White Rose' to London, usually a Pacific turn.
21	11.53am Euston – Crewe parcels derails at Watford Jct. and blocks all four main lines. Trains diverted into Marylebone include 10.10am ex-Manchester (D306), 2.5pm ex-Liverpool (D298) and 12.50pm ex-Bangor (D28), both new types to Marylebone, plus 46170 *British Legion* on the 9.50am ex-Llandudno. Up 'Merseyside Express' proceeds to Paddington with 46240 *City of Coventry* still in charge! Up 'Royal Scot' and 'Caledonian' both terminate at St Pancras, as does the 10am from Blackpool, behind a 9F.
25	43888 (16A) is a rare sight at Oxford, and 61204 also comes in on a Peterborough – Torquay football special.
25	SR diesels D5009 + D6523 work through from Dartford to Ashton Gate on an 11-coach football excursion.
25	WR 5-car diesel Pullman travels from Tyseley to Swindon for attention via Stourbridge, Worcester and Cheltenham – first sightings here of these units.
28	45723 *Fearless* (5A) is a surprise choice for the 'Cambrian Coast Express' between Shrewsbury and Wolverhampton (LL).
28	CR 0-4-4T 55225 is seen making good speed at Shields Road (Glasgow) hauling a new 'Blue Train' set, delivered from Pressed Steel at Linwood.
30	D859 *Vanquisher*, new ex-NBL, seen on trials at Gushetfaulds, Glasgow.
30	46162 *Queen's Westminster Rifleman* pays an unexpected visit to Salisbury on the 9.32am Bromford Bridge – Fawley oil tank empties. A 9F takes over.
30	O4 2-8-0 63617 (36C) is an outstanding arrival at Heaton; oil train from York.

U/D 60918 heads the 4.56am Crewe – Manchester (Central) parcels; surprise loco!

U/D D6556/59 are on short term loan to New England (34E) for crew training prior to the introduction of the Cliffe – Uddingston cement workings. (See Dec 4th).

U/D 0-6-0Ts 1501/2/9 arive at Andrew Barclay's Works at Kilmarnock from Swindon via Bagnall's Works at Stafford. They are to be reconditioned for further use by the NCB's Durham Division.

U/D Down 'Caledonian' makes a special stop at Lockerbie to allow a party of wool merchants and tailors to disembark and attend a conference at a Lockerbie mill. When the party return to London the 'Caledonian' is again stopped specially at Lockerbie, and both driver and fireman are presented with high-quality suit lengths (made at Lockerbie).

The following table shows the rolling stock position in mid-1961 compared with 1954 and repays further study.

Locomotives	End of 1954	Mid-1961
Steam	18420	12676
Diesel	316	2822
Electric	71	147
Coaching Stock		
Locomotive hauled	53062	44195
Diesel multiple unit	70	3978
Electric multiple unit	4632	6743
Wagon Stock		
Total	1,124,710	960,446
Fitted or piped	179,788	322,511

At the end of 1954 the overall availability of the steam fleet was 86%, with
4.5% under or awaiting repair in works, and
9.5% in shed under repair.

The DMU/EMU fleet of 4702 had 8.4% 'under or awaiting repair'.
The wagon fleet of 1,124,710 had 6.5%   do.

DECEMBER 1961

1ST 'Birmingham Pullman' = rake of corridor stock that has just arrived in Paddington as the 8.38am from Henley! Pullman itself has engine problems in the platform and 5043 *Earl of Mount Edgcumbe* is quickly acquired to work this stock to Birmingham, and back, on the Pullman timings.

3 92210/47 are found under repair in Oswestry Works, surprisingly, as is 1025 *County of Radnor*, neither being types regularly encountered here.

4   2.30am Cliffe (SR) – Uddingston (ScR) cement train begins operation, worked by SR BRCW Type 3s to York and back. D6528/66 have no return empties on the first day and so head south from York light engine.

4   (Two weeks beginning). Load trials carried out between Doncaster and New England with classes 9F, WD, V2, B1 on 67 wagons plus dynamometer car.

4-8   Sheffield Pullman services are again 'Deltic' hauled, strengthened to 8 cars.

5   Ivatt 2-6-0 43040 (21A) is an unprecedented sight at Wells on the 5.20pm from Bristol, returning on the 7.15pm coupled to a 3MT 2-6-2T.

5   72005 *Clan Macgregor* reaches St Pancras (only the third 'Clan' here) on the 10.5pm sleeper ex-Edinburgh, from Leeds.

5   70035 *Rudyard Kipling* (40B) works the 8.13am to Barking from Tilbury (Riverside), undoubtedly the first Pacific to head an LTS local passenger train!

6   0-6-2T 69568 (34A) seen at Royston – first N2 here for many years.

7,9   80113 (64G) brings the 10.5pm Edinburgh – St Pancras sleeper into Carlisle after D29 fails at Hawick (7th). D5312 fails here on 9th and 78047 heads the 12noon from Waverley forward to Carlisle.

9   60108 *Gay Crusader* (tender-first) works the 7.38am from Peterborough into King's Cross, a 6-coach suburban set! Strange sight.

9   60074 *Harvester* stalls between Cross Gates and Wetherby on the 3pm Liverpool – Newcastle. 73168 then propels all the way to Harrogate!

10   60008 *Dwight D. Eisenhower* (34A) is a highly unusual occupant of Holbeck shed, after heading the 'Harrogate Sunday Pullman' from London.

13   10.43am Hull – Liverpool 'Trans-Pennine' set fails at Farnley Jct. (Leeds), where passengers make a lineside transfer into a 3-car Met-Cam DMU.

14   60525 *A. H. Peppercorn* (61B) is a rarity at King's Cross with a mid-day arrival from Sunderland. Aberdeen engines scarcely ever get this far south.

15   70011 *Hotspur* (31B) brings the surprising sight of a March engine into Euston – of all places – working in on a parcels train.

15-17 Quadruple freight collision near Huntingdon blocks all East Coast tracks.
Diversions bring 60088 *Book Law* through Lincoln on the down 'Yorkshire Pullman' (16th) and down 'Harrogate Sunday Pullman' (17th), Pullmans being uncommon here. March/St Ives/Cambridge line also sees D9001 *St. Paddy* and 60067 *Ladas*, both making class debuts over this stretch (17th). D6520/79 head through March on the SR – ScR cement train.

16   Due to the above disruption, first northbound train to reach Newcastle is the 4am King's Cross to York, extended to Newcastle, arr. 2.40pm. Passengers for Edinburgh are shepherded into two coaches added to the 3.15pm parcels train.

17   45651 *Shovell* (89A) works into Paddington on a Christmas mail special.

17   61938 (41A) is surprise power for the 8pm Manchester (Victoria) to Normanton, the class being unusual on this route

19   70016 *Ariel* (12C Carlisle Canal) works the 4.5am Niddrie – Heaton freight. Most surprisingly this is the first recorded sighting of a 'Britannia' on the East Coast main line between Edinburgh and Newcastle!

19   8P 71000 *Duke of Gloucester* works the up 'Cambrian Coast Express' between Shrewsbury and Wolverhampton, followed by the 4.45pm Stourbridge – Kidderminster and the 7.50pm Worcester – Burton parcels!

19   30862 *Lord Collingwood* passes through Westbury with oil tanks for Fawley.

20   D1000 *Western Enterprise* emerges brand new from Swindon Works in an innovative livery called 'desert sand'.

21   60857 (36A) appears at Skipton on a special Leeds – Barrow freight.

22   The sole blue-liveried D5578 leaves York on the 2.30pm to Colchester.

23   61053 (50A) reaches Heysham with freight from Stourton (Leeds).

25   44798 (67A) is an unexpected visitor to Hawick shed.

26   Driver of a relief St Pancras – Manchester express is knocked out when his diesel hits icicles hanging from the roof of Dove Holes Tunnel (Peak District).

27   D0280 *Falcon* heads the down 'Inter-City', introducing diesel locomotive traction to a Paddington – Birmingham express for the first time.

27   2-8-0 2841 (81D) is sent to Stratford for repair after failing on an oil tank train from Thames Haven to Immingham. GWR locos rarely reach 30A depot.

28   43947 (14A) exits St Pancras with a Swedish Lloyd boat train for Tilbury.

28   D9013 arrives in Queen Street on the down 'North Briton'.

29   D96 travels through the Severn Tunnel on the 6.44am Derby – Bristol, routed this way due to a derailment at Yate. D29 runs round its train at Severn Tunnel Jct.

30   60872 *King's Own Yorkshire Light Infantry* heads a namesake troop train all the way from Pontefract to Southampton Docks, an extremely rare working.

31   Up 'Atlantic Coast Express' terminates at Clapham Jct. due to heavy snow.

31   42757 (12A) appears on 61B; 'Crabs' are rare in Aberdeen.

U/D   SR locos in Yorkshire: 30931 *King's Wimbledon*, H 0-4-4Ts 31177, 31261, C 0-6-0 31579 and C2X 0-6-0 32534 all end up in a scrap yard near Swinton.

JANUARY 1962

1ST   Up 'Night Ferry' (N 2-6-0 31412 + 34100 *Appledore*) is cheered through Canterbury (East) by passengers waiting for local trains 'lost' in the snow.

1   Up 'Caledonian' seen at Preston behind D132, first 'Peak' on this service?

2   Haywards Heath – Brighton is formed of a 10-coach steam set with 75074 in place of an EMU. Heavy snow dislocates Central Division trains.

2   12.15pm Perth – Euston (due Watford 9.38pm, seen at 1.3am) passes behind an EE Type 4 + Stanier 2-6-0 42960, an uncommon combination.

2   46141 *The North Staffordshire Regiment* reaches Scarborough with ECS.

2   92205 (71A) works between Exmouth Jct. and Salisbury on the 11.50am Meldon Quarry ballast train, a rare class on the West of England main line.

3   700 class 0-6-0 30325 works the 2.45pm Eastbourne – Tunbridge Wells, the first '700' seen on passenger duty on this route.

3   B16 4-6-0 61438 is unusual power for a northbound Waverley route freight.

4   44527 (17B) takes over the 12.20pm Swansea (Victoria) – Shrewsbury at Pontardulais. (But why is a Burton 0-6-0 here anyway?)

6   Enthusiasts' Special is run from Eastleigh to Swindon Works behind 30901 *Winchester*. Stock carries 'Ocean Liner Express' roofboards. First 'Schools' to reach Swindon.

6   D6706/12 (ER-allocated) work a football special into New Street for the FA Cup tie between Birmingham and Spurs, an infrequent type in this station.

8   72004 *Clan Macdonald* enters Southport on the 6.10pm from Manchester (Victoria).

9	5.29pm Leeds (Central) – King's Cross arrives behind D35 (82A Bath Road!).
9	45661 *Vernon* heads the 9am Liverpool – Newcastle throughout, most unusual.
9	45554 *Ontario* (5A) appears at Eastleigh on the Fawley oil tank train.
10	30906 *Sherborne* brings the Channel Islands Boat train into Waterloo.
10	4.5pm Liverpool – Euston leaves Lime Street with E3065 + 44758 hauling 15 coaches, the '5' providing steam heating.
10	Manchester portion of the 'Pines Express' arrives in Crewe with 2-6-4T 42372 bunker first in front of a failed electric.
11	45634 *Trinidad* (3B) is in charge of the up 'Cambrian Coast Express' between Shrewsbury and Wolverhampton. More LMR power on an ex-WR main line.
12	45685 *Barfleur* (82E Bristol Barrow Road) finds distant employment on the 4.30pm Glasgow (Central) – Manchester.
12	0-6-0PT 3742 (82F) works the Bournemouth (West) portion of the 1.30pm from Waterloo round from Central, and the 6.40pm in the reverse direction.
16	Birkenhead – Paddington express makes special stop at Chirk to pick up the Duchess of Kent and Princess Alexandra, in accordance with a provision of the 1848 agreement drawn up between the railway and Chirk Castle Estate.
16	45515 *Caernarvon* is surprise power to bring the ECS of the 12.30pm to King's Cross into Leeds (Central).
17	60526 *Sugar Palm* reaches Derby on the 3.30pm Newcastle – Birmingham.
17	Northbound 'Devonian' appears in New Street behind the unprecedented combination of 0-6-0PT 9493 + 92248 + D38, all of which give way to a 'Jubilee'. (The trio also had three bankers to ascend the Lickey!).
18	Cliffe – Uddingston cement train passes Newark with 92044 + D6513.
18	70045 *Lord Rowallan* (14D Neasden) heads the 4.20pm local from Chesterfield (Central) into Sheffield (Victoria). Unusual (mis-)use of a 7MT.
18	Sister engine 70005 *John Milton* reaches Skegness on an 18-coach ECS train.
19	Q1 0-6-0 33026 works a failed EMU set through Cheshunt towards London.
19	60054 *Prince of Wales* (34F) is very strange power for an ECS train arriving at Luddendenfoot (in the Calder Valley) from Edinburgh.
21	'Harrogate Sunday Pullman' diverts into Leeds (City), then Bradford (Forster Square), where Pullman cars are an extreme rarity.
22	Up 'Yorkshire Pullman' provides the extraordinary sight of D9009 *Alycidon* piloting 60109 *Hermit* (short of steam at Hitchin, D9009 attached).
22	B16 4-6-0 61418 (50A) works a special freight Neasden – Temple Mills, runs LE Stratford to King's Cross, then a down freight. A rare class in London.
23	Unidentified 2-8-0 hauls Metropolitan electrics 4,6,8,10,13 northbound through Kettering, for disposal.
26	46200 *The Princess Royal* graces Lostock Hall with its unexpected presence.
27	5020 *Trematon Castle* has 'heavy' repairs at…Caerphilly Works, unusually.
30	70009 *Alfred the Great* (31B) is an unprecedented arrival at Laisterdyke carriage sidings (Bradford) with ECS from Stratford!
U/D	Experimentally, EE Type 4s from Crewe work the 'Royal Highlander' through to Inverness.
U/D	'Robin Hood' leaves St Pancras behind 45739 *Ulster* piloted by a 'Peak'.
U/D	Gresley SK coach SC12972E only loses its varnished teak livery during overhaul at Cowlairs – long lasting livery!

FEBRUARY 1962

2ND Holbeck shed hosts 60057 *Ormonde* and 60024 *Kingfisher* (both 64B). The A3 leaves Leeds (City) on the 3.30am to Glasgow (9.25pm ex-St Pancras), and the A4 (which came in on the overnight sleeper from Edinburgh, the 10.5pm to St Pancras) departs Leeds on the 5.38pm Manchester – Newcastle.

3 70006 *Robert Burns* (32A) exits Hull (a rarity here) on a York-bound freight.

3 30863 *Lord Rodney* works the 11.20am Hither Green – Tonbridge freight, then goes to Ashford for scrapping. Not a regular type on this line nowadays.

4 70044 *Earl Haig* (55A) heads the 8.40am Bradford (Forster Square) to Morecambe, diverted via Ilkley to Skipton, due to PW work at Shipley.

5 E6001, the first 600/1600hp Bo-Bo electro-diesel, emerges from Eastleigh.

6 V3 2-6-2T 67641 reaches Wetheral (near Carlisle) + NER Iinspection Saloon.

7 73101 (67A) appears at St Andrews + Inspection Saloon, from Perth.

9 2-8-2T 7217 (86E Severn T. Jct.)) makes a surprise appearance at Weymouth.

10 Cliffe – Uddingston cement train passes Newark with 60106 *Flying Fox* as pilot to D6517 (73C Hither Green), a new combination, surely!

10 46112 *Sherwood Forester* is most unusual power for the down 'Waverley' between Carlisle and Edinburgh, returning with the 10.5pm Sleeping Car train to St Pancras, at least as far as Carlisle. 'Scots' are rarities on this route.

11 11.50am Newcastle – Manchester (Red Bank) parcels leaves York with 60809 *The Snapper* piloting D40, yet another interesting pairing.

12 70022 *Tornado* departs Buchanan Street on the 10.15am to Aberdeen.

12,13,16 6.25pm Hitchin – Huntingdon 2-coach local is headed by 60017 *Silver Fox*, on these three days!

13 B16 4-6-0 61463 heads the 5.30pm Sheffield (M) – Manchester (C), only the second ever visit of this class to the Hope Valley line.

13 46208 *Princess Helena Victoria* appears at Bescot depot to have its tender wheels turned. First sighting of a 'Princess Royal' here?

14 Stanier 2-6-0 42950 hauls three sets of Wirral EMU stock from Hooton to Horwich for repairs, via Ellesmere Port, Warrington.

14,15 'Dukedog' 4-4-0 9017 comes out of store at Oswestry and runs LE to Old Oak Common. Continues LE to Brighton next day to turn and go to Sheffield Park on the Bluebell Railway. Unique sight on the Central Division of the SR.

15 45685 *Barfleur* (82E), remarkably, reaches Basingstoke on a freight from the Southampton area bound for Feltham!

16 D9006 runs out of fuel beyond Berwick on the 11.35pm to Edinburgh from King's Cross. 60089 *Felstead* is attached to take the train on, but itself needs assistance from St Margarets into Waverley by Ivatt 2-6-0 46462, the train arriving treble-headed!

17 60097 *Humorist* (64B) pays a unique visit to Darnall shed (41A).

18 61252 (32A) runs into Birkenhead LE from Ellesmere Port, having worked a special freight from Guide Bridge, all strange places for a Norwich engine!

19 SR – ScR cement train is worked from Heaton to Berwick by 60529 *Pearl Diver* + 60900, the train being split at Berwick.

22 60027 *Merlin* (64B) – on loan to St Rollox – makes test runs each way between Buchanan Street and Aberdeen on a 3 hour schedule, with net times of 164min/155min northbound/southbound.

24   45504 *Royal Signals* (82B) leads the 3-coach local to Wolverhampton out of Snow Hill at 6pm, an unexpected type on this service.

24   70016 *Ariel* heads the 1.30pm Niddrie – Thornton. First 7MT in these parts?

26   10.5pm Edinburgh – St Pancras sleeper leaves Hawick with 78046 most unusually piloting 60093 *Coronach*, rather than banking at the rear. On the same day 70018 *Flying Dutchman* heads the down 'Waverley' between Carlisle and Edinburgh.

U/D   D7007 (82A) reaches York. Crew training run?

U/D   Park Royal railbus appears on the Highland main line working the 7.25am Aviemore – Inverness and 5.10pm return working.

U/D   During seven days, ten V2s work through to New Street, either on the 12.43pm or 3.30pm Newcastle – Birmingham trains, workings taken over very soon after by 'Peaks'.

U/D   D0280 *Falcon* is tested over the South Devon banks between Exeter and Plymouth. Also on the Lickey incline, being stabled overnight at Worcester on these occasions. The new WR dynamometer car records the results.

MARCH 1962

2ND   46163 *Civil Service Rifleman* (6J Holyhead) heads the 11am Liverpool to Newcastle throughout, yet another substitute for a Type 4 diesel.

2   35013 *Blue Funnel* is a surprise visitor to Chichester yard, reason unknown.

3   Up 'Thames-Clyde Express' is worked to Leeds by 60089 *Felstead* (64A); 60011 *Empire of India* (64B) also brings the up 'Waverley' over the S&C.

4   1pm Newcastle – King's Cross via West Hartlepool performs an involuntary circuit; King Edward Bridge/High Level Bridge/platform 10/King Edward Bridge before being correctly routed for Sunderland, not Gateshead West!

5   Up 'Thames-Clyde Express' departs St Enoch, probably uniquely, behind 46203 *Princess Margaret Rose* as far as Carlisle. As the S&C line is blocked by a derailment, both this train and the up 'Waverley' terminate at Penrith, where road transport is provided for onward travel. Added interest today!

6   5.48pm Euston – Watford local fails to stop at Harrow, Hatch End or Bushey and runs non-stop Willesden – Watford! A blackboard apology appears the following morning at the stations omitted.

7   After a violent storm in South Devon, the sea wall at Teignmouth is damaged and a 'Warship' diesel is reported 'drowned' in a tunnel!

7   46122 *Royal Ulster Rifleman* is noted passing Southampton (Central) on the 10.24am Fawley – Bromford Bridge oil tanks. Most unusual power.

10   D810 *Cockade* is a surprise sight at Gloucester in the 9.5am from Paddington.

10   Specials for the women's hockey international at Wembley bring 60121 *Silurian*, 60123 *H. A. Ivatt*, 60158 *Aberdonian*, 60071 *Tranquil*, 70040 *Clive of India* plus D5657 into Neasden from the NER – a most unusual congregation here.

11   92232 (88A) spotted on York MPD. First Canton engine seen here?

11   Schools excursion from High Wycombe brings a 6-car WR Cross-Country DMU through to Doncaster, another first appearance.

13   U 2-6-0 31631 strays onto Bath (Green Park) depot, again reason unknown.

13	3.30pm Manchester – Plymouth arrives at Pontypool Road minus the through coaches from Glasgow. These two appear much later behind 78060 (27D Wigan), which continues with them right through to Bristol, amazingly!
14	46248 *City of Leeds* (5A) puts in a rare appearance at Callander on the 7.52am to Buchanan Street. (Though 46244, 46247 (twice) did the same in July 1961).
14	J27 0-6-0 65849 heads a passenger train from Whitby to Middlesbrough when a DMU fails. Has a J27 ever been known to work a passenger train before?
15	46200 *The Princess Royal* heads the 'Comet' out of Manchester (Piccadilly), a rare event nowadays, as this is usually a diesel turn.
19	60078 *Night Hawk* (52A) is a welcome sight on the GC at Rugby on the 5.22pm Leicester – Banbury, returning north on the 7.30pm Swindon – York.
19	D367 derails on the down 'Northumbrian' blocking the King Edward Bridge at Newcastle. Down 'Queen of Scots' (close behind) is stopped at Low Fell, takes 0-6-0 65645 as pilot to D348 and proceeds to Newcastle via the Norwood loop. A J25 on a Pullman!
19	CR 0-6-0 57266 (67D) – in its 80th year – is turned out for the 5.10pm Ardrossan – Kilmarnock, usually a railbus.
19	Adams 4-4-2T 30582 is a long way from its usual haunt (Axminster – Lyme Regis) when seen working a special at Windsor & Eton (Riverside).
20	O2 0-4-4T 30199 (72A) reaches London in preparation for a railtour on 25th.
20	'Crab' 42790 reaches Millbrook with the empty oil tanks for Fawley.
21	L&Y 'Pug' 0-4-0STs 51222/24 (without wheels) pass through Huddersfield on flat wagons within a Mirfield – Crewe freight.
23	A Bolton – Goole freight is seen between Rochdale and Oldham headed by 46142 *The York & Lancaster Regiment* – a class previously unknown here.
24	The largely disused Rugby Testing Station contains WR gas turbine 18000 and 46201 *Princess Elizabeth* – this being the subject of a preservation appeal.
24-27	During commissioning of the new signal box at Perth, Inverness diesels work through to Glasgow e.g. D5116 + D5325 are used on the 9.30am Queen Street to King's Cross as far as Edinburgh.
26	70043 *Lord Kitchener* is surprisingly in charge of the down 'Mid-day Scot', a train on which 'Britannia' power is seldom, if ever, used.
27,28	Two 'Coronations' appear at Stoke; 46254 *City of Stoke-on-Trent* on the 2.10pm Piccadilly – Euston (27th), and 46228 *Duchess of Rutland* on the up 'Lancastrian'. These locos are usually severely restricted on this route.
28	D153 works through from Edinburgh to Inverness and returns on the 17-coach 'Royal Highlander' as a test for their use on the York – Inverness Car Sleeper.
30	60031 *Golden Plover* (65B) heads the up 'West Riding' into King's Cross, replacing D9015 *Tulyar* at Doncaster. First St Rollox loco seen in London?
31	60015 *Quicksilver* and 60021 *Wild Swan*, plus 60039 *Sandwich* all head FA Cup semi-final specials to Sheffield (Victoria) from King's Cross.
31	Immaculate 61017 *Bushbuck* works the up/down Bradford portions of the 'White Rose' to/from Wakefield (Westgate), with a large circular headboard reading 'Wool Wins' as part of a Yorkshire Woollen Industry campaign.
31	Grand National special from Hull/Cleethorpes is, at 17-coaches, probably the longest ever run; includes the usual Pullman and ex-'Devon Belle' observation car at the rear and

reaches Aintree Central behind 76087 + 44868.

U/D   Railway Exhibition at Manchester (Central) has 46256 *Sir William A. Stanier, F.R.S.*, Compound 1000, preserved 4-4-0 506 *Butler Henderson*, D63 and E3058 on display.

U/D   D9021 is used in high-speed tests from Longsight, on the Manchester – Crewe electrified line sandwiched (dead) between two electrics. (Rail-end stress tests).

APRIL 1962

1ST   Privately preserved GNR J52 0-6-0ST 1247 hauls a 6-coach excursion from London Bridge to Sheffield Park and back, having run LE from Marshmoor to Bricklayers Arms the day before.

1   2.42pm Eastleigh – Waterloo is diverted via Staines (Central) with 34011 *Tavistock* piloting 75077. 'Bournemouth Belle' also comes this way.

2   46104 *Scottish Borderer* (66A!) is a big surprise at Cardiff, on 2.50pm from Liverpool. Any 'Scot' is rare in Cardiff, but a Polmadie example…!

2   2-6-4T 42325 (in disguise and equipped with German-type smoke deflectors) is wrecked by saboteurs south of Elstree Tunnel, the train of (condemned) wagons also being destroyed. As part of the film *The Password is Courage* Radlett station becomes a Polish wartime station, much to the surprise of the passengers on the 11.25am from St Pancras, which stopped specially.

4   Directors of the North British Locomotive Co. Ltd announce its liquidation.

4   Football excursions from Hull bring 61893/99, 61906 into Bradford (Exchange), where K3's are almost unknown.

4   D8021 pilots 60047 *Donovan* on an up sleeper between Hitchin and King's Cross, an incongruous pairing.

6   J37 0-6-0 64626 has a pick-up freight at Ayr (Harbour), totally out of place.

7   D6733 is a new class to arrive at Leeds (City), with a parcels train from Hull.

9   D5349/59 are seen west of Glasgow double-heading the ScR Television train.

9-14   Exhibits in the north bay platform in Snow Hill are D1002 *Western Explorer*, a Cafeteria Car, Camping Coach W9887W – part of 'Western Railway Week'.

13   70040 *Clive of India* (40B) appears at Hitchin on…an up pick-up goods!

13   60534 *Irish Elegance* (64A) works the 'Queen of Scots' throughout from Leeds (Central) to Edinburgh, after reaching Leeds via the S&C days earlier.

14   Up 'Golden Arrow' is in the hands of D6536 + BR/Sulzer Type 2, unusually.

14   20002 on the 5.14pm Newhaven – Victoria is assisted from Three bridges by E5006, an unusual pairing of the two types of DC electric locos.

14   D163 named *Leicestershire and Derbyshire Yeomanry* in a ceremony at Derby.

14   46141 *The North Staffordshire Regiment* is the first 'Scot' to reach March.

18   46106 *Gordon Highlander* is the first 'Scot' to reach Harrogate, heading an overnight farmers' special from the West Country, to Barlby.

18   GWR brakevan branded 'Marazion, for use on perishable traffic only' arrives at.. Newcastle (!) on parcels traffic from York.

19   Restored T9 4-4-0 (30)120 in LSWR livery heads the 12.10pm Southampton (Central) – Bournemouth (Central) service train, and return working.

20   CR 4-4-0 54468 steams from Inverness to Polmadie (for moving EMU stock).

20   (Good Friday) 60802 leaves St Enoch with a 'Starlight Special' for St Pancras via

Edinburgh.

20 72001 *Clan Cameron* appears at Barrow; heads an oil train to Millom next day.

21 D320 (5A) noted heading a 14-coach train southbound out of Inverness.

21,22 60103 *Flying Scotsman* works the Grantham duty to Edinburgh, probably its first Scottish visit since pre-war days, returning next day on the 11.5am to King's Cross as far as Newcastle.

22 46143 *The South Staffordshire Regiment* (9E) is seen in Snow Hill with an excursion from Manchester (C) to Stratford-on-Avon. Uncommon class here.

23 61281 (40E) arrives in Weston-super-Mare; excursion from Nottingham.

23 Evening special from Cleethorpes reaches New Holland Pier behind 70039 *Sir Christopher Wren* (40B). Largest engine ever seen on the Pier?

23 'Royal Scots' 46109/12/18/50/61 all come into Blackpool on excursion traffic, as do K3s 61853/56 plus several diesels.

23 Two excursions are run to Grassington (closed 1930) behind 44041 and Ivatt 2-6-0 43030 from Bradford (via Ilkley) and Leeds (via Keighley).

23 2-6-4T 67754 takes the Bradford portion of the 11.50am Harrogate – King's Cross to Wakefield, first L1 on a passenger turn in this area.

24 46161 *King's Own* passes through Harrogate, working the 3.30pm Manchester to Newcastle relief throughout, first 'Scot' to do so on a scheduled express.

24 46121 *Highland Light Infantry* (66A!) astonishingly works through to Bristol with the 12.52pm from York. Polmadie engine in Temple Meads!

25 6.32pm from Leeds to Newcastle (ex-Liverpool) is powered by an EE Type 4 which fails in the platform; D237 takes over but comes to a standstill at Headingley. 60053 *Sansovino* is sent to assist and propels the entire train through to Harrogate!

25 35021 *New Zealand Line* passes through Goring (unusual here) on the 11.5am Wolverhampton – Bournemouth (West).

26 60891 (52B) heads over the S&C with an up milk train, a rare type here.

26 D9009 *Alycidon* returns to traffic, from Robert Stephenson & Hawthorn's Works at Darlington.

26,27 800 West Indian immigrants travel from Southampton Docks to London, not by boat train but, curiously, by road to Victoria Coach Station, with baggage following (also by road)!

27 72006 *Clan Mackenzie* is a surprise arrival at Leicester on freight, ex-Carlisle.

27 D5379 (14A) heads a Tilbury boat train out of St Pancras; first diesel usage?

28 6000 *King George V* reaches Ruabon on the 'Festiniog Railway Special', only the third time on record a 'King' has travelled to Ruabon.

28 D41 (82A) on the 10.30am Bristol – Newcastle via Stockton, bursts a fuel pipe at Ryhope. J39 0-6-0 64846 (tender first) is attached as pilot to Sunderland where V3 2-6-2T 67687 (bunker first) is added; the trio then go to Newcastle.

29 'Railjoint Test Train' passes through Goring, a 'Castle' sandwiched between D601 *Ark Royal* and D804 *Avenger*, another very strange trio.

U/D D65xx runs trials between Fawley and Didcot. First diesel over the DNS line.

U/D All 'Baby Deltics' reported taken out of service.

U/D Official statement to the Press (by BR) regarding the late arrival of the promised diesel units on the Oxted line explains that this due to mass resignations of Eastleigh Carriage Works staff following the Minister of Transport, Ernest Marples' announcement of the intended closure of the plant in 1963.

U/D   BTC spokesman, quoting 1960 figures;
UK   41% of heavy goods traffic by rail, 59% by road
Germany   55% of heavy goods traffic by rail, in ½ number of wagons!

MAY 1962

5TH   FA Cup Final specials bring 5072 *Hurricane* (84A) and 46130 *The West Yorkshire Regiment* (56F Low Moor, especially rare) to Wembley (Central).

4   34064 *Fighter Command* is fitted with a Giesl oblong ejector at Eastleigh Works, only the second BR loco to receive this device (92250 has the other).

10   New NBL Type 2s D6344/45 pass Crewe coupled LE on delivery to WR.

11,12   Three Farnley Jct. 'Jubilees' 45646/95, 45708 reach Marylebone on RL Cup Final specials; six others 45562/82/97, 45605/63/94 work to Wembley Hill.

12   46160 *Queen Victoria's Rifleman* takes the 4.10pm Paddington – Birkenhead forward from Leamington Spa when 6011 *King James I* fails there, becoming the first 'Scot' to reach Snow Hill!

13   30925 *Cheltenham* pilots 4-4-0 40464 on the RCTS railtour from Nottingham (Victoria) which reaches as far north as…Darlington! The return run to York is made in 39min 21s for the 44.1 miles, start to stop. Participants visit the shed and Works at Darlington, plus shed and Museum at York. Quite a tour.

13   D97 heads the down 'Thames-Clyde Express' which is diverted via Low Gill, Sedburgh to reach Tebay, and thence Carlisle. First 'diesel' diversion?

13   O2 0-4-4T 30199 (72A) found in the small shed at Redbridge wagon works.

16   O2 2-8-0 63984 (34F) is a most unexpected sight at Blisworth, light engine.

17   72005 *Clan Macgregor* reaches Sutton Coldfield on the Inverness car sleeper.

16-22   30925, working temporarily from Neasden, heads the 6.10pm Marylebone to Woodford Halse, runs LE to Banbury, then the milk train back to Marylebone. These turns take place on 17/18/21/22 May. Also runs M'bone – Nottingham.

19   D834 *Pathfinder* on the 8am Plymouth – Liverpool, is piloted into Pontypool Road by 48463, a surprising combination.

20   E6 0-6-2T 32408 appears at Basingstoke shed, looking like a stray.

20   45713 *Renown* + a few '5's seen in Waverley. (Princes Street closed on Sundays)

20   D45 runs through Sedburgh Station on the diverted down 'Thames-Clyde Express'. Locals turn out for the occasion! (See 13th also).

22   O4 2-8-0 63686 (9G) is a rarity at Rhyl, turning there after working a freight to Mostyn from Birkenhead.

26   61389 (34F Grantham!) reaches Blackpool on an excursion from Newark.

27   Glasgow 'Blue Trains' begin running south of the Clyde.

27   Two excursions from Sheffield bring D5805, D5825 to Rhyl.

29   0-6-0T 1501 (now maroon) noted passing over Stainmore Summit (by road) to reach the Durham Division of the NCB.

30   34070 *Manston* makes a rare Pacific appearance at Budleigh Salterton with a return excursion to Bristol.

30   Afternoon 'Talisman' has the following catalogue of power: at Waverley a 'Deltic' fails to start, so steam to Newcastle; 60006 *Sir Ralph Wedgwood* to York; 60121 *Silurian* to Doncaster and 60136 *Alcazar* to King's Cross!

31	D1000 *Western Enterprise* heads the Wolverhampton – Worcester at Dudley.
U/D	D813 *Diadem*, on loan to 5A (crew training) is seen on the Chester line.
U/D	D0260 *Lion* (BRCW experimental 2750hp Co-Co) conducts trials between Shrewsbury and Wolverhampton. DP2, the EE prototype 2700hp Co-Co starts work from Camden.
U/D	Ex-Works Pacifics 60530 *Sayajirao*, 60535 *Hornet's Beauty* and 60037 *Hyperion* (all 64A), are rare visitors to King's Cross during the month.
U/D	Four special trains carrying Bertram Mills Circus are run from Hull to Scarborough; then on to York. K3s and B16s provide the power.

JUNE 1962

1ST	60123 *H. A. Ivatt* (56C) reaches Leicester (C) on 5.53pm ex-Sheffield (V).
1	60918 appears on Old Oak Common after working an overnight pigeon special from Newcastle as far as North Acton Jct. First V2 at 81A?
1	46247 *City of Liverpool* is an unprecedented visitor to Grangemouth on a freight from Stirling, reaching here on the car sleeper from Sutton Coldfield.
2	45660 *Rooke* brings a pigeon special into Weymouth, returning north on a train of tomatoes from the Channel Islands. First 'Jubilee' at Weymouth?
2	(Week ending) D0260 *Lion* seen on load trials on the Lickey incline.
2,3	RCTS 'Aberdeen Flyer' railtour is A4-hauled throughout to Aberdeen; 60022 *Mallard* King's Cross – Edinburgh; 60004 *William Whitelaw* onwards. Return is 'Princess Royal' hauled all the way; 46201 *Princess Elizabeth* to Carlisle and 46200 *The Princess Royal* thence to Euston. Again, quite a tour!
4	Lancing Carriage Works shunter A1 0-6-0T DS680 is sent to Brighton for presentation to the Canadian Railway Historical Association, for shipping to Canada in due course.
5	6.55pm Fawley – Eastleigh freight is powered by D6505 + 82014, the first steam/diesel combination seen in this area.
5	D286 + D223 *Lancastria* double-head the 9.45am Newcastle – Liverpool through Huddersfield, first tandem pairing seen here.
5	7.54am Castle Cary – Weymouth is pulled by 7829 *Ramsbury Manor*, unusual.
6,7	The unique Ballater branch battery MU has trial run Aberdeen – Arbroath, and then runs non-stop Aberdeen – Dundee and return next day.
7	15-car DEMU works from Eastleigh to Lancing, comprising four Oxted units.
8	U1 2-6-0 31899 + 34019 *Bideford* work a 17-bogie pigeon special from Newcastle into Crowborough. 31899 + 34055 *Fighter Pilot* head the ECS.
9,10	45690 *Leander* (82E) brings a 'Starlight Special' into Marylebone, and 46138 *The London Irish Rifleman* (with 6J shedplate) arrives with another next day.
10	45580 *Burma* pilots 61161 out of Blackpool, on a return special to Ossett.
10	D5811/27 double-head an excursion from Chesterfield into Southport.
10	Excursion from Staines to Brighton is composed of 'Ocean Liner Express' stock headed, incongruously, by Q1 0-6-0 33006.
10	61013 *Topi* + 61980 form an unlikely pair to power a Whit Sunday relief from Leeds (Central) through to King's Cross.
10	61292/3 (62B) both work specials from Dundee through to Wemyss Bay.
11	60146 *Peregrine* unexpectedly arrives in Scarborough, apparently for storage, but leaves five days later.

12	35002 *Union Castle* pilots 30934 *St. Lawrence* out of Weymouth on the 3.50pm to Waterloo, an exceptional pairing.
13	46151 *The Royal Horse Guardsman* is equally unexpected at Lincoln (Central) on the 4.48pm from Sheffield (Victoria).
14	45683 *Hogue* pilots D169 into Newcastle on the 8.5am from New Street, and most unusually, 45635 *Tobago* + 45652 *Hawke* head the 3.16pm to Liverpool.
15	9.40am Swindon – York reaches Leicester (C) behind D7005, a 'Hymek' first.
17	60870 heads the 'Lincolnshire Poacher' charter special from Alford to the Lake District, working the train from Grimsby to Penrith via Leeds, Low Gill and Shap on the outward run, from Carnforth on the return. Rare workings!
17	46244 *King George VI* enters Waverley with Perth – King's Cross car sleeper.
18	D9000 is named *Royal Scots Grey* in a ceremony at Waverley. Colonel-in-Chief of the Regiment is presented with a nameplate from namesake loco 46101. D9000 then leaves on the inaugural run of the accelerated 'Flying Scotsman', on its centenary as the 10 o'clock 'Scotch Express' between the English and Scottish capitals. In contrast...
18	Glasgow – Aberdeen expresses revert to steam haulage on accelerated timings with A4 haulage (supplemented by A3s) on 3-hour schedules.
19	70021 *Morning Star* acts as Broad Street station passenger pilot!
19	T9 4-4-0 120 (restored to LSW livery) hauls a dead 4-CEP unit as the 11.50am Eastleigh – Stewarts Lane freight, to Clapham Jct.
20	E3071 is towed to Derby and put in the Research Dept sidings by 45285.
20	2-8-2T 7250 is unusual power for an up ECS working at Reading.
21	60525 *A. H. Peppercorn* (61B) is a rare sight in Princes Street with an excursion from Aberdeen.
22	45618 *New Hebrides* (17B Burton!) is observed on the Central Wales line working southbound oil tanks through Llandrindod Wells.
22	Pigeon special (from Glasgow to Chichester, 22 bogies) reaches Eastleigh behind a 'Hall' + 1017 *County of Hereford*. Both are removed here (as 1017 is banned on the SR!). 76014 + U 2-6-0 31794 take the train forward.
22	5043 *Earl of Mount Edgcumbe* also penetrates to Eastleigh from Salisbury on a Swansea to Portsmouth special, is removed and runs LE back to Salisbury.
23	Two 'Warships' reach Crewe; D850 *Swift* on the 8.27am Bristol – Liverpool and D867 *Zenith* on the 9am Plymouth – Liverpool.
23	46203 *Princess Margaret Rose* is a complete surprise at Waverley, arriving on the 6.25am from Perth, taking out the 2.10pm to Dundee. Class debut here!
23	A2/3 60522 *Straight Deal* arrives in Scarborough on the 4.41pm ex-Glasgow via Pilmoor and Malton (two reversals here). Runs LE tender first to York.
23,29	46255 *City of Hereford* finds itself at Windermere on an afternoon local service – first 'Coronation' on the branch for ten years. Six days later 46252 *City of Leicester* appears on the 11am relief from Euston!
24	D5698 (30A) gets as far as Oxford on a Colchester – Lavington troop train.
24	30850 *Lord Nelson* exits Paddington with an enthusiasts' special to Swindon, the first time this class has visited Paddington (or Swindon!).
25	RMS 'Queen Elizabeth' docks at Southampton and three boat trains run to Waterloo behind D6526/35/83. First use of this type from the docks?
28	The Wolverhampton – Portsmouth through train arrives at its destination behind

6823 *Oakley Grange*, which had worked it from Basingstoke.

29,30 46208 *Princess Helena Victoria* arrives in Liverpool (Exchange) on the 2pm from Glasgow, a class first in this terminus. The very next day 46201 *Princess Elizabeth* appears on the same working!

30 Reigate – Redhill EMU fails and is hauled to Redhill by a WR 2-6-0 – rare!

U/D 39 additional or special trains are run over the Whitsun period in the Huddersfield area – all steam hauled.

U/D LMS diesel 10000 seen on crew training between Oxford and Bletchley.

U/D EE Type 1s in pairs, work two excursions between Glasgow and Oban with the ScR TV train.

U/D 6.12pm King's Cross – Leeds is, uniquely, booked to be piloted between Doncaster and Wakefield by a Low Moor '5', which then heads the Halifax portion through to Bradford. (60136 *Alcazar* is so piloted on 16 July).

U/D Recent LMR weekly notice contains 4 whole pages devoted exclusively to the prohibition of 46170 *British Legion* from specific sections of the LMR!

JULY 1962

1ST 70049 *Solway Firth* (16D) is an unusual visitor to Swindon shed.

1 First named diesel appears at Scarborough – D221 *Ivernia* (9A).

2 46200 *The Princess Royal* is unlikely power nowadays to bring the 'Royal Scot' into Glasgow (Central).

2 72006 *Clan Mcakenzie* heads the Aberdeen – King's Cross fish at Dundee.

5 Beattie 2-4-0WT 30586 works the 5.24pm Padstow – Wadebridge, a class very rarely seen on a passenger turn.

7 75068 is a surprise loco for the 8.12am Bournemouth (West) – Waterloo.

7 46203 *Princess Margaret Rose* heads the down 'Bon Accord' and 72009 *Clan Stewart* the up 'Saint Mungo' between Glasgow and Aberdeen.

7 70034 *Thomas Hardy* + 70014 *Iron Duke* double-head the 9.46am to Yarmouth out of York, an infrequent pairing of 'Britannias'.

10 70004 *William Shakespeare* observed heading the 6.5pm Broad Street – Tring.

10 35027 *Port Line* is a surprise choice for the 3.5pm Weymouth – Cardiff tomato train, providing Westbury with the rare sight of a 'Merchant Navy'.

12 WD 2-10-0 90757 is a unique visitor to Ilkley, having worked LE from Manningham via Guiseley.

12 D1006 *Western Stalwart* heads the 'Birmingham Pullman' substitute stock as the Blue Pullman unit is unavailable.

13 45741 *Leinster* (12B) provides an unexpected, but welcome sight at Grimsby.

14 1.15pm Blackpool (Central) – Leeds/Bradford departs behind the uncommon 'same class' pairing of 45633 *Aden* + 45741, which didn't stay long at Grimsby!

14 Glasgow Fair holiday train (1M73 to Euston) passes through Carlisle station non-stop with 46227 *Duchess of Devonshire*; 46230 *Duchess of Buccleuch* on 1M30 to Liverpool (Exchange) relief works right to Exchange, both unusual.

14 30856 *Lord St. Vincent* reaches Willesden, returning a Colne Wakes Week special from Portsmouth & Southsea.

14 61205 (31B) materialises in Euston on the 8am from Colne, working up from Blisworth following a diesel failure, a rare sight nevertheless.

14   2.25pm Waverley – Perth is unusually headed by 46201 *Princess Elizabeth*.

14   D52 reaches Buchanan Street, working through on the 11.10am ex-Inverness.

14,15   46250 *City of Lichfield*, 46255 *City of Hereford* reach Aberdeen on successive days, a very infrequent happening.

15   CR 0-4-4T 55269 is a surprise sight at Aviemore, dead on the shed (60B).

16   70039 *Sir Christopher Wren* passes LE through Derby (Friargate) southbound.

16   9.10pm St Pancras – Edinburgh sleeper is double-headed (rarely so on this route) between Carlisle and Hawick by 61007 *Klipspringer* + 60940.

17   46105 *Cameron Highlander* (66A) is an unexpected occupant of Hillhouse shed (Huddersfield). Polmadie engines rarely venture here.

19   2-6-0s 6312 + 6319 double-head a Marlborough – Colchester troop train. Locos are not changes at Oxford and set off for Bletchley only when fitters have lifted the WR ATC equipment on both engines.

19   Strangest double-headed pairing yet recorded is that on the 5.38pm Snow Hill to Lapworth, when 2-6-2T 41xx is piloted by…a single unit railcar. Bizarre!

21   73095 (89A), in spotless green ex-Works livery arrives in Scarborough, exactly two years since working here previously in similar condition!

21   1.55pm Paddington – Pembroke Dock enters Newport behind the impressive trio of 2-8-0T 5243 + 2-6-2T 4145 (bunker-to-bunker) + D7031, the extra help coming on at Magor.

21   W 2-6-4T 31924 is unusual power for Waterloo – Clapham Jct. ECS work.

22   RCTS railtour to the Festiniog Railway from Leeds/Bradford includes haulage by 46200 *The Princess Royal* both ways between Chester and Llandudno Jct.
The DMU from here to Blaenau Festiniog breaks an axle beyond Betws-y-Coed with participants walking the track to redirected road coaches. Now late, the RCTS special on the FR is joined to a service train, forming a double-length train headed by 'Fairlie' *Earl of Merioneth*, with *Prince* in the middle!

23   Car sleeper leaves St Enoch with 45727 *Inflexible* + 60086 *Gainsborough*, another unusual combination.

23   D0280 *Falcon* heads the up 'Master Cutler', Sheffield (V) – King's Cross.

27   60071 *Tranquil* arrives at King's Cross with an additional train from Keighley, a most unusual starting point for a through train to King's Cross.

28   46226 *Duchess of Rutland* is a surprise arrival in Waverley on the 6.25am from Perth. Its departure is even more surprising however, working a troop train from Heaton over the Forth and Tay Bridges to Barry Links, beyond Dundee! Then heads the ECS back to Dundee tender first, then the 7.35pm freight to Perth, also tender first. Event of the month!

U/D   Type 2 D6112 (65A) appears in Colchester on its way to Paxman's Works.

U/D   11.10am (SO) Windermere – Leeds (City) runs via Hincaster Jct. to Arnside (reverse), then to Carnforth (reverse) before proceeding via Wennington to Leeds. Uniquely, it is *scheduled* to reverse twice in six miles!

U/D   70048 *The Territorial Army 1908-1958* reaches Morecambe, from Leeds.

U/D   E2001 (formerly 18100) moves to Rugby for instructional purposes. 18000 still resides in the former Testing Station; several years since both have been together in the same place.

| U/D | Broad Street is used for film making, with one departure indicator showing several trains leaving for destinations in Lancashire, to the astonishment of regular travellers! |
| U/D | 61033 *Dibatag* appears at Gloucester on the 10.10am Newcastle – Cardiff. |

AUGUST 1962

1ST	60528 *Tudor Minstrel* (62B) is an ex-Works arrival in Leeds (Central) on the 1.15pm ex-King's Cross. Dundee locos are rare here, whatever the reason.
1	Brighton – Portsmouth line is blocked at Barnham and the 11am to Cardiff is diverted into Littlehampton. 34101 *Hartland* runs round its train, proceeds tender first to Horsham where Ivatt 2-6-2T is attached at the rear. Train reverses, runs 'top-and-tailed' to Woking (reverse), thence to Salisbury.
3	7.20pm Waterloo – Bournemouth stock is largely in WR chocolate & cream!
4	Bank Holiday Saturday. 61864 (34E) is a notable visitor to Holbeck depot.
4	The strange pairing of 43969 + 61252 (31B) is observed at Melton Mowbray on the 8.4am Gorleston-on-Sea to Leicester.
4	Margate – Wolverhampton reaches Oxford behind Q1 0-6-0 33033 (70C).
4	75007 (81F) surprisingly appears at Sandy on an Oxford – Cambridge route troop train. Few WR-allocated locos appear on the East Coast main line.
4	D175 + D50 bring the 6.5am Birmingham – Newcastle into York, rare pairing.
5	East Coast excursion from Leeds (City) behind D348 runs via Garforth to Castleford, loading passengers at Kippax, Ledston – both closed since 1951.
6	2-8-0 4704 (81A) has the 4.30pm Birkenhead – Paddington from Shrewsbury to Wolverhampton, a very rare type on passenger work north of here. 6016 *King Edward V* heads the up 'Cambrian Coast Express' between the same places – first time since 1959 that this has happened.
6	D6743 pilots 70003 *John Bunyan* out of York on the 12.38pm southbound.
7	'Queen of Scots' is worked Leeds (Central) – Waverley throughout by 60086 *Gainsborough* (55A), only 6min late on a 'Deltic' schedule. Holbeck engines are uncommon arrivals in Waverley.
9	High-speed test runs are made between Manchester (Piccadilly) and Euston, three cars only (including the Civil Engineers' recording car). Haulage is by AC electric to Crewe, then D2 *Helvellyn* to Euston.
10	34023 *Blackmore Vale* (72A) reaches Cricklewood to take ECS to Southampton Docks.
10	45662 *Kempenfelt* is a considerable rarity at Frome, working a Weymouth to Wolverhampton train.
10	46244 *King George VI* is a big surprise at Grangemouth, on freight ex-Perth.
10	Annual Station Gardens Competition (Sheffield area) special comprises one Officer's saloon for the judges, headed by D8059.
10	45566 *Queensland* (56F) travels through to Marylebone from Huddersfield on a Holiday Week special. Low Moor engines are eye-openers at this terminus.
11	Marsden (NER) – Blackpool, fare 33s. Diggle (next station, LMR) – B'pool, fare 13s. 9d. Solution, buy a Marsden – Diggle ticket (1s. 2d.) and re-book!
11	8.45am Leeds (City) – Edinburgh via York departs behind 46109 *Royal Engineer* (55A), surprisingly. As far as York?

11	12.52pm Waverley – Dunbar is worked by 'Crab' 42832 (12A), making a rare appearance of this type on the East Coast main line, ex-Inverurie Works.
11	75078 (70D) reaches Wolverhampton on the 9.32am from Portsmouth (Harbour). Extraordinary to see a Basingstoke engine so far north.
11	34051 *Winston Churchill* works into Bristol from Salisbury, and departs piloting 4960 *Pyle Hall* on the 10.50am to Portsmouth, interesting pairing!
13	Shoeburyness shed and yard contains 22 withdrawn locos, amongst which is 0-6-2T 69461, the last N1 by several years, having been a stationary boiler in the carriage sidings for a long time, still carrying a 37A shedplate (Ardsley).
13	60954 passes through Loughborough on a relief to the down 'Thames-Clyde Express', most unusual power on the Midland main line.
14	D0280 *Falcon* makes its debut in Plymouth on a 16-coach test train.
15	34036 *Westward Ho* heads the 11.10am Plymouth – Brighton via the WR route to Exeter, a type now rarely seen on the South Devon banks.
17,18	60871 reaches St Pancras (a big surprise here) from Derby on the 3.25pm from Manchester, and returns next day with an extra at 2pm, to Sheffield.
18	60529 *Pearl Diver* is a shock observation at Beattock shed with damage to its left-hand cylinder, having failed at Lockerbie.
18	9.5am Liverpool (Lime Street) – Penychain (for Butlin's Camp) travels from Bangor to Afon Wen with 75050 (tender first) piloting 2-6-4T 42211. 11.25am Penychain – Castleton (Lancs) has 75032 + 78034 tender-to-tender on the same stretch, both interesting loco combinations.
18	Holbeck 60038 *Firdaussi* arrives in Newcastle with the 9.30am from Manchester and departs on the 1.10pm Craigendoran – Leicester CTAC train.
19	45009 (66B) brings a rare Motherwell shedplate to Blackpool on an excursion.
19	92153 + 92158 seen at Loughborough with a test train of 70 fully-fitted 21-ton mineral wagons, recording coach and van. Double-headed 2-10-0s are rare!
20	5.49pm Victoria – Oxted fails at Riddlesdown and the following 6.10pm service couples up, forming an 18-coach diesel train. This proceeds to Oxted where passengers on the crippled 5.49pm (including Dr Beeching!) transfer to the 6.10pm, now 2 hours late.
22	D6573 (solo on the Cliffe – Uddingston cement train) fails at Stevenage. 'Baby Deltic' D5903 assists to Hitchin, but fails there itself!
23	D5340 (60A) appears at Newcastle hauling dead D355, a failure on the York to Inverness car sleeper. Inverness engines are like hen's teeth in Newcastle.
23,25	6841 *Hazeley Grange* and 6941 *Fillongley Hall* (both 83D!) appear at Woodford Halse on the 3.20am freight from Old Oak Common, respectively.
25	Beattie 2-4-0WTs 30585/6 noted on Yeovil Town shed, having been finally supplanted at Wadebridge by 0-6-0PTs 1367/8/9.
25	3.35pm King's Cross – Leeds is hauled throughout, uniquely (?) by 61845 (40A).
25	D0280 *Falcon* is surprise power for a Sheffield – Southport excursion.
25	The interesting combination of 80047 + 60038 *Firdaussi* heads the car sleeper out of St Enoch.
26	0-6-0PT 7762 visits Springs Branch shed (8F) *en route* to a local scrap yard.
30	92128 takes a pigeon special through Poole, bound for Weymouth.
31	O4 2-8-0 63837 passes through Lancaster (Green Ayre) with empty ICI tanks from Immingham to Heysham – an unprecedented loco in these parts.
U/D	A DMU working for several years, the Rhyl – Llandudno 'Welsh Dragon'

temporarily reverts to a steam push/pull set, complete with loco headboard.

U/D   New diesel shunter for the Docks holds up traffic in Southampton by being delivered…by road!

U/D   During the month the 6.25am ex-Perth brings 'Jubilees' 45588, 45734/38/42; 7MT 70050 and 6MT 72002 into Waverley.

U/D   Pullman car *Joan* is attached to the down 'Thames-Clyde Express' for General Eisenhower's visit to Scotland. First Pullman car seen on a train on the Midland for many years.

U/D   34043 Combe Martin + 92245 head the 7.43am Bradford-Bournemouth (west) from Bath, the most powerful combination yet seen on the S&D.

SEPTEMBER 1962

1ST   Q1 0-6-0 33039 is unusual power for the 3.50pm Weymouth – Waterloo, at least as far as Bournemouth.

1   70008 *Black Prince* reaches Newcastle; first 7MT here for some time.

2   'Trans-Pennine' DMU strengthened to 8 cars, forms an excursion from Leeds/Bradford – Ravenglass for a trip on the 'Ratty'. Return is via Whitehaven, Keswick, Penrith, Carlisle and the S&C line. Lots of new ground for a TP unit.

2   Sunday 'Royal Highlander' leaves Inverness behind D5342 + D5346 + D5115 (16 cars, including 8 Sleeping Cars and Restaurant Car), travelling via Forres.

2-9   6002 *King William IV* is put on show at Snow Hill to mark the end of their use on Paddington – Wolverhampton expresses. (On the 4th, 6002 is requisitioned to work to Wolverhampton to cover for a failed diesel!). Services 'go diesel' on 10th, start of winter timetable.

4   46203 *Princess Margaret Rose* is at St Enoch on the Eastbourne car sleeper.

6   New Brush Type 4 2750hp Co-Co D1500 reaches Crewe Works for weighing, returning same day back to Loughborough.

7   2-6-4T 42639 + 6857 *Tudor Grange* form an eye-catching combination at the head of the 9.10am Crewe – Banbury freight.

7,8   K 2-6-0 32345 (75E Three bridges) is a surprise arrival at Andover on freight; even more unusual next day on the 2.47pm Salisbury – Waterloo semi-fast.

8   44847 (15E) arrives in Guildford with a Doncaster – North Camp special for the Farnborough Air Show.

8   D290 + D170 double-head the 3.16pm Newcastle – Liverpool, excessively.

8   Due to a collision at Offord on 7th which blocks the East Coast main line, the up 'Scarborough Flyer' is diverted from York to St Pancras via Normanton (where 60803 gives way to D85) and Chesterfield. Up 'Northumbrian' travels via Sheffield to St Pancras (73053 on arrival). Up 'Queen of Scots' terminates at Leeds and forms the down service. D6743 works into Marylebone with an extra service from Sheffield, and several 'Deltics' travel via Cambridge, Ely, and March on East Coast trains.

8   70034 *Thomas Hardy* (31B) enters Leeds (Central) on the 2.40pm ex-London.

8   On the last day of passenger working on the Chard branch, the 10.25am mixed train carries one person to Chard Central behind 0-6-0PT 8783, still lettered 'GWR' on its tanks. So endeth one unchanging scene.

9   61156 (30A) heads the last steam working from Harwich into Liverpool Street, a relief train carrying nine passengers! East Anglia thus becomes the first major area to become entirely dieselised. So endeth another.

9   D6740 (40B) brings a special ex-Goole into Blackpool, first EE Type 3 here.

10   Prototype Clayton Type 1 900hp Bo-Bo D8500 reaches Polmadie, for service.

12   77001 (51L), ex-Works, is employed on a Crewe – Healey Mills freight.

14   73000 (17A) arrives in Halifax on the 5.30pm from St Pancras.

15   34096 *Trevone* takes an excursion from Portsmouth to Coventry as far as Willesden, running via the Direct line and serving principle stations to Surbiton, a steam-powered semi-fast on a long-electrified line!

15   3-car DMU forms a special from Bristol to Frome, only the second DMU to visit the North Somerset branch, closed to passenger traffic over 3 years ago.

15   'Devonian' enters New Street behind 43958, complete with headboard, after D36 catches fire on the Lickey and is detached at Blackwell.

15   D6521 runs through from Southampton to Parkeston Quay with a 4-coach special conveying President Tubman of Liberia, *en route* to Sweden.

15   A 'Royal Scot' is turned out to work the 2-coach 5.6pm Bristol – Bath stopper.

15   45660 *Rooke* (89A) is an unprecedented arrival at Exeter (St Davids) on the 3.32pm Bristol – Plymouth parcels. 45660 turns, then heads north light engine.

17   70028 *Royal Star* (9A) appears in St Enoch on the car sleeper ex-Marylebone.

17   61204 (31B!) brings a horse-box special into Chester from North Wales.

22   LNW 0-8-0 48930 (21A) heads a railtour from Luton (Bute Street) to Banbury via Bletchley south curve, returning via the Bletchley flyover.

22   34050 *Royal Observer Corps* steams out of Paddington (!) with an enthusiasts' special to Weymouth. This is then taken from here (!) to Hamworthy Jct. and over the S&D to Bath by 2-8-0 53808. 4992 *Crosby Hall* takes the train to Cheltenham from Green Park, with 2-6-2T 5154 + 2-6-0 7335 to Notgrove before 7335 completes the return to Paddington solo.

23   72004 *Clan Macdonald* reaches Morecambe on an excursion from Glasgow.

23   W 2-6-4T 31924 passes LE through Crewkerne. Rarely seen this far west, it is heading to Exeter for banking duties, St Davids to Central. 31921 joins it later.

27   60160 *Auld Reekie* heads the 10.15am Edinburgh – Leeds over the S&C but fails at Hellifield. 2-6-4T 42051 takes the service into Leeds.

27,28 70000 *Britannia* and 70002 *Geoffrey Chaucer* (both 31B) reach Newcastle, being seen on a freight for Heaton, and on Gateshead depot, respectively.

29   D5377, propelling a brake tender, works through Ilkley on ammonia tanks from Teesside to Skipton. First sight of a brake tender on this line.

29   L&Y 0-6-0 52518 + 44408 work the 'South Yorkshireman' special to/from Sowerby Bridge to Doncaster, York, Darlington, York and Leeds.

29   D1008 *Western Harrier* on the 6.40pm Shrewsbury – Paddington fails near Stafford Road; 6000 *King George V* banks the train into Wolverhampton (LL) runs round and is placed inside D1008 to work through to Paddington!

30   'Britannias' 70017/22/26 (all 21D) all reach Blackpool on illuminations specials from Wolverhampton.

U/D D1500 arrives at Cricklewood for a BTC inspection in London.

U/D Sunderland shed hosts A4 60020 and A3s 60082/92/107 for boiler attention.

U/D (Sundays 16/9 to 4/11). Leeds – King's Cross services run via Low Moor. 'Harrogate Sunday Pullman' runs to Leeds (City), Bradford (Forster Square).

OCTOBER 1962

2ND   1023 *County of Oxford* turns up at Walsall!

2   60116 *Hal o' the Wynd* (52D) is a surprise choice for the 5.15pm 3 hour Aberdeen – Glasgow train.

4   44807 (6J Holyhead) arrives at Malton on a horse-box special.

4   D179 fails at Tuxford on the up 'Yorkshire Pullman'. 60032 *Gannet* then pilots D179 plus train through to King's Cross, quite a sight!

4   D9004 fails at Retford on the 9.40am ex-Newcastle. 61208 is attached in front and takes the express at least as far as Grantham.

4   61395 (9G) works a special van train between Carlisle and Oldham, over the S&C. 61093 (41D) heads the 3.40pm Bradford (Forster Square) – Carlisle. Two B1s over Ais Gill on the same day – unheard of!

5   D8502 is seen at Holbeck; D8501/3 at Shipley (10th), and D8500/04/05 changing crews at Holbeck (17th). All new locos bound for Polmadie.

5   60531 *Barham* (61B) noted on Heaton shed, whilst Aberdeen stablemate 60527 *Sun Chariot* comes into Newcastle on the up 'Queen of Scots' and departs on the King's Cross – Aberdeen fish empties (what a contrast!).

8   8.10am King's Cross – Hull leaves with D1500 + 61389 (to Grantham).

8   D336 (5A) reaches Plymouth (a first for this type) on the 12.5pm from Manchester. D156 also arrives on the 'Cornishman'. Both are sent specially to test Laira's new loco washing facilities, for LMR's guidance.

9   Cliffe – Uddingston cement train is worked by 92186 as far as York.

10   45555 *Quebec* (5B) is an extreme rarity over the Waverley route, working a Millerhill – Carlisle freight.

10,11   D9018 *Ballymoss* is involved in high-speed test runs (with dynamometer car) from King's Cross to Doncaster and back. D1500 repeats these runs next day. These are fuel consumption and train timing tests on a 385 ton load.

12   A 'borrowed' Derby lightweight DMU is a rare sight at Reading, from Oxford.

12   L&Y 0-6-0 52515 (56E) heads 40 empty coal wagons, and later 28 full ones, each way on the Calder Valley line, a sight not seen for many years.

12   70029 *Shooting Star* (5A) arrives at Oxford (Morris Cowley) from Crewe with a train of commercial vehicles from the BMC plant at Bathgate.

13   D1041 *Western Prince* pilots D7010 out of Paddington on the 'Pembroke Coast Express', an unusual combination.

13   'Top Shed' 60015 *Quicksilver* is an astonishing deputy for a pair of BRCW Type 2s on the 11.40am Millerhill – Carlisle freight over the Waverley line.

14   2pm King's Cross – Edinburgh has D9016 replaced at Newcastle by 60535 *Hornet's Beauty*, which runs hot and is replaced at Drem by 80006 which is double-headed from St Margarets into Waverley by D5340 (60A)!

15   Redbridge works shunter O2 0-4-4T 30199 gets rare passenger mileage, taking the 11.35am Southampton (Old Docks) boat train portion to Central.

16   King Olav of Norway lands at Leith for a State visit to Scotland. Travels from Leith to Princes Street in a 5-coach special, which includes two Pullmans and a NER Royal Saloon, headed by D368, which also takes him to/from Glasgow during the week.

17   30930 *Radley* heads the 8.47am Tunbridge Wells (West) – London Bridge.

First 'Schools' to travel the Forest Row line?

17   O4 2-8-0 63685 (41A) makes a surprise trip to Hitchin with a pick-up freight.

21   D5116 (60A) gets a run to Montrose with a football special from Perth.

22   9.30pm St Pancras – Glasgow sleeper fails at Shipley; D27 is removed and replaced by 90721, which takes the train on to Skipton.

23   4.55pm Newcastle – King's Cross arrives at Hitchin with D5059/94 hauling a defunct D279 plus train.

24   D9018 *Ballymoss* dies at Tollerton on the afternoon 'Talisman' and is propelled by a V2 for 20 miles to Northallerton, where it springs to life again!

24   77004 (50E Scarborough) visits Tutbury after overhaul at Crewe.

26   Royal train arrives at Newport behind D7023/24 and proceeds into Richard, Thomas and Baldwin's Spencer steel works at Llanwern for the official opening by the Queen. Two specials are run for guests, from Paddington to Magor, headed by 6000 *King George V* and 6018 *King Henry VI*, the latter with a large circular headboard and a train of 12 x 1st class diners and Kitchen Cars of both WR and ER stock. 'Kings' go to Ebbw Jct. shed for servicing.

26   D65xx heads the 10.30am Southampton (Old Docks) – Waterloo despite having no steam heating, but no suitable steam loco is available.

27   Three Newbury race specials are worked by 6000 *King George V*, 6005 *King George II* and 6011 *King James I*, a unique triple occurrence.

27   'Pines Express' (now running via Oxford) is seen at Southampton with 5933 *Haydon Hall* in charge.

28   34010 *Sidmouth* noted at Petersfield on the diverted 'Bournemouth Belle'.

29   Unattended 4-car EMU runs away from Bromley North for 1½ miles before crashing into a road bridge abutment north of Grove Park station.

U/D   80038/65/83 appear at Westbury on the 9am ex-Weymouth and 8.31pm return. 57xx 0-6-0PTs work Weymouth – Bournemouth (Central) local trains. Tank engines are drafted in as Weymouth turntable is out of action.

U/D   Annesley (16D) receives the novel allocation of 'Royal Scots' 46112/43/53/58.

U/D   D178 heads the 7.30am Edinburgh – Aberdeen, 7.15pm Aberdeen – King's Cross, first 'Peak' north of Edinburgh on East Coast main line.

U/D   Shrewsbury portion of the 'Inter-City' forms the 11.15am Shrewsbury to Chester local and 2.10pm return, complete with carriage roofboards!

U/D   60011 *Empire of India* (61B) receives attention at Inverurie Works, the first time an A4 has been north of Aberdeen.

U/D   (Sundays) East Coast diversions from Newcastle to Morpeth via Bedlington involve all diesels running round their trains at Morpeth.

NOVEMBER 1962

1ST   'Hampshire' DEMU 1116 forms the 10.54am Waterloo – Basingstoke, a first.

1   Due to Pacific failure, 30934 *St. Lawrence* takes over the 3.20pm Waterloo to Weymouth at Basingstoke, piloted by 80039 Brockenhurst to Bournemouth.

2   Football special from Dartford brings D5009 + D6570 to Yeovil Jct., with 76018 working it to Yeovil Town. These diesels are an unusual pairing.

3   34087 *145 Squadron* heads a Bournemouth – Coventry football special. Loco travels to

Nuneaton for servicing. Return is via Salisbury and Fordingbridge.

3 Two further soccer specials are of note; A2/3 60519 *Honeyway* (64A) works a Morecambe – Blyth train from Carlisle onwards, and 60128 *Bongrace* (36A) reaches South Shields with Doncaster fans.

3 61853 (56B) is a big surprise on Gloucester (Barnwood shed, 85E).

4 6011 *King James I* + 6018 *King Henry VI* are used for weight-bearing trials on the new bridge over the river Wye at Chepstow.

5 46128 *The Lovat Scouts* exits Waverley on the 10.3am to Perth, unusual power.

5 Helston Branch (8¾ miles from Jct. at Gwinear Road) closes, first closure of a branch line to passengers in Cornwall since 1929 (Par – Fowey).

5 J39 0-6-0 64801 + 90500 double-head the 3.30pm Skipton – Thornaby ammonia tanks. Some years since a J39 passed through Ilkley.

6 Restored D11 4-4-0 506 *Butler Henderson* is seen being towed through Sheffield (Victoria) by a Bo-Bo electric, *en route* Gorton – Clapham Museum.

9 43979 is strange power for a local freight from Gloucester to Swindon.

10 D5687 heads an excursion from Bury St Edmunds, into Stratford-on-Avon.

11 30926 *Repton* pilots restored T9 4-4-0 120 on a Waterloo – Southampton Docks enthusiasts' special, an interesting choice of motive power.

11 46170 *British Legion* is taken out of store at Llandudno Jct. and sent to Rugby to form the centrepiece of the Remembrance service. Loco is then withdrawn.

12 2-6-2T 41255 is a rare type to be seen working a Halifax – Huddersfield goods.

16 Allegation of 'Reckless Driving' is made against the driver of the 9.30am Portsmouth – Waterloo by passengers experiencing a 'violent ride' *en route*. SR is investigating this first-ever such complaint.

16 48356 (15B) works a Whitemoor – Norwich empty van train for the sugar beet traffic. First steam seen at Norwich since June.

19 45522 *Prestatyn* heads the (overpowered) 2-coach 8.5am Carlisle – Hellifield!

19 73101 (67A) unusually noted in the Calder Valley, with eastbound goods.

20 60892 (64A) enters Leeds (City) on the 10.15am Edinburgh – St Pancras.

21 M7 0-4-4T 30131 is set in motion by an irresponsible person at Eastleigh shed and derails at catch points, blocking the up Portsmouth – Eastleigh line, which is reduced to single-line working for 7 hours whilst 30131 is removed.

22 61409 (40A) reaches New Street on four coaches as a DMU replacement. Return (to Nottingham) has to be tender first due to short turn-round time.

24 Strangely, 73031 (82E) works the 7.50pm Hunslet – Carlisle goods.

25 D855 *Triumph* passes Ross-on-Wye on the diverted 8.45am Plymouth to Liverpool. First 'Warship' to be routed this way?

26 44848 + 44911 run to York from Nantwich on a 15-coach football special.

26 O4/8 2-8-0 63914 (36E) brings Power Station coal into Elland from Worksop.

26 9.50pm York – Swindon mail reaches Huddersfield with 70054 *Dornoch Firth* piloting a 'Jubilee', an unusual combination.

29 Astonishingly, 92239 (71A!) brings empty oil tanks into Stanlow and goes LE to Birkenhead shed, to local disbelief!

DECEMBER 1962

1ST   45535 *Sir Herbert Walker K.C.B.* arrives in Waverley (rare class here) on the 6.25am from Perth, returning with the 10.3am back to Perth.

2,16   H16 4-6-2T 30517 heads an RCTS/SLS suburban railtour through Raynes Park, a type rarely seen on passenger workings of any sort. Beattie 2-4-0WTs 30585/7 work the Waterloo – Hampton Court section, and Wimbledon to Waterloo on the return (both days). Remarkably, these engines had worked London suburban services some 60 years ago, hence their choice for the tours.

4-7   Severely cold weather causes all Gatehead's 'Deltics' to be put onto fitted freight duties, due to train heating boiler deficiencies. A 'Deltic' is even seen on the Cliffe – Uddingston cement train between York and Heaton!

5   0-6-0PT 1649 leaves Dingwall when 0-4-0 shunter D2444 arrives – last steam engine north of Inverness is now displaced.

5   Thick fog delays all overnight trains heavily. 9.45pm ex-Euston is 7¼ hours late into Glasgow; the 12.10am ex-Euston has still not arrived after 16½ hours.

5,6   61156 (31B) heads out of Preston on a 3-coach relief train from Rugby to Barrow. Then pilots 'Crab' 42778 on a Workington – Carnforth freight next day. Has a March loco been seen on this stretch of coast before?

7   'Palatine' reaches Manchester (Central) with 70002 *Geoffrey Chaucer* (31B), doubtful if a March engine has reached here before, either.

8   D5395 appears on the Chesham branch of the LTE in order to rescue a 2-6-4T which is out of water on the branch parcels train.

8   60160 *Auld Reekie* (64B) reaches Holbeck depot, having worked into Leeds over the S&C line. Haymarket engines are rare at any Leeds shed.

8,12   61251 *Oliver Bury* + 61361 double-head the Cliffe – Uddingston cement train as far as York (8th). 60835 *The Green Howard* works the empties south from York on the 12th. Further unusual workings on this train.

11   61044 (41A) arrives in Newmarket with horseboxes, first steam on the Hitchin – Cambridge line for several weeks.

12   D1005 *Western Venturer*, travelling at 75mph in a blizzard, kills six cows at Cropredy. Damage to brake system applies full emergency brakes, causing skidding that wears several 'flats' on carriage wheels. D1005 retires to Banbury shed, *hors de combat*. Train is 2 hours late into Birmingham.

18   A2/3 60522 *Straight Deal* (64A), ex-store at Scarborough, is used at Leeds (City) for pre-heating the Sleeping Car train to St Pancras.

19,20   D6758 (51L) makes a class debut in Scotland by working into Waverley from Newcastle, and returning on the 2.25pm on both days.

21   D41 works through to Paignton on the (extended) 11.53am York – Bristol.

22   70051 *Firth of Forth* reaches Bristol on an excursion from Richmond (N.Yks).

22   34016 *Bodmin* + 34104 *Bere Alston* provide an extremely rare sight at Waterloo by double-heading the 4.5pm from Salisbury into the terminus.

24   The Type 4 hauling the 4.42pm Newcastle – Liverpool expires at Darlington. 60045 *Lemberg* replaces it, working through to Lime Street, an unprecedented occurrence! Leaves Liverpool on Boxing Day as pilot on the 10.35pm York mail as far as Leeds. Subsequently heads the 10.25am to St Enoch on the 27th.

24	44891 heads a 3-coach set of dedicated (!) Maryport & Carlisle stock between Manchester and Leeds, as replacement for the 7.42am DMU service.
25,26	60146 *Peregrine* is surprise Christmas Day power for the 3.30pm Aberdeen to Glasgow, as is A2/3 60512 *Steady Aim* on the 5.15pm to Glasgow next day.
28	46133 *The Green Howards* visits Ayr; used as station pilot for part of the day.
30	D70xx travels the Chippenham – Calne branch, fitted with a snowplough.
30	C 0-6-0s 31271/80, tender-to-tender with a snowplough on each loco, run between Ashford and London, clearing the SE Division main line.
31	2.5pm King's Cross – York/Hull, booked for D352 is replaced in the platform by D275, which is replaced by 60026 *Miles Beevor* and leaves 43min late!
U/D	V2s 60833/859/929/944 all reach March from the NER with seed potato trains from Scotland.
U/D	7.25am Bedford – St Pancras DMU engine seizes up near Harpenden with much smoke. 650 passengers decant onto the track, walk back to Harpenden!
U/D	Paddington is newly repainted in terracotta and grey. To reduce discolouring from steam engine exhausts, two D63xx are enlisted for ECS workings, as is 0-6-0PT 3711, which is fitted for oil-burning.
U/D	(Christmas period, 20-27 Dec). 109 special long-distance 'extras' augment services from Paddington.

JANUARY 1963

1ST	D7004 complete with snowplough, works over the Witham – Wells branch and later heads the 3.17pm Frome – Yatton.
2-4	10.10am Paddington – Shrewsbury and 4.45pm return is an 8-car DMU rake including a London suburban set, an extreme improvisation measure!
4	34032 *Camelford* pilots W 2-6-4T 31917 on the 10.45pm Yeovil Jct. – Exeter (Central). These tanks hardly ever see use on passenger trains.
4-7	New Clacton EMU stock makes special run from Liverpool Street to Clacton for officials and civic dignatories; goes on exhibition at Colchester (St Botolphs) (5th), commences regular service on the 7th.
6,7	South Tyneside 650V DC electric service between Newcastle and South Shields runs for last time (6th), DMUs taking over next day. Electric stock is transferred to SR Central Division for further use after modifications.
7	Aston – Glasgow (Gushetfaulds) overnight 'Condor' freight service begins.
7-9	9.30pm Bradford (Forster Square) – St Pancras is hauled to Leeds by 72008 *Clan Macleod*, and by 72006 *Clan Mackenzie* the next two days. Unexpected!
8	61329 (36A) noted at Chepstow with the 10.45am York – Cardiff empty ore wagons, which it works to Severn Tunnel Jct. First Doncaster engine here?
10	Lickey banker 0-6-0PT 9453 pilots 61337 into New Street (2½ hours late) on the 7.35am Bristol – Bradford. Bankers 'never' get to New Street!
10	46149 *The Middlesex Regiment* (9A) is seen turning on the Shipley triangle, a manoeuvre very rarely necessary or witnessed.
11	44417 finds itself heading the 7.30am Bournemouth (West) – Eastleigh.
11	Up 'Inter-City' leaves Snow Hill behind D1049 *Western Monarch* with 45699 *Galatea* coupled inside, a double-header to savour!

| 12 | 70037 *Hereward the Wake* is most unusual power for the Hull portion of the 'Yorkshire Pullman' between Hull and Doncaster. |

12 70037 *Hereward the Wake* is most unusual power for the Hull portion of the 'Yorkshire Pullman' between Hull and Doncaster.

12 D6118 + 60535 *Hornet's Beauty* power the 12noon Dundee – Glasgow.

13 45190 + 'Castle' bring an express into Paddington, another new combination?

13 Derby station witnesses the passage of the coupled quintet of light engines, 90115/503/518/682 + 61138, an unusual sight.

14 9.18am New Street – Ely, usually a DMU turn, is found to be 70011 *Hotspur* (31B) plus coaching stock.

14 Plymouth Laira is overwhelmed by the number of steam engines, and WR types ('Castles/Halls/Granges') are sent to the SR Friary shed for servicing.

14 60103 *Flying Scotsman* performs its last 'official' BR duty by hauling the 1.15pm King's Cross – Leeds as far as Doncaster. New owner is Alan Pegler.

16 D9016 is named *The Black Watch* at Dundee (West) station, running LE from, and back to, Haymarket.

16,21 46128 *The Lovat Scouts* (5A) arrives in Morecambe on the 8.30am from Bradford (Forster Square), as does 61084 on the 21st, both unusual locos.

17 S15 4-6-0 30842 (72A) surprisingly brings the 'Pines Express' into Oxford.

17 6868 *Penrhos Grange* causes consternation at New Street by arriving with the 6.46am Gloucester – Sheffield!

18 Two 'Merchant Navy's' reach Oxford: 35027 *Port Line* with the northbound 'Pines' and 35029 *Ellerman Lines* on the 11.16am Bournemouth – York.

18 D8206 reaches Ely with the 5.16pm from Liverpool Street, despite having no train heating on one of the coldest evenings!

18-20 Delay of the month: inward Channel Islands service on Friday reaches Waterloo on Sunday evening!

19-24 10.5pm Waverley – St Pancras sleeper becomes stuck in a snowdrift at Dent. Passengers transfer to the rear coaches, which are hauled back to Carlisle for onward travel via Newcastle to King's Cross (19th). The S&C is now blocked, with diversions in force between Low Gill, Clapham resulting in down 'Waverley' (21st, 60082 *Neil Gow*), 10.25am Leeds – Glasgow (23rd, 60085 *Manna*) and up 'Thames-Clyde Express' (24th, 60802) all passing through Kirkby Lonsdale. A red 'Coronation' is also seen (23rd).

20 Rochdale – Oldham DMU becomes snowbound...for two days!

21 Up 'Master Cutler' is powered by 60119 *Patrick Stirling* throughout, a rare class on this (diesel priority) working.

21 D5561 + snowplough is seen on the Thetford – Watton/Swaffham branch, first of its class to be seen here.

21 12.30am Manchester sleeper leaves Marylebone behind D81, unusually.

22 60157 *Great Eastern* hauls the Ampleforth College special throughout from King's Cross to Malton, with 60968 working the train to Gilling and back to Malton, from where 60157 takes the ECS to York, tender first.

23 70052 *Firth of Tay* (5A) is an astonishing visitor to Plymouth (nearly 4 hours late) on the 12.5pm ex-Manchester, working through from Shrewsbury.

23 44411 is an exceptional choice for the 3.2pm Salisbury – Eastleigh freight.

23 60027 *Merlin* (ex-Works) brings the novel sight of a 65B engine to Leeds (Central), working the 1.15pm from King's Cross.

23-25 60945 (50A) reaches Bristol from Birmingham via the Lickey. Works east on the WR main line with the 10.15pm freight to Woodford Halse (24th), and to Didcot on the 25th. Notable wanderings!

24   7.46am Accrington – Bury DMU takes 117min (instead of 19). Icy rails and wheelslip cause a stall on the 1 in 38/40 near Baxenden; '5' comes as banker.

24   12.10am Euston – Glasgow sleeper, due Central 9.30am arrives 9¾ hours late behind 60532 *Blue Peter* (62B), which worked it from Carlisle.

24   61156 (31B) heads the 4.40pm Grimsby – Stoke Gifford to Leamington Spa, from where 0-6-0 2211 reaches Nuneaton (Trent Valley) on parcels.

24   61105, 61399 both make most unusual appearances in St Pancras.

26   45218 (27C Southport) is a surprising arrival in Edinburgh on the 11.38am Carlisle – Craiginches freight.

27   All trains are diverted onto the slow line at Ampthill whilst giant icicles are removed from the tunnel's air shafts.

27-29   Up arrivals into Leeds (City) include D345 as unusual power for the 'Thames-Clyde Express'; 60001 *Sir Ronald Matthews* unexpectedly on the 'Waverley' next day, and even 60147 *North Eastern* – again on the 'Waverley' – turns up the day after.

31   2-8-0T 4242 (88A Canton) arrives in Plymouth on freight, eventually leaving LE on 4 February. Unusual visitor from South Wales.

U/D   60036 *Colombo*, 60092 *Fairway* (both 56B Ardsley) are rarities in Waverley.

U/D   Traffic from Middleton Colliery (Leeds) is to be diverted over the Middleton Railway; first instance of BR putting freight over a privately owned preserved line.

U/D   7.55am Swansea – Newcastle has train heating problems, resulting in a 'Peak' having 78009 (85A!) coupled inside all the way from Gloucester to York, where 78009 remains on shed for two days recovering! Amazing.

U/D   61257 (51L Thornaby!) is 'borrowed' by Northampton to make at least two trips into Euston on diesel workings!

FEBRUARY 1963

2ND   Scotland v Wales rugby international brings 46251 *City of Nottingham*, 70053 *Moray Firth* into Princes Street on specials; both go to Haymarket and are joined by 46167 *The Hertfordshire Regiment*. St Margarets hosts 45721 *Impregnable*, 46157 *The Royal Artilleryman* and 70050 *Firth of Clyde*, these also having worked in on rugby specials.

2   46224 *Princess Alexandra* is an outstanding departure from St Enoch on the up 'Thames-Clyde Express', only the second 'Coronation' to haul this train.

3   Edinburgh – Pyle returning rugby excursion leaves Shrewsbury behind the contrasting combination of Ivatt 2-6-0 46516 (89D) + 48732 (87F Llanelly).

3   D9009 Alycidon is a (unique?) overnight occupant at Farnley shed (55C).

4   61002 *Impala* (50A) is yet another surprise B1 arrival into St Pancras, on the 6.20pm ex-Nottingham.

5   60861 hauls a Mirfield – Marsden freight, returning with another, rare for this type to reach so far west on this line.

5   45660 *Rooke* comes into Paddington on the 7.10am from Oxford. LMS locos are only occasional visitors to this GWR terminus.

5   Numerous weather-related cancellations cause 'Jinty' 0-6-0T 47335 to work an

improvised special between Watford and Euston.

5   5.10pm Glasgow – Stranraer DMU becomes stuck in a snowdrift at Barrhill. Some passengers are rescued by helicopter next day, rest travel back to Girvan by special train.

6   Newcastle enjoys the unprecedented sight of the down 'Flying Scotsman' and up 'Royal Scot' in adjacent platforms, as snow blocks the line at Shap. Up 'Royal Scot' passes York (D300) about ten minutes after D162 on the up 'Thames-Clyde Express', as the Ais Gill route is also blocked. Interesting!

6   Blizzards across Devon cause five trains and three engines to be buried in snowdrifts near Tavistock, on the SR line between Exeter and Plymouth.

7   61402 (40A) is the first loco of an LNER class to be seen at Shrewsbury for two years on the 6.30am parcels from Crewe, and 8.52am return.

7   Fowler dock tank 47165 (26C Bolton) raises eyebrows at Castleton working local freight from Bury. A rare 'main line' excursion for this 0-6-0.

7   46220 *Coronation* (12B) is another unprecedented sight, this time at Bristol (Temple Meads), working from Crewe via Pontypool Road and the Severn Tunnel with the through coaches from Glasgow that missed the connecting train. 46220 runs LE back to Pontypool Road shed, then Shrewsbury.

8   Q1 0-6-0 33012 (70B) heads the 11.50am freight east out of Exmouth Jct., probably the first time a Q1 has been so far west.

8   9am Liverpool – Newcastle sets off behind D179 + D183 – which fails at Leeds. D179 fails at York, 60154 *Bon Accord* completes the run!

9   60096 *Papyrus* (64B!) takes the 10.25am to St Enoch out of Leeds (City).

10   34094 *Mortehoe* exits Marylebone on an enthusiasts' special to Crewe, via High Wycombe, Wolverhampton, Market Drayton. Return is via the GC main line through Nottingham (Victoria). Lots of rare track for a SR Pacific!

11   2-8-0 3808 passes through Nottingham (V) on a Woodford Halse – Annesley goods, unprecedented to see a GWR freight loco in Nottingham.

11   45585 *Hyderabad* is an uncommon type to visit Lincoln shed.

12   34067 *Tangmere* works to Taunton from Exeter (Central) via Salisbury and Westbury on an officer's saloon.

12   60084 *Trigo* reaches New Street on the 8.20am from Newcastle.

12-14 D9012 *Crepello* + dynamometer car is seen working the 'West Riding' and 12.55pm up from Leeds. (Train heating boiler performance test).

13   61208 (36E) brings the 'Master Cutler' into King's Cross, the first time this train has been B1-hauled since week ending 20 January 1961.

15   16-car ECS train (3 x 4-CEP + 4-EPB) is an unusual sight, Ford to Selhurst.

15   5078 *Beaufort* (Neath, officially withdrawn) arrives in Weymouth (a rare visitor here) from Westbury and returns north on the 8.57am next day.

15   Steam again at Elgin. 61400 + 76104 pair up to haul a special Naval train from Lossiemouth, 14 coaches (including 5 Sleeping Cars) plus 11 container wagons.

16   11am Liverpool – Newcastle is hauled throughout by 45531 *Sir Frederick Harrison*, steam rarely does this nowadays.

16   Special demonstration run is put on between Liverpool Street and Clacton, conveying 520 invited guests and enthusiasts.10-coach train of new EMU stock reaches Clacton in 69½min, back in 70min 10s. Demo repeated on 23rd.

16	D8064/67 bring the down 'Thames-Clyde Express' into Leeds, from Sheffield, the first time this type have been recorded on this train, even as substitutes.
17	70024 *Vulcan* works throughout from Kensington Olympia to Stratford-on-Avon on a theatre scenery special.
18	70027 *Rising Star* reaches Southport, from Preston. First 7MT since 1958.
19	'Crab' 42819 (26B Agecroft!) reaches Glasgow on a local from Carlisle.
22	70022 *Tornado* comes into Marylebone on a parcels train from Crewe.
24	60022 *Mallard* heads an enthusiasts' special from Waterloo (first A4 since 1948) to Exeter (Central), back to Paddington (first A4 since 1957).
25	11.35am Sheffield (M) – Nottingham (M) 3-car DMU fails and the (over-powered!) replacement is a 3-coach train headed by D154 + 2-6-4T 42636.
26	Special freight train leaves Kemble at 8pm conveying a complete farm, bound for Dunragit (near Stranraer), arriving noon on 27th; 25 wagons, one coach. BR charges £1,000 to convey Sir Charles Cooper's herd of pedigree Hereford cattle (and everything else).
27	3-cyl. 2-6-4T 42501 bids farewell to Shoeburyness, last steam on the LTS.
28	6.52am from Sandy arrives in King's Cross with 90439 piloting an ailing D5653. Has a WD engine ever worked a train into this terminus before?
U/D	(since 6 Feb) Pairs of Brush Type 2s work through between Purfleet and Rowfant, requiring special authority to work the single line between Three Bridges and Rowfant whilst this tank wagon traffic lasts.
U/D	Special cross-London coal trains to Redhill or Three Bridges bring D53xx from 14A, D50xx (1A), D55xx (30A) and an 8F through from Willesden.
U/D	D1500 works a 17-coach test train over the South Devon banks, and a 19-coach train over the Lickey incline, including restarts on the most severe gradients. The WR dynamometer car officiates.
U/D	O4/8 2-8-0 63705 (41H Staveley GC) works a York – Taffs Well special coke train through to Washwood Heath, serviced at Saltley. 63705 later reaches Cardiff East Dock and hauls local freights before returning north. A remarkable visitor to South Wales.
U/D	South Tyneside electric parcels car E68000 seen at Mirfield whilst being hauled to Liverpool from Newcastle.
U/D	L&Y 'Pug' 0-4-0ST 51218 is found dead in Severn Tunnel Jct. shed, where it stays at least a week.
U/D	46141 *The North Staffordshire Regiment* reaches Southampton Docks to take out a banana special for the Midlands via Salisbury and Westbury.

MARCH 1963

1ST	ECS train passes Wimbledon with D6526/03 hauling the extraordinary consist of 2 wagons, D6502 (dead), 4-EPB, E5006 (dead), 4-SUB, brake van.
1	70050 *Firth of Clyde* (5A) appears at Neath on freight from Severn Tunnel Jct.
4	BRCW Type 3s take over the Fawley – Bromford Bridge oil tank trains.
6	Q 0-6-0 30536 arrives at Oxted on the 5.20pm from London Bridge.
8	Holbeck depot hosts 60098 *Spion Kop* (64A) – recently ex-store – and D6123 *en route* to Davey Paxman at Colchester for a new engine.
8	92000 (84E Tyseley) is a surprise at Huddersfield on a special freight from Crewe to

Seaham Harbour. Locos from WR sheds rarely pass this way.

8   70050 now seen at Neasden on an up sleeper for Marylebone. Varied work!

9   61308 (64A) is noted with surprise at Egremont, on down coke empties.

9   E5023 puts in a first appearance for the class at Eastbourne, on freight.

12   61337 (50A) reaches Bristol (St Phillips Marsh, 82B). A rare visitor.

16   Two interesting football specials arrive in Manchester; D5536 brings one from Norwich into Central, and 45736 *Phoenix* into Piccadilly, from Euston.

17   60022 *Mallard* heads a Southampton/Bristol/Swindon/Westbury/Southampton railtour organised by the LCGB. Lots of new mileage for an A4!

18   5-5-5! Five football excursions run through from Leicester to Leyton for the FA Cup tie behind five immaculate Stanier Black '5's.

22   6995 *Benthall Hall* (88L Cardiff East Dock) works a rugby special throughout from Cardiff to Southampton Old Docks for the France v Wales game in Paris. 6995 heads the train back two days later, being at Eastleigh in between.

23   Saltley (21A) hosts 2-8-0 2809 and 6844 *Penhydd Grange*, unusual locos here.

24   Leeds – Crewe Works enthusiasts' special is worked from Leeds to Tyseley by 72008 *Clan Macleod*, piloted to Wolverhampton by 7929 *Wyke Hall*, a unique combination.

25   60856 (50A) is serviced at Nuneaton shed after working a 'Cathedral' special from Newcastle to Coventry.

27   1.54pm Kettering – Leicester is a 2-car DMU headed by 92078!

28   21 Presflo cement wagons + brake are laboriously hauled up the bank from St Davids to Central (in Exeter) by 2-8-0 3812 piloted by 80038/64 and banked by Ivatt 2-6-2T 41320 + W 2-6-4T 31916. A wet day, slippery rails = 5 locos!

29   45568 *Western Australia* (55A!) reaches Feltham on a cross-London freight.

29   61097 arrives in King's Cross with a special from Grimsby conveying the Chinese Trade Delegation. 3-coach loco-hauled trains are rare sights here.

30   34042 *Dorchester*, 34054 *Lord Beaverbrook*, 34102 *Lapford* all work specials from Southampton through to…Nottingham (Victoria) for the 6th round FA Cup tie with Forest! (Only the third time SR Pacifics have appeared here).

30   70005 *John Milton* reaches Reading on a parcels train from Blisworth.

30   14 specials are run to Aintree (Central or Sefton Arms) for the Grand National, all steam hauled, from as far as London/Glasgow/Newcastle/Cleethorpes.

31   E4 0-6-2T 473 (privately owned, Bluebell Railway) works from Victoria to Sheffield Park on an excursion, piloted by 80084 to Haywards Heath.

U/D 2251 class 0-6-0s work local freights between Exmouth Jct. and Honiton.

U/D Several steam locos are seen running coupled to diesel brake tenders, on the Midland Division close to London.

U/D Parkhead shed (Glasgow) stores many of the new Clayton Type 1s awaiting modification. £1 million worth of immobilised power.

U/D Beeching Report *The Reshaping of British Railways* is published this month.

APRIL 1963

1ST 2-8-2T 7249 visits Weymouth on a coal train, a class rarely seen here.

2   5014 *Goodrich Castle* appears on Exmouth Jct. shed, now in WR territory.

2,4 D1004 *Western Crusader* heads the 'Birmingham Pullman' loco-hauled set of Pullmans;

7019 *Fowey Castle* powers this substitute rake two days later.

3   46125 *3rd Carabinier* brings the 'Pines Express' into Wolverhampton from Crewe.

3   45592 *Indore* pilots D1013 *Western Ranger* through Cosford on the 8.55am Birkenhead – Paddington, an interesting LMR/WR steam/diesel combination.

4   45580 *Burma* (24E) works through to Stratford-on-Avon with an excursion from Nelson. First Blackpool engine to reach here?

6   Ivatt 2-6-0 43133 (67B), ex-Horwich Works, heads the 3.20pm Blackpool (Central) – Manchester (Victoria), where Hurlford engines are rarely seen.

7   D9010 is noted at Garforth with a diverted Sunday King's Cross – Leeds train.

8   45269 (21A) heads the 10.5am Hereford – Paddington, and looks wrong here.

8   For the FA Cup replay at Tottenham, one of the specials from Southampton to Waterloo is formed of three 'Hampshire' DEMU sets.

9   Express from Sheffield arrives in St Pancras behind 61093 + 45435 instead of the usual 'Peak' diesel, an uncommon LNER/LMS pairing of 4-6-0s.

12 L&Y 0-6-0s 52275 and 52456 are strange sights at Hurlford, Dumfries respectively, but are only in transit to a Scottish scrap merchant.

13 D139 (17A) makes a class debut on SR territory by working a cross-London freight through to Feltham.

14 A Blue Pullman set is used for a society special from Bristol to Plymouth, out via Okehampton to Saltash, then Millbay, and back via the WR route.

14 D5381 (14A) is another class debutant, at Brighton, on a Bedford special.

15 70037 *Hereward the Wake* (40B) heads the 9.30am Liverpool (Exchange) to Glasgow, at least as far as Carlisle, where Immingham engines are noteworthy.

15 46 Easter Monday specials arrive in Blackpool, including D5542 (32A!).

15 D1008 *Western Harrier* breaks new ground by working a football special through to Peterborough (East) from Swindon, via Northampton (both ways).

15,16 72008 *Clan Macleod* and 72006 *Clan Mackenzie* both reach Morecambe with excursions from Leeds/Bradford, on successive days.

17,18 34031 *Torrington* heads specials on both days between St Pancras and Derby, organised by Ian Allan Ltd. 34031 is still at Cricklewood depot on 20th.

18 D8530 runs a test train from Derby to Millers Dale, unseen here previously.

18 0-6-0PT 6400 tows 35012 *United States Lines* from Axminster (where it had failed the previous day) to Exmouth Jct. – contrasting loco sizes!

18 46247 *City of Liverpool* is excess power for the 8am Dundee – Buchanan St.

19 60105 *Victor Wild* heads the Cliffe – Uddingston cement train, surprisingly.

20 45358 (67B) brings the unique sight of a Hurlford engine to Toton shed.

20 Alan Pegler's 4472 *Flying Scotsman* heads the Festiniog Rly Society special out of Paddington, and works it to Ruabon. 2,000 people are estimated to be at Snow Hill to witness the passage, its first non-BR public excursion.

20 Manchester – Marylebone sleeper arrives with the unexpected pairing of 76041 piloting 46143 *The South Staffordshire Regiment*.

21 Swindon-built 'Inter-City' DMU makes trial run to Plymouth.

22 B16 4-6-0s 61454/61 both pass south through Derby with hopper wagons.

23 Two LNW 0-8-0s discovered on Haymarket! – though only in transit to local scrapyards.

24 Astonishingly, 70006 *Robert Burns* (31B) appears in Bristol (Temple Meads) on a relief from Birmingham. Has a March engine reached Bristol before?

24	4705 sets off towards Worcester on a parcels train, but as this class is barred beyond Oxford it is removed at Honeybourne.
26	D123 (17A) operates the 5.29pm Snow Hill – Knowle & Dorridge local as a crew training exercise.
27	12 SR Pacifics at Snow Hill! All work football specials from Southampton for the FA Cup semi-final at Villa Park; 9 travel via Oxford and Leamington Spa, 3 are routed via Oxford, Worcester and Stourbridge where 8Fs are taken as pilots, the pairings being 48478 + 34009, 48430 + 34046, 48417 + 34049. The 9 are 34028/40/42/45/50/52/88/94/98. Six Pacifics each go to Stafford Road, Tyseley for servicing. 7919 *Runter Hall* heads a 13th special.
27	61105 (41A) runs through from Manchester to Stratford-on-Avon, also via Snow Hill, which therefore sees GWR/SR/LMS/LNER engines in one day.
28	34007 *Wadebridge* (70A) reaches Temple Meads from Southampton with passengers from Bordeaux who are on a social exchange special.
30	60017 *Silver Fox* works through to Malton on the Ampleforth College special, returning the ECS tender first to York piloted by 77014, an engaging tender-to-tender spectacle!
U/D	(First week). 46228 *Duchess of Rutland*, 72006 *Clan Mackenzie*, 72007 *Clan Mackintosh* all work the 6.25am Perth – Waverley, all head the 10.3am back.
U/D	(Sundays). West Coast traffic is diverted via Morecambe (Promenade) and the electric line through Lancaster (Green Ayre).
U/D	60042 *Singapore* becomes the first A3 to be allocated to 61B (Ferryhill).
U/D	'Silver Princess' (Budd, 1947) – now no longer so named – is in service on the 'Shamrock' (Euston – Holyhead express).
U/D	Gorton Works is to close in May after 113 years of operation. 48520 is the last loco to be repaired, and will leave at the end of the month.

MAY 1963

1ST	D7001 makes the class debut in Cornwall on a freight out of Plymouth.
2	45562 *Alberta* (55A) appears on Slough shed after heading a special from Leeds to Windsor. First 'Jubilee' at Slough for many years.
3	70027 *Rising Star* heads the Aston – Gushetfaulds 'Condor' express freight, first time steam has been seen on this service.
3	35027 *Port Line* reaches Portsmouth & Southsea with an excursion originating in Northampton. 'Merchant Navies' are infrequent visitors to Portsmouth.
4	Preserved 46203 *Princess Margaret Rose* is towed from Crewe along the North Wales coast to its new home at Butlin's Holiday Camp near Pwllheli.
4	6-car 'Hastings' DEMU 1005 forms the 9.45am Eastbourne – Tonbridge.
4	Lord Garnock's restored K4 3442 *The Great Marquess* (ex-61994) hauls 'The Dalesman' railtour from, and back to, Bradford (Forster Square).
7	'Hastings' gauge D6588, unusually, powers the 3.8pm Tonbridge – Brighton.
7	72005 *Clan Macgregor* and 72008 *Clan Macleod* both work to Coventry with excursionists from Barrow, who visit the new cathedral.
9,10	Ivatt 2-6-2T 41312 (75A!), ex-Works, is seen at Newport, and working the 6.50pm freight from Severn Tunnel Jct. to Bristol next day.
10	44774 reaches Southampton Docks on an educational special from Luton.

11 Extras for the Rugby League Cup final arrive at St Pancras behind well-polished 'Jubilees' 45597 *Barbados*, 45634 *Trinidad*, 45698 *Mars*, 45739 *Ulster* despite almost total dieselisation of the Midland main line.

11 34094 *Mortehoe* arrives in Saltley to work an excursion from Birmingham to Doncaster next day. Yet another SR Pacific well out of bounds!

11 The (now largely disused) Rugby Test Plant houses stored locos 18000, E2001 plus 44833 under repair, with 42854 outside. At the station 76067 (71A!) is a notable stranger returning south from Horwich Works.

12 10.50am from Edinburgh reaches King's Cross with D5064 piloting D9006.

14 70054 *Dornoch Firth* comes into Bury (Knowsley St) on a football special from Stoke. 'Britannias' are uncommon at Bury.

17 Two diverse Holbeck engines arrive in Newcastle on specials; 60038 *Firdaussi* (Wetherby to Alnwick), and 45573 *Newfoundland* (from Skipton).

18 Privately-owned 4472 *Flying Scotsman* heads a special from Lincoln throughout to Southampton, assisted on the return by a 4F as pilot between Pye Bridge and Mansfield! Much new mileage here for an A3.

18 D800 *Sir Brian Robertson* heads an excursion from St Austell to Weymouth, via Castle Cary. First 'Warship' to reach this resort?

19 34044 *Woolacombe* works unchanged from Poole to Wolverhampton on an excursion. Another SR escapee!

20 D1008 *Western Harrier* travels as far west as Milford Haven with fish empties.

21 44715 runs down the East Coast main line with the 4.30am freight from New England to Ranskill (north of Retford). Unusual power on this route.

21,22 46115 *Scots Guardsman* is a surprising engine to work the 4.40pm Manchester (Central) – Northwich stopper on successive days.

21-23 D5711/14 are tried on the ICI limestone train from Peak Forest to Northwich.

23 D6565 fails at Streatham Common on the 4.48pm Victoria – Groombridge, and W 2-6-4T 31921 proceeds to haul everything to East Croydon. Rare to find a W class on any sort of passenger work.

23 60061 *Pretty Polly* works a special throughout from King's Cross to Rowntree's Halt (York), a private halt for chocolate factory employees.

23 44167 arrives at Exmouth Jct. shed from Templecombe, for retubing. First 4F here.

25 73071 heads a St Albans – Littlehampton excursion throughout. First steam 'foreigner' so far this year.

25 61367 (34F) visits Blackpool on a special from Newark consisting of four coaches and a van. Grantham engines are rarities at west coast resorts.

26 4074 *Caldicot Castle* is paired with oil-burning 0-6-0PT 3711 to run (in steam) from Slough to Swindon Works.

27 46224 *Princess Alexandra* is the first class visitor to Ayr since 23 October 1961 (46252) on a relief from St Enoch, and returns the ECS itself.

27 60038 *Firdaussi* hauls two diesel shunters from Hull to 56G (Bradford Hammerton Street), where an A3 is an exceptional sight.

28,29 D6538/49 (both 73C) bring excursions to Coventry (for the new Cathedral) from Folkestone, and Portsmouth a day later.

29 60952 visits Manchester with the 2am freight from Normanton. Taken off at Middleton Jct., the V2 proceeds to Newton Heath (26A) for servicing.

29	61394 (34A) arrives at Windsor & Eton on a Letchworth schools' special.
29	D6123 is seen running on the Clacton line after fitting with a new Paxman 'Ventura' engine of 1350hp.
31	70028 *Royal Star* (21D Aston) is a rarity on a King's Cross – Peterborough.
31	D8047 + D5640 power a Lourdes pilgrimage train through Hadley Wood.
U/D	Former Tyneside 2-car EMU seen beginning a new life at Gatwick Airport.
U/D	GSW 0-6-0T (LMS 16379), sold to the NCB in 1934 to work Hafod Colliery (Wrexham), is overhauled at Oswestry Works, presented to the BTC, runs under its own steam to St Rollox Works (Glasgow) for painting into its original livery, reaching here on 25th.
U/D	Extra run of the 'Brighton Belle' is to depart Victoria at 11pm, with meal service commencing about one hour before departure. Novel!
U/D	BR grants the Hunslet Engine Co. (Leeds) permission to use BR tracks to test a modified NCB 0-6-0ST, between Yarnton and Kingham. Hunslet's gas-producer firebox and exhaust arrangements are under test, and the WR dynamometer car officiates. 10 May 1963 is therefore the very last day that a steam engine is scientifically tested in this country.

JUNE 1963

1ST	Steam returns to the West Highland line; D34 4-4-0 256 *Glen Douglas* + J37 0-6-0 64632 (Glasgow – Fort William), J37s 64636 + 64592 on to Mallaig.
1	D1038 *Western Sovereign* reaches…York (!) on a special from the West Country, returning the same evening. The interloper arouses much interest!
2	'Trans-Pennine' unit is loaned to the Furness district for a special to North Wales.
2	D7067 works a Cardiff – Portsmouth (Harbour) excursion throughout, first 'Hymek' seen here.
3	46115 *Scots Guardsman* heads a special from Heckmondwike to Morecambe, piloted on the return by 'Crab' 42719, an unusual pairing.
3	80133 is provided for the 12.55pm Blaengwnfi – Porthcawl excursion, a 4MT 2-6-4T being unprecedented at Blaengwynfi.
3	92224 (88L Cardiff East Dock) appears at Coventry from Newport with a train of BICC electrification material, a rare through working for a 9F.
1,2,3	Whitsuntide specials;

Skegness receives	57 over the three days	
Blackpool	58 on Sunday + 52 on Monday	
Scarborough	24 on Sunday (17 diesel)	

4	60876 reaches Chesterfield on a schools' excursion from Jarrow.
4	46255 *City of Hereford* (9.43am to Glasgow) and 46238 *City of Carlisle* (9.30am from Glasgow) both seen in Liverpool (Exchange), a unique double.
6	60157 *Great Eastern* (36A) finds itself at Millhouses shed, Sheffield.
6	9.32pm Bradford (Exchange) – King's Cross leaves behind 2-6-4T 42650 piloted by D1515, yet another new combination?
7	46250 *City of Lichfield* appears on 84A (Stafford Road) having worked a pigeon special to Wolverhampton from the North West.
8	35030 *Elder Dempster Lines* is a rarity at Exeter (St Davids) taking over a 13-coach troop train from Plymouth (via Newton Abbot). Two W 2-6-4Ts are added as bankers,

but the train goes forward to Exeter (St Thomas) – bankers attached – to allow an up Waterloo service to precede it up to Central. Troop train then reverses back to St Davids and tries again.

8   45597 *Barbados* (55A) works a special for the Provident Clothing Co. Ltd throughout from Bradford (Forster Square) to…King's Cross (!) – only the second time a 'Jubilee' has ever made it to this terminus. Two Sleeping Cars are included in the 11-coach consist. After servicing, 45597 runs north LE to work a New England – Doncaster freight in the evening.

9   46245 *City of London* heads out of King's Cross with an enthusiasts' special to Doncaster for the Works Open Day. First 'Coronation' to do so since 46236 *City of Bradford* worked to Leeds in the 1948 Interchange Trials.

9   60134 *Foxhunter* is a stranger at Huddersfield, departing on the 7.7am special to Castle Douglas, of all places!

10   'Birmingham Pullman' unit fails at Bicester, only second trip after overhaul. Service is maintained by the spare 'Bournemouth Belle' loco-hauled set, a 'Midland Pullman' unit, and a 'South Wales Pullman' unit.

10   92231 is surprise power for the 5.5pm Southampton (Terminus) – Wimborne.

12   Swindon-built Cross-Country DMU works two trips on the Exmouth branch.

12   Preserved 6100 *Royal Scot* resides on Boston shed in transit to Skegness, and eventual display at Butlin's Holiday Camp at Ingoldmells.

13   D7084 observed at Ambergate, heading towards Buxton (on clearance tests?).

13   Scottish restored locos, HR 4-6-0 103 + CR 4-2-2 123 head a private special from Edinburgh to Pitlochry, out via the Forth Bridge, back via Stirling.

14   Leeds – Oban 13-coach special is worked through to Stirling (and back) by 60086 *Gainsborough*, with 45535 *Sir Herbert Walker, K.C.B.* piloting over Ais Gill, from Hellifield. An astonishing duo!

14   34079 *141 Squadron* works an excursion from Torrington to Totnes, with D63xx assistance from Newton Abbot. 34079 returns the train from Paignton.

15   Restored T9 120 bring a 3-coach special from Southampton (with students in Victorian dress) into Winchester (Chesil); King Alfred's College centenary.

15   1.15pm Bristol – Manchester relief departs for Pontypool Road with the rare pairing of 6821 *Leaton Grange* + 6829 *Burmington Grange* in charge.

16   4 x 2-car Derby lightweight DMUs form a Bletchley – Eastbourne excursion.

16   Last scheduled steam-hauled express from King's Cross is the 10.45pm to Leeds, with 60158 *Aberdonian* as power. 'Top Shed' (34A) now closes.

17,22   5026 *Criccieth Castle* leaves Crewe with the 'Pines Express' as far as Oxford, via Shrewsbury. 45644 *Howe* does the same five days hence.

18   D5617 (31B) enters Coventry on a 'Cathedral' special from Hunstanton.

19   D6847 pilots D40 into Plymouth on the 'Cornishman'. First EE Type 3 here.

19   D172 (52A) heads 24 miscellaneous coaches and vans forming the 12.22pm Scotswood – Holloway ECS train, the heaviest yet seen.

19   92239 enters Brighton on freight ex-Eastleigh, first 9F here in ordinary traffic.

20   Swindon Cross-Country DMU has trial run Exeter (C) – Salisbury and back.

21   'Condor' arrives at Hendon behind 45669 *Fisher* + 45228, reliable pairing.

22   60038 *Firdaussi* heads a Leeds – Filey special via York, Market Weighton; takes the ECS to Scarborough, turns on the Filey Holiday Camp triangle and returns the special via Beverley, Hull and Selby. First A3 through Beverley.

22	J37 0-6-0 64562 (64A) reaches Newcastle on freight ex-Edinburgh. Unusual.
22	10.25am Manchester (P) – Bournemouth (W) has 45529 *Stephenson* (1A) as far as Wolverhampton (Low Level). 45529 also heads the return working.
22	60086 and 'Patriot' 45535 both work to Ayr with specials from Glasgow.
22	60083 *Sir Hugo* noted at Beattock on the 10am Euston – Perth.
23	Q1 0-6-0 33016 stalls on a PW train near Billingshurst. The following Bognor Regis – Victoria EMU buffers-up and propels the train to Christ's Hospital.
24	60157 *Great Eastern* (36A) makes a surprise appearance at Buchanan Street at the head of the 5.30pm (3 hour train) to Aberdeen.
25	78030 (5A) noted at Harlech on an inspection train.
25	5050 *Earl of St. Germans* reaches Portsmouth on a schools' special from Bristol; impounded at Fratton shed as 'Castles' are banned here! 73002 works the return, but the WR have to wait 4 weeks to get their engine back.
29	60080 *Dick Turpin* heads the 9.20am Scarborough – Leeds, providing the first sight of a Gresley Pacific on a timetabled passenger train from here.
29	60002 *Sir Murrough Wilson* arrives in St Enoch on the Sleeping Car train from St Pancras; then works the 1.30pm to Ayr, only the second time an A4 has reached here; 60012 *Commonwealth of Australia* did so on 29 May 1951.
29	Caprotti 44749 brings an overnight arrival from Balloch into Marylebone.
29	D1000 *Western Enterprise* reaches Basingstoke on a Paisley – Weymouth troop train, is taken off and returns LE to the WR.
30	'Three Summits' railtour brings 60004 *William Whitelaw* and 60023 *Golden Eagle* alongside each other at Carlisle station, probably a first here.
U/D	D70xx works through to Exmouth on the 10.44pm (FO) from Manchester (P).
U/D	N 2-6-0 31412 + 75075 double-head an 18-vehicle pigeon special out of Newhaven, bound for Newcastle. An uncommon combination of locos.

JULY 1963

2ND	J36 0-6-0 65293 is a surprise arrival at Gourock (to be a stationary boiler?).
3	62035 seen passing through Wolverhampton (Low Level), with up freight.
6	45635 *Tobago* reaches Skegness on an excursion from Bury, a rare visitor here.
6	60007 *Sir Nigel Gresley* heads the LCGB '*Mallard* Commemorative Railtour' from King's Cross to York and back, visiting Doncaster Plant, York Museum and MPD, achieving 102mph at Little Bytham on the way back.
9	34004 *Yeovil* appears on Oxley depot, having worked an extra from the south.
10	Up 'Granite City' (Aberdeen – Glasgow 3hr train) is worked by 44923, which keeps time throughout! (Who needs Pacifics?)
11	70035 *Rudyard Kipling* observed at Spalding hauling a very mixed train consisting of D8401/two-car DMU/railbus E79962/guards van. Eyes widen!
12	45584 *North West Frontier* appears at Westbury, heading a train from the West Country to the West Midlands (i.e. northbound!).
12	70037 *Hereward the Wake* (40B) arrives in Coventry from Scunthorpe, with visitors to the new Cathedral.
12	D8518 heads an Isle of Man boat train from Ardrossan into Glasgow (Central).
13	EE Types 1 + 4 pair up to power the 'Mid-day Scot' out of Glasgow (Central), D8125

(with the headboard!) piloting D309, most unusual. Two more EE Type 1s double-head a train for Blackpool, a Glasgow Fair special.

14 46229 *Duchess of Hamilton* is a rare sight at Newton Heath shed (26A).

15 60871 provides an unprecedented vision at Euston, working in on the 8.17am from Nuneaton, and taking out the 12.10pm to Rugby. Amazing!

15 46223 *Princess Alice* reaches Ayr on a race special, a highly unusual arrival.

17 60034 *Lord Faringdon* graces the ScR – SR cement train, seen passing York.

18 5039 *Rhuddlan Castle* reaches Weymouth on a special from the London area.

18 Preserved 6100 *Royal Scot*, after spending a fortnight in Skegness yard, is moved by road the remaining 3 miles into Butlin's Camp. It is piped into position by a band of the Royal Scots Regiment.

19 D6522 (73C) is a unique arrival in King's Cross with the boat train from Tyne Commission Quay, having hauled it from Hitchin, at least. Extraordinary!

20 Bathgate – Morris Cowley car transporter train is worked over the Waverley route by 61345 + 46157 *The Royal Artilleryman*, an uncommon pairing.

20 80147 + 35011 *General Steam Navigation* head a Waterloo train out of Weymouth, seen at Upwey. A fascinating combination.

20 45526 *Morecambe and Heysham* enters Marylebone on an extra from Preston.

20 D5902/8 noted at Cambridge, in transit to Vulcan Foundry.

20 Down 'Queen of Scots' comes into Newcastle with D274 piloting D9016.

20 44422 (82G Templecombe!) seen LE at York, southbound. (How? Why?)

22 W 2-6-4T appears on Exmouth branch for the first time, on the 12.23pm Exmouth Jct. – Topsham freight and 2.10pm return working.

23 90393 heads a train between Derby (Friargate) and Nottingham (Victoria), rare and unsuitable choice for a passenger working.

24 Cliffe – Uddingston cement train is diverted north of York, and sports the eye-catching combination of diesel brake tender + D6787 + D350 at the head end.

25 D1524 (34G) heads the 10.5am Marylebone – York parcels forward from Nottingham (Victoria), a class debut on the GC main line.

27 62024 (well cleaned!) hauls 3 empty WR Royal Saloons between Durham and Newcastle for attachment to the front of the 1.10pm Edinburgh – King's Cross (HRH Prince Philip, HRH Princess Alexandra are visiting).

27 11.30am Peterborough – Edinburgh arrives in Newcastle behind the extraordinary combination of D5103 + D5151 + brake tender + D172 (failed)!

27 46160 *Queen Victoria's Rifleman* seen working ECS on the Edinburgh suburban line, a very unusual sight.

28 46223 *Princess Alice* is, surprisingly, serviced at St Margarets (64A).

28 34087 *145 Squadron* heads SR stock from Wolverhampton (LL) to Snow Hill.

29 70019 *Lightning* (21D) leaves Marylebone with a troop train for Gleneagles.

30,31 60023 *Golden Eagle* visits Redcar on a race special; 60036 *Colombo* follows suit next day. Gresley Pacifics are infrequent visitors here.

31 75022 (81E Didcot) travels to Cambridge on a troop train from the WR.

U/D 60008 *Dwight D. Eisenhower* is withdrawn for preservation in the USA.

U/D 11.55pm King's Cross – Newcastle is powered by TWO 'Deltics'!

U/D Builders' plate on 350hp shunter D3209 reads 'LMS Built 1956 Derby'!

U/D 5.16pm Glasgow (Central) – Princes Street produces a variety of motive power e.g.

46223 *Princess Alice* (66A) on 2nd, D8086 (66A) on 11th and D239 (52A) on 16th. Unpredictable!

U/D   (Saturday, small hours). Northbound passenger train (with banker) fails just short of Shap; following train buffers up, but fails itself. Banker, trapped between these two trains, throws out its fire. Third train called up from Scout Green, also buffers-up and entire formation surmounts Shap successfully. No recollection locally of anything similar happening previously!

U/D   Regarding Railtour on 6th; 25 years since *Mallard* hit 126mph on 3 July 1938, 60022 itself now withdrawn for preservation, end of diagrammed steam to/from from King's Cross, all being commemorated.

AUGUST 1963

2ND   45732 *Sanspareil* (9B) brings the 11am ex-Liverpool into Newcastle. Works a short trip with the Gateshead breakdown crane, then returns LE to York.

2   34057 *Biggin Hill* heads one of the very few boat trains to be steam hauled this year between Newhaven and Victoria – the 6.26pm relief.

3   5-coach 10.22am (SO) Malton – Whitby is headed by 44800; first is roof-boarded 'Cardiff-Birmingham-Newcastle' and the third 'Flying Scotsman'!

3   8.43am Wolverhampton – Portsmouth changes engines at Basingstoke, with 6839 *Hewell Grange* taking over from…6812 *Chesford Grange*, unusual.

3   73116 *Iseult* (70A) reaches Oxford (where Nine Elms locos are rarities) on the 10.34am Bournemouth – Bradford.

4   7.55am Tunbridge Wells West – Victoria consists of 4 x 3-car units, rare to see 12-car trains in normal service on this line.

6   45287 (21B Bescot) noted at Chippenham taking a relief to Weymouth, any LMS loco is a rare sight at Chippenham.

6   Newcastle – Red Bank ECS train passes through the Calder Valley behind 60932 piloting 45712 *Victory*, an interesting LNER/LMS pairing.

6   D7048 fails leaving Kingham on a Paddington – Worcester service. Train is drawn back the station by…a 3-car DMU which had arrived from Oxford!

8   Great Train Robbery takes place. 6.50pm (7th) Aberdeen/Glasgow – Euston mail train (D326) is stopped near Cheddington. £2,631,784 is stolen.

9   Scenes of almost unprecedented chaos result at Waterloo when a cable fire at Lambeth Road cuts all power at about 4pm.

10   6.25am New Street – St Enoch is headed by 60071 *Tranquil*, from Leeds.

10   80039 is used on the Yeovil Jct. – Town shuttle, a WR 2-car rail-motor unit!

10   D7018 is an innovation at Snow Hill on the 11.15am from Ilfracombe, whilst 73114 *Etarre* (70A) is a rare arrival on the 9am from Portsmouth.

12   46201 *Princess Elizabeth* leaves Kingmoor and travels LE over the S&C to Leeds, then via Derby to Saltley, arriving 15th. After partially dismantling its motion, 46201 is towed by 44045 down the Lickey to Dowty Bros, Ashchurch for preservation. Put on show to the public at the end of the month.

13,20   D6123 (65A), with new Paxman engine, is given a two-way trial on the Aston – Gushetfaulds 'Condor' fitted freight. 45644 *Howe* repeats this a week later.

16   First diesel at Ilfracombe is D6340 on the WR General Manager's Saloon. Returns to

Exeter piloting 34110 *66 Squadron* on the 12.15pm, a rare duet.

16 1016 *County of Hants* passes through Basingstoke with freight, ex-Reading.

17 60017 *Silver Fox* is observed at Ais Gill with a down fitted freight.

18 Relief train from Bournemouth arrives in Huddersfield behind 73031 (85C Gloucester Barnwood), an unlikely shed to be represented here!

19 6913 *Levens Hall*, 5936 *Oakley Hall* are both noted on Annesley shed (16B).

19 80113 + V2 power the 11.34am Carlisle – Millerhill freight to Hawick.

21 2-8-2T 7207 runs over part of the GC main line, bringing freight to Woodford.

22 60045 *Lemberg* reaches Mirfield with freight from Tyne Yard.

23 43963 (21A) is acting banker for the day on the Lickey, as 92079 is in need of attention. A one-day only spectacle!

23 'Castle' at Cambridge! Only for scrap however, as 5099 *Compton Castle* + 0-4-2T 1473 + 2-6-2Ts 4106/63 are in transit to King's at Norwich.

24 60942 brings a football special into Huddersfield, ex-Newcastle. Rare visitor.

24 D6811 leaves York on the 5.30pm Scarborough – Swindon which includes, strangely, a Pullman car and a Royal Mail van.

24 B16 4-6-0 61457 reaches Carlisle on the 8.15am Newcastle – Heads of Ayr, and 70011 *Hotspur* (31B) – well out of bounds – appears on a military special.

25 60112 *St. Simon* leaves Waterloo on a chartered special bound for Weymouth, back via Westbury and Salisbury. New territory for an A3.

25 D7048 reaches Brighton (via Kensington) on a special from High Wycombe, making a class debut in Brighton.

26 D7032 descends the Lickey on a southbound steel train.

27 Stanier 2-6-0 42977 (5B) heads a banana train from Barry Docks through Cardiff (General). This class is rarely seen in South Wales.

31 61394 (41F Mexborough) ascends the Lickey on a Poole – Sheffield.

31 72009 *Clan Stewart* is a rare visitor to Euston, bringing in the 12.20pm from Llandudno.

U/D 4.49pm Leeds – Doncaster stopper is rostered to be a 'Deltic'/Brush Type 4 combination, to facilitate engine movements. (That's 6050hp for a local!)

U/D 'Hymeks' work into Bournemouth on Saturdays with the 9.45pm overnight train from Leeds, departing on the 8.5am to Leeds.

U/D Restored A1 0-6-0T (formerly 32654) travels in the 4.30am Eastleigh Works to Feltham freight and on to Tilbury Docks. Engine is shipped to Canada on 23rd, heading for Montreal and the Railroad Museum in Delson, Quebec.

U/D Passenger between Worksop and Mansfield is issued with an LNER ticket of a style dating from the late 1920s/early 1930s!

U/D 45419 (6A) and 73073 (6G) both work through to Cambridge on horsebox specials. Interesting cross-country journeys.

U/D A1s have previously been almost unknown on the S&C, but with Neville Hill (55H) receiving an allocation, several workings have been observed e.g.

3rd – 60146 *Peregrine* on the 6.35am New Street – St Enoch via Leeds

3rd – 60134 *Foxhunter*, 6.29am New Street – Gourock CTAC express

10th – 60131 *Osprey*, on the same CTAC train

17th – 60134 *Foxhunter*, 4.10pm St Enoch – Leeds

24th – 60118 *Archibald Sturrock*, again on the CTAC train,

plus appearances on the London – Stirling car sleeper

SEPTEMBER 1963

1ST   60802 works the 9.50pm Perth – Euston as far south as Carnforth, where the coal supply is dangerously low. Heads north two days later on freight.

2   D8237 is a strange beast to arrive at Eastbourne, charged with towing D5596 back to Stratford – having failed on an Enfield excursion the day before.

3   3-car Met-Cam DMU is a surprise at Aberystwyth on a special from Derby.

3   60119 *Patrick Stirling* reaches 'steam-less' King's Cross, ex-Doncaster.

4   1.45pm Coventry – New Street local has D8121/27 (66A) as power!

4   D6860 is tested on the Lickey incline with 15-coach load, including the WR dynamometer car. 505 tons restarted from milepost 55, impressive.

5   D8500/01 (in tandem) undergo trials on iron ore trains from Tyne Dock to Consett, also on coal trains on the Blyth & Tyne line. Loaned to Ardsley,13th.

6   The 'Waverley' is unexpectedly hauled between Carlisle and Edinburgh by 60131 *Osprey* (55H). Returns to Leeds next day on 8.35am from St Enoch.

7   44661 (6G) appears at Rugby (Central) working the up, and later the down, Newcastle – Bournemouth service, in place of an EE Type 3.

7   Tiverton Jct. station waiting room still boasts furniture bearing the initials of the Bristol & Exeter Railway! (Amalgamated with the Great Western in 1876).

8   72008 *Clan Macleod* heads the Stourton – Bradford (Valley) pick-up freight, then runs LE to Skipton shed, unusual power for this type of work.

8   70039 *Sir Christopher Wren* is noted at Sowerby Bridge on a Scunthorpe to Blackpool excursion.

9   7.30am New Street – Euston has a pair of Type 4s, D330 + D375, unusually.

9   J37 0-6-0 64571 heads a relief passenger train from Falkirk to Buchanan Street.

10-15   Restored CR 4-2-2 123 arrives at Norwood Jct. LE from Willesden (10th). T9 4-4-0 120 (also restored) joins it on 12th, both work the 'Blue Belle' railtour on the 15th to/from Haywards Heath, being serviced at Brighton in between.

11   'Crab' 42812 and 45690 *Leander* are two strangers on Southall depot after working coal trains from Woodford Halse.

12,19,20   Excursions to Coventry Cathedral; 73155 (71A) from Portsmouth (12th), D6519 (73C) from Croydon (19th), D5667 (32B) from Ipswich (20th). Variety!

13   60006 *Sir Ralph Wedgwood* reaches Mirfield on freight from Tyne Yard.

15   45690 *Leander* is now a stranger at Exeter (St Davids) on a train from Bristol.

17   D1533 is unusual power on the York – Bournemouth, at Nottingham (Victoria).

17,19,20   60530 *Sayajirao* (66A) works the 7.22am Kilmarnock – Glasgow via Dalry on all three days, unusual motive power for a local train.

19   U 2-6-0 31801 surprisingly arrives at Waterloo on the 7.30am ex-Basingstoke.

19,20   D5623, D5591 next day, both head westbound troop trains through Reading from the ER. Both return later with the ECS.

20   (For two weeks). D6123 (with new engine) works test trains between Carlisle and Hurlford with the LMR No.3 dynamometer car + two Mobile Test Units.

23   61250 *A. Harold Bibby* (34F Grantham!) springs a surprise at Huddersfield by working the Wakefield – Lockwood goods.

23   D8501 (66A) – on loan to Ardsley (56B) – reaches Bradford (Valley) via the Idle branch to Shipley, a unique sight here.

25	O4/6 2-8-0 63913 is a rarity at Hull (Alexandra Dock), leaving tender first with a train of imported timber.
26,27	46238 *City of Carlisle* appears at Shipley from the north, turns on the triangle and heads off to Skipton, to work an RCTS/SLS railtour next day, to Carlisle. First 'Coronation' over the S&C since 46247 on 9 July 1961 on another RCTS train.
27	60017 *Silver Fox* works a single horsebox from Hitchin to Crews Hill!
28	51A hosts ScR 'Clans' 72000/1/2/3 prior to scrapping at the local Works.
28	60114 *W. P. Allen* hauls the Gainsborough Model Railway Society excursion to Blackpool throughout from Lincoln, via the Calder Valley. First A1 seen over much of the route, certainly at Blackpool!
28	Southbound 'Pines Express' arrives in Oxford behind 45660 *Rooke*.
28	46140 *The King's Royal Rifle Corps* heads an excursion over the Manchester to Altrincham electrified line, bound for Bournville.
28	34064 *Fighter Command* (fitted with a Giesl ejector) exits…Paddington (!) taking the Talyllyn Railway Preservation Society special to Ruabon.
28	D7022 works a 14-coach football special from Swindon to Northampton throughout (via Oxford, Bletchley), and the return. New ground for a 'Hymek'.
28	46245 *City of London* departs Snow Hill on a special to Crewe Works. First 'Coronation' seen at Snow Hill since Jan/Feb 1956.
U/D	46247 *City of Liverpool* (condemned) is hauled dead through Shipley heading for the Birmingham area.
U/D	D63xx, D70xx, D8xx classes are all trialled on the Callington branch.
U/D	BRCW 2750hp Co-Co D0260 *Lion* noted at Leeds (Central) on the up 'Yorkshire Pullman'.
U/D	0-6-0PTs 1646/49 (ex-Dornoch branch) are scrapped at Cowlairs.
U/D	7.55am Tunbridge Wells – London Bridge and 5.20pm return is a 7-coach set of a new formation composed of a de-motored 2-BIL EMU with five steel trailers from SUB units inserted. Set is air-braked and D6529 is dedicated to these workings, supplying both light and heat.

OCTOBER 1963

2ND	WD 2-10-0 90763 (12A) is a rare sight at Gateshead, albeit in transit to Darlington Works for cutting up.
4	60010 *Dominion of Canada*, 60026 *Miles Beevor* both seen in 'steam-less' King's Cross, on the 6.12pm to York, 10pm return special to Doncaster.
4	D34 arrives at Newton Abbot to test the new washing plant.
5	46251 *City of Nottingham* operates the 'Duchess Commemorative Rail Tour' from Crewe to Princes Street and back, having been brought out of store for the occasion, and returned to store afterwards.
5	61572 has a last fling on the 'Wandering 1500' rail tour from Broad Street to Stratford-on-Avon and return, organised by the M&GN Society. Engine was withdrawn in 1961, stored, and put into working order at Devons Road during the previous month, even displaying '1J' on the buffer beam! On the return run the B12 hits 70mph on the WCML. Eyes blinked at this foreign apparition.
6	45552 *Silver Jubilee* exits Paddington on an enthusiasts' special.

7	0-6-0PT 3759 heads the 5.50pm Exmouth – Tipton St Johns, unusual power.
9	Rarity of the month is the arrival of 60021 *Wild Swan* at Derby on the 12.15pm Newcastle – Bristol! 60021 returns on the 6.30am Derby – Sheffield local next day.
10	More steam at the Cross! 60139 *Sea Eagle* on the 1.47pm ex-Doncaster.
12	Woodford Halse sports ten WR locos, 6 to the south of the station, 4 on shed.
13	Restored T9 4-4-0 120 pilots U 2-6-0 31790 on an LCGB special from Waterloo through Reading, bound for Banbury and Woodford Halse.
14,15	3.30pm up 'Postal' out of Aberdeen has 72009 *Clan Stewart* as far as Carstairs and 46157 *The Royal Artilleryman* the following day (both 12A).
15	60146 *Peregrine* (55H) is another surprise at Derby on the 4.5pm Newcastle to Bristol. Works LE to Royston next day, then a coal train to Normanton (!).
15	60010 *Dominion of Canada* heads the 3.34am York – Hull freight, then the 6.25am Hull – Gascoigne Wood mineral empties. Menial work for an A4.
16	0-6-0 2214, fitted with snowplough, makes test runs from Exeter to Okehampton. First of this class seen on this route.
16	Five WR locos, 'Counties' 1007/8 + 6109 + 7324 + 5746 set off in convoy from Didcot to the scrapyard at...Norwich, not the obvious destination!
17	D166 + D170 power the 9am Liverpool – Newcastle, rare 'same-class' double.
18	72008 *Clan Macleod* brings visitors to Coventry cathedral, from Maryport.
19	45735 *Comet* is a rarity at St Pancras, working to/from Manchester on a Belle Vue special; a whisp of steam in a diesel atmosphere.
19	4472 *Flying Scotsman* works an Ian Allan 10-coach Pullman special between Paddington, Taunton via Devizes, and the return from Exeter (C) to Waterloo, the train going to Ilfracombe in between. 4472 is coaled at Exmouth Jct. with a wagon-load of Yorkshire coal brought down specially!
19	Swansea East Dock (87D) is host to L&Y 0-4-0ST 51218, MR 0-4-0T 41535 and LMS 0-4-0ST 47003, all for local work on the tightly-curved dock lines.
20	D7065 is a first-time arrival in Eastbourne with a special from Oxford carrying members of the Covent Gardens Opera Co. in 3 coaches and 7 vans.
21	Bo-Bo E3030 works a Press special as far south as Lichfield (Trent Valley).
22	46110 *Grenadier Guardsman* pulls away from Durham, working through on the 3.9pm Liverpool – Newcastle, another diesel substitute.
23	61155 arrives in Swindon on the overnight empty parcels train from York.
24	D1545 works as far as Rugby (Central) with the up, and later returns with the down, Newcastle – Bournemouth through train.
24	Whilst towing 'Jubilees' 45624/70/72/84 to Coventry shed for storage, sister engine 45563 *Australia* is called upon to push the failed 3.12pm Rugby to Coventry 6-car DMU into Coventry station. An intriguing ensemble!
25	70050 *Firth of Clyde* works an ECS train throughout from Tyseley to Laisterdyke (Bradford), where 'Britannias' are an extreme rarity.
25	Down 'Waverley' fails at Garsdale. 44386 is sent to the rescue, puts D229 *Saxonia* into a siding, hauls the express over Ais Gill at 45mph, reaches 80mph at Newbiggin and covers the 51¼ miles from Garsdale to Carlisle in 57min including the Appleby stop! Amazing.
26	Uniquely, 46110 *Grenadier Guardsman* works a Newcastle – Edinburgh freight over the East Coast main line! Astonishing.

27 Last regular run of the 6.16pm Haywards Heath – Seaford is, most unusually, formed of 6-PAN unit 3033. Bluebell line is now isolated.

28 Northbound 'Pines Express' leaves Wellington for Crewe behind a pair of 'Halls' a most unusual sight.

28 New D8550 (66A) travels from Derby to Colchester with 7 BR coaches flanked by two brake vans, all ex-Works. Placed at the Davey Paxman Works whilst a group from the Institution of Locomotive Engineers visits the Works, train is then exhibited at St Botolphs before returning to Derby on 1 November.

29 60017 *Silver Fox* passes though Newark on the Uddingston – Cliffe cement empties; then works the 6.40pm King's Cross – Leeds, 9 days after official withdrawal. Last ER A4 recorded at work.

31 45620 *North Borneo* is seen on the East Coast main line at Hitchin on a coal train for Barford Power Station. Very few 'Jubilees' ever reach here.

U/D D8536/01 + D5300 triple-head a northbound freight through Drem, an uncommon combination.

U/D 60024 *Kingfisher* (64C) is noted on various turns between Princes Street, Carstairs, Carlisle and Stirling, and is joined by 60012 *Commonwealth of Australia* transferred from England, Dalry Road being the least likely of Edinburgh's sheds to receive an allocation of A4s!

NOVEMBER 1963

2ND D1514 (failed) arrives at Hitchin with the 7.22am ex-Peterborough, piloted by...48221 (16A)! Both locos removed, train terminates here.

3 60528 *Tudor Minstrel* (62B) is an unusual sight in Queen Street.

3 S15 4-6-0 30512 retires to Brighton shed after working the LCGB 'Hayling Island Special' from Waterloo to Fratton.

5 Southbound 'Pines Express' arrives in Wolverhampton with 2-8-0 3855 piloting D1000 *Western Enterprise*, a very unexpected combination.

6 Three 'Warship'-hauled expresses are diverted via Okehampton between Exeter and Plymouth, due to a landslip at Teignmouth.

8 O1 2-8-0 63725 (31B) surprisingly reaches Newcastle on freight from York.

9 'Crab' 42789 (55F Manningham!) somehow arrives at Grangemouth with freight from the Motherwell area.

13 73007 (63A) is a rarity at Newcastle, on a seed potato train from Scotland.

16 46118 *Royal Welch Fusilier*, 46162 *Queen's Westminster Rifleman* bring 25 coaches-worth of fans through from Carlisle to York for the FA Cup tie.

17 46245 *City of London* heads the Crewe – Paddington via Snow Hill return leg of a Euston – Crewe enthusiasts' excursion.

17 WR route Exeter – Plymouth is flooded, and a Cardiff – Plymouth Inter-City DMU runs via Okehampton, making a debut over this SR line.

18 6819 *Highnam Grange* + 70018 *Flying Dutchman* – a pairing reminiscent of scenes on the South Devon banks a decade ago – bring the down 'Pines Express' into Wolverhampton (Low Level).

19 6.55am Penistone – Bradford DMU becomes a total failure after hitting two cows in a tunnel between Stocksmoor and Brockholes. Line closed for 2½ hours.

20	D6747 heads the 8.30am Cleethorpes – King's Cross but is replaced at Peterborough by 61314, itself in poor shape, which stops for assistance at Hitchin by…D6747 (!) running up LE. This then pilots 61314 through to King's Cross.
21	A private special to Eastbourne (five Pullmans) departs Cannon Street behind 20001.
24	Unofficial strike by motormen causes 7.25pm Brighton – Victoria and 9.47pm return to be formed of six diesel-hauled coaches, to passengers' surprise.
24	45527 *Southport* (12A) heads the 9.20am to Carstairs out of Waverley, where 'Patriots' are rarely seen.
26	Diesel hauling the 1.55pm Penzance – Plymouth stopper fails at Truro. D63xx on the Plymouth Inspection Saloon (with engineering personnel on board) is commandeered, a passenger coach added to this, which then substitutes for the 1.55pm and runs to Plymouth, where eyebrows are raised at this apparition!
27	45632 *Tonga* (26A) works through from Manchester to Newcastle on the 5pm from Liverpool. Newton Heath engines are uncommon in the North East.
28-30	72006 *Clan Mackenzie* (12A) brings an up freight into Banbury, heads another into London next day, and is seen on Old Oak Common on 30th. Rare!
28,29	Three 'Castles' 5065 + 7013/30 are towed via Bletchley flyover to King's scapyard in Norwich (28th); three 'Halls' 5910/60/66 repeat this next day.
29	D9021 is named *Argyll & Sutherland Highlander* by the Colonel of the Regiment in a ceremony at Stirling. First 'Deltic' seen here.
29	Unidentified 'Deltic' observed at speed north of Forfar on the 9.30am Aberdeen – Glasgow.
29	61354 noted at Keith in steam, and 76xxx is at Elgin to work to Keith via Buckie. Steam (working from 61A) still sometimes seen on the GNS lines.
U/D	D57xx seen on crew training to Todmorden, on the Calder Valley main line.
U/D	80081, 80147 initiate through workings by tank engines over the 71 miles between Bath and Bournemouth via the S&D line.
U/D	Preserved locos currently in store at Dawsholm; 49/103/123/256 plus 54398 *Ben Alder* and 62712 *Morayshire*.
U/D	7818 *Granville Manor* works through on freight from Banbury to Redhill and penetrates to Merstham once/twice to pick up the return load.
U/D	HRH Duke of Edinburgh travels in four Royal coaches attached to the 11pm from Paddington, these being berthed overnight on the Abingdon branch. D1069 *Western Vanguard* brings these four into Oxford next day for the Duke's visit, and returns the ECS through to Wolverton, rare type here.
U/D	Application of 'diesel' numbers to steam locomotives at Eastleigh Works. During 1963, 4 x Departmental USA 0-6-0Ts have been given hand-painted 6½" high yellow numerals in the 'Grotesque' font usually applied to diesel engines. These are; DS 237/238 (Ashford Works shunters) – Nov/August and DS 235/236 (Lancing Carriage Works shunters) – April/May. Earlier, all 3 Beattie 2-4-0WTs and one A1X 0-6-0T also received this font, which is considerably narrower than Gill Sans and fits these small engines more easily. These numbers are white transfers. 30586 (2/60) and 32670 (5/60) have the numerals on the bunker sides, but 30587 (5/60) and 30585 (1/61) have them on the cabsides. *(Information courtesy Barry Fletcher).*

DECEMBER 1963

3RD 92231 (71A) brings the rare sight of an Eastleigh engine to Nottingham (V).

5,6 48170, 48750 (respectively) both reach Norwich on freights from Peterborough and return LE immediately (as East Anglia is steam-free!).

6 60100 *Spearmint* takes the 9.15am to Carstairs out of Princes Street.

7 (Week ending). 61162 (40A) seen working Rugby – Euston locals!

9 72006 *Clan Mackenzie* departs Paddington with an enthusiasts' special for Swindon, only the second 'Clan' to appear at this terminus. (See 28-30 Nov.)

9 8.40am Bristol – Sheffield leaves Temple Meads behind 45674 *Duncan* + 45675 *Hardy*, double-headers with consecutive numbers are exceedingly rare!

9 92220 *Evening Star* enters Eastleigh with freight from Washwood Heath, and is then used on the 11.25am Southampton Docks – Temple Mills banana train as far as Basingstoke.

10 60004 *William Whitelaw* (61B) passes Newcastle towed by 61216 in transit to Darlington Works, but in error ends up at Doncaster instead, not reaching Darlington until eight days later!

11 D290 on the 'Pines Express' at Wolverhampton (from Crewe), is the first EE Type 4 seen on this train.

12 'Counties' 1017/22/26 are moved from Hereford to Ince (Wigan) for disposal via Shrewsbury and Stockport, where they occupy the shed for the weekend.

12 D1072 *Western Glory* noted on trial at Preston with a 7-coach ECS train to Penrith and back. First 'Western' seen north of Crewe on the West Coast line.

12 45685 *Barfleur* heads a football excursion from Bristol to Coventry complete with GWR-type reporting number plates on the smokebox door, rare sight here.

12 9.30am Gloucester (Eastgate) – Bristol (a Derby 'Peak' duty for some time) suddenly produces 5018 *St. Mawes Castle*! A further 8 x GWR locos appear over the next 12 days, all returning LE to Worcester.

13 70052 *Firth of Tay* (5A) takes over the 2.35pm Birkenhead – Paddington at Shrewsbury and reportedly works it right to Paddington, rare working, if so.

13 48386 (Woodford Halse) is a surprise arrival in Plymouth, on freight.

14 After an M7 0-4-4T fails, the 5.57pm Brockenhurst – Lymington Pier and later services, are operated by a DEMU, very much an emergency move.

17 10.35am (WFO) Bridgewater – Mold ICI empty tanks is the longest through working for a 2-8-0 from Taunton, and 2882 (83B) appears at 6B on this duty.

18,23 2.43pm Three Bridges – East Grinstead special parcels is graced by double-headed H 0-4-4Ts 31518 + 31551. Same train on 23rd has 31263 + 31551.

19 4pm down 'Talisman' takes pilot 60063 *Isinglass* at Hatfield to assist D9007 *Pinza*.

21 82026 is a total stranger to be seen shunting at Redhill.

21 92061 makes a rare appearance for this class on the East Coast main line between Newcastle and Edinburgh, working a Heaton – Millerhill freight.

23 45237 noted at Prestatyn towing LNW 0-6-2T 1054 (ex-58926) for eventual display at Penrhyn Castle.

24 D7037 heads the 12.20pm Cardiff – Derby throughout, and the 5.20pm return.

24 Re-engined D6123 exits Waverley on the down 'Queen of Scots' to Glasgow.

26 D1517 (34G) makes a class debut on the Waverley route, heading the 2.43pm Edinburgh

– Hawick. D1549 makes another first appearance, on the GSW line, with the up 'Thames-Clyde Express'.

27   35019 *French Line CGT* brings the 14-coach 9.21am from Weymouth into Waterloo, thought to be the longest train in Waterloo since the war!

28   Northbound 'Devonian' headed by D37 receives 61275 (50A) as pilot from New Street to Sheffield (to avoid LE movement).

28   60816 (64A) – in immaculate external condition – is an interesting choice to power the 9.25am Crewe – Perth from Carlisle, via Beattock and Carstairs.

30   7.32am ex-Doncaster reaches Leeds (Central) with 45739 *Ulster*, surprisingly.

U/D D6553 (73C) is at Derby for tests hauling air-braked Liner Train stock between Derby and Leicester.

U/D 70006 *Robert Burns* reaches Scotland at last! – spotted on St Margarets depot.

JANUARY 1964

3RD D29, due to work the 12.15pm Newcastle – Bristol, is replaced at the last minute by D256. This works to York, where 60847 takes over to…Derby. Crews change but the loco doesn't. New driver has never driven a V2, new fireman never seen one, but they set off for Birmingham!

4   FA Cup, 3rd round specials: 45531 *Sir Frederick Harrison* reaches Hull with Everton supporters; D151 arrives in Cardiff with Leeds fans; 34088 *213 Squadron* works to Birmingham from Aldershot; 34037 *Clovelly* gets to Leamington on a Portsmouth – Stoke special; D7059 seen in Southampton, but return train to Manchester has communication cord pulled 47 times (4 hours late back); 46155 *The Lancer* comes to Highbury & Islington from Wolverhampton; D7004/28/41 make it to Crewe (a first) as do 4079 *Pendennis Castle* and 5002 *Ludlow Castle* on trains from Bristol heading for Manchester. An interesting day!

4   D5713 mysteriously spotted at Chinley South Junction.

6   61319 (50A) is surprise power on the 12.35pm Longsight – Buxton goods.

7   92235 (86B Ebbw Jct.) runs through Nottingham (Victoria) with a Woodford to York freight. Newport engines rarely reach these parts.

7   78000 is unexpectedly employed on the 5.8pm Derby – Chesterfield.

7   70016 *Ariel* passes Shipley on northbound freight, an engine not seen here for more than a decade, when it was on loan to Holbeck.

7   60120 *Kittywake* causes a stir at Mirfield on a parcel train from York.

8   D7015 (86A Canton) works through to Derby on four coaches, substituting for an Inter-City DMU. Cardiff locos are rare in Derby.

9   8456 is cut up at a private yard at Plaistow, the 14th 0-6-0PT scrapped here.

9   Carlisle: 60535 *Hornet's Beauty* arrives on mineral empties from Glasgow, and 61007 *Klipspringer* has charge of the 6pm to St Enoch.

11   Two Coventry – Reading football specials are worked throughout by 70025 *Western Star* and 45048 + 45392 double-headed.

12   Stanier 2-6-0 42978 (5E Nuneaton) reaches Cardiff on freight. Most unusual.

13   8.50am Waterloo – Portsmouth fails near Godalming and short-circuits the traction current. 8.27am Portsmouth stopper is immobilised behind this, south of Guildford from where a steam engine is sent to propel the 8.27 up to the 8.50 and push both trains to Witley. Fuse is replaced and current restored.

14 0-8-0 63426 makes an unprecedented first appearance of a Q6 at Huddersfield, in order to work a special freight back to Neville Hill.

14,15 70011 *Hotspur* (12A) heads the up 'Postal' out of Aberdeen on both days.

16 Up 'Master Cutler' seen passing Hitchin with two Brush Type 4s at the head.

18 'Royal Scot' is diverted via Dumfries, passing through behind D312 (8A).

18 70000 *Britannia* reaches Darlington with an enthusiasts' special from B'ham.

20 0-6-0 41835 heads the 7.35am Barrow Hill – Chesterfield goods, and then works the freight-only Brampton branch. Most unusual to see a Staveley Works shunter out on the 'Main' lines.

20 45484 (66A) tows 60077 *The White Knight* (64A) from Kingmoor to Gateshead (for light repairs at Darlington) and returns towing 70013 *Oliver Cromwell* back to Carlisle. A first for a Polmadie loco to reach Gateshead?

21 34091 *Weymouth* runs light engine from Bournemouth to Salisbury, via Fordingbridge. Pacifics are a rarity on this stretch of line.

22 73009 (67A) + 73057 (66A) head the 'Thames-Clyde Express' out of St Enoch.

24 70025 *Western Star* arrives at Bradford (Exchange) on a parcels train from Manchester, and is then used as station pilot!

25 J72 0-6-0T 69016 works the weekly signal cabin supply train from Heaton via the Riverside branch to Tynemouth and back via Benton, an extremely rare occurrence as this is usually a B1 or V3 turn.

26 0-6-2T 6696 noted at Barry shed still lettered BRITISH RAILWAYS in full, 1948 style!

26 D9000 *Royal Scots Grey* becomes immobile north of Durham on the 7.15pm (25th) Aberdeen – King's Cross. The following 8.20pm from Aberdeen, also 'Deltic'-hauled, couples onto the rear and the two engines plus 25 coaches proceed the 7 miles to Durham, where the 7.15 is pushed into a siding to await a replacement locomotive.

28 11.50am Newcastle – Lincoln fails at Sunderland. V3 2-6-2Ts 67620/40 then double-head the train to West Hartlepool, to be relieved by 60847.

28 First 'Hymek' to reach Waterloo is D7008, which arrives with the ECS of a Brentford v Oxford football special. Stock cleaned as evening match is played.

30 4.25pm Euston – Wolverhampton is, most surprisingly, worked throughout by 'Crab' 42900 (1A).

30 60063 *Isinglass* (34E) heads the 7.10pm Neville Hill – Skipton freight. Unheard of for a Peterborough engine to reach these parts.

FEBRUARY 1964

1ST Football special arrives in Coventry from Hull behind D6737 (50B).

4 61002 *Impala* and 'Crab' 42799 both work freights into Cardiff.

5 Pullman car 70 is a surprise attachment to the rear of the 10.45am Sheffield (Victoria) – Manchester (Piccadilly) and the return working. (70's batteries need recharging).

6 70003 *John Bunyan* arrives at Embsay to collect ballast hoppers for Burnley, an extreme rarity for a 7MT to be on the Skipton – Ilkley line.

6 Electro-diesel E6004 seen near Bickley Jct. sandwiched between 4-CEP unit and eight loco-hauled coaches.

8 72005 *Clan Macgregor* comes into Chester off the CLC line with freight to Shotton Steelworks. Serviced at Mold Junction, then heads a Carlisle freight.

9	44660 (2E Saltley) appears at Hitchin on an up coal train, surprisingly.
9	In Glasgow, 73005 is seen paired with the green tender ex-72002, and 44723 has the green tender ex-45677 (both withdrawn locos).
10	6822 *Manton Grange* (2A Tyseley) pilots 70044 *Earl Haig* on the southbound 'Pines Express' from Crewe to Oxford, a most unusual combination.
12	'Crab' 42904 (16D Nottingham) is a startling sight on the Grantham to Doncaster pick-up goods. LMS engines rarely encroach onto this line.
12	'Thames-Clyde Express' leaves St Enoch behind the eye-catching pairing of 72009 *Clan Stewart* + 60535 *Hornet's Beauty*! Unique?
14	30928 *Stowe* is delivered by road from Millbrook to Beaulieu Abbey for display at Lord Montague's Museum.
15	FA Cup 6th round: special from Hull to Wrexham is a 2-car DMU; Preston v Carlisle match entices 40 coaches-worth of fans onto three trains, 46238 *City of Carlisle* brings 14 of these into the East Lancs platform at Preston (a rare sight), whilst 45512 *Bunsen* and 45545 *Planet* have a further 12,14 each.
17	60877 is an imposing visitor to Bedford shed, off the Leicester goods.
17	Derailment at Cumbernauld causes the 8.25am Buchanan Street – Aberdeen to depart with an A4 at both ends! Train reverses at Sighthill (engine detached) and takes the NB line to Greenhill to join the CR route.
17	Two 6-car 'Hastings' DEMUs form a Deal – Wembley Hill special, first inter-regional use of these vehicles.
17	Fawley – Bromford Bridge oil tanks has 80015 + D6528, to Eastleigh.
20	820xx makes a class debut at Ilfracombe, with an Inspection Saloon.
24	CEGB 0-4-0T travels on BR tracks from Sandy to Bedford, a rare movement.
25	Darlington – Crook parcels (one full brake) is worked by 75046 (27A!).
25	Preserved A4 4468 *Mallard* travels from Doncaster to Nine Elms via Mexborough, Neasden and Kew. Moves to Clapham Museum by road on 29th.
25	D8120/26 (66A!) seen as a pair on goods duties at...Leamington Spa!
26	2-8-2T 7221 works an up freight at Southall, uncommon in the London area.
27	73092 in ex-Works green livery is a cheerful sight at Kingmoor shed.
27	D6123 (65A Eastfield!) arrives at Coventry on the car train from Linwood.
28	46254 *City of Stoke-on-Trent* works the up 'Condor' fitted freight and is serviced at Aston before heading the 10.10pm Birmingham – Glasgow.
29	FA Cup: Swansea fans charter a WR Blue Pullman unit for the match at Liverpool; ten specials are run from the North East for the Sunderland game in Manchester, headed by seven A3's (to Leeds), two EE Type 4s, one DMU.
U/D	5.52am Doncaster – Lincoln is headed by an EE Type 3 with Pacific pilot; 60119 *Patrick Stirling* on 20th, A1 (?) on 21st, 60054 *Prince of Wales* on 22nd.
U/D	GWR locos for scrapping at Norwich include three 'Halls', 4095 *Harlech Castle* and 2-8-0 4705.
U/D	Contrasting motive power for the Scotswood – Red Bank ECS
	27th Stanier 2-6-0 42960 piloting 78041
	29th 70008 *Black Prince* piloting 44858, and 90380 solo 11 March.

MARCH 1964

1ST   35003 *Royal Mail* at St Pancras! Chartered special to Derby and back. First 'Mecrchant Navy' to run on the Midland main line.

4   LNW 'Coal Tank' 0-6-2T 1054 (BR 58926) leaves Bangor shed and travels to Menai Bridge station, thence by road to Penrhyn Castle for display.

4   70042 *Lord Roberts* works the Leeds – Bradford (Forster Square) leg of the 'Devonian', and 70041 *Sir John Moore* heads the 3.40pm to Carlisle. Two (consecutive) 7MTs in Forster Square on the same day must be unique!

5   46256 *Sir William A. Stanier, F.R.S.* arrives at Nuneaton, gingerly, from Rugby with northbound freight. As the coal-pusher is not working, fireman is barred from bringing coal forward when 'under the wires', so E3029 pilots 46256 to Stafford, where 46256 is removed to bring coal forward safely.

8   Oxted line 3-car DEMU breaks new ground by working between Horsham and Brighton, usually a steam push-pull service.

8   70020 *Mercury* reaches Bournemouth (Central) with a special from Waterloo.

9,10   2.11pm up fish train departs Aberdeen with D6110 piloting 60836, and D6117 pilots 70003 *John Bunyan* next day.

11   Eastleigh shed (70D) hosts seven withdrawn 'Terrier' 0-6-0Ts awaiting purchase decisions with preservation in mind.

12   Surprise of the year? 7912 *Little Linford Hall* appears at Sheffield (Victoria) having worked the Bournemouth – York from Banbury. Only the third 'Hall' to reach this far north. *(See 15 August!)*.

14   FA Cup semi-final at Villa Park, Preston v Swansea: two Blue Pullman sets arrive, a South Wales unit via New Street to Witton, and a Bristol set to/from Snow Hill. D7057/92 also work to Witton via the Lickey, on further specials.

14   6.50pm Cleethorpes – King's Cross is, unusually, double-headed by D6800/6.

16   60002 *Sir Murrough Wilson* heads the 'Waverley' from Edinburgh through to Leeds via the S&C, an unexpected direction for an A4 to reach Leeds.

18   Preserved A3 4472 *Flying Scotsman* works a private 3-coach special from Doncaster to Cardiff and back, with 'Devon Belle' observation car M280M (ex-Doncaster C&W shops the previous day), bringing up the rear. Welsh Tourist Board awards Alan Pegler its Certificate of Merit, personally.

18   60121 *Silurian* appears in Sheffield (Midland) with ECS from York.

21   12 specials are run to Aintree (Sefton Arms) for the Grand National, including four from Euston behind 'Coronations' 46228/39/40/51 to Crewe, with 'Britannias' 70018/50/51/54 from there. 70021/47 come in from Coventry, Watford and a Blue Pullman set arrives from Swansea. 45522 *Prestatyn* brings in a special from Cleethorpes, with a Pullman car and ex-'Coronation' beaver-tail at the rear.

21   Manchester (Piccadilly) – Marylebone sleeper headed by 45735 *Comet* fails north of Rugby. 61275 (with its own freight) then pushes the cavalcade into Rugby (Central). A fitter attends to 45735, which proceeds to London.

23   Q1 0-6-0 33027 heads a railtour out of Waterloo, where Q1s are rarely seen.

25   6229 *Duchess of Hamilton*, in LMS livery, is in Crewe Works paint shop, ready to go to Butlin's at Minehead for static display.

25   D6553 is seen heading out of Bristol towards Filton with Liner Train vehicles.

26	Leeds – Doncaster train is headed by 60843 piloted by EE prototype DP2.
26	6811 *Cranbourne Grange* (2C Stourbridge) passes Winchester with the Fawley – Bromford Bridge oil tanks.
27	(Good Friday) 34010 *Sidmouth* works a special from Glasgow throughout between Willesden, Newhaven.
28	12.26pm Bournemouth (West) – Brockenhurst via Ringwood is hauled by 34045 *Ottery St. Mary*, which also works the return 2.8pm service, tender first.
28	62058 powers the 4.31pm Sheffield (Midland) – Chinley and the 6.32pm back. First K1 seen on the Hope Valley line.
28	'Regency Belle' luxury Pullman special (utilising redecorated 5-BEL unit 3052) begins running between Victoria and Brighton. Departs 7.15pm, returns from Brighton 2.15am Sunday morning, breakfast served *en route* (!) included in the fare of 7gns.
29	46256 *Sir William A. Stanier, F.R.S.* is noted at Portobello on a railtour that had originated in Birmingham. 'Coronations' are rare in Edinburgh on any pretext.
30	44915 reaches Brighton heading an excursion from Rugby.
31	D5512 surprisingly arrives in Paddington, with a parcels train from Didcot.
U/D	Two 3-car Euston – Watford EMUs are seen between Ely and Thetford en route to King's scrapyard at Norwich, which also receives 11 GWR locos including three 'Castles' 5065, 7017/30.
U/D	George Cohen of Kettering buys 30 SR engines for scrap, 15 of which arrive from Feltham, and three 'Schools' 30902/29/35, from Nine Elms.
U/D	Officials of the Hayling Island Railway Society travel to Brussels to negotiate the purchase of some of their tramcars. Line expected to open later this year.

APRIL 1964

1ST	60847 noted at Cricklewood depot, looking very much out of place.
1	60150 *Willbrook* reaches Mirfield on a York – Wavertree parcels train.
3	D336 on the 9pm Perth – Euston fails at Motherwell, with D8541/8 pairing up to forward the train to Carstairs, where 60813 takes over to Carlisle.
3	92220 *Evening Star* arrives at Three Bridges shed from Eastleigh, to work an enthusiasts' special forward to Paddington. First 9F seen at Three Bridges?
3,4	61165 (34E New England) leaves Temple Meads on the 8.40am to Sheffield. Next day, 61104 (41D Canklow) heads the 9.30am Gloucester – Bristol and the 6.30pm slow to Birmingham, whilst 61002 *Impala* (50A) reaches Severn Beach with a block freight for ICI. All strange engines in these parts.
4	'Hymek' appears in Cornwall, arriving in Truro on freight from Plymouth.
4	'Regency Belle' is steam hauled by 34088 *213 Squadron*, with five Pullmans between two full brakes. East Coast Met-Cam car 334 is in the rake.
4,5	Tetbury branch closes (4th). Coffin addressed to Dr Beeching is loaded at Trouble House Halt and transferred at Kemble onto the London connection. It is later delivered to Dr Beeching. On the 5th, the Cirencester branch closes. Farewell party outside station burns effigy of Mr Marples in protest.
7	S&C line blocked at Cumwinton, hence up 'Waverley' climbs Shap behind immaculate 60041 *Salmon Trout en route* to Leeds via Low Gill, Clapham.
8	Both the 8.40pm and 8.50pm Euston – Holyhead departures are 'Coronation' hauled, by

46239 *City of Chester* and 46245 *City of London* respectively, an extremely rare event nowadays.

9 9.31am Victoria – Newhaven boat train leaves behind 73115 *King Pellinore* piloted by a D65xx, and the 5.14pm return working by 73115 piloted by DC electric E5018, a rare pairing of steam/electric motive power.

9 45694 *Bellerophon* (56F Low Moor) tows condemned Derby light-weight DMU's through Doncaster for scrap.

10 60139 *Sea Eagle* reaches Derby on the 11.50am York – Bristol, returning next day with the 6.30am Derby – Sheffield. A1s are most unusual here.

10,11 70009 *Alfred the Great* (12A) is unprecedented power at Harrogate to work the 11.30am to King's Cross as far as Leeds, on both days.

13 3-coach BBC special departs Cross Gates for Malton and Whitby behind preserved K4 3442 *The Great Marquess* with filming taking place at Pickering and Goathland. Return into York is heralded by the ringing of 3442s bell, a gift to Viscount Garnock, ex-Pennsylvania RR K4 4-6-2 loco.

14 Shakespeare 400th Anniversary Celebrations at Stratford-on-Avon bring 70030 *William Wordsworth* and 70052 *Firth of Tay* through from Manchester, with 6926 *Holkham Hall* piloting 70030 from Gresty Lane to Snow Hill. 34044 *Woolacombe* also arrives on an excursion from Poole.

14-17 D8589, D8593 – the latter in grey primer – work test freights between Manchester and Derby via Chinley.

15 'Clan' invades South Wales! 72006 *Clan Mackenzie* reaches Margam on the overnight Carlisle – Milford Haven oil tank empties.

15 45379 is the first of its class to reach Chichester, working an excursion to Bournville. It had brought the ECS from Willesden two days earlier.

16 92137 (2E Saltley) brings a fertilizer train to Weymouth. Few 9Fs visit here.

17 60051 *Blink Bonny* (52B) arrives at Huddersfield shed to work an enthusiasts' special to Crewe and Derby next day.

18 35008 *Orient Line* and 35011 *General Steam Navigation* are the first 'Merchant Navy' class locos to reach Stratford-on-Avon, with specials from Bournemouth (West). Engines go to Tyseley for servicing.

18 Preserved A3 4472 *Flying Scotsman* heads an excursion from Manchester (Central) to Marylebone via High Wycombe, and proceeds through the Woodhead Tunnel with its fire damped down, hauled by 26001. On the return leg 4472 is removed at Penistone, with 26052 taking the train forward.

18 5.15pm Gloucester – Chalford 2-coach auto-train causes a minor sensation by arriving at Stroud with 0-4-2T 1472 piloted by D39! 45633 *Aden* also passes through LE westbound, most unusual to see a 'Jubilee' on this line.

20 D6557 is, strangely, employed as station pilot at King's Cross, where a 73C (Hither Green) loco makes a second-only, very surprising, appearance.

20 6825 *Llanvair Grange* tows 6229 *Duchess of Hamilton* through Bristol *en route* to Butlin's at Minehead, reached by road on 7 May after being towed from Taunton by 0-6-0PT 9647 on the 29 April .

20 Up 'Mayflower', powered by D10xx, is diverted via Okehampton between Plymouth and Exeter. First 'Western' over this former SR route?

22,29 D209 (30A) reaches Coventry with a 'Cathedral visitors' excursion from Ipswich. Next

	week D5556 (32A) comes in from Norwich, and immaculate 45694 *Bellerophon* (56F) from Bradford, with more sightseers.
24	60012 *Commonwealth of Australia* heads the 5.45pm Aberdeen – Edinburgh. First time in months an A4 has been on an Edinburgh express.
24-27	60008 *Dwight D. Eisenhower* is towed overnight from Doncaster to Eastleigh, and thence by 35012 *United States Line* to Southampton New Docks. Dr Beeching hands over 60008 on behalf of BR to the National Railroad Museum Green Bay, Wisconsin before loading as deck cargo on the 'American Planter' three days later.
25	With the Alnmouth – Berwick section blocked, Carlisle sees (amongst others) D9019 on the up 'Flying Scotsman' and D174 with the up 'Queen of Scots', providing the rare sight of Pullman cars over the Waverley route.
25	Five of the return specials for the Schoolboys' International Soccer match at Wembley are diesel hauled, first use of diesel power on trains for this event.
25	70038 *Robin Hood* (40B) is an uncommon visitor to Leeds (City).
25	B16 4-6-0 61435 departs, most unusually, from platform 4 at Leeds (City Wellington, the LMS part) towards Harrogate, taking out a railtour train.
28	D1573 heads the 3.16pm Leeds – Morecambe but fails at Shipley. 90711 takes the train on to Skipton, contrasting power!
30	70054 *Dornoch Firth* reaches Stratford-on-Avon with an excursion from Accrington, via Snow Hill.
U/D	ER Pacifics go to Crewe Works for minor repairs. 60118 *Archibald Sturrock*, 60131 *Osprey* and 60134 *Foxhunter* are seen in the Works yard.
U/D	73070 tows 3213/9 + 6133 + 6380 via Bletchley to Cambridge for scrapping at King's of Norwich. Stanier 2-6-0 42963 tows 31851/96 + 32337 over the same route, and 48361 likewise takes 31894 + 32343.
U/D	GE line suburban EMU's are overhauled at Wolverton, and are steam-hauled over the Cambridge – Bletchley line, with pantographs removed.

MAY 1964

2ND	FA Cup Final brings a 'Midland Pullman' set to Wembley Hill with fans from Preston. Three specials run for West Ham fans, a short cross-London trip!
2	2-8-0 4707 reaches Exeter (Central) on a cement train from Taunton. First (and last!) visit of this class to Central.
3	34002 *Salisbury* makes the first appearance of an SR Pacific in Penzance, and is probably the last steam worked express passenger train in Cornwall, on an enthusiasts' special from Plymouth.
5	60118 *Archibald Sturrock* arrives LE at Huddersfield in order to take an excursion to…Castle Douglas of all places!
6	78020 (5A) seen between Bala and Ruabon with an Inspection Saloon.
6,7	HR 'Jones Goods' 4-6-0 103 runs LE overnight from Dawsholm to Bedford to take part in the filming of *Those Magnificent Men in their Flying Machines* on the Bedford – Hitchin branch.
7	D7013 is a class first over the Netley line, with a Swindon – Portsmouth (Harbour) educational excursion.
9	High-speed run from Paddington to Plymouth (an Ian Allan special) has 4079 *Pendennis*

Castle to Westbury, 6999 *Capel Dewi Hall* to Taunton and 7025 *Sudeley Castle* to Plymouth. Return is with 7029 *Clun Castle* to Bristol and 5054 *Earl of Ducie* to London. A memorable day!

9   46251 *City of Nottingham* appears in its home city to work a railtour as far as Banbury, where 34038 *Lynton* takes over for the run to Eastleigh, thence to Swindon. 46251 is in charge again from Swindon back to Nottingham.

10   Preserved K4 3442 *The Great Marquess* works onto the North Wales coast line – where these engines were never seen – with a special from Leeds.

13   A1X 0-6-0T 32626 (plus LBSC milk van) runs from Haywards Heath through Ardingly to Horsted Keynes – the line closed in October 1963 and this is the last movement over this section – to their new home on the Bluebell Railway.

14   D1586 – in works grey – noted on a 15-coach test train in the Lune Gorge.

16   (Whit Saturday) 70017 *Arrow* (5A) surprisingly heads the up 'Cambrian Coast Express' from Shrewsbury, as far as Snow Hill.

16   Special car train from Halewood to Bathgate is worked over the Waverley route by the uncommon combination of 45018 piloting 60042 *Singapore*.

16   75002 (6F Machynlleth), in green livery ex-Eastleigh Works, is seen running-in on Waterloo – Basingstoke trains. Where's Machynlleth, they ask?

16-18 D1073 *Western Bulwark* reaches Bournemouth on the 12.15pm relief from Wolverhampton; visits Brighton on a through working from Stourbridge (17th) and arrives in Portsmouth (Harbour), again from Stourbridge the day after.

19   4-coach Hull portion of the 'Yorkshire Pullman' is worked throughout to King's Cross as a separate train, headed by D6738 (50B) all the way.

20   73028 tows 5018 *St. Mawes Castle* down the Midland main line to Kettering. First 'Castle' on this line, if only for scrap!

22   D59 is named *The Royal Warwickshire Fusilier* at Snow Hill and afterwards heads a special train for guests to Stratford-on-Avon.

22   'Pines Express' stops specially at Winchester (Chesil)! Basingstoke – Reading line is blocked, so train is diverted via Chesil, Newbury and Thatcham. First titled train ever to call at Chesil, over 2½ years after its complete closure!

22   34034 *Honiton* exits Victoria on a Southampton Docks boat train that includes three Restaurant Cars in its 9-coach formation.

23   60818 seen on a 2-coach train at Callander. V2s are prohibited here!

22/23 D9004 hauls the overnight sleeper from Edinburgh through to Inverness in order to be named *Queen's Own Highlander* at the Highland capital. Returns south as far as Perth on the 5.45pm 'Royal Highlander' to Euston.

22,26,27 7034 *Ince Castle*, 4093 *Dunster Castle* and 92135 respectively are seen on the Portishead branch on the single track through the Avon Gorge, with freights for Oldbury (Birmingham).

23   72007 *Clan Mackintosh* is unusual power to appear at Lancaster (Green Ayre) on the electrified branch, with a RCTS special.

25   5.30pm Waterloo – Bournemouth (West) suffers a Pacific engine failure at Eastleigh. 80064 takes over and doesn't lose any time on schedule!

27   D1710 is the first of its class to reach Plymouth, working the newspaper train from Paddington and returning on the 7.25pm perishables to London.

27,28 Interesting arrivals at Coventry with visitors to the Cathedral are D1735 (86A Canton) on an excursion from Barry, and D389 (52A) with a special from Pocklington next day.

28   46240 *City of Coventry* is highly unusual power for the 4.30pm Manchester (Exchange) – Llandudno club train.

28   D1733 plus 8-coach train of XP64 stock are officially unveiled at Marylebone and run to High Wycombe and back. Stock is booked to work the 'Talisman' service from 15 June; a West Riding train from September, Euston – Heysham from January, and a South Wales express from March '65.

29   4080 *Powderham Castle* passes Leamington Spa assisting failed D1695 on the 6pm from Paddington.

29   46238 *City of Carlisle* runs through Lancaster (Castle) in charge of...2 x Mk1 coaches/ Restaurant Car/3 x Sleeping Cars/10 x conflats (loaded)/3 x open wagons (loaded with bright yellow equipment)/brakevan. Quite a mixture!

30   70000 *Britannia* (5A) works the 10.50am pigeon special from Heysham right through to Milford Haven (!), and adjourns to Llanelly for servicing.

30   Torrential rain floods all the Standedge Tunnels to a depth of five feet, stranding the 7.45pm Leeds – Liverpool Trans-Pennine DMU mid-way through the tunnel. A steam-hauled relief train is brought alongside and passengers transferred by improvised planking! (The lower level canal tunnel allows flood water to escape eventually).

30   45696 *Arethusa* is unusual power for the 12noon Hawick – Edinburgh.

U/D   Experimental washing plant at Rugby depot hosts a number of diesel types, plus Co-Co 27002 *Aurora* and Bo-Bo E3043.

U/D   70041 *Sir John Moore* is an unexpected guest at Eastfield (65A).

U/D   Equally so is S&D 2-8-0 53807 at Swindon, for minor repairs.

U/D   0-4-0T 41535 finally reaches Swansea (East Dock) 6 months after setting off from Derby Works!

U/D   Whitsun holiday period excursion workings include;
        D602 *Bulldog*, D837 *Ramillies* both appear in Bournemouth. Three specials to Seaton Carew are run from Bishop Auckland via Spennymoor and Ferryhill, (normally closed to passengers). 12-coach Doncaster – Blackpool return run; D6748 takes a 2-6-4T as pilot between Bolton and Rochdale, first steam/diesel pairing seen on this line.

U/D   A3 4472 *Flying Scotsman* operates 'Pegler's Pullman' between Doncaster and Edinburgh. On 16 May heads University of St Andrews charter train Waverley – Aberdeen, 4472s first visit to the Granite City since newly-built in 1923!

JUNE 1964

2ND   60929 arrives in Huddersfield with the Eastbourne – Leeds/Bradford which it had worked from Leicester, and goes forward on the Leeds portion. Rare sight.

4   Scotswood – Red Bank ECS is a fine sight behind a brace of 'Crabs'.

4   70002 *Geoffrey Chaucer* (12A) arrives in York on the 5.38pm from Manchester (Exchange). Carlisle 'Britannias' are uncommon in York.

5   45379 is the first steam engine to be seen at Rye for two years, coming in on an 11-coach excursion.

5   Carlisle – Edinburgh schools' special is worked over the Waverley route by 45363 + 45588 *Kashmir*. LMS pairings over this former NB line are rare.

6	D5348 appears at Queen Street bearing a large headboard declaring 'Clan Cameron Gathering', which will be held near Fort William. (See 16/6/56).
7	Newark witnesses the southbound passage of the coupled LE trio of D5660 (31B) + D5559 (32A) + D5543 (32B), all ex-Doncaster Works.
7	7023 *Penrice Castle* is the first 'Castle' to reach the S&D terminus at Bath (Green Park) to work an enthusiasts' special to Gloucester.
11	61308 takes the stock of the XP64 train from Waverley to Queen Street to be exhibited there before entering service on the 'Talisman' on the 15th.
11	D7099 heads a 20-vehicle special from Wadebridge to Kensington, conveying the Household Cavalry from the Royal Cornwall Show, via the SR main line.
12	Bathgate – Halewood car train empties is worked over the Waverley route by the powerful combination of 70038 *Robin Hood* + 70008 *Black Prince*.
12	60114 *W. P. Allen* heads a school's excursion from Mexborough to Beaconsfield, through Nottingham (Victoria). Few A1s travel the GC line.
12-14	35012 *United States Line* heads LE down the Midland main line to Leeds to work a railtour to Carlisle and back, out via Shap returning via Ais Gill, on the 13th. Retraces its steps to Nine Elms on the 14th.
14	34079 *141 Squadron* ascends the Lickey in running a Bristol – Crewe special, outward via Derby back via Rugeley and Birmingham.
16	90529 passes through Nottingham (Victoria) towing Q 0-6-0 30547, to join Qs 30536/44 for scrap at Killamarsh, Sheffield.
17	D393 (51L Thornaby) arrives at Coventry on a 'Cathedral' special from Bishop Auckland.
17	D9018 *Ballymoss* fails at Durham on the up morning 'Talisman'. V3 2-6-2T 67628 assists to Darlington, where 60036 *Colombo* takes over to York, with D263 thereafter. King's Cross is reached 1½ hours late, on the third day of the new-image XP64 stock usage. An unfortunate start.
17	61319 reliably hauls Dr Beeching's Inspection Saloon throughout his Yorkshire tour.
18	D5518 (30A) brings a 4-car ER EMU into Eastleigh Carriage Works.
19	48603 is serviced at Redhill shed after working a Manchester – Horley pigeon special. LMR 8F's are almost unknown here.
20	Eastbourne depot hosts a Canklow B1 61313, which has come in on another pigeon special (to Lewes), and 45617 *Mauritius* – which is impounded, being unauthorised on the Central Division!
20	70045 *Lord Rowallan* works over the Oldham branch on a Manchester to Blackpool originating at Shaw, for local holidays.
20	45672 *Anson*, after working into Newhaven on the car sleeper from Glasgow, is used on an Eastbourne – Romsey excursion as far as Haywards Heath. Rare!
20	'Royal Scot' (D298) enters St Pancras. Euston building work is the cause.
20	34080 *74 Squadron* + 34066 *Spitfire* double-head the 10.28am Exeter to Waterloo out of Central. Most unusual for SR Pacifics to be seen in pairs.
20	Bristol (Barrow Road) has, for the first time, representatives of all four pre-nationalisation Companies' locos on shed. In addition to the usual LMS and GWR inmates, 61153/67 and 34079 *141 Squadron* (which worked the special on the 14th) are also on view.
20,27	60134 *Foxhunter*, 60118 *Archibald Sturrock* work into Carlisle on successive Saturdays with the northbound CTAC Scottish Tours Express from Leeds over the S&C. Both then

work the up CTAC trains back to Leeds.

20,27 5971 *Merevale Hall* and 6911 *Holker Hall* both reach Nottingham (Victoria) on the 10.38am Bournemouth (West) – Bradford (Exchange), handing over to 45562 *Alberta* and 45581 *Bihar and Orissa* respectively.

21 46251 *City of Nottingham* sensationally arrives into Paddington on a special from Shrewsbury.

21 The full length of the Shrewsbury – Aberystwyth line is opened specially (no Sunday service) for the passage of a Leeds (City) – Towyn 'Trans-Pennine' DMU excursion and a Snow Hill – Aberystwyth DMU special.

22 Up 'Bristol Pullman' loco-hauled Pullman replacement set is noted at Reading behind 7916 *Mobberly Hall*.

22 34079 *141 Squadron* leaves Bristol, heading for Taunton with a cattle train. SR Pacifics are rarities on this route.

24 The unprecedented combination of 60535 *Hornet's Beauty* piloted by 92249 heads a down freight on the CR route between Carlisle and Glasgow!

24 48388 passes Chesterfield towing Bo-Bo AC electric E3048 northwards!

25 Nottingham (Victoria) witnesses the unusual coupled LE trio of 46122 *Royal Ulster Rifleman* + 61210 (36E Retford) + 44226 (2E Saltley).

26 9.25pm St Enoch – St Pancras sleeper is worked to Leeds by 60527 *Sun Chariot* piloted by 44887. The 9.25pm Glasgow (Central) – Kensington sleeper leaves behind D304 piloted by 70013 *Oliver Cromwell*.

27 60051 *Blink Bonny* departs Whitley Bay with a returning special to Liverpool (Riverside). 60106 *Flying Fox* also leaves Walker on a naval special, both unusual visitors to the North Tyneside electric line.

27 75051 (8F Springs Branch, Wigan) surprisingly reaches Silloth on the 6.30pm from Carlisle.

28 Ex-Crosti boilered 92029 is spotted at Old Oak Common, rare here.

28 D7053 is a first time 'Hymek' visitor to Clacton, on a special from the WR.

28 Single-unit railcar is used for an enthusiasts' special, Plymouth to Eastleigh.

29 Swansea East Dock shed – now closed – is immediately filled by ten SR locos bound for scrap at Cowan's (Morriston). Classes U, N, Q1 are present.

29 70047 (6J) hauls an excursion from Watford throughout to Portsmouth, where Holyhead engines are a long way from home!

30 Sister engine 70017 *Arrow* is seen heading a Southampton – Nine Elms freight after receiving attention at Eastleigh shed.

U/D LMR conducts high-speed tests with 100mph running between Euston and Liverpool using D2 *Helvellyn* on six coaches plus track recording car. The 1966 electrification is in mind.

JULY 1964

1ST The unusual combination of 45162 + 60882 is seen on a down special freight at Longtown on the Waverley route.

4 9.50am (SO) Edinburgh (Waverley) – Leeds via Hawick arrives at Carlisle behind D8558/9, making their debut on passenger workings over this line.

4 D261 + D212 *Aureol* leave Princes Street on the 10.10am to Birmingham via Carstairs. Unusual for these Type 4s to double-up.

4	10.35am Blackpool – Perth is worked by 45736 *Pheonix*, without change.
5	Seven weeks after the class is officially extinct, M7 0-4-4T 30053 arrives at Victoria with a railtour that had covered the Caterham, Tattenham Corner branches with a 6-coach Buffet Car special.
7,8	61313 (41D Canklow) arrives at Redhill shed from Eastbourne for repairs, and is joined by 44951 (56D Mirfield) following its failure on the Newhaven to Glasgow car sleeper (8th). Together with the daily 'Manor' from Reading plus its own SR locos, all the 'Big Four' Companies are represented at Rehill!
11	Coventry annual holiday begins and 30 extras are run; a DMU goes to Great Yarmouth, the other 29 are all steam hauled including the 5am to Eastbourne headed by, appropriately, 46240 *City of Coventry*.
11	46241 *City of Edinburgh* gets through to Morecambe, from Glasgow (Central).
11	44832 powers the 4am Nine Elms – Basingstoke freight. 92215 had been equally unusual on the same working on the 7th.
12	A1 at Worcester! 60114 *W. P. Allen* heads a Sheffield – Cardiff special, but fails on shed before the return journey, (still there at the end of the month).
14	60001 *Sir Ronald Matthews*, the last English-based A4, makes a trial run after repair from Newcastle to Morpeth via Bedlington, returning on the main line.
16	D865 *Zealous* causes excitement at Leicester (Central) on a special ex-Bristol.
18	73113 *Lyonnesse* (70A) is the first named 5MT to be observed at Eastbourne.
18	61400 (61B) works the returning Heads of Ayr – Aberdeen holiday train all the way back to its home city.
19	D7091 arrives in Newport (High Street) with the Plymouth – Cardiff, which consists of four Hawkesworth coaches plus a 4-car DMU!
20	5pm Birmingham – Euston noted at Watford behind EE Types 1 + 4, paired.
22	7pm Glasgow (Central) – Manchester departs with 46225 *Duchess of Gloucester* being piloted by D8113, a really odd sight.
25	Holiday relief train is brought into Wolverhampton (Low Level) by a BRCW Type 3, the furthest north a D65xx has reached on a passenger train.
25	60816 (62B) leaves St Enoch on the 5.30pm to Carlisle via Dumfries, a surprising choice for this service and route.
25	78047 pilots 60052 *Prince Palatine* from Hawick to Riccarton Jct. on the 9.50am (SO) Waverley – Leeds. An eye-catching combination!
25,26	92233 (12A) visits Ayr on excursion traffic, the first 9F to be seen here. 60927 (56B) arrives next day, a class not seen at Ayr for six years, and an Ardsley example probably never before.
27	35005 *Canadian Pacific* finds unprecedented employment on the Chessington branch, hauling the block coal train for Charrington's.
28	D9016 is named *Gordon Highlander* at Aberdeen in the presence of the preserved GNS 4-4-0 49 of the same name. 49 had arrived at Aberdeen pulling 246 *Morayshire* (ex-62712) from Dawsholm to Inverurie for repainting.
28	Preserved A1X 0-6-0T 32636 arrives at Minehead, for exhibition at Butlin's Camp, as part of a regular goods train and conveyed on a low-loader wagon, not on its own wheels.
28	46112 *Sherwood Forester* is towed through Derby (Friargate) in transit to the breaker's yard – first and last 'Scot' to be seen here.

29	75013 (1E) reaches Scarborough on the 10.11am freight from York, the first Bletchley engine to be seen here.
30	Preserved A1X 0-6-0T 32640 is hauled through Snow Hill in a goods train. It will join 6203 *Princess Margaret Rose* at Butlin's, Pwllheli.
31	D6530 fails near Southampton on the 11.30am Brighton – Plymouth. 76007 propels the train to Dean, runs round, and hauls the entire consist to Salisbury.
U/D	Up 'Thames-Clyde Express' leaves St Enoch 'Coronation'-hauled at least once during the month.
U/D	The last 47xx class 2-8-0s 4703/4/7 go to Norwich for scrapping.
U/D	4950 *Patshull Hall* and 4976 *Warfield Hall* go to the Central Wagon Company at Ince, Wigan, for scrapping.

AUGUST 1964

1ST	(August Bank Holiday Saturday) 48737 (82F) is a rarity to power the Bournemouth (West) portion of a Waterloo express round from Central.
1	Ivatt 2-6-0 43074 (55F) is another rarity at Westbury (together with its Manningham shedplate), running-in after Works attention at Swindon.
1	Returning ECS trains from Glasgow Fair holiday traffic leave Law Jct. for the south behind 92249, 45371, 60118 *Archibald Sturrock*, 46128 *The Lovat Scouts* and 70038 *Robin Hood*. Variety!
1	The 'Royal Scot' arrives at Glasgow (Central). 70002 *Geoffrey Chaucer* is at the head, most unusual for a 'Britannia' to be on this service – ever!
1	Further variety at Glasgow. 8.35am St Enoch – St Pancras departs with 70003 *John Bunyan* piloting 45626 *Seychelles,* and the 9.56am relief from Central to Euston has 73075 piloting 70007 *Coeur-de-Lion*, both trains via the GSW route. Arrivals at St Enoch include 60131 *Osprey* on a relief from Leeds and 60976 (52A) on the 9.30am from St Pancras, the A1, V2 both working from Leeds. Steam still very much in evidence!
1	10.5am Glasgow (Central) – Birmingham departs behind the unusual Crewe/York pairing of D391 (50A) + D337 (5A). The same train on the 8th has D8115 piloting D311 through to Carlisle.
1	Stanier 2-6-0 42955 works from Scarborough to York on a relief to Glasgow.
1	73088 *Joyous Gard* (70A) heads the 8.48am New Milton – Swansea as far as Dorchester.
8	34071 *601 Squadron* passes Dorchester (West) on an up troop train. SR power rarely ventures along this line.
8	70049 *Solway Firth* (1A) heads the 6.35am Birmingham – Glasgow north from Leeds. Willesden engines are infrequent over the S&C, to say the least.
8	60114 *W. P. Allen* (having eventually been repaired at Worcester) heads the 11.40am relief to Newcastle out of New Street.
8	D6516/18/25 all reach Wolverhampton (Low Level) on returning holiday traffic from Margate, Eastbourne and Portsmouth respectively.
10	D5590 (31B) is an astonishing arrival at Euston on the 5.22pm from Bletchley.
10	D7593 reaches Brighton (first of class here?) on a 'City of Leicester Holiday Express' day excursion.

11	D5605 pilots D9016 *Gordon Highlander* at Stevenage on the down 'Talisman'.
12	12-coach Royal train (taking the Queen to Balmoral) is noted on the Ballater branch entrusted to the consecutive pairing of D6145/46.
15	45562 *Alberta* (55C Farnley Jct.) turns up at Basingstoke on a pigeon special!
15	46257 *City of Salford* leaves Princes Street with the 10.10am to Birmingham, which it works throughout, surprisingly.
15	Carlisle, north end; 60052 *Prince Palatine* comes in on the 2.50pm from Waverley, 60134 *Foxhunter* (55H Neville Hill) appears LE for the return working whilst 60535 *Hornet's Beauty* waits on the adjacent road with the 7.40pm to St Enoch, all three seen together. LNER Pacifics rule OK?
15	'Grange' at Huddersfield – event of the year! 6858 *Woolston Grange* (2B Oxley) on the 8.55am Bournemouth (West) – Leeds gets to Nottingham (Victoria), but is not replaced and proceeds to Sheffield (Victoria) – on time – where it scrapes the platform edge but is again not replaced. 6858 leaves driven by an ER Loco Inspector in blue pin-stripe suit, homburg hat (plus briefcase!) and is finally changed at Huddersfield for 45048. Astonishing! 6858 is then impounded on Hillhouse shed until the 26th when it departs for Oxley, restricted to 35mph, under the bell-code 2-6-1 'out of gauge load'. (GWR 2-6-0s 6398/9 when new, were delivered through Huddersfield from Stephenson's in 1 921).
16	D6540 passes through Basingstoke hauling LT Central Line stock for use on the Isle of Wight.
20	D349 makes a foray north of Inverness with a mid-day freight, at least as far as Dingwall, a filling-in turn before working the car sleeper back to York.
22	10.53am Workington – Euston is seen at Dalton behind the astounding pairing of 'Jinty' 0-6-0T 47675 piloting D5717!
22	1pm Liverpool – Leeds 6-car 'Trans-Pennine' unit is so full that many of the 160 passengers trying to board at Earlestown are left behind. The next 2pm T-P to Hull (5-cars) therefore has 156 standing passengers (44 in the Griddle car) between Earlestown and Manchester (Exchange), with only four exits available due to the mountains of luggage in the vestibules.
22	Privately restored 2-6-2T 4555 hauls local goods trips around Birmingham and makes several appearances in Snow Hill.
22	Two pairs of EE Type 1s arrive in Scarborough on excursions. D8067 + D8058 from Elsecar, and D8059 + D8006 with the 12.40pm ex-Chesterfield.
26	D1690 passes High Wycombe with a Blue Pullman replacement Pullman set.
26	Astonishingly, 73006 (63A Perth!) appears on Basingstoke shed – a strong contender for surprise of the year!
26	V2s from the NER travel all the way to Swindon for scrapping; 60812/916/975 are present, with others to follow.
29	Oswestry Works hosts a 9F for repair, a class first here.
29	5pm Buchanan Street – Dundee headed by 73150 is banked up to Cowlairs by…60031 *Golden Plover*, tender-first, which had brought in the stock as the 4pm arrival!
29	46245 *City of London* presents itself at Derby Works Open Day, where this class never reached in normal service.
U/D	D7026 and D6343 are seen on early morning freights from Old Oak Common to Aylesbury, both types new to the GC line.

U/D	Ward's scrap yard (Sheffield area) contains 'Castles', 'Counties', GWR 2-8-0s and 2-6-0s, as well as SR S15 4-6-0s (but not for long!).

SEPTEMBER 1964

1ST   46245 *City of London* works an 'Ian Allan' Paddington – Crewe special and back. 'Coronations' have always been rare visitors to this terminus.

2   70052 *Firth of Tay* (5A) and 70005 *John Milton* (2J Aston) arrive at Derby in quick succession, on football excursions from Coventry for an evening match.

4   45595 *Southern Rhodesia* reaches Weymouth on a pigeon special from Preston. Heads a tomato train to Westbury next day, back light engine, before working the pigeon empties north again on the 9th. All notable movements.

4   70026 *Polar Star* (6J) arrives in York on the 5.38pm from Manchester (Exchange). Holyhead engines seldom work this far east.

4   Last run of the down 'Caledonian' is headed (specially) by 46238 *City of Carlisle* in recognition of this class's performances on this non-stop express.

5   'Denby Dale Pie' event attracts ten extra trains from Huddersfield, all full!

5   Penultimate day of Queen Street – Kirkintilloch service sees the 5.18pm climb to Cowlairs behind D6120 + D6105, with D6129 banking!

5   45600 *Bermuda* drags E3065 and its Liverpool – Euston express along an un-electrified diversion near Winwick.

6   Railtour of the West Riding brings a 5-car DMU to Bradford (City Road) goods depot, the only time a passenger train has ever reached here.

6   A last steam-hauled enthusiasts' special over the Romsey – Andover line begins at Winchester (Chesil, closed September 1961), out via Southampton, back to Eastleigh via Chandlers Ford. 82029 provides the motive power.

6   70037 *Hereward the Wake* is seen tender-first at Lochmaben, between Dumfries and Lockerbie, with the diverted Carlisle – Perth milk train.

7   XP64 stock commences running on the 'West Riding' – the 7am Bradford (Exchange) to King's Cross, and arrives 28min late on its first day. Oh dear!

7   Single-unit railcar enters Euston! 8.15am from Rugby fails at Bletchley and passengers are transferred to the Buckingham branch railcar to reach London.

9   D8043 (1A) makes a class-first visit to the GW main line by arriving at Stoke Gifford with the 3.25am freight from Carlisle.

12   8-car DMU is utilised for a football special from Derby to Newcastle.

12   Blackpool – Lincoln relief is headed throughout by 44947. Even '5's don't make it to Lincoln very often.

12   Up 'Mid-day Scot' and 'Red Rose' (amongst others) are diverted round Rugby via Nuneaton/ Wigston/Market Harborough/Northampton, as the new signalbox is being commissioned at Rugby. Quite a detour.

13   D6706 reaches Farnborough with an Air Display special from Southend. The 11.32am Woking – Basingstoke starts back at Waterloo (for Air Display passengers), bringing the rare sight of a 'Hampshire' DEMU to Waterloo.

14,18   45346 (16D Nottingham) works the 3.4pm Redhill – Reading; 45299(1A) heads a similar train on the 18th. Both are fill-in turns off the Newhaven car sleeper service.

15   Down 'White Rose Pullman' limps into Hitchin, where 61105/38 are attached ahead of failed D1514, forming a most unusual trio.

15 Restored 6233 *Duchess of Sutherland* (in LMS livery) arrives at Ayr for temporary storage until facilities at Butlin's Heads of Ayr Camp are ready for it. A1X 0-6-0T 32662 is also expected shortly.

15 62057 brings a 17-coach ECS train into Scarborough from York, where shunter D3874 just managed this load from Clifton Sidings to the station.

16 A 'Clan' passes Longtown on special freight to Edinburgh. Rare power here.

17 5056 *Earl of Powis* heads a freight from Oxley into Basingstoke. Believed to be the first double-chimneyed 'Castle' seen on SR territory.

17 Q1 0-6-0 33026 reaches Weymouth on an FA Cup special from Fareham.

18 5.47pm Bradford (Exchange) to London parcels (but including two Pullman cars) sets off behind the rare combination of Ivatt 2-6-0 43070 + 61173.

18,19 A1X 0-6-0T 32650 travels LE from Eastleigh to Eastbourne, and on to Robertsbridge next day, for use on the Kent & East Sussex Railway.

19 46155 *The Lancer* appears at Peterborough (East) on a special from St Pancras. 60128 *Bongrace* takes over for the run to Sheffield (Victoria).

19,26 38 specials go to Blackpool for the illuminations on the 19th, 40 next week. Visitors include 44974 (67B), 44768 (Hamilton) (19th) and 73005 (67A), 45183 (64C) (26th).

20 92220 *Evening Star* leaves Victoria with an enthusiasts' special to Seaton via Alton/ Southampton/Salisbury, returning direct to Salibury, Wimbledon.

20 Taunton shed is host to, surprisingly, 48039 (9L). 8F's are not exactly ten a penny at Taunton, but a Buxton example must be a unique occurrence.

21 Ivatt 2-6-0 43066 (40E Colwick) is a sensational arrival at Chichester on a freight from Salisbury. First of this class to penetrate Sussex?

22 45660 *Rooke* (55A) comes into Weymouth from Crewe, but is employed on banking duties before being allowed to return north!

23 60138 *Boswell* (50A) is an unexpected sight on Nottingham shed (16D).

25 A1X 0-6-0T 32662 commences its journey to Ayr in an Eastleigh – Oxley freight, giving observers a unique view of a 'Terrier' on its passage north.

26 70051 *Firth of Forth* (5A) retires to Eastleigh for servicing after working a football special from Coventry to Southampton. 90660 (40B) is a most unexpected stablemate on the shed.

26 Last run of the 'Coronation' class. 46256 *Sir William A. Stanier, F.R.S.* heads the Crewe – Carlisle – Crewe legs of a special that goes to Edinburgh behind 60007 *Sir Nigel Gresley* and which returns to Carlisle via Glasgow with 60009 *Union of South Africa*.

27 Last 'County' 1011 *County of Chester* is used to head a special between Wolverhampton (Low Level) and Ruabon, where these were always rare.

U/D SR locos stored at Fratton are moved to Stratford; 30120, 30245, 30587, 30777 *Sir Lamiel*, 30850 *Lord Nelson*, 30925 *Cheltenham*. LNW 0-8-0 49395 also arrives from Crewe.

U/D 61313, having been repaired at Redhill, works trains to Reading, and an ECS train to Brighton, at the end of the month.

U/D 15 x V2s arrive at Swindon for scrap, though Stanier 2-6-0s 42945/54/75 are repaired here.

OCTOBER 1964

1ST   6233 *Duchess of Sutherland* and A1X 0-6-0T 32662 seen together on Ayr shed. During the month both move to Heads of Ayr, 32662 + 6233's tender then 6233 itself are plinthed outside the Camp, next to the main road.

1   61319 works an Inspection Saloon from York – Whitby and back. Prospective buyer for the Scarborough – Whitby line?

2   Most unusually, D5900 pilots D264 on the 7.54am from Sunderland into King's Cross.

3   61313 (41D) finally leaves Redhill and runs light engine to Clapham Jct., Cricklewood and back towards Canklow.

3   3442 *The Great Marquess* + 4472 *Flying Scotsman* double-head a special from Harrogate to Darlington. 4472 left King's Cross at 8am with the main train, 3442 left Leeds at 11.40am with a Leeds portion, joining at Harrogate. Southbound, the train splits at York, 3442 to Leeds, 4472 to London.

3   92021 passes Ayr with ECS for Stranraer, new ground for a 9F.

4   70020 *Mercury* enters King's Cross on a special, returning from York. Another welcome entry into the steam-free zone!

6   Special freight on the GC sees 92025 tow 35002 *Union Castle* + 35015 *Rotterdam Lloyd* + U 2-6-0 31793 towards Sheffield for scrapping.

7   4.20pm King's Cross – Leeds (the XP64 train) fails at Marshmoor. The following 4.22pm to Royston terminates at Brookmans Park, is then run on the down main line and pushes the 4.20 to Hatfield.

9   Down 'Aberdonian' limps into Hitchin behind D1568 (40B) – itself rare on a 'Deltic' diagram – and is replaced by D5903 to Peterborough, even rarer!

10   Preserved CR 4-2-2 123 heads a Buchanan Street – Callander return working.

10   The 'Warship' on the 9am from Waterloo fails and is assisted from Seaton Jct. to Sidmouth Jct. by 82030, a memorable pairing.

9-12   35007 *Aberdeen Commonwealth* heads LE along the Midland main line to Saltley (9th) to work a Birmingham – York special and back on the 11th. 35007 is then seen at Bedford (12th) on a fitted freight from Lawley Street (Birmingham).

12   4472 *Flying Scotsman* passes Reading (West) on a 'Farnborough Flyer' excursion. More new territory for the preserved A3.

12   Very late southbound 'Condor' noted at Bedford behind 70050 *Firth of Clyde*.

12   92002 reaches Weymouth on a parcels train from Wolverhampton, and
73093 (85B) + 45250 (9K Bolton) bring in a pigeon special from Crewe. All three locos depart together, coupled light engine, on the 15th.

13   Privately owned 2-6-2T 4555 makes a last run on Snow Hill – Stratford trains before going to Totnes for work on the preserved Ashburton branch.

15   D1624 breaks new ground for the class by reaching Barrow with a special BR party from Euston visiting Vickers-Armstrong.

15   U 2-6-0s 31616/24/21 observed being towed east along the LTS line to a scrapyard at Grays.

15   60154 *Bon Accord* noted at Shipley working a Hunslet – Carlisle freight. A1s are uncommon on this route.

17   Withdrawn WR gas turbine 18000 is seen dumped outside Market Harborough shed, formerly stored at Rugby Testing Station.

19	35001 *Channel Packet* appears on the WR line to Weymouth assisting D7090 from Evershot on the Kensington – Weymouth parcels. Unprecedented.
19/20	Scottish preserved locos 123/49/103/256/54398 all move from Dawsholm to Parkhead for storage, on closure of Dawsholm depot.
20	D6714 arrives at Feltham (first reported here) with freight from Purfleet.
21	60885 is a surprise guest at Manningham shed prior to working the 7.45pm Bradford (Valley) – Carlisle freight. Probably a unique occurrence.
21	Preserved locos V2 4771 *Green Arrow* + J15 0-6-0 1217E are towed from Doncaster to Hellifield for storage.
22	7808 *Cookham Manor* pilots D5287 (16A Toton) into Weymouth on a special freight working. The diesel returns straight away, but 7808 stays a few days for banking and station pilot duties.
23	D828 *Magnifcent* appears on the Hounslow loop with the diverted 7.45pm Exeter – Waterloo van train.
24	D7010 arrives in Waterloo from the West of England trailing stock of LMS/LNER/GWR origin, including a GWR 12-wheeled Buffet Car!
24	60009 *Union of South Africa* (61B) exits King's Cross with the 'Jubilee Requiem' railtour to Newcastle and back, the last A4 departure from London. 100mph reached on return run at Essendine.
24	70040 *Clive of India* brings the 'Royal Scot' into Glasgow – a rare event for this class – returning south with the 11.15pm to Birmingham.
24	Cliffe – Uddingston cement train is diverted via the GN/GE line through Lincoln behind D6558, the first seen here.
24	60130 *Kestrel* reaches New Street on the 9.20am Newcastle – Bristol. ER Pacifics do not often appear in Birmingham.
24	44558 is a stranger on Yeovil Town shed. S&D locos rarely stray this far.
26	45742 *Connaught* heads the 2pm Bradford (FS) – St Pancras as far as Leeds.
27	73080 *Merlin* (70G Weymouth!) seen on the Avonmouth line with the Clifton Down pick-up freight, an unexpected engine on this branch.
28	D1723 + D1032 *Western Marksman* combine to head the 10.45am from Paddington at Chippenham, not a regularly seen pairing.
28	70040 *Clive of India* arrives in Bradford (Forster Square) with the 1am from St Pancras. Later the 9.30pm to St Pancras is taken out by 72005 *Clan Macgregor*, both engines notable here, and only running from/to Leeds.
29	62005 is another notable sight at Forster Square on a parcels train from Leeds, and today the 9.30pm has 46160 *Queen Victoria's Rifleman* to Leeds, which is even more unusual than a 'Clan'!
29	70028 *Royal Star* works into Euston on the 10.15am from Birmingham, first steam on this train for many months.
30	2-6-4T 42410 + one brake/second deputises for the 8.17am Huddersfield to Penistone 2-car DMU. The four compartments available are somewhat full!
30	HM the Queen travels from Waterloo – Guildford in 4-CEP unit 7207, only the second time a SR Royal train has not included Pullman stock. (First was on 30 July, Arundel – Victoria and back).
U/D	Smoking accommodation reduced on WR expresses to South Wales and West of England from 70% (1st class) and 75% (2nd class) to 60% throughout.

U/D	A3s 60054/63 find their way to East Anglia at last, for scrap at Norwich.
U/D	Last week of the Chalford branch sees 'Hymek' Type 3 and Brush Type 4 diesels on the one-coach train, which is somewhat overpowered!
U/D	SR locos heading for South Wales scrapyards, currently at capacity, are held back at Bristol, with 30048/5, 31913, 34052/62/75/63 being recent arrivals.
U/D	Preserved locos assembling in Stratford for official storage includes 6000, 30120, 30245, 30587, 30777, 30850, 30925, 33001, 42500, 49395, 63460, 63601 and L&Y 1008.

NOVEMBER 1964

2ND	From this date, the 11pm working of the 'Brighton Belle' from Victoria calls at Haywards Heath, giving this station an all-Pullman train for the first time.
4	D5902 undergoes trial runs between Doncaster and Grantham before re-entering traffic. Rare to see these on other than London suburban workings.
7	70027 *Rising Star* takes the 11am Liverpool – Newcastle as far as Leeds.
9	9am Liverpool – Newcastle leaves with D181 piloting D172, unusually.
10	Ivatt 2-6-0 43072, with 21 wagons behind the tender, becomes out of control downhill and enters Adolphus Street Goods yard at 50mph. Engine turns on its side, falls 30 feet onto the road below, and is cut up on the spot. Sixth (and worst) such incident in Bradford area over the last eight years.
11	Up 'Thames-Clyde Express' passes through Shipley with D379 (1B) piloting 45254. Camden engines are rare sights between Leeds and Carlisle.
11	3pm Crewe – Banbury freight is headed by the odd combination D1685 + 48346.
12	Montrose witnesses the unusual trio of 80090/123/124 all present together, the first two on potato train workings. Two days earlier, J36 0-6-0 65319 (62B) arrived to return failed D5317 to Dundee.
12	61250 *A. Harold Bibby* (40B) arrives in King's Cross with a parcels train and 60112 *St. Simon* comes in with ECS – probably the last A3 to be seen this far south on a regular turn. Steam workings are few and far between now.
15	Ward's scrapyard at Killamarsh contains LT electric locos nos. 4, 6, 8, 10.
15	Remembrance service at Rugby shed has Stanier 2-6-0 42969 decorated with poppies. Engine itself is stored unserviceable awaiting withdrawal.
16	48646 (9M Bury) enters Scarborough on an extra coal train. First steam loco to arrive here for 47 days.
20	Remarkably, 60837 (50A) reaches St Pancras on a parcels train ex-Leicester. Only the second appearance here for this class.
24	61406 (40B) brings 18 parcel vans from Hull into Bradford (Forster Square), another rare class to reach this terminus.
26	D8586, in Works primer only, seen at Spondon on acceptance trials.
29	GWR railcar W4W observed at Swindon labelled 'To be moved to Hellifield for storage, thence to York Museum'.
30	Filming in Poole Harbour involves BR steamship *Roebuck* (renamed *Galtesund*) – first visit of a BR steamship here.
U/D	35029 *Elder Dempster Lines* is an extraordinarily unexpected sight at Bath Spa heading west on a parcels train!
U/D	61275 (50A) passes through Carstairs on the 1pm Carlisle – Millerhill freight. York

steam engines here are most unusual.

U/D   Several Sunday trains from Waterloo – Bournemouth/Weymouth are diverted via Romsey from Eastleigh, involving no less than three reversals. Southampton tunnel engineering works are the cause.

U/D   Departmental J72 0-6-0Ts 58, 59 are to be employed at Blyth shipping staithes to defrost coal wagons during winter weather to facilitate tipping.

U/D   45198 noted at Cowlairs Works paired with tender 9002 (built 1933 and equipped with roller bearings) which went to America in that year behind 'Royal Scot' 6152 – masquerading as 6100 – on its official tour.

U/D   D9003 *Meld* and D9014 *The Duke of Wellington's Regiment* are used on water pick-up tests at 80, 90, 100mph on Wiske Moor troughs (York – Darlington).

DECEMBER 1964

2ND   60140 *Balmoral* heads the 2.39pm Carlisle – Stourton freight throughout.

4   61010 *Wildebeeste* arrives in Scarborough on the 1.20pm from Hull. First steam on a passenger train into the resort for 3 months.

4   O4 2-8-0 63607 (36E) reaches Hitchin on an up coal train, a rare class here.

5   D9006 is named *The Fife & Forfar Yeomanry* at a ceremony at Cupar station.

5   44334 (15E Leicester Central) appears at Cardiff (General) on the 12noon from Cheltenham! 4F's are rare anyway, but one from 15E is unheard of.

5   FA Cup 2nd round brings two football excursions, each of 12-coach 'Hastings' line DEMUs, through from Gillingham (Kent) to...Luton!

5   Seven SR Pacifics 34020/30/65/78/80, 34106/7 reach Llanelly for scrapping.

6   70020 *Mercury* leaves Broad Street with an enthusiasts' special, which it works to Havant, and back from Eastleigh. In between, train has 34072 *257 Squadron* to Southampton, then USA 0-6-0Ts 30069/73 tour the docks and take the train to Eastleigh.

7   Up morning 'Talisman' is diverted via Carlisle; 'Deltics' are rarely seen here.

7   60112 *St. Simon* is an unprecedented visitor to St Pancras (Goods) on the 4.55am freight from Derby. The A3 is serviced at Cricklewood before leaving Marylebone on the 8.28pm to Preston, as far as Sheffield.

9   J38 0-6-0 65929 is surprise power for the 11.15am Carlisle – Millerhill freight. J38s almost never reach Carlisle.

9   62044 (51A) passes through Derby on a southbound freight, whilst D5696 (30A) arrives with GE line EMU stock for the C&W Works and returns with a train of repaired EMUs an hour later.

11   D1021 *Western Cavalier* comes into Weymouth on a train from Bristol, deputising for a DMU set.

12   D1568 (40B Immingham) is observed juxtaposed with a BR/Sulzer Type 2 (60A Inverness) at Waverley. A rare pair of shedplates to be seen together.

13,20,27 70002 *Geoffrey Chaucer* departs Waverley with the 11.10am (SuO) to Liverpool. 72006 *Clan Mackenzie* has this train on the 20th, and 70005 *John Milton* on the 27th. BR Pacifics are generally uncommon in Edinburgh.

14   D173 (52A) hauls the 9.15am freight from Whitemoor through to Yarmouth. First 'Peak' seen east of Ely.

15   D1719 (86A Ebbw Jct.) astonishingly appears in the loco yard at King's Cross at 9.50am,

but leaves Paddington at 5.10pm for...Wolverhampton. Is it lost?

16   45303 (6A) arrives in Paddington, with a parcels train from Birmingham.

16   7026 *Tenby Castle* brings a football special from Hereford into Weymouth.

17   82024 seen at Hastings (a first) on a parcels train from Eastbourne.

18   'Western' diesel arrives in New Street (unusual here) on a relief ex-Plymouth.

20   73009 (67A) is returned to Corkerhill ex-Works from...Darlington!

20   92241 reaches Redhill on a special, coming in from the Reading direction.

20   70021 *Morning Star* crosses Ribblehead viaduct on the up 'Thames-Clyde Express', standing-in for a Type 4 diesel.

21   Q1 0-6-0 33006 heads a Brighton – Hastings parcels train, followed by the local freight from Lewes to Crowborough, first Q1 seen on this turn for years.

21,23,26   44770 (6J!) brings a parcels train into Weymouth. Then works local services to Bournemouth (23rd), and heads north on one coach forming the 6.8pm Weymouth – Westbury on 26th, in lieu of a failed DMU.

22   73113 *Lyonnesse* + N 2-6-0 31831 head the 4.4pm Redhill – Reading. Most unusual power.

22   48374 powers the Feltham – Alton special fertiliser freight which the 8F then proceeds to work through to Farringdon, an unprecedented sight in the Meon Valley.

23   72005 *Clan Macgregor* (12A) arrives Marylebone (rare here) on the 2.35am ex-Leicester (London Rd.), departing on the 2.38pm to Nottingham (Victoria).

24   D9017 *The Durham Light Infantry* runs through Newark piloting 60124 *Kenilworth* on the 10.15am Newcastle – King's Cross, very unusual pairing.

24   62059 brings the 8.50am Manchester (Exchange) – Newcastle into its destination, having replaced 60118 *Archibald Sturrock* at Darlington.

25   72006 *Clan Mackenzie* + 60007 *Sir Nigel Gresley* double-head the 1.30pm Aberdeen – Glasgow, a unique combination! (72006 had been booked to work the fish train, cancelled on Christmas Day).

26   34042 *Dorchester* works through to Bristol on the Portsmouth – Cardiff.

27   73088 *Joyous Gard* (70A) noted on Willesden shed!

28   61337 (50A) brings some variety to Liverpool (Lime Street) with the ECS for the 12.15pm to Bridlington.

28   34038 *Lynton* + D1073 *Western Bulwark* pass through Feltham with an empty parcels train towards London. Another combination thought to be unique!

30   7.17am East Grinstead – London Bridge is headed by 80068. First steam passenger train on the Oxted line (and at London Bridge) for many months.

30   73029 (2B Oxley) reaches Nutfield (east of Redhill) on freight.

30   61327 heads the 7.40am Bristol – Bradford between Leeds (City) and Forster Square. First B1 on a passenger train here for some time.

U/D   Snowplough tenders, ex-'Schools', converted at Eastleigh, are sent to Salisbury, Ashford, Basingstoke and Redhill. Five converts from V2 tenders go to Banbury, Shrewsbury and three to Crewe.

U/D   8.5am York – Derby parcels brings the following to Derby during the month; 60146 *Peregrine*, 60877/884, 60106 *Flying Fox* and 60112 *St. Simon*. All return LE to York, except 60112, which goes to St Pancras on the 7th!

U/D   NER DC Bo-Bo electrics 26500/1, due to be towed to Tweedmouth shed for storage, in fact go to Hellifield MPD instead.

U/D	70035 *Rudyard Kipling* breaks new ground by working throughout on the 10.30am Aberdeen – Edinburgh (Millerhill) freight.
U/D	Bo-Bo 10800 emerges from Brush Works (Loughborough) in green with 'Research Locomotive' painted on each side.
U/D	Severe gales cause Vauxhall cars to be blown off a northbound car carrier whilst crossing the exposed Ribblehead Viaduct!

JANUARY 1965

1ST	10.8am from York arrives in Bournemouth (Central) with 76012 piloting 6996 *Blackwell Hall*, and 35029 *Ellerman Lines* pushing in the rear!
1-7	35026 *Lamport & Holt Line* heads the 2pm Weymouth – Yeovil daily, a stranger on this WR route.
3,4	60007 *Sir Nigel Gresley*, 60106 *Flying Fox* appear on Kingmoor shed. Both work freights next day to Millerhill, Leeds respectively.
4	BR's ban on steam locos south of Crewe now operates. Big rise in steam workings in the London area noted! A 'Britannia' seen on Euston ECS duty!
5	246 *Morayshire* (ex-62712) leaves Kittybrewster (61A) after restoration at Inverurie Works, and is towed south towards Glasgow.
9	Three Shrewsbury – Manchester (Piccadilly) football specials are headed by 73053/90/95 throughout. Two specials reach Sheffield (Mid) with 70004 *William Shakespeare* and 70030 *William Wordsworth*, from Birmingham, all notable workings nowadays.
11	60004 *William Whitelaw* heads the 12.7pm Aberdeen – Edinburgh. A4s are normally confined to the Glasgow route, so this is unusual.
13	Variety at Yeovil; on view are a 3-car cross-country DMU, 75001, 76005, 82035, 80xxx, 0-6-0PT 6419, WC Pacific, 0-4-2T 1442, Ivatt 2-6-2Ts 41283/90, D7069 and railbuses W79975/8. Interesting!
17	46241 *City of Edinburgh* seen at Oxley, for scrap at Cashmore's, nearby.
20	5.11pm Leeds – Manchester stopper is a Lincoln-based 2-car Derby unit displaying 'Pinxton' on the destination blind!
23,24	45674 *Duncan* arrives at Bournemouth with a parcels train from Crewe, then pilots 35030 *Elder Dempster Lines* to Weymouth on the 'Royal Wessex'! 45674 leaves Weymouth (24th) with freight for Wolverhampton.
25	7.40pm Holyhead – Birmingham has D327 as pilot to 80132 (for steam heat) between Llandudno and Chester, strange sight nonetheless.
28	Inter-City DMU set makes a trial run from Glasgow to Aberdeen in 2 hours 35 minutes, with one stop at Perth.
30	34051 *Winston Churchill* hauls its namesake's funeral train of five Pullmans and one van, from Victoria to Handborough, north of Oxford (Evesham line).
30	70000 *Britannia* (5A) arrives in Weymouth with empty vans from Crewe.
30	60952 is observed on Skipton shed, surprisingly.
30	D302, with brake tender, arrives at Willesden on a coal train. First brake tender seen this far south on West Coast main line.
30	D1659, in undercoat, takes empty coaching stock over Shap.
30	One of four football specials for the Southampton v Crystal Palace match is formed of two 6-car 'Hastings' sets, which had worked up to London Bridge as the 6.43am from

	Eastbourne and Eridge. 12-car trains rare on this route.
30	NBL Type 2s used on the Sidmouth/Exmouth branches, a new class here.
U/D	Ivatt 2-6-2Ts 41248/9 are used to power DMU replacement services between Taunton and Barnstaple. First of this class seen on this line.
U/D	The two oldest vehicles in BR stock are both GWR bullion vans, W819/20 built 1904/5 and last overhauled at Swindon 9/64 and 1/65 respectively.
U/D	BR launches its 'Corporate Identity' image at the Design Centre in the Haymarket, London Jan. 5-23. 'British Rail' and the new double-arrow symbol are introduced.

FEBRUARY 1965

3-7	44867 (9B) (ex-Cowlairs Works) seen on ECS duties at Waverley on 5th; works football special Waverley – Falkirk and back (6th), heads 10am Waverley – Treherbert piloted by 45364 (7th). This special had arrived on 3rd for the rugby International; the last to arrive (on 6th) enters Waverley behind 61099 piloting 70038 *Robin Hood*, which then leaves on the 10.40am to Merthyr double-headed by 80113 (64G) on 7th. All return specials are diverted via Hellifield/Blackburn due to theft of telegraph wires between Carlisle and Penrith.
4	XP64 stock now forms the 'Ulster Express' (Euston – Heysham). Stock will transfer to South Wales services from Paddington on 1 March.
4,6	Ivatt 2-6-0 43006 (12D Tebay) surprisingly works the 10.36am Cardiff to Portsmouth out of Eastleigh. Arrives in Andover with freight off the MSWJ line two days later, whilst running-in from Eastleigh Works.
6	60157 *Great Eastern* works the Uddingston – Cliffe cement train. Rare!
10	7029 *Clun Castle* brings the 7am Reading – Southampton into Basingstoke.
11,12	D1727 pilots 45689 *Ajax* (5A) into Weymouth on a troop train. 45689 itself pilots a 'Hall' out of Weymouth on next day .
13	Double-heading day! 9am Liverpool – Newcastle exits Huddersfield behind D186 + D272; the 11am behind D277 + D346 and the 3pm has Caprotti duo 73144 + 73136.
13	Hellifield shed (now under the Curator of Historical Relics) contains V2 4771 *Green Arrow*, J17 1217E, NER electrics 26500/1, LNWR 1439.
15,19	60835 *The Green Howard* (64A) pilots D381 (1B) on the Thornton – Milford Haven oil tanks over the Waverley Route. Is this St Margarets/Camden pairing unique? Combination is 60052 *Prince Palatine* + 60835 on 19th.
17	70047 (6J) noted at Cardiff (East Dock) shed, having hauled 46168 *The Girl Guide* + 45577 *Bengal* + 34099 *Lynmouth* to Swansea for scrap.
19	Up 'North Briton' fails at Morpeth. D6793 is coupled ahead of D1578 as far as Newcastle, an uncommon pairing.
22-24	34051 *Winston Churchill* hauls 34045 *Ottery St. Mary*, 34056 *Croydon*, 34096 *Trevone*, 34105 *Swanage*, to scrapyards in South Wales, in two trips.
22-24	45660 *Rooke* (55A!) seen on Old Oak Common, then Southall (23rd) and works the 12.50am Southall – Crewe freight (24th), an out of place 'Jubilee'!
23,24	D5244 arrives in Weymouth with freight ex-Nottingham, departing next day as pilot to 35028 *Clan Line* on the 5.20pm to Westbury!
26	No fewer than 20 LMS locos are at Eastleigh, either for scrap or overhaul.
27	70051 *Firth of Forth* enters Paddington, from Wolverhampton. Uncommon!

27	Darlington Works has, uniquely, examples of A1/2/3/4's all at once. 60131 *Osprey*, 60528 *Tudor Minstrel*, 60532 *Blue Peter*, 4472 *Flying Scotsman*, 60019 *Bittern* and 60034 *Lord Faringdon* respectively.
U/D	0-6-0 3208 (the snowplough loco at Llandudno Junction) works through Blaenau Festiniog to Trawsfynydd, first GWR engine from this direction.
U/D	Progress? 12noon Manchester – Holyhead was an 8-coach steam train (with Miniature Buffet), is now a Derby lightweight DMU on a 4½ hour run.
U/D	Former Duke of Sutherland's 0-4-4T *Dunrobin* and private saloon, (on the RH&D since 1950) are sold to Canada, and exported from London Docks.

MARCH 1965

1ST	44853 works a fish-empties special to Immingham to meet the arrival of a whale boat. Similar train runs next day behind D6803.
2	J38 0-6-0 65901 noted at Insch, first steam north of Inverurie for some time.
3	9.42am Newcastle – Liverpool finally leaves at 11.15! Booked 'Peak' fails on Heaton, replacement also fails. 60810 is supplied but refused by the driver, 60146 *Peregrine* is then commandeered and train departs.
4	Heavy snow falls and…down 'Cambrian Coast Express' is formed of a Blue Pullman set and terminates at Shrewsbury; points freeze at Rugby, some trains are 7 hours late into Euston, up 'Condor' arrives at Hendon 12 hours late, and there's a complete power signalling failure at Woking.
5	7816 *Frilsham Manor* (tender lettered GWR!) reaches Eastleigh with vans.
6	Down 'Mid-day Scot' passes Warrington behind, unusually, D119.
6	45694 *Bellerophon* (56A) reaches Oxford on the York – Bournemouth.
6	D5100 (50A) brings a Hull football special into Bristol (Stapleton Road); York locos are rare here.
6	Preserved K4 3442 *The Great Marquess* + 62005 seen at Whitby double-heading a last-day tour of local lines before their closure.
7	35022 *Holland America Line* heads an Exeter – Waterloo special non-stop from Yeovil Junction – 122.9 miles, a new SR record. (No water troughs).
7	35014 *Nederland Line* occupies Redhill shed until 23 April. (Hot-box).
7	U 2-6-0 31639 + Q1 33006 appear at Rugby (Midland) double-heading an enthusiasts' excursion. Unprecedented sight here!
10	5.5pm Baldock – King's Cross is surprisingly worked by D9020 *Nimbus*.
11	'Crab' 42751 (9G) passes Hereford with banana vans for Barry Docks.
12,13	Two school specials from Plymouth, Paignton are worked throughout to Gatwick Airport by D806 *Cambrian*, D822 *Hercules* respectively.
13	8-car 'Birmingham Pullman' set forms a RU supporters' special from Coventry to… West Hartlepool (!) for the County Championship Final. 70020 *Mercury* is another strange arrival on a RU excursion ex-Coventry.
13	D7058 (81A) heads a circus train from Ascot to Tyseley, throughout.
17	Preserved MR 2-4-0 158A and 4-2-2 118, and LTS 4-4-2 80, ex-store at Derby Works, are hauled to Hellifield by a Type 2 diesel.
18	Surprise! D870 *Zulu* is seen at New Street on the 'Devonian'.
20	D1661 is named *North Star* by Ray Gunter (Minister of Labour) at Paddington and pulls

a 10-coach special to Temple Meads, where D1662 is named *Isambard Kingdom Brunel* by the Lord Mayor of Bristol.

20 70043 *Lord Kitchener* (5A) + 9F double-head a freight into Cardiff.

22,28 Steam in Victoria. U 2-6-0 31809 arrives with ECS for a 1st class-only special to Brighton. On 28th 73022 works a Highbridge train, returning with 35023 *Holland-Afrika Line*, only the second MN here since 1959.

26,28 Cardiff – Paris excursion is hauled to Newhaven by D1737. This works the 4.40am Eastbourne newspaper train from London Bridge as far as Haywards Heath, then LE to Newhaven for the return working in two days time.

27 7029 *Clun Castle* reaches Nottingham (Midland) on an enthusiasts' special from Paddington via the Lickey incline; returning via Northampton, Bletchley and High Wycombe. 7029 is serviced at Nottingham shed.

27 Excursions to Aintree for the Grand National include four running non-stop from Euston; a Swansea train formed of a Pullman diesel set, and one from Grimsby with three Pullman cars plus a 'Devon Belle' observation car.

27 D1064 *Western Regent* heads the 7.40am Birkenhead – Paddington between Chester and Wolverhampton (despite a 'hydraulic' ban on LMR lines).

29 6830 *Buckenhill Grange* propels a new-build snowplough north through Basingstoke.

30 48671 runs light through Portslade – first 8F seen here since a batch was built new at Brighton in 1943 – having been for weighing at Brighton MPD.

31 92214 (86E Severn Tunnel Junction) pulls a Healey Mills – Aston goods.

U/D Brush Type 4s from 86A (Ebbw Junction), 87E (Landore) run through to Edinburgh via the Waverley Route on Milford Haven – Thornton oil trains.

U/D Good progress is being made installing 16¾ miles of 1500V DC wiring that extends the Manchester – Sheffield electrification into Tinsley yard.

U/D 60062 *Minoru*, 60106 *Flying Fox* arrive at Norwich – for cutting up.

U/D 46163 *Civil Service Rifleman* reaches Pontymister – again for scrap.

U/D 6831 *Bearley Grange* found in steam at Crewe North shed, rare visitor here.

U/D 'Peak' appears for repair at Brush Works (Loughborough), first to be dealt with on a four-year Brush/BR contract for repairs to Type 2,3,4 diesels.

U/D 90686 (8F Springs Branch Wigan) reaches Weymouth on a perishables train from Wigan – and is then used on station pilot duties!

U/D LMS Co-Co 10000 works a Neasden – Woodford Halse goods.

U/D Leeds Corporation Transport prohibits railway guards from carrying detonators while travelling by bus!

U/D Butlin's Holiday Camps now have all of the following on show:

Ayr	6233 *Duchess of Sutherland*	A1X 0-6-0T 32665
Minehead	6229 *Duchess of Hamilton*	A1X 0-6-0T 32678
Pwllheli	6203 *Princess Margaret Rose*	A1X 0-6-0T 32640
Skegness	6100 *Royal Scot*	B4 0-4-0T 30102

U/D 10 March-6 April. BR sends 5-man team to the Southern Pacific Railroad (USA) to investigate and report on the maintenance of diesel locos.

APRIL 1965

3**RD** 7029 *Clun Castle* heads a special from Snow Hill to Swindon, returning via Gloucester and the Lickey bank to King's Norton, with diesel into New Street.

3 6819 *Highnam Grange*, unusually, works a Wrexham – Brymbo freight.

4 D5695 (30A) leaves King's Cross on a special to Hull for the Hudson Bay Launch Co., with a 'Devon Belle' observation car at the rear.

6 D1036 *Western Emperor* reaches Crewkerne; ballast from Menheniot quarry.

8 70042 *Lord Roberts* works a Chester to Stratford-on-Avon special throughout.

8 D6507 stalls on Falmer bank with the 6.25am Victoria – Brighton. 80034 assists in the rear, all the way to Brighton!

9 London Transport 0-6-0PT L94 runs light from Lillie Bridge to Eastleigh for Works attention, a surprising movement.

9 9.40pm St Enoch – Euston sleeper departs behind 73101 + 73102. Consecutively numbered double-headers are always noteworthy!

10 Snowplough sandwich! N 2-6-0 31405 leaves Brighton for Eastbourne propelling one and hauling another.

11 4079 *Pendennis Castle*, now in GWR livery, is received by the GWR Society at Swindon. Prior to this 4079 had worked Swindon – Gloucester trains and the 4.15pm Paddington – Banbury, the only steam duty out of the terminus.

14 D1742 (86A Canton) reaches Newcastle on a Gloucester extra.

15 D8005/44 depart Euston on a 14-coach Good Friday relief to Liverpool.

15 D9001 *St. Paddy* fails at Welwyn Garden City on the down 'Heart of Midlothian'. D5062 assists, forming an unusual pairing.

17 Hellifield receives GWR railcar W4W and 44027, for official storage.

19 34089 *602 Squadron* enters Stratford-on-Avon with an excursion from Poole.

19 Six 'Jubilee' hauled excursions pass through Mirfield, (five for Belle Vue).

19,20 45006 heads a Wolverhampton to Weston-super-Mare excursion all the way, takes the ECS to Bridgwater and is serviced at Taunton. 45006 reaches Bournemouth (Central) next day on a relief to the 'Pines Express'.

19,20 44915 (1E Bletchley) works the 3.35pm Waterloo – Bournemouth, returning to London (20th) on the 6.22am from Central. Shades of 1953!

20 D6938 is a surprise arrival in Weymouth on a train from Bristol.

21 Steel Co. of Wales's diesel shunter derails at Margam on the main line. Down 'Capitals United Express' (headed by D1060 *Western Dominion*) is hauled at slow speed by a BR shunter through Margam yard to avoid the blockage.

24 70052 *Firth of Tay* heads the last steam tour out of St Pancras, to Nottingham. 70052 is serviced at Toton whilst 44401 + 61406 continue the tour.

24 D1576 heads an FA Amateur Cup special from Whitby – King's Cross (via Middlesbrough) with assistance from an EE Type 4 to Battersby.

27 70030 *William Wordsworth* reaches Llanelly with condemned coaches.

27 Surprise steam on the Merton branch; N 2-6-0 31873 with a weed-killing train.

30 'Pines Express' arrives in Snow Hill behind the exceptional combination of 6856 *Stowe Grange* piloting 70011 *Hotspur*.

U/D Bristol (Barrow Road) hosts 35001 *Channel Packet*, *en route* for scrap.

U/D   Green SR coaches transferred to WR appear on 6.55am Taunton – Bristol and 8.40am Bristol – New Street, adding colour to the scene.

MAY 1965

1ST   Cup Final day. Twenty five specials run Liverpool – Euston (electric to Rugby, then diesel). Six run Sheffield – King's Cross, all EE Type 4s.

4   60154 *Bon Accord* passes Shipley on an excursion from Edinburgh.

4,5   61030 *Nyala* (56B) is a rarity on the 6.57pm Sheffield (Midland) to Manchester (Central) and return working, on successive days.

5   LMS Co-Co 10001 + brake tender heads a down freight through Willesden.

5   D1801 is a rare pilot to D9012 *Crepello* on the 9.30am from Queen Street, seen at Newark.

6,7,14   Ivatt 2-6-0 43063 (9F Heaton Mersey) works into Brockenhurst on a ballast train; is seen at Nine Elms (70A) on 7th, heads 1.35pm van train from Southampton Docks to Waterloo (14th). Running-in ex-Eastleigh Works.

7   D175 (52A) is a surprise arrival Exeter (St Davids), having worked the car train from Newcastle throughout.

8   Rugby League Cup final attracts 21 specials into King's Cross from Leeds, including D31 (55A). Another reaches St Pancras behind D277 (52A). Holbeck, Gateshead engines are rare in King's Cross, St Pancras respectively.

8   45531 *Sir Frederick Harrison* seen at Harrogate, heading the 5-coach portion of the 11.34am to King's Cross as far as Leeds. Unprecedented.

8   70046 *Anzac* appears at Severn Tunnel Junction on a pigeon special.

8   60024 *Kingfisher* fails at Larbert with the 1.30pm Aberdeen – Glasgow and is taken to Grangemouth for attention, first A4 noted here.

8   D9010 is named *The King's Own Scottish Borderer* at Dumfries and then works the 2.58pm troop special to Inverness, as far as Perth.

9   0-6-2T 6604 uses the wheel-drop facility at Llandudno Junction MPD.

9   Restored A3 4472 *Flying Scotsman* powers a special from Paddington to Gobowen for 550 overseas visitors to celebrate VE-day and to see the 'real' Britain, including a civic welcome at Shrewsbury.

10   Clapham Junction signalbox gantry sags and threatens immediate collapse, at 8.35am. Chaos ensues with all trains in/out of Waterloo stopped. Boat trains diverted to Victoria and other services start/finish at Surbiton, Wimbledon or Woking. Emergency repairs completed for next day's traffic.

10   D9013 *The Black Watch* is seen at Newark on train 4E02, the up 'Presflo' cement empties!

12,19   'Coventry Cathedral' special arrives from Portsmouth behind 73115 *King Pellinore* (70D). One from Bexhill (19th) has D6529 (73C).

14   D5531 (32A!) seen at Euston on 12.50pm ex-Bangor. Rare!

15   Restored A3 4472 *Flying Scotsman* reaches Dumfries on a special from Lincoln, returning the train to Carlisle via Lockerbie and the CR main line.

15   2.50pm Edinburgh – Carlisle fails at Hawick. 78047 + 76049 combine to take the service forward, a pairing rarely, if ever, seen before.

16   'Peak' on the Bristol – Sheffield fails at Gloucester; D7004 + 48095 take the train on to New Street. Surprise arrival!

16   Two 4-car sets of London Underground stock go to Micheldever for storage.

16,30 Three Territorial Army specials are run to/from Stranraer behind. 45573, 72006/8 (*Newfoundland, Clan Mackenzie, Clan Macleod*) to Carlisle. They return to Stranraer (30th) behind 72006/8, 72007 *Clan Mackintosh.*

19 Horsham; 3-car set of Waterloo & City tube stock arrives on a trial trip from Stewarts Lane! A remarkable sight.

20 'Royal Scot' is diverted via Leeds and the S&C line due to a derailment at Hest Bank. Down train passes Shipley behind D210 *Empress of Britain.*

21 44680 (5A) reaches Eastbourne shed after working to Hastings on a pigeon special from York. Steam on Central Division is banned from 14 June.

22 D5228, D7584 both take excursions to Skegness, a rare class here.

23 Two 'Merchant Navy's reach Westbury; 35005 *Canadian Pacific* passes on an Eastleigh – Swindon special and 35017 *Belgian Marine* comes in from Exeter, with 7029 *Clun Castle* taking over to Bristol.

26 S15 4-6-0 30838 heads the Bournemouth (West) – York through Eastleigh.

26 Three educational excursions arrive in Southampton; D7040 from Bridgwater, D5527 (Enfield), D5399 (Bedford), all unusual types here.

27 Ivatt 2-6-0 43007 is pressed into service after overhaul at Eastleigh Works, working the 4.40pm Bournemouth (Central) – Eastleigh. Unusual power!

29 73021 (85B) brings the first steam-hauled passenger train for a long time into Bognor Regis – an excursion from Slough. 73021 is serviced at Fratton.

29 D225 *Lusitania* (9A) is the first EE Type 4 seen on the South Eastern Division, with ECS to Folkestone (including the SR Ambulance car) forming a pilgrimage special Lourdes – Workington, which D225 takes to Barrow.

29 Restored A3 4472 *Flying Scotsman* brings a special from Nottingham into Clapham Junction and proceeds via Richmond, Reading to Swindon before returning to Nottingham by ascending the Lickey incline.

30 12-car DMU excursion train fails at Seamer on the way to Scarborough. 61123 is attached to the rear and pushes the ensemble to its destination.

U/D Last regular steam-hauled passenger train in South Wales is the Severn Tunnel car-ferry to/from Pilning; usually a number of carflats and two coaches headed by a WR 2-6-2T.

U/D Green 73026 seen in Cowlairs Works, and 75012 at St Rollox, a type hitherto unknown north of Carlisle. St Rollox Works also contains, surprisingly, D8236 (34G Finsbury Park!).

U/D EE Type 3s in pairs, run trials between Bristol and Paddington, down on the 'Bristolian', up on the 12.15pm from Temple Meads.

JUNE 1965

1ST D251 passes Otley (uncommon here) on a Newcastle – Ilkley charter.

4 48544 (1E) works a 20-van pigeon special from Newcastle down the Brighton main line to Hove, a rare sight; returns with the empties on 8th.

4 'Tees-Tyne Pullman' arrives in Durham behind D5589/95 following a 'Deltic' failure. Unusual to see Brush Type 2s so far north.

5 60835 *The Green Howard* heads a military special from Dundee throughout between Edinburgh and Appleby (!) via Hawick and Carlisle.

5 70033 *Charles Dickens* reaches Bournemouth (West) on the Liverpool portion of the 'Pines Express'.

5	62057 and 70053 *Moray Firth* both seen at Cardiff East Dock shed after working special coal trains, aftermath of miners' strike 24 May to 2 June.
6	D5904 arrives in Skegness with an excursion from London. Most unusual to see this type outside the London suburbs.
7	0-6-0PTs 9669, 4683 both work Wrexham – New Brighton services on retimed DMU workings consisting of five non-corridors.
7	Blackpool (North) – Central now closed – sees departure of 39 returning Whit Monday specials, 34 of which are steam-hauled.
7	2.11pm fish train leaves Aberdeen with a NBL Type 2 piloting an A4.
7	Polmadie contains 60124 *Kenilworth*, 60134 *Foxhunter* and 60154 *Flamboyant*, the last two being surprising visitors from Neville Hill.
7	D1766 on a return Preston – York excursion is the last passenger train between Arthington and Skipton.
8	Brush Type 4 D1660 is named *City of Truro* at Truro station.
9	D89 is named *The Honourable Artillery Company* at Broad Street.
9	First through working from Penzance to Edinburgh since 1920s (?) is for a Jehovah's Witnesses party, arriving in Waverley behind 60027 *Merlin*.
9,11	44666 (2E Saltley) leaves Paddington on the 4.15pm to Banbury. 7029 *Clun Castle* heads the last steam duty – the 4.15pm – on the 11th.
12	0-6-2T 6604 seen shunting at Chester after its long stay at Llandudno Jct.
13/14	Another Jehovah's Witnesses party special leaves Waverley at 8.55pm with a complete set of SR green coaches behind D1510 bound for Bournemouth, where it arrives next day behind D12, uncommon diesels here.
14	Summer timetable starts. **BR now uses the 24 hour clock in all timetables.**
14	'Pines Express' is 'Hymek'-hauled between Bournemouth and Oxford.
16,17	48408 (1E Bletchley) works the following; 16.12 Southampton – Bournemouth, 18.40 Bournemouth – Woking, plus the 08.21 Basingstoke – Waterloo and 17.09 Waterloo – Basingstoke commuter services next day, a class of train an 8F would never be chosen to work on home territory!
19	D7059/76 both visit the East Anglian coast on excursion traffic.
19,20,27	Excursions to Cleethorpes. On 19th,20th Ollerton, Edwinstowe run five specials. On 27th Ollerton runs four more – 50 coaches, 2,800 passengers plus extra buses! Both originating stations are 'closed', though no statutory notices have been posted, contrary to the 1962 Act, and the timetabled service withdrawn without notification. Langwith, Whitwell (both also 'closed') send four specials on 20th as well. All miners' holiday traffic.
20	'Trans-Pennine' DMU operates a Leeds – Towyn excursion. Section from Shrewsbury to Towyn opens specially as no Sunday trains usually run.
21	'Britannia' 70047 works the pick-up freight at Evesham, an odd sight!
22	6841 *Marlas Grange* pilots 44691 into Weymouth on a pigeon special, an uncommon combination.
24	61022 *Sassaby* (56A) penetrates to Shrewsbury on empty wagons from the NER. Wakefield engines are complete strangers in Shropshire.
26	45627 *Sierra Leone* is piloted from Carstairs to Carlisle by D8122 on the 14.00 Glasgow – Liverpool, and D8085 pilots 70009 *Alfred the Great* as far as Kilmarnock on the 13.35 Glasgow – Morecambe, both uncommon pairings.
26	6861 *Crynant Grange* arrives LE from the north (Annesley?) into Nottingham (Victoria),

and departs on the 11.15 parcels to Marylebone, a big surprise!

28 Queen visits Clydeside and – for the first time – uses 2nd class accommodation on the Glasgow blue train between Helensburgh (Central) and Dalmuir Park.

30 45398 hauls GE-line EMU stock through to Eastleigh Works for repair.

U/D Bo-Bo AC electrics E3088, E3114 observed being towed through Castleford to Darlington for bogie rotation tests on the turntable at the MPD. E3068/174 do the same; very strange to see these away from electrified lines

U/D 'South Wales Pullman' noted formed of replacement loco-hauled stock consisting of only three Pullman cars plus XP64 stock.

JULY 1965

2ND Weymouth portion of the down 'Royal Wessex' is headed by 80138.

2 34086 *219 Squadron* arrives in Cardiff on a returning miners' holiday special.

3 Scarborough sees D360 (64B) leave on the 10.25 to Glasgow, D5048 (32B) on the 12.37 to Sheffield and D1585 (87E) arrive on the 14.12 ex-King's Norton. That's Haymarket, Ipswich, Landore diesels in one day – at Scarborough!

3 73042 (70G) works the Weymouth – Wolverhampton (Low Level) throughout. Weymouth engines rarely venture so far afield.

3 Ramblers' excursion from Bradford (Forster Square) to Whitby fails to stop at Shipley, and is held in Leeds for those left to join the 09.10 Bradford – Bristol. 'Peak' hauling this fails and is rescued by 2-6-4T 42138. Walking replanned.

3 11.10 ex-Ilfracombe arrives into Snow Hill behind 7912 *Little Linford Hall* piloted by Ivatt 2-6-0 46442, a really odd combination.

4 Ex-Crosti 92028 brings freight into Basingstoke; a type rarely seen here.

4 D7026/46 are infrequent visitors to Ramsgate, on specials ex-WR.

6 35014 *Nederland Line*, 35019 *French Line CGT* both arrive in Feltham yard on well-loaded freights from Southampton, unusual work for this class.

6 D5837 (41A) is a rarity in Waverley on a special from Doncaster, as neither Brush Type 2s nor Darnall engines ever normally reach here.

9 70010 *John of Gaunt* (12A) works the 14.10 Tees Yard – Doncaster freight, and D1727 (81A!) heads the 21.40 Doncaster – Bounds Green.

11 Strangely, 2-6-4T 42161 (16J Rowsley) appears in Doncaster station.

14 'Peak' hauling the 17.10 Newcastle – Liverpool fails and another, D175, then propels the service from Leeds to Huddersfield, where D175 goes to the front!

16 17.00 ex-Paddington reaches Carmarthen with D1660 *City of Truro* + D1642, a 5500hp combination!

16/17 D1707 (81A!) powers the 19.00 ex-Glasgow into Marylebone.

16/17 D382 takes the 22.05 Hull – Paignton down the Lickey.

17 Derailment causes the up 'Thames-Clyde Express' and the up 'Waverley' to be diverted into Euston behind D45, D73 respectively.

17 Ivatt 2-6-0 46511 heads the 14.35 Birkenhead – Paddington between Chester and Shrewsbury, a small-engine choice for an express!

17 46115 *Scots Guardsman* exits Waverley on the 09.50 to Leeds via Carlisle, whilst 60836 departs Princes Street on the 10.55 relief to Manchester piloted by a '5'. Regional role-reversal in Edinburgh!

18,19	D206 (30A) heads the up 'Condor' and the return working next day, failing on Polmadie. First Stratford loco on 'Condor', and at 66A?
20	All traffic in/out of King's Cross halted for a while due to torrential rain and severe thunderstorms causing flooding in Gasworks Tunnel.
21	Ivatt 2-6-2T 41301 powers the 18.55 Weymouth – Feltham freight all the way, but has to take extra coal at Basingstoke! Odd choice for long-distance work.
24	70045 *Lord Rowallan* (2B Oxley) reaches Basingstoke on the 08.47 Wolverhampton – Portsmouth, returning on the 10.42 Poole – Sheffield.
24	King's Cross – Hull train is headed by D1870 + D6742, a rare combination.
24	10.50 Inverness – Glasgow has D8032 (60A) working solo, as is D8092 (65A) on the 14.00 Dundee – Glasgow. Shortage of diesels also cause DMUs to form 10.35 Glasgow – Inverness, 11.00 Glasgow – Aberdeen the week before.
24	D119 brings the 22.02 overnight service from Keighley into Paignton, where 'Peaks' are unusual arrivals.
27	34089 *602 Squadron* appears at Bristol with a van train, then heads the 18.40 freight to Cambridge via the WR main line to Swindon, Oxford. Unexpected!
28	61030 *Nyala* (56B) reaches Millerhill yard with the 14.10 freight from Carlisle. Ardsley engines are statistically rare in Edinburgh.
29	44691 works the 11.25 Weymouth – Waterloo throughout, and the 18.30 back to Weymouth, 'borrowed' power from the LMR (again).
29	D6943 tows an ailing Cardiff – Birmingham DMU into Snow Hill, first EE Type 3 seen here.
29	'Pines Express' enters Bournemouth with D1710 (81A Old Oak Common!).
29	Up 'Royal Scot' is diverted via Edinburgh and Hawick to reach Carlisle due to flooding on the Caledonian main line.
31	15-coach Euston – Glasgow pounds up Shap behind 70013 *Oliver Cromwell* + 70039 *Sir Christopher Wren* double-heading, a wonderful sound!
31	NBL Type 2s D6325/22/49 work the 10.05 Newquay – Paddington as far as Par. Instances of triple-heading are few and far between!
31	10.20 Ilfracombe – Cardiff sets off behind D6344 with four coaches of LMR, ER, NER, SR ownership respectively, on a WR service!

AUGUST 1965

2ND	73119 *Elaine* (70D Eastleigh) is surprise power on the 11.15 Nottingham (Victoria) – Neasden parcels.
3	34100 *Appledore* leaves Worcester (!) with a Birmingham-bound freight.
4	D233 takes a 'City of Birmingham Holiday Express' to Weston-super-Mare, where EE Type 4s are rare commodities.
4,6	21.45 Glasgow – Euston sleeper requires steam-heat to five coaches, causing '5's to be coupled inside AC electric locos between Crewe and Rugby. Pairs are E3073 + 45297 (4th) and E3019 + 44839 (6th).
7	D6788 reaches Edinburgh on 13.23 ex-Newcastle; EE Type 3s are uncommon in Waverley.
7	92001 arrives in Banbury with the 11.10 Bournemouth – Newcastle.
8	D6533 heads a cadet special from Clapham Junction to Tavistock and takes the 12-coach ECS up the 1 in 37 between the two Exeter stations unaided!

9	BR/Sulzer Type 2 (from 1A, ex-St Rollox Works) makes a guest appearance on the 08.25 Buchanan Street – Aberdeen and 17.15 return working.

9 BR/Sulzer Type 2 (from 1A, ex-St Rollox Works) makes a guest appearance on the 08.25 Buchanan Street – Aberdeen and 17.15 return working.

10 Preserved CR 4-2-2 123 sets off from Glasgow to Elstree for a part in the film *Gordon of Khartoum*. Filming cancelled as 123 reaches Hellifield.

11 09.45 Yeovil Junction – Exeter arrives at Axminster behind 80039 hauling failed D6341, itself 'pulling' the failed DMU service stock!

11 70013 *Oliver Cromwell* seen southbound at Lancaster hauling a TPO coach and a Derby 2-car DMU, an unexpected formation!

13 7029 *Clun Castle* drags 92220 from Cardiff (East Dock) as far as Gloucester. The 9F is on its way to Swindon for renovation.

14 D1696 (87E Landore!) leaves Glasgow on the 10.05 to Birmingham.

14 70045 *Lord Rowallan*, 70053 *Moray Firth* both appear at Snow Hill, on the 10.05 Kingswear – Wolverhampton and 11.10 Ilfracombe – Wolverhampton. Two 'Britannias' in a day at Snow Hill!

14 80012 is allocated the 19.20 Bournemouth – Waterloo; four coaches only, but non-stop from Southampton. Water is taken at Basingstoke!

17 Unidentified passenger train is seen heading east between Severn Tunnel and Bristol with 70048 *The Territorial Army 1908-1958* piloted by D6926.

17 D9013 *The Black Watch*, D9003 *Meld* head the Hull – King's Cross fish, and the King's Cross – York parcels respectively.

18 'Minnie' (the Hillhouse shed cat) leaves the depot on the tender tank of 44829, is soaked by water taken from Standedge troughs, climbs over the coal to the warmth of the cab – surprising the crew! Returns home from Stockport to Huddersfield in cardboard box on footplate of 48437.

19,20 LT 0-6-0PT L94, ex-Eastleigh Works, runs LE to Woolston to haul a failed 2-6-4T back to Eastleigh. Strange sight! Returns to Lillie Bridge next day.

20 Sheffield – Bournemouth relief (SR green liveried stock) headed by D5681 (40B) is seen diverted through Nuneaton, an unusual sight in these parts.

21 N7 0-6-2T 69621 noted at Wakefield. For storage at Neville Hill?

21 45675 *Hardy* reaches Scunthorpe on freight from Toton. Unexpected power.

21 Giesl ejector fitted 92250 exits Huddersfield with a Leeds parcels train.

21-30 Highland Railway Centenary week. 'Jones Goods' 4-6-0 103 plus two restored CR coaches leave Perth for Inverness on 21st, work specials between Inverness and Forres all week, and return to Perth on 30th.

22 6849 *Walton Grange* exits Crewe on a Liverpool (Riverside) – Andover troop train.

22 D7058 piloted by a Brush Type 2 is seen leaving Cambridge heading a 14-coach train towards London. WR hydraulics are rare in East Anglia.

25 Preserved K4 3442 *The Great Marquess* arrives in Snow Hill with a special publicity train for Carpet Trades, Kidderminster.

27 72008 *Clan Macleod* works both the 08.25 and 17.15 3-hour trains between Glasgow and Aberdeen, and 60052 *Prince Palatine* heads the 19.45 Aberdeen – Edinburgh, all noteworthy occurrences.

28 Preserved D34 4-4-0 256 *Glen Douglas* leaves St Enoch on a tour train, returning to Queen Street, which closes to steam on 4 September, so 256 may be the last to arrive.

29 Euston-Lairg newspaper train has TWO EE Type 4s to work 4 vans only, to Crewe. Extravagant provision of motive power!

31	70011 *Hotspur* (12A) is a surprise visitor to Scarborough on the 11.06 from Wakefield. 'Britannias' rarely reach the coast here.
U/D	Swindon 0-6-0s D9521/2/3/4 based on Reading, work parcels trains to Didcot, Newbury, Southall, Paddington and Basingstoke.
U/D	E2001 (formerly E1000, converted from gas turbine 18100) is employed on freight trains south of Crewe on several occasions.
U/D	60012 *Commonweath of Australia* visits Inverurie Works for light repairs, the second A4 to do so. 60052 also receives attention here (see 27th and U/D October 1962).

SEPTEMBER 1965

3RD	6991 *Acton Burnell Hall* arrives in Bournemouth (West) on the 10.08 ex-York, last GWR loco here. West closes temporarily on 4th, forever on October 4th.
4	7029 *Clun Castle* arrives in Snow Hill on the 12.30 ex-Penzance, with 7029 provided by Bristol at the specific request of the RCTS, Cheltenham branch.
4,5	60145 *Saint Mungo* works a Birmingham – Leeds return special. It also hauls a special from Moor Street to Banbury (5th), where the A1 is seen serviced alongside 34051 *Winston Churchill*, before returning to Moor Street.
4	Two 3-car Metro-Cammell DMU's arrive in Cardiff as the 10.30 excursion from Wolverhampton, a rare DMU type in South Wales, or on the WR at all.
5	D290 exits Snow Hill on the diverted 11.33 New Street – Glasgow.
6	0-4-0ST *Bonnie Prince Charlie*, (owned by Corralls, Coal Merchants) runs on BR from Hamworthy to Dible's Wharf, Southampton – a rare movement.
8	Accident causes track damage at Goring; 19.45 Paddington-Bristol takes 1¾ hours Reading to Didcot, running *a few yards* behind the 19.25 to Worcester, with the 20.00 to South Wales *buffered up* to the 19.45 for much of the way.
11	D9019 is named *Royal Highland Fusilier* at Glasgow (Central) amidst military and pipe bands and a guard of honour. The last 'Deltic' to receive its name.
11	Green liveried 75024 (6C Croes Newydd!) seen running-in at Buchanan Street following a visit to Cowlairs Works.
11	Coventry – Bristol football special is equipped with a loudspeaker system, playing pop music and relaying bingo sessions, a successful experiment!
11,12	Restored A3 4472 *Flying Scotsman* heads up the Midland main line on a Lincoln – Olympia special, and works a Waterloo/Bournemouth/Weymouth/Westbury/Paddington excursion throughout, next day.
13	D1067 *Western Druid* arrives in Weymouth on a troop train; works 11.25 to Waterloo as far as Bournemouth and 14.52 back, and finally assists 34001 *Exeter* with the Channel Islands boat train, to Dorchester. Rare workings.
13	Stanier 2-6-0s 42953/63/77 all work through Preston, one is usually a rarity!
14	70026 *Polar Star* is seen at High Wycombe on the 09.35 ex-Wolverhampton.
15	D5637 (31B March!) passes Stafford on a horsebox special to Holyhead.
16-18	73000 (6D Shrewsbury) heads the 17.00 Glasgow – Dundee, the 23.00 Glasgow – Aberdeen (17th) and the 13.30 Aberdeen – Glasgow (18th).
17	45081 heads a Sedburgh School special, between Sedburgh and Low Gill.
18	Holiday special from Scotland arrives at Blackpool behind 45477 (64C).
19	D320 (1E Bletchley) noted at Faversham on a 12-coach excursion of LMR stock heading

for Ramsgate. EE Type 4s are not often seen in Kent.

19 60004 *William Whitelaw* leaves Leeds (City) on a railtour to Darlington Works via Harrogate, returning via Pelaw and Stockton to York, Leeds. A4s are suprisingly rare on the Leeds Northern line through Harrogate.

19 48309 heads the 10.50 Weymouth – Waterloo at least as far as Bournemouth!

20 73035 fresh from Cowlairs Works, brings the 17.14 relief from Queen Street into Waverley. First green liveried 5MT to be seen in Edinburgh?

20 60532 *Blue Peter* is surprise power for the 18.20 Montrose – Edinburgh.

21 D1725 (82A Bath Road) passes Newark on the 'Anglo-Scottish Car Carrier'.

21 Bo-Bo E3023 is the first electric loco seen in Euston, being towed in and marshalled into a parcels train, bound for Crewe to receive attention.

23 Up 'Cornish Riviera Express' leaves Par with D6311/15 + D601 *Ark Royal* triple-heading as far as Plymouth.

25 35010 *Blue Star* reaches Brighton light engine from Eastleigh, for weighing.

25,27 Ivatt 2-6-2T 41264 + 45307 form an unusual combination heading a Glasgow – Morecambe extra south from Carlisle, and D1664 *George Jackson Churchward* (87E Landore) leaves on the 19.06 to Appleby! (25th). Another 'rare shed Brush', D1556 (31B March) arrives in Carlisle on the 10.35 from Euston two days later.

27 75063 (6D) works throughout to Cardiff on the 07.02 from Shrewsbury.

28-30 16.52 Tring – Watford is a Bo-Bo electric hauling an LMS non-corridor suburban set, a service soon to be formed by an electric multiple unit.

29 Announcement at Waverley station: "Due to a derailment at Shankend 'The Waverley', due 16.52, is running early and will arrive at 16.25". (Train is diverted via the faster Carstairs route!).

30 45050 takes the 09.15 to Hereford out of Paddington, where few '5's reach.

U/D D5370 (51L Thornaby) is surprisingly seen heading north out of London on the Midland main line on a freight for Leicester, very much out of place.

U/D A long van train is seen (in appalling weather) between the tunnels at North Queensferry heading towards the Forth Bridge behind a J37 0-6-0 piloting a NBL Type 2, with two further J37's (both tender first) banking at the rear, quite a sight!

OCTOBER 1965

2ND 70012 *John of Gaunt* reaches New Holland Pier (!) on an RCTS railtour.

2 72008 *Clan Macleod* is at Chester on the 07.30 parcels from Pontypool Rd.

2 0-6-2T 6613 brings freight from West Wales into Margam yard, the first steam to arrive here since the beginning of the year.

2 D9015 *Tulyar* (on one engine) tows D8235 + D5900 from Finsbury Park to Doncaster Works. Notable trio!

3 'Merchant Navy'-hauled special from Waterloo – Ilfracombe runs non-stop Basingstoke to Exeter, only the second time since 1906 this has happened!

3,31 09.10 Waterloo – Southampton Docks boat train runs via Cobham, Guildford, Havant and Netley behind D1598, a rarity on these lines. D827 *Kelly* travels the same route on the 31st with the 08.45 boat train, even more unexpectedly.

6 All seven southbound tracks at Nottingham (Victoria) are occupied by; 63644, 63675, 90241, D7507 on freights and 70046 *Anzac*, 70047 plus a Grantham DMU on passenger turns – at the same time!

7	6947 *Helmingham Hall* is seen – uniquely – on Lickey incline banking duties when D6939 derails at Bromsgrove and no other loco is available.
8,9	4079 *Pendennis Castle*, A3 4472 *Flying Scotsman* both appear on Southall shed. 4472 fails at Swindon on a Paddington – Cardiff special (9th) and afterwards ascends the Lickey light engine, bound for Doncaster.
13	1600hp Bo-Bo electro-diesel E6007 (first of 30 from Vulcan Foundry) passes through Newton-le-Willows *en route* to Derby, then the SR.
16	LMR Blue Pullman diesel set makes a trial run between Leeds (Central) and King's Cross and back, stopping only at Doncaster. The unit worked to Leeds from Reddish via Huddersfield, Halifax and Low Moor returning the same way. Train carries high-ranking BRB and Regional Officers.
16	61199 heads a northbound evening freight through Skipton, to…?
16	(Week ending). Public are invited to sample new EMUs on Rugby to Stafford services, for free!
17	Preserved 0-6-0PT 6435 pilots 7029 *Clun Castle* between Gloucester and Bristol. 6435 is in the process of transferring to the Ashburton branch.
17	D854 *Tiger* passes Aller Junction with a British India Line 7-coach Pullman special from Paddington to Falmouth conveying guests for the 'shakedown' cruise of the 'Nevasa' to Tilbury. D858 *Valorous* takes over at Plymouth. First Pullman train over the Saltash Bridge.
21	Most unusually, the 'Mid-day Scot' pulls into Glasgow (Central) behind 70009 *Alfred the Great*. (Diesel failure at Carlisle is the cause).
21	London-bound freight is halted specially at Coventry as the cargo of prize cows requires milking. Stop had been arranged for Rugby, but the train is an hour late and the cows can't wait!
22	Sleeping Car train runs from Paddington to Weymouth for an Association of British Travel Agents' meeting in the Channel Islands.
22,23	02.15 Cardiff – Corby is worked by diesel-hydraulics throughout to Corby; D7043 and D1055 *Western Advocate* on successive days.
23	Up 'Flying Scotsman' travels over the Waverley route behind D9000 *Royal Scots Grey* due to a derailment at Chathill.
23,24	Midland line trains run via the Skipton – Ilkley line again. This closed in July but is still used for diversions e.g.19,26 September and 16 October – so far!
24	60007 *Sir Nigel Gresley* (61B) operates an enthusiasts' special from Manchester (Exchange) to Paddington and back, outwards via Chester, Shrewsbury and Snow Hill. Much new track mileage for an A4!
24,25	Strangers seen at St Rollox shed; 75071 (6C Croes Newydd), and D1601 (86A Cardiff Canton) next day.
27	D303 (1A) reaches Portsmouth with the Royal train from Aberdeen conveying the Duke of Edinburgh.
27	Churchill's funeral van (sold by BR for £350) is exported through London's Royal Victoria Dock to Los Angeles' City of Industry.
27	'Midland Pullman' suffers a rare failure when the rear power car engine seizes up working the 18.10 St Pancras – Manchester (Central). Train proceeds three hours late from Bedford without this power car, but with the rear tail lamp partially supported by string from last coach.

28	D1047 *Western Lord* (83A) passes Bedford (St Johns) on a coal train from Cardiff to Cambridge. Jaws drop, eyes are rubbed.
28	34079 *141 Squadron* and its train of SR stock arrive at Worcester for servicing after taking a special to Stratford-on-Avon, both uncommon workings.
29	D1015 *Western Champion* brings the northbound 'Devonian' right through to Derby. Heads are shaken, ABCs examined.
30,31	Unidentified 'Baby Deltic' appears on the LTS section heading the 21.25 Royston – Thames Haven oil tank empties, and the 01.45 return, loaded.
30	70039 *Sir Christopher Wren* heads the 'Thames-Clyde Express' through Shipley towards Leeds, a diesel replacement, probably at Carlisle.
U/D	Kipps depot now houses the ScR preserved locos 49/103/123/256 plus 54398 *Ben Alder* and GSW 16378, all formerly at Parkhead or Dawsholm sheds.

NOVEMBER 1965

4TH	D1672 (86A Canton!) heads the up 'Royal Scot' into Carlisle.
6	60041 *Salmon Trout* takes the Caledonian main line to Carstairs on the 06.11 freight from Carlisle to Leith.
6	34044 *Woolacombe* works the 09.37 Bournemouth (Central) – Bath (Green Park) and the 19.55 return. Once frequent on the S&D, Pacifics are now rare.
7	35028 *Clan Line* heads the 10.34 Bournemouth – Waterloo via the Netley line and the Portsmouth direct, a route over which this class is banned.
7	17.10 Newcastle – Liverpool arrives into Huddersfield 4 hours late, beating all previous records for lateness on this service!
9	Bo-Bo E3132 (new) is hauled from Doncaster to the Derby Research Centre.
10	84010/5/6/28 are towed from Lostock Hall to Fratton, for possible use on the Isle of Wight.
15	61350 reaches Glasgow (Central) on the 12.45 from Liverpool (Exchange).
16	45694 *Bellerophon* brings the 17.30 Leeds (Central) – King's Cross into Doncaster, but no further as D1509 takes over.
19,30	07.15 Glasgow – Dundee and 12noon return, are surprisingly worked by 45530 *Sir Frank Ree* on the 19th and by 70008 *Black Prince* on the 30th.
20	Derailment causes 22.20 Glasgow – Euston to traverse part of the Cathcart Circle, probably the only time Sleeping Cars have been seen here.
21	D8022 + D5028 form an unexpected combination double-heading an oil tank train at Chislehurst towards Tonbridge.
23	72008 *Clan MacCleod* is, rarely, at Huddersfield on the 11.00 ex-Liverpool.
23	60052 *Prince Palatine* (64A) arrives in Newcastle (last in-service visit of an A3 here) on the 08.40 ex-Birmingham, returning with the 14.35 to York.
24	D6774 (51L Thornaby), propelling a brake tender, passes Newark with an up special steel train. A working worth noting.
27	35022 *Holland America Line* reaches Crewe on an enthusiasts' special from Waterloo via Bletchley and Wolverhampton, going to Oxley for servicing.
27	7029 *Clun Castle* works the 'last steam out of Paddington' excursion to Gloucester via Bristol, and hauls the return to Swindon.
27	Swindon-built 650hp 0-6-0 D9521 gets a rare turn on a passenger working, the 17.10 Gloucester – Cheltenham, when a steam loco fails.

| 28 | D7098 + 73037 double-head an up parcels diverted via Staines between Byfleet Junction and Waterloo. |

28   D7098 + 73037 double-head an up parcels diverted via Staines between Byfleet Junction and Waterloo.

29   60970 + 60976 double-head the 08.16 freight from Millerhill at Hawick, an unusual same-class pairing on this route.

U/D   70036 *Boadicea* is an unusual type to visit Cowlairs Works for attention.

Euston electrified. Energised 25 October regular electric services begin 22 November.

     6th   First scheduled departure, E3110 with pantograph test car.

     9th   E3182 leaves with invited guests in Project Officer's Saloon.

     15th   E3094 brings in the 12.55 ex-Bangor, takes out 'Northern Irishman'.

     17th   E3090 conducts high-speed test run; ten coaches, two inspection cars.

     U/D At least twice, electric locos haul peak-hour residential trains to Bletchley. The non-corridor stock is only steam-heated and passengers are condemned to freeze in one of the coldest weeks of winter so far!

DECEMBER 1965

3RD   D9010 *The King's Own Scottish Borderer* works the 18.40 York – Swindon as far as Sheffield (Victoria). First sighting of a 'Deltic' here.

3   70039 *Sir Christopher Wren* is paired with an Inverness Type 2 on the 21.20 Aberdeen to Kilmarnock freight – a rare 12A/60A pairing.

4   FA Cup tie brings an excursion from Peterborough behind D5624 (34G) into Shrewsbury, first Brush Type 2 to reach here. Another tie at Grantham sees D1657 (86A Canton) arrive, having worked through from Swindon.

4   45654 *Hood* + 45596 *Bahamas* double-head the 'Jubilee Commemorative Railtour' between Manchester and York. 45694 *Bellerophon* is also at York, hence the sight of three 'Jubilees' – never to be repeated – all in the vicinity of York coaling plant.

4   60129 *Guy Mannering* arrives in Norwich, but only for scrapping.

11   D375 brings an up parcels train into Reading; few EE Type 4s seen here.

11   44311 is seen at Blea Moor with a northbound train of lime wagons, rare nowadays on a main line working as the class is nearly extinct.

11   7029 *Clun Castle* noted on banking duty at Sapperton!

11,12 60034 *Lord Faringdon* (61B) works an Edinburgh – York chartered special. Returns on the 09.00 additional parcels to Waverley next day.

12   48309 (82F) operates an 8-coach special from Oxford to Bedford (St Johns) and back. Doubtful if a Bath engine has ever reached Bedford before.

12   Holbeck hosts SR 73112 *Morgan Le Fay*, which is towing 34051 *Winston Churchill* to Hellifield for storage. Double astonishment!

14   61131 (56A) works the Whitehaven – Northwich freight as far as Carnforth, rare to see a B1 on the Furness line.

15   D5623 (34G) heads the King's Cross – Waverley parcels throughout!

17   D1637 (87E Landore) heads an Immingham – Colwick freight.

17,18 Landslip and subsequent collision at Bridgend causes substantial detours. Fishguard boat trains and Milford Haven oil trains and some parcels trains run via Aberdare and Vale of Neath line. Heavy rain and a further landslip closes this route as well, forcing the above trains plus milk trains and the Carmarthen – PDN sleeper to be routed from Port Talbot via Tondu to Treherbert. This line also suffers subsidence

(18th) and milk trains have to take the Central Wales line to Craven Arms and Shrewsbury!

18	70004 *William Shakespeare* arrives at Darlington Works for light repairs.
24,27	D1500 (34G!) heads the up 'Pines Express', spends Christmas at Reading and works the 23.50 Southampton – Oxley goods (27th). Do Finsbury Park know?
28	N 2-6-0 31816 brings the ECS for the 18.00 to Salisbury into Waterloo.
28	70013 *Oliver Cromwell* arrives in Newcastle at 12.50 towing the 4-car DMU that forms the 07.35 from Carlisle, somewhat late!
28	2-6-4T 42269 + 61386 double-head the Bradford portion of the 09.25 Bradford (Exchange) – King's Cross as far as Wakefield (Westgate).
28	60528 *Tudor Minstrel* (62B) is a surprise choice to work the 10.05 Edinburgh – Birmingham via Carstairs, through to Carlisle.
29	D59 heads the 11.30 Wemyss Bay – Glasgow, rare work for this class.
29	D1761 (31B) raises eyebrows at Paddington heading the 10.35 from Wolverhampton. You just don't get March engines at Paddington!
31	61058 appears on Gloucester (Horton Road) shed, most unusual.
U/D	D860 *Victorious* reaches Swanbourne on the Oxford – Cambridge line, but D1021 *Western Cavalier* makes it to Cambridge with freight from Oxford.
U/D	The ten 840xx 2-6-2Ts transferred to the SR for possible use on the IOW are rejected as being in poor condition, returned to the LMR and withdrawn!

JANUARY 1966

1ST	D380 reaches Ashford Works on an empty freightliner train from the LMR, returning via Tonbridge. EE Type 4s are uncommon in Kent.
1	35011 *General Steam Navigation* travels over part of the S&D with a closure special, the first 'Merchant Navy' to do so.
1	D1570 heads a passenger working from Pontypridd to Cardiff. First Brush Type 4 seen on such a train in the Valleys.
3	72008 *Clan Macleod* (an A4 deputy) exits Aberdeen on the 17.30 to Perth.
3	Full electric working commences in/out of Euston. A landmark date!
4	2-coach 08.04 Rugby – Euston has E3068 + E3130 as motive power!
4	76069 hauls the 12.30 Southampton (Eastern Docks) – Water Orton as far as Worcester, an unusual engine for such a train.
4	No engine appears at Buchanan Street for the 17.50 to Stirling. 60009 *Union of South Africa*, having arrived from Aberdeen at 17.30, takes out the 17.50 running tender first! Unprecedented.
4,5	Sheffield (Midland) sees the arrival, on successive days, of 45130 (6C Croes Newydd) and 76033 (70D Eastleigh) respectively, both hauling special banana trains from Southampton to York.
5	60824 departs Leeds (City) with the northbound 'Thames-Clyde Express', an extremely rare occurrence for this class to work this train.
8	61121 (36A) takes the 17.45 freight to Leeds out of Carlisle, another rare class to work over the Settle & Carlisle.
12	USA 0-6-0T 30071 heads a Southampton Central to Eastern Docks boat train portion, most unusual for a USA, which is rarely seen on any passenger duty.

12	D9000/14 *Royal Scots Grey/The Duke of Wellington's Regiment* pass northbound, coupled light engine, through Newark – an intriguing sight.
13	D825 *Intrepid* is employed on the 12.36 Cardiff – Portsmouth (Harbour) throughout, and the 17.28 return – usually a DMU service.
14	D10xx works the Thames Haven – Rowley Regis oil tank train through Evesham, where 'Westerns' had been previously unknown.
15	75010 (6A) ex-Cowlairs Works, is a big surprise at the head of a Scotland v France rugby special from Queen Street to Edinburgh, where this class had also been previously unknown.
16	D817 *Foxhound* heads the 09.10 Waterloo – Southampton (Western Docks) boat train via the Portsmouth direct and the Netley line, unexpected.
16	06.27 Faversham – Charing Cross is formed of a 4-CEP unit, + 2-HAP from Strood. This 6-car set then runs all day between Charing Cross and Ramsgate.
16	2-8-0 2818 (due for preservation) arrives at Eastleigh from Swindon.
17-20	De-icing car runs from Ramsgate to Dover and Faversham sandwiched between two 4-CEP units, very peculiar formation.
17,20	'Night Ferry' is worked from Dover to Victoria by a pair of BRCW Type 3s, in blizzard conditions, in place of the regular electric loco.
21	61232 makes a surprise arrival into St Pancras on the 07.37 local from Luton as the booked DMU was not available. (So 70052 was not the last!)
21	D6546 appears in Hull on a freight from York, between Cliffe – Uddingston cement train workings. This SR-allocated class is a rarity in Hull.
22	13.20 Waverley – Lanark has the notable pairing of D5318 + 2-6-4T 42058.
22	D7088 reaches Crewe (uncommon here) on the 08.45 Cardiff – Manchester, returning south on the 12.45 Manchester – Penzance.
22	'Cambrian Coast Express' arrives in Paddington with D1923 piloting 44760 (for steam heating). Similar duo of D1686 + 45436 arrives later.
22	D1041 *Western Prince* brings the 18.10 Paddington – Birkenhead into Shrewsbury, where this class are infrequent visitors.
22	75058 (10G Skipton) unexpectedly works through to Carlisle on the 15.40 from Bradford (Forster Square). D2726 (200hp 0-4-0 shunter) is seen at Upperby, having failed in transit from 64A to Wolverton Works, a most unusual transfer.
23	34093 *Saunton* reaches Cricklewood (a rare visitor here) with a Southampton to Hull excursion.
23	Closure of Snow Hill tunnel means that the 09.45 Snow Hill – Birkenhead (in lieu of 08.45 ex-Leamington Spa), and 19.17 return are formed of two 3-car 'Cross-Country' DMUs, types rarely seen on the Wirral.
23	70046 *Anzac* found under repair at Perth (63A), on one of its very rare appearances in Scotland.
25	10.05 to Birmingham via Carstairs leaves Edinburgh behind 73108 + 73151, an uncommon pairing to be seen in Waverley.
29	45593 *Kolhapur* ('Miraculously overhauled and repainted at Crewe Works') is seen at Preston working the 06.30 Morecambe – Crewe!
30	LNER 0-6-0 diesel shunters 15000/1/2/3 are noted working from Crewe.
U/D	Large variety of mainline diesels have now infiltrated into Oxford. Those seen recently include D267, D1040 *Western Queen*, D5520, D6342/47/50/52, D7037/48/49/85 and Brush type 4s on the 'Pines Express'.

U/D 45643 *Rodney*, 45675 *Hardy*, 45694 *Bellerophon* (all 55A) noted working on ECS trains between Leeds (Central) and Copley Hill sidings, with stock from the 07.32 ex-Doncaster, not previously tasks for Holbeck engines.

U/D 75061 (8L Aintree) pays several visits to Doncaster on freight workings.

U/D 76096 heads an 8-coach Prestwick – London special for fog-bound airline passengers, as far as Carlisle.

U/D With the permanent diversion of Immingham – Avonmouth freights via Newark (Castle), Newark is one of the few places in the country to see engines of all six Regions appearing on regular diagrammed workings.

U/D BRB announces it is no longer interested in retaining 4-4-0 54398 *Ben Alder* for preservation. It was withdrawn in February 1953.

FEBRUARY 1966

2ND 61173 surprisingly reaches Severn Tunnel Jct. with freight from York.

3 45633 *Aden* appears at Feltham (!) on a goods train from the Staines direction.

3-5 62005 (50A) noted at Chester on a Manchester – Rhyl parcels and on the 16.25 Birkenhead – Paddington between Chester and Shrewsbury. Goes to Holyhead (4th), works 11.45 Holyhead – Broad Street meat train along the North Wales coast (5th). All unexpected workings for a York K1!

11 22.05 Edinburgh – St Pancras sleeper is worked through to Leeds by D1972 (64B), not many Haymarket engines travel over the S&C.

12 13.18 Edinburgh – Carstairs/Lanark leaves Waverley behind the unusual combination of D1541 piloting 2-6-4T 42058.

12 'Britannia' 70047 heads the 07.40 Shrewsbury – Chester, a rarity on this line.

12 Norwich v Walsall FA Cup tie attracts three specials from Walsall, one of which is a WR Blue Pullman unit – first sighting of these in East Anglia.

12 Football excursion from Cardiff to Southport is hauled throughout by D1638 (87E Landore). Returns at 18.30 first stop Newport, something of a record?

13,26 61013 *Topi* appears at Cheltenham LE off the Honeybourne line.
61035 *Pronghorn* passes Cheltenham working an ammonia tank train (26th), and is later seen on Gloucester shed. B1s rarely visit these parts.

15 D5615 (34G!) heads the Stafford – Kilburn parcels into Coventry, 4hr late!

15 Motherwell; 70053 *Moray Firth* heads south with a dozen Camping Coaches newly painted cream/green. 75010 (6A) passes at high speed with an engineers' Inspection Saloon from Glasgow. Both notable abnormal workings.

16 Banbury (Merton Street) – Buckingham (closed 12/63 to all traffic) sees a further special movement when private diesel shunter, LMS 7063, runs from Brackley to Buckingham *en route* to Hams Hall power station.

17 34017 *Ilfracombe* (at Banbury overnight after working Poole – York on 16th), is appropriated to head the 09.10 Paddington – Birkenhead forward to Wolverhampton as no diesel is available. Astonishing!

18 Hull portion of 'Yorkshire Pullman' is brought into Doncaster by 48357, towing a failed EE Type 3 plus train. Has an 8F worked a Pullman before?

19 45647 *Sturdee* (55C Farnley) is strange power for the 14.30 Chester (General) to Paddington at least as far as Wellington, and probably Wolverhampton.

19	D7085 heads the 18.23 Southampton – Bournemouth, most unusually.
23	D148 (supposedly on crew training at Worcester) brings the 'Cheltenham Spa Express' into Paddington instead!
23,24	York – Poole service is worked forward from Banbury by 48276 (5D Stoke) through to Eastleigh, with no steam heating! 48276 is seen next day on a coal train from Eastleigh to Weymouth, where LMR 8Fs are rarely noted.
24	Derwent Valley Light Railway sees a 'passenger train' when 0-6-0 shunter D2062 heads the NER Inspection Saloon from York (Layerthorpe) to Wheldrake conveying the DVLR directors.
26	72008 *Clan Macleod* waits at Bradford (Forster Square) with the 15.40 to Carlisle. Few Pacifics reach this terminus.
27	Ivatt 2-6-2Ts 41284 + 41301 (both 70G Weymouth) evade the WR's steam ban by working an enthusiasts' special over the Bridport branch, then Yeovil.
U/D	A 'Britannia' leaves Dundee LE for Perth, where the turntable is out of action. 7MTs don't often get to Dundee, for any purpose.
U/D	New 8-car Pullman train to work (from 18 April) Euston – Manchester and Liverpool, undergoes high-speed trials on the West Coast main line.
U/D	Royton – Royton Jct. (to be closed 16/4/66) still has some LMS Child Single tickets to Manchester (Victoria), fare 2s 9d, 18 years after Nationalisation!
U/D	Evesham goods yard sports examples of both RENFE and Italian railways' wagons, for tomato/onion traffic.
U/D	Leaflet is distributed stating that electrification of the Bournemouth line in 1967 will bring 28 trains a day from Boscombe to London, with 35min quicker journey times. Boscombe station closed in 1965!
U/D	The Sunday 14.25 Victoria – Worthing is formed of three 4-PUL units i.e. three Pullman cars spread out along the 12-coach train, an unusual sight.
U/D	Nine small tank engines (stored at Canklow) cannot be condemned until an 1866 agreement between the Midland Rly and Staveley Works is repealed!
U/D	LMS Co-Co diesel 10001 heads a Willesden – Hither Green freight, its first visit to the SR, SE Division.
U/D	Railbus E79964, found to be unsuitable for Alston/Haltwhistle branch, returns to Cambridge for further work in East Anglia.
U/D	No less than eight 'Britannias' are seen in the Aberdeen district during the month, including 70041 *Sir John Moore* and 70010 *Owen Glendower* deputising for A4s on the 13.30 to Glasgow and 17.30 to Perth respectively.

MARCH 1966

1ST	D5520 + brake van appear at Reading, route learning from Stratford depot.
2	70041 *Sir John Moore* arrives in Waverley on 17.16 from Glasgow (Central). These engines are still infrequent visitors to Edinburgh.
4	D6505 (73C!) reaches Bristol with condemned coaches for South Wales.
5	Hull v Southport FA Cup match brings four specials from Southport including the surprising sight of 70014 *Iron Duke* at Paragon, where 7MTs are rare.
5	WR Blue Pullman set is chartered by Coventry City fans for the FA Cup tie in Liverpool.

5,6	Final S&D closure specials are run, with 34006 *Bude* + 34057 *Biggin Hill* seen crossing Midford Viaduct on the 5th, 35028 *Clan Line* at Templecombe next day – only the second of this class ever to venture onto the S&D.
6	60019 *Bittern* (61B) heads a Williams Deacon's Bank Club railtour from Manchester (Piccadilly) to Crewe, Derby and back. The A4 then goes on display at Piccadilly as a 'Rail Week' exhibit (2 days). Returns north on 9th.
8,9	D7007 conducts banking tests on the Lickey incline. D1050 *Western Ruler* is also here next day with the WR dynamometer car, on loco bogie tests.
9	Astonishingly, 60532 *Blue Peter* (62B Dundee!) pulls into Bradford (Forster Square) with a special parcels train from Edinburgh. Witnesses are agog. The A2 returns to York light engine. Definitely the event of the month!
9	Nameplates from SR Pacifics 35005/04, 34042 – *Canadian Pacific/Cunard White Star* and *Dorchester* respectively – are presented (at Charing Cross Hotel) to the Canadian Railroad Historical Association for display in the National Railway Museum in Quebec. (Samuel Cunard was a Canadian, and Lord Dorchester was a Governor of Canada).
11	Ayr observes the odd spectacle of 0-6-0 shunter D3207 + D414 double-heading an oil tank train!
12	11.00 special from Wolverhampton to Wembley Hill (for the womens' international hockey match) has D1687 piloting 45287 (for steam heat). 16 specials in all are run for this fixture.
12	35027 *Port Line* is an unprecedented arrival in Wolverhampton (Low Level) on a football excursion from Southampton, having worked it throughout!
15	D1584 (81A!) reaches Durham on the 08.20 Cardiff – Newcastle. First ever Old Oak Common engine seen in the North East?
17	60868 (64A) gets through to Doncaster on the 09.00 Tees Yard – Ferme Park freight. St Margarets' locos are rarely seen at Doncaster nowadays.
17	77014 (8E Northwich, last of its type on the LMR) is surprisingly transferred to… Guildford (70C!) and is seen passing Basingstoke, in transit. First of this class to appear in the South of England.
17,21	D1876 (41A) hauls the Blue Pullman substitute train (of Pullman cars) from Bristol to Old Oak Common (17th), which is also reached by D1978 (52A) on a freight ex-Margam (21st). Tinsley, Gateshead locos on 81A, whatever next?
19	D357 (64B) heads the 14.10 Aberdeen – Elgin, first use of this type on GNS passenger work. Also seen two days later at Insch with 16 bulk grain wagons.
21	D859 *Vanquisher* reaches Shrewsbury on the 09.10 Paddington – Birkenhead.
21,22	60024 *Kingfisher* (61B) departs Kingmoor for Banbury via the S&C, Leeds, Sheffield and Birmingham. Heads the 11.10 Banbury – Eastleigh freight, then special freight to Woking, and LE to Nine Elms the following day. (See 26,27). Returns Nine Elms to Birmingham via High Wycombe, on 29th.
23	61030 *Nyala* (56A) is a rare sight on a down freight passing Preston.
23	06.58 Edinburgh – Carlisle noted at Longtown with the unusual pairing of D8579 + D5308 at its head.
24	61035 *Pronghorn* (50A) is spotted at Smethwick, shunting empty cable wagons in the yard of the Westinghouse Brake & Signal Co.
25	Preserved A3 4472 *Flying Scotsman* visits Cuffley for filming purposes. First steam for many months on the south end of the GN system.

26	70025 *Western* Star, 70031 *Byron* both arrive (from Edge Hill only) at Aintree (Sefton Arms) on Grand National specials originating at Euston. Nine specials are run, that from Grimsby including an observation car, ex-'Coronation'.
26,27	60024 *Kingfisher* operates two specials from Waterloo on successive days; firstly to Weymouth, and then to Exeter. First A4 to leave Waterloo since 1948.
30	Last vehicle on both the 09.00 Liverpool – Newcastle and the 09.45 Newcastle to Liverpool, between Liverpool and Leeds, is the Chief Civil Engineer's track recording coach, squirting much blue liquid onto the track at relevant places!
31	D6895 (87E Landore) turns up at…King's Cross with a parcels train. Unexpected power from an unexpected depot!
U/D	(from 20th) BR uses the Stone – Colwich Jct. branch to test an export order of 40 railbuses for Mexico. These are built by Metro-Cammell at Stoke, and are brought to Stone on low-loaders.

APRIL 1966

1ST	D1049 *Western Monarch* surprisingly works through to Crewe on the 11.50 Plymouth – Manchester, and returns with a troop train to Plymouth at 17.00.
2	Darlington Works closes. (Last steam repair was 76040, left 3 Feb.)
2	D7069 used on trains between Sidmouth Jct., Tipton St Johns and Exmouth, an unusual class on these services.
2	17.05 Liverpool – Newcastle arrives in Leeds double-headed by 73035 + 73077, instead of the usual Type 4 diesel.
2	48730 + 2 coaches form the 11.55 Blackpool (North) – Blackburn and 14.15 return, as the exit from Accrington DMU depot is blocked by snow.
3	D1010 *Western Campaigner* reaches Bletchley (a type rarely seen here) on a Royal train working from Windsor, returning next day.
3	2-6-0s U 31639 + N 31411 pause briefly in Reading (General) with an enthusiasts' special from the Redhill direction, and then head for Basingstoke.
4	77014 is seen at Waterloo with the ECS for the 18.30 departure.
7	(Maundy Thursday) 75050 + 73092 (an unusual pairing of standards) double-head the 18.09 Waterloo – Basingstoke.
8	17.35 relief Buchanan Street – Aberdeen has unexpected power in the shape of 62045 as far as Perth. This class is something of a novelty at Buchanan St.
10	60532 *Blue Peter* (62B) interrupts its passage from Montrose to Glasgow (Central) on a returning railtour, to assist (in the rear), from Inverkeithing, the stalled Inverness – York car sleeper before resuming its own progress.
10	D314 appears at Weston-super-Mare (a first?) on an excursion from Coventry.
11	Football special pulls into Southampton (Central) behind D7077.
11	Five 'Jubilee'-hauled, Easter Monday specials to Blackpool from the West Riding all travel via Copy Pit, a spectacular procession of 45562 *Alberta*, 45565 *Victoria*, 45647 *Sturdee*, 45694 *Bellerophon* and 45739 *Ulster*.
12	60019 *Bittern* (61B) brings a Millerhill – Tyne Yard freight into Newcastle and is serviced at Tyne Dock (an A4 first?), before heading north again.
12	16.25 Birkenhead – Paddington noted at Oxford with D1010 *Western Campaigner* piloting D1589, an extravagant combination of 5450hp!

14	70051 *Firth of Forth* takes a northbound freight out of Tyne Yard. 7MTs are an extreme rarity on the Newcastle – Edinburgh section, probably only the second occasion, surprisingly, and neither on passenger trains!
15	Southbound parcels train leaves Barrow with D5703 piloted by D1850, one or the other would be normal, both is notable.
16	Last Bradford/Leeds – Morecambe 'residential' is run. 2-6-4T 42394 brings the Leeds portion into Skipton, attaching to the 17.10 from Forster Square. 44926 takes the combined train forward, and the service, which has been timetabled since Midland Railway days, now ceases.
16,30	Longmoor Military Railway WD 2-10-0 600 operates a special railtour from Woking to Liss, thence to Borden, Bentley and on to Aldershot, Ascot and Staines. Tour originates at Waterloo and is repeated on the 30th, when U 2-6-0s 31791 + 31639 power the train as far as Woking. LMR locos rarely work over BR tracks.
18	The last HR 4-4-0 54398 *Ben Alder* is finally broken up. A long and lingering death, as it was withdrawn for preservation 13 years ago!
18	New timetable begins, and the full high-speed AC electric services from Euston to Manchester and Liverpool commence. Opening of a new era!
18	'Deltics' start working the 07.35 Bradford (Exchange) – King's Cross.
18	Up 'Master Cutler' arrives in King's Cross behind D131 after no less than four (!) failures in Sheffield prior to the train even departing.
19	D209 (32B) appears, ex-Crewe Works, at Carnforth, where Ipswich engines 'never' reach!
20	D1732 (82A) brings the 09.13 from Bradford into St Pancras, where Bristol engines 'never' reach!
20	LMR Blue Pullman unit arrives in Hull, and its crew return home. As nobody else knows how to drive it, it is dumped at Botanic Gardens depot until the 28th when a driver arrives and takes it to…Swindon!
22	44880 (66B) arrives in Doncaster just after midnight. (Motherwell engines aren't supposed to reach here either!).
23	Football specials for the Chelsea v Sheffield Wednesday FA Cup semi-final at Villa Park bring D820 *Grenville* and D7057/78/80 into Snow Hill from Paddington, uncommon types in the West Midlands.
23	60528 *Tudor Minstrel* (62B) heads a railtour from Manchester (Exchange) to Edinburgh via Shap and the Waverley route. A rare loco south of Carlisle.
24	'Bournemouth Belle' is diverted via Alton and arrives in Southampton with D6556 piloting 34017 *Ilfracombe*, an interesting pairing.
28	60010 *Dominion of Canada* reaches Hellifield, for temporary storage!
29	61012 *Puku* is surprisingly observed at Wellington (Salop) on a freight.
30	Bristol (Bath Road) Open Day attracts 80043, 48706/60 and 0-6-0PTs 3681, 3758 (despite the whole of the WR being dieselised on 6 March), plus eight diesels including the Brush D0280 'Falcon'.
U/D	WR runs 120 long distance 'extras' over the Easter period.
U/D	16.33 Waverley – Inverness is provided with 'Deltic' haulage to Perth, the engine returning on the Perth – King's Cross car sleeper.
U/D	Convent near Llandovery purchases over a dozen GWR brake vans (from Birds of Morriston) for conversion to living quarters for nuns. Planning permission has to be obtained before the vans can be delivered.

MAY 1966

3RD   D7025 heads an Oxford – Harwich car-carrying train throughout.

4   SR electro-diesel reaches Cricklewood on a cross-London freight, ex-Feltham.

5   Dortmund FC supporters' special (for the European Cup-Winners Cup final in Glasgow) has 70046 *Anzac* to Carlisle, and 70040 *Clive of India* to Glasgow.

5   15.54 Waterloo – Exeter leaves with D6527 piloting D820 *Grenville*. Unusual!

6   'Crab' 42700 is towed from Birkenhead to Hellifield, for official storage.

9   Returning football special (22.45 Waterloo – Southampton) is formed of three 'Hampshire' units, whereas the outward train had loco-hauled stock. Strange!

10   E6012 + Inspection Saloon tour lines in the Bournemouth area, visiting the Fawley, Lymington and Swanage branches, plus Dorchester (South).

10-12   Naval special from Elgin travels overnight (10th/11th) to Crewe, where 70002 *Geoffrey Chaucer* then works the Sleeping Car train through to Portsmouth & Southsea. 70002 takes the ECS to Willesden, and then goes to Nine Elms for servicing (11th). Heads 09.20 Waterloo – Southampton Docks boat train and ECS back to Clapham Jct., then LE to 70A (12th). Heads north a week later.

12   Despite electrification, D225 *Lusitania* reaches Euston on a Glasgow sleeper.

14   D26 powers a Halifax – Largs excursion throughout, a 12-coach train with two Kitchen Cars in the formation. A long day out!

14   D6741 (50B) brings a RL excursion from Hull into St Helens (Shaw Street), which sees its first visit of an EE Type 3.

15,22   45493 (off Saturday's York – Poole) heads the 08.55 Bournemouth – Waterloo on both days, diverted via Alton on both days, and twice returns on the 20.30 back from Waterloo. Has a '5' been 'over the Alps' before?

16   D1926 (82A!) passes through St Helens on ECS towards Wigan. Rarity!

20   46235 *City of Birmingham* is towed from Crewe to Birmingham (through Snow Hill) for display at the Birmingham Science Museum.

20,21   60024 *Kingfisher* (61B) works to Doncaster on an Edinburgh – King's Cross American Tourist Special. Returns on enthusiasts' excursion next day.

21   77014 heads a railtour train between Totton, Blandford and Broadstone. 34006 *Bude* then takes it on to Ringwood, first train here since May 1964.

22   Two specials mark the complete closure of the Montrose – Inverbervie branch, closed to passengers 1/10/51. Lord Provosts of both towns travel on the trains and constables are called upon to control the crowds!

23,24   70046 *Anzac* heads the 17.15 Glasgow – Aberdeen 3hr train and the 13.30 back from Aberdeen next day. Infrequently seen class on these services.

25   D5530 is a most unusual type at Worcester, on freight from Washwood Heath.

25   D1723 climbs the Lickey with a 60-wagon load, banked by three (!) EE Type 3s. That's 8000hp actively employed on one train – a British record?

26   Ex-Crosti 92021 is a rarity on the 20.15 Leeds (City) – Edgeley parcels.

26   Harwich – Liverpool Street 'Day Continental' boat train is powered by the very unusual combination of D8214 + D204.

27   The 08.55 ex-Grimsby arrives at King's Cross behind D6810 + D5672, the latter fitted with tablet exchange apparatus, an extremely rare sight here.

29   (Whit Sunday) D1744 (81A) reaches Blackpool on an excursion from the Midlands.

Surely a first for an Old Oak Common engine to appear here?

31   Surprise! The 14.56 Wrexham – Paddington is headed by 70014 *Iron Duke*.

U/D   Privately-owned 7029 *Clun Castle* regularly works the 08.25 Bordesley to Banbury pick-up goods, returning to Tyseley on Saturdays.

JUNE 1966

2ND   D309 leaves Gloucester with oil tanks for South Wales, where this class is rare.

4   Preserved A3 4472 *Flying Scotsman* arrives in Llandudno having worked through from Lincoln on a Gainsborough Model Railway Society excursion.

5   'Royal Highlander' departs Euston behind D308 + D330 (four coaches of the Royal train are attached at the rear) despite 'full' electrification.

5   D26 (55A Holbeck!) reaches Tavistock Jct. with freight from Bristol.

9   Surprise! 62067 (52F Blyth ex-Works) heads the 15.57 Glasgow – Gourock.

10   73089 *Maid of Astolat* appears at Coventry on an excursion from the SR.

11   34012 *Launceston* works a Blandford (closed!) – Brighton special throughout.

11   Three excursions from High Wycombe to Clacton bring D1615 (81A) and two 'Hymeks' through to the Essex resort, where an Old Oak loco is a novelty.

11   11.03 Paddington – Pwllhehi has 76041 as power all the way from Wolverhampton (Low Level) to destination, a surprising through working.

11   D5632 (31B March) is seen unexpectedly conducting trials at Blyth.

12   6-car 'Trans-Pennine' unit operates a Leeds – Towyn Sunday excursion. The Cambrian line west of Shrewsbury again opens specially for this train.

13,14 'Bournemouth Belle' consists of the 'Golden Arrow' stock (part Pullman, part MkI coaches) following a shunting mis-hap. (Due to the seaman's strike, 'GA' stock is available). Next day, the 'Belle' is a mix of Pullmans from both trains.

13   Channel Tunnel Co. runs special test train with D1996 through both the single bore tunnels at Standedge, at various speeds. Tests repeated next three days.

14   61199 reaches Gloucester on a steel train, then heads freight via Worcester.

15-17 'Jinty' 0-6-0T 47447 is deputed to work 19.30 Birkenhead – Chester parcels train three nights running! Motive power shortage is the cause.

16   70004 *William Shakespeare* makes a rare appearance at Mirfield shed.

18   Last day of steam working on the Alnwick branch produces 92099 on the afternoon workings complete with wreath and 'Norseman' headboard!

19   70003 *John Bunyan* is first 7MT in Bristol area for a year, at Stoke Gifford.

25   09.10 Dundee – Blackpool reaches Carlisle behind D8608/06, surprisingly.

25   D6984 makes the class debut on the Cambrian, working the 10.15 Shrewsbury to Aberystwyth, a driver training turn for Shrewsbury crews.

25,26 35026 *Lamport & Holt Line* heads an enthusiasts' special from Waterloo through to Manchester, piloted by 92113 (!) between Dudley and Snow Hill. (35026 runs LE to Doncaster via Huddersfield; works special back to London next day via Nottingham). Train goes on to Aberdeen and includes J37 0-6-0s 64570 + 64618 (on 10 green SR coaches!) between Edinburgh and Dundee.

26   6-COR 3043 + 5-BEL 3051 work the 19.00 'Brighton Belle' from Victoria.

26   Budd 'Silver Princess' car, (ex-'Mancunian' set), seen condemned at Derby.

27   WR 'Boardroom' car W9004W – in chocolate & cream livery – reaches Inverness conveying American millionaires on a golfing holiday!

28   0-6-0 shunter D2262 operates a parcels train trial (five vehicles) to Healey Mills from Huddersfield via Halifax and Cleckheaton. An unusual experiment.

28   60007 *Sir Nigel Gresley* passes Tebay (towed) for restoration at Crewe.

29   Piccadilly Line tube stock for use on the IOW (designated 4-VEC, 3-TIS) seen undergoing crew training runs between Stewarts Lane, Wimbledon, Woking.

29   0-6-0PT 1638 (6C Croes Newydd) heads the 20.25 Chester – Ellesmere Port via Hooton freight. First visit of 16xx class to Chester?

U/D   A number of electrically-hauled freights on the West Coast line arrive in London with AC locos coupled to 'diesel' brake tenders. A really odd sight.

JULY 1966

1ST   73137 + 70015 *Apollo* bring the 11.00 Liverpool – Newcastle into Leeds.

1   ECS from Wolverton arrives at Swindon behind D301. This class is rare here.

1   D830 *Majestic* on a special from Paignton, and D804 *Avenger* on another from Plymouth, both arrive in Tilbury in connection with a cruise ship sailing.

27 June-6 July   60919 (62B) departs Scotland (27th) to work a railtour out of Waterloo. Seen passing Oxford LE (30th) in transit to Nine Elms. Fails here, is repaired, runs LE to Eastleigh, runs hot, returns to Basingstoke. Leaves here on 6th heading north on the 15.35 Southampton – Water Orton banana train.

3   21.56 Edinburgh – St Pancras has D365 + D22 to Carlisle. Unusual.

3,10   06.00 Weymouth – Waterloo boat train passes through Swindon behind D6548, D6508 respectively, diverted due to engineering works.

4   Much activity at St Enoch (closed to passenger traffic 27 June) as a lengthy military special of men, horses and guns departs for Kensington Olympia with 73120 + 45126.

9   2-car DMU forming the 13.15 Thornton Jct. – Edinburgh has to be banked from Inverkeithing to North Queensferry by a J37 0-6-0 when a motor fails.

10   92064 (52H Tyne Dock, but bearing a 54B shedplate – which had been recoded 52H seven years ago!) reaches Heaton Mersey on parcels from York.

11   NER Bo-Bo electric 26500 is hauled from store at Hellifield to Rugby for presentation to AEI (ex-BTH) for their museum, though stored again, initially.

15   Royal train (ex-Truro, overnight stop at Mottisfont) with D806 *Cambrian* reaches Bournemouth, first 'Warship' here. D806 takes the ECS to Willesden.

15   90677 (50B) heads Hull – Morris Cowley carflats at Leamington Spa.

16   D5706 is a big surprise at Durham, surely a first, heading an up troop train.

19   D7062 reaches York (!) on a troop special from Windsor to Newcastle via Gloucester and Derby. Returns piloting D1992 on 12.25 York – Bristol.

20,21 44710 appears on a weed-killing train on the Hampton Court branch. In contrast, it works the next day's 09.30 Waterloo – Bournemouth express!

21   45562 *Alberta* heads a cattle special for Alnwick, from York to Newcastle.

22   D1663 *Sir Daniel Gooch* (87E Landore!) leaves Immingham for Avonmouth.

22   D1044 *Western Duchess* appears at Dorking on a freight towards Redhill.

22   70000 *Britannia* is moved from Newton Heath to Stratford for preservation.
           26501 (see 11th) leaves Hellifield for scrapping, near Blyth, via Kingmoor.

23   45593 *Kolhapur*, 45697 *Achilles* and 45675 *Hardy* all work through to Glasgow from

Leeds on trains originating in Birmingham, St Pancras (two).

23   07.06 from Edinburgh reaches Carlisle 1¾ hours late with D5310 (failed) at the front, and D8080 (65A) propelling from the rear!

25   61344 is unexpectedly at the head of the 17.50 Buchanan Street – Stirling.

27   Early morning Ramsgate – Cannon Street service is diverted from Faversham via Canterbury, Dover, Ashford and covers the 101½ miles non-stop in 109 minutes, a record over SR electrified lines.

U/D   In summer timetable, 17.25 Hull – Doncaster is diagrammed for EE Type3 + Brush Type 4 in multiple on Saturdays; 4500hp for 8 coaches. But 'Deltics' work the Bradford portion of 'White Rose Pullman' from Leeds (Central), that's 3300hp for 3 coaches!

U/D   0-6-0 Shunter D2554 ex-Parkeston Quay, is allocated to Ryde, IOW. Pre-shipping crew training for island drivers takes place from Fratton shed.

U/D   SR Bulleid stock (sent to the ScR in exchange for BR Mk1s, used for the Bournemouth electrification) is seen at work on the Highland main line!

AUGUST 1966

2ND   19.00 to Euston is triple-headed out of Inverness by D5126/23 + D5333.

2,4   EE Type 4s reach Folkestone Harbour on returning Lourdes Pilgrimage traffic. D228 *Samaria* heads for Liverpool on the 2nd and D225 *Lusitania*, D384 both work specials to Birmingham two days later.

4   4-wheeled SNCF wagon seen at King's Cross on a down parcels train still with Customs' seal, guarded by railway police, for 'Edinburgh Art Council'.

5   'Royal Scot' unexpectedly arrives in Glasgow (Central) behind a 'Britannia'.

6   D5004 is rare power for the 18.10 Paddington – Birkenhead from Leamington due to loco failure there. D5004 had been 'acquired' from a parcels train.

11   46115 *Scots Guardsman* departs Kingmoor for the Worth Valley line.

11,12   70004 *William Shakespeare* surprisingly heads the 07.05 Basingstoke to Waterloo, whilst the other former 'Golden Arrow' engine 70014 *Iron Duke* is seen on Skipton shed next day, another surprise.

13   Next in sequence 70015 *Apollo*, reaches Bradford (Exchange), where 7MTs are rare, on a 3-coach special from Southport, a working repeated on the 20th.

13   34002 *Salisbury* reaches Nottingham (Victoria) on a special from Waterloo to Sheffield, is serviced at Colwick and returns up the GC line to Marylebone. At Sheffield, two Cravens-built blue coaches for Ghana enliven the scene.

13   7808 *Cookham Manor* reaches the Dowty Works preservation site, Ashchurch.

13   Ramsgate – Victoria service is made up (strangely) of Buffet Car sets 7011/17.

14   60532 *Blue Peter* (61B) sets off from Waterloo on a railtour to Exeter but stalls on Honiton bank, adjourns to Exmouth Jct. for attention, but works the return leg Exeter to Westbury, with 70004 running the tour back to Waterloo.

14   D6115 (65A) noted on Kingmoor, a most unusual type in Carlisle.

16   70004 heads the 17.23 Waterloo – Southampton Docks boat train, followed by a northbound banana train out of the docks. Quite a Southern tour for 70004!

17,21   60532 observed heading north from Tyseley to Manchester. Then used to haul a Manchester – Holyhead special on the 21st. Diverse routes for an A2!

18   D1603 (82A!) exits Liverpool Street on the 17.30 departure. Has a Bristol engine ever been here before?

18,19 62046 is a stranger at Derby, appearing on successive days on freight.

20 92002 leaves Southampton on the Poole – Newcastle, surprise power.

23 61306 (50B) passes Harrow on ECS – first B1 in London area since 8/11/65.

23-25 Long distance season ticket holders are invited to see the progress of electrification works by travelling in an ER Inspection Saloon at the rear of the 07.24 Bournemouth – Waterloo and the 16.35 Waterloo – Weymouth.

26 The Waverley route sees the passage of D9000 *Royal Scots Grey* on the down Newton Abbot car sleeper, and a highly unusual performer on the 11.40 Bathgate – King's Norton empty carflats, D1790 (41A Darnall!).

27 70021 *Morning Star* heads a Shrewsbury – Newcastle special into York.

29 'Crab' 42942 works a Rock Ferry – Llandudno day excursion, probably the last appearance for this class on a public 'long distance' passenger train.

U/D 60010 *Dominion of Canada* arrives in Crewe for overhaul, from Hellifield.

U/D Cowlairs Works to close shortly; last steam repair is 62059.

U/D 1-6 August. 75016 takes over the Cambrian diagram of an EE Type 3 and runs approximately 400 miles per day!

U/D 92220 *Evening Star* is moved to Pontypool Road for official storage.

U/D 9Fs work block soda ash trains twice/week from Cheshire through to Larbert. This class is rarely seen in the Scottish Lowlands.

SEPTEMBER 1966

3ᴿᴰ 35030 *Elder Dempster Lines* heads a last-day railtour of the GC, arriving at Nottingham (Victoria) from Waterloo, and is serviced at Colwick before hauling the return. Special proceeds to Sheffield and back in the mean time.

3 92227 is sent to Marylebone to pick up 44865, 45298 and 61306.

3 60019 *Bittern* makes last public run between Glasgow/Aberdeen and back on a special ScR excursion; BR decrees that after this date, **steam haulage of all timetabled passenger trains ceases,** except on the Southern Region.

4 Aberdeen – York private excursion is A4 hauled throughout, with 60024 *Kingfisher* covering the first leg to Edinburgh, and 60019 south to York.

4 D1737 runs out of fuel on the 11.40 Paddington – Bristol at Dr Days Jct. D32 is sent out from Bath Road to rescue the ensemble.

4 Test train of LT 1938 tube stock runs Ryde St Johns – Shanklin and back.

10 Preserved A3 4472 *Flying Scotsman* heads a Farnborough Air Display special up the Midland main line.

13 Dover (Priory) sees the unexpected arrival of D1910, on a troop train.

15 D5376 (borrowed from Leicester) is highly unusual power for the 09.10 Burton – Banbury coal train and 13.25 return empties.

15 0-6-0 shunters D2201/2/3 are transferred from March (31B) to 5A, the first two of which are 'tram engines' (with enclosed motion) formerly used on the Wisbech harbour branch. 'Skirts' at Crewe North!

17 *Flying Scotsman* operates a Victoria – Brighton special excursion, and on to Eastleigh via Chichester, and the return working. A few 'first occasions' here!

17 D119 brings the 'Cheltenham Spa Express' into Paddington. Unusual power.

18	77014 pilots 34102 *Lapford* on the down 'Bournemouth Belle', at Alton, diverted.
18	16.50 Goodrington Sands – Exeter (St Davids) 6-car DMU is made up of three single-unit railcars + a 3-car set, a very strange combination.
19	75075 is promoted to working the 14.10 Exeter (Central) – Waterloo.
19,22,23	45222 (16B Annesley) heads the 08.35 Waterloo – Weymouth on all three days. Déjà vu, since 45222 was on loan to 70A in 1953!
23	D5302 makes a rare foray up the East Coast main line, by working the 17.00 relief Edinburgh – Newcastle, where this type is rarely seen.
23	44898 + 60532 *Blue Peter* work the first leg of an Aberdeen – Blackpool.
23	2-6-4T 42691 (64A) reaches York shed on its short-lived transfer from the ScR to Holbeck (55A).
24	7029 *Clun Castle* heads a 9-coach Paddington – Towyn special, to Shrewsbury.
25	60010 *Dominion of Canada*, 60007 *Sir Nigel Gresley* and 60026 *Miles Beevor* are all to be found in…Crewe Works!
25,26	Blackpool North shed hosts 'Britannias' 70008/9/13/29/31/34/49/54, having arrived (mostly) for Glasgow Fair holiday traffic. 11 specials return to Glasgow + 2 for Aberdeen (26th) – all steam, 11 via Shap, 2 via Ais Gill.
26	Last steam loco, 47000, descends Sheep Pasture incline, to store at Cromford.
29	70010 *Owen Glendower* departs Leeds on the 10.25 to Glasgow, with 70034 *Thomas Hardy* taking over at Carlisle, in contravention of BR's decree (3rd).
29	60007 in Works grey, passes through Huddersfield on a 4-coach special to Doncaster Works for repainting. First A3 seen in traffic at Huddersfield.
U/D	A3 4472 acquires a second tender, from 60009, converted to be gangwayed at both ends and to carry water only, with '4472' on the sides.
U/D	Squirrel jumps onto overhead wires at Rochford, causing short-circuit and 90 minute delay to Southend services!

OCTOBER 1966

3RD	34089 *602 Squadron* leaves Eastleigh – last steam loco to be repaired there.
5	D65xx is seen at New Barnet hauling new TC units 415/6 (ex-York Carriage Works), for the Bournemouth electrification.
6	09.33 Edinburgh – Perth is hauled by 70038 *Robin Hood*, despite the ban.
8	A3 4472 *Flying Scotsman* reaches Blackpool; illuminations special ex-Lincoln.
8	60532 *Blue Peter* heads a railtour, Edinburgh/Hawick/Carlisle/Beattock and back to Waverley via Carstairs. A2s don't often traverse Beattock.
10	62059 (52F Blyth) noted southbound over the Waverley route, the last steam engine to be repaired at Cowlairs Works, Glasgow.
11	J36 0-6-0 65345 stars in an episode of *Dr Finlay's Casebook* – filmed at Uplawmoor station with the two restored CR coaches.
11,13	D6116/36 (65A) appear at Kingmoor depot for crew training purposes.
14	D1025 *Western Guardsman* is surprise power for a Poole – Salisbury freight.
15	Steam special to Exeter has 35023 *Holland-Afrika Line* Waterloo – Westbury and back from Salisbury, with 35026 *Lamport & Holt Line* on to Taunton, Exeter and back to Salisbury. Two 'Merchant Navy's in a day at Westbury!
18	Heavy coal train out of Kirby-in-Ashfield is powered by D1803 + D1826 with two brake

tenders between the locos, most unusual.

19   Ivatt 2-6-2T 41298 heads the afternoon freight on the Merton Abbey line, a class not previously seen here at all! (Rostered for a 350hp diesel shunter).

20   22.30 Edinburgh – King's Cross fails near Connington and is run into by the engine coming to assist it!

20   EE Co-Co DP2 + D1515 provide 5450hp for the 08.35 Hull – King's Cross!

22   Bristol Bath Road Open Day display includes USA 0-6-0T 30064, 7029 *Clun Castle* and 7808 *Cookham Manor*, plus Longmoor MR 0-6-0 196.

22   A3 4472 (with two tenders) heads a King's Cross – Newcastle special as far as York, with 35026 *Lamport & Holt Line* going on to Newcastle and making a class debut there.

26   Hull – Morris Cowley special train of carflats reaches its destination behind, surprisingly, 61289; returns to the LMR post haste (Banbury shed closed).

27   34051 *Winston Churchill* leaves Hellifield for Eastleigh via Wigan and Crewe.

28,29   Royal train runs overnight from Uckfield to Merthyr Vale (Queen to visit Aberfan disaster site). D1054 *Western Governor* works the train throughout, with D1019 *Western Challenger* as stand-by, both seen briefly on adjacent lines at Lewes station.

29   D800 *Sir Brian Robertson* heads the Waterloo – Weymouth mail, via Alton.

29   Holbeck depot hosts surprise guest D9015 *Tulyar* (34G), a first here.

29   92220 *Evening Star* is towed to Crewe Works for storage, initially.

31-17 Nov   Due to dredging works at Dover, 'Golden Arrow' runs to/from Folkestone Harbour headed by an electro-diesel, which takes 11 vehicles up the incline from the Harbour unassisted.

U/D   'Western' Type 4 reaches Thames Haven, rare here, with freight from the WR.

U/D   Three 3-car WR DMU sets are transferred to…Glasgow (!) for further use.

U/D   During October, nine 'Britannias' work through to Aberdeen on freight, where these engines were once uncommon.

U/D   Since January, the 13.46 Barrow – Euston has been worked to Preston by every 'Britannia' except 70007/19, mostly on running-in turns from Crewe.

NOVEMBER 1966

1ST   Ivatt 2-6-0 46431 heads through Garsdale northbound with an Inspection Saloon, and passes D8123 at Kirkby Stephen (West) on a 9-coach test train.

4   D9003 *Meld* works the 07.25 Lincoln – King's Cross.

5   4079 *Pendennis Castle* moves from Southall, on its own, to Didcot for storage.

5   Last passenger train to Oswestry, a 2-car DMU, is given a rousing send-off from Gobowen – especially as it is Guy Fawkes night !

5   08.34 Corstorphine – Waverley DMU fails. 'Deltic' + 6 coaches takes over!

8   0-6-0PT 3625 passes through Coventry, coupled to 76042 and towed by D1635, *en route* to Cohen's of Kettering for scrap. An interesting trio.

10   D1921 on the 08.30 Waterloo – Bournemouth starts in reverse (!) and is in danger of backing the SR Inspection Saloon attached at the rear of the train (plus a full complement of senior engineers) into Ivatt 2-6-2T 41298, which had brought in the empty stock.

12   Railtour takes 34015 *Exmouth* out of Waterloo to Reading (a rare engine change point); 35023 *Holland-Afrika Line* thence to Banbury, 7029 *Clun Castle* to Stratford-on-Avon and 70004 *William Shakespeare* to Stourbridge (via Snow Hill). Then 7029 to Banbury and 35023 back to Victoria. Variety!

13	Withdrawn 0-6-0 diesel shunter D3122 is seen at Derby Works with the old BR crest upside down on both sides!
14	Up 'Bournemouth Belle' is diverted from Eastleigh to Salisbury (reverse). 34019 *Bideford* then runs non-stop to Waterloo, a rarity nowadays from here.
16	E3040 is the first AC electric loco into New Street, for testing circuits.
16,17	60532 *Blue Peter* brings the 19.15 Aberdeen – King's Cross into Waverley. 70005 *John Milton* heads the 09.33 to Perth next day. What steam ban?
17,18	35026 *Lamport & Holt Line* works the 12.00 Basingstoke – Manchester (Red Bank) ECS special for a railtour next weekend. Seen on 9B the day after.
18	92063 heads the last steam Tyne Dock – Consett return empties.
18	'Crab' 42942 powers the 20.55 Birkenhead – Paddington (with Sleeping Car) as far as Chester. Has a 'Crab' hauled a Sleeping Car before? Ban?
18	D1073 *Western Bulwark* fails at Gomshall on the 13.15 Severn Tunnel Jct. to Norwood freight, and is assisted by 77014 to Redhill. Unique pairing.
19	75074 is trusted with the 15.23 Bournemouth – Waterloo.
20	D5362 (65A!) observed in the sidings at Crewe North, surprisingly.
20	35026 heads a railtour from Manchester (Piccadilly) to Doncaster and York via Huddersfield – only the second seen here – and back to Manchester.
22	The unlikely pairing of 44675 piloted by D1609 (86A Cardiff Canton) bring the 16.05 from Glasgow into Leeds (City). ('Steam-heat' avoids ban?)
24	Up 'Heart of Midlothian' arrives in York with D1983 + D9007 *Pinza*.
24/25	D1578 (52A) arrives in Kensington with the 20.40 milk train (on 24th) from Whitland, and later leaves Paddington on the 12.10 to Birkenhead. Wanderer!
26	SR electro-diesel E6024 is observed running south LE through Finsbury Park.
27	45562 *Alberta* turns up at Shrewsbury, in immaculate condition, pleasingly.
U/D	D9007/16/18 take part in 'horn-position' trials between Arlesey and Great Ponton on the ECML, bearing headcodes 1B01 ('18), 1B02 ('07) and 1B03.
U/D	D221 *Ivernia* is a most unexpected sight at Eastleigh on the 14.05 freight from Warrington. Returns next day on 01.05 Eastleigh – Carlisle freight.

DECEMBER 1966

3RD	70004 *William Shakespeare* (9B) heads the 08.55 Birkenhead – Paddington from Chester to Shrewsbury (which BR says it shouldn't be doing!)
5	Full electric working of all main line passenger trains through New Street begins, and complements the Manchester/Liverpool services.
7	76064 arrives in Waterloo on the 18.35 from Salisbury.
8	Eastleigh sees the arrival of 8 'Warships' and 3 'Hymeks' on freights from/to Westbury, Bristol and Severn Tunnel Jct., as a result of further stages of the National Freight Train Plan being inaugurated.
9	D1584 (87E Landore!) appears at Preston on a parcels special from Liverpool.
11	73020 brings the 'Bournemouth 'Belle' into Waterloo. Short of Pacifics?
15	D7087 gets right through to Derby on the Swindon – York parcels!
17	45593 *Kolhapur* (55A) passes through Wrexham on a down freight. Lost?
17	NCB 0-6-2T 67 (TVR 28, GWR 450) seen at Slough in an up freight train.

22	E3162 is towed to Cricklewood for tyre turning, from Willesden.
22	First 'Peak' recorded on Birkenhead depot is D186 (52A!), surprisingly.
23	D1746 (81A!) heads the 09.20 out of King's Cross, for Leeds. Was the last Old Oak engine in King's Cross 6018 *King Henry VI* in 1948?
23	D294 enters Paddington on the 12.35 from Wolverhampton, returning thence on the 17.05 relief. EE Type 4s rarely reach Brunel's terminus.
23	20 reliefs depart King's Cross and 7 come in, including 1A83 from Edinburgh which had been stopped at Hitchin and met by police – fight in the Buffet Car!
24	92131 heads the 08.55 Birkenhead – Paddington into Shrewsbury, after an engine failure at Wrexham. More illicit steam! And...
24	61199 (50A) appears at Preston on a Manchester – Blackpool train.
27	16.54 Carlisle – Edinburgh conveys through coaches from St Pancras plus, surprisingly, the regular van of yeast from Burton-on-Trent to Elgin.
30	Train Guard reports having seen a man by the track at the Devon end of Calstock viaduct. The escaped Dartmoor prisoner is thereby recaptured!
31	6000 *King George V* is removed from store at Stratford and towed to Swindon for restoration.
31	D9020 *Nimbus* (34G) is unexpected power for the 03.15 Millerhill – Hawick goods, returning on the 06.58 Hawick – Edinburgh passenger turn.
31	'Crab' 42942 is specially provided to work the 14.45 Birkenhead – Paddington as far as Chester, and the return working, the 12.10 from Paddington.
31	(Midnight) Steam locos on Shrewsbury shed 'whistle-in' the New Year, a traditional chorus here, and (probably) the last.
U/D	Bo-Bo electro-diesel E6043 undergoes clearance trials in Southampton Docks.
U/D	Y9 0-4-0ST 68095 (ex-64A) arrives by road at...Lytham! Bought privately for possible use in Lytham dock area.
U/D	D5561, D5624 both reach Scotland on Dagenham – Bathgate coal trains. This class rarely gets so far north.
U/D	Father Christmas comes to Aberystwyth by special train from Devil's Bridge, using the narrow-gauge terminus for, probably, the last time.
U/D	70013 *Oliver Cromwell* is the last steam engine to be overhauled at Crewe, or anywhere else on BR, as steam repairs cease at the end of the year. 70013 is in the paintshop on 31st, as are 60007/10 and 92220. 60026, 71000 lie derelict.

JANUARY 1967

2ND	EE DP2 heads train 1A01, diverted through Lincoln – first sight of DP2 here.
2	09.00 Liverpool (Exchange) – Glasgow leaves with 45330 piloting 75059, the unusual pair working to Lancaster, where D334 takes over.
3	Up London train passes Kingmoor with D6841 + 70009 *Alfred the Great*, another unusual combination.
4	Ivatt 2-6-0 46454 reaches Gloucester on freight from the Honeybourne line, an uncommon visitor here.
7	EE DP2 enters Bradford (Exchange) with the 'White Rose' from King's Cross in place of the usual 'Deltic', and returns on the 16.10.
7	4-LAV unit 2925 makes a rare appearance at Waterloo in the formation of the 09.27 to Portsmouth.

7 Walsall v Gillingham FA Cup match brings 6-car 'Hastings' DEMU set 1033 into Walsall, carrying the away team's supporters.

8 D1811 (86A Cardiff Canton) appears at Kirkby shed (16E), surprisingly.

9 73100 arrives at Fairlie Pier on the 16.44 relief from Glasgow (Central).

12 D1569 (40B Immingham!) heads the 00.15 to Birkenhead out of Paddington.

13 17.47 London Bridge – Portsmouth is switched to a non-electrified line at Redhill. Train grinds to a halt, but with one shoe still on conductor rail, so train reverses, very slowly! 40min delay incurred.

14 D9015 *Tulyar* is found under repair at Holbeck depot, most unusually.   .

16 D7028 reaches Bedford with a football special from Oxford, via Bletchley. 'Hymeks' rarely venture so far east.

17 D330 brings the 'Cambrian Coast Express' into Paddington, a rare class here.

17,18 E3074 is towed to York by 45005 and seen at Heaton next day, strange sight.

19 E6048 is noted running light engine through Wigston Magna, near Leicester.

21 73006 (9H Patricroft) works the 11.00 Liverpool – Newcastle to Leeds and only loses 2½min on the diesel schedule.

22 Due to a derailment Marylebone is closed. Three trains from High Wycombe divert to Paddington, bringing LMR 4-car DMUs here for first time.

28 60009 *Union of South Africa* is in steam on 62A, first visit of an A4 here?

28 E3160 found inside Darlington steam shed, for bogie rotation tests on the depot turntable. (See also E3074 above).

28 FA Cup 3rd round day. Huddersfield v Chelsea brings three specials from King's Cross to Huddersfield headed by D1502/22 and D1874; Carlisle v Blackburn also attracts three specials, 70014 *Iron Duke* via Hellifield and the S &C line, plus 70003 *John Bunyan* and 70012 *John of Gaunt* via Preston and Shap – all specially cleaned; Bury v Walsall generates three specials as well, one of which is an 8-car WR Blue Pullman set. However, Divisional Manager at Stoke refuses to provide stock to take Stoke fans to Liverpool, due to past hooliganism. Several fans walk all the way in protest!

29 York shed contains 60019 *Bittern* (in the diesel shop), 45675 *Hardy* (in steam) and D1681 (86A), amongst others.

FEBRUARY 1967

1ST-5TH Nine Brush Type 4s work into Edinburgh over the Waverley route with specials for the Scotland v Wales rugby match. Five are seen returning from Carlisle via Ais Gill, Hellifield and Blackburn, four behind 70014 *Iron Duke* and 70010 *Owen Glendower* (both for Cardiff), 70003 *John Bunyan* (Carmarthen) and 70039 *Sir Christopher Wren* (Swansea), plus D1931 (86A) also to Swansea. Others pass in the early hours.

4 An 'Annual Dinner' special train is worked from Guildford to Redhill by USA 0-6-0T 30072, setting down participants at Deepdene and collecting them after the function concluded. A unique working for a USA tank.

4 'Britannia' 70047 heads the 21.25 Edinburgh – St Pancras, as far as Carlisle.

7 Inspection train travels over the Taunton – Barnstaple line (closed completely 3/10/66). NB Type 2 pulls two coaches, and at least 50 officials find cause to make the trip!

8 Peak Forest – Healey Mills freight arrives behind D399 + 92203.

11-13	D327 + D318 bring Mr Kosygin's train into Glasgow (Central), where 80116/120 in immaculate condition are turned out to work the empty stock. Train goes on to Kilmarnock, Edinburgh and finally Euston. Soviet Prime Minister leaves Victoria for Gatwick in 5-car Pullman train headed by E6036.
11	12.45 Heysham – Neville Hill oil tank train is worked by 61123 + 92212, and the 10.55 Morecambe – Manvers Main coal empties has another unlikely pairing in 75058 + 48454.
11	D67 brings the 14.56 from Weston-super-Mare into Taunton, most unusually.
16	70041 *Sir John Moore* is surprise power for the 07.15 Perth – Aberdeen local.
17	S&D dismantling train at Shillingstone is headed by D6330 (82A), not a type seen on the line before closure!
18	FA Cup 4th round day. Special leaves Southampton for Bristol behind D800 *Sir Brian Robertson* which fails at Salisbury, D813 *Diadem* takes over. Match at Liverpool brings an 8-car WR Blue Pullman set from Snow Hill into Lime Street as a privately-chartered special.
18	D1874 (34G Finsbury Park) is an uncommon depot to be represented working the 09.35 Carlisle – Millerhill freight.
19	11.20 from New Street reaches Glasgow with D183 + 44884, another unusual combination, though the '5' is probably there for steam heat.
20	(All week) 7029 *Clun Castle* works the Knowle car train to Banbury, returning LE to Tyseley each evening. (Running-in for railtour on 4 March).
23	D169 is surprise power for the down morning 'Talisman', seen 70min late at Drem, a 'Deltic' presumed to have failed further south.
26	7029 *Clun Castle* passes Shrewsbury on a test run prior to working the special.
U/D	Roughly 115 Brush Type 4s visit Vickers engine works at Barrow over the last six months. About six are present at any time, each staying approximately four days. All Regions send locos here for refurbishment.
U/D	Bromsgrove; poster advertises Day Return fare to Worcester…but the only train is at 17.59 and there's no return service until next day!
U/D	12-coach Blue Pullman trains run trials in Bristol area (i.e. 2 x 6-car former 'Midland Pullman' sets, redundant from St Pancras – Manchester route).
U/D	W55000 (a single unit railcar), plus AC Cars railbus W79995, both ex-WR, arrive at…Ayr (!) for use on Kilmarnock services.
U/D	Last shunting horse 'Charlie' is withdrawn from work at Newmarket, shunting horseboxes.

MARCH 1967

4TH	Last 'Cambrian Coast Express' has 75033, Aberystwyth to Shrewsbury.
4,5	4079 *Pendennis Castle*, 7029 *Clun Castle* both run specials from Paddington to Chester and back, last Saturday of through working to Birkenhead, where 7029 arrives (5th) on a 'last day special'. Woodside has probably its busiest day since opening in 1878! Final steam departure, 21.40 to Paddington, has 44690 to Chester, and is last Sleeping Car train out of Woodside.
6,7	70028 *Royal Star* brings the ECS of the 14.20 Edinburgh – Newcastle into Waverley; 70012 *John of Gaunt* repeats this next day.
8	70032 *Tennyson* brings train 1X82 – a naval personnel special originating at Plymouth – into Waverley from Carlisle.
8	D5342 (60A) passes through Hawick, northbound, with an officers' special.

10	(and all week). Newly restored in LNER blue livery at Crewe Works, A4 4498 *Sir Nigel Gresley* makes trial runs between Crewe and Shrewsbury.
11	FA Cup 5th round day. Specials from Swindon reach Nottingham (Midland) behind D7030/37 – first seen here in service. For the Spurs v Bristol City match, specials arriving at Northumberland Park include a 12-car Blue Pullman formation.
11	Excursion returning from the womens' hockey international at Wembley, to Bradford (Exchange), has D6741/82 (50B Dairycoates) throughout.
12	K4 3442 *The Great Marquess* operates a Victoria – Southampton special via Brighton and Chichester. Return is from Eastleigh by same route, 3442 coming off at East Croydon and running LE to 70A; diesel to Victoria.
12	'Night Ferry' has unusual motive power in the shape of two electro-diesels.
15	D6794 heads the Cliffe – Uddingston cement train both ways. (Hastings gauge D6597 (73D St Leonards) works it on the 28th).
17	Royal train to Shropshire is headed from Euston to Wellington by D217 *Carinthia*, and to Donnington where train is stabled overnight, by 44680. Last steam on an occupied Royal train?
17	Special from Carlisle to Gatwick arrives behind D232 *Empress of Canada*.
18	70025 *Western Star* reaches Hull on a rugby special from Barrow. Has to return via Goole and Knottingley, as Selby route blocked by a Dutch cargo vessel stuck under the swing bridge preventing its proper closure!
20	IOW electric services begin, on time, between Ryde (Pier head) and Shanklin.
20-22	A4 4498 *Sir Nigel Gresley* works the 23.40 Crewe – Preston parcels, and the 05.30 3-coach local return. More running-in turns.
23	Freight seen between Nottingham and Annesley is powered by D8198/9 + brake tender + D5264 + D7512, total 4500hp! A quadruple-header.
23	08.03 from Poole enters Waterloo behind 76006 + 75068, noteworthy!
25	(Easter Saturday) Ivatt 2-6-2T 41320 heads a 5-coach excursion from Bournemouth to Blandford (where coal traffic still reaches).
25	Up 'Flying Scotsman' passes Newark with D9004 *Queen's Own Highlander* + D9019 *Royal Highland Fusilier*, the latter having failed.
25	BR lays on an 18-coach special for a tour of Scotland, which departs from Edinburgh behind D368 + D1973; from Perth behind 44997 + 60009 *Union of South Africa*; from Aberdeen behind D5070 + D5127; from Aviemore behind D5070 + D5127 + D5122; from Perth to Edinburgh 44997 + 60009. Swansong for *Union*, which retires to its private line at Lochty.
27	0-6-0 shunter D2251 is used to transfer a boat train portion from Southampton (Central) to the Western Docks – most unusual.
28	D5134/5 both work holiday reliefs through Huddersfield, first of this type seen here on passenger work.
28	Noted at Wolverton Carriage Works; LNW 12-wheeled Sleeping Car repainted in rail blue/grey and displaying 'Cinema Coach' on its sides. Only pre-grouping vehicle to receive the latest livery?
31	D6855 (66A) heads the 13.00 Carlisle – Edinburgh and 17.54 return. First EE Type 3 to work a passenger train over the Waverley route.
31	Railway Technical Centre (Development & Design) extension opened at Derby by Minister of Transport. (12,000 railway employees now in Derby).
U/D	LTS 4-4-2T 80 is moved from store at Hellifield, and spends several days at Carnforth.

U/D   (Easter period) Exeter – Waterloo trains are strengthened and banked between St Davids and Central by…D1010 *Western Campaigner* and D1036 *Western Emporer*, rare duties for this type!

APRIL 1967

1ST   Restored A4 4498 *Sir Nigel Gresley* makes its inaugural public run on a Crewe/Shap/Carlisle/Ais Gill/Blackburn/Crewe railtour in snowy conditions!

1   First revenue-earning electric to Southampton (Central) is a special from Folkestone Harbour with an Italian shipping crew. 4-CEP's 7174/7122 used.

4,10   Preserved A4 60010 *Dominion of Canada* is towed from Crewe Works to London Docks via Shrewsbury, Wolverhampton and Worcester (4th). BRB presents 60010 to the Canadian High Commisioner for display at the Canadian Railroad Historical Association's museum in Montreal, and the engine is loaded aboard the MV 'Beaveroak' at Victoria Docks for shipment (10th).

4   Strike by guards at Paddington cancels the 16.45 and 18.45 services to Bristol; hence the 17.45 12-car 'Bristol Pullman' is made available to all passengers.

7   10.25 ex-Leeds enters Glasgow (Central) with 70011 *Hotspur* piloting D7612.

8   'Grand National' race day attracts nine specials to Aintree, five from London, one each from Birmingham, Grimsby, Glasgow and Newcastle.

8   70022 *Tornado* reaches Swinton on a 12-coach RL Cup special from Barrow.

10,11   44767 hauls 0-6-0 shunters D2595/97 between Carlisle and Millerhill in course of their transfer from Bradford (Hammerton Street). Run is repeated next day, with 44767 towing D2593, D2608/17.

13   D6547 leaves Preston Park (Brighton) pulling preserved M7 0-4-4T 30053 + 926 *Repton* + GWR coach 6705 to Willseden. Trio are later observed at Edge Hill sidings, Liverpool before reaching Gladstone Dock for shipment to Canada (Montreal Exhibition), then on to Bellows falls, Vermont.

14   Ex-Crosti 92024 makes a rare appearance on the Neville Hill – Ellesmere Port oil tank empties.

16   SR electric locos E5006/15/16/17/19/23/24 are noted in Crewe Works for conversion to electro-diesels in the E6101 series.

16   Four return specials from the England v Scotland soccer international are routed from Crewe to Carlisle via Hellifield, and pass Ais Gill in quick succession behind 'Britannias' 70013/34/35/38.

16   Restored K4 3442 *The Great Marquess* is piloted by 45377 between Bolton and Blackburn on a Euston/Stockport/Keighley/Leeds/King's Cross railtour, 3442 working Stockport – Leeds (Central).

18   E5011 fails at Faversham on the 22-vehicle 'Night Ferry', which eventually proceeds to Victoria behind electro-diesels E6028/49.

19   Electro-diesels E6020/47 also double-head, surprisingly, the 07.30 Bournemouth – Waterloo.

21   Preserved 2-8-0 2818 departs Eastleigh Works destined for Bristol City Museum (yet to be built), and arrives at Avonmouth for storage in the docks, heavily cocooned to prevent damage!

29   11.50 St Pancras – Bradford (Forster Square) is diverted to Leeds (Central) on the day of its closure (!) and heads for Bradford (Exchange) with 44662.

U/D   A letter, posted in Jamaica and addressed 'The Bridge School, First 2nd class Carriage, 08.45 Haywards Heath – London Bridge train' is handed over by the Station Manager at Haywards Heath! (From a former commuter on this train to his ex-companions).

MAY 1967

1ST   D9006 *The Fife and Forfar Yeomanry* heads the 08.55 Hull – King's Cross, first 'Deltic' seen in Hull. D9007 *Pinza* repeats this three weeks later.

2   D45 hauls a Senior Citizens' special from Newcastle to Eastbourne throughout.

2,5,16   09.45 Farington Jct. – Chorley freight (over 60 wagons) is double-headed by 73157 + 43019 on 2nd, 43019 + 73127 on 5th, and 75009 + 43033 on 16th.

2   0-6-0 shunter D2173 works a 5-coach mail/parcels special from Huddersfield to Stockport (in 1hr 50min). Driver retires next day after 50 years service.

5   Huddersfield gets a rare sight of D8511/12 as they pass through to York, which has 0-6-0s D9507/10/11/34 on shed (ex-WR) bound for Hull.

6   A3 4472 *Flying Scotsman* seen at Thetford with a special from Doncaster to Norwich and Yarmouth. First A3 to grace East Anglian metals in steam.

7   Railtour makes two round trips on the Swanage – Wareham branch, 'topped and tailed' by 34023 *Blackmore Vale* + 76026, and 34023 + 80011.

9   D1994 works a trial freightliner between King's Cross (Goods) and the docks at Felixstowe. First Brush '4' to run on the privately-owned Dock Railway.

10   D8615 arrives in Carlisle towing a failed DMU, the 06.41 from Hawick.

10   90373 hauls a 3-car EMU set for the Glasgow – Wemyss Bay line through Keighley, a most unusual sight here.

14   A3 4472 heads a 3-coach private special from Doncaster to Gleneagles, which includes the *Hadrian Bar* Pullman car. Takes stock to Heaton, runs south LE.

14   23.25 Waterloo – Chessington comprises 4-GRI 3086 + 4-COR 3119. First known use of Portsmouth line stock on this branch.

15,16   Restored A4 4498 *Sir Nigel Gresley* works the 12.30 Crewe – Glasgow parcels to Carlisle, and 17.25 Carlisle – Perth parcels next day, in preparation for railtour duty between Glasgow and Aberdeen on the 20th.

17   11.00 Liverpool – Newcastle arrives in Leeds behind 73011 + 45307 on the day of the official opening of the rebuilt station by the Lord Mayor.

18   77014 is highly unusual power for the 16.46 Weymouth – Bournemouth.

20   D326 arrives at Southampton Ocean Terminal hauling a special of LMR stock which it has worked through from Birkenhead.

24   LNER 8-wheeled tender 5642 (in green) appears at Huddersfield shed on its way to Hunslet Engine Co. (Leeds) as possible second tender for A4 4498. Last in use with 60026 *Miles Beevor*, this was the tender behind *Mallard* on its record breaking run in July 1938. (*Information courtesy of Melvin Haigh*).

25   D6537 reaches Stratford-on-Avon with an excursion from New Cross Gate.

26   0-6-0 shunter D3669 is employed on the 00.45 van train from Three Bridges to Chichester, an unusually long trek for a slow-speed (20mph) loco.

27   D9010 *The King's Own Scottish Borderer* exits Perth on the up car carrier.

30   45562 *Alberta* takes the Royal train from York to Nidd Bridge for overnight stabling; also works the ECS to Ripon and York, next day.

31   Down 'Devonian' reaches Plymouth behind D1107 (50A York!).

31   90362 + 92048 (the first such combination for some time) passes through Huddersfield on an oil train from Stanlow.

U/D   Down 'Master Cutler' is several times headed by a pair of Brush Type 2s.

U/D   High-speed braking tests with Bournemouth line stock produces a 108mph maximum with a 12-car set, possibly higher with a solo 4-REP unit.

U/D   General level of steam-running between Southampton and Waterloo is claimed *never* to have been higher than in April/May!

JUNE 1967

3RD   D7028 (84A Laira) works an excursion from Maidenhead into Margate.

3   15-coach Bournemouth – Waterloo train is formed of four TC units headed by electro-diesel E6042, which propels the set back as the 13.30 to Weymouth.

3,4   Tyne Dock shed services 45562 *Alberta* and A3 4472 *Flying Scotsman* , both on railtour duties. Not a shed that often sees express passenger steam power! 4472 works back to King's Cross, but retires to Nine Elms for coal, so that, early on the 4th both 4472 and 4498 are on 70A. 4498 had worked Waterloo to Bournemouth special on 3rd and was to head a Waterloo – Weymouth on 4th.

5   21.15 St Pancras – Edinburgh (on 4th) arrives in Carlisle from Leeds behind D1541 (34G!) and proceeds to Edinburgh piloted by 70013 *Oliver Cromwell*.

10   Three WR excursions reach Clacton behind D1607, D1731 (both 81A) and D7028 (84A borrowed by 81A).

10   Notably unusual is the sight of 80145 on the 07.18 Waterloo – Salisbury.

11   The Sunday 09.50 Liverpool – Glasgow is diverted via Southport and Burscough North curve, and is joined to the Manchester portion at Blackburn instead of Preston, stopping at Lostock Hall for Preston passengers to alight.

14   E5014 takes the Portsmouth line, unusually, at Woking with an ECS train.

17   A3 4472 works a King's Cross – Newcastle special which is brought back over the Settle & Carlisle by D9005 *The Prince of Wales's Own Regiment of Yorkshire* – first 'Deltic' over the S&C since the test runs in 1956?

17   North Tyneside electric services end, with a special 8-car formation on the 18.15 Newcastle – Wallsend – Newcastle. Twelve DMU sets are drafted from Scotland to Gosforth to replace the old NER electric units.

18   Reading – Ramsgate excursion is formed of three WR Pressed Steel DMUs.

18   34108 *Wincanton* + 34089 *602 Squadron* head a 'Farewell to SR Steam' special though Hinton Admiral. Pairs of Pacifics are rare, even on specials.

24   D7021 is in charge, surprisingly, of the 06.15 Exeter (St Davids) – Waterloo.

24   82019 (70A) appears at Marylebone (first steam here since last September) probably for a filming contract next day.

25   D1608 (81A) brings a WR excursion into Margate, first Brush '4' seen here?

25   34102 *Lapford* reaches Westbury on a Weymouth – Crewe tomato train.

29   'Tees-Tyne Pullman' set appears at Scarborough conveying a Consett Iron Co. staff outing. D271 heads the train. (This set is also used for other Saturday specials from Newcastle to Scarborough during the summer).

U/D   7029 *Clun Castle* works LE from Tyseley to head the 19.10 Banbury to Bordesley goods for several days, running-in after piston valve attention.

U/D LTS 4-4-2T No. 80 is still at Carnforth, bound, eventually for the Pullman Car Co.'s works at Preston Park, Brighton.

U/D D6706 is fitted with a flashing headlight and, apparently, a chime whistle similar to an A4s!

JULY 1967

1ST 75074 takes a Portsmouth Harbour – Bolton special through to Willesden.

1 D6519 noted at Weston-super-Mare on an excursion of SR stock.

2 SR's official 'Farewell to Steam' special has 35007 *Aberdeen Commonwealth* + 35008 *Orient Line* double-heading between Weymouth and Bournemouth, an extremely rare combination under any circumstance.

2 Railtour from Birmingham reaches York behind 70038 *Robin Hood*.

2-16 A3 4472 *Flying Scotsman* and A4 4498 *Sir Nigel Gresley*, plus E3036 are on display at Chester station for the Arts Festival. 4472 is absent on 9th, in charge of a Chester – Blackpool special. 4498 hauled both the others from Crewe.

3 Granada TV shoots a re-creation of an 1840s 3-coach train at Park Bridge, Manchester. Two replica 1838 coaches are constructed and painted but the 'loco' is a blown-up photo of 2-2-2 *Cornwall* mounted on blockboard and propped up on the track!

4,5 D1062 *Western Courier* appears twice on the Windsor line, passing Whitton on both days with condemned coaches from Clapham Jct. to South Wales.

6 D1029 *Western Legionnaire* is piloted from Newton Abbot to Plymouth by D1988 (52A Gateshead!) on the 09.35 from Cardiff – an improbable pairing.

8 D8304/02 power the 09.20 Scarborough – Manchester as far as Leeds.

8 Wandering D1988 now heads the 17.35 Paddington – New Street, an equally unexpected service to be seen working.

8 D8121 reaches Stranraer with an annual special from Aberdeen.

8 07.18 Waterloo – Salisbury is surprisingly headed by 82029!

9 Final day of SR steam. 73029 works over the Portsmouth direct line with ECS to Clapham Jct. from Fratton. Frome sees the passage of 34095 *Brentor* on the 10.20 Weymouth – Crewe; 34052 *Lord Dowding* on the 14.20 Weymouth – Bescot and 73092 on the 15.00 ex-Weymouth, all three on perishables traffic from the Channel Islands, working as far as Westbury. 77014 with vans from Bournemouth is the last steam to arrive at Weymouth. Last ever 'Bournemouth Belle' is powered by a grimy D1924 despite being diagrammed for steam. Bournemouth line 'Goes Electric' next day.

10 BRB official party returning from inauguration celebrations on the 16.40 from Bournemouth are ¾ hour late into Waterloo.

11,12 60019 *Bittern* is run-in on the 16.27 York – Newcastle parcels and 22.27 parcels back to York both days, prior to a Leeds – Glasgow special (16th).

12 Through Aberystwyth – Euston train is worked to/from Wolverhampton (HL) by D5084 + D5145, the pair running round the train at Shrewsbury, an innovation on these services.

14 An EE Type1 pilots 70028 *Royal Star* on the 21.05 relief out of Glasgow (Central).

15 53 steam-hauled passenger trains pass through Preston, of which 43 are '5's.

15 Wagons-Lits Sleeping Car 3985 of the 'Night Ferry' formation (built 1952 but newly

overhauled) is on display at Old Oak Common diesel depot Open Day. Bears plates for the London – Basle service due to start in December. First W-L vehicle to go on show to the public in UK for 20 years. Worked from Paris two days earlier and is returned on 16th.

15   Failure of a semi-fast at Brockenhurst causes the 10.05 ex-Weymouth to be formed from E6009/22 in the middle of the train, propelling one TC set and hauling two more, from Brockenhurst onwards.

15-17   Waverley route sees the passage of 64 trains in 33 hours (15 is the usual total) including 15 'Deltics' as East Coast line is blocked north of Newcastle.

18   70023 *Venus* + 70025 *Western Star* noted at Grayrigg on an up parcels.

18   General Manager's 2-coach inspection special traverses the Catterick Camp railway, hauled from York by D8312.

19   D7035 reaches as far as Ipswich on a special train of carflats from Hinksey to Felixstowe, and returns light engine. Rare class in East Anglia.

19   70035 *Rudyard Kipling* arrives in Tyne Yard on freight from Carlisle, and returns immediately.

20   Bradford portion of ex-King's Cross train is worked forward from Leeds by 45027 + D5098, the unlikely pair returning to Leeds with 1E73 to London.

22   Relief to the down 'Devonian' runs non-stop through New Street, most unusual as the Camp Hill line is normally used to avoid New Street if not stopping. Main train is worked by, surprisingly, D1566 (31B).

25   SR Co-Co electric 20001 arrives at Winchester on a 3-coach Royal train working from Waterloo.

29   09.30 Paddington – Penzance leaves Exeter with D1028 *Western Hussar* piloted by D7032, unusual to be double-headed at this location.

30   D5630, D5682 both reach Crowborough on army cadet specials from Norwich and Lowestoft respectively, and return with the empty stock.

31   Collision at Thirsk causes the 14.00 down 'Heart of Midlothian' to run via the S&C line and the Waverley route. By 18.45 the Northallerton/Harrogate line (closed 4/3/67) is passed for use with 30mph speed limit north of Melmerby. This route is then used for down trains for the next three days.

U/D   D193 reaches Felixstowe on a freightliner train from King's Cross.

U/D   Summer Saturdays 10.00 Liverpool Street – Sheringham and 14.42 return, is formed of two 3-car DMU sets.

U/D   During the last two weeks of steam to Bournemouth, 35008 *Orient Line* is recorded at over 100mph between Grateley and Andover.

AUGUST 1967

1ST   Crew training for Midlands drivers on D800-class diesels begins when 8-coach ECS trains are run between Oxley and Chester.

2   D176 on the 16.42 ex-Newcastle is 'raced' upgrade out of Huddersfield by 48070 on a short freight. D176 is overtaken in no uncertain manner!

3   26014 is towed from Reddish to Soho electric depot Birmingham, for possible conversion to AC/DC – to be carried out by GEC of Witton.

4   D602 *Bulldog* is noted at Cardiff. Long confined to the Plymouth – Penzance route, D601/2/4 are now transferred to 87E (Landore).

| 10 | 17.00 from Waterloo is so late into Exeter that westbound passengers are catered for by putting platform seats into the van of the 18.55 Kensington to Plymouth milk empties. A 'Please return the platform seats' note is attached! |

10   17.00 from Waterloo is so late into Exeter that westbound passengers are catered for by putting platform seats into the van of the 18.55 Kensington to Plymouth milk empties. A 'Please return the platform seats' note is attached!

10   D1973 (64B!) unexpectedly reaches Reading on the 08.30 from Newcastle.

11   12.10 Euston – Perth is worked through from Carlisle by 70051 *Firth of Forth*.

11   LTS 4-4-2T No.80 leaves Carnforth for Hellifield after its dome cover had been reduced in height to clear catenary on the run to Brighton. MR locos 118 and 158A depart Hellifield for Leicester, but 158A is at Holbeck on the 19th.

16-21   7029 *Clun Castle* arrives at Derby (for weighing) from Tyseley. Departs for York next day and undergoes platform clearance tests at Newcastle the day after, being serviced at Gateshead – first steam engine here for two years (18th). 7029 also conducts further clearance tests in the Aire Valley (21st) prior to working over the S&C line at the end of next month.

17   62005 arrives LE at Holbeck, for a boiler exam at Hunslet Engine Co.'s works, with a view to transferring the boiler to preserved K4 3442.

20   12.05 Penzance – Paddington is, unusually, powered by D1653 with D808 *Centaur* as pilot, which is not detached at Newton Abbot.

21   Up West of England train arrives at Bristol with D601 *Ark Royal* piloting D1017 *Western Warrior*, a rare combination. (D601 is in course of transfer).

22   D602 *Bulldog* is noted at Llandrindod Wells, conducting clearance tests.

25   70013 *Oliver Cromwell* arrives at Derby for display at the Works Open Day on the following day, the only steam engine on show.

26   D6597 passes through Tiverton Jct. towards Exeter with the 09.57 Brighton to Exeter relief. First 'Hastings' narrow-bodied loco to reach the West Country.

26-28   D842 *Royal Oak* runs through Cheltenham on the 12.35 Sheffield – Cardiff, first 'Warship' here? D842 also reaches New Street two days later on a Plymouth – Bradford relief (Bank Holiday Monday).

28   Bournemouth – Dover (Marine) special is worked throughout by a 4-VEP unit.

28   D5214 + D5241 reach Southend (Central) with an excursion from Bedford.

28   70045 *Lord Rowallan* pulls out of Liverpool (Lime Street) on an excursion to Windermere; 70039 *Sir Christopher Wren* also heads a special to Blackpool.

30   Northbound 'Devonian' leaves Newton Abbot behind the unexpected pairing of D827 *Kelly* piloted by D830 *Majestic*.

U/D   Official announcement is made of plans to close St Pancras.

U/D   MR preserved locos 118 and 158A arrive at Leicester shed for storage prior to entering Leicester Museum.

U/D   Up 'Royal Scot' is powered by D5348 + D1806 between Glasgow and Carlisle, an unusual combination.

U/D   'Hymek' Type 3s begin to replace EE Type 3s on banking duties on the Lickey incline, resulting 'in a crash programme of crew training being pushed through' – to quote an official source!

SEPTEMBER 1967

1ST   Caterham receives a 'Peak' to work a troop special to Morpeth – any loco hauled train is rare at Caterham.

2   08.00 Waterloo – Exeter (St Davids) arrives with D832 *Onslaught* as pilot to D6533, the

unusual pair also taking out the return working.

4   17.45 Liverpool/Manchester – Glasgow arrives in Central behind 45345 + 70031 *Byron*. Double-headers into Central are always rare (the pilot is usually detached at Polmadie), but especially as steam has almost ended in Scotland.

4   7029 *Clun Castle* reaches Hitchin on a test train of eight bogies, takes water from the DMU hydrant and returns north again, in preparation for the 9th.

8   Pullman car special runs from Leeds to Blackpool for the switching on of the illuminations. D385 powers the arrival, fails, and 'Peak' D35 heads the return.

9   7029, on a railtour originating at King's Cross, stands on King Edward Bridge, Newcastle and changes engines to 62005. 7029 returns LE to 55A.

14,15   Remains of 60026 *Miles Beevor* are towed through Huddersfield eastwards (from Crewe) by a diesel. Next day, roles are reversed when A4 4498 *Sir Nigel Gresley* tows a dead diesel through Huddersfield *en route* to Crewe!

17   7029 arrives in Leeds on a special from King's Cross, and is serviced at 55A(Holbeck), which celebrates an Open Day for the occasion.

18   Train 1A91 leaves Newton Abbot for Paddington with D1042 *Western Princess* piloting D1732, an unusual and powerful combination of 5450hp.

19   Preserved 0-6-0 3205 + two coaches is watered by the fire brigade at Evesham station, returning to Bridgnorth from an Open Day at Taplow. Local TV network covers 3205's progress.

20-22   34002 *Salisbury* (withdrawn but in good external condition) spends three days on Gloucester shed attracting attention, and visitors.

22   WR excursion to the Trossachs leaves Cheltenham behind D1675 on a train of ten vehicles including a Buffet Car and two Sleeping Cars.

23   61306 (last working B1) heads the 14.49 Leeds – Heysham parcels train.

23   A3 4472 *Flying Scotsman* reaches Norwich, Ipswich on special from York.

25   16.00 Blackpool (North) – Glasgow return special is powered by 70045 *Lord Rowallan* to Carlisle (via Ais Gill) and by 70012 *John of Gaunt* onwards.

29   70011 *Hotspur* heads a special van train from Doncaster to Leeds.

29   48729 runs through Wigan (Wallgate) hauling three 4-car sets of Lancaster to Morecambe EMU stock, for scrapping at Long Marston.

29   D5242 hauls privately-owned 45596 *Bahamas* from Stockport to the Hunslet Engine Co., Leeds, for overhaul.

30   70023 *Venus* works an up troop train of SR stock through Preston; D1675 (82A) heads for Blackpool on a special, as does D1555 (40B) hauling a Cambridge Buffet Express set with 'King's Cross – Cambridge' roofboards.

30, 1 Oct   Peterborough – Carlisle railtours are steam hauled between Doncaster and Carlisle, with 7029 going north, A4 4498 coming south on the 30th; reversed on 1st October.

U/D   A number of trains between Wolverhampton, Chester are formed of failed DMU sets hauled by Brush Type 4s.

U/D   D601 *Ark Royal*, D602 *Bulldog* both reported working coal trains from South Wales as far as Llandrindod Wells.

U/D   62 year-old porter at Croston (Liverpool/Preston) discovers the early morning trains each way are cancelled due to the unofficial dispute; cycles off to tell the 7 or 8 regular passengers of this and save them an exasperating wait!

OCTOBER 1967

3RD A4 4498 *Sir Nigel Gresley* returns south from Carlisle after railtour duty as pilot to 48727 on the 05.10 freight to Bescot!

5 D8206/38 head a Temple Mills – Hoo Jct. freight passed Dartford, first of this type seen on this service.

6 D1661 *North Star* (87E!) arrives in St Pancras on the 08.55 from Sheffield.

8 Unprecedented event – a Sunday train over the St Andrews branch! Excursion from Glasgow is run in connection with a golf tournament, headed by D5369 to Leuchars, where D5122 (60A) attaches at the rear to 'top & tail' the train.

14 92091 works a Liverpool – Carlisle railtour to Preston; 7029 *Clun Castle* takes over, northbound via Shap, returning via Ais Gill to Hellifield. Here 92091 resumes command; 7029 runs LE to Lostock Hall, then Tyseley.

14 45596 *Bahamas* noted under repair at Hunslet Engine Co. (Leeds).

15 Oct-19 Nov Marylebone and Kensington Olympia become temporary additional termini for services to/from Paddington whilst the latter is being resignalled. First arrival at Olympia is D7076 on 10.10 from Worcester (15th); Marylebone sees D841 *Roebuck* arrive from Snow Hill (16th), D7060 and D1672 come in two days later, and ECS workings are handled by D6327/48/52.

16,19 18.00 Waterloo – Salisbury is formed of a BRCW Type 3 (push/pull fitted) + two TC sets + electro-diesel propelling from the rear, on both days. An uncommon arrangement.

19 45562 *Alberta* seen on Royal train duty, firstly providing steam heat in Newcastle, then taking the train to South Gosforth to stable overnight.

20 Romiley Golf Club hires a 3-car DMU to travel from Hazel Grove to a dance at Buxton, leaving at 19.15 returning 02.00, the line being kept open specially.

21 Bristol (Bath Road) Open Day display includes 7029, 7808 *Cookham Manor*, 46201 *Princess Elizabeth* and 0-6-0PT 1638 (towed from Tyseley by 7029), plus 34013 *Okehampton*, 34100 *Appledore, en route* to South Wales for scrap, but 'borrowed' for the occasion. 10,000 people attend.

21 Colour-light signal between Merchiston and Slateford Jct. still shows red, despite all track having been removed!

28 D178 reaches Bishop Auckland on an FA Amateur Cup special.

28 Cheap Day tickets introduced Euston – Birmingham/Coventry for 10s return to popularise the electric service.

28 70013 *Oliver Cromwell* appears on a railtour on the Penistone line out of Huddersfield – first steam seen on this route for some years.

28 BR embargo on steam hauled specials comes into force. Only those organised before this date are allowed to run after the cut-off date. So…

30 Nottingham – Carlisle special has D145 to Crewe, A4 4498 to Carlisle via Shap attaining 96mph at Hartford and running Carnforth – Shap 5min quicker than the 'Caledonian', with 11 coaches instead of 8. Returns via Ais Gill, Accrington to reach Crewe, where D145 takes over.

31 14.05 ex-Euston arrives into Glasgow (Central) behind a Type 4 with 70013 *Oliver Cromwell* coupled inside for steam heating purposes.

U/D WR Inspection Saloon W80969W – in faded carmine & cream livery – is noted at Waverley, of all places.

U/D   Six AL4s E3036/38/41/42/44/45 are observed stored in Bury shed, with the remaining four of this class expected shortly.

NOVEMBER 1967

4TH   60019 *Bittern* heads a Leeds – Edinburgh railtour via Newcastle, both ways.

4   D5642 (34G) noted at Darlington – a class rarely seen north of York.

5   D6122 (65A but ex-store at Inverurie) turns up, most surprisingly, at Hither Green, where jaws drop in disbelief!

5   D9010 *The King's Own Scottish Borderer* passes Portobello with the President of Turkey's train, consisting of Royal Saloons plus LMR Sleeping Cars.

6   92203, with a 'Summer Ore' headboard pulls the last steam-hauled Bidston to Shotton iron ore train, with Sir Richard Summers on the footplate. 92203 is then sold into private hands for preservation.

7   70011 *Hotspur*, returning LE from Edinburgh, fails at Newcastleton and is conveyed to Carlisle in the 21.30 Millerhill – Oldham freight.

15   D850 *Swift* (81A) breaks new ground, working an engineering train from Oxley, via Walsall and Nuneaton, onto the Coventry line.

18   A3 4472 *Flying Scotsman* departs St Pancras on a special for Chesterfield, returning it to King's Cross.

23   D1514 (34G!) is unexpected power for the 08.30 Plymouth – Paddington and the 16.00 thence to Swansea.

25   0-6-0PT 1638 is the last loco to take water at Newton Abbot's column, when running LE from Bristol to Totnes and the Dart Valley Railway.

25 Oct – 19 Nov Marylebone sees the following engines on trains diverted from Paddington;

          D6326/32/41/45/50/54/57 on ECS workings
          D7035/60/64/73 on 07.35 ex-Banbury, D7063/66 – other trains
          D836/38/40/41/46   D5216/17/18/22
          D1674/86/87/90   D1712/39

almost all of which will never reach Marylebone again!

25   60019 *Bittern* heads a Leeds/Carnforth/Wigan/Manchester/Bolton/Rochdale/Leeds railtour. Has Rochdale ever seen an A4 before?

25   D9008 *The Green Howards* on the 21.24 Bradford (Exchange) – King's Cross is diverted to run via Gainsborough, Lincoln and Sleaford.

27   D363 (64B) is an unusual loco to work the up 'Hull Pullman'.

27   Iced-up conductor rail strands the 12-car 07.27 Eastbourne – London Bridge EMU north of Haywards Heath. The following 12-car EMU forming the 07.37 Littlehampton – Victoria couples at the rear, and the 24-car ensemble proceeds to Purley, where the trains are split and pursue separate paths. Longest passenger-carrying train since the war?

28   Derailment at Raynes Park causes the 10.07 and 11.13 arrivals at Waterloo from the West of England to be diverted into Paddington. Return workings at 11.00, 13.00 also start from here.

U/D   King's scrapyard at Norwich receives 75074, 75075, 75077 from Salisbury, yet another type rarely seen in East Anglia in normal service.

DECEMBER 1967

2ND 6998 *Burton Agnes Hall* tows 0-4-2T 1466 + 3 preserved coaches belonging to the GW Society, from Plymouth to Didcot.

2 D6948 + brake tender noted at Edge Hill goods yard – first EE Type 3 seen in the Liverpool area.

5 D828 *Magnificent* heads the 19.13 Paddington – New Street. These services are usually in the hands of Brush Type 4s.

5,6 D1665 (87E Landore!) observed on the Waverley route with the Kings Norton to Bathgate car train, and return working next day.

6 D816 *Eclipse* appears on the Fawley branch with the 11.20 Hillsea – Fawley and 13.15 Fawley – Eastleigh, whilst D207 reaches Hamworthy on a special roadstone freight, returning light engine. Both rare loco workings.

8 Heavy snow paralyses all train movements around Brighton for 4 hours. 08.30 from Waterloo takes 8 hours to Bournemouth amidst memorable disruption.

9 23.59 (8th) Victoria – Brighton leaves at 01.00 and after several reversals and detours *en route*, reaches Brighton at 06.25. The 06.15 from Exeter is very late into Salisbury, so 'Hampshire' DEMU 1133 forms an extra to Waterloo.

9 06.45 Plymouth – Paddington fails at Newton Abbot. D1051 *Western Embassador* is removed and replaced by the 4900hp combination of D823 *Hermes* + D1063 *Western Monitor* on 5 coaches plus one van! The 14.00 Penzance – Paddington calls all stations Plymouth – Exeter (as local services cancelled), meaning Exeter (St Thomas) is served (uniquely?) by a Penzance – Paddington express.

9 Cheap shopping excursions are run from Birmingham and Coventry to Euston. 3,600 people travel thus up to London in 4 x 12-coach EMUs.

12 All Weymouth services start/finish at Bournemouth, with two 'Hampshire' units working a shuttle service between the two towns. At this time the SW Division has never been in such a bad state, especially the Bournemouth line.

14 Exeter (Riverside) – Newton Abbot freight is triple-headed by D6331/36/37!

22 06.30 Hull – Liverpool 'Trans-Pennine' finds Standedge Tunnel blocked, so reverses from Huddersfield to gain the Calder Valley route via Rochdale. First time a 'TP' has run to Manchester this way?

23 D5116 (60A) is surprisingly found working coal trains out of Ayr!

23 D9010 *The King's Own Scottish Borderer* heads the 04.00 newspaper train Edinburgh – Hawick, and the 06.58 return passenger service.

26 70013 *Oliver Cromwell* hauls a 13-coach football special Carlisle – Blackpool (South) and is serviced at North shed 21 miles by rail, 2 miles by sea breeze. All other 7MTs are withdrawn at the end of the month.

27 D1902 (86A Canton!) is a surprise to work the 10.45 King's Cross – Sheffield.

27 75043 is coupled inside D221 *Ivernia* to steam heat the 11.00 Windermere to Euston. The pair is replaced at Carnforth.

28 D1781 noted at Hither Green sidings, the first of this class seen here.

29 70013 steam-hauls the 17.47 (FO) Manchester –York for the last time.

U/D Congestion at New Street causes Cardiff, Hereford and Worcester trains to re-use what remains of Snow Hill. Many complaints ensue regarding 'own transfer' between stations and missed connections at New Street.

U/D   Blizzard conditions further south cause the Birmingham – Edinburgh to arrive 2½ hours late behind D8558, i.e. no train heating from Carstairs!

U/D   Part of the recently opened car park at St Enoch is closed due to the pigeon population fouling the parked cars!

JANUARY 1968

3RD   Train from Epsom Downs hits fallen tree near Sutton. Passengers de-train and walk 100yd along track to Sutton station.

4   D1834 (ML) is well off the beaten track on a Swansea – Paddington express.

6   SR 'Hastings' 6-car DEMU set 1001 undergoes riding tests out of King's Cross as far as Grantham. Later in the month, D1938 is seen propelling an 11-coach test train (with dynamometer car) between Sandy and Doncaster.

7   USA 0-6-0T 30064 is hauled from Salisbury to Knowle Jct. for transfer to Doxford and the Sadler Rail Coach Company.

9   Bad weather effects. Overnight blizzard brings New Street to a standstill, 06.00 – 09.00; several trains divert to Snow Hill (!). Difficulty in despatching ECS to Euston forces AM10 EMUs to be used on through express workings to Manchester. Floodwater at Exeter (St Davids) causes delays and Barnstaple line closed. Bideford road bridge collapses; single-unit railcar provides (free!) shuttle service Bideford/Torrington (line closed 10/65). Dover portion of the 22.10 to Victoria consists of E6005 plus 2-HAP + 4-CEP + 2 x 2-HAP sets, terminating at Faversham. Ramsgate portion proceeds solo.

9,19,23 V2 4771 *Green Arrow* and 44027 leave Hellifield (9th), as do LTS 4-4-2T No.80 and J17 0-6-0 1217E on 19th, heading for Preston Park, where 45000 and 92220 *Evening Star* arrive on the 23rd – all for storage.

12   D1020 *Western Hero* is a most unusual visitor to reach Redhill.

12,13 Strangers at King's Cross. D153 (55A) arrives on the morning 'Talisman'. Next day D7573 (55A) comes in on the 4-coach 08.25 from Leeds; Up 'Yorkshire Pullman' has D387 (8F Springs Branch, Wigan – surely a first here) and D1893 (56A Knottingley) heads the down Aberdeen freightliner.

13   (Week ending) Wagons-Lits Sleeping Car 3805 is on view in platform 15 at Waterloo as part of 'Holiday Ideas' exhibition on concourse.

15   Disastrous overnight storm brings Glasgow Blue Trains almost to a standstill.

16   D9002 *The King's Own Yorkshire Light Infantry* breaks new ground, working LE from Leeds to Bradford (Forster Sq.), returning with one van for Heaton!

18   D1607 (82A!) arrives in Whitemoor yard on freight from Temple Mills.

19   D233 *Empress of England* enters Paddington from Oxford, surprising power.

20   Research Dept (Derby) hosts D1961, D7055, D6700, D7559. Recent visitors include AC electrics E3066/163/200.

22   21.44 parcels train from Halifax comprising Pullman car *Amber* as the sole load, passes through Huddersfield where any such vehicle is a rare sight.

22   Southampton – Waterloo boat train has D857 *Undaunted* as surprise loco.

22   07.57 from Folkestone is only 7min late into Charing Cross, its best performance since 17 July last year!

24   14.55 Manchester – Plymouth arrives in Exeter behind D7017 piloting D1066 *Western Prefect* (on one engine). An uncommon pairing.

25	Former North Tyneside articulated twin EMU noted at Worthing, strangely.
U/D	Clayton Type 1s take over banking duties on Shap, from steam.
U/D	D9004 *Queen's Own Highlander* operates a train of air-braked stock twice daily between Edinburgh and Dundee.
U/D	New EE Type 4 D404 seen on crew training turns, Perth – Stirling.
U/D	Rebuilt Buffet Cars (nos S69319-29) running in REP sets are named after places associated with the SR, shades of the 'Tavern Cars' of earlier years.
U/D	From Christmas Eve, for six weeks, 62005 is used as a steam raiser at North Tees works of ICI at Port Clarence. Loco was officially withdrawn on 30/12/67.

FEBRUARY 1968

1ST	J17 0-6-0 1217E (in transit to Brighton) suffers a hot tender axlebox, retires to Bedford MPD for 3-4 weeks but is moved out into the sun for photographers!
1	14.10 Worcester – Paddington is double-headed by a 'Hymek' + 'Warship' pairing, most unusually.
2,3	D853 *Thruster*, D837 *Ramillies* both work special freights between Bescot and Stoke (class debuts here?) returning light engine.
3	D9004 *Queen's Own Highlander* noted at Cupar on braking trials, and D9010 *The King's Own Scottish Borderer* heads the 19.59 Aberdeen – Waverley. 'Deltics' begin to appear more frequently north of Edinburgh.
5	WR Brush Type 4s have a regular rostered daily visit to…Liverpool Street! Canton diagram 10 (M-F) includes working the 17.30 to Yarmouth (Vauxhall) as far as Norwich, then the 20.20 freight to Bristol.
6	D1773 (34G!) reaches Exeter (Riverside) on 7N58 ex-Manvers Main Colliery.
8	D1988 (52A!) spends the day as standby loco at…Paddington, after hauling the 20.00 Cardiff – Acton on the 7th.
8	NCB 0-4-0ST takes water at Huddersfield *en route* from Hartley Bank Colliery to Emley Moor Colliery under its own power, a rare sight.
9	D1920 (70D Eastleigh!) departs Whitemoor yard with freight to Temple Mills. (Another instance of 'foreign' Brush Type 4's turning up just about anywhere).
13,20,27	Arrivals at Preston Park, towed from Stratford via Stewarts Lane are: M7 0-4-4T 30245, 30850 *Lord Nelson* (13th); 30925 *Cheltenham*, L&Y 2-4-2T 1008, LSWR 4-4-0 120 (20th); 2-4-0WT 30587, 70000 *Britannia* on 27th.
14	D6700 conducts trials between Doncaster and Peterborough with a 9-coach push/pull set (+ ER dynamometer car). Riding, braking in 'push' mode tested.
17	Crew training takes place between Stewarts Lane and Orpington, with a Brush Type 4 hauling two 4-CEP units.
19	Rebuilt electro-diesel E6102 is tested with 35 air-braked coal hoppers from Hither Green to Dover and back.
21	D5821/56 are observed descending the Lickey (not a type often seen in these parts) on a coal train from Wath.
24	D5702 seen between Chinley and Cheadle Heath, a very rare sight here
28	D1525 (34G) arrives in Glasgow (Central) on the 'Thames-Clyde Express'. Has a Finsbury Park diesel ever reached here before (or pulled this train)?
27,29	D15, D190 (both 55A) arrive at Exeter (Riverside) on the 07.00 freight from Severn Tunnel Jct. Have Holbeck locos ever reached here before?

29   Restored 7029 *Clun Castle* heads the 16.10 Knowle – Banbury freight and the 19.10 back to Bordesley. Unexpected!

29   D6700 commences push/pull trials between Glasgow, Edinburgh on five coaches, E34500 being fitted with driving controls. High-speed trials follow.

U/D   Southampton – Newcastle freightliner service brings 70D (Eastleigh) Brush Type 4s to Newcastle on a regular basis. D1926 is also used on the 11.30 to Edinburgh and 16.10 return, on the 25th!

U/D   21.55 Dringhouses – Tyne Yard freight, plus 08.15 Cardiff – Newcastle passenger working, bring Brush Type 4s from 87E, 82A, 81A to Tyneside on a regular basis.

MARCH 1968

4TH   E3014 appears at Tyseley for minor repairs and weighing.

4   The 'North Briton' arrives in Edinburgh from Leeds behind D220 *Franconia* (8J). First time that an Allerton-allocated diesel has reached Edinburgh?

5   More arrivals at Preston Park from Stratford are; 30777 *Sir Lamiel*, Q1 0-6-0 33001, and 2-6-4T 42500 all towed via Stewarts Lane.

8   Last passenger train to use Kings Road station, Devonport, consists of four Royal Saloons + D1023 *Western Fusilier* for stabling, before D821 *Greyhound* takes the Duke of Edinburgh into Plymouth.

9   06.32 Newport – Portsmouth is a 3-coach train headed by D7069 instead of the usual 6-car Cross-Country DMU

9   Leeds United v Bristol City FA Cup match generates seven specials from Bristol, one of which is a coupled pair of WR diesel Pullman sets. This runs over the Lickey, and makes its first appearance in the West Riding. (See also 16 October 1965).

10   D854 *Tiger* is unusual power for a Bournemouth – Weymouth parcels train.

12   D1771 (30A) makes it to Edinburgh on a car transporter train. Few Stratford engines ever reach this far north.

13   A4 4498 *Sir Nigel Gresley* is the first steam to arrive in Shrewsbury for four months, coming in LE from Crewe, returning two hour later.

16   9B (Stockport) hosts 5596 *Bahamas* (recently arrived from Hunslet Engine Co., restored and repainted), A3 4472 *Flying Scotsman* and 70013 *Oliver Cromwell* – these last two to work rail tours to Carnforth next day.

18   D7012 heads the 19.00 to Exeter out of Waterloo, noteworthy power.

21   SR DC electric 20001 appears at Faversham with a 7-coach set, crew training.

22   Due to a signalling error, the 15.25 Liverpool – Euston is turned onto the Aston line on leaving New Street. Train is sent round the LNW circle line, and passes through New Street again 20min after first departure!

23   USA 0-6-0Ts DS 237/8 (ex-Ashford Works shunters) are towed to Tonbridge and are still there a week later.

23   A3 4472 *Flying Scotsman* exits St Pancras heading a special to the KWVR.

24   D1957 on the Glasgow – Birmingham fails at Dent Head (S&C line). D1623 on the following Glasgow – Liverpool buffers-up and pushes & pulls the two trains (26 coaches) to Hellifield, where D223 tows D1957 + train to Preston.

25   Privately-owned 5596 *Bahamas* runs LE from Longsight to Buxton and back.

28   D5580 (32A) runs through Coventry and Nuneaton (Trent Valley), where Norwich

engines rarely appear, on the diverted Birmingham – Yarmouth.

28   16.15 Windermere – Euston passes Warrington behind D318 + D1951, an infrequent combination.

30   D1556 (40B) is a surprise arrival at Reading on the 16.00 Avonmouth to Thames Haven oil train.

30   Nine 'Grand National' excursions are run to Aintree (Sefton Arms) including one from Grimsby, as usual with a Pullman car + observation car at the rear.

U/D   Vale of Rheidol locos 7,8,9 are the only BR steam engines to receive the new blue livery and 'double-arrow' symbol.

U/D   DC electrics 27000-6 are to be stored at Bury along with E3036-45.

U/D   D5714 observed on Toton depot, the first seen here.

U/D   J17 0-6-0 1217E finally reaches Stewarts Lane, and is still there on 1 April.

APRIL 1968

1ST   J27 0-6-0 65827 noted at the NCB shed at Philadelphia (Co. Durham); repairs.

3   'Night Limited' sleeper from Euston is taken forward from Motherwell by D8533 + D8548, round the Cathcart circle to reach Glasgow (Central), due to a derailment at Shawford. Unique power for such a train.

6,7   92203 + 75029 (both in steam) run coupled LE from Crewe to Cricklewood continuing, separately, to Liss and Longmoor MR next day.

7   Camping Coach at Glenfinnan is former SEC Royal Saloon 7930, surprisingly.

8   D1997 (34G) is unlikely power on the 17.15 Kingmoor – Tyne Yard goods.

11   10.30 'Cornish Riviera Express' leaves Paddington behind D1740 (WL = Western Lines of LMR), a most unlikely locomotive.

11   13.10 Glasgow – Euston arrives at Carlisle with D5307 + D5070 (both 64B) in charge, very unusual types for this service. D413 replaces both, heads south.

11   D5061 + D5276 (both 9A) substitute for a Type 4 on the 17.47 Manchester (Exchange) – Newcastle.

12   Operational problems occur at Carlisle (especially) as the ScR is running a weekday service and the LMR a Sunday service! (It is Good Friday).

13   Vale of Rheidol 2-6-2T 9 *Prince of Wales* works the first train of the season from Aberystwyth, repainted in BR blue with 'double-arrow' symbol.

14   60532 *Blue Peter* is noted in store outside Thornton depot (62A).

14   08.55 Cardiff – Paignton excursion is formed of a 6-car Swindon-built Inter-City DMU, the first seen in the South West for many months.

14   D405 conducts high-speed push/pull tests between Glasgow and Edinburgh. Speeds in excess of 100mph are achieved.

16   Due to the late running of other services, a special train is put on between Ely and Cambridge consisting of D5699 + DMU power car E51263, which is normally reserved for parcels traffic.

16   D5573 (32B) works a York – Tyne Yard freight, uncommon class so far north.

20,27   Railtour arrives at Stalybridge behind 45110 + 44949, departing with 73134 + 73069 for the next stage to Bolton. Next week 44781 + 45046 hand over to 73050 + 73069 on a repeat tour.

22   D1758, bearing a 'London – Paris Freightliner' headboard, inaugurates the service by working the Stratford – Dover leg of the journey.

24	Train of four Pullman cars plus brake van passes through Worcester, towards Hereford Pullman cars are extreme rarities hereabouts.
30	Prior to A3 4472 *Flying Scotsman's* commemorative run next day, the LMR stages a 6-hour Euston – Glasgow test run, with a D400 class north of Crewe.
U/D	Preserved MR locos 118, 158A are moved to a former tram depot in London Road, Leicester along with NER electric 26500. The roundhouse at Leicester still contains 49395, 63601, 4771 *Green Arrow*, 44027 – all stored.
U/D	A Brush Type 4 conducts early morning tour of underground Mersey electric lines. These clearance tests last 5 hours, to see if this type could be used on engineering trains.
U/D	Since October 1967 the WR has had the use of a French-built (1965) 0-4-0 diesel hydraulic loco designed for the laying, inspection and maintenance of track. This shunter arrived in the UK in September 1966 on loan to the SR, for evaluation during the Bournemouth electrification work, and saw use in the Woking and Shalford PW yards moving track panels. After completion of this project it transferred to the WR, and has now been returned to France to work on the SNCF. (*Information courtesy of Barry Fletcher*).

MAY 1968

1ST	A3 4472 *Flying Scotsman* exits King's Cross on the 40th anniversary of its first non-stop 'Flying Scotsman' run to Waverley, next to D9021 *Argyll & Sutherland Highlander* on the 10.00 'F.S.'. 4472 is met at Waverley by the Lord Provost, pipe band and large crowd having again achieved a non-stop run.
4	'Viscount' airliner overshoots the runway at Southend at 20.20, with a wing beneath the catenary and wreckage on the line – which re-opens next morning.
4	D401 appears at Darlington for wheel-balancing after a derailment last week.
6	Final steam-hauled 'Belfast Boat Express' is worked from Heysham to Manchester by 45025, complete with headboard. This was the only entire rake of blue/grey stock worked regularly by steam, and the last train titled in the timetable to be worked by steam.
6	D296 noted at Worting Jct. with the 00.55 Washwood Heath – Southampton Eastern Docks freight. EE Type 4s are infrequent visitors to this route.
8	D73 is a surprise arrival at Paddington on the 07.05 ex-Cheltenham.
8	A bigger surprise is D1574 + D9016 *Gordon Highlander* double-heading the 'Yorkshire Pullman' throughout from King's Cross to Leeds.
9	D5302 (64B) comes into Newcastle with freightliner empties from Edinburgh. These Type 2s rarely reach Newcastle.
9	Royal train is worked from St Pancras to Nottingham and returns through Banbury. D5223/6 are entrusted with the duty.
10	5-car DMU forms the 09.00 ECS train from Newton Abbot to…Edinburgh!
12	Rare working at Bexleyheath as down ECS train passes through formed of 3 x 4-CEP units with two Motor Luggage Vans bringing up the rear.
12	4472 heads an excursion to Norwich, its second 'live' GE lines appearance.
15	D7598 + brake tender, works a Banbury – High Wycombe freight, usually a 'Warship' duty.
16	D416 brings the 08.14 from Perth into Waverley, an unusual type here.
16	2-6-4T 42085 + 61306 are hauled to Carnforth from Neville Hill.

16	Eastbound freight passes through Sittingbourne with a Brush Type 4 piloting an E5000-series DC electric, a most unexpected sight.
18	D835 *Pegasus* heads an Andover – Liverpool (Riverside) troop special as far as Crewe, via Bescot and Stafford. First 'Warship' to work Stafford – Crewe.
18	D5337 (60A) is a rarity at Carlisle arriving on the 12.50 ECS from Perth.
18	D6956 reaches Southall on the 06.30 special ballast train from Newport.
20	V of R line begins using part of the main line station at Aberystwyth as its terminus, and the old GWR steam depot as a combined loco and carriage shed.
23	07.45 Truro – Penzance is worked by D6306 + D6315 in multiple, with the corridor connections joined together, a relatively rare occurrence.
25	A3 4472 *Flying Scotsman* works over the Forth Bridge, believed to be only the second or third time it has ever done so!
26	WR mystery excursion from Reading is formed of a 9-coach rake of DMUs.
30	Up relief 'Thames-Clyde Express' runs through Keighley behind the unprecedented sight of triple-headed EE Type 1s!
31	D1111 heads an Edinburgh – Felixstowe special train of 15 SNCF containers.
31	75019 reaches Appleby with a lime train from the Grassington branch.
U/D	Two 'Hymeks' pass Berkswell on the 18.25 Southampton – Edge Hill freight.
U/D	D5115/122/125/128 all 60A, all work over the Waverley route in May.
U/D	New SuO service, 15.40 Edinburgh – Newcastle with southbound connections is a Swindon Inter-City set. This, and the return are not in the new timetable!

JUNE 1968

1ST	D8128 (41E Staveley) is unexpectedly found being repaired at…Inverurie!
1	D6507 brings ECS into Paignton, making a class debut here.
1	Hellifield shed contains 'Crab' 42700, Q7 0-8-0 63460 and ECJS 3rd class corridor coach no.12.
2	D1672 *Colossus*, D1675 *Amazon* (both from Weston-super-Mare), plus D235 *Apapa* (from Rugby) provide interest at Brighton on excursion traffic.
3	Oxford – Ramsgate special is formed of 3 x 3-car Pressed Steel suburban sets.
4	D1662 (87E Landore!) enters Newcastle on the up 'North Briton'.
4	D6540 reaches New Street on a relief train from Bournemouth, and D7034 comes in on the 16.29 from Poole, both unusual types in Birmingham.
5	D6905/19/36/37 are all noted on the West Highland line, from which this class has since been banned.
7	70013 *Oliver Cromwell* passes Barrow station on a down freight, and later heads the 20.28 Barrow – Huddersfield parcels.
8	D9003 *Meld* also works a parcels train, from Edinburgh to Dundee, then retires to Eastfield depot for tyre turning.
8	Centenary of the Midland line is celebrated with a railtour from St Pancras to Manchester (Central), headed by 70013 north of Derby.
8	D221 *Ivernia* (8J) miraculously appears on 1E71 Leeds – King's Cross plus the return working. Surely the first Allerton engine to reach King's Cross?
8	DC electric 20002 exits Waterloo on an enthusiasts' train, as far as Seaford.
9	Wakefield – Bridlington excursion calls at Featherstone (closed 2/1/67), which is opened

specially. (It had also re-opened 13/5/67 when several trains stopped here in connection with the RL Cup Final at Wembley).

10   D1016 *Western Gladiator* is a shock arrival at Leeds (!) on an atomic pile train, which must surely qualify as the event of the month.

11   Mr H.S. Monks (of Parbold, near Wigan) is treated by BR to a special trip from Liverpool to London (with his wife) in recognition of his 75 years as a Season Ticket holder!

11   Heysham – Neville Hill oil tanks is hauled by 92167 with its rear driving wheels uncoupled, thus running as a 2-8-2!

14   D9020 *Nimbus* heads an up freightliner train out of Portobello, unexpectedly.

15   Up goods runs through Huddersfield with D215 *Aquitania* + D255. Rare sight.

15   Excursion from Blandford Forum to Kew Bridge calls at the closed stations of Bailey Gate and Broadstone. Return is to Bournemouth, as only 'daylight working' is allowed on the remaining portions of the S&D.

15-22 Platform 8 at Brighton is used to shoot scenes for the film *Oh, What a Lovely War*. M7 0-4-4T 30245 is recovered from store at Preston Park to star, repainted, lined out and lettered 'LSWR 245' on one side only (not steamed).

18   D9003 *Meld* heads 3Z29, a King's Cross – Edinburgh pigeon special!

21   Ex-Departmental B1s 30, 32 (61050, 61315 respectively) are hauled from Barrow Hill to Derby Works, an unexpected sight.

22   D6505 heads a Romsey – Plymouth special as far as Newton Abbot. The train is formed of air-braked coaching stock, the first noted in the West of England.

22,23 Activity at Margate. D5506 arrives from Romford (first of this type here for 3 years) piloted by E6033 – a strange pairing. Second special comes in from Bristol with D1754 (87E Landore). Next day D854 *Tiger* (the first 'Warship' seen here) and D1590, D7011 (both 82A) all arrive on excursion traffic.

27   D256 (50A) noted in Liverpool Street, first EE Type 4 here since last August.

28   D416 passes Craigentinny on 1S65 Euston – Glasgow, diverted via Hawick.

28   Four coupled LEs pass through Exeter towards Newton Abbot; D6329 + D7037 + D811 *Daring* + D867 *Zenith*, a notable sight.

29   D6122 (ex-Hither Green) reaches Cadoxton yard *en route* to Barry for scrap.

29   KWVR opens from Keighley to Oxenhope. Ivatt 2-6-2T 41241 + USA 0-6-0T 72 power the inaugural train.

29   Platforms at Exeter (St Davids) are manned entirely by Inspectors from various parts of the WR, due to the 'work-to-rule' dispute.

29,30 Due to the NUR/ASLEF dispute and overtime ban, BR suspends all services from 22.00 on Saturday, to 06.00 Monday 1 July. During this period of closure, London main line termini are used for stabling trains.

U/D   J17 0-6-0 1217E is still at Stewarts Lane, awaiting transfer to Preston Park.

U/D   BR sells off its four observation cars as follows;
          'Devon Belle'   280 to Dart Valley, 'Coronation' SC1719E to Lochty,
          Cars   281 to Alan Pegler.   Cars   SC1729E to Gresley Soc.

JULY 1968

1ST   'Golden Arrow' is diverted into London Bridge (High level), terminating here.

2   06.25 Oxted line service from Victoria is operated by a class 33 hauling two out-of-fuel

3-car DMUs, a consequence of the 'work-to-rule'.

3   D1936 (86A) works a Millerhill freight into Temple Mills, and only five trains run over the Thames Haven branch, powered by D1106 (51L), D1645 (87E), D1986 (52A) and D6701 (41A), all strangers 'borrowed' by Stratford.

10   Heavy rain, flooding forces the Whitland – Kensington milk train to divert to the Worcester – Hereford route, where class 52s are seldom seen.

10,11   22.45 Paddington – Bristol is unable to proceed (due to flooding) beyond Didcot. Train is abandoned by crew and passengers about 03.30 as they descend on a local transport café for sustenance. Train struggles on to Oxford, Worcester and Gloucester, where defeat is declared (more flooding), and Bristol is eventually reached by road 15 hours after leaving Paddington!

11   Car sleeper from Newton Abbot reaches Edinburgh 10 hours late (a record) due to disastrous flooding down south.

12   D6894 heads the 14.20 Edinburgh – Newcastle, a type rare on passenger workings on this stretch of the East Coast main line.

13   Edinburgh – Birmingham leaves Waverley behind D411, still uncommon here.

15   70013 *Oliver Cromwell* travels LE from Carnforth to Crewe for repainting only, in preparation for the final railtours.

17   Local Aberdeen and Inverness newspapers report a suggestion that a steam service ought to be operated between Aviemore and Grantown-on-Spey (West) as a tourist attraction.

20   D9019 *Royal Highland Fusilier* runs LE through Huddersfield for tests between Stockport and Crewe; loco returns to ER next day.

20   07.45 Paddington – Bristol (and 13.15 return) comprises 3 sets of DMUs.

20   Paignton train arrives in Paddington with D1654 + D1938, that's 5500hp!

20   Intensive diesel utilisation; D1893 (55G Knottingley) reaches Paignton overnight, heads the 08.25 Newton Abbot – Kensington Motorail and 15.05 return working, then the 20.55 Newton Abbot – Edinburgh Motorail.

25   D433 makes a class debut at Newton Heath and is the focus of much attention.

26   D5376 + D5373 form a surprise pair on the 15.05 Banbury – Burton freight.

27   D5280 + D5281 work the 11.06 Blackpool (North) – Birmingham. Consecutively numbered double-headers are still rarities.

27   D1662, D1756 (both 87E) both pass through Preston on up expresses.

27   Weymouth trains from Birmingham, and from Wolverhampton are formed of Metro-Cammell DMU sets, due to a shortage of rolling stock.

28   D18 appears at Southend (Central) on a special from Bedford, a rare working for this class.

29   11.00 Oxford – Banbury (plus 12.43 return) is formed of D6327 (81A) towing DMU set 418.

30,31   A4 4498 *Sir Nigel Gresley* undergoes a test run from Crewe to Shrewsbury and back, prior to running light to Newcastle for storage at NCB, Philadelphia.

U/D   July visitors to Haymarket (64B) include D1866 (30A), D7575 (ML Midland Lines), D5414 (D16 Nottingham), D1564 (31B).

AUGUST 1968

3RD   21.25 Preston – Liverpool (Exchange) headed by 45318 is the last normal-service passenger train on BR to be hauled by steam.

3	75019 hauls the last steam-hauled freight, a van train from Heysham to Carnforth, which passes through Hest Bank at about 16.00.
3	6-coach 08.05 Carlisle – Birmingham has the luxury of D385 + D248!
3	14.15 Exeter (Central) – Ilfracombe arrives at St Davids carrying a red flag instead of a tail light. The flag is promptly replaced!
4	No fewer than six 'End of Steam' specials are run in and around Lancashire, mostly double-headed as follows; 1Z78 = 44871 + 44894, 1Z74 North = 70013 *Oliver Cromwell* + 44781, 1Z74 South = 45390 + 73069, 1Z79 = 44874 + 45017, RCTS train = 48476 + 73069, plus 45156 *Ayrshire Yeomanry* + 45305 on BR's own Manchester – Southport special.
5	Q7 0-8-0 63460 leaves Hellifield, heading for Stewarts Lane.
7	15.05 Penzance – Paddington stops specially at Dawlish to pick up the Prime Minister's newly-married son and daughter-in-law.
8,9	AC Cars railbus W79978 leaves Grangemouth and travels to Gosforth carriage sidings, Newcastle. Runs to Grosmont (9th), for future NYMR use.
9	6000 *King George V* is rope-hauled out of Swindon stock shed and handed over by the Mayor of Swindon to Mr B. Bulmer (Chairman of the Hereford cider firm that have undertaken to restore the engine at the United Wagon Works in Newport). 6000 is on a 2-year loan to Bulmers.
10	WR 8-car diesel Pullman set reaches Milford Haven on a special working for a Gulf Petroleum Co. party, who open the new refinery there.
11	BR's '15 Guinea Special' leaves Liverpool (Lime Street) 09.10 behind 45110, with banking assistance from E3083, on a 314 mile tour. 70013 *Oliver Cromwell* operates the Manchester – Carlisle leg, with 44871 + 44781 on the southbound leg and 45110 back to Lime Street. **Official end of BR steam services.**
11-16	70013 runs LE Carlisle – Norwich via Doncaster *en route* to Bressingham, reaching Norwich on the 12th (pm). Leaves early on 16th for Diss in company of LTS 80 *Thundersley*, ex-store in the goods shed at Attleborough. 80 goes (by road) to Bresssingham on 17th, 70013 next day – steamed here on 22nd.
16	J17 0-6-0 1217E is towed from Stewarts Lane to Preston Park, finally.
17	08.30 ex-Paddington arrives at Exeter (St Davids) 2 hours late behind D813 *Diadem* + D6319 + D1004 *Western Crusader*. D1004 develops engine fault, D6319 is sent to assist but catches fire, D813 rescues the ensemble.
17	10.45 Holyhead – Kensington Olympia Motorail reports having a car wind-screen smashed by a dog jumping from a bridge north of Crewe! Two other windscreens are also found to be broken.
17	6-car 'Trans-Pennine' set forming the 10.00 Liverpool – Hull is turned on the triangle at Earlestown, complete with passengers. Leading cab was out of action and the set had been driven from the rear cab since Liverpool!
18	16.30 Inverness – Edinburgh (14 vehicles) has D5345 + D5341 + D5121.
18	Reading – Barry excursion is formed of 3 sets of London suburban DMUs.
21	16-coach train arrives at Southend (Victoria). The 17.04 ex-Liverpool Street fails at Rayleigh and the following train pushes the defective to its destination.
21	Cheap excursion is advertised (at 10s) from Richmond to Bognor Regis. Two trains are run, carrying 2,300 passengers!
22	Midnight Euston – Crewe mail train is stopped at Berkswell when a signalman spots

an open door; 12 mail bags have fallen out! Other traffic halted whilst shunter D3108, the Coventry pilot, plus wagon and men are sent to search for the bags, which are duly located and restored to the Crewe train.

22 60532 *Blue Peter* goes to York for storage in the 01.35 freight from Millerhill.

24 Privately owned 45428 travels under its own steam from Holbeck via Derby (water stop) to Tyseley, to join 5593 *Kolhapur* and 7029 *Clun Castle*.

24 Hawker Siddeley 4000hp Co-Co 'Kestrel' noted in the Research Dept yard at Derby. Runs trials to Nuneaton and back 27/8/9 August with LMR dynamometer car No.3 and E3132 at the rear.

24 E6044 works an assorted train from Stewarts Lane to Preston Park, comprising Q7 0-8-0 63460, preserved coaching stock, steam crane and vehicles containing relics, including early Stockton and Darlington wagons.

27 Leicester Museum of Industrial Technology opens; scheduled to receive seven locos on permanent loan, 118, 158A, 26500, 49395, 63601, 44027, 4771 *Green Arrow*, though only the first three can be exhibited at present.

28 10.20 Exeter – Waterloo passes Templecombe with D6573 + D818 *Glory*, a most infrequent combination.

U/D D5623 is a most unusual visitor to Edinburgh.

U/D AL3s E3024/32/33/34/98 are also moved to Bury for storage.

SEPTEMBER 1968

1ST 6-car 'Trans-Pennine' set in blue/grey works the 11.35 Sheffield – Liverpool (Lime Street) via Chinley, a most unusual occurrence on this route.

1,15,29 D1674, D1652 (both 82A) and D1866 (41A) all reach Aberdeen at the head of the 17.50 (SuO) from Edinburgh respectively, far-flung visitors!

6 A3 4472 *Flying Scotsman* arrives in Huddersfield (LE from Doncaster via Sheffield, Penistone) to work a special to Tyne Dock and back.

7 Narrow-bodied D6586/94 power the Brighton – Exeter throughout, and the 08.30 Plymouth – Paddington surprisingly has three working 'Warships' at its head; D860 *Victorious* piloting D823 *Hermes* + D819 *Goliath* (in multiple).

8 In Brent yard, shunter D3177 still has the 'Lion & Wheel' emblem!

8 BR officially discontinues the use of the 'D' prefix for diesel locos, though 'E' prefix is to remain for electrics. *(NB This account continues to employ the D prefix for the remaining months as implementation on BR is gradual).*

9 14.05 Euston – Glasgow appears at Crewe headed by the unexpected combination of D248 + D422.

9 D6939 hauls a train of prefabricated track panels over the Buxton – Stockport line, the first class 37 seen here.

10 43924 is the first engine to leave Woodham Bros (Barry) scrapyard, for restoration on the KWVR.

12 80002 resumes carriage heating duties at Cowlairs.

14 Excursion to Windermere from Durham has D258 (55B York) in charge of 9 Pullman cars, 4 of which are in the old (umber & cream) livery.

14 A class 33 reaches Abergavenny on a troop train from Ludgershall, and returns with the ECS.

14+ Exceptional rain and subsequent flooding, landslips etc. cause chaos to SR services.

	Arrivals indicator at Waterloo is abandoned for 10 days!
15	Torrential rain forces 08.40 Charing Cross – Hastings to be diverted via Redhill, but on reaching Edenbridge is trapped by floods fore and aft; the town itself is largely awash and no road relief is possible. Helicopter called in to transfer stranded passengers but cannot land due to poor visibility! When dark, a bus gets passengers to Town station, where some trains are running, and Hastings is reached around midnight!
18	Two 'Westerns' head a long freight towards Cardiff from the Barry direction.
19	73050 runs LE from Patricroft along the Calder Valley (to Peterborough).
19	2-coach special from Newcastle conveying the ER Board on an official visit, is run over NCB tracks between Woodhorn and Lynemouth Colliery.
21	Carnforth still holds 30 steam locos for disposal, plus 42073/85, 44871, 45231, 61306, 75027/48 and 46441 for preservation.
22	Farnborough Air Show special from Exeter is powered by D822 *Hercules* complete with a large circular headboard reading 'Royal Observer Corps Special Train'. Another special, from Southend has D1665 (87E) both ways.
27	(For two weeks). D46 is on loan from Toton depot to the CEGB at Willington (between Burton, Derby) to assist in maintaining power from the major generator as a feeder generator is defunct. Power cuts are thus avoided.
29	Tyseley Open Day attracts 20,000 visitors; 7029, 7818, 3205, (4)5593, 45428, 48773 are on view, plus rolling stock exhibits. A3 4472 arrives on a special from Retford, and D1020 *Western Hero* on another, from Paddington.

OCTOBER 1968

1ST	Exhibition at Bedford (centenary of MR to St Pancras) has Metropolitan 0-4-4T L44 on show, plus brand new D444, the first seen in this area.
2	3-coach special for Shiek Zaid of Abu Dhabi's shooting party (Restaurant Car + Sleeping Car + brake) arrives in Waverley from Bonar Bridge with D6129. Immaculate D1971 takes the train overnight to London.
3	Class 47 works into Barnstaple Jct. on clearance tests for possible use on coal trains between Exeter and Yelland power station.
6	Express arrives in St Pancras with D5216 + D5241 piloting D130 which had sustained fire damage.
6	A3 4472 *Flying Scotsman* departs King's Cross with a special to York in aid of funds to restore the Minster.
7	The 'Euro-Scot Freightliner' is inaugurated by D9021 *Argyll & Sutherland Highlander*, seen heading north complete with headboard.
11	D1926 (70D Eastleigh) heads south on the East Coast main line with a special train of cement wagons.
12	D1614 (82A) reaches Liverpool (Lime Street) on the 15.42 from Newcastle. Few Bristol engines ever work into Liverpool.
17,23	D834 *Pathfinder*, D1053 *Western Patriarch* (respectively) exit Radstock yard on coal traffic to Portishead, two class debuts for the North Somerset line.
19,21	Bristol (Bath Road) Open Day display includes 7808/6697/46201 (in red undercoat from Ashchurch), plus 2818 from Avonmouth Docks. Also E3044, the first time an AC electric has travelled west, which is seen two days later being towed north through Gloucester

by D837 *Ramillies*.

22 11.43 arrival from Norwich comes into Liverpool Street at 12.50 behind D8237, highly unusual power on any passenger train, for any reason.

23 Belgian Railways books a special excursion from Dover (Marine) to Leeds, returning next day.

25,26,27 A3 4472 appears in Huddersfield three days running in connection with the 'Moorlands' railtour and journeys to/from Doncaster. Railtour takes 4472 to Liverpool for the first time, leaving Lime Street for Carlisle, then Leeds, Wakefield, Huddersfield and Manchester on the return leg.

26 Football special returning to Portsmouth from Bristol is an 11-TC formation propelled by D6519 in push/pull mode.

27 D1902 (86A) arrives in Waverley on the 09.30 (SuO) ex-Aberdeen, then heads the 19.14 back again. Has a Cardiff Canton engine reached Aberdeen before?

27 10.50 Edinburgh – Birmingham is diverted via Hawick and headed by D215 *Aquitania* + D264, an uncommon same-class combination.

28 15.10 from Weymouth arrives in Bristol behind D1011 *Western Thunderer* pulling the usual 3-car DMU.

28 D5386 (D16 Nottingham) is a rare class to reach Stockport, on freight.

29 21.50 ex-York mail train is seen at Huddersfield with D156 piloting D1707, another uncommon combination.

U/D 44767 cannot proceed from Kingmoor to Carnforth for subsequent preservation as its tender is unserviceable. Another therefore has to be obtained from Draper's scrapyard at Hull, fortunately that from 44950 (with Timken roller bearings) which had previously run behind 44767. BR Regulations do not permit movement of an engine without a tender, as the tender handbrake is the only effective brake on a dead steam engine.

NOVEMBER 1968

1ST 3-coach special ex-Aberdeen is piped out of Aviemore on the return by a piper in Highland dress as D5313 takes the last train back over the Speyside line.

2 30 withdrawn steam engines are still present at Rose Grove shed.

3 0-6-0 shunter 15219, on an engineering train, runs out of water at Herne Bay and is filled up with the hose normally used to clean the toilets there.

3 D9005/13/19, D153 all work over the Blyth & Tyne freight route on diverted ECML expresses, due to engineering works south of Morpeth.

4 Rolling stock from the Midland Centenary exhibition is towed from Bletchley to Aylesbury, resulting in the strange sight of L44/LNW saloon/3 preserved freight wagons crossing the Bletchley flyover.

7 D7056 heads a Morris Cowley – Immingham car train as far as Colwick, the first class 35 seen here.

7 Hampshire unit 1131 reaches Exeter as the 12.44 ex-Salisbury (i.e. 11.10 ex- Waterloo, which failed at Andover). 1131 returns as the 16.05 (to Salisbury).

11 'David & Goliath' seen at Hunslet Engine Co. Works when A3 4472 *Flying Scotsman* is in for attention alongside *Linda* from the Festiniog Railway!

12 Surprisingly, D7560 (D08 Liverpool) works through to Wareham on the 20.05 from

Ellesmere Port, returning with the 08.28 Fratton – Trafford Park.

13   6000 *King George V* is steamed at Bulmer's, Hereford to celebrate the inauguration of new rail facilities. Five refurbished Pullman cars, 64/76/83/36 and *Aquila* make their debut, and 0-6-0 shunter D2578 is named *Cider Queen*.

20   'Night Ferry' makes a daylight publicity run Victoria – Dover for London travel agency staff to familiarise themselves with Wagons-Lits travel.

21   D5535 heads the 10.50 Ipswich – Bridgwater sugar beet pulp train to Old Oak Common, and stays there for crew training purposes.

22   07.59 Orpington – Victoria is signalled into an already occupied platform at Victoria, leaving part of the train outside the station; some passengers climb down and walk along the (electrified) track to reach the platform!

23   Triple-header arrives in Exeter (St Davids); D7041 piloting D869 *Zest* + D807 *Caradoc* in multiple. Rare sight. Pilot comes off at Newton Abbot.

25   Duke of Edinburgh ceremonially presents two historic carriages to the US Ambassador, at Kensington Olympia. These are Pullman car *Isle of Thanet* (from Winston Churchill's funeral train) and LNER coach 1592 (from General Eisenhower's train in GB, France and Germany), and are gifts from BR to the National Railroad Museum at Green Bay, Wisconsin.

28   A WR single unit railcar is a curious sight, speeding towards... Edinburgh!

28   3-car LMR DMU set appears at Exeter, running from Birmingham to Plymouth in the timings of the 07.06 Bradford – Penzance, the down 'Cornishman'. The set returns from Plymouth straight away.

28,29   14.55 Edinburgh – Carlisle is worked by D5332 (60A), and by D1873 (34G) next day, diverse power from diverse depots!

30   Coventry v Ipswich football special brings D6724 (31B) through to Coventry.

U/D   Clearance tests take place to determine whether 3-car Manchester (Piccadilly) to Hadfield/Glossop EMUs could work through Woodhead Tunnel to operate a possible Penistone – Manchester service if closure proposals are rejected.

DECEMBER 1968

7TH   3-cyl 2-6-4T 42500 leaves Preston Park behind D6557 to Clapham Jct., *en route* to Attleborough, for Bressingham Gardens, where it arrives on 21st.

7   Football special from Dartford to Kettering is formed of Hastings unit 1034, and Luton receives two more Hastings units on another special ex-Gillingham.

8   LT 0-6-0PT, ex-GWR, works an engineering train onto the King's Cross suburban lines outside the station.

10   D5515 heads the 09.40 Dagenham – Severn Tunnel Jct. throughout, returning with the 16.05 back to Acton. Furthest west that a class 31 has reached?

11   D6712 (30A) is a surprising sight passing LE east through Huddersfield.

12   D9021 *Argyll & Sutherland Highlander* goes to Perth to head the 09.45 to Euston which is to pick up the 'Save the Argylls' petition at Stirling.

16   E2001 (ex-gas turbine) is hauled through Northampton by a class 86 *en route* to store at Market Harborough.

18   22.25 (17th) Fawley – Grangetown (Cardiff/Barry) is headed throughout by a class 33, the first to be seen so far west.

18	D1020 *Western Hero* appears at Norwood Jct. on a cross-London freight.
20	London – Basel Sleeping Car service inaugurated.
21	70000 *Britannia* departs Preston Park behind D6554 as far as Redhill, where it is to be inspected by East Anglian Locomotive Preservation Society.
22	D9011 *The Royal Northumberland Fusiliers* heads 1A38 King's Cross to Edinburgh diverted via Knottingley, where this class is rarely seen.
26	'Mid-day Scot' leaves Glasgow (Central) behind D405 + D418. First pairing?
U/D	Two of the three class 37s used as Lickey bankers can now be used in multiple, by one crew; 3rd remains a single unit. At least 11 freights require assistance of all three bankers (that's about 7800hp including train engine!).
U/D	Closure notice for the Darlington – Richmond branch (effective 3/3/69) is displayed at…Liverpool Street!

Appendices

APPENDIX I – STEAM DATABASE (major classes only)

GWR: 4-6-0 classes

County	6MT	1000 – 1029
Star/Castle	6P/7P	4000 – 4072
Castle	7P	4073 – 4099
		5000 – 5099
		7000 – 7037
Hall	5MT	4900 – 4999
		5900 – 5999
		6900 – 6999
		7900 – 7929
King	8P	6000 – 6029
Grange	5MT	6800 – 6879
Manor	5MT	7800 – 7829

SR: 4-6-0 classes

King Arthur	5P	30448 – 30457
N15		30736 – 30755
		30763 – 30806
Lord Nelson	7P	30850 – 30865

4-4-0 class

Schools V	5P	30900 – 30939

4-6-2 classes

West Country	7P	34001 – 34048
WC		34091 – 34108
Battle of Britain		34049 – 34090
BB		34109 – 34110
Merchant Navy	8P	35001 – 35030

LMS: 4-4-0 class

Compound	4P	40900 – 41199

2-6-0 class

Crab	5MT	42700 – 42944

0-6-0 class

	4F	43836 – 44606

4-6-0 classes

'5'	5MT	44658 – 45499
Patriot	6P/7P	45500 – 45551
Jubilee	6P/7P	45552 – 45742
Royal Scot	7P	46100 – 46170

4-6-2 classes

Princess	8P	46200 – 46212
Coronation	8P	46220 – 46257

2-8-0 class

	8F	48000 - 48775

LNER: 4-6-2 classes

A4	8P	60001 – 60034
A3	7P	60035 – 60112
A1	8P	60113 – 60162
A2	8P	60500 – 60539

2-6-2 class

V2	7P	60800 – 60983

4-6-0 classes

B1	5MT	61000 – 61409
B12	4P/3F	61501 – 61580
B2/B17	4P/5P	61600 – 61672

2-6-0 classes

K1	5P/6F	62001 – 62070
K2	4MT	61720 – 61794
K3	5P/6F	61800 – 61992
K4	5P/6F	61993 – 61998

4-4-0 class

D49	4P	62700 – 62775

BR: 4-6-2 classes

Britannia	7MT	70000 – 70054
Clan	6MT	72000 – 72009

4-6-0 classes

	5MT	73000 – 73171
	4MT	75000 – 75089

2-6-0 class

	4MT	76000 – 76114
	3MT	77000 – 77019
	2MT	78000 – 78064

2-6-4T class

	4MT	80000 – 80154

2-6-2T classes

	3MT	82000 – 82044
	2MT	84000 – 82029

2-8-0 class

	WD	90000 – 90732

2-10-0 class

	9F	92000 – 92250
	WD	90750 – 90774

Wheel arrangement; Power classification (revised 1950);
4-6-2 = Pacific   P = Passenger
4-4-2 = Atlantic   F = Freight
                   MT = Mixed Traffic

APPENDIX II – DIESEL DATABASE (major classes only)

			hp		intro	class
Type 5						
Deltic	D9000 – 9021	Co-Co	3300	EE	1961	55
Type 4						
Peak	D1 – D193	1Co-Co1	2500	BR/Sulzer	1959	44-6
	D200 – 399	1Co-Co1	2000	EE	1958	40
	D400 – 449	Co-Co	2700	EE	1967	50
Warship	D600 – 604	A1A-A1A	2000	NBL	1958	41
Warship	D800 – 870	B-B	2200	BR/NBL	1958	42/3
Western	D1000 – 1073	C-C	2700	BR	1961	52
	D1100 – 1011	Co-Co	2750	Brush	1962	47
	D1500 – 1999	do.		do.		
Type 3						
	D6500 – 6597	Bo-Bo	1550	BRCW	1959	33
	D6600 – 6608	Co-Co	1750	EE	1960	37
	D6700 – 6999	do.		do.		
Hymek	D7000 – 7100	B-B	1700	BP	1961	35
Type 2						
	D5000 – 5150	Bo-Bo	1160	BR/Sulzer	1958	24
	D5151 – 5299	Bo-Bo	1250	BR/Sulzer	1961	25
	D7500 – 7677	do.		do.		
	D5300 – 5346	Bo-Bo	1160	BRCW	1958	26
	D5347 – 5415	Bo-Bo	1250	BRCW	1961	27
	D5500 – 5699	A1A-A1A	1365	Brush	1957	31
	D5800 – 5862	do.		do.		
	D5700 – 5719	Co-Bo	1200	MV	1958	28
Baby Deltic	D5900 – 5909	Bo-Bo	1100	EE	1959	23
	D6100 – 6157	Bo-Bo	1100	NBL	1958	21
	do.	do.	1350	do.	1963	29
	D6300 – 6357	B-B	1100	NBL	1959	22
Type 1						
	D8000 – 8199	Bo-Bo	1000	EE	1957	20
	D8300 – 8327	do.		do.		
	D8200 – 8243	Bo-Bo	800	BTH	1957	15
	D8400 – 8409	Bo-Bo	800	NBL	1958	16
	D8500 – 8616	Bo-Bo	900	Clayton	1962	17
	D9500 – 9555	0-6-0	650	BR	1964	14

Builders;

EE = English Electric
BP = Beyer Peacock
MV = Metropolitan Vickers
BRCW = Birmingham Railway Carriage & Wagon

NBL = North British Loco.
BTH = British Thomson Houston
BR = British Railways

APPENDIX III – ELECTRIC LOCOMOTIVE DATABASE (major classes only)

DC Types

20001/2/3	Co-Co	1470hp	SR	1941	class 70	
26001 – 26057	Bo+Bo	1868	BR	1950	EM1 76	
27000 – 27006	Co-Co	2490	BR	1953	EM2 77	
E5000 – 5024	Bo-Bo	2552	BR	1957	class 71	
E6001 – 6049	Bo-Bo	600/1600	BR	1962	class 73	
E6101 – 6110	Bo-Bo	650/2552	BR	1967	class 74	

NB 26000 was an LNER prototype built in 1941. Class 74 was rebuilt from class 71

AC Types

E3001-3023, 96/97	Bo-Bo	3200	BRCW	1959	AL1, class 81
E3046 – 3055	Bo-Bo	3300	BP	1960	AL2, class 82
E3024-35, 98/99/100	Bo-Bo	2950	EE	1960	AL3, class 83
E3036 – 3045	Bo-Bo	3300	NBL	1960	AL4, class 84
E3056 – 3095	Bo-Bo	3200	BR	1960	AL5, class 85
E3101 – 3200	Bo-Bo	3600	EE/BR	1965	AL6, class 86

APPENDIX IV – TITLED EXPRESS DATABASE

WR to/from Paddington	**Destination**
Bristolian	Bristol
Cambrian Coast Express	Aberystwyth
Capitals United Express	Cardiff
Cathedrals Express	Worcester
Cheltenham Spa Express	Cheltenham
Cornish Riviera Express	Penzance
Inter-City	Wolverhampton
Mayflower	Plymouth
Merchant Venturer	Bristol
Pembroke Coast Express	Pembroke Dock
Red Dragon	Carmarthen
Royal Duchy	Penzance
South Wales Pullman	Swansea
Torbay Express	Kingswear
(Cornishman Wolverhampton – Penzance)	
(Devonian Bradford – Paignton)	

SR to/from Waterloo	
Atlantic Coast Express	Padstow
Bournemouth Belle	Bournemouth
Devon Belle	Ilfracombe
Royal Wessex	Weymouth

to/ from Victoria	
Brighton Belle	Brighton
Golden Arrow	Dover
Night Ferry	Dover
Thanet/Kentish Belle	Ramsgate
to/from Charing Cross	
Man of Kent	Margate
(Pines Express Manchester – Bournemouth)	

LMR to/from Euston	
Royal Scot	Glasgow
Mid-day Scot	Glasgow
Caledonian	Glasgow
Northern Irishman	Stranraer
Royal Highlander	Inverness
Midlander	Wolverhampton
Mancunian	Manchester
Lancastrian	Manchester
Comet	Manchester
Merseyside Express	Liverpool
Red Rose	Liverpool
Manxman	Liverpool
Shamrock	Liverpool
Irish Mail	Holyhead
Emerald Isle Express	Holyhead
Welshman	Holyhead
Ulster Express	Heysham

Lakes Express	Windermere

to/from St Pancras	
Thames-Clyde Express	Glasgow
Waverley	Edinburgh
Palatine	Manchester
Robin Hood	Nottingham

ScR internal services to/from Glasgow	
Irishman	Stranraer
Bon Accord	Aberdeen
Granite City	Aberdeen
Saint Mungo	Aberdeen
Fife Coast Express	St Andrews

ER to/from King's Cross	
Flying Scotsman	Edinburgh
Capitals Limited	Edinburgh
Heart of Midlothian	Edinburgh
Elizabethan	Edinburgh
Talisman	Edinburgh
Night Scotsman	Edinburgh
Queen of Scots	Glasgow
North Briton (from Leeds)	Glasgow
Aberdonian	Aberdeen
Fair Maid	Perth
Tees-Tyne Pullman	Newcastle
Northumbrian	Newcastle
Norseman	Newcastle
Tynesider	Newcastle
Yorkshire Pullman	Leeds/ Bradford
West Riding	Leeds/ Bradford
White Rose	Leeds/ Bradford
Harrogate Sunday Pullman	+ H'gate
Scarborough Flyer	Scarborough
Tees-Thames	Middlesbrough

to/ from Marylebone	
Master Cutler	Sheffield
South Yorkshireman	Bradford

to/from Liverpool Street	
Hook Continental	Harwich
Scandinavian	Harwich
Day Continental	Harwich
East Anglian	Norwich
Norfolkman	Norwich
Fenman	King's Lynn
Broadsman	Cromer
Easterling	Yarmouth
Essex Coast Express	Clacton

APPENDIX V – SHEDCODE DATABASE (unchanged codes)

1A	Willesden	52A	Gateshead	83A	Newton Abbot
1B	Camden	52B	Heaton	83B	Taunton
1D	Devons Road	52C	Blaydon	83C	Exeter
1E	Bletchley	52D	Tweedmouth		

5A	Crewe North
5B	Crewe South

60A	Inverness
60B	Aviemore
60C	Helmsdale
60D	Wick

84A	Wolverhampton (Stafford Road)

6A	Chester
6B	Mold Jct
6G	Llandudno Jct
6J	Holyhead

61A	Kittybrewster
61B	Ferryhill
61C	Keith

85A	Worcester
85B	Gloucester

86E	Severn Tunnel Junction
86G	Pontypool Road

8A	Edge Hill
8B	Warrington
8C	Speke Jct

62A	Thornton Jct
62B	Dundee Tay Br.

87A	Neath
87G	Carmarthen
87H	Neyland

9A	Longsight
9B	Edgeley
9E	Trafford Park
9F	Heaton Mersey

63A	Perth

64A	St Margarets
64B	Haymarket
64C	Dalry Road
64G	Hawick

NB Selected depots only. Codes valid to depot closure, or 1966. See text for later alterations.

14A	Cricklewood
14B	Kentish Town

65A	Eastfield
65B	St Rollox
65C	Parkhead
65D	Dawsholme
65F	Grangemouth

30A	Stratford
30E	Colchester
30F	Parkeston

31A	Cambridge
31B	March
31C	Kings Lynn

66A	Polmadie
66B	Motherwell

32A	Norwich
32B	Ipswich
32C	Lowestoft
32D	Yarmouth (South Town)

67A	Corkerhill
67B	Hurlford
67C	Ayr
67D	Ardrossan

33A	Plaistow
33B	Tilbury
33C	Shoeburyness

70A	Nine Elms
70B	Feltham
70C	Guildford
70D	Basingstoke

34A	King's Cross
34G	Finsbury Park

73B	Bricklayers Arms
73C	Hither Green

36A	Doncaster
36E	Retford

75A	Brighton
75B	Redhill

40A	Lincoln
40B	Immingham
40F	Boston

81A	Old Oak Common
81D	Reading
81E	Didcot
81F	Oxford

50A	York
50D	Starbeck

82A	Bristol Bath Rd
82B	St Philip's Marsh
82C	Swindon
82D	Westbury

51A	Darlington
51L	Thornaby

APPENDIX VI – SHEDCODE DATABASE (changed codes)

Selected sheds only. Codes valid until closure of depot, or 1966. Most changes made in 1963, some earlier.

2A	Rugby	later 1F		35B	Grantham	34F
38E	Woodford Halse	2F		35C	Spital Bridge	31F
					(Peterborough)	
3A	Bescot	21B, 2F		36B	Mexborough	41F
3B	Bushbury	21C				
3D	Aston	21D		37A	Ardsley	56B
				37B	Copley hill	56C
6C	Birkenhead	8H		37C	Bradford	56G
10A	Springs Branch	8F		38A	Colwick	40E, 16B
10C	Patricroft	26F		38B	Annesley	16D
11A	Carnforth	24L		39A	Gorton	9G
				39B	Darnall	41A
12B	Carlisle Upperby	12A, 12B				
12A	Carlisle Kingmoor	68A, 12A		50B	Neville Hill	55H
68E	Carlisle Canal	12C				
				53A	Dairycoates	50B
34E	Neasden	14D		53B	Botanic Gardens	50C
15A	Wellingborough	15B		63D	Fort William	65J, 63B
15C	Leicester (Midland)	15A				
38C	Leicester (GC)	15E		71A	Eastleigh	70D
				71B	Bournemouth	70F
16A	Nottingham	16D		71G	Bath (S&D)	82F
17A	Derby	16C		71H	Templecombe	82G
18A	Toton	16A				
				72A	Exmouth Jct	83D
19A	Grimesthorpe	41B		72B	Salisbury	70E
19B	Millhouses	41C				
19C	Canklow	41D		73A	Stewarts Lane	75D
20A	Holbeck	55A		74A	Ashford	73F
				74C	Dover	73H
21A	Saltley	2E				
				83D	Laira	84A
22A	Bristol Barrow Road	82E		83G	Penzance	84D
22B	Gloucester Barnwood	85E				
				84B	Oxley	2B
25A	Wakefield	56A		84C	Banbury	2D
25F	Low Moor	56F		84E	Tyseley	2A
25G	Farnley Jct	55C		84G	Shrewsbury	89A, 6D
26A	Newton Heath	9D		86C	Canton	88A, 86A
27A	Bank Hall	8K		88A	Cathays	88M
28A	Blackpool	24E, 10E		89A	Oswestry	89D
				89C	Machynlleth	6F
35A	New England	34E				

APPENDIX VII – ABBREVIATIONS DATABASE

BR	British Railways
WR	Western Region
SR	Southern Region
LMR	London Midland Region
ER	Eastern Region
NER	North Eastern Region
ScR	Scottish Region
GWR	Great Western Railway
SR	Southern Railway (context)
LMS	London Midland & Scottish
LNER	London North Eastern Railway
LBSC	London Brighton & S. Coast
SEC	South Eastern & Chatham
LSW	London & South Western
L&M	Liverpool & Manchester
CLC	Cheshire Lines Committee
LTS	London Tilbury & Southend
S&D	Somerset & Dorset
MR	Midland Railway
LNW	London North Western
L&Y	Lancashire & Yorkshire
GER	Great Eastern Railway
GNR	Great Northern Railway
GCR	Great Central Railway
NER	North Eastern Rly (context)
NBR	North British Railway
GNS	Great North of Scotland Rly
HR	Highland Railway
CR	Caledonian Railway
GSW	Glasgow South Western
DNS	Didcot Newbury Southampton
MSWJ	Midland & South Western Jct
M&GN	Midland & Great Northern
NLR	North London Railway
CKP	Cockermouth Keswick Penrith
SMJ	Stratford & Midland Jct
MSJA	Manchester South Jct & Altrincham
LDEC	Lancashire Derbyshire & East Coast
SHT	Swansea Harbour Trust

RH&D	Romney Hythe & Dymchurch
S&C	Settle & Carlisle (line)
ECJS	East Coast Joint Stock
LTE	London Transport Executive
RE	Railway Executive
BTC	British Transport Committee
SNCF	French National Railways
TUCC	Transport Users' Consultative Committee
CTAC	Creative Tourist's Association Conference
LCGB	Locomotive Club of Great Britain
RCTS	Railway Correspondence & Travel Society
SLS	Stephenson Locomotive Society

PT = Pannier tank		T = tank engine	
ST = Saddle tank		WT = Well tank	

up = towards London
down = away from London

ECS	empty coaching stock
DMU	diesel multiple unit
DEMU	diesel electric multiple unit
EMU	electric multiple unit
LE	light engine (ie. running solo)
MPD	motive power depot (shed)
PW	permanent way (track)
AC	alternating current
DC	direct current
DE	diesel electric
DH	diesel hydraulic
GT	gas turbine

TPO	Travelling Post Office

London stations are not prefixed 'London', neither are
<u>Birmingham</u>
Snow Hill, New Street
<u>Edinburgh</u>
Waverley, Princes Street
<u>Glasgow</u>
Buchanan Street, Queen Street, St Enoch